BLOOD, TOIL, TEARS AND SWEAT

Also by Roger Parkinson:

Peace For Our Time

Roger Parkinson

BLOOD, TOIL, TEARS AND SWEAT

The War History from Dunkirk to Alamein, based on the War Cabinet papers of 1940 to 1942

David McKay Company, Inc.
New York

BLOOD, TOIL, TEARS AND SWEAT

COPYRIGHT © 1973 BY ROGER PARKINSON

First published in Great Britain, 1973

First American Edition, 1973

LIBRARY OF CONGRESS CATALOG CARD NUMBER: 73-77296

MANUFACTURED IN THE UNITED STATES OF AMERICA

Contents

Maps

Abbreviations and Code Names

ABDA   American, British, Dutch, Australian (Command)
AFV   Armoured Fighting Vehicle
CCS   Combined Chiefs of Staff
CIGS   Chief of the Imperial General Staff
C-in-C   Commander in Chief
GOC   General Officer Commanding
COS   Chiefs of Staff
JIC   Joint Intelligence Committee
JPS   Joint Planning Staff
MT   Motor Transport
OPD   Operations (Planning) Division
PRU   Photographic Reconnaissance Unit

ABC 1, 2   Anglo-American Staff plans, 1941
Acrobat   Advance from Cyrenaica into Tripoli after 'Crusader', 1942
Barbarossa   German campaign against Russia, 1941
Battleaxe   Operations in Western Desert to relieve Tobruk, 1941
Bolero   Build-up in UK of American forces and supplies
Brevity   Attempted capture of Sollum and Capuzzo, 1942
Brisk   Proposed occupation of Azores, 1940-41
Catapult   Naval operation against French Fleet at Oran, 1940
Claymore   Raid on Lofoten Islands, 1941
Compass   Operation in Western Desert against Italians, 1940
Crusader   Operations in Western Desert, 1941-2
Dynamo   Dunkirk evacuation, 1940
Exporter   Operations in Syria, 1941
Felix   German plan for seizure of Gibraltar
Gymnast   Allied occupation of French North Africa, 1941, also 'Super-Gymnast' and later 'Torch'
Hats   Fast convoy through Mediterranean, 1940
Imperator   Proposed large raid on enemy Channel coast, 1942
Ironclad   Capture of Diego Suarez, 1942

Jaguar   Air reinforcement of Malta, 1941

Jubilee   Dieppe raid, 1942, formerly 'Rutter'

Jupiter   Suggested operations against airfields in North Norway, 1942

Lightfoot   Operations in Western Desert, October 1942

Lustre   Troop movement from Egypt to Greece, 1941

Magnet   Movement of US troops to Northern Ireland, 1942

Mandibles   Proposed occupation of Dodecanese, 1940-41

Marita   German attack on Greece, 1941

Matador   Proposed movement into Thailand to forestall Japanese, 1941

Menace   Operation against Dakar, 1940, formerly 'Scipio'

Mercury   German attack on Crete, 1941

Pedestal   Convoy to Malta, 1942

Plan D (Dog)   Memorandum on American strategy by Admiral Stark, 1940

PQ   Convoys to North Russia; QP for return journeys

Puma   Proposed operation to occupy Canary Islands, 1941

Round-Up   Plan for allied invasion of Europe, 1943

Rutter   Original name for Dieppe raid, later 'Jubilee'

Scipio   Original name for operations against Dakar, later 'Menace'

Sealion   Proposed German invasion of Britain, 1940-41

Sledgehammer   Plan for limited invasion of France, 1942

Sunflower   Movement of German troops to North Africa, 1941

Thruster   Proposed capture of Azores against Portuguese opposition, 1941

Tiger   Fast convoy of tanks and aircraft to Egypt, 1941

Torch   Invasion of Vichy African territories, 1942

Tube Alloys   Atomic bombs

Typhoon   German attack on Moscow, 1941

Whipcord   Proposed capture of Sicily, 1942

Workshop   Proposed capture of Pantelleria, winter 1940-41

Introduction

Yard after yard of War Cabinet files have now been released from security restrictions and are open for public inspection. This book concentrates upon the Minutes and Memoranda of the main wartime decision-making bodies – those concerned with the central direction of strategy and Grand Strategy during the perilous years of 1940, 1941 and 1942. Much material from other committees is left unexplored; nor does the book claim to be the first to reveal the contents of the formerly top-secret War Cabinet files – a privilege given to the official histories. Instead, this is the first attempt to take the official documents and marry them to the memoirs and diaries written by the participants in those great events, an aim which was outside the scholarly terms of reference of the official historians. The book therefore deals with both personalities and policies; the official documents and the private diaries complement each other. The unemotional, outwardly dry Minutes and Memoranda come alive when placed in context and linked with diaries and memoirs; some puzzling personal declarations in the latter are better explained. The two different sources allow an excellent opportunity for comprehensive description.

The book could have been written in two ways. One would be to treat events topic by topic, dealing with one then going back to deal with another. This method has been used by the official historians and is found in some of the personal accounts, notably Churchill's. Alternatively, events could be treated chronologically in almost day by day fashion. The latter has been chosen despite the obvious additional strain imposed upon the reader in having to follow a number of different threads simultaneously. This strain itself perhaps conveys a better idea of the daily stresses which Churchill and his colleagues had to endure, when incredible resilience was needed to overcome the dreadful depression of almost daily defeats. The strength displayed by Churchill in those everlasting grey months of 1941 and most of 1942 was greatness beyond even his performance in the black days of 1940. The records of the War Cabinet, Defence Committee and Chiefs of Staff meetings show a relentless, apparently unending series of setbacks; nor is it possible to describe the full pressure upon the Prime Minister and his Ministers – I have not dealt with the hours of discussion on Ireland or India.

Any book on the Second World War of course owes a tremendous debt to Churchill's histories. In addition, I have taken quotations from the following in my effort to link the personal experiences of those involved with the official records: Bryant's brilliant revelation of Lord Alanbrooke's thoughts and opinions in *The Turn of the Tide*; the fascinating *Diaries of Sir Alexander Cadogan*, edited by Dilks; Lord Avon's *The Reckoning*; Ismay's typically modest *Memoirs*; Kennedy's *The Business of War*; Nicolson's *Diaries and Letters*; Hull's *Memoirs*; *The White House Papers of Harry L. Hopkins*, edited by Sherwood. Details of the quotations and of other books consulted are to be found in the source lists and bibliography.

My thanks go to the staff of the Public Record Office and the London Library for their customary invaluable help. This book is dedicated to my wife Betty, as fervent but insufficient recognition that it results from my partnership with her.

BLOOD, TOIL, TEARS AND SWEAT

Dunkirk

Thick black smoke still billowed high into heavy air. Sporadic rifle-fire burst staccato from last pockets of resistance; prisoners shuffled in long lines, hands clasped above heads, or squatted on the dirty sand in sullen, silent groups. The fields, roads, dunes and streets were clogged with abandoned trucks, tanks and guns. German advance patrols were setting up gun positions and English dead were being collected. Waves lapped gently on to the beach. And everywhere the sickly stench of burning rubber, the smell which, for those British survivors now safely back across the water, would forever bring back the memory of that terrible place – Dunkirk.

Over the English Channel the remains of the British Expeditionary Force were choking the streets of coastal towns, and filling the troop trains which were to take them home for a snatched seven days of rest. The tiny station at Headcorn, Kent, with a staff of three, had to feed 145,000 soldiers; gallant members of the Women's Voluntary Service exhausted themselves washing feet, serving food and mending socks. In London, the War Office appealed for foot ointment, handkerchiefs, shaving soap, razorblades and cigarettes. The *Daily Mirror* carried a banner headline on Dunkirk: 'BLOODY MARVELLOUS.'

Also in the British capital, the emergency quarters for the War Cabinet stood prepared for the expected holocaust; this underground nerve centre spread six acres beneath Whitehall, and survivors in 'The Hole' could last a week if bombing blocked all exits. To lessen the danger from flooding – the quarters were far below the level of the Thames – rooms had high thresholds and tight-fitting doors, as in a warship. The Cabinet Room itself, where about one in ten meetings would be held, was forty feet square, austere, with ugly eighteen-inch red girders slung across the ceiling. On one wall hung a Navy League map of the threatened British Empire. The black baize Cabinet table was surrounded by tubular-metal chairs with green leather upholstery. One chair was slightly different, made from dark brown wood with rounded arms. In front of it lay a large, clean blotter and four inkwells, and a small pile of red labels boldly marked 'Action This Day'. A small card stood to one side, upon which was written Queen Victoria's declaration: 'Please understand there is no pessimism in the house and we are not interested in the possibilities of defeat: they do not exist.' Above the door were two bare bulbs, one green, one red, to show whether an air raid was in progress in the streets overhead. Behind the Prime Minister's seat was a fire bucket, into which would be tossed large, fat cigar butts, always thrown without aim, but with unerring accuracy.

'This is the room from which I will direct the war,' Winston Churchill declared. He pointed with stubby finger at his chair. 'And if the invasion takes place, that is where I shall sit. And I shall sit there until the Germans are driven back – or they carry me out dead.'

Operation 'Dynamo', the evacuation of allied troops from Dunkirk, was officially declared finished by the British Admiralty at 2.23 p.m., Tuesday, 4 June 1940. About 338,226 troops had been rescued, of whom 225,000 were British. They brought back little more than rifles, bayonets and a few machine-guns; left behind were 90,000 rifles, 2,300 guns, 120,000 vehicles, 8,000 Bren-guns and 400 anti-tank rifles, with 7,000 tons of ammunition.[1]

A complete French collapse, discreetly referred to in all British Cabinet discussion as 'a certain eventuality', seemed daily more inevitable. The Chiefs of Staff in London had already considered Britain's position should this disaster occur, and their report, discussed by the War Cabinet on 27 May when members doubted whether more than a small part of the army could be lifted from the Continent, had been exceedingly gloomy. Within a few weeks of a French defeat, they predicted Britain would be exposed to short-range concentrated attack from bases from Trondheim in Norway, to Brest in France. Britain's avoiding defeat would depend on her people's capacity to withstand air bombardment, on the continued import of food and supplies, and on her ability to resist German airborne and seaborne assault. The existing Civil Defence organization was insufficient they declared, and should the Germans succeed in gaining a foothold, the British army would be unable to drive them out. All depended on the ability of the Royal Air Force to reduce the scale of attack to a manageable size – 'the crux of the matter is air superiority'.

The Chiefs of Staff could find only minimum grounds for hope. A logical view of the British and German positions showed that the enemy had every chance of success. But the Chiefs of Staff avoided the hopeless verdict by turning with desperate faith to intangibles: '*Prima facie* Germany has most of the cards: but the real test is whether the morale of our fighting personnel and civil population will counter-balance the numerical and material advantage which Germany enjoys. We believe it will.'[2]

Winston Churchill had been Prime Minister for twenty-three days when the Dunkirk evacuation was officially ended that terrifying Tuesday. Since his takeover from Neville Chamberlain, Whitehall had been thrust to a new level of activity. Leading civil servants later described Churchill's acquisition of power: 'I doubt if there has ever been such a rapid transformation of opinion in Whitehall and of the tempo at which business was conducted,' wrote John Colville, Assistant Private Secretary at 10 Downing Street; Lord Bridges, Cabinet Secretary since 1938, agreed: 'Within a very few days of his becoming Prime Minister, the whole machinery of government was working at a pace, and with an intensity of purpose, quite unlike anything which had gone before.' 'The effect of this influence was immediate and dramatic,' added Lord Normanbrook. 'The machine responded at once to his leadership. It quickened the pace and improved the tone of administration. A new sense of urgency was created...'[3]

Upon this organizational machine depended Britain's survival. Decisions taken during these days, with so few resources spread over such a wide area, were of utmost consequence for the free world. 'In these days the War Cabinet were in a state of unusual emotion,' understated Churchill.[4] This Cabinet met under conditions of terrible strain; paperwork alone meant Ministers reading the equivalent of almost two full-scale novels each day. Only five Ministers were originally invited from all political parties to become full War Cabinet members, and the number never rose above eight. 'I can remember no case where differences arose between Conservative, Labour and Liberal along party lines,' wrote Attlee. General Ismay agreed: 'I can testify that the War Cabinet was a band of brothers.'[5] Not that tempers were always restrained; on the contrary, even the cold, unemotional official Minutes hint at heated arguments and acid comments. The Prime Minister was difficult to bridle and often impossible to comprehend fully; Lord Halifax wrote in his diary after one War Cabinet session: 'It is the most extraordinary brain, Winston's, to watch functioning that I have ever seen ... a curious mixture of a child's emotion and a man's reason.'[6] He used his Ministers as a captive audience while he talked out his thoughts, frequently appearing irrelevant, and often impatient of intervention. Attlee, who stood in for Churchill, was often considered a better chairman, but according to Bridges, the Prime Minister varied his behaviour. 'At times of crisis, when

3

big issues had to be settled promptly, Churchill was always superb and most businesslike.... But when matters on the Agenda were less important or pressing, Churchill's love of argument, and his enjoyment in following up some point ... could lead to a far longer meeting than was necessary.' To Churchill, 'such a meeting was like a good dish – something to be enjoyed and savoured and not gulped down.'[7] But the thrust-forward chin was 'a sure sign of impending conflict and of a late hour for bed', commented Oliver Lyttelton.[8]

Despite his dominance and personality, Churchill was by no means dictatorial at War Cabinet meetings: the official Minutes are not full of the Prime Minister's monologues. He had utmost respect for the constitutional position of this body, just as he had for the ultimate power of the Houses of Parliament. And he had hand-picked his team; he trusted his Ministers; collectively they would direct Britain's fight for survival. Halifax continued as Foreign Secretary, the position he had held under Chamberlain since early 1938: austere, always diplomatic and outwardly aloof, Halifax was held in high respect by the ebullient Churchill, but never became an intimate friend. The same applied to Chamberlain himself, who remained in the War Cabinet as Lord President of the Council: old conflicts were forgotten, and nobody was more sincere than Churchill in his consideration of Chamberlain during the latter's last, agonizing illness. Clement Attlee, leader of the Labour Party, joined the War Cabinet as Lord Privy Seal. Modest, concise, Attlee's business-like efficiency became well known and welcome among civil servants. Another Labour man, Arthur Greenwood, became Minister without Portfolio.

Churchill, Attlee, Halifax, Chamberlain and Greenwood – this was the inner core. Just outside the War Cabinet itself, for the moment, stood Anthony Eden, Secretary of State for War and closest of all to Churchill. With an aristocratic ease of manner, yet with strong natural reserve, he was a man of inflexible principles who often differed from Churchill – yet the Prime Minister felt that when a grave situation arose Eden and he, though perhaps many miles apart, would automatically reach the same conclusion.[9] Vying with Eden for closest intimacy with Churchill was Lord Beaverbrook, Minister of Aircraft Production, whose creeds could be discerned from the three texts displayed in his room: 'Organization is the enemy of improvization.... It is a long jump from knowing to doing.... Committees take the punch out of war.' Ernest Bevin, the tough and abrasive head of the massive Transport and General Workers' Union, and now Minister of Labour, was later to become Beaverbrook's staunch enemy in Cabinet meetings, where 'Ernie' Bevin would become so annoyed with the starchy Beaver-

4

brook that he would snatch out his false teeth and stuff them into his pocket lest he bit his tongue in temper.[10] In complete contrast was Sir John Anderson, ex-under Secretary and Treasury representative in Ireland, Chairman of the Board of Inland Revenue, Permanent Under Secretary of the Home Office, Governor of Bengal, and Lord Privy Seal under Chamberlain – in which office, as virtual Minister for Civil Defence, he had given his name to the famous shelter upon which thousands now relied to protect them from Hitler's bombs. Anderson had become Home Secretary in Chamberlain's war administration, although not in the War Cabinet, and he agreed to remain Home Secretary and Minister for Home Security under Churchill. Intensely serious and self-denying, he was nicknamed 'Pompous John' and 'Jehovah'; but he represented all the best qualities of a skilled and loyal civil servant – Churchill called him 'my automatic pilot'.

Despite Churchill's opposition to Chamberlain's Government, he had thought it expedient and wise to give 22 of the leading Ministerial posts to men who had served under his predecessor. Apart from Halifax and Anderson, these included Sir Kingsley Wood, who became Chancellor of the Exchequer, and the popular Lord Woolton, who stayed at the Ministry of Food. Sir John Simon became Lord Chancellor. Duff Cooper, who had resigned as First Lord of the Admiralty in opposition to Chamberlain, became Minister of Information. Apart from Attlee and Greenwood, other Labour members who received prominent posts included the adroit and caustic Herbert Morrison, who took over the Supply Ministry, and Hugh Dalton, Minister of Economic Warfare. Albert Alexander, the strong supporter of the Co-operative movement, succeeded Churchill as First Lord of the Admiralty, while the Liberal leader, Sir Archibald Sinclair, received the Air Ministry. Two other men, without Ministerial posts, exerted influence upon Churchill. The witty, red-haired Brendan Bräcken, who loved Churchill as a father – indeed, he let it be rumoured that he was Churchill's illegitimate son[11] – refused to become entangled in Ministerial responsibility, and caused constant apprehension among the staff at 10 Downing Street through the private confidence he enjoyed with the Prime Miniser. So, too, did Professor F. A. Lindemann – 'the Prof' – nominally adviser to Churchill on scientific matters, who used his intelligence and influence to brief the leader on matters ranging from new building to the shortage of matches, from the Russian problem to rationing, inflation, raw materials and a whole host of subjects concerned with the armed forces. Yet at this time he had no official position – and no one to answer to except Churchill.

Churchill, as Prime Minister of a Coalition Government, and as Defence Minister, had a unique position of complete authority. Through his latter appointment, conferred upon himself, he was more closely involved than Chamberlain had ever been with the supreme and equally unique military body, the Chiefs of Staff (COS) Committee. His involvement was increased through the activities of General Hastings 'Pug' Ismay, a Committee member and head of the Defence Minister's Office. With his amazing ability to smooth over clashes of temperament, 'an interpreter, one among a thousand', Ismay was to perform invaluable work during these crucial weeks. Since April 1940, a Vice-Chiefs of Staff Committee had been established to deal with much of the routine, departmental work, but the COS were still overburdened and had to attend both to urgent immediate matters and to broad future policy. Churchill entrusted these service leaders with awesome power. A later member of the Committee wrote: 'Anything which might affect the running of the war, even in the slightest degree, was referred to them for an opinion ... anyone criticizing the Chiefs of Staff, no matter how high his position, was likely to find the Prime Minister's heavy guns turned against him.'[12] Churchill himself exercised restraint towards the COS. 'Not once during the whole war,' wrote Ismay, 'did he overrule his military advisers on a purely military question.'[13]

Service Chairman of the Committee was Admiral of the Fleet Sir Dudley Pound, imperturbable and brave, but suffering from a brain tumour which was to kill him. His illness was unknown to his colleagues, who privately and with later regrets ridiculed his symptomatic sleepiness. 'He looked,' said one, 'like an old parrot asleep on his perch.'[14] Yet the Admiral was the only member of the Committee responsible both for operational control of his own service and its actual direction in battle; after a hard day of conferences and top-level decisions, he had to return to the Admiralty to supervise the hourly struggle against enemy warships. At most, he snatched moments of sleep on a camp-bed near the War Room. Sir Cyril Newall, soon to be succeeded by Sir Charles Portal, was Chief of Air Staff, and the remaining Committee member had only recently arrived: at the end of May, General Sir John Dill had taken over as Chief of the Imperial General Staff (CIGS) from General Sir Edmund Ironside, now C-in-C, Home Forces. Dill, modest, unassuming, was to experience a steadily deteriorating working relationship with Churchill, and was soon to suffer terrible personal sadness. Beneath the COS Committee were the Joint-Planning Sub-Committee, which also reported direct to the War Cabinet. Churchill frequently seemed unable to establish agreement with this sub-committee, and referred to it as 'the whole

machinery of negation'; according to Sir Ian Jacob, 'so often...
they produced papers which proved conclusively that what he
wanted to do was out of the question.'[15]

As a further link between the COS and War Cabinet, Churchill
had established the Defence Committee, which replaced the Military Co-ordination Committee. This group was itself split into two,
one dealing with Operations, the other with Supply, the first of
which had greater predominance. Composition of the Defence
Committee (Operations) varied, but always included the Deputy
Prime Minister, and the three Service Ministers – who were not
members of the War Cabinet, and who were now mainly occupied
with organization and administration, although still responsible to
Parliament for all business of their departments. When Anthony
Eden left the War Office and returned to the Foreign Office, he
remained a member of the Defence Committee. Meetings were
always attended by the COS.

The COS Committee usually met at about 10 a.m., ready to
present papers to the War Cabinet meeting at about noon. The
Defence Committee usually gathered in the afternoons or late
evenings, although the number of sessions fell in 1942. From 10
May until the end of 1940, 52 meetings of the Defence Committee
were held, 322 of the Chiefs of Staff, and 196 of the War Cabinet.
Figures for the first six months of 1941 were respectively, 44, 229
and 64. Frequency varied according to the state of affairs.

And now this colourful mixture of types, classes, parties, politicians, servicemen, and civil servants, had to merge into a team
capable of successfully conducting the war effort. This direction
at this crucial time could not even be aimed at overthrowing
Hitler; instead it had to concentrate on the more immediate,
infinitely more desperate task of finding a way to prevent Britain's
own destruction. Plans had to be prepared, dispositions made, in
an unreal, murky atmosphere. Uncertainty prevailed. The West
had been completely surprised by the spectacular German
successes in Scandinavia and the Low Countries; German planning
and execution had proved superb – would they continue to be so
deadly? What were Hitler's next moves – and what weapons, perhaps so far secret, would be used? From which direction would
the assault on Britain be launched – through neutral Eire, against
Scotland, or the South-East? Too few troops existed and insufficient
arms were available, to guard against all contingencies. Time would
probably be too short to undertake fully those preparations which
were possible.

The weather in those early June days persisted in its perverse
beauty. Sunsets were crimson and gold, each dawn promised an
even better day. Temperatures tipped 90 degrees and England had

never looked more lovely. But the sense of foreboding mingled with the scent in the light summer air; and Ministers went uneasily to War Cabinet meetings, fearful of news which might be revealed.

The Battle for France

The War Cabinet's most urgent and painful problem was the question of aid to France, intimately bound to Britain's own survival. How much of Britain's precious and inadequate strength could be sent to help her ally? The dilemma was constantly voiced of whether the battle of France was the decisive clash and, therefore, all efforts and all sacrifices should be made to succour the French, or whether the expected invasion of Britain would be the operation to give Hitler ultimate victory or deal him utter defeat. If the latter were true, then nothing could be spared for France which would help Britain; if France were lost, she would be restored when Nazi swords had been broken against Britain's island defences.

The War Cabinet meeting of Monday, 3 June, the day before the Dunkirk operation officially ended, saw the most agonizing discussion of all on this issue. Another desperate appeal had come from Paris for more troops and more aircraft. The COS had hurriedly prepared a report on further assistance Britain could give, and recommended sending two divisions. Churchill told the War Cabinet that 'his personal view was that the proposed assistance was not sufficient.... We should promise to send a third division, provided that the French could supply the artillery for it.' Attlee asked whether simultaneous attack on both France and Britain could be ruled out; Newall and Dill thought dual attack possible but not likely. The Germans would probably attempt first to knock out France. Chamberlain saw a possible compromise: a third division could not anyway be sent immediately: 'The whole situation may have changed considerably by the end of the next three or four weeks.... There is no harm in promising to send a third division.' In the event, Chamberlain was correct: by the time the third division could be assembled and embarked, all would be finished.

The War Cabinet, at this meeting, then turned to the more immediate question of air support. Britain herself was desperately

Map 1. Europe, Scandinavia and Russia

short of fighters, all of which would soon be urgently required, and Newall stressed that the British position had been seriously weakened by the German success in the Low Countries. 'Our fighter defences were organized to meet the bomber threat on the United Kingdom from bases in Germany, and are inadequate to meet short range bomber attack accompanied by fighters.' Germany could achieve this from newly acquired airfields in Belgium. He added that against the advice of Dowding, C-in-C Fighter Command, Britain had sent to France, in addition to squadrons of the original commitment, 'first four squadrons (64 aircraft), then eight flights (48 aircraft), then 32 aircraft from the first line at home, making a total of 144 aircraft to operate "for a few days", in addition to six squadrons which had been ordered to operate in relays over France and Belgium at an early stage of the battle.' Dowding was at this meeting and now produced a graph to illustrate the Hurricane aircraft wastage in the ten days 8-18 May, when intensive operations had been carried out against the initial German advance. A total of 250 Hurricanes had been lost – 25 a day, against only four a day received from production.

There is sharp conflict between this official account of Dowding's plea that no more fighters be spared, and his official biographer's, containing Dowding's own comments. In this, the date for the dramatic intervention is given as 15 May, not 3 June. Dowding therefore claims he made his plea soon after the German offensive had begun; his graph warning was thus infinitely more grim, because it referred to future wastages, should losses be allowed to bleed away Britain's fighter strength. 'I said: "If the present rate of wastage continues for another fortnight we shall not have a single Hurricane left in France or in this country." '[1] The Minutes for 15 May make no mention of any graph; clearly, 3 June, three weeks later, the Air Marshal made his case. According to the Minutes for this meeting, Dowding declared 'had this rate of wastage continued throughout May, we should have expended all our Hurricanes by the end of May'. He referred to a past not future situation, and in fact the high wastage of 8-18 May had subsequently dropped. The graph had therefore far less impact than claimed in the biography. Evidence that his figures were outdated came in answer to a Minister's question: Hurricanes were still left. 'The number of fighters serviceable on 2 June,' said Dowding, 'was 244 Hurricanes and 280 Spitfires,' although he added that 'a number of pilots now in fighter squadrons had not yet done their first solo on 8-gun fighters, and it would take some six weeks before they were sufficiently proficient to take part in active operations'.

In Dowding's account, the graph is the most prominent presentation of Fighter Command's weakness. The official account proves it far less important than a verbal statement also made by Dowding: 'That very day,' the Minutes record him as saying, 'the last of three squadrons of Fighter Command which had not yet been engaged in the battle, were being withdrawn from Scotland to take part in the operations.... If the enemy developed a heavy air attack on this country at this moment, he could not guarantee air superiority for more than 48 hours.'[2] This was indeed stern, despite Newall's view that immediate German air attack was unlikely.

Yet the discrepancy between Dowding's later account and the official Minutes remains important, and not merely because it shows the biography to be inaccurate. It helps reveal the way in which issues, later black-and-white, were then clouded by uncertainties, conditions, vague predictions. Moreover, in the biography Churchill is taken to task for not having referred, in his memoirs, to Dowding's 15 May presentation. 'He made no mention of the appearance of Dowding before the Cabinet, of Dowding's statement....'[3] In fact, while giving no specific dates, Churchill gives Dowding considerable credit when he refers to events in early June; and this weakens Dowding's claim that his appeal angered Churchill and contributed to his ultimate fall from favour. 'After the meeting of 15 May there was no chance of our ever becoming friendly. I had opposed him and he had had to change his very stubborn mind.... I've always felt that he didn't like it.'[4]

The allegation is also made that although the War Cabinet decided not to send more fighters, Churchill personally reversed this decision immediately afterwards. Sir Ian Jacob, Military Assistant Secretary to the War Cabinet, seems to support this claim, while giving no specific dates, and his words are quoted in the biography: 'The Prime Minister then went out into the garden with a few others, and second thoughts prevailed. The decision was reversed, and I think it was decided to send four squadrons.' The allegation, if true, would show Churchill to have disregarded War Cabinet authority and procedure; as Sir Ian Jacob commented: 'The scene is clearly stamped on my memory, more so than the actual decision, but I believe it was the only occasion in the whole war on which, a firm decision having been reached, the Prime Minister changed his mind.'[5]

Sir Ian's recollections were inaccurate. The War Cabinet Minutes show that a firm decision had not been reached at the 3 June meeting – discussion continued next day. Churchill did not therefore reverse any conclusion. Four more squadrons were indeed allocated to help the French, but not until two days later, under certain restrictive conditions and after more War Cabinet meetings – and after further French appeals and more momentous events.

* * *

Paul Reynaud, the French Premier, sent for the British Ambassador on the morning of 4 June; Sir Ronald Campbell was handed a letter from General Weygand, in support of an appeal from General Joseph Vuillemin, head of the French Air Force, for the immediate despatch of 10 more RAF fighter squadrons, and of a further 10 as soon as possible. All these aircraft were to be based in France. The Ambassador hastily conferred with General Edward Spears, military liaison officer sent by Churchill to Paris, and told Reynaud that the request put the British Government in an impossible position. How, he asked the French leader, would you react if the situation were reversed? Would any French Government act in the way Britain was now asked to do? Reynaud insisted that the coming battle would decide the war, and strong British aircraft reinforcements would make the difference between victory and defeat.[6] An account of this conversation had still to reach London when the War Cabinet met at 11.30 a.m., when discussion on air support for France continued. The meeting opened with the latest situation report, read by Dill: the final measures of French evacuation from Dunkirk had been carried out the preceding night; 'no further operations have taken place'; about 20,700 troops, mainly French, remained unaccounted for. A message had come from the French Admiral, Abriel, which had been read to the COS Committee just before the War Cabinet meeting. 'Last night's evacuation was most successful. English were magnificent.'[7] Churchill now told Ministers that Britain could not refuse to maintain in France the same number of squadrons as before the last battle started, while keeping a larger number of squadrons than ever in Britain. 'At one time ... we had been down to 29 fighter squadrons in the air defence of Great Britain, whereas we now had about 45. According to Beaverbrook's figures, we now had more aircraft available in this country than we had had before the German invasion of the Low Countries began. We could never keep all that we wanted for our own defence while the French were fighting for their lives.' Beaverbrook told the War Cabinet that he hoped to keep up a rate of production of 400 aircraft of all types a week, at least throughout June.

But Sinclair, Air Secretary, pointed out that although the total number of fighter aircraft now available might be 'slightly' greater than on 10 May, overall efficiency was very much less. 'Owing to the very heavy losses which our fighters had sustained squadrons were now greatly disorganized, and many of the leaders had been lost.' Sinclair continued: 'The strength of the fighter forces in this country had been originally fixed at 56, on the assumption that the Germans would not be in possession of the Low Countries. We were now down to 45 squadrons, with the enemy in possession of all the Channel ports, even if we did not send any additional squadrons to France.' To make good losses in pilots, the two existing operational training units would have to be enlarged and another created, all of which required more aircraft. A somewhat negative compromise was reached after long discussion; a telegram was sent to Spears for Reynaud, which read in part, '... as regards fighters, the three squadrons now in France were being brought up to strength immediately. In view of the very serious losses of the last three weeks it must take some little time to overhaul our squadrons, seek to replace our losses, and determine what further help we can send and when....'[8]

Parliament reassembled during the day; immediately after the War Cabinet meeting finished Churchill completed preparations for a major policy speech, dictating, revising, breaking down the structure into pauses and points on the exact lines that the sentences would be delivered. He intended to cover a number of important topics, from the need to guard against hostile aliens in Britain, to the situation in France, and the need for an offensive spirit. This latter topic was the subject of a Minute to Ismay for the COS. 'We are greatly concerned – and it is certainly wise to be so – with the dangers of the Germans landing in England.... But if it is so easy for the Germans to invade us ... why should it be thought impossible for us to do anything of the same kind to them? The completely defensive habit of mind which has ruined the French must not be allowed to ruin all our initiative.'[9] From this Minute, at such a time of peril, originated the cross-Channel operations aimed at harassing the enemy – and which provided valuable lessons for the eventual Normandy landings.

Anxious MPs gathered in the lofty House of Commons Chamber. Churchill walked slowly in, sat hunched on the Front Bench, displayed hints of nervousness as he twisted his fingers, shuffled his papers, and abruptly stooped to pick scraps of paper from the floor. His apprehension was unfounded; he rose to make perhaps the greatest speech of his war career. He began his delivery at a slow, measured pace. He came to his description of Dunkirk: 'We must be very careful not to assign to this deliverance the attribute of a victory. Wars are not won by evacuation.' Churchill had heard reports of some soldiers saved from Dunkirk criticizing the apparent lack of protection from air attack; the RAF had seemed absent from the skies above the beaches. But Churchill knew how desperately and bloodily the RAF had been engaged. 'There was a victory inside this deliverance which should be noted. It was gained by the Air Force. Many of our soldiers coming back have not seen the Air Force at work; they saw only the bombers which escaped its protective attack. They underrate its achievement.' Then,

15

prophetically and perhaps mindful of the War Cabinet discussions three hours before, Churchill added: 'I will pay my tribute to these young airmen. The great French Army was very largely, for the time being, cast back and disturbed by the onrush of a few thousands of armoured vehicles. May it not also be that the cause of civilization itself will be defended by the skill and devotion of a few thousand airmen?' The speech was intended to declare not only to the British people, but to the world – and especially France and America – that Britain would continue the struggle, if necessary alone. In his memoirs Churchill stressed that the possibility of Britain seeking peace was never considered in the War Cabinet, and the official Minutes now support this boast. But others might have doubted Britain's resolve, and Churchill intended to make clear the country's determination. First, he added a light touch to emphasize the magnificent peroration to follow. 'When Napoleon lay at Boulougne ... he was told: "There are bitter weeds in England." There are certainly a great many more of them since the British Expeditionary Force returned.' And then came the mighty, resounding climax. 'Even though large tracts of Europe and many old and famous States have fallen or may fall into the grip of the Gestapo and all the odious apparatus of Nazi rule, we shall not flag or fail. We shall go on to the end. ... We shall fight on the beaches, we shall fight on the landing grounds, we shall fight in the fields and in the streets, we shall fight in the hills; we shall never surrender, and even if, which I do not for a moment believe, this island or a large part of it were subjugated and starving, then our Empire beyond the seas, armed and guarded by the British Fleet, would carry on the struggle, until, in God's time, the new world, with all its power and might, steps forth to the rescue and the liberation of the old.'[10]

The speech was broadcast during the evening, with an announcer reading Churchill's text. Such was the impact, and so famous did the speech become, that many listeners were later convinced they had heard Churchill deliver the words over the radio. It mattered little; the speech united Prime Minister and people – 'Winston' entered British homes. His words excited the free world, as intended, although the French Embassy in London criticized his 'tactical error' in stressing Britain's determination to fight alone. 'This is not exactly encouraging the French to fight on against fearful odds.'[11]

Discreet discussions had been taking place at the Foreign Office of which the French were kept strictly uninformed. These talks centred on the situation should France collapse, and especially on the future of the powerful French Fleet. France had the second greatest navy in the world and a constant fear – to become increasingly predominant – was the danger that a combined German-

French naval power would sweep the Royal Navy, upon which Great Britain so desperately depended, completely from the surface of the seas. The British Ambassador at Paris had been asked for his opinion on 3 June and he now replied on the 4th. If France collapsed, the French air force would have practically ceased to exist and would not therefore be of any use to Britain; he thought the Germans would demand the surrender of the fleet, and the French Government might agree. The only way to avoid this would be to persuade Admiral Darlan, Commander of the French Navy, to order the whole fleet to British waters in defiance of his Government.[12] Next day, Campbell cabled another gloomy assessment; he did not believe the French could hold the Germans; it was necessary to be ready for the worst 'more quickly than we expect'.[13]

Just after noon that day, Churchill opened the War Cabinet meeting. 'A German attack has been launched this morning on a seventy-mile front, extending from Amiens to the Laon-Choissons road.' Dill, CIGS, added that the Germans appeared to be making a push for Paris. The next stage of the German offensive had begun – and the French need for air help was immediately even more urgent. At 3.45 p.m. the COS were hastily gathered to consider the latest situation: in the short time since the War Cabinet meeting two telegrams had arrived from General Spears, which the Chiefs of Staff now considered. The first telegram read: 'Reply from M. Paul Reynaud to Mr Winston Churchill's message of 4 June. (1) Despatch of British divisions. General Weygand's opinion is that if no way can be found of keeping the battle going, there are grave risks that it will be lost.... You tell me [Reynaud] that the first division will only embark seven days from now. A further eight days will be taken up between this disembarkation and the date on which it could be used on the front. Even this first division is therefore likely to arrive too late.... (2) Fighter Aircraft. You tell me in view of the heavy losses sustained by the British fighter strength you are only in the position at the moment to re-equip the three squadrons at present in France. You thus reject the request put forward on 3 June and forwarded by me yesterday, 4 June ... to the effect that there should be despatched to France (i) immediately, ten squadrons of fighters, (ii) as soon as possible, ten further squadrons. These 20 squadrons representing one-half of the total fighter strength based in the United Kingdom. I cannot believe that your decision will be adhered to in the presence of the new factor of the German offensive.' The second telegram, from General Spears, was even more desperate. 'Following was handed by Weygand to Reynaud as he entered the Council Room. Begins: "The Commander-in-Chief is compelled to record that the appeals addressed to the British Government have remained fruitless. We are now facing the

German attack without having received any further support from England. No fighter aircraft and no fresh divisions." ' The COS therefore agreed that Dill should draw up a programme showing the rate at which troops already promised could be sent to France and, as a further aid to War Cabinet discussion, Newall would draw up a programme showing how many squadrons would have to be amalgamated to send up to four to France.[14]

French pressure was now infinitely harder to bear; and unknown to the Prime Minister the American Ambassador at Paris, William C. Bullitt, had already sent a highly adverse comment to Washington on Britain's apparent lack of co-operation. He feared 'the British might be conserving their Air Force and Fleet so as to use them as bargaining points in negotiations with Hitler'. But if Bullitt had not taken note of Churchill's 4 June speech, President Roosevelt fortunately, had. Cordell Hull, US Secretary of State, wrote later: 'France was finished, but we were convinced that Britain, under Churchill's indomitable leadership, intended to fight on.... Only the day before Bullitt's telegram Churchill had made his magnificent speech.'[15]

At 10.35 p.m. a cable was received at the Foreign Office from Sir Ronald Campbell and immediately shown to the Prime Minister. 'M. Reynaud, when I saw him this evening, told me that Marshall Pétain, on learning of the Prime Minister's reply to the latest French appeal for further help in the air exclaimed, "Well, there is nothing left but to make peace. If you do not want to do it you can hand over to me." M. Reynaud had of course scouted the idea and said he only mentioned it to me to show how grave the situation was. He asked whether I thought that His Majesty's Government completely realized it. I said that I was quite certain they did and that they were going, and would continue to go, as far as was *possible*. If they denuded the British Isles of all their air defences on the eve of invasion by all of the enemies' devices they would incur an unforgiveable responsibility.' The Ambassador added: 'I am deeply distressed by the reiteration of these appeals at a time when I know you are doing all you can, but the very grave danger in which the French stand in this hour must be their excuse.'[16]

Churchill had already decided to offer more to the French; his decision early this evening, 5 June, was the one Sir Ian Jacob must have mistakenly remembered as following the War Cabinet meeting two days before. It followed repeated appeals from Paris, when, because of this new German push towards the French capital, an immediate air offensive against Britain was even less likely. In addition to the nine squadrons of all types in France, Britain would now make available four squadrons of day bombers and two of Hurricane fighters. But these would be committed only on a day-by-day

18

basis and would fly from British airfields, in order to have them ready at hand in case of British need. This offer, sent at 5.35 p.m. after the COS meeting, was addressed to Reynaud and Weygand, and the telegram included some sharp comments in answer to French criticisms. 'Permit me to observe that your divisions picked out at Dunkirk are not to enter the line for a month. We are trying to send one of our seasoned divisions in a fortnight.... You don't seem to understand at all that British fighter aviation has been worn to a shred and frightfully mixed up by the need of maintaining a standing patrol of 48 fighters over Dunkirk, without which evacuation would have been impossible.'[17]

Church bells rang in Berlin next morning, Thursday, 6 June, and swastikas were unfurled at Hitler's orders, to celebrate the Flanders victory. Berliners seemed unimpressed. At 10 Downing Street, Churchill had a busy morning in bed, dictating, as normal, countless Minutes while dressed in a flamboyant robe and surrounded by papers, breakfast dishes, champagne glasses and cigar butts. Notes were addressed to the Minister of Supply, Herbert Morrison, to Beaverbrook, the Admiralty, War Office, COS and Halifax. The multitude of Minutes having been sent, the Prime Minister dressed for the War Cabinet meeting at 12.30, where he informed Ministers of the telegrams received the previous day from Paris, and of his latest limited offer to Reynaud. Ministers agreed with his decision. The War Cabinet heard that the French appeared to be fighting better than expected: German armoured formations had penetrated in some places to a depth of 10 or 12 miles between Anizy and the mouth of the Somme but, Dill commented, the French strongholds seemed to be holding out. 'Generally speaking, the position seemed more satisfactory than we had expected'; however, the CIGS warned that there were no signs as yet of large enemy armoured formations. 'The enemy was probably testing the strength of the front all along before launching his main attack.' Churchill reported that General Spears believed an improvement had occurred in 'the tone of the French command, which seemed to be gaining more confidence. If the fighting developed into old style infantry battles the Germans might not relish the prospect of pressing home their attacks.'[18]

British air help on a day-to-day basis would continue, said a message sent early that evening to Reynaud. Considerable bomber sorties would also be maintained during the night on objectives specified by the French High Command.[19] But the brief flare of optimism began to fade. Campbell, in a cable sent next morning, 7 June, doubted the French would hold up the Germans long enough to change the military situation. Although the French Army was fighting magnificently, he said, the French High Command continued to be greatly depressed, from Weygand downwards, by

divisions.'[26] The German advance in this area was also the subject of a pessimistic discussion in Paris, at the same time that the War Cabinet met in 10 Downing Street. Immediately after the conference Reynaud saw Campbell and revealed he had 'won the day' by obtaining a decision that the French would struggle as long as anything remained with which to fight. 'There had been a moment when he had been alone in feeling like that.' Together with this sombre warning, Reynaud gave the Ambassador a message for Churchill, which was cabled at 2 p.m. 'Rouen and Le Havre are definitely threatened, and with them the supplies for Paris and for half of the army. I thank you for your effort, but the situation calls for a greater one.... I feel bound to ask you to throw all your forces into the battle as we are doing.'[27] The Defence Committee met at 10 Downing Street immediately this fresh appeal reached London. 'Two alternatives are open to us,' explained Churchill. 'We could regard the present battle as decisive for France and ourselves, and throw in the whole of our fighter resources in an attempt to save the situation and bring about victory. If we failed, we should then have to surrender. Alternatively, we should recognize that whereas the present land battle is of great importance, it will not be decisive one way or the other for Great Britain.... One thing is certain. If this country were defeated, the war would be lost for France no less than for ourselves, whereas, provided we are strong ourselves, we could win the war and, in so doing, restore France.' Churchill therefore judged it fatal to yield to French demands to the detriment of Britain's own safety. There was unanimous agreement. A telegram was drafted to Reynaud, that it would be a great strategic blunder to throw away, in a battle depending mainly on troops and tanks, the force with which Britain hoped to break the *Luftwaffe* when invasion was attempted. But this communication was reconsidered at the close of the meeting and, a milder message substituted, despatched at 9.30 p.m. 'We are giving you all the support we can in this great battle short of ruining the capacity of this country to continue the war. We have had very heavy and disproportionate loss in the air today but we shall continue tomorrow.'[28]

Deadlock now existed between Paris and London and tightened dangerously during Sunday, 9 June. The German advance accelerated and the French IX Corps and British 51st Division were threatened by an east encircling movement. Reports reaching London were confused. At that time, full implications of the danger to the British troops do not seem to have been appreciated, but Churchill realized he would soon have to visit Paris to clarify the general situation – he mentioned to Eden during this Sunday that he wanted the War Secretary to accompany him.[29] The War Cabinet

22

did not meet until 7 p.m. when Ministers were told that a battle was in progress along the whole Western Front, and the French were again appealing for air support. Churchill described a conversation he had had during the afternoon with General Charles de Gaulle, who had arrived in London earlier in the day. Four days before Reynaud had made this young officer Under-Secretary of State for National Defence, but at this time the General was unknown in London: Cadogan had confided to Foreign Office colleagues: 'I can't tell you anything about de Gaulle, except that he's got a head like a pineapple and hips like a woman.'[30] Churchill now told the War Cabinet that de Gaulle had given a 'more favourable impression of French determination and morale', and had urged further British Divisions should be sent as rapidly as possible. Churchill said he had outlined plans to de Gaulle and had also explained why Britain could not engage the whole of the RAF in the battle; de Gaulle had replied that speaking for himself 'he agreed with our policy'.[31]

Reynaud, in a message received during the afternoon, also urged British reinforcements should be sent as soon as possible; Churchill replied at 11.40 p.m. – British forces were giving maximum support and the RAF had been continuously engaged. Fresh forces had landed in France during the last few days; further reinforcements were being organized and would shortly be available.[32] Yet by now he was fully aware that these troops would arrive too late; their despatch was more of a diplomatic than a military gesture. During the day he had replied to a telegram from the South African leader, General Smuts, urging all possible forces should be concentrated at the decisive point – in France. Churchill disagreed. 'I see only one sure way through now, to wit, that Hitler should attack this country and in so doing break his air weapon. If this happens he will be left to face the winter with Europe writhing under his heel, and probably with the United States against him after the Presidential election is over.'[33]

News from another European capital – Rome – suddenly deteriorated. Late on Sunday night, 9 June, a telegram arrived from Sir Percy Loraine, the British Ambassador: Ciano, the Italian Foreign Minister, had told the French Ambassador that the 'die was cast'. The Allied Ambassadors would probably be leaving on 11 or 12 June after an Italian declaration of war.[34] Italy clearly wished to be present to pick at the French carcass.

'The 10th of June was a ghastly day,' wrote Ismay. The weather suddenly switched from blazing sun to lowering, leadened skies; lights burnt in Whitehall offices throughout the day. This Monday began with a long meeting of the Defence Committee, at which the Minister of Information revealed that a very strong broadcast

23

offensive had been launched by the Germans, backed by the Italians, with the object of convincing the French now was the time to make peace, as they had been led astray by the British – who were not giving support. Certain French circles, commented Churchill, felt Britain had given inadequate land support, and had only paid attention to rescuing her own army from Dunkirk. 'We, on the other hand, have some reason to feel that matters have not been very well handled by the French; and that recent events on the left flank in France have been a repetition of what occurred in Flanders. It is nevertheless essential that nothing should be said here which might be construed as criticism.' General Ironside, Commander of Home Forces, informed the Defence Committee of progress made in anti-invasion measures and in doing so revealed serious deficiencies. A complete system of coast-watching had been instituted, with communications to divisional headquarters; 32,000 men were allotted to holding positions in places where ground could not be lost to the enemy; 'very rapid progress' was being made in the preparation of beach defensives. Next in the defensive system came the field force, for which 15 divisions were available: these troops were organized in brigade groups to act as mobile columns to strike the enemy wherever he might land. The arming of these divisions with rifles, bren-guns, anti-tank rifles and armoured carriers was on the whole fairly complete. 'There are, however, two chief weaknesses. First, the men in these divisions are not yet adequately trained for attack.... Second, there is a great shortage of artillery and anti-tank weapons.' Static defences and protection of vital points would be the responsibility of 33,000 troops of the Home Defence Battalions and 471,000 men of the Local Defence Volunteers – soon to be called the Home Guard. But, General Ironside confessed, the latter only had about 100,000 rifles, less than one for every four men: the remainder would have to make do with 80,000 shot-guns. To help make up this gross deficiency 75,000 Ross rifles were being brought from Canada and one million 'Molotov' cocktails were being issued against tanks.[35] At this time, according to the Defence Committee (Supply), Britain only had 103 cruiser and 114 infantry tanks in the United Kingdom.[36]

At Monday lunchtime Campbell received the disconcerting news that the French Government intended to flee from Paris; the Foreign Ministry would evacuate the capital at 3 p.m. The British Ambassador decided to go with the Government and to hand over the care of the Embassy to his American colleague: his staff hurriedly crammed suitcases and burnt secret cyphers. Yet he still retained some optimism: he telegraphed that he was more satisfied with the general situation than he had expected; although the Germans had made progress on the previous day, 9 June, the French seemed to be fighting better than had been believed possible and wanted to continue to a finish. Reynaud had ordered defence lines to be prepared in Brittany, added the Ambassador, and Weygand was now 'calm and resolute'.[37] This same shadowy optimism was reflected in War Cabinet discussions at 10 Downing Street, starting at 12.30 p.m. before this latest news from Campbell had been received. Dill reported that the German attack in the Rheims area had only succeeded in establishing two bridgeheads south of the river Aisne. 'Generally speaking, the French High Command was reasonably satisfied with this situation ... although the position was undoubtedly serious, there was not much enemy progress reported.' But far more serious was the situation in the Seine sector. 'Our own 51st Division, with two other French Divisions, had been ordered to retire on Le Havre. The two French Divisions, which were equipped with horsed transport, were making slow progress.' The CIGS summed up: 'The French army might be said to be still holding the German attack. The real anxiety lay in whether the French had adequate reserves to stem the German advance. On the other hand the strain on the German communications, which were now very long, must be very great indeed, and was undoubtedly increased by our air operations.' Churchill said he had considered whether he should go to Paris at once to attend an early meeting of the Supreme War Council; but, he went on, if he went to Paris now the French would press Britain to give fighter help beyond that which she could agree to. Churchill therefore favoured sending a personal message to Reynaud, and the War Cabinet agreed.[38]

But, soon after the War Cabinet meeting, the telegram from Campbell arrived – and Churchill read to his consternation that the French Government would no longer be in Paris anyway; he immediately changed his mind about not seeing Reynaud and signalled a request for a meeting. Meanwhile, the French leader despatched an urgent appeal to Roosevelt, seeking a public announcement by the President that America would give France all possible moral and material aid short of sending an expeditionary force. France would fight on, insisted Reynaud, if necessary from North Africa or from French possessions in America.

Then, late on this Monday afternoon, came the expected Italian decision. A cable reached Whitehall from Loraine at 5.58 p.m.: just over an hour before he had been told by Ciano that the King of Italy would consider himself in a state of war with Britain as from midnight on 11 June. A similar communication had been made to the French Ambassador. Sir Percy sent a further message at 7 p.m.: in answer to a question, the Italian Foreign Minister had informed him the communication was the actual declaration of war, not a preliminary to such a declaration.[39] In his diary, Ciano described the British Ambassador's reaction as 'laconic and inscrutable. He received my communication without batting an eyelid or changing colour ... he withdrew with dignity and courtesy. At the door we exchanged a long and cordial handshake.'[40] The Italian Minister made no mention in his journal of Sir Percy's supposed exit-line: 'I have the honour to remind Your Excellency that England is not in the habit of losing her wars.' Mussolini appeared on the balcony of the Palazzo Venezia to announce the news of war to a bewildered Roman crowd. Ciano moaned: 'I am sad, very sad. The adventure begins. May God help Italy.'[41]

As Loraine was preparing to quit Rome, Campbell was leaving Paris for Touraine. He reached the Château de Champchevrier at Cléré next morning, 11 June, at 4 a.m. Meanwhile, Reynaud had replied to Churchill's plea for a meeting; the French leader discouraged the idea on the grounds that he was visiting the Front. Churchill immediately sent another urgent telegram renewing his request. The British Prime Minister then walked to the Admiralty War Room; the time was about midnight; Churchill, sitting with a group of officers in the smoky, tense atmosphere, listened to a broadcast by Roosevelt speaking at Charlottesville. The American President promised 'to extend to the opponents of force the material resources of this nation'. Production would be increased in the United States so that 'we in the Americas may have equipment and training equal to the task of any emergency and every defence'. Churchill wrote: 'When he uttered the scathing words about Italy, "on this 10th day of June, 1940, the hand that held the dagger has struck it into the back of its neighbour", there was a deep growl of satisfaction.' Roosevelt, with the presidential elections five months away, had gone as far as he could. Before going to bed Churchill sent a note of thanks – in which he also appealed for 'the 30 or 40 old destroyers you have already had reconditioned.... The next six months are vital.'[42]

Within hours, Italy began her war operations. Pound told the COS at 10 o'clock next morning, 11 June: 'Malta was bombed at 05.00 hours.' This appeared to be the first act of aggression in the Mediterranean area, he added, and Turkey would now probably enter the war on the British side, in implementation of the Anglo-Turkish Treaty – an assumption soon proved incorrect. While the COS meeting was continuing a message was brought in from the French High Command. 'Compelling needs in the south-east oblige us at once to modify our air dispositions and lead me to request the co-operation of British air forces, amounting to six fighter squadrons.... May I stress that the giving of this aid be urgent.' A copy of the message was immediately taken to the Prime Minister. The COS then discussed the danger to the Channel Islands from the renewed German advance, and decided two infantry battalions should be sent immediately.[43]

Militarily, the situation in France was becoming hourly more desperate. British forces from the 51st Division had been separated by a German thrust from the south-east: some were being evacuated from Le Havre, while others had fallen back after sharp fighting to the perimeter of St Valéry, also to seek safety from the sea. Politically, the French Government and administration was rapidly slipping into complete confusion. Owing to fear of air attack, departments were dispersed over a wide area of Touraine, and telephonic links were chaotic. During the morning Campbell managed to see Baudouin, Under-Secretary for Foreign Affairs, but the latter said he had had no news since leaving Paris the previous afternoon. Reynaud was at Weygand's HQ 100 miles away. Sir Ronald believed many top French officials only considered the move to Tours had been the first stage, and a further evacuation would soon take place to Bordeaux or Brittany. At the Foreign Office in London, where officials anxiously awaited scraps of information from Campbell, a report was being prepared on 'the considerations which arose and the demands we should make' if France collapsed. Churchill, in requesting the memorandum, had stated: 'There is, I think, no need to anticipate an immediate collapse, but the matter must be watched.' Within three hours, the report had been completed: Britain should attempt to persuade the French Government to take refuge outside France, and, if this was successful, no difficulty would be experienced in securing the transfer of the French fleet to colonial or British ports. But if the French asked the enemy for an armistice, the Germans would almost certainly demand the handover of the fleet; if the French refused this, they might be exposed to great sufferings until the fleet was surrendered. Britain's best policy would be to urge the sinking of the fleet before an armistice request was made.[44] The COS, in another report, came to a similar conclusion, and also stressed the great dangers of allowing the French fleet to fall into German control.[45]

The War Cabinet met at 12.30 p.m. The Prime Minister revealed that, 90 minutes before, a reply had been received from his second request to Reynaud for an early meeting – the French leader now agreed and a conference had been fixed for 6 p.m.; Churchill told the War Cabinet: 'We shall have to concert with them a grand strategic plan for the future conduct of the war and find out what their intentions are.'[46] At 2 p.m. Churchill was driven to Hendon airfield, with the Foreign Office report in his briefcase, concerning the French fleet. The Prime Minister, Eden, Dill and Ismay – the last in defiance of Churchill's instructions – boarded a flimsy Flamingo aircraft which, later in the war, was to explode over

London and kill all the senior Russian officials who were passengers.

The yellow Flamingo lifted into unbroken blue sky. Below, the colours of the English countryside seemed unnaturally bright in the brilliant June sun. Escorted by 12 droning Hurricanes, whose use made Eden feel 'almost ashamed', the Prime Minister soon crossed the water separating Britain from her enemy, then travelled on over the flat, wide fields of tortured France. Paul Reynaud had agreed to meet Churchill at Briare on the Loire, about 60 miles east of Orleans, and the Flamingo landed at a small, rough airfield covered with a confusion of dismembered aircraft. Churchill clambered on to French soil for the fourth time since taking office exactly one month before. The reception at the airstrip was depressing and ominous, but the atmosphere slightly improved at the small château where talks began at 7 p.m. 'There were no reproaches or recriminations,' wrote Churchill. 'We were all up against brute facts.'[47] To and fro discussions, to be described by the Prime Minister to the War Cabinet next day, lasted until 9 p.m.

During the night, while Churchill slept in the French château, thick sea mist swirled around the small port of St Valéry, 200 miles to the north. Trapped British troops, awaiting evacuation, could not be lifted to safety; by the early morning of Wednesday, 12 June, Germans had reached the cliffs and opened direct fire upon the beaches. At 10.30 a.m., as Churchill and Reynaud were starting another session of talks, the remains of the British 51st Division were forced to surrender. Over 8,000 Highland troops filed away into captivity. News of this disaster had still to reach London when the War Cabinet met at 11.30 a.m. with Chamberlain in the chair. The Vice-CIGS said the situation west of Rouen was very obscure and the general picture was 'certainly not promising'. There were signs of a heavy German attack east of Rheims, and the French, having fallen back on to the Marne, had opened up a line of advance for the enemy on to Paris. General Haining added: 'German advanced elements must be expected in the capital within the next 24 to 48 hours.'[48]

The second session of Anglo-French summit talks concluded at Briare before lunch and Churchill prepared to fly back to London. Clouds had drifted over, and the dozen Hurricanes were unable to provide protective escort. The Flamingo flew alone. As the small aircraft passed eight thousand feet above smoking Le Havre, and crossed the Channel – narrowly missing the attentions of two enemy aircraft – General Alan Brooke was on his way over to France on the most desperate mission of his military career: to command the British forces left on the Continent, mainly the 52nd Division and the 100,000 men from the original BEF.

Hitler might soon be able to turn his full force upon Britain;

but one important defensive measure was now announced completed. Sir John Anderson told the Commons during the afternoon that the shelter programme, launched 19 months before, had been finished: 20 million people, over half the civil population, could now find shelter space simultaneously.

Churchill and his party landed safe at Hendon and separated for an hour before the War Cabinet meeting. Eden, finding no time to celebrate his birthday, hurried to the War Office and scribbled down his thoughts in a letter to the Prime Minister. 'I am more than ever convinced that the chances of Reynaud's survival and of France staying in the war are to a large extent dependent upon the attitude of the United States.' He suggested the Prime Minister, using his excellent relations with the President, might urge Roosevelt to break off relations with Germany without declaring war.[49] Eden then crossed the road to 10 Downing Street where, at 5 p.m. a shocked War Cabinet heard Churchill's report on the Anglo-French talks. Reynaud, Pétain and Weygand had been 'studiously polite and dignified,' said Churchill, 'but it was clear that France was near the end of organized resistance.' The Prime Minister continued: 'The main points in General Weygand's report had been as follows.... The French armies had been fighting for six days, night and day, and were now almost completely exhausted. In some places two divisions were holding 120 kilometres of front and some divisions had been reduced to two battalions. The enemy seemed to have overmatched and outwitted them.... Enemy armoured forces had caused great disorganization among the headquarters of the higher formations.... The French army was now on its last line, which had already been penetrated, but not decisively, in two or three places. General Weygand had expressed the opinion that the allies had entered upon the war very lightly without making the necessary preparations.... The present position was the last on which the French forces intended to offer a co-ordinated and determined resistance. If it collapsed, he (Weygand) would not be responsible for any attempt to carry on the struggle, but would be willing to serve under any other officer.'

Churchill told the War Cabinet that de Gaulle, who had been sitting with Reynaud, 'was all in favour of carrying on a guerrilla warfare. He was young and energetic and had made a very favourable impression.' But Reynaud had said Pétain had 'quite made up his mind that peace must be made with the Germans. His view was that all France was being systematically destroyed ... it was his duty to save the rest of the country from this fate. He had gone so far as to write a memorandum on this subject.' Churchill added that 'Pétain was a dangerous man at this juncture; he had always been defeatist, even in the last War.... Reynaud seemed quite determined to fight on, and Admiral Darlan had said quite emphatically that he would never surrender the French navy to the enemy.' Churchill commented that the danger existed of Darlan being overruled by the politicians; he himself had emphasized to the French that if the situation deteriorated and important decisions had to be taken, Britain must be informed immediately and given an opportunity of consultation.

Eden told Ministers that the effect of Churchill's visit on the French had been remarkable. 'Where they had first appeared as men who had abandoned hope, they were now inspired to bend their minds to see what could be done if their lines were broken.' The chief danger, he believed, was that apart from Pétain, Reynaud's Cabinet had no strong personality. Summing up, Churchill thought that 'a chapter in the war was now closing'. Effective resistance by France as a great land power was coming to an end. 'We must now concentrate everything on the defence of this island, though for a period we might still have to send a measure of support to France.' Churchill 'viewed the new phase with confidence'. The Prime Minister sent a warning message to Roosevelt after the meeting; perhaps prompted by Eden's letter, he wrote: 'The aged Marshal Pétain ... is, I fear, ready to lend his name and prestige to a treaty of peace for France. Reynaud, on the other hand, is for fighting on, and he has a young General de Gaulle who believes much can be done. This therefore is the moment for you to strengthen Reynaud the utmost you can, and try to tip the balance in favour of the best and longest possible French resistance.'[50]

But time had almost run out. During the evening, just after the British War Cabinet had dispersed, French Ministers met near Tours, and Weygand, supported by Pétain, urged the Government to start armistice negotiations. The desperate Reynaud hastily appealed to Churchill. Chamberlain described this appeal, and Churchill's reaction, when he chaired a War Cabinet meeting at noon next day, Thursday, 13 June. The Prime Minister had received the message late the previous night, he said, and he reminded Ministers of Reynaud's undertaking that if any new major decision had to be taken, Britain would be consulted. The Prime Minister and Foreign Secretary had left by air that morning for a meeting with Reynaud. Dill told the War Cabinet that the German attack was spreading eastwards to the Meuse. Large enemy concentrations were located near Sedan and would probably drive towards Verdun; Rheims was being cut off to the east by the enemy advance across the Marne at Chalons, and to the west by the enemy crossing the river at Château Thierry.[51]

While the War Cabinet sat in London, Churchill, Halifax, Beaverbrook and Ismay landed at bomb-cratered Tours airfield – for the last visit the Prime Minister would make to France for four years. Thunder clouds hung heavy overhead and rain splattered; Churchill wrote later: 'Immediately one sensed the increasing degeneration of affairs.'[52] No one was there to receive the British party, which had to cram into a small borrowed Citroën. Roads were jammed with refugees and the car had to bump across sodden fields to reach the town. When the British arrived at the *Préfecture*, where talks were to be held, no one knew of Reynaud's whereabouts: Churchill and his group went to a nearby café for a cold chicken lunch. Reynaud finally appeared, showing signs of tremendous strain – his eyes kept twitching from left to right with a nervous tic – and the meeting began. Churchill lit a cigar at the start of the conference, but soon allowed it to go out, and the absorbed Prime Minister made no attempt to re-light it or remove it from his mouth.

Brooke was struggling along 340 miles of refugee-clogged roads to reach Weygand's HQ, a journey he described as 'an unbelievable ordeal'. Evacuation from Le Havre had been completed during the morning, with 2,200 British troops brought away and another 8,800 carried round to Cherbourg to continue to fight. In London, the decision had been taken to change previous instructions that no further evacuation of children from cities should be started before air raids, and in the next five days nearly 100,000 youngsters would be moved from in and around the capital. An order was issued during the day banning the ringing of church bells; these would be needed to sound airborne attack alarms. Signposts were being ripped down to confuse enemy paratroopers. The COS, meeting at 4 p.m. finalized a telegram to be sent to Dominion Prime Ministers concerning plans to meet 'a certain eventuality'. 'We must expect widespread destruction, considerable dislocation of industry and communications, and heavy casualties. Chances of Germany achieving success depend mainly on our ability to maintain in being our air forces, their sources of supply, and the fleet and its base.... Providing we can prevent enemy gaining high degree of air superiority we think we should be able to prevent large-scale invasion.'[53] This session was the second held by the COS that Thursday; during the first, at 10 a.m., it had been decided to reverse the decision to send battalions to the Channel Islands: the islands would now be demilitarized and spared devastation.[54]

Churchill sped back to London during the evening and immediately called the War Cabinet; he began his account at 10.15 p.m. Reynaud had at first seemed 'very depressed'. General Weygand had reported that the French armies were exhausted and the line was pierced in many places; refugees were pouring through the country; many of the troops were disordered. Reynaud had said that 'the French had suffered as much as they could bear and had done their best as a loyal ally. He now asked whether Great Britain would release France from the pledge which she had made not to make a separate peace.' Churchill said that he felt 'on rather weak ground', as Britain had so few troops in the battle; nevertheless, he had told Reynaud that 'we were determined to continue to give all the help in our power, and believed Hitler could not win the war without overcoming us.... We were, therefore, not in a position to release France from her obligation. Whatever happened, we would level no reproaches or recriminations at France; but that was a different matter from consenting to release her from her pledge.' Churchill had told Reynaud that a new message should be sent to Roosevelt, urging him to intervene. 'This appeal would be backed up from here [London] by a statement of the position.... M. Reynaud had agreed to do this and proposed to make an appeal for maximum help which the President could give.' Churchill told the War Cabinet that the French had agreed to hold on until the results of this final appeal were known.

Churchill now revealed that since returning to London a further 'remarkable' message had been received from President Roosevelt, and he read the telegram to the War Cabinet: the President, in this reply to Reynaud's message of 10 June, repeated his previous statement that the American Government were doing everything possible, and Roosevelt said he was 'personally, particularly impressed by your [Reynaud's] declaration that France will continue to fight on behalf of Democracy even if it means slow withdrawal, even to North Africa and the Atlantic. It is most important to remember that the French and British fleets continue in mastery of the Atlantic and other oceans; also to remember that vital materials from the outside world are necessary to maintain all armies.' This message, said Churchill, 'came as near as possible to a declaration of war and was probably as much as the President could do without Congress. The President could hardly urge the French to continue the struggle, and to undergo further torture, if he did not intend to enter the war to support them.... This message would have been quite sufficient as an answer to M. Reynaud's final appeal, but it would be observed that it had come in advance of it, which made the effect even more striking.' Discussion followed as to the precise interpretation which could be put on President Roosevelt's latest telegram. 'It was generally felt, although the implications of the message might be clear to the Anglo-Saxon mind, they might appear in rather a different light to the French, who would be looking for something more definite. It would be necessary to point out to them that the message contained two points which were tantamount to a declaration of war – the first, a promise of all material aid, which implied active assistance; and the second, the call to

32

go on fighting.' Churchill suggested he should say to Reynaud that the message fulfilled every hope and could only mean America would enter the war. 'If the French continued the struggle, Hitler would enter Paris within a day or so, but he would find an empty shell. Though he might occupy much of her country, the soul of France would have gone beyond his reach.'

Attlee urged that 'a statement in dramatic terms should be issued to hearten the people of France'. Other Ministers agreed and the suggestion was made that 'we might say "France and Great Britain are one"'. Churchill then left the War Cabinet Room to speak to Kennedy, the American Ambassador, and during his absence a summary of Reynaud's broadcast appeal to Roosevelt, as reported on the news agency tapes, was brought in and read. The Prime Minister then re-entered and reported that Kennedy had spoken to the President: Roosevelt agreed to the publication of his message, but Cordell Hull was against the idea. 'The President had heard that the meeting at Tours had been very successful, and it seemed he did not realize how critical the situation was.' Kennedy had gone back to the Embassy to communicate with the President and give him an account of the meeting, based on notes supplied by Churchill. Churchill then read drafts of three messages: a telegram to Reynaud on the lines he had already mentioned; a message to the French Government from the British Government, and a telegram to Roosevelt. The texts were agreed by the War Cabinet. The second of these documents, significant in itself, was to lead to further developments within a few hours: 'In this solemn hour for the British and French nations and for the cause of freedom and democracy, to which they have vowed themselves, His Majesty's Government desire to pay to the Government of the French Republic the tribute which is due to the heroic fortitude and constancy of the French armies in battle against enormous odds. Their effort is worthy of the most glorious traditions of France and has inflicted deep and long-lasting injury on the enemy strength. Great Britain will continue to give the utmost aid in her power. We take this opportunity of proclaiming the indissoluble union of our two peoples and our two Empires.... We shall never turn from the conflict until France comes safe and erect in all her grandeur, until the wronged and enslaved states and peoples have been liberated, and until civilization is free from the nightmare of Nazidom. That this day will dawn we are more sure than ever; it may dawn sooner than we now have right to expect.'[55] Churchill's message to Roosevelt was also despatched during the night; he described the Tours meeting – 'They were very nearly gone.... I urged that this issue [appeal for an armistice] should not be discussed until a further appeal has been made by Reynaud to you.' He then referred to

Roosevelt's 'magnificent message', but added: 'Mr President, I must tell you that it seems to be absolutely vital that this message should be published tomorrow, 14 June, in order that it may play the decisive part in turning the course of world history. It will, I am sure, decide the French to deny Hitler a patched-up peace.' Churchill concluded: 'We realize fully that the moment Hitler finds he cannot dictate a Nazi peace in Paris he will turn his fury on to us.' The Prime Minister who, according to Ismay, had never looked harassed or tired throughout the day, finally went to bed in the early hours of Friday, 14 June.

Sir Ronald Campbell was active throughout the night. At 12.30 a.m. he reported German tanks might reach Tours during the day; at 3.30 a.m. he cabled that some officials at the French Foreign Ministry had been told to be ready to move at dawn; at 5.15 a.m. the Ambassador added that the French Government had indeed decided to leave Tours – a move would be made to Bordeaux within a few hours, although Ministers did not expect to be safe there for more than a short time and advised the early despatch of a British warship to evacuate the British Embassy staff. Brooke, who had noted in his diary the previous evening: 'I can see no hope of the French holding out longer than the next few days,' had all his suspicions confirmed at his meeting with Weygand at 8.30 a.m. on the 14th. The French military leader, his neck painfully stiff from a car accident the night before, admitted that the French army was unable to offer organized resistance; Paris had been abandoned; no French reserves remained. He informed Brooke of a plan, which he incorrectly claimed had been agreed by the Allies, to hold Brittany as a last defence. Brooke was appalled: the Brittany line would be about 150 kilometres long and there would be little more than four divisions to stem the German advance. No defences had been prepared; and the Germans might well arrive before troops could be deployed. The British commander immediately drafted a message to be taken back to London.[56]

While this alarming discussion took place, German forces filtered into undefended Paris. Tanks squealed down cobbled streets; troop carriers whined along boulevards. Giant swastikas were immediately unfurled on the *Chambre des Députés* and the Eiffel Tower, and in Berlin the High Command issued a triumphant statement: 'The second phase of the campaign is over with the capture of Paris. The third phase has begun. It is the pursuit and final destruction of the enemy.'

Churchill opened the War Cabinet meeting at 12.30 p.m. with further disastrous news: a message had now been received from Kennedy to say Roosevelt was unwilling to allow his 13 June message to be published, and Kennedy had asked whether Churchill would explain the position to Reynaud. 'I declined to do so and stressed strongly that, if President Roosevelt appeared now to be holding back, this would have a disastrous effect on French resistance.' Ministers discussed a telegram sent by Campbell the previous night, which reported rumours that, if America did not declare war, Britain would liberate France from her treaty commitment not to seek a separate peace. The War Cabinet agreed that a telegram should be sent to Reynaud denying this suggestion. Halifax told Ministers of a conversation he had had the previous evening with Corbin, who had urged more dramatic British help: ironically, in view of the confusion and apprehension at Weygand's HQ, he had asked: 'Were we, for example, concerting plans to help the French defend some last corner of their country?' Corbin had also suggested Britain ought to receive two or three millions of the six or seven millions of refugees now in southern France, and 'had not taken kindly to the reply that, from the blockade point of view, it was more advantageous to us that these millions should be where they were'. He added: 'Altogether it had been a confused and not very satisfactory conversation.' Later in the meeting Halifax reported that according to a telegram from Tangier, Spanish troops were about to occupy Tangier territory. It had long been contemplated that Britain and France should invite Spain to take such a step in the event of war with Italy, and 'very likely some indication of this had reached the Spaniards from the French'. He proposed any press statement should take the line that the Spaniards had been invited by the French to occupy the city; the War Cabinet agreed.[57]

Meanwhile, discussions were taking place at the Foreign Office on a desperate, last-chance move to succour the French, Sir Robert Vansittart, chief diplomatic adviser to the Foreign Secretary, and Major Desmond Morton, met Monnet and Pleven during the day, joined by de Gaulle soon afterwards. Between them they evolved the framework of a fundamental Franco-British union to merge the two countries; proof would thus be given of the common struggle against Hitler. Discussions were to continue the following day.

Brooke's message reached London, expressing his consternation at the situation revealed by Weygand. 'Weygand had stated organized resistance has come to an end. French Army disintegrating disconnected groups. He told me of decision taken by Governments yesterday to attempt to hold Brittany. He, [General] Georges and I are in complete agreement as to military impossibility of this with troops which can be made available. Strongly recommended decision should be reconsidered.'[58] At 4 p.m. Brooke, now at Le Mans, managed to telephone Dill and requested the flow of troops to France should be stopped immediately: the CIGS said this had already been done. Brooke then described his profound fears of 'the Brittany scheme', and added that the Expeditionary Force should be re-embarked as soon as possible. In reply, the CIGS confessed he had not heard of the Brittany plan and would consult the Prime Minister. The facts, it transpired, were that a plan to hold Brittany had been discussed at the talks on the morning of the 12th, but no decision had been taken.[59]

The sad misunderstanding and the urgent need to take drastic action with regard to the BEF led to a hastily summoned meeting of the Defence Committee at 10 Downing Street, starting at 6.30 p.m. and attended by the Chiefs and Vice-Chiefs of Staff. The Committee agreed to a telegram to Brooke, ordering him to act independently but in co-operation with French forces in his vicinity. Another telegram was approved for transmission to Reynaud, via Campbell, in which the French leader was informed of Weygand's statement to Brooke, and that 'in these circumstances I [Churchill] feel sure you will agree that the Allied cause would best be served by stopping the disembarkation of any further British forces in France till the situation is more clear'. The Prime Minister then pointed out to the Defence Committee that 'although organized resistance by the French Armies might be coming to an end, the French Government were not suing for an armistice as we had feared. They were apparently falling back into the country and continuing to fight, although action was unco-ordinated. It was essential, therefore, that if the French 10th Army was still fighting, General Brooke should co-operate with them as long as they were putting up any resistance at all.' Dill said Brooke intended to do so, but also wanted to send back the two brigades now in the Le Mans area: Churchill disagreed with this last intention and insisted the two brigades should be put into the battle if the French were continuing to fight. Then, at 8.20 p.m., as the meeting was breaking up, Brooke was contacted by Dill by telephone and spoken to by the Prime Minister. The argument over the two brigades in the Le Mans area continued; according to the official Minutes: 'It was suggested to him, both by the Prime Minister and the CIGS, that he should leave these two brigades in their present position to assist the retirement of the forward brigade and the line of communication troops. It was emphasized that we were in honour bound to fight alongside the French as long as we possibly could. Brooke said that, in view of the gap in his right flank, to maintain the two brigades in their present position was to run the risk of losing them altogether. In these circumstances, the Prime Minister agreed that the brigades should be moved back, but that this operation should be regarded not as one of general policy, but as one imposed by local conditions.'[60] Brooke's own account of this telephone conversation is considerably more colourful than the official version. The talk began, wrote Brooke, with him giving Dill an account of dispositions already agreed upon during their previous telephone conversations, to which Sir John replied: 'The Prime Minister does not want you to do that.' General Brooke's description continues: 'I think I answered: "What the hell does he want?" At any rate, Dill's next reply was: "He wants to speak to you."' The effort to persuade Churchill that the brigades should be moved lasted half an hour, 'and on many occasions his arguments were so formed as to give me the impression that he considered that I was suffering from "cold feet". This was so infuriating that I was repeatedly on the verge of losing my temper.' Brooke added: 'He was endeavouring to force a commander to carry out his wishes against the commander's better judgment.'[61] This, the first personal contact between the Prime Minister and the future CIGS, was hardly auspicious.

Stricken France seemed unlikely to survive the weekend. The British War Cabinet met at 10 a.m. next day, Sunday 15 June, and Churchill opened by revealing a further disappointing message from Roosevelt. The President hoped it was realized the United States was doing all it could to furnish materials and supplies, but his message of the 13th had in no sense been intended to commit his country to military participation: this could only be done by Congress. He was unable to agree to publication of the message, since misunderstandings must be avoided. Churchill's draft reply was given War Cabinet approval: this stressed the disappointment felt at the refusal to publish the message of the 13th, although Churchill said he understood Roosevelt's position. 'I am personally convinced that America will in the end go to all lengths, but this moment is supremely critical for France. A declaration that the United States will if necessary enter the war might save France. Failing that, in a few days French resistance may have crumpled and we shall be left alone.' Churchill warned Roosevelt of the dangers to America if Britain herself should fall. 'If we go down you may have a United States of Europe under the Nazi command far more numerous, far stronger, far better armed than the New World.' The chief weapon in this armament, should Hitler conquer Britain, could be the British Fleet under German control. Churchill appealed once again for American destroyers.

The situation had deteriorated badly in France the previous day, Churchill now told the War Cabinet. He described Brooke's message and the telephone conversation and read the telegrams to Reynaud and the British Commander. Ministers believed the War Cabinet meeting to be almost finished; then Chamberlain introduced a new and dramatic subject. He began by referring to the message which had been issued early the previous morning, proclaiming the 'indissoluble union' of the French and British people, then he said that a memorandum had since been handed to him proposing a still greater degree of unity – including references to a joint Parliament and joint War Cabinet. Churchill, who later mistakenly wrote that the first he heard of the scheme had been at a lunch on this day, was initially against the idea. But he told the War Cabinet that 'the real question was what action we could take to uphold the French. If means were found to prepare a statement as to English and French unity, in a dramatic form which would make a big appeal to the French, so much the better.' Attlee pointed out the difficulties of having any kind of joint Cabinet, having regard to the position of the Dominions. Other Ministers also had doubts, and discussion was deferred until the following day.[62] But the need for some final, desperate action to keep the French going was becoming overwhelmingly imperative. Campbell, struggling with chaotic telephone facilities, contacted the Foreign Office with information regarding Reynaud's 14 June 'final appeal' to Roosevelt: whether France continued the conflict depended on an assurance from Roosevelt that America would enter the war at a very early date. Reynaud had so far received no reply. At 2.45 p.m. Sir Ronald reported: 'Things are slipping fast.' Also at 2.45, he was instructed by the Foreign Office that the British Government felt very strongly 'the absolute necessity of [the French Government] refusing to take any action by way of negotiations with Hitler for a separate peace'. An armistice was preferable and was 'entirely different from the Government formally consenting to negotiate a peace or surrender. We have the example of Holland of the army surrendering while the Government yet survives.' This statement was not received by Sir Ronald until early the following morning.

At 4 p.m. he told the Foreign Office that Pétain and Weygand were determined to resign unless the French Government asked for an armistice or the United States declared war. But in Washington, a disappointing discussion took place between the British and French Ambassadors, and Roosevelt and Cordell Hull. The question of entering the war rested with Congress, repeated Roosevelt, and a campaign in favour of a declaration would destroy his Government's authority. Lord Lothian gave London his opinion of the talks: the American Government realized nothing more could be done at the moment, but the Government had still to face the fact 'that the only way in which it can save itself from being confronted by totalitarian navies and air forces three or four times as powerful as its own in the near future, is by setting the situation in all its stark brutality in front of Congress without

38

delay and inviting it to go to war'.[63] Meanwhile, Campbell was again seeing Reynaud, just before the French leader faced a Council meeting. The British Ambassador, in his 6.5 p.m. report of the conversation, revealed that Reynaud had said he could not withstand further pressure. Reynaud added that he would tell Ministers of his determination to resign if he failed to receive support and he had expected four or five Ministers, including Pétain, to walk out in opposition to him. During the short talk Reynaud had said he would never agree to the surrender of the French fleet, from which Sir Ronald suspected some of Reynaud's Ministers might approve such a move.[64] In turn, the Ambassador had informed Reynaud of the British Cabinet's decision to stop British troop disembarkation.

Reynaud then went to the fateful Council meeting, declared his position and appealed to Pétain to persuade Weygand to continue the struggle. But Pétain supported Weygand who, moreover, rejected as dishonourable the suggestion that the French Army should follow the Dutch action and surrender while the Government fought on from overseas. If the army ceased fighting, then the Government should also admit defeat. Chautemps suggested an apparent compromise: the British should be asked to agree to a French inquiry – no more than an inquiry – of German armistice terms. After a confused discussion, this fatal step was agreed. Reynaud immediately contacted Campbell and told him the position; the British Ambassador had still to receive instructions sent to him at 2.45 p.m. that Britain would prefer the French to follow the Dutch example. While Sir Ronald was attempting to contact London with Reynaud's urgent inquiry, Churchill sent another appeal to Roosevelt: 'We are now faced with the imminent collapse of French resistance. If this occurs, the successful defence of this island will be the only hope of averting the collapse of civilization as we define it. We must ask, therefore, as a matter of life and death to be reinforced with ... destroyers.'[65]

Just before Saturday midnight, Sir Ronald managed to talk direct to Whitehall, and told officials that three cypher telegrams would be telephoned: the first arrived at 1.5 a.m. on Sunday and merely stated that a second would soon be sent containing a message from Reynaud to Churchill. The French leader insisted upon an early reply. The message reached London at 1.20 a.m. and stated the French Ministerial Council's decision to seek Britain's authority for an inquiry of German armistice terms: this inquiry would be made through the American Government, and Reynaud warned that without such a move public opinion in France might react violently to the idea of the French Government fleeing abroad, leaving France to 'cruel privations and sufferings'. Reynaud added that if Britain granted the request, the French fleet would not be surrendered to Germany; if Britain refused he, Reynaud, would have to resign.[66] Before Sir Ronald's third cypher message reached London, he telephoned again, at 2 a.m., to ask whether a further meeting between the French and British leaders would be practicable; he was informed this could probably be arranged. Two hours later, the Ambassador's third message came through, containing his personal views: Reynaud seemed to have put up a good fight, but had been overwhelmed by weight of numbers and could not guarantee that, if he had to resign, his successor would maintain the decision that the surrender of the fleet would be an unacceptable condition of an armistice.

Members of the British War Cabinet met at 10 Downing Street at 10.15 on Sunday morning, 16 June, to consider Reynaud's request. Churchill said the decision to inquire about armistice terms 'seemed to imply that there was some possibility that if the terms were too harsh, the French Government might be willing to carry on the struggle outside France'. Chamberlain believed no more hope existed of the French continuing the struggle from inside France. 'Our objectives must now therefore be, first, to save the French fleet ... second, to ensure that a French Government of some sort continued in being which would, at least nominally, carry on the war.' Attlee agreed, and Ministers realized that if British consent were refused, Reynaud would resign and, as Halifax pointed out, 'we should then be faced with the greater of two evils'. Some discussion took place as to whether Britain should refuse to give *formal* consent while unofficially approving the French request, but 'it was suggested that refusal of such formal assent might give M. Reynaud the excuse for resigning, and this it was most important to avoid'. Churchill thought that 'we should send a brief message to the French Government which would make it clear that our treaty was not with M. Reynaud or any other individual Prime Minister, but with France herself. We were prepared to release France from that treaty to the limited extent necessary to allow of the inquiry ... but only provided that the French fleet was ordered to sail immediately for British harbours.' Churchill then went into the next room and himself drafted a message embodying these points. During the meeting two more messages were received from Sir Ronald, supported by another from General Spears: Reynaud would welcome talks with Churchill sometime in the afternoon and suggested Nantes as a rendezvous. The War Cabinet decided to inform the British Ambassador that a message was on its way from Churchill to Reynaud and the question of a meeting would be considered later.

Discussion turned to the invasion problem. Eden said he had

seen a report prepared for the Ministry of Information on the state of public opinion. 'This report is not very encouraging. Bearing in mind the stern times ahead of us, I would like to have seen a firmer note of resolution.' Criticism was made of the press, with Ministers considering it unfortunate that 'there is a certain tendency to encourage inquests rather than to concentrate on the tasks ahead'.[67]

Churchill's reply to Reynaud was despatched to Campbell at 12.35 p.m. A second message was prepared for the French leader, which was also, as Churchill commented, 'stiff'. This, demanding consultation as soon as armistice terms were received, was not available for transmission until 3.10 p.m.; within a minute or so after it had left the Foreign Office, an urgent telegram was sent to Sir Ronald instructing him to ask Reynaud to suspend action on the 12.35 message; at 4.45 p.m. a further order told the Ambassador that the same applied to the 3.10 signal. The suspension stemmed from a meeting Churchill had now had with de Gaulle; the latter had been disturbed by the 'sharpness' of the War Cabinet decisions that morning, and supported the idea of a proclamation of the indissoluble union of the French and British people, as discussed at the War Cabinet the previous day. De Gaulle had already taken the initiative and had telephoned the general terms to Reynaud, who had replied that such an announcement would 'make all the difference'. De Gaulle intended to return to Bordeaux during the evening and could take a copy of the final text. So, at 3 p.m., the War Cabinet met again, with de Gaulle waiting in the lobby outside. Churchill described his meeting with the French General, and Halifax reported a meeting with Vansittart, who had 'previously been asked to draft some dramatic announcement which might strengthen M. Reynaud's hand'. De Gaulle had also urged a meeting of Churchill and Reynaud, if possible on the next day, Monday. The draft proclamation was then read to the War Cabinet. It was recognized that 'such a proclamation raised some very big issues with which it was difficult to deal at such short notice'. The issues were indeed massive, including subjects such as common citizenship, restoration of war damage, abolition of customs, fusion of currencies, unification of Government and military command; and, to increase the pressure on the harassed Ministers, news was received at 3.55 that the French Council of Ministers would meet at 5 p.m. to decide whether further resistance was possible. Ministers were told that de Gaulle had been informed by Reynaud on the telephone that 'if a favourable answer to the proposed proclamation of unity was received by 5 p.m., M. Reynaud felt he would be able to hold the position'. A number of amendments were made to the document, none of which substantially altered the wording, after which the War Cabinet decided that 'while the draft declaration was not free from difficulty, the draft as amended did not present any insuperable difficulties; and that the right course was to proceed with it'. The text was immediately taken to de Gaulle in the next room and he hurried off for Bordeaux – only pausing to telephone the news to Reynaud in time for the French Council meeting, less than 30 minutes away. The War Cabinet decided Churchill, Attlee and Sinclair, the three party leaders, should meet Reynaud at the earliest possible moment, and they also made preparations to leave.[68]

The War Cabinet, in a discussion lasting just over 60 minutes, had agreed to a document which could have affected Britain's independent sovereignty more than any other declaration in the island's long history. 'At this most fateful moment in the history of the modern world,' read the declaration, 'the Governments of the United Kingdom and the French Republic make this declaration of indissoluble union and unyielding resolution in their common defence of justice and freedom, against subjection to a system which reduces mankind to a life of robots and slaves. The two Governments declare that France and Great Britain shall no longer be two nations but one Franco-British Union. The constitution of the Union will provide for joint organs of defence, foreign, financial and economic policies. Every citizen of France will enjoy immediate citizenship of Great Britain, every British subject will become a citizen of France.... During the war there shall be a single War Cabinet and all the forces of Britain and France ... will be placed under its direction. It will govern from wherever it best can. The two Parliaments will be formally associated.... And thus we shall conquer.'[69]

But events followed in tragic and rapid succession. Campbell was discussing with Reynaud the two earlier telegrams from London, containing the reply to the request for permission to discover armistice terms, when de Gaulle telephoned with the War Cabinet's decision. News of the declaration immediately transformed the despairing Reynaud. 'For a document like that I would fight to the last,' he told Sir Ronald, and he left 'with a light step' for the Council meeting. Sir Ronald informed the Foreign Office of Reynaud's reaction and, as a result, was instructed at 6.45 p.m.: 'The Prime Minister, accompanied by the Lord Privy Seal, Secretary of State for Air, the three Chiefs of Staff and certain others, arrives at Concarneau at noon tomorrow, the 17th, in a cruiser, for a meeting with M. Reynaud.' Meanwhile, inside the French Council Chamber, the final blow had been dealt to French freedom. Reynaud had read the declaration, twice. Violent suspicions, accusations and protests rang out from panicked members. Britain herself was virtually defeated: Pétain described the declaration as 'fusion with a corpse'. Arguments, recriminations and allegations continued: the proposal was never even graced with a vote. The British demand that the French fleet should sail to British ports as a prelude to negotiations was never considered. Reynaud suffered terrible personal defeat. And, at 8 p.m. he sent in his resignation to the President, with the advice that Pétain should be chosen as his successor.

Winston Churchill was sitting in the special train at Waterloo station, waiting to leave for Southampton. A delay occurred; just after 10 p.m. the Prime Minister's private secretary ran down the platform with a signal from Campbell. 'Ministerial crisis has opened.... Hope to have news by midnight. Meanwhile meeting arranged for tomorrow impossible.' The Prime Minister, fearing the worst, returned to wait for further information at 10 Downing Street; within minutes Sir Ronald telephoned Reynaud's decision to resign; British Ministers were told to be ready for a sudden War Cabinet meeting; at 11.30 p.m. the French radio declared Marshal Pétain had been asked to form a new administration in which Weygand would be Vice-President of the Council and Defence Minister. Churchill immediately attempted to contact Pétain, and after long delays caused by telephonic confusion, managed to speak to him at 2 a.m. on Monday, the 17th. He implored the new French leader not to hand over the fleet to the Germans and, according to General Hollis, the Military Secretary to the Cabinet: 'It was the most violent conversation I ever heard Churchill conduct. He only spoke so roughly because he felt that anger might sway the old Marshal when nothing else would.'[70]

A more detailed report of the ruinous French Council meeting arrived from Sir Ronald at 4.05 a.m. The Ambassador and General Spears had seen the desolate Reynaud and had tried, in vain, to persuade him to be rid of 'the evil influences among his colleagues', and Sir Ronald had also seen President Lebrun in a futile attempt to persuade him to insist that Reynaud should form a new government. Sir Ronald commented that Pétain and Weygand were 'living in another world, and imagined that they could sit round a green table discussing armistice terms in the old manner'.

At 1 a.m. Sir Ronald was granted an interview with the new Foreign Minister, Baudouin, and he reported this meeting to London at 4.40 a.m. The British Ambassador had been told that the French Government, under Pétain, was now to ask for the German armistice terms. The request was an admission of Hitler's victory. The British, who had not been consulted over this last decision, had now to stand alone; 'a certain eventuality' had arrived.

3

━━━━━━━━━━━━━━━━━━━━━━━━━━━━━━━━━━━━━━

Alone

German *Panzers* pierced the shattered French while, to the north, the Russian Red Army started to overrun the Baltic Republics, and to the south, Italy cast her groping shadow across the blue Mediterranean, and, across the Atlantic, America remained impotent. Britain's War Cabinet had to deal with two immediate problems: to bring forces back from France, and to throw all effort into defence against invasion. Two assumptions were taken for granted: the French would agree to the German terms and, second, Britain would never consider a similar step. Ernest Bevin experienced the typical British reaction: addressing a Trade Union audience he somewhat foolishly remarked that the Government, although the situation looked bleak, had decided to carry on the fight; a voice from the front row immediately bellowed: 'We'd knock your bleedin' 'ead off Ernie, if you'd decided anything else.'

Before dawn on Monday, 17 June, Guderian's tanks had reached the Swiss frontier, isolating the Maginot Line from the rest of France. To the north, the French 10th Corps was in full retreat; British troops were already being embarked from Cherbourg and General Brooke ordered this withdrawal to be accelerated. The War Cabinet met at 11 a.m. 'There was general agreement that, now that the French Government under Marshal Pétain was suing for an armistice, we should be sacrificing our men to no purpose if we told them to fight on. The French would no doubt reproach us for evacuating our troops while fighting was still in progress, but further sacrifice would serve no useful purpose and would not prevent the French from blaming us in any case.' Churchill, having only managed to snatch two hours sleep, said General de Gaulle was coming to England, 'as he had apparently been warned that, as things were developing, it might be as well for him to leave France'. Dill warned that the retreats and withdrawals which British forces had recently been compelled to carry out must have left their mark on the psychology of the troops. 'We must once and for all cast behind us the spirit of "looking over one's shoulder" and of looking for a position to fall back on.' Another warning came from Eden: the local Defence Volunteers were, he said, largely a 'broomstick' army, although rifles were being provided as quickly as possible. A message was brought into the War Cabinet room: most French troops had ceased firing at 12.40 p.m. The communication also gave an account of Pétain's broadcast at noon, in which the new French leader was reported to have said: 'It is with a broken heart that I tell you today that fighting must cease. I addressed myself last night to the enemy, to ask him if he is prepared to seek with me, as between soldiers after an honourable fight, the means of putting an end to hostilities.'[1]

Dill immediately tried to contact Brooke, and succeeded at 1.15 p.m. Brooke, asked if he had heard of the French ceasefire, 'told him that I had not heard a word about it.... Here I was operating with Allies, and in command of a force sent to their assistance in their final struggle. And when the end came, they never even had the decency to inform me.'[2] Within a few minutes Brooke discovered German advance units had pushed forward between his own HQ and the bulk of the British being evacuated from Cherbourg; the General closed down his HQ and headed for St Nazaire.

Concern continued to mount over the fate of the French fleet. At 1 p.m. Sir Ronald was told to remind the French that a 'necessary pre-condition' of Britain's assent to the application for armistice terms had been that the French warships should sail for British ports. At 4.25 p.m. a message came from Sir Ronald: he had seen Pétain immediately before a French Council meeting and had emphasized Britain's position. The Marshal apparently believed the fleet should be scuttled. When asked if the Government would go to North Africa if German terms were unacceptable, Pétain had said he would stay but he supposed a small Government might go overseas. An hour later Sir Ronald was instructed to see Pétain again: the exhausted Ambassador saw Baudouin, Chautemps and other Ministers, and emphasized 'most strongly' the British demand to be consulted before a reply was sent to the Germans and also that the fleet be sent to British ports.[3]

Diplomatic activity also remained constant across the Atlantic. Roosevelt told the British Ambassador that, if he were asked to act as intermediary, he would make the transfer of the French fleet to Britain a condition of his mediation. At a second interview Lord Lothian pressed for American destroyers to be sent as soon as possible; Roosevelt replied that he was already having great difficulty in persuading the Senate Naval Affairs Committee to release motor boats, about which the Admiralty had inquired on 28 May and that, in the present anxiety about American defence, it would be almost impossible to obtain Congressional approval for the release of the destroyers. The British Ambassador urged the President to make a completely frank statement to Congress about the gravity of the naval position and the consequences to America of a British defeat. During the night of 17-18 June Lord Lothian was instructed by London to make a further appeal to Roosevelt in view of Pétain's noon broadcast; the Ambassador replied that the President had agreed to telegraph a strong message to Pétain and a private message would also be sent to Darlan.

Two broadcasts went over the air from London that evening, 17 June. De Gaulle, who had slipped from his country in a small aircraft – carrying, wrote Churchill, 'the honour of France' – spoke to the French people. 'France is not alone. She has a vast Empire behind her. She can unite with the British Empire, which holds the seas and is continuing the struggle. She can utilize to the full, as England is doing, the vast industrial resources of the United States.' Churchill also conveyed a defiant message. 'We have become the sole champions now in arms to defend the world cause. We shall do our best to be worthy of this high honour. We shall defend our island home and with the British Empire we shall fight on unconquerable until the curse of Hitler is lifted from the brows of mankind. We are sure that in the end all will come right.'[4]

Fighting died in darkened France except for scattered engagements and in the small vulnerable corner where British troops were still struggling to extricate themselves from the German mesh. At 4 p.m. on the 17th the SS *Lancastria* had been bombed and sunk in the Loire; over 3,000 men had been drowned or burnt to death in the burning oil. Churchill had received the news as he sat in the dark and deserted War Cabinet Room; he refused to allow publication of the tragedy: 'The newspapers have got quite enough disaster for today.'[5] The destroyer which was to have evacuated General Brooke was diverted to seek survivors, and the General had to embark on a small armed merchant ship which herself had assisted in the *Lancastria* rescue operations. Her decks were slimy with oil from discarded uniforms, planks were littered with blood-stained bandages, cotton-wool and tattered clothes. The vessel stank of iodine, cordite and fuel. Soon before dawn on Tuesday, 18 June, the 125th anniversary of the Battle of Waterloo, the British Commander-in-Chief set sail for England in the battered, smelly trawler.

First item on the agenda for the COS meeting at 10 a.m. on the 18th simply stated: 'Urgent measures to meet invasion.' People in the South-East were undoubtedly apprehensive, the Committee decided, whereas 'in the industrial North there was a more robust outlook. There was little realization of the danger, but on Tyneside and in Lancashire people were full of fight.' The response to the appeal to evacuate children from the danger areas was considered unsatisfactory – only 100,000 out of a possible 500,000 had gone from London. The Prime Minister intended to make a Commons speech later in the day and this would 'probably have a good effect on morale'. But danger remained of morale being broken through intensive bombing and, from the point of view of avoiding panic, 'the more men under discipline the better'.[6] During the morning a long statement was despatched to Lord Lothian for communication to Roosevelt. 'The final issue will ... stand at first on our ability to withstand the great effort which the enemy is likely to make against Great Britain in the *immediate* future.' Suggestions had been made that, in the event of Britain being overrun, the struggle could be continued by the British fleet from America. But the assessment made clear that all naval forces would be thrown into repulsing invasion; if the latter were successful, then the Royal Navy would itself have been destroyed. Britain once more asked for American destroyers.[7]

Churchill spent the morning preparing his speech for the Commons and was therefore absent from the War Cabinet meeting at 12.30 p.m., when Dill reported that evacuation was being carried out from Cherbourg, Brest, St Malo and St Nazaire. He informed Ministers of the tragic loss of *Lancastria*. Halifax suggested that during the coming critical two days it would help the Ambassador in France to have a British Minister with him, and the War Cabinet decided to ask Alexander, First Lord of the Admiralty, and Pound, who had already gone to Bordeaux to see Darlan, to stay there for the moment.[8] Brief optimism had been shown in a telegram from Sir Ronald early in the morning: he expected the French Council of Ministers to take a 'satisfactory decision' about the fleet. But, as the War Cabinet meeting closed, at 1.50 p.m., he reported that the Council had merely agreed to refuse German terms involving the surrender of the fleet. French warships would not therefore sail to British ports; the French believed it a point of honour to receive German terms while the fleet and army were still fighting – regardless of the fact that the army had been told to cease fire the previous day.[9]

Adolf Hitler and Benito Mussolini were locked in close conference at Munich. Ribbentrop, Nazi Foreign Minister, told his Italian counterpart: 'We must offer lenient armistice terms to France, especially concerning the fleet; this is to avoid the French fleet joining with the English.'[10] Up to this date Hitler had planned to kill Britain through slow strangulation: her supply routes could be easily severed once France and the Low Countries offered bases for German air and naval forces. Now, on 18 June, Hitler first mentioned the possibility of invasion to Mussolini.

While Hitler and Mussolini continued their Munich conference, Churchill shuffled his notes in the House of Commons, adjusted his spectacles and declared: 'What General Weygand called the Battle of France is over. I expect that the Battle of Britain is about to begin.' Big Ben had solemnly struck the hour of four as the Prime Minister began his speech; and, at that very moment, the last evacuation ship had left Cherbourg – 136,000 British troops had been snatched from French harbours. 'The whole fury and might of the enemy must very soon be turned on us,' warned Churchill. 'Hitler knows that he will have to break us in this island or lose the war. If we can stand up to him all Europe may be free and the life of the world may move forward into broad, sunlit uplands.' He paused. 'But if we fail, then the whole world, including the United States, including all that we have known and cared for, will sink into the abyss of a new Dark Age, made more sinister, and perhaps more protracted, by the lights of perverted science.' He approached his thunderous conclusion. 'Let us therefore brace ourselves to our duties and so bear ourselves that, if the British Empire and its Commonwealth last for a thousand years, men will still say: "This was their finest hour!" '[11]

Next day, 19 June, the COS warned that the dangers foreseen in the 27 May report on the effects of a French collapse now confronted the country. The Chiefs, at a 10 a.m. Defence Committee meeting, recommended that all measures which had not so far been carried out should be put into force immediately. Perhaps only a few days remained. But much had already been done through crude improvisation and by extending existing resources: the meeting was told that arrangements were now complete for watching the whole coast by coastguards and special observers: every stretch would now be scanned every half-hour throughout day and night; behind this system lay the Observer Corps network over most of the country. The Royal Navy had drawn up a list of ports most likely to be invasion targets, and all round defence was being arranged for each. Mobile reserves were being hastily provided with all types of transport, including civilian coaches, and each division now had vehicles for the conveyance of one brigade. Churchill inquired whether the idea of Storm Troops, so successfully used by the Germans, had been accepted by the British Army: General Ironside, Commander of Home Forces, said he was against the idea as a whole, but he was proceeding on the principle that a large number of smaller units should be trained on special lines, for example tank hunting platoons, independent companies and special irregular units. 'Steps were being taken to inculcate throughout the army the offensive spirit which was so important, but it should be realized that effective counter-attack could not be carried out without the requisite weapons.' The official Minutes of this meeting coldly reveal the deplorable extent of these arms deficiencies. 'The Committee were informed of progress in the issue of infantry tanks. A total of 80 would be in the hands of the troops by evening.... Artillery. The Committee were informed, (a) 710 field guns were in the hands of the troops. This represented two-fifths of the establishment. (b) Preparations were being made for dealing with French 75s, which it was hoped to receive from America. The ammunition would require reconditioning as it was very old, but it would be quite good enough for use at point-blank range against tanks.... Anti-tank guns. 167 anti-tank guns were now available in the artillery of the various divisions.'[12]

Once again came a brief spurt of optimism over the crucial French fleet situation. Churchill opened the War Cabinet meeting at 12.30 p.m. by telling Ministers he had received a telegram from Alexander, then at Bordeaux with the First Sea Lord, and the signal had given 'a more encouraging picture than we had been led to believe possible' – fighting was still continuing at sea and the French navy was 'in good heart'. The First Lord had been favourably impressed with Admiral Darlan, who was confident the French fleet would obey him and seemed determined the warships would not be taken by the Germans. Churchill added that he had been approached by Monnet the previous day, who had urged another member of the British Government should fly to Bordeaux; the Prime Minister had agreed and Lord Lloyd had left early in the morning. Only a few minutes later, Pound hurried into the meeting. He had just returned from Bordeaux, and told Ministers that when he had been about to leave the French Government, the Germans were only 120 kilometres away and, as far as he could see no attempts were being made to defend the city. But Admiral Darlan had seemed very calm and determined and during the talks had steadfastly maintained that 'in no circumstances would the French fleet be surrendered'.[13] Lord Lloyd arrived in Bordeaux at lunchtime, while the War Cabinet was still waiting in London. He immediately discussed with Campbell a message he had brought for the French from Churchill, in which Britain urged the Government to go abroad and undertook to transport as many French personnel and as much material as possible to North Africa; the offer to transform the Anglo-French alliance into a complete union was confirmed. Lloyd arranged to see President Lebrun, Pétain and Baudouin.[14]

The Germans tightened their military hold upon the French and, at the same time, they pushed forward armistice arrangements. Sir

Ronald reported during the afternoon that Pétain had informed him of a message from the Spanish Ambassador, received in the morning, that, if the French would nominate plenipotentiaries, the Germans would indicate a time and place for a meeting. The French had nominated delegates without plenipotentiary powers thus reserving a final decision on the terms. The British Ambassador was also told that leading members of the Government were preparing to move overseas, probably to Algiers, where the struggle would be continued; steps had already been taken to send aircraft and stores to North Africa.[15]

During this Wednesday evening a bomb fell on the fringe of London, the first time damage had been caused so near the capital. Bordeaux was subjected to an air raid: a telegram from Campbell and Lloyd describing talks with Lebrun had to be drafted by candlelight. Alexander was on his way back to London, where he arrived in time to report to the War Cabinet at noon on the 20th. He, Campbell and Lloyd had seen the French President at 7.30 the previous evening; Lebrun, 'very depressed and unable to cope with the situation,' had made a long statement on France's suffering. At 10 p.m. they had seen Pétain and Baudouin, and the British offer of help had been repeated, 'in a somewhat better atmosphere'. The French Ministers had apologized for seeking an armistice. Lloyd had referred to the French fleet and he, the First Lord, had emphasized Britain's need for French destroyers. The French leader had apparently forgotten his previous conviction that Britain was already a corpse: according to the First Lord, 'Pétain, who had taken the view that Great Britain would have no difficulty in resisting invasion, had said that he understood our point of view, but had not thought it likely that the French Government would agree to turning their destroyers over to us. He had repeated that he would never allow them to fall into German hands.' Churchill suggested that as there seemed considerable risk of the French scuttling much of their fleet, they might be persuaded to make greater efforts to get the vessels away if America would offer to buy them.[16] Apparently unknown to the Prime Minister, this same startling thought had occurred to President Roosevelt.

The Foreign Office was becoming increasingly anxious lest during this time of sensitive relations with the French Government, the actions of the impetuous young de Gaulle should result in fatal complications. 'We ought to be careful not to ride two horses at the same time,' declared a Memorandum. The General had therefore been asked not to broadcast on 19 June as he had wished. Yet now, on the 20th, General Spears sent a Minute to Churchill suggesting as a matter of 'utmost urgency' that de Gaulle should broadcast during the evening. But during the War Cabinet meeting a statement had been issued on the French wireless disowning the General and so, when de Gaulle visited the Foreign Office in the afternoon he was informed by Cadogan of Weygand's possible departure for North Africa; in the circumstances, Sir Alexander pointed out, it would be better if no controversial statements were issued from London. De Gaulle apparently understood.[17]

Campbell, suffering from seven days of virtually no sleep, kept up a constant flow of messages during the evening and night of the 20-21 June. First he reported that the French Government were to move to Perpignan and that French representatives would receive armistice terms at Tours during the night; he then telephoned a 'last minute' change of plan: the Government had decided to remain in Bordeaux to receive the terms, as the Germans had offered to restore the telephone line from that city to Tours. Just after midnight he reported the terms had still not arrived. Thereafter, communications were considerably delayed, sometimes by 10 hours, and the War Cabinet, meeting at noon on the 21st, lacked fresh information. Before discussing the French situation Ministers were informed that the withdrawal of troops from France could now be regarded as complete and that military evacuation of the Channel Islands had been carried out. During the day as many of the civilian inhabitants as wished to leave the Channel Islands would be brought to England.

Halifax then said the French Ambassador had been to see him during the morning. Corbin had claimed there was a growing French belief that it would be better to continue the struggle, and had urged Britain to do all possible to encourage this movement. German propaganda that Britain was already treating France as an enemy or as a colony should be strongly countered. Corbin had therefore proposed the sending of aircraft to drop food to French troops. But Sir Archibald Sinclair, Air Secretary, thought 'the results that would be obtained were quite inadequate to justify the risks and diversion of effort'. Other Ministers agreed. Corbin had also urged Britain to allow French food ships to proceed to ports in Metropolitan France not occupied by the enemy. Ministers also objected to this idea: the ports might be taken by the Germans. Churchill pointed out that 'the policy of the French Government would be determined not by any action which we might take, but by the terms offered by the Germans'. Halifax voiced disapproval: he did not disagree with this nor the conclusions reached 'but he could not help regretting that it was not possible even to a limited extent to follow the advice given by the French Ambassador'.[18]

Churchill was more correct in his assessment: two hours after the War Cabinet Ministers dispersed Franco-German armistice talks began. The site chosen by the Germans for discussion was an extremely pleasant one, among the stately elms and sturdy oaks of the forest of Compiègne, in the gentle June sunshine. The site was also that chosen by the French when they had received the defeated Germans at the close of the Great War: nearby stood a giant granite block on which was carved, in proud, high letters, this inscription: 'Here on the eleventh of November 1918 succumbed the criminal pride of the German Empire – vanquished by the Free Peoples which it tried to enslave.' Within hours the monument would be dragged to the ground; meanwhile, Adolf Hitler, who arrived at 3.15 p.m., strutted over and read the outdated message. Talks were held in the same railway carriage used in the armistice discussions of 1918, and Hitler lounged in the chair occupied by Foch in those far-gone days. The Führer left the carriage after the preamble had been read; Keitel began to announce the terms to the dignified French. General Charles Huntziger, Commander of the French Second Army at Sedan, and leading French delegate, telephoned Bordeaux during the late evening. The telephone cable ran through both German and French battle lines, but this miracle of German engineering was almost insufficient: when the French General contacted Bordeaux and spoke to Weygand, the latter claimed he was unable to receive the terms because all secretaries had gone home and nobody could take the details down. This farcical situation was solved; by midnight the French Government had possession of the armistice treaty of 24 clauses.[19] Campbell telegraphed news of the terms to London, but transmission was again badly delayed: meanwhile, the French despatched their initial acknowledgement.

The British War Cabinet had once more to rely on outdated information when Ministers met at 10 a.m. on Saturday, 22 June. Churchill had driven down to his country home at Chequers, and Chamberlain took the chair; Halifax commented on latest telegrams from Sir Ronald: the French Government's move to Perpignan having been cancelled, the Ambassador had feared the idea of sending a Governmental nucleus overseas might be abandoned. A number of Parliamentarians had been put on board ship at Bordeaux and were now 'hung up' somewhere at the mouth of the Garonne. Unfortunately, these were mainly men who stood for resistance and the defeatist element, including Laval, was still active. Alexander said Admiral Odend'hal, head of the French naval mission in Britain, had received orders from Darlan that French vessels now at British ports should leave for Africa. Halifax was called to the telephone to speak to Churchill; he then told Ministers that the Prime Minister was anxious to send a further message to the French Government, reminding them that Britain was entitled to be taken fully into their confidence at this critical moment. But later in the meeting another telegram arrived from Campbell', despatched at 4 a.m. The German terms had now been received at Bordeaux. These filled nine pages of type, reported the Ambassador, and the text was too long to be telegraphed verbatim: conditions regarding the French fleet would be transmitted separately. The Franco-German armistice would come into force as soon as the French Government had concluded an armistice with Italy, and the German Government would notify the French by wireless of the ceasefire. The War Cabinet agreed to a message containing points Churchill had mentioned to Halifax, sent after receiving Churchill's approval. The effort was wasted: the signal arrived at Bordeaux far too late.[20]

Difficulties of communication continued to hamper discussion throughout this strained Saturday. Sir Ronald had despatched a telegram at 10 a.m. giving details of Article 8 in the armistice convention which dealt with the French fleet, but this was not received in London until 2.40 p.m., and had been overtaken by a wireless message, which described his actions after he had heard by telephone about midnight on 21 June that the German terms had arrived. Sir Ronald had hurried to the Council Presidency, where he had been given a rough outline of the terms, and he had immediately written a note calling attention to the insidious conditions with regard to the fleet, which relied heavily upon German promises. He had insisted that this note should be taken into the French Council meeting. After this 1 a.m. session the Ambassador had waylaid Baudouin in a corridor: the Foreign Minister, according to Sir Ronald, had been rude and unco-operative and merely revealed that the Government was to make a counter-proposal about the fleet and wished it to sail for North Africa. Sir Ronald had insisted on seeing Baudouin 'somewhere where we can talk quietly', and the Foreign Minister had eventually shown him into the Council Room; only after repeated requests had he handed over a copy of the German terms, saying the French reply would 'put questions'. 'The French have completely lost their heads,' commented Sir Ronald, 'as witnessed by the shameful scene as above described, and are totally unmanageable.'[21]

Having studied the terms, the British Ambassador believed them to be 'diabolically clever'. Especially so was the article referring to the French fleet, details of which were contained in Sir Ronald's telegram received at 2.40 p.m. Warships, except those safeguarding French colonial interests, were to be assembled in specified ports; the fleet would be demobilized and disarmed in these ports under German or Italian control. The German Government 'solemnly declared' they had no intention of using for their own purposes the French fleet stationed in ports under German command, except those vessels necessary for coast surveillance and mine-sweeping. The Germans also stated their intention of not making any claim in respect of the French fleet at the time of peace term negotiations.[22] To the French, bewildered and exhausted, these conditions might appear eminently reasonable – but all depended upon the German word, and what vessels would be considered 'necessary' for coast surveillance? At 5.50 p.m. the Foreign Office despatched a cable to Sir Ronald: the only hope seemed to rest with Darlan, and if the fleet could not sail to British or American ports, warships should be scuttled. Campbell probably never received this message.

While the British feared for the future of the French fleet, concern was mounting in America about the Royal Navy. US experts were anxious that it should sail to America if the worst came; Lord Lothian, at the request of the United States naval authorities, had asked whether fleet ammunition and material should not be sent, ready for further use. Churchill sent a stern reply during the day: 'There is no warrant for such precautions at the present time.'[23] The answer did nothing to allay American fears; and ambiguity surrounded various statements Churchill had already made and would continue to make. In his 4 June speech Churchill had declared that if the worst came to the worst, the Royal Navy would fight on from overseas; in his message to Roosevelt on 15 June Churchill had warned of the dangers to America if Britain herself should fall – and he had added that a chief weapon in the enemy armament, in such an eventuality, would be the British fleet under German control. American naval authorities clearly had every justification for feeling worried in view of such a warning. Yet in the long assessment sent to Roosevelt on the 18th, it had been stressed that suggestions to send the fleet to America, if Britain were overrun, were irrelevant because all naval forces would be thrown into repulsing invasion, and if invasion were successful the Royal Navy would have been destroyed. Would the Royal Navy sail to America, or would it have been destroyed – or would it have been taken over by the Nazis? Americans were soon to increase their efforts to clarify this important point.

Churchill returned from Chequers to chair a second War Cabinet meeting starting at 9.30 p.m., on this Saturday, 22 June, and Ministers discussed the crucial Article 8. During the meeting a message was brought into the Cabinet Room: according to the Germans an armistice had been signed by the French. This agreement would not, however, take effect until six hours after a Franco-Italian armistice had been concluded. Time had almost come to switch support from the French Government and to 'ride the other horse'. Duff Cooper, Minister of Information, read to the War Cabinet the draft of a broadcast which de Gaulle proposed to make. The day before, a Cabinet committee had been set up to examine and co-ordinate plans for continued resistance in France; at a noon meeting on the 22nd, the Committee had decided a broadcast appeal should be made to French troops to come to Britain. The War Cabinet now invited Duff Cooper to arrange for de Gaulle to broadcast at 10 p.m. Ministers then agreed upon a statement to be issued to French colonies, calling on them to continue the war: 'We appeal to them to do this even if they receive orders from the Government in France to surrender to the enemy, for that Government is already under the control of the enemy and can no longer be regarded as representative of France.'

A long discussion followed on the French fleet situation, and Churchill revealed himself in favour of the strongest possible action, despite the risk of bloodshed. Pound gave details of the present dispositions of the French warships: the *Richelieu*, 'the most powerful battleship afloat in the world today', had sailed with a full crew and ammunition for Dakar, where she was expected to arrive very shortly. The *Jean Bart*, the other modern battleship, was proceeding to Casablanca, where she would arrive soon: she was not complete, however, and probably had no fighting value. The two battle-cruisers *Dunkerque* and *Strasburg* were at Oran and the French 8-inch cruisers were at Toulon and Alexandria. Pound maintained that Darlan 'had taken all possible steps to safeguard our interests', but Churchill retorted that 'in a matter so vital to the safety of the whole British Empire we could not afford to rely on the word of Darlan. However good his intentions might be he might be forced to resign, and his place taken by another Minister who would not shrink from betraying us. The most important thing to do was to make certain of the two modern battleships, *Richelieu* and *Jean Bart*.' Churchill continued: 'A strong force must be sent and *Richelieu* must be dealt with first. If the Captains refused to parley they must be treated as traitors to the allied cause. The ships might have to be bombed by aircraft from *Ark Royal*, or they might be mined into their harbours.... In no circumstances whatsoever must these ships be allowed to escape.' But Churchill, at this War Cabinct meeting, was in the belligerent minority. Pound had already stressed his belief that Darlan should be trusted; Halifax thought that 'we should exhaust every means of persuasion before using force.' He therefore suggested that 'at this stage we should concentrate all our efforts on making the parleys a success.' Other Ministers concurred, and Churchill modified his outspoken view. 'The Prime Minister agreed,' recorded the Minutes, 'but stressed that at all times we must keep in view our main object, which was that in no circumstances must we run the mortal risk of allowing these ships to fall into the hands of the enemy. Rather than that we should have to fight and sink them.' Ministers decided to send a further appeal to Darlan and also an appeal to Admiral Estava at Oran – the latter should be conveyed by the Vice-Chief of Naval Staff and Lord Lloyd, who should fly out immediately.[24]

Confirmation came of the French armistice signature as the War Cabinet Ministers were preparing to disperse; Churchill and Halifax decided to postpone Lloyd's visit to Oran for at least 24 hours to await developments. The Franco-Italian armistice would be signed two days later, at 7.35 p.m. on 24 June. But already, as this War Cabinet closed on Sunday, 22 June, Free France was dead. A large part of the country, including all the crucial northern and Atlantic coast, was to be occupied; French forces, except those needed to maintain internal order, would be demobilized; nationals would be forbidden to fight against Germany; the convention could be denounced at any time by Hitler. The terms were hard, but they were by no means harsh. By not demanding the surrender of the French fleet as the British and French had feared, Hitler skilfully slipped a wedge between the former allies. With the powerful French fleet still available as a glittering prize, relations between France and Britain would suffer and deteriorate – perhaps even to the point of open conflict. And Churchill's attitude at this second War Cabinet meeting on 22 June showed this conflict might not be many hours away. 'I have had a most scarifying 48 hours,' wrote Cadogan in his diary. 'Everyone all over the place and WSC endorses any wild idea.'[25]

Lord Halifax read the latest telegram from Bordeaux to War Cabinet Ministers next morning, Sunday, 23 June: the Ambassador was finally leaving France for Britain, and Ministers expressed their 'high appreciation of the great courage and resolution which Sir Ronald Campbell had displayed in those difficult and often distasteful circumstances'. A previous telegram from Sir Ronald reported French personalities who had already embarked and, Halifax told Ministers: 'These people would form a nucleus for the continuation of the struggle in the French Empire.... General de Gaulle might well be the centre around which the most resolute French statesmen might rally.' Churchill read a letter from de Gaulle outlining proposals for a Council of Liberation which Britain was asked to recognize. De Gaulle was a 'fine fighting soldier', commented Churchill, with 'a good reputation and a strong personality', and might be the right man. But before approving the proposals it would be well to find what French personalities were available to serve on the Council and which of them de Gaulle had in mind.[26] Churchill, Halifax and Cadogan therefore interviewed de Gaulle soon after the War Cabinet meeting and various names were proposed by the General, including that of Reynaud, who he thought should head a provisional Government. Churchill then promised Britain would make a declaration to announce the Council and the Government's support; de Gaulle would make a broadcast during the evening. The Prime Minister issued another statement during the day, as agreed by the War Cabinet the previous night: 'HM Government have heard with grief and amazement that the terms dictated by the Germans have been accepted by the French Government at Bordeaux. They cannot feel that such or similar terms could have been submitted to by any French Government which possessed freedom, independence and constitutional authority.... HM Government call upon all Frenchmen outside the power of the enemy to aid them.'

Eden was visiting defensive positions in Kent, Sussex and Surrey while the defiant declaration was being published and, after his inspection of this most likely German invasion district, the War Secretary hastily sent an alarming report to the Prime Minister. 'There is no anti-tank regiment nor anti-tank gun in the whole of this Corps area.' Nor were there any tanks; air defences were lacking; only minimum co-operation existed between the British army and the RAF.[27]

Corbin became increasingly apprehensive as the time approached for de Gaulle's evening broadcast, and contacted Halifax to declare his grave concern over Britain's proposed support for the General's movement, but his request that the broadcast should be cancelled was refused. During the evening he visited Vansittart's home; at 9.15 Vansittart telephoned Cadogan at his request, asking that the broadcast should be altered. Halifax said it was too late. So de Gaulle announced the formation of a French National Committee in agreement with Britain. 'The war is not lost; the country is not dead; hope is not extinct. *Vive la France!*' A statement immediately followed, in French, confirming British recognition of the Committee. Corbin wasted no time in telephoning his alarm and insisted Britain was making the wrong approach to the question of continuing French resistance, and maintained his pressure next morning, Monday, 24 June. 'I've never been so nearly driven *mad*,' exclaimed Cadogan.[28] Corbin told Halifax that to the French people a Committee on British soil with British support would appear no more independent than the Bordeaux Government; no one would pay attention to it; resistance was impossible. Halifax's argument that the Committee would form a nucleus failed to reassure the Ambassador. But the man believed by de Gaulle as most suitable to head a provisional Government, Reynaud, was soon deemed untrustworthy by the Prime Minister. Churchill read a message from Reynaud to the noon War Cabinet meeting, in which

57

he pleaded there should be no recriminations, and attempted to argue that Britain would be safeguarded against Germany gaining the French fleet. The message clearly showed, commented Churchill, that 'M. Reynaud could be no more relied on than any of the other members of the Bordeaux Government.... This Government had broken their solemn treaty obligation with us and were completely under the thumb of Germany. They would allow their resources to fall into the hands of the enemy and be used against their previous allies.'

Ministers discovered Churchill was persisting in his desire for strong action over the French fleet. 'There is grave danger that the rot will spread from the top through the fleet, army and the air force and all the French colonies.' Ominously, Churchill added: 'In the near future we shall have to solve the problem of our future relations with the present French Government.' Halifax still sought caution – 'it might be desirable that we should go rather slowly for the present in withdrawing recognition for the Pétain Government. To do so would give food for enemy propaganda that we were treating France as an enemy, and might extinguish the will to resist.' But Churchill scorned this diplomatic approach; he declared he would send a reply to Reynaud 'setting out the position as I see it', and he would make clear that no trust could be put in the German word: no limit existed to the danger which Germany would thrust upon France. 'It is not a question of recrimination, but of things which are to us matters of life and death.' Sir John Anderson reported that although the numbers of refugees from France were so far small, reports had been received that up to 40,000 might soon come to Britain. 'This was an alarming prospect, both from the point of view of home security and accommodation; we were approaching the limit of civilian accommodation available.'[29]

Discussion took place on the French fleet, but no decisions were made; Ministers agreed to hold a further meeting later in the day. The War Cabinet therefore met again at 6 p.m, and now, due mainly to Churchill's firm attitude, a number of critical conclusions were reached. Pressure on the War Cabinet to take strong action was increased early in the meeting, when a message was received from Rome: an armistice had been signed between France and Italy, although no details were available. Halifax read a reply which had arrived from Lebrun to a message sent by the King on 3 June: he insisted that the fleet would not be used against Britain. But Ministers now agreed that Britain should 'make a formal communication to the French Government that it was clear there was a grave risk of the French ships falling into German hands and that this was a risk that we could not accept'. Churchill and Halifax were asked to draft an ultimatum in which Britain would demand the ships should be scuttled within a specified time, otherwise Britain would take action by force against them. On receipt of such an ultimatum some of the French ships might put to sea – but this would make them easier to deal with. Ministers did not believe French crews would offer serious resistance, but the War Cabinet asked for a Naval Staff appreciation of action involved if force had to be used. Churchill described talks with those closely connected with de Gaulle, including Vansittart and Spears. 'It had been suggested that the British declaration following on de Gaulle's broadcast had gone too far, and that it implied intention to sever relations with the Bordeaux Government.' The declaration had not stated this intention, continued Churchill, 'but in any event those present at the discussion had agreed that we could not draw back. The waverers would only be influenced by strong action on our part.'[30]

The Naval Staff appreciation of action involved in using force against the French fleet was completed within two hours. A third meeting therefore opened at 10.30 p.m. And those advocating force now received a setback: the naval experts advised against such a drastic step. As soon as British forces made any attempt to take over or sink units of the French fleet, crews of remaining ships would probably become actively hostile; chances would thereby be reduced of securing more than a small part of the fleet. Pound maintained the attitude he had shown throughout the French fleet discussions: he reminded Ministers that Darlan and other French Admirals had consistently declared that in no circumstances would the fleet be surrendered. Pound believed Britain's object would be more likely achieved through trusting in these assurances, rather than by attempting to use force, and the naval experts 'did not therefore recommend the proposed operation'. Presented with this cold conclusion, Ministers modified their views; it was pointed out in discussion that if the operation were to result in the loss or disablement of two of Britain's capital ships, Britain would be in danger of losing command of the Western Mediterranean and Ministers also felt that 'the decision to order the destruction of people who only 48 hours before had been allies would be hard to make'. The War Cabinet therefore agreed to detain French warships in British ports as long as possible, but deferred a decision on the rest of the French fleet. Halifax read a message from Rabat, saying former members of Reynaud's Cabinet had arrived there reportedly on their way to England. Sinclair suggested British representatives should be sent by flying boat to Rabat to establish contact; Duff Cooper offered to go and Ministers decided he should be accompanied by Gort.[31]

Meanwhile, Darlan had made a top-secret cypher signal to the French fleet, ordering sabotage preparations for any attempt to seize vessels. 'The demobilized warships are to stay French, under the French flag.'[32] War Cabinet ministers remained unaware of this message; but reports received in London late on 24 June and on 25 June did indicate a decline in the will to resist the Germans throughout the French colonies. Further disappointment came in a telegram from Madrid, read to the War Cabinet at 11.30 a.m. on Tuesday, 25 June, and reporting that Reynaud would probably accept the offer of post of Ambassador in Washington. Halifax then read a statement in which the Bordeaux Government had presented their case to the American Government: Britain had failed to mobilize her manpower for the struggle against Germany and had failed to send 26 promised divisions to France; war production in England had been inadequate; Britain believed more in the blockade than in helping her ally; Churchill, on his last visit to France, had been expected to attend a French Council meeting, but had failed to do so; originally Britain had said she would not reproach Paris if the French sued for peace. Churchill indignantly condemned the statement as 'false from beginning to end', and explained points he intended to make in a House of Commons speech.[33]

The Vice-Chiefs of Staff had held an important meeting just before the War Cabinet session; Ironside revealed detailed plans for Britain's defence – and the exposition was to cause short-lived but nevertheless unsettling alarm. Three main elements were being built up in the defensive system, he said: a 'crust' on the coast acting as outposts; a line of anti-tank obstacles running down the centre of England to the Blackwall Tunnel, thence to Maidstone and south to the sea; mobile reserves in the rear of this anti-tank line. Beach defences were progressing well and concrete block-houses were being built by civilian contractors – in Kent alone there were about 900. 'Frontages held by divisions on the coastline were admittedly very long indeed, but it would not be sound to lock up too many troops in a static role.' Between the coast and the anti-tank line were located mobile columns to deal with any enemy tanks breaking through the coastal crust. Armoured fighting vehicles were very short, he admitted, but a large amount of improvisation was being carried out.[34] The Vice-Chiefs of Staff went away to study the detailed plans and doubts and misunderstandings were to grow under this close scrutiny.

Admiral Odend'hal, head of the French naval mission, contacted the Admiralty during the day with a message from Darlan: the French had accepted the armistice only on condition that the French fleet remained French and Darlan therefore regretted

Britain should have found it necessary to detain French ships in British ports: this detention was 'almost an unfriendly act'. The Admiralty immediately passed this message to the Foreign Office, where it was pointed out that Darlan's statement about safeguarding the French fleet was 'quite contrary' to their information. The last part of the message could be ominous: Darlan might claim he was released from all obligations to Britain since the British had taken matters into their own hands.[35] Within hours, this pessimistic assessment seemed correct. Signals flashed to the Admiralty War Room concerning the movement of the giant *Richelieu* – 'the most powerful battleship afloat'. A meeting of the War Cabinet, hastily called at 6 p.m., was informed that the *Richelieu* had slipped from Dakar at 2.5 p.m. Ministers authorized the Admiralty to take 'the best measures in their power to capture the *Richelieu* and also the *Jean Bart* if she should put to sea. Every step should be taken to avoid bloodshed and no more force should be used than was necessary.' No communication would be made to the French Government until the operation had been completed.[36] France and Britain edged closer to conflict: signals were immediately made to HMS *Dorsetshire*. 'The two vessels ought to have met about midnight,' Pound told the War Cabinet next morning, 26 June, 'but no signal confirming this has been received.'

While the anxious wait continued, Ministers were informed of a further disintegration in French resistance. Duff Cooper, accompanied by Lord Gort, had arrived at Rabat by flying boat to see former French Ministers. Rabat was in mourning, with flags at half-mast and church bells tolling. Permission to see the Ministers was refused and General Auguste Nogues, C-in-C French North Africa, declined to meet the British mission. Dill reported that the morale of French troops in Britain was deteriorating: 'several men in the Foreign Legion have been put in custody as Communists by their Generals, and they wish to shoot three of them.' The CIGS also revealed some brighter developments: operations in the Middle-East confirmed the Italian reluctance to fight. In recent raids at Kassala, on the White Nile, Italian forces had sustained considerable losses, while British units had not suffered a single casualty.

Halifax referred to a number of telegrams reporting German intentions. A message from Belgrade claimed the German General Staff had had to change their minds about invasion, in view of the fighting qualities of British troops and the Dunkirk evacuation success. According to a Bucharest telegram, Hitler would soon make a determined effort to break British morale using 'some new weapon'; invasion was not contemplated: if the new weapon failed, he would announce that for every bomb dropped on Germany, ten would land on Britain. Another telegram reported a Polish informant as giving 8 July as the invasion date. Ministers agreed with a suggestion by Chamberlain that the COS should give further study to methods of collecting, collating, and acting upon invasion reports.[37]

Churchill had been absent from the War Cabinet meeting, but he had also been considering improvements in Britain's defence organization. He wrote to Eden: 'I don't think much of the name "Local Defence Volunteers" for your very large, new force. The word "local" is uninspiring. Mr Herbert Morrison suggested to me today the title "Civic Guard", but I think "Home Guard" would be better.' During this Wednesday Churchill sent a Minute to the Information Minister. 'The Press and broadcast should be asked to handle air raids in a cool way and on a diminishing tone of public interest.... Everyone should learn to take air raids and air raid alarms as if they were no more than thunderstorms.'[38]

The Vice-Chiefs of Staff held a special meeting at 3.30 p.m. to discuss the Home Defence plans revealed by General Ironside the previous day, 25 June; and the 'gravest concern' was expressed by Air Marshall Peirse, Vice-Admiral Phillips and General Haining. 'The coast was to be held by a crust, and it appeared that the main resistance might only be offered after the enemy had overrun nearly half the country, and obtained possession of aerodromes and other vital facilities.' This policy, as expressed by Ironside, would be disastrous, they claimed: the enemy must be resisted 'with the utmost resolution from the moment he set foot on the shore. Once he established himself firmly on land, experience had shown that the German was extremely difficult to dislodge.... We should have to dispute every inch of the ground at the landing places themselves.' The Vice-Chiefs added that very little mention had been made in Ironside's plan for the defence of the south coast, 'which was now quite as liable to attack as the east and south-east coasts'. They therefore declared that 'the plan was completely unsound and needed drastic and immediate revision', and they requested the COS to have a meeting with them, as a matter of urgency, to discuss the situation.[39] Faced with this alarming reaction, the COS summoned the Vice-Chiefs of Staff to a meeting at 9.45 that evening: if the Home Defence plan were indeed 'completely unsound' the country's defence against the expected imminent invasion would have to be revised in a matter of hours. Dill hurried to see Ironside before the meeting took place.

But the COS found, to their relief, that much of the criticism stemmed from a misunderstanding. The beach defences, which the Vice-Chiefs considered too flimsy, would be stronger than had been believed: the words 'outposts' and 'crusts' gave the wrong impression; 'foremost defended localities' would be a better term. These positions would be held to the last and Ironside fully intended that the battle should be fought on the seashore, as the Vice-Chiefs advocated. 'This intention was fully appreciated by troops manning the coastal defences. Ironside's explanation and certain paragraphs in his operational instructions gave a rather different impression.' Ismay, who had accompanied Churchill that day on a visit to East Anglia, said troops and commanders whom they had visited 'undoubtedly intended to fight on the seashore and had no thought of withdrawal'.[40] The disturbances subsided and the Vice-Chiefs expressed themselves satisfied.

A distressing telegram arrived from Lord Lothian late in the evening. He reported a wave of pessimism passing over the United States; many believed the defeat of Britain was inevitable and even the President might possibly be affected by this attitude. A 'resolute and cheering broadcast' by the Prime Minister might help dispel this mood. Churchill hastened to reply: he would broadcast presently, meanwhile Lothian should remember words did not count for much and undue attention should not be paid to 'eddies of Unites States opinion.... Your mood should be bland and phlegmatic. No one is downhearted here.'[41]

The French Ambassador, Corbin, felt he could no longer cope with the situation and now resigned on his own initiative. The business of the Embassy was conducted for a while by the Chargé, Cambon. Meanwhile, off the coast of Africa, contact had at last been made with the elusive French battleship; Pound reported events to the War Cabinet at noon next day, Thursday, 27 June. 'The *Richelieu* was located by aircraft from the *Devonshire* at 3 p.m. yesterday, the 26th.' A confrontation had seemed inevitable, with all resulting possibility of full-scale hostilities. 'At that moment, however, the *Richelieu* altered course 180 degrees and returned to Dakar under orders from the French Admiral at Dakar.' The crisis had passed, but Ministers, in their reaction to the *Richelieu* scare, now abruptly switched again to a policy of firm action against the French fleet. 'The real question,' decided the War Cabinet, 'was what to do with regard to the French ships at Oran.' Magnetic mines could be laid, using aircraft from Britain, but Ministers agreed it would be better to wait until 3 July before taking action, when the *Hood, Nelson, Valiant, Resolution* and *Ark Royal* would be deployed outside the port – a far stronger force than the French fleet in the harbour. 'On arriving off the port the following courses would be open to us: (a) We could demand that the ships should be demilitarized under our control. (b) We could ask the French ships to come to sea and proceed to British ports. (c) We could say that unless the ships had been sunk within three hours, we should bombard them.' Pound, despite his reluctance to use force, did point out that the French warships were believed to be moored with their sterns to the breakwater, making it impossible for them to fire to sea. Churchill thought the War Cabinet 'approved in principle'.[42]

Friday, 28 June, marked the 21st anniversary of the signing of the Versailles Treaty. Hitler planned to mark the occasion with a victory parade before Versailles Palace, but pressure of business persuaded him to abandon this further French humiliation. In London the Government decided to announce full official recognition of de Gaulle, and a short statement was made at the time of an evening broadcast by the General. 'HM Government recognize General de Gaulle as the leader of all Free Frenchmen, wherever they may be, who rally to him in support of the Allied cause.'

On the same day the War Cabinet discussed further details for dealing with the French fleet, by force, and these talks continued next morning, 29 June, when Ministers met at 10 a.m. Alexander said messages had been received revealing that the French Admirals at Dakar and Martinique had been told by Darlan not to offer British warships facilities. The Commander at Martinique had also been instructed that 'French ships should be prepared to resist attack by British ships'. Pound said it could be assumed similar instructions had been received at Oran and other French colonial ports. Nevertheless, and despite their advice on 24 June that French ships should not be attacked, the Naval Staff was at work on contingency plans for action at Oran. Halifax told the War Cabinet that the Under-Secretary of State in the American State Department had declared that the US Government believed the surrender of the French naval fleet would be 'the most degrading surrender in history'. 'It seems safe to assume,' added Halifax, 'that any action which we might do in respect of the French fleet would be applauded in the United States.'[43]

Churchill, with a forecast of terrible bombing campaigns soon to come, sent a Minute to Professor Lindemann. 'It seems to me that the blockade is largely ruined, in which case the sole decisive weapon in our hands would be overwhelming air attack upon Germany.'[44] And as if to emphasize their freedom of movement, and hence the ineffectiveness of blockade, German troops casually stepped ashore on to the Channel Island of Guernsey next day, Sunday, 30 June. Jersey was to be similarly occupied on 1 July. A total of 29,000 people from the islands, about one-third of the population, had been evacuated between 21 and 24 June.

The French, insisted Darlan, were trying to persuade the Germans to accept modifications of the fleet armistice terms; Darlan telephoned Odend'hal on the 30th to say the Italians had approved the stationing of the 'effective fleet' either at Toulon or in North Africa, and he hoped the Germans would also agree. But the British did not consider the North African ports, still less Toulon, to be sufficiently out of German reach and, at a meeting in the evening of the 30th, the COS agreed that an attack on French ships in Algerian waters should be carried out as soon as possible. The decision marked a complete reversal of the naval advice tendered six days before.[45] Operation 'Catapult', as the plan was called, went before the War Cabinet for final consideration next evening, Monday, 1 July. Meanwhile, at 2.25 a.m. on the Monday, a preliminary order left the Admiralty for Vice-Admiral Somerville with Force H at Gibraltar: 'Be prepared for "Catapult" on 1 July.'[46]

A War Cabinet meeting was held on this Monday morning to deal with other matters. Sinclair reported steps taken to increase the store of pilots in the immediate urgency and for the future: training courses had been shortened, training units increased and pilots had been borrowed from the Fleet Air Arm. Churchill drew attention to the scheme for evacuating children to North America, and warned that 'a large movement of this kind encouraged a defeatist spirit which was entirely contrary to the true facts of the position and should be strongly discouraged'.[47] In Berlin Hitler commented: 'I cannot conceive of anyone in England still seriously believing in victory.' The Führer was discussing possible operations in the Mediterranean, and told the new Italian Ambassador, Dino Alfieri, that Gibraltar and Suez should be attacked.[48] Nor, apparently, did the new French leaders expect, or hope, that Britain would last many months: also on 1 July, the same day that the French Government moved to Vichy, the American Ambassador sent an illuminating report to Washington. Mr Bullitt believed the 'physical and moral defeat' of the new French leaders had been 'so absolute that they have accepted completely for France the fate of becoming a province of Nazi Germany ... they hope England will be rapidly and completely defeated by Germany and that the Italians will suffer the same fate. Their hope is that France may become Germany's favourite province.'[49]

British Ministers met at 6 p.m. to give final approval for the destruction of the French fleet. The Vice-Chief of Naval Staff reported a conversation with Admiral Odend'hal: the latter had said a telegram had been received from Darlan asking Britain to reserve final judgment until details of the latest armistice talks were known. Churchill dismissed this reason for delay: 'Discussion as to the armistice conditions could not effect the real facts of the situation.' Ministers agreed the operation should take place. The War Cabinet considered whether demilitarization should be offered to the French Admiral at Oran, as one of the alternatives put to him. Against this idea was the possibility that any demilitarization which could be carried out quickly could also be quickly repaired, although the First Sea Lord believed such an offer was most likely to appeal to the French Navy. Ministers finally decided that while Britain should not declare this alternative, the Flag Officer should be authorized to accept it to avoid bloodshed if other alternatives were refused. As far as French warships at Algiers were concerned, Ministers agreed that a separate operation should not be undertaken, in view of the strong port defences.[50]

Churchill and Alexander left to write the final draft of orders to Admiral Somerville at Gibraltar and the instructions which he was to hand to the French Admiral at Oran. Ismay commented later: 'All who were present when that message was drafted could not but feel sad and, in a sense, guilty.... To Churchill, with his deep love of France, it must have been an agonizing moment. But he never flinched.'[51] The document to be given to the French declared: 'It is impossible for us, your comrades up to now, to allow your fine ships to fall into the power of the German or Italian enemy.... HM Government have instructed me to demand that the French fleet now at Mers-el-Kebir and Oran shall act in accordance with one of the following alternatives: (a) Sail with us and continue to fight for victory. (b) Sail with reduced crews under our control to a British port. The reduced crews will be repatriated at the earliest moment... (c) Alternatively, if you feel bound to stipulate that your ships should not be used against Germans or Italians, since this would break the Armistice, then sail them with us with reduced crews to some French port in the West Indies ... where they can be demilitarized to our satisfaction, or perhaps be entrusted to the United States.... If you refuse these fair offers, I must with profound regret require you to sink your ships within six hours. Finally, failing the above, I have orders of HM Government to use whatever force may be necessary....'[52] At 1.08 on the morning of 2 July, orders and this message were signalled to the British Admiral at Gibraltar. Ismay commented: 'I pictured the horror on the face of James Somerville, a typical British sailor and the soul of chivalry, as he read these instructions.'

During this Tuesday, a top secret military directive was issued by the German High Command. 'The Führer and Supreme Commander has decided: That a landing in England is possible, providing that air superiority can be attained and certain other necessary conditions fulfilled. The date of commencement is still undecided. All preparations to be begun immediately.' But Hitler still hesitated; the directive added: 'All preparations must be undertaken on the basis that the invasion is still only a plan and has not yet been decided upon.' Churchill spent Tuesday afternoon with Bernard Montgomery, commander of the Third Division deployed

66

in the South Downs. The two men had never previously met. The Prime Minister then returned to 10 Downing Street, preoccupied with the thought of the Oran operation due to take place next day and, at 10.55 p.m. he sent a personal message to Somerville: 'You are charged with one of the most disagreeable and difficult tasks that a British Admiral has ever been faced with, but we have complete confidence in you and rely on you to carry it out relentlessly.'[53]

British warships sailed at dawn on Wednesday, 3 July. By 9.30 they lurked silently off Oran and the ships of the French fleet, which only 11 days before had been fighting alongside the British, were within range of the Royal Navy's massive and loaded guns.

The Battle of Britain

Admiral Gensoul at Oran gave an inflexible answer to Britain's demand: French honour decreed that an ultimatum backed by force should be met by force. War Cabinet Ministers heard latest events when they met at 11.30 a.m. French warships at Portsmouth had been taken over without bloodshed, but one British leading seaman and one French officer had been killed during the occupation of the *Surcouf* at Plymouth. The Oran deadlock was described, and Ministers discussed whether demilitarization should now be included in the list of alternatives open to the French; but the War Cabinet decided that 'demilitarization not having been included in the alternatives first offered, we should not offer it now as this would look like weakening'. The French Admiral had been given a time limit within which to comply with British demands; meanwhile, various French warships had furled their awnings, from which it appeared they might intend to put to sea. Ministers agreed that another signal should be sent to Somerville, stating: 'If you consider that the French fleet are preparing to leave harbour, inform them that if they move you must open fire.' Later in the meeting Ministers were told a telegram had been received from the British Admiral. 'Gensoul's reply refuses our conditions and repeats previous assurances re sinking of ships. States he will fight. I am prepared to fire at 1.30 p.m.' Another telegram had arrived from Washington. And this revealed that Roosevelt had previously made an astonishing attempt to solve the French fleet problem. Lothian had asked Roosevelt whether American opinion would support forcible seizure of French warships. 'He said "Certainly." They would expect them to be seized rather than that they should fall into German hands ... and he said he had offered to buy the French fleet from the French before the Reynaud Government fell.' This novel solution was now impossible – 'there was nobody from whom he could buy it today'.[1]

Gensoul, having taken his firm line, apparently deemed it unnecessary to signal more than this intention to the French Admiralty: he made no mention of the various alternatives Somerville had presented to him. The French Admiralty replied that all available forces in the Mediterranean had been ordered to Gensoul's support. Churchill sat in the cold and cheerless War Cabinet Room during the afternoon until, just before the warm Mediterranean dusk, the finish came. Confusion surrounds the actual sequence of events: Churchill's own account specifies that a signal was despatched to Somerville at 6.26 p.m.: 'French ships must comply with our terms or sink themselves or be sunk by you before dark.' But, Churchill's version continues, bombardment had already begun when this message reached the British fleet.[2] The official British War Histories give a different timetable, in which Gensoul informed Somerville late in the afternoon that he proposed to demilitarize all his ships but, according to the official account, by then it was too late: 'Somerville had instructions to finish off the affair before nightfall and shortly afterwards Force H opened fire.'[3] The French retaliated; the unwilling bombardment lasted for about 10 minutes, followed by attacks by aircraft launched from the *Ark Royal*. The *Dunkerque* was driven aground, the battleship *Bretagne* blew up, and the battleship *Provence* and a large destroyer were disabled. The *Strasbourg*, damaged by torpedo aircraft, escaped to Toulon. Nearly 1,300 Frenchmen died.

Negotiations with the French at Alexandria had started well, but, the War Cabinet were informed next day, 4 July, the situation had deteriorated. The French Commander, Admiral Godfroy, had at first agreed to discharge his fuel oil, until news of events at Oran reached him and he refused to continue this demobilizing process. Admiral Cunningham rejected forceful action: the French were on the alert, he claimed, and if the French ships were sunk the valuable port of Alexandria might be blocked. Any damage to British ships would be difficult to repair in view of the poor facilities in the eastern Mediterranean, and Britain was not therefore in a position at Alexandria to take the strong action used at Oran. A signal had been sent to Cunningham giving two possible courses: either he should deliver an ultimatum, or the French should be starved into surrender. Churchill told Ministers he disagreed with this second choice: a quick solution had to be found so that the eastern Mediterranean fleet could regain its mobility; and the spectacle of a deadlock in the harbour would do great harm to Egyptian opinion. But, Churchill admitted, no decision could be taken until an answer had been received to the latest Admiralty telegram.[4] All turned out well. Largely due to Cunningham's tact, to good relations between the two fleets, and the fact that Alexandria was under British control, agreement was reached before the War Cabinet met at noon on

5 July and Ministers were told all French fuel oil was to be discharged immediately. Pound also told this 5 July meeting that Admiral Somerville intended to deal with the disabled Oran warships during the afternoon, after which he would proceed to Dakar to handle the *Richelieu*. And, on the subject of Dakar, Churchill made first mention of a future controversy: he said Spears was interviewing de Gaulle to find out 'whether he [de Gaulle] was prepared to put ashore somewhere behind Dakar with a view to rallying French forces'.[5]

Next day, the 10 a.m. War Cabinet meeting was told of a torpedo air attack on disabled French vessels at Oran: six hits had been obtained and one heavy explosion had been heard. 'It had not been thought necessary to give warning of this attack. The risk to life was far less in an attack by torpedo bombers than by bombardment. In any event, Admiral Gensoul had stated ... that the ships had been evacuated.'[6] Two days later, on 8 July, Somerville's fleet launched the strike against the *Richelieu* at Dakar, after an ultimatum had been presented and ignored. The massive battleship was severely damaged from depth charges and torpedoes, although not beyond repair. Consequently, at the 11 July War Cabinet meeting Ministers approved the Admiralty view that 'we should now inform the French naval authorities that we proposed to take no further action with regard to the French ships in French colonial or North African ports'.[7]

Operations were considered successful: seven out of the nine French capital ships had been put outside the enemy's power. But throughout these sad days War Cabinet Ministers had feared the possible French reaction; on the first day, 3 July, the Defence Committee had sent a telegram to all Colonies, Dominions, India, Burma and C-in-Cs abroad, warning them 'to take every precaution in case the French declared war against us'.[8] A few bombs were dropped on Gibraltar by French aircraft, but the French protest remained mainly verbal. Baudouin described Darlan's anguished behaviour on 4 July: 'The Admiral was not the same man as yesterday when, soberly and without raising his voice, he told us his sad news. This morning his voice trembled.... "I have been deceived by my brothers in arms. They have betrayed the trust I reposed in them."' Darlan intended to launch a surprise attack on the Royal Navy, but, according to Baudouin, was overruled by Pétain after much persuasion.[9] Cambon, the French Chargé, delivered a protest note during the evening of 4 July, and told Halifax that 'the situation between the French and British Governments was so grave that it was impossible to foretell what decision his Government would come to'. Halifax told the War Cabinet next day that Cambon had just been to see him again and had stated he was resigning, 'as he feared he might have to make a communication on behalf of his Government which, after having lived in this country for over 25 years, he would not wish to make'.[10] The Marquis de Castellane, temporary French Chargé, called at the Foreign Office on Sunday, 7 July; Halifax informed the 7 p.m. War Cabinet meeting that the Marquis had given an informal warning of a communication to be presented shortly: this would announce the French Government's decision that unilateral diplomatic relations with Britain must be broken. The War Cabinet decided the British answer should point out that the reason for the unilateral relationship was because 'we had had to withdraw our Ambassador to prevent him being captured'.[11] The French communication was delivered next morning, 8 July, and the British answer was handed over on the 9th.

By now operations were over; Churchill told the 11 July War Cabinet meeting that he intended to make a broadcast on Sunday evening, 14 July, in which he would refer to Anglo-French relations. 'He proposed to strike a restrained and friendly note, and might refer to the French as an oppressed people, who would be liberated by the defeat of Germany.' 'In any public statement,' commented Lord Halifax, 'it would be better to describe any Frenchmen who were well disposed towards us as anti-Nazis or anti-German, rather than as pro-Ally or Free Frenchmen.'[12] The War Cabinet approved the final text of Churchill's broadcast at 7 p.m. on the Sunday, and a few minutes later the Prime Minister went on the air. This phase of the war was at an end, Churchill declared, and he emphasized: 'We are fighting by ourselves alone; but we are not fighting for ourselves alone.' The French were, for the moment, slightly appeased; next day the Marquis de Castellane told Halifax that 'there was now a more hopeful outlook for Anglo-French relations, as a result of the Prime Minister's broadcast'.[13]

One incident, recounted by Churchill in his memoirs, would surely have been included in his speech if known at the time: two French peasant families, both of whom had lost sons at Oran, insisted on Union Jacks lying side by side with the Tricolors draped across the coffins. The gesture provided a symbol of one of the most pitiful events of the Second World War. But operations against the French fleets achieved more than the reduction of the risk presented by these warships: Britain's determination to continue the war, by all desperate means, was dramatically underlined; the message was well perceived by Ciano, who noted in his diary on 4 July: 'It proves that the fighting spirit of His Britannic Majesty's fleet is quite alive.'[14] Fighting spirit was stressed in Churchill's 14 July broadcast. 'Now, it has come to us to stand alone in the breach and face the worst that the tyrant's might and enmity can do.... We shall defend every village, every town, and every city.' And unknown to Churchill the country's supreme trial had begun: four days before, 10 July, is the date now used by historians to mark the opening of the Battle of Britain.

Indications of some imminent German action reached London on the very day British warships first clashed with the French. The COS, meeting on this tense Wednesday, 3 July, had been given a strong warning by the Army Director of Intelligence: considerable evidence pointed to an early invasion. An increase in German troops had been identified in southern Norway, including large numbers of parachutists. Sufficient merchant shipping had been gathered in Norwegian ports to transport two divisions and Norwegian craft had been requisitioned and armed. 'We could not hope to get any long warning of an invasion from this quarter.' Troops had also been concentrated in Denmark and large amounts of shipping had been observed at Baltic ports. Other troop concentrations were reported in Holland and two parachute regiments had moved to Belgium, where German air wings had been strengthened. Stocks of petrol were being built up; a German fighter patrol was continuously maintained above Calais, presumably to cover some activity. A Paris parade fixed for 7 July had been postponed; Hitler might want to use this occasion for a ceremonial entry into the city and also to announce his intention of carrying the war into Britain, while postponement of the date indicated German measures were not quite ready – this view was supported by evidence that *Luftwaffe* wings had not been made up to full strength. The COS were reminded that they had always believed a large-scale invasion would not be practical without German air superiority, but the enemy possibly intended to throw all resources at Britain and hope to get considerable troops ashore in the confusion.[15] At 11 p.m. this same day, 3 July, the Defence Committee also heard a report on early invasion possibilities. The Chief of Air Staff said the Joint Intelligence Sub-Committee believed grounds existed for expecting such an attempt to be imminent – 'there was nothing that could be taken as definite evidence, but there were indications from a number of directions which it would be unsafe to ignore'. Churchill called for more facts to be placed before the War Cabinet. Meanwhile, the Defence Committee also discussed Ireland: a Zurich message reported allegations of aggressive intentions by Britain on Eire, and action was threatened by Germany to forestall any British move. Committee members agreed 'that these articles followed the usual German techniques and might well be a prelude to a German move'.[16] Churchill, in a statement approved at the 3 July War Cabinet meeting, gave a strong warning to the fighting services and civil servants. 'On what may be the eve of an attempted invasion or battle for our native land, the Prime Minister desires to impress upon all persons holding responsible positions ... their duty to maintain a spirit of alert and confident energy.... They should check and rebuke any expressions of loose and ill-digested opinion. ... They should not hesitate to report, if necessary remove, any officers or officials who are found to be consciously exercising a disturbing influence, and whose talks are calculated to spread alarm and despondency.'[17]

The contents of this communication were included in a speech Churchill gave to the Commons on the 4th. News of the attack upon French warships had been released at 3 a.m.; Churchill now explained the operation to horrified MPs. 'I leave the judgment of our action, with confidence, to Parliament. I leave it to the nation, and I leave it to the United States. I leave it to the world and history.' Gradually, the House of Commons seemed to respond to Churchill's words and the effect of the speech was apparently to have a significance greater than its content. Until then Churchill, once the Conservative outcast, had never seemed fully accepted back by his own party, now, however, 'there occurred a scene unique in my own experience', remembered Churchill. All members, on all benches, stood to shout and cheer the Prime Minister, who sat trembling with tears streaming down his heavy cheeks. One newspaper correspondent later claimed credit for this reception: he had warned Chamberlain of the ill-effect on outside opinion of the Conservative attitude, and Chamberlain had hinted in a reply on 1 July that he would do something about it. The Conservatives' Chief Whip, Margesson, was rumoured to have pressed Tory members into enthusiastic action.[18]

Britain's main defence against invasion still rested with the Royal Navy – and the fleet still desperately needed destroyers; Churchill accordingly told the War Cabinet next day, Friday, 5 July, that he proposed to send another appeal to Roosevelt.[19] But a telegram arrived from Lord Lothian later in the day which indicated remaining obstacles in the way of destroyer transfer. Informed American opinion was at last beginning to realize the danger to America if the British fleet were lost and, Lothian continued, a number of influential people were considering a demand that America should enter the war immediately in order to give more effective help during the critical months. But, the Ambassador added, these sympathetic Americans believed it would be hard to swing public opinion unless Britain gave an assurance that, in the event of America coming into the war, remaining British warships would cross the Atlantic if Britain were overrun.[20] Churchill vehemently disagreed with Lord Lothian's opinion that this assurance should be given.

Ciano conferred with Hitler on Sunday, 7 July. 'He is rather inclined to continue the struggle and to unleash a storm of wrath and of steel upon the British. But the final decision has not been reached.'[21] Keitel explained to Ciano the difficulties involved in invasion – but an easy and essential operation, he continued, would be a major air attack upon the airfields, factories and principal communication centres.

Meanwhile, Air Marshall Dowding, head of Fighter Command, had been worrying about his retirement date. Since February 1937, his relinquishment of command had been the subject of last-minute changes of plan; at the end of April he had been asked to stay until 14 July; on 5 July he was asked, for the fifth time, to defer leaving. Dowding immediately wrote to Newall, Chief of Air Staff, seeking clarification. 'I am anxious to stay,' he stated. Dowding sent a copy of the letter to Sinclair, from whom he received a note on Wednesday, 10 July, confirming Dowding's retention of command at least until October.[22]

The War Cabinet met at noon on this Wednesday, and discussed the role of volunteers in the event of invasion. As the conference was continuing at 10 Downing Street, a Channel coastal convoy steamed south-west through the Straits of Dover. Six Hurricanes had been ordered to provide escort. Just before 1.30 p.m. the leading vessels came abreast of Dover and nearby RDF (radar) stations reported enemy aircraft gathering behind Calais. Further enemy air activity was identified, and the operations table at Dowding's Fighter Command HQ began to plot the first stage of the Battle of Britain.

The German aim during this preliminary period, lasting until about 18 August, was to harry the Channel convoys and draw out and weaken Fighter Command. At the same time, damage would be inflicted upon the coastal towns which would be important objectives in the eventual invasion. The 10 July engagement set the pattern for following days. The six RAF Hurricanes found themselves grossly outnumbered by long-range Messerschmitt 110s and short range 109s, both escorting about 20 Dornier bombers. The skirmish was hectic, short and deadly; and other RAF squadrons were called out to deal with enemy activity elsewhere in the Channel area. Teleprinter reports at Fighter Command HQ that evening showed over 600 sorties had been flown, twice as many as the daily average during the Dunkirk withdrawal.[23] Wear and tear was consequently increased and the next two days, 11 and 12 July, saw continuation of this high effort: no large German attacks on vital targets were attempted, but Fighter Command nevertheless became increasingly stretched. Dowding's resentment rose at having to divert precious strength to coastal duties. Although far below the level they would soon reach, night air attacks had shown an increase

– Aberdeen was hit on the night of 12 July, and over 50 people killed or seriously injured. At any moment the main enemy offensive could be launched; Dowding needed to keep all resources fully prepared and he criticized the Admiralty's demand that fighter escort should be provided for the mass of Channel shipping.

Much had still to be done to prepare for the main land and air battle. There was often administrative confusion – no air raid warning had been sounded when Aberdeen was attacked, yet on other occasions warnings were issued when no enemy bombers were near. As the War Cabinet had already noted, mysterious ground flares led to the belief that parachutists had landed, and on 10 July an official denial had to be issued. Civilians were uncertain as to action they should take in the event of invasion; also on 10 July the noon War Cabinet meeting discussed a leaflet titled: *If the Invader Comes*. The CIGS said that since this had been issued many inquiries had come for further details, but it was essential to decide whether defence arrangements should include civilian active resistance. Ironside believed civilians should keep out of actual fighting; and the War Cabinet agreed that 'armed civilians acting independently might well upset the plans of a military commander by their unexpected and unorganized activities'.[24] A 'Stay Put' campaign was launched, with messages conveyed in official advertisements such as that carried in *The Times* on 11 July. 'What do I do? I remember that this is the moment to act like a soldier. I do *not* get panicky. I *stay put*.... I remember that fighting men must have ·clear roads.'

Hitler's preoccupation with plans for crushing Britain began to grow – and his naval and military advisers were increasingly concerned about difficulties involved. On 11 July, Hitler ordered his service chiefs to a conference at Obersalzberg; on the same day, Admiral Erich Raeder, head of Naval Staff and responsible for the sea-borne invasion forces, urged the defeat of Britain through 'submarine warfare, air attacks on convoys and heavy air attacks on her main centres'.[25] Hitler's military conference took place on 13 July: the Führer could not understand why Britain did not seek peace; perhaps, he said, she still set her hope on Russia. In which case, 'England will have to be compelled by force'. Hitler wrote to Mussolini and declined his offer of help in the invasion of Britain; but his hesitation seemed to be ending. 'I am now convinced that any new appeal to reason would meet with ... rejection.'[26] And on Tuesday, 16 July, Hitler issued Directive No 16. Only seven copies were made. 'Since England, in spite of her hopeless military situation, shows no sign of being ready to come to an understanding, I have decided to prepare a landing operation against England and, if necessary, to carry it out. The aim of this operation will be to eliminate the English homeland as a base for the prosecution of the war against Germany and, if necessary, to occupy it completely.' Preparations for the operation had to be completed by mid-August. But heading the list of essential preliminary steps was the condition that 'the English Air Force must be so reduced morally and physically that it is unable to deliver any significant attack against the German crossing'.[27]

Hitler's directive specified the main assault would be on a wide front from about Ramsgate to the area west of the Isle of Wight. But on 17 July, the day after this directive, the British COS approved a report stating the main enemy seaborne assault would probably be aimed between the Wash and Newhaven. Southwold in Suffolk was among the most likely beach landing targets. The COS, in approving this report by the Joint Intelligence Committee, therefore envisaged the main enemy attack would come more towards the east coast, whereas Hitler's thoughts concentrated upon the south. The British report also reached conclusions considerably in advance of German plans at that time, declaring that beaches would be selected for the landing of a wave of tanks carried in small, flat-bottomed craft, and these tank waves would be supported by troops in specially equipped merchant ships which could be run ashore. Hitler made no detailed comments on the use of paratroopers; the Joint Intelligence Committee warned that up to 15,000 men might be air dropped in one day in East Anglia or Kent. By sea, the British report estimated, up to five divisions might be landed as an initial strike force.[28]

During this Wednesday, 17 July, Churchill toured Southern Command, leaving Chamberlain to chair the noon War Cabinet meeting. Brooke, who escorted him around his command area, discovered him 'in wonderful spirits and full of offensive plans for the next summer'. Churchill and Brooke now found themselves in close agreement; the Prime Minister gave the General's opinions much attention and two days later Brooke was to discover the reason for this careful scrutiny.[29]

On 18 July, for the first time since 1871, German troops strutted in victory parade through the Brandenburg Gate, Berlin. German soldiers had last marched through the gate on the drizzling, cold day of 16 December 1918, slouched in dejected defeat. Now a holiday spirit prevailed among Berliners – who were waiting with interest for a scheduled speech by Hitler to the Reichstag the following evening, Friday, 19 July. Churchill addressed the House of Commons during the Thursday afternoon. Excellent chances existed for defeating a German invasion, he declared, and the larger the attempt, the greater the target. 'There would be very great possibilities, to put it mildly, that this armada would be intercepted long before it reached the coast and all the men drowned in the sea or, at the worst, blown to pieces with their equipment while trying to land.'

Luftwaffe attacks on Channel convoys and south coast ports had continued, despite considerable casualties: at the end of the first nine days the Germans had lost 61 aircraft to Fighter Command's 28. But next day, 19 July, came a sharp reversal: in an engagement off Dover, six of nine RAF aircraft were lost and during the day Fighter Command suffered eight aircraft losses to only two for the *Luftwaffe*.[30] The German policy of draining RAF fighter strength might now start to succeed. This strategy was so far unrealized by the War Cabinet; no discussions took place during this initial period on the air conflict, and only later was it appreciated that the Battle of Britain had quietly begun. Meanwhile, at the War Cabinet meeting on the 19th, approval was given to General Brooke's appointment as C-in-C, Home Forces, in succession to Ironside.[31] 'I had done my best,' wrote Sir Edmund. 'And so my military career comes to an end in the middle of a great war.... I don't suppose Winston liked doing it, for he is always loyal to his friends.'[32] A War Office announcement declared that the decision had been taken to 'place the command of Home Forces in the hands of a Commander-in-Chief who has had immediate experience of command in France and Belgium'. 'I find it very hard to realize fully,' wrote Brooke in his diary after an evening interview with Eden, 'the responsibility that I am assuming. I only pray to God that I may be capable of carrying out the job. The idea of failure at this stage of the war is too ghastly to contemplate.'[33]

But as Brooke was seeing Eden, Adolf Hitler was addressing the Reichstag – and he extended to Britain the laurel branch of peace, albeit stained with French blood. 'In this hour I feel it to be my duty before my conscience to appeal once more to reason and common sense in Great Britain.' Hitler's voice was lower than usual and his words calm. 'I consider myself in a position to make this appeal since I am not the vanquished seeking favours, but the victor speaking in the name of reason. I can see no reason why this war must go on.' Less than an hour later the BBC had broadcast a rejection of this offer, without waiting for authorization. Indeed, the War Cabinet did not discuss the speech until the following week; no meetings were held during the Saturday and Sunday – for the first time since the start of the offensive in the west Ministers had been offered a weekend free from sessions. Hitler's speech was not deemed sufficient to alter arrangements. Churchill's reaction was to write to Chamberlain and Attlee on the 20th with a tentative suggestion that the speech might be answered by Parliamentary resolutions.[34] The idea was rejected by the War Cabinet on Wednesday, 24 July, and Ministers decided the Press 'should be discouraged from suggesting that there was anything in Hitler's speech which called for an official reply'.[35] Meanwhile, on the evening of the 22nd, Halifax had broadcast a confirmation of the BBC statement on the 19th: 'We shall not stop fighting until Freedom is secure.'

The three chiefs of the German forces were called to a conference with Hitler on Sunday, 21 July, and the Führer once more displayed his mixed doubt and determination – he also, for the first time, ordered plans for operations against the Soviets: Britain, he believed, pinned her hopes on Russia and America. 'The invasion of Britain is an exceptionally daring undertaking. Operational surprise cannot be expected; a defensively prepared and utterly determined enemy faces us.' The time of year was an important factor, 'since the weather in the North Sea and in the Channel during the second half of September is very bad, and the fogs begin in the middle of October. The main operations must therefore be completed by 15 September.' But, Hitler added, 'as air co-operation is decisive it must be regarded as the principal factor in fixing the date'. German naval staff planners had already made provisional estimates of the invasion force required, and Raeder confessed to Hitler on 22 July, the day following the conference, that the task was impossible. Hitler insisted plans should continue, at the same time his thoughts now dwelt increasingly upon Russia.

British War Cabinet discussions ranged wide on 22 July, over both offensive and defensive topics. Approval was given to a COS report, describing possible alternative bases should Gibraltar become unusable, and suggesting that a force should be ready to seize Cape Verde Island and the Azores if Spain or Portugal seemed intent on intervening against Britain. The War Cabinet also approved a new offensive department: the Special Operations Executive, presided over by Hugh Dalton, Minister of Economic Warfare, and aimed at co-ordinating all subversive and sabotage action.[36] Churchill's attention was also becoming fixed upon the Middle East. On 10 July, at his request, a Cabinet committee had been established to deal with problems concerned with this area, presided over by Eden. Other members were Leo Amery and Lloyd, representing India and the Colonies, and meetings were also attended by Lord Caldecote, the Dominions Secretary, the COS, and R. A. Butler, Under-Secretary at the Foreign Office. General Sir Archibald Wavell, C-in-C, Middle East, was committed to pushing back the Italians from their North African territories and from Abyssinia, but the British were heavily outnumbered and suffered from lack of equipment – which was also desperately needed at home. Wavell had so far adopted a policy of minor offensives, but even these were in danger of curtailment through ammunition shortages. On 23 July a depressing signal reached London from Wavell, warning that unless critical shortages could be made up within three months, his army's position would be at risk.[37] Churchill reacted with an explosive Minute to the COS. 'What is happening to the concert of the campaign in the Middle East? What has been done by the Committee of Ministers I recently set up? ... Make sure I have a report about the position which I can consider on Thursday morning.'[38] The Prime Minister became increasingly critical of Wavell, whom he had never met. Explanations put forward by the COS and the War Secretary failed to satisfy him, and Eden noted in his diary on Thursday, 25 July: 'Dined with Winston. Violent tirade after about Middle East and Wavell and at times heated altercation.... Bed at 1.30 a.m.'[39]

Earlier on this Thursday, the French Government put further obstacles in the way of the establishment of a British diplomatic representative at Vichy; Churchill sent a Minute to Halifax: 'I want to promote a kind of collusive conspiracy in the Vichy Government whereby certain members of the Government, perhaps with the consent of those who remain, will depart to North Africa in order to make a better bargain for France from North African shores and from a position of independence.'[40] The Minute provided a foretaste of the gigantic future operation, 'Torch'.

By now, 25 July, the impact of the German air strategy over the Channel had been realized in Whitehall. The previous day had seen teasing, simultaneous attacks on small convoys in the Thames Estuary and in the Dover Straits. Thursday brought a far more serious clash. A convoy of 21 merchant ships had left Southend in the morning; steaming off Deal, the slow ships were attacked by a wave of 35 dive-bombers, with other strikers following soon afterwards. RAF Spitfires found themselves heavily outnumbered and Hurricanes from the forward base at Hawkinge had to climb in full view of the enemy; Dowding reported to the Air Ministry: 'You never had time to gain height before you were attacked.' Five ships in the convoy were sunk and another six crippled; German E-boats later sank three of the latter.[41] Some means had clearly to be found to ease the Fighter Command burden. So, early on Friday the 26th, Dowding drove to London from his HQ at Bentley Priory, Stanmore, to attend a Defence Committee meeting at 11.30 a.m. Churchill opened this conference, held in the Admiralty's Upper War Room. 'We could hardly go on allowing convoys to sustain casualties on the scale experienced on the previous day.' Pound said some of the better armed Hunt class destroyers were now becoming available and could be used as escorts. 'It might be found that the Germans would concentrate on the destroyers and they might, or might not, succeed in withstanding these attacks.' This rather nebulous answer failed to satisfy the hard-pressed Fighter Command chief, and Dowding told the Committee that 'at times there were over 100 aircraft over the Channel.... This meant that most of the energies of our fighters were taken up in engaging enemy fighters, and the bombers often had a comparatively straight-forward task.' Dowding came to the main argument. 'He would like to point out, however, that the Channel convoys consisted of small ships, mostly engaged in the coal trade on the south coast, and it would not be a national calamity if it ceased.'[42] A compromise was eventually reached: merchant ships' sailings were stopped while the Admiralty worked out new arrangements for passing convoys through the most dangerous areas by night and escorting them more effectively by day for the remainder of their voyage.

Churchill had left the Defence Committee before the close of the discussions to attend the War Cabinet session starting at noon, when Ministers considered a memorandum by the Minister of Information, pointing out that while the morale of the people was very high, 'the present mood might not endure indefinitely'. Should such a deterioration develop, said the paper, the Government must be in a position to convey a clear and definite picture of the cause at stake. Halifax reminded the War Cabinet that at the start of the war Britain had taken the view that, if Germany would get rid of Hitlerism, no reason existed why Germany should not take her place in a new and better Europe. Later, he continued, this line had been dropped at French insistence and he thought it was important that Britain should return to it.[43]

This busy Friday continued with a special meeting of the COS, called to discuss the role of the three services in the event of invasion. Principal commanders concerned with the island's defence considered an Air Staff Memorandum, which was approved and became the main instructional directive. The paper maintained that invasion by sea was not a practical operation until Fighter Command had been defeated; consequently the preliminary invasion stage was likely to be a large-scale air offensive against fighter defences and a heavy air attack might simultaneously be made on naval forces and their bases. Discussion at the meeting also touched upon the Royal Navy's difficulties in preparing for counter-invasion operations while at the same time safeguarding essential overseas supplies.[44] As a result, one participant at this conference came away considerably perturbed; Brooke, upon whose forces the responsibility for dealing with a successful landing would fall, wrote in his diary: 'The attitude of representatives of the Naval Commander brought out very clearly the fact that the Navy now realizes fully that its position on the sea has been seriously undermined by the advent of aircraft.' He added : 'Sea supremacy is no longer what it was and in the face of strong bomber forces can no longer ensure the safety of this island. This throws a much heavier task on the Army.'[45] Next day, 27 June, German aircraft seemed to underline Brooke's point. Now that the Channel convoys had been temporarily stopped, the *Luftwaffe* turned upon Royal Navy warships : two destroyers were sunk and a third damaged. On Sunday, 28 July, the Admiralty admitted that command of the Straits in daylight had been lost and Dover destroyers were withdrawn to Portsmouth.

During this Sunday troops intended for the first wave of the German invasion began to arrive in the coastal areas facing England and, in London, the Middle East Committee decided more British troops and valuable equipment should be sent to help Wavell in Egypt, although this reinforcement would not leave until invasion dangers had lessened.[46] *Luftwaffe* formations came back again during the afternoon to prey above the Channel, and the resulting clash was described to the War Cabinet next morning, Monday, 29 July – this session was held in the War Room deep underground at Storey's Gate. One hundred enemy aircraft had been engaged by four RAF squadrons, Ministers were told. 'During the day the enemy had lost nine machines for certain. Our losses amounted to two machines, plus two more damaged.' Another air engagement had taken place over Dover early that morning and information was still being received. Four RAF squadrons had been directed against the raiders, and 'the latest report was that the enemy had lost eight machines for certain, eight more probable, and six possible. One of our pilots had been killed and several machines had been damaged.'

Much of the remainder of this War Cabinet meeting was devoted to the struggle for allies and for co-operation from foreign nations. Diplomatic activities with America had followed two main lines, which before long were to converge. Lothian had suggested at the end of May that Britain should consider making a formal offer to allow America to construct airfields and naval stations on British islands of strategic importance to the United States, perhaps in Newfoundland and Trinidad. The War Cabinet had hesitated, believing it undesirable to make an offer unless Britain could be assured of substantial advantages, but Lothian had persisted; communications on the subject passed between the Ambassador, the War Cabinet and the Foreign Office throughout June and July. The Foreign Office supported Lothian and, at Halifax's request, had drawn up a Memorandum for the War Cabinet. The COS had agreed that it would be desirable to meet US requirements, and necessary approval had been obtained from the territories concerned. Now, on 29 July, the Foreign Office Memorandum was put before the War Cabinet. Meanwhile, the question of obtaining destroyers from America had remained prominent. Lothian had told Churchill on 5 July that US opinion had at last begun to realize America might lose the British fleet if Britain were successfully invaded. On 22 July he added that with the end of the Presidential election conventions, public attention was again concentrated upon the war and he had been asked by Americans what action the US should take, to which Lothian had replied that 100 destroyers should be sent. A few days later the Ambassador made a broadcast referring to Britain's need of these warships and, on the night of 27 July, Churchill told him this shortage was more acute than ever.[47]

The Memorandum submitted to the War Cabinet on the 29th proposed that Britain should offer America, 'without asking for any *quid pro quo*', facilities on specified British territories. In discussion, reported the official Minutes, Ministers 'argued that it was doubtful whether the facilities, once granted, could be withdrawn at the end of the war and that this might prove the thin end of the wedge'. Lord Lloyd, the Colonial Secretary, was firmly against the idea and considered it might result in loss of sovereignty. But, the Minutes continued, 'the United States had supplied us with so much that it was difficult to refuse their request; and their attitude was increasingly favourable towards us.' Some Ministers also argued that caution should be exercised with a Pan American Airways request for facilities – Pan American 'had shown itself in the past to be hostile to British interests'. The War Cabinet therefore agreed in principle to the grant of aircraft landing facilities in Jamaica, Georgetown and Trinidad, a lease to Pan American of a small area near Trinidad airport, a lease for an airfield in British Guiana, permission for Pan American to construct an airfield near Kingston, and authority for the US army to send training flights to Newfoundland. Final approval would be given after consideration of any special conditions with regard to the Pan American grant.[48]

Ministers emerged from the underground HQ. Eden, who specially disliked this stuffy War Room, had already complained about meeting there, 'not least because I sat in line with the Prime Minister and not opposite him as in the Cabinet Room, where I could see his expression. I did not like to argue out of the corner of my mouth.' Soon after this meeting Churchill asked to see Eden alone and spoke of a Government reshuffle: Chamberlain was finding it increasingly difficult to attend meetings and keep pace with Cabinet work – illness was rapidly overtaking him. One answer, Churchill now said, was to bring Eden into the War Cabinet proper, but he added that he thought Eden would prefer to stay where he was 'since there was no more important work to be done anywhere'. Eden agreed, and no more was said at that time.[49] The War

Secretary was pre-occupied with the Middle East and with trying to improve Churchill's opinion of Wavell. Next day, Tuesday, 30 July, the COS agreed with suggested reinforcements as detailed by the Middle East Committee two days before. Also on this Tuesday another desperate telegram arrived from Wavell: 'We cannot continue indefinitely to fight this war without proper equipment and I hope the Middle East requirements will be delayed no longer.'[50] And within 24 hours the British had been obliged to evacuate Sollum, on the Egyptian-Libyan border: British advance posts were pulled back to the fortified position at Mersa Matruh. Eden commented: 'Sad, but not unexpected.'

Churchill warned a secret session of the House of Commons on 31 July that a crisis might soon be imminent. 'Winston surpassed himself,' observed Harold Nicolson. 'The situation is obscure. It may be that Hitler will first bomb us with gas and then try to land. At the same time, Italy and Japan will hit us as hard as they can. It will be a dreadful month.'[51] The Prime Minister wrote to Roosevelt during the evening. 'It has now become most urgent for you to let us have the destroyers, motor-boats and flying-boats for which we have asked ... Mr President, with great respect I must tell you that in the long history of the world this is a thing to do *now*.'[52]

Hitler was holding a military conference. Two days before the German Naval Staff had drawn up a memorandum advising 'against undertaking the operation [invasion] this year,' and Raeder now expanded this opinion: the weather was unpredictable and a calm sea would be essential – even if the first assault wave crossed successfully, weather conditions might deteriorate before the second and third could make their attempt. Moreover, the Army wanted a wide front from the Dover Straits to Lyme Bay which, said Raeder, was far too broad. He pressed again for a delay until May 1941. But Hitler had other plans for 1941; according to notes jotted down by Halder, the Chief of Staff, 'if Russia is smashed, Britain's last hope will be shattered.... Decision. In view of these considerations Russia must be liquidated. Spring 1941.' Despite this conclusion, plans for the assault on Britain – now termed Operation 'Sealion' – would go forward, with 15 September as a target date; a final decision would be made after the *Luftwaffe* 'had made concentrated attacks on southern England for one week. If the effect of the air attacks is such that the enemy air force, harbours and naval forces etc., are heavily, damaged, Operation "Sealion" will be carried out in 1940. Otherwise it is to be postponed until May 1941.'[53]

Next day, 1 August, the Soviet Foreign Minister declared that Russo-German relations were in excellent shape and scorned 'attempts to frighten us with the prospect of an increase in German strength'. He did however call for 'increased military preparedness'. Molotov, opening the seventh session of the USSR Supreme Council, said that after the hostile British acts towards Russia, it was difficult to expect a favourable development of Anglo-Soviet relations, although Sir Stafford Cripps' appointment as Ambassador might be a sign of a desire to improve these relations. The War Cabinet meeting on this Thursday discussed a telegram from Sir Stafford, dated 31 July. He had complained of the great difficulty he was experiencing in obtaining an interview with Molotov and suggested Halifax should see the Russian Ambassador, Maisky, and 'indicate to him that it was hardly necessary to maintain an Ambassador to a Government whose Minister for Foreign Affairs declined to receive him'. Halifax told the War Cabinet that while he was perfectly willing to see Maisky, he did not feel inclined to go so far as to threaten withdrawal. The War Cabinet agreed.

Newall told the War Cabinet that 'there was nothing of importance to report in regard to air operations'.[54] But during this same day, Hitler issued his Directive No 17, one of the briefest he wrote. 'In order to establish the necessary conditions of the final conquest of England I intend to intensify air and sea warfare against the English homeland. I therefore order.... The German Air Force is to overpower the English Air Force with all the forces at its command.'[55] Date for the start of the battle was on or after 5 August – four days away.

Late on the day of Hitler's directive, 1 August, German bombers droned over Hampshire and Somerset dropping green and yellow leaflets. Titled *The Last Appeal to Reason*, these sheets contained the text of Hitler's Reichstag speech: they became popular purchases at Red Cross auctions. Next morning Hermann Göring issued orders to his *Luftwaffe* wings: RAF fighter defences in the south must be smashed in four days, and the whole RAF defeated within four weeks. Operation 'Eagle' would begin when the weather was favourable and final preparations were completed.

During the first week of August, the last days of comparative quiet, the War Cabinet found time to look further than Britain's threatened beaches. Relations with France and America led to long and complicated discussions. Lord Lothian cabled on the night of 1-2 August that Roosevelt's advisers wanted to sell Britain up to 60 destroyers, but necessary legislation would be opposed by isolationists in Congress and the issue would bog down in the Presidential election campaign. One possible solution was for America to sell the destroyers to Canada, with whom Britain would make some arrangement. A better answer might be for the destroyers to be purchased in exchange for the sale to the US of defence bases in Newfoundland, Bermuda, Trinidad and possibly elsewhere. Churchill sent a cable to the Ambassador on Saturday, 3 August: 'Second alternative, i.e. bases, is agreeable, but we prefer that it should be on lease indefinitely and not for sale. It is understood that this will enable us to secure destroyers and flying boats at once.... Go ahead on these lines full steam.'[56] But only three hours later Lothian telegraphed that the President had now made it clear there was no way of selling destroyers except by Congressional legislation and Congress would only approve if 'molasses' were offered – a public assurance from the British Government that if events went badly the fleet would leave British waters if necessary, and continue to fight overseas.[57] The War Cabinet met at noon on Tuesday, 6 August, to consider Roosevelt's statement, and a reply was ready late on 7 August and eventually sent to Lothian on the afternoon of the 8th. The discouraging message was written in Churchill's most haughty tone. 'Our position is not such as to bring the collapse of Britain into the arena of practical discussion. Pray make it clear at once that we could never agree to the slightest compromising of our full liberty of action, nor tolerate any such defeatist announcement, the effect of which would be disastrous.' Churchill did open one chink of compromise: if Britain were overrun the position of the fleet would be as described in his 4 June speech – in which Churchill declared that if 'this island, or a large part of it, were subjugated and starving' the British Empire, armed and guarded by the British Fleet, would continue the struggle until 'the New World, with all its power and might, steps forth to the rescue and the liberation of the Old'. This previous statement was as far as Churchill would go and there, for the moment, the matter rested.[58]

Relations with France had been discussed by the War Cabinet on Friday, 2 August, when Duff Cooper thought negotiation with Vichy was inconsistent with British policy elsewhere. Halifax agreed, but believed any break should come from the French rather than from Britain.[59] Discussion was resumed three days later, 5 August, when the Prime Minister informed the War Cabinet that de Gaulle proposed to form a Council of Defence of French possessions beyond the sea, composed of those qualified authorities which decided to join the General. Churchill said he intended to give Britain's approval, and the War Cabinet agreed. On the same day Ministers also approved the final text of an agreement with the Free French leader; de Gaulle wanted a clause specifying his troops would not have to 'take up arms against France', and had asked that the agreement should also include mention of 'the full restoration of the independence and greatness of France'. Churchill commented that 'it was undesirable that we should agree to phrases

85

the interpretation of which might land us in difficulties', and it was therefore proposed to accept the text but to protect Britain's position by an exchange of letters. The agreement was nevertheless soon to lead Britain into difficulties linked with another decision taken at this 5 August meeting. The War Cabinet had before them memoranda by Churchill and the COS on the possibilities of Free French action overseas. Churchill said Britain should give 'every encouragement', and a number of possible operations had been mentioned, including landing troops in Morocco, Algeria and Tunis. Each of these projects, continued Churchill, had been dismissed 'for the sufficient reason that Britain would have to supply land forces to carry it out; we did not wish to embark on the course of active conquest of any part of the French Empire.... De Gaulle had himself taken the view that a landing in one of the French West African possessions would offer better prospects.' A plan had therefore been drawn up: de Gaulle's force should be ready to sail for West Africa on 15 August, 'with a view to hoisting the Free French flag in French territories in West Africa, the occupation of Dakar and the consolidation under the Free French flag of the French Colonies in West and Equatorial Africa'. Some Ministers had doubts; according to the official Minutes: 'De Gaulle's plans were being drawn up on the assumption that he would be able to make an unopposed landing, but there could be no certainty that this would be possible.... Duala seemed to be the most hopeful port of disembarkation and Dakar the least hopeful. Dakar had formidable fixed defences.' Alexander, in a statement which within hours was to grow in impact, stressed that Britain would be providing the naval escort and 'we should be committed to action at sea if French warships should attempt to stop the expedition'. But Ministers agreed in principle to the operation, known then as 'Scipio', and emphasized 'it was of the utmost importance to conduct the preparations in secrecy'.[60]

The COS, lukewarm over the idea from the start and believing it contradicted Britain's continued attempts to improve relations with Vichy, became even less enthusiastic later this day, 5 August. To their consternation they found that de Gaulle had taken no account of the possibility of French Vichy naval forces interfering with the Dakar landing. Moreover, in talks between Churchill and de Gaulle on the 6th, the General asked Britain to guarantee his expedition against any forces sent by Vichy by sea.[61] The new situation was considered by the COS at 11 p.m. on 7 August; they stressed the conflict between this operation and relations with Vichy, and emphasized the danger of war with Metropolitan France. But the Chiefs agreed that the Dakar operation should be attempted – if reports from local agents indicated de Gaulle would be welcomed.[62] Early on the 8th, Churchill called for plans to be drawn up. 'It would seem extremely important to British interests that General de Gaulle should take Dakar at the earliest moment.' Now, however, Churchill's enthusiasm for the idea seemed to rule out the possibility of the operation being cancelled if local reports were unfavourable. 'If his [de Gaulle's] emissaries report that it can be taken peaceably so much the better. If their report is adverse an adequate Polish and British force should be provided and full naval protection given. The operation once begun must be carried through.'[63] The scheme had therefore escalated far beyond the original idea. Nevertheless, the COS went ahead with the planning and Churchill approved the appointment of Vice-Admiral John Cunningham and Major-General Irwin as the commanders. These officers visited Churchill at Chequers on the night of 12 August and, in Churchill's words: 'I drafted their instructions myself.'[64]

Full details were put before the War Cabinet at noon next day, Tuesday, 13 August, when Churchill explained that under the revised scheme, now code-named 'Menace', it was proposed to establish de Gaulle at Dakar by a *coup de main*. Only about 2,500 Senegalese troops were believed stationed at Dakar, with about 200 French officers. 'The forces which we sent would be sufficient to overcome the garrison if it came to a fight. The whole operation would be completed between dawn and dusk.' Vichy might declare war, admitted the Prime Minister. 'It would not perhaps matter very much if they did, but on the whole it was unlikely that they would do so.' Attlee said he liked the scheme, but Halifax had doubts: he asked for a day in which to consider possible Vichy reactions. Subject to this further study by the Foreign Secretary, the War Cabinet approved the plan outlined by the Prime Minister.[65] So, under the new scheme, British troops would now be openly used and the operation would be carried through regardless of opposition – which was not expected to be strong. Churchill recognized the danger of prolonged fighting; on the other hand, Britain was rapidly coming to need some kind of victory: so far British war efforts had seemed to lead to purely defensive measures, or to negative results – or to failure. The Dakar expedition might help to restore some British prestige; moreover, as Churchill commented in writing of the Dakar operation, 'these were days in which far more serious risks were the commonplaces of our daily life'.[66] And these serious risks were looming.

Thirteen crack German divisions for the first invasion wave had completed deployment on Saturday, 3 August – the same day that Churchill issued a statement to the Press: 'The Prime Minister wishes it to be known that the possibility of German attempts at invasion has by no means passed away. The fact that the Germans are now putting about rumours that they do not intend an invasion should be regarded with a double dose of suspicion which attaches to their utterances.' Halifax told the War Cabinet on 7 August: The German Military Attaché at Angora has reported the attack on England is due to start on 11 August.'[67] Next day the COS considered and approved a long Minute on defence against invasion which had been completed by Churchill earlier in the week. 'Complete agreement' existed between the Chiefs' assessment and that drawn up by the Prime Minister. 'Indeed,' Churchill was informed, 'it is remarkable how closely the present distribution of Home Defence divisions corresponds with your figure.'[68]

At the War Cabinet meeting on the 8 August Newall said there was little to report; yet within minutes the bloodiest Battle of Britain engagements so far were to take place, and the tragic preliminaries had already begun. The previous evening the first large Channel convoy since the end of July had assembled in the Thames estuary. The merchant ships would sail west under new protective plans drawn up by the Admiralty: two destroyers would provide escort; the merchantmen would slip through the most dangerous waters during darkness; specially modified vessels carried barrage balloons; a strong fighter escort would meet the ships at first light on the 8th. But, during the convoy lull the Germans had erected a radar set on the Wissant cliffs – and this detected the convoy moving during the night. E-boats streaked across the Channel to lay ambush and, in the small hours of the 8th, hell and destruction erupted. German surface craft chased and harried the stricken merchantmen along the Sussex coast: two were sunk, a third damaged, and before daylight two ships collided causing one to sink. Fighter Command aircraft rose to give the planned protection, but by now the convoy had ceased to exist. Scattered, vulnerable merchant ships wallowed below as the RAF and *Luftwaffe* clashed in vicious, individual dogfights. By the end of the day more than half the 25 vessels had been damaged and six sunk. But in the air the RAF claimed a victory, to be described to the War Cabinet next morning, Friday, 9 August.

Throughout Thursday Churchill was handed minute by minute accounts of the fighting above the Channel. But his attention was also directed towards the Middle East, as he met, for the first time, General Wavell. Described by Eden as 'not a man who could be drawn out', Wavell was never able to establish an easy, give and take relationship with Churchill, despite common private interests – especially painting and poetry. The C-in-C Middle East had arrived in London the previous day, Wednesday, and early on the Thursday he talked alone with Eden; the War Secretary described him as 'in good heart, but the deficiencies are shocking. We shall have

88

to make him up, a parcel of what we can scrape together and send it out soon.'[69] Wavell then attended the COS meeting and a session of the Middle East Committee: he gave a long report of his position and chronic shortages. The real danger would be the introduction of German armoured and motorized units; moreover, owing to lack of pre-war preparations, British Intelligence sources in Libya were deficient – German troops might therefore arrive without British knowledge. Extensive operations against the Sudan could not begin before the end of the rainy season in October, he continued, but he did not consider the Italian capture of Kassala important. In Kenya, the post of Moyale on the Abyssinian escarpment had been lost and plans for an early advance into Italian Somaliland had been set back, but Kenya itself should be in no danger. In British Somaliland an Italian force was advancing from Abyssinia, and Wavell reminded his listeners that it had been the original British intention to evacuate this dependency, which was of little strategic importance. He added, however, that he should like to hold the territory and he had moved a British battalion from Aden to reinforce the Indian and African troops holding the garrison.[70] At the end of Wavell's report, described by Eden as 'masterly' the Middle East Committee and the COS strongly recommended the speeding-up of convoys to Cairo. Wavell then went for his first discussions with Churchill. Ciano, in Rome, was also discussing the Middle East on this Thursday; Rudolfo Graziani, the Army Commander, informed him that the proposed Italian attack on Egypt was 'a very serious undertaking ... our present preparations are far from perfect'. Graziani added: 'We move towards a defeat which, in the desert, must inevitably develop into a rapid and total disaster.'[71]

Newall told Ministers next day, 9 August, that 'the fighting which had taken place off the Isle of Wight on the previous day had been the biggest air action off our coast so far. The enemy's main effort had developed into three successive attacks, involving at least 300 aircraft.... Our fighters had achieved great success.' Losses were estimated at 18 RAF aircraft to 66 German, with 52 of the latter confirmed. The War Cabinet 'congratulated the Secretary of State for Air and the Chief of the Air Staff on this fine achievement'.[72] After the war, however, the respective losses were in fact shown to have been 31 German and 20 RAF aircraft. Eden drove to Chequers later in the day, after inspecting positions in East Anglia, and the War Secretary, Churchill and Wavell continued discussions; Eden wrote: 'Churchill still kept, I think, his reservations about Wavell.' Agreement was reached that the War Office should prepare a list of forces which could be sent to the Middle East immediately, despite risks of invasion.[73]

Next morning, Saturday, 10 August, in Berlin Göring decreed that the *Luftwaffe* should launch Operation 'Eagle' on the 13th; in Somaliland one of the four main British positions was captured after heavy Italian artillery bombardment; in London Dill passed to Churchill a list of items for Middle East reinforcement. The CIGS recommended that 102 cruiser and infantry tanks should be sent – leaving only about 250 in Britain. In addition, 52 of the less effective light tanks should be despatched, together with anti-tank, anti-aircraft, field and Bren-guns. Staff discussions in the morning resulted in unqualified approval; Churchill wrote: 'The decision to give this blood-transfusion while we braced ourselves to meet a mortal danger was at once awful and right. No one faltered.'[74] But disagreement now arose over the route these reinforcements should take: through the short but dangerous Mediterranean, as Churchill ardently advocated, or around the safe Cape route, as the Admiralty vehemently insisted. The conflict was to continue, strong and sometimes bitter, for the next week.

Meanwhile, preliminaries had begun for the main phase of the Battle of Britain. Newall reported to the War Cabinet at 12.30 p.m., Monday, 12 August: 'At 10.30 yesterday morning five raids started against Portland and Weymouth on a 20-mile front, in which 200 enemy machines took part, of which 150 crossed the coast. This raid was met by seven of our fighter squadrons. Attacks were made on the Dover balloon barrage, resulting in the destruction of seven balloons. Attacks by two waves of 100 enemy aircraft were made on convoys in the Thames estuary.' Twenty Hurricanes and five Spitfires were estimated to have been lost, compared with 60 enemy aircraft. He concluded that 'a number of enemy raids are in progress at this moment, including one at Portsmouth, but detailed information is not yet available'.[75] Göring was in fact throwing the *Luftwaffe* against Fighter Command's forward airfields at Manston, Lympne and Hawkinge, at six RDF south coast stations, and at Portsmouth and Gosport naval installations. His aim was to destroy the RAF's radar screen, without which Fighter Command would be half blind: one RDF station, at Ventnor in the Isle of Wight, was so effectively hit that a gap was torn in the radar station chain which could not be bridged for 10 days. But during the evening the *Luftwaffe* chief made a severe mistake: instead of ordering the continuation of this offensive against vital RDF posts, he issued final instructions for the all-out attack on Fighter Command itself.

Late on this night of 12 August, as *Luftwaffe* pilots readied their machines, Churchill was conducting a hectic meeting of the Defence Committee. The subject was the Middle East; Wavell was in attendance. Discussion began at 10 p.m. and was first taken up with the continuing argument over the Middle East convoy route.

Pound laboriously repeated his case: relatively slow MT ships would render the fleet vulnerable to air, submarine and surface attack. The Italians would be ready; chances of getting through were remote. Churchill retorted that 'the Admiralty appeared to be taking an unduly pessimistic view of the risks involved. In his opinion it should be possible to pass a convoy of three fast ships through to Egypt.... The presence of the ships would act as bait and should draw down upon them concentrations of Italian naval units and thereby afford the desired opportunity to inflict serious damage upon the Italian navy.' But he added that 'he felt bound to accept the opinion of the Naval Staff although he was not in agreement with it'. Wavell said that much as he wanted the reinforcements quickly, 'the risks of losing them in passage through the Mediterranean, and the fact that if this equipment were lost much of it could not be replaced for several months, would not in his opinion justify the gain in time'. The meeting decided to defer a decision for the moment. Wavell then gave an account of his military dispositions; Churchill immediately took vigorous exception to his plans, and Wavell sat silent, astonished by the Prime Minister's aggressiveness. The Prime Minister continued to vent his views after the meeting had officially finished, long past midnight, with Churchill striding up and down the garden at 10 Downing Street. 'All this was not novel to Dill or me,' wrote Eden, 'but to Wavell it was.'[76] Finally, at 2 a.m. Churchill went to his bed.

Dawn broke on Tuesday, 13 August, with a thick bank of murky cloud reaching down to 4,000 feet over the wet green countryside of south-east England. Nervous pilots in Messerschmidt, Dornier and Junker aircraft raced their engines on airfields in Belgium and France. RAF Fighter Command aircraft were receiving their daily oiling and tuning and thick belts of glinting ammunition were being fed into guns. Dowding was completing a letter which he would remember to send during the day to Newall, thanking him for a recent note which had confirmed he would not be retired for the moment. And 'Eagle' day had come.

5

Day of Eagles

Operation Eagle almost failed to begin on 13 August; the thick cloud continued to cling and thus spoilt Göring's plan for a combination of bombing and high-level fighter sweeps. The cloud would slice between the fighters above and the German bombers below, around which Dowding's pilots would be able to swarm unmolested. So, soon after sunrise, the morning attacks were cancelled. But the instructions came too late: Dornier 17 and Junker 88 bombers were already airborne. Some fighters wheeled back to base, but the bulk of the bombers, unaware of the change of plan, headed unprotected for their targets. Fighter Command aircraft, given 30 minutes warning from radar stations, scrambled to intercept. Bombers bound for Sheerness were pounced upon soon after breaking cloud and Hurricanes forced them to drop their bombs well short of target. Sixty miles to the west, two more enemy bomber formations were crossing the Sussex coast: Hurricanes were sent in at exactly the right moment, meeting the enemy near Bognor and near Worthing. A third German force had more success: after having to navigate by dead reckoning through thick cloud, they managed to break cover so close to their target at East-church that Spitfires had insufficient time to catch them before they shed their bombs.[1]

While harsh dogfights were continuing in the heavy skies and bombs burst upon Fighter Command bases, the War Cabinet met at 10 Downing Street and Ministers heard the first reports of 'considerable air activity'. One raid had come over the Thames estuary, said Sir Cyril Newall, and another, estimated at 250 aircraft, had entered over Selsey Bill as far as Horsham. 'According to reports so far available, the casualties were as follows: our own – 3 aircraft crashed, 2 unaccounted for; enemy – 6 confirmed, 11 unconfirmed, 19 damaged.'[2] With news of the German air effort came renewed invasion fears: during the morning General Brooke was given Admiralty information of a German embarkation from Nor-

92

way on the night of the 11th: an invasion was to be expected, directed against Scotland.[3] Brooke spent the afternoon inspecting coastal defences from Exmouth to Weymouth, accompanied by Churchill, while German aircraft returned at 3.30 p.m. to hit airfields north and south of the Thames estuary with about 50 bombers, this time strongly escorted, and another 40 bombers struck at airfields on the Salisbury Plain and at Southampton dockside buildings. Activity dwindled; since dawn 1,000 German sorties had been flown, and 700 RAF. But Göring's initial onslaught, muted by the weather, had failed.

Churchill returned to London in time to meet Eden and Sir John Dill at 6 p.m. Wavell was not present at this continuation of Middle East talks, and Churchill now made plain his low opinion of the Commander. At the War Cabinet meeting earlier in the day, Churchill had said that 'he had taken a great liking to General Wavell', yet now, according to Eden, he judged him to be no more than 'a good average colonel'. Dill, on the other hand, agreed with Wavell's dispositions and believed, with Eden, he had 'exceptional ability'.[4]

War Cabinet Ministers were informed at their meeting next day, Wednesday 14th, that air raids the previous day had been 'on a heavier scale than any yet experienced. The raids had been on a front from Weymouth to the Thames estuary, and some of them had penetrated from 25 to 30 miles inland.' All attacks had been intercepted and heavy losses inflicted with few RAF casualties; figures were, according to Newall, 13 RAF machines lost – out of which 10 pilots had been saved – compared with 78 German aircraft destroyed 'for certain', 33 probable and 49 damaged. Official totals after the war were to put these at 45 German aircraft lost, against 13 RAF aircraft but only 7 pilots. Anthony Eden told the War Cabinet of police reports of 45 parachutes having been found, apparently abandoned by the enemy, in various parts of Scotland, Derbyshire, Staffordshire and Yorkshire. A box with maps and instructions was also said to have been discovered; two parachutists were reported captured. Ministers discussed whether a reward should be offered for the capture of parachutists, but decided against the idea; however, they believed the widest publicity should be given to this landing of enemy agents, if it was confirmed, in order to enlist civilian help.[5] These paratroop drops were later discovered to be fakes, but the publicity and general rumours led to considerable apprehension and the persecution of innocent civilians suspected of being enemy troops.

Also on this Wednesday morning the Defence Committee met to discuss 'pilot wastage'. The session heard cold, dispassionate details of this very human problem: 'the postulated wastage, which was

93

taken as a basis for planning the production of pilots from training establishments, was at present fixed at 746 per month.' The unemotional exposition continued: 'this figure was reduced to 650 net by excluding those pilots who returned subsequently to duty. On the other hand, the actual figures for loss of pilots, in action and accidents, for June/July were as follows: June – 318 killed, 43 wounded; total 361. July – 208 killed, 70 wounded; total 278.' The number of pilots available was obviously as important as the number of machines for them to fly; the high wastage could therefore be disastrous if the Air Ministry figures proved correct. Churchill disbelieved the 746 monthly total and asked Sir Christopher Courtney, of the Air Ministry, how the figure had been obtained. Sir Christopher replied that 'it was necessary to estimate the intensity of fighting which might take place. If this estimate were too low then the training output, which was based on the wastage figure, would prove too small. If it were too high then the output of pilots would be too large, but this would enable us to build up surplus.' The Prime Minister asked for more details.[6]

Clouds had closed even further down upon the Kent and Sussex countryside, and Göring decided not to repeat the mistake of the previous day. He marshalled his forces for a massive all-out attack due to start at dawn the following day. So, on Thursday, 15 August, more *Luftwaffe* aircraft were thrown at Britain than at any time in the battle. For the first time, German aircraft were used from *Luftflotte 5* based in Norway – these would strike at the north of England, while *Luftflotten* 2 and 3 slashed again at the south. The plan was daring – the aircraft from Norway would be almost at the end of their range and incapable of attacking well-defended targets – but Göring believed Dowding had lost so many aircraft on the 13th that he would have to take fighters from the north to guard against the southern attacks. Dowding refused to oblige. Spitfires from Acklington, led by a young flight-lieutenant, closed in on the enemy raiders off the Farne Islands. The weather was fine and clear; 13 miles from the Northumberland coast, the 12 Spitfires sighted 100 enemy bombers. The outnumbered RAF pilots swooped in from the sun and stared disbelievingly at the enemy reaction: the bombers hurriedly split into two formations, one heading rapidly east, the other making for Tyneside. The latter were intercepted by Spitfires from Catterick and forced to flee; the first was engaged by remaining Spitfires from Acklington, by the Tyne guns, and by southern Hurricane pilots on 'rest and recuperation' from heavy work during previous days. Fifteen enemy aircraft were destroyed without a single RAF casualty. German bombers attacking across the North Sea at an airfield near Great Driffield had more success, but eight were nevertheless brought down. In the south Fighter Command 11 and 10 Groups frantically tried to deal with German marauders reaching for vital airfields. Aircraft were wheeling, fighting, retiring, fighting again – all 22 squadrons were engaged. The enemy filtered through the defences at a number of points: bases in Suffolk, at Eastchurch, Hawkinge, Worthy Down, Middle Wallop, West Malling and Croydon received varying damage, and the Short Aircraft factory, Rochester, also suffered.[7] The *Luftwaffe* flew nearly 1,800 sorties, the RAF almost 1,000; 75 German aircraft had been destroyed to the RAF's 34. Dowding had used his resources brilliantly, and Churchill gave him full credit: 'We must regard the generalship here shown as an example of genius in the art of war.'[8] But the War Cabinet, meeting at noon at 10 Downing Street, heard of a new complication with regard to the air war. Lord Halifax drew attention to a telegram from Washington, in which Lord Lothian said the claims made by the British and Germans as to the number of aircraft destroyed were so contradictory that 'there was a risk that it might be thought both sides were telling lies'. The Air Secretary told Ministers that the existing practice was to treat as destroyed an aircraft which the pilot saw crash or break in pieces in the air, or go down in flames. He admitted the possibility of mistake, or of two pilots seeing the same aircraft. 'On the other hand, our published figures of enemy aircraft destroyed were almost certainly under the mark, since they did not include any aircraft which did not comply with this test, or aircraft known to be seriously damaged and probably unable to get home. Again, no allowance was made for aircraft brought down by our own pilots who failed to return.'

Ministers were told that the argument over the route for Middle East supplies was still continuing, but 'it had been arranged to defer the decision until the 26th' when more information would be available.[9] During the day the British commander in Somaliland sought permission for withdrawal – 'the only course to save us from disastrous defeat and annihilation'.[10] Middle East HQ gave authorization. Wavell left London in the late afternoon to return to Cairo, after Churchill, who wanted more talks, had reluctantly given permission. The Prime Minister had asked Eden for a possible alternative for Wavell as Middle East C-in-C and had agreed General Auchinleck was the best choice. 'But we both felt,' wrote Eden, 'that we had not sufficient evidence to compel a change which at the moment might have had a very bad effect on morale'.[11] Italy, now free to occupy British Somaliland, also seemed to be threatening in another direction: a Greek cruiser, the *Helle*, was sunk by an unidentified submarine, and the Italians were immediately – and correctly – suspected. At the same time, Rome newspapers and radio broadcasts opened a violent campaign demanding the cession of Epirus and accusing Athens of 'unneutral' behaviour in favour of Great Britain.[12]

Also on 15 August, Churchill wrote to President Roosevelt: he was unable to go beyond his speech of 4 June with regard to the British fleet sailing to America, despite the need for a destroyer agreement. 'In any use you may make of this repeated assurance [of 4 June] you will please bear in mind the disastrous effect from our point of view, and perhaps also from yours, of allowing any impression to grow that we regard the conquest of the British Islands and its naval bases as any other than an impossible contingency. The spirit of our people is splendid.' Next day, Friday, 16 August, Roosevelt held a press conference at which he revealed America and Britain were holding talks on the acquisition of bases: America would give something in return, but destroyers were not involved.[13]

Friday saw another all-out *Luftwaffe* offensive, with over 1,700 sorties launched. German intelligence mistakenly believed RAF Fighter Command would only have about 300 serviceable aircraft left: in fact, the 47 operational Hurricane and Spitfire squadrons were fully equipped and over 200 aircraft were ready in reserve. But these reserves, and supplies of pilots, were nevertheless dwindling fast. Göring ordered concentration on eliminating the RAF in the air and on the ground. West Malling, Brize Norton, and especially Tangmere, were bombed, although none were put out of operation. On Saturday, 17 August, came a lull, despite reasonably good weather, during which Dowding urged for pilots to be transferred from Bomber Command – he had had 150 men killed, wounded or reported missing in the last ten days. Soon after Sunday lunch, enemy raiders returned, aiming at Biggin Hill and Kenley airfields. The former was to be attacked by a combination of high level bombing, followed by aircraft streaking in below radar coverage and guided on to the target by smoke raised from the first assault. But high-level bombers failed to arrive in time, and low-level aircraft ran into disastrous fire from ground defences and waiting Spitfires. Only two of the nine aircraft arrived back at base, and one of these had a dead pilot. Kenley, seven miles from Biggin Hill, suffered far more; West Malling and Croydon were also hit; during the evening further raids were directed at Thorney Island, Ford and Gosport airfields. But, during this cloudy, drizzling Sunday, 71 *Luftwaffe* aircraft had been destroyed – the Vice-Chief of Air Staff was to tell Ministers next morning that the total was about 126. Göring and his pilots were becoming increasingly concerned; on Monday, 19 August, the *Luftwaffe* chief issued a further, desperate order: 'We have reached the decisive period of the air war against England. The vital task is the defeat of the enemy air force. Our first aim is to destroy the enemy's fighters.' And then, the same day, the weather blackened and aircraft on the Continent and in Britain were grounded. In Rome, Mussolini believed the German air offensive to be going well and that invasion would take place 'within a week or within a month', he therefore instructed Marshal Graziani to attack Egypt on the day that the first German platoon set foot on British soil.

The War Cabinet, when it met at noon on the 19th for the first time in three days, heard that American support now seemed more likely. Mackenzie King, the Canadian leader, had cabled the day before to say he had seen Roosevelt and had been given his permission to report that destroyers might start leaving for Britain by the end of the week. Fifty would be sent and he hoped special authorization would not be needed from Congress; Roosevelt would be satisfied if Churchill made a statement on the lines of the 4 June speech. The Prime Minister therefore told the War Cabinet that he proposed to deal with the 'assurance' in a speech next day, 20 August.[14] But a new complication came on the night of the 19th. Lord Lothian reported a suggestion by Sumner Welles for an exchange of letters from the British Ambassador and Cordell Hull – otherwise it would be legally impossible for the destroyers to be sent without legislation, except in exchange for a definite consideration and unless the Chief of Naval Staff certified the warships as not essential for American defence. Welles had drafted the text of the letters; Lothian had immediately objected to the inclusion of a reference to Churchill's 4 June statement in a letter intended for publication. Alternative texts had been proposed by Lothian, which he sent to London for approval. These made a distinction between the transfer of bases and destroyers; this, said the Ambassador, was necessary because the 'far-reaching and tremendous concessions' which Britain had made could not be compared with 50 old destroyers. Unless this division were made, said the Ambassador, British public opinion would think America had driven an intolerably hard bargain at the moment of Britain's greatest difficulty.[15] Despite the drawback revealed by Lothian, Churchill intended to go ahead with his planned speech: his statement was aimed at more than relieving American apprehension.

An idea for one sentence in his address had come to him five days before. During the hectic afternoon of the 15th he had visited Operations Room, 11 Group, Fighter Command, accompanied by Ismay, at a time when all squadrons were engaged and nothing remained in reserve – and the map table continued to indicate fresh *Luftwaffe* waves lapping the coast. Ismay commented afterwards: 'I felt sick with fear.' But the RAF pilots continued to claw up to dive down upon the enemy, and safe darkness came. Churchill turned to Ismay: 'Don't speak to me. I have never been so moved.' Five minutes later he leant forward and broke the silence. 'Never in the field of human conflict has so much been owed by so many to so few.'[16] Churchill, on the 20th, repeated these words to the House of Commons. Despite the fame which the sentence soon acquired, the speech was not intended to be a rousing, oratical call-to-arms. 'It was a moderate and well-balanced speech,' commented Harold Nicolson. 'He did not try to arouse enthusiasm, but only to give guidance.'[17] The Prime Minister continued his review of the first year of the war by hinting at possible German action against Russia, and then raised the question of Anglo-American co-operation; he referred indirectly to the fleet: if Britain had been put in France's terrible position, it would have been the duty of the war leader to fight to the end, but it would also have been his duty 'to provide, as far as possible, for the naval security of Canada and our Dominions and to make sure they had the means to carry on the struggle from beyond the oceans'. Churchill described America's need for naval and air facilities, and revealed the Government's decision, 'without being asked or offered any inducement,' to inform the American Government that she would be glad to place such defence facilities at their disposal by leasing suitable sites. This would mean British and American organizations being 'somewhat mixed up'. Churchill concluded: 'Looking out upon the future, I do not view the process with any misgivings. I could not stop it if I wished; no one can stop it. Like the Mississippi, it just keeps rolling along. Let it roll. Let it roll on full flood, inexorable, irresistible, benignant, to broader lands and better days.'[18]

After this plea for Anglo-American co-operation, attention turned again to liaison with another ally, Free France. Late that night the Vice-Chiefs of Staff met to discuss the Dakar operation. A number of conversations had been held during the past few days, including interviews with de Gaulle, and the plans which the War Cabinet had provisionally approved on 13 August, for full British participation, had been found steeped in difficulties – tactical, logistical and topographical. So, at Churchill's suggestion, the Vice-Chiefs recommended a return to the original plan: the garrison should be invited to receive de Gaulle, and the British force would remain in the background; only if opposition became serious would the British ships open fire. The plan now went back to the Commanders and to de Gaulle for further discussion.[19] Lothian's draft letters over the destroyer deal were discussed by the War Cabinet on the 21st and Ministers agreed with the Ambassador's comments. It was pointed out that Roosevelt had previously not intended to establish any open connection between the measures which the two

Governments were to take, and a formal bargain on these lines was out of the question: Britain was offering far more than America. The War Cabinet believed the Prime Minister's speech of the previous night might increase American confidence and soften the U.S. Administration to less vigorous terms, and Ministers therefore decided to wait a few days before sending a reply. The War Cabinet next discussed the rising tension between Italy and Greece; Lord Halifax said that according to his advisers, 'though Signor Mussolini was heating up the atmosphere, he was unlikely to declare war against Greece at the present time'. This view was apparently shared by the Turkish Foreign Minister.[20] Optimism seemed to be reinforced at the War Cabinet meeting next day, 22 August; a telegram had been received from Belgrade: the Yugoslav General Staff had informed the British Naval Attaché that Italian troop movements in south Albania were of little importance, and relations between Italy and Greece had improved during the last three days. Also on 22 August, Ciano wrote in his diary: 'Actions against Yugoslavia and Greece are indefinitely postponed. It appears that the Germans have renewed their pressure, even on our headquarters, in this sense.'[21]

Daily the struggle against the *Luftwaffe* was expected to be resumed; each dawn, anxious eyes scanned the weather; meteorological reports were impatiently awaited. But clouds continued to give protection and Newall told the War Cabinet on the 22nd that enemy operations on the previous day had mainly consisted of small raids, usually by single aircraft along the east and south-east coasts. Ministers at this meeting approved a draft letter from Churchill to Roosevelt, which stated the British objections to a 'contract, bargain or sale'. Churchill saw difficulties and even risks in an exchange of notes. 'People will contrast on each side what is given and received.'[22] This message was sent to Roosevelt later in the day. Churchill gave a dinner at 10 Downing Street that Thursday night to visiting American generals; after midnight he talked to Eden and expressed his concern over the composition of the War Cabinet. Bevin, still outside the actual War Cabinet, would make an excellent member, believed Churchill, and Eden agreed; the Prime Minister then asked Eden if he himself would like to become a full War Cabinet member, as Foreign Secretary. 'I replied I would prefer to stay where I was,' wrote Eden in his diary. 'Winston seemed relieved. "I know where I can find another Foreign Secretary, he is here in the room with me; but where am I to find another Secretary of State for War?" '[23] Earlier in the evening the COS had considered the Dakar operation; rumours of a leak of British intentions had been brought to their notice, but the COS, despite the need for complete secrecy for the operation, decided planning should still go ahead.[24] Also on the 22nd, risks of Britain becoming involved in yet another dangerous venture had suddenly increased; Lord Halifax told the War Cabinet next day that the Ambassador at Athens had been asked by the Greek President of the Council, General Metaxas, what help Britain could give if the country were attacked by Italy. Metaxas feared this attack might happen within the next few days. The Chiefs of Staff considered Britain should not go beyond a general assurance, which had already been given, that the most valuable help she could offer would be the ultimate defeat of Italy; Britain should not therefore undertake to send forces, but would try to prevent an Italian occupation of Crete. The War Cabinet agreed that the Ambassador at Athens, Sir Michael Palairet, should reply along these lines.[25]

All major affairs and topics seemed to be hanging in suspense, and the *Luftwaffe* lull continued. Discussion was resumed at the Defence Committee meeting held on the 23rd over the rate of pilot wastage, and Ministers heard that recent fighting had taken a heavy toll of pilot strength. Churchill, in continuation of remarks he had made at the Defence Committee meeting on the 14th, said he was not prepared to accept the figure of 746 as the rate of pilot wastage to be expected throughout the winter months. But Sinclair pointed out that in the last 16 days the casualties had been far higher than the Air Ministry's postulated wastage. At the current rate the figure of 746 would in fact be too low, although he admitted that the present strain was unlikely to continue. Churchill retorted that 'if it were assumed that 600 out of the 746 postulated casualties were in battle, and if the claim made by the Air Ministry to destroy German aircraft in a ratio of three to one were accepted, then the German postulated wastage in battle would be 1,800 per month. To this figure we should add the German accident casualties which, if their force were double ours, would work out at about 280 per month, giving a grand total of 2,080 lost each month. The Germans would thus have to produce over 14,000 pilots in the next seven months to make good their wastage.' Churchill sarcastically asked whether the possibility of such an output of pilots by the Germans had been investigated. An Air Ministry official pointed out that it was not a sound argument to discount Britain's wastage by referring to that of the enemy. 'The enemy could control to some extent this wastage by refraining from raiding in this country, whereas we might feel bound to continue and increase the bombing of Germany.' Churchill replied that 'if the Germans did not come here we should not lose fighter pilots,' and he added that a figure of about 500 per month, rather than 746, would be a more accurate forecast of the wastage during the winter.[26]

Saturday, 24 August, was an unsettling and unfortunate day. The most important subjects which had been preoccupying the War Cabinet seemed fated by misfortune: negotiations with America, Greece, Dakar. The *Luftwaffe* offensive was at last resumed – and London was bombed.

On the first subject, American negotiations, Lothian had telephoned Sir Alexander Cadogan during Friday afternoon to report his conversations with Welles: Roosevelt had still been adamant that Congress must be given 'molasses' and recognition would have to be given to the link between the bases and destroyers. If Britain failed to agree, warned Lord Lothian, she would probably lose the destroyers. Churchill still believed the two offers were unmatched and he was now even prepared to believe that the destroyers were not, after all, essential. He therefore drew up a draft agreement, which he sent to the Foreign Office on the 24th, in which Britain made an unconditional offer of the base facilities and the destroyers were not mentioned. But a letter to Roosevelt contained one suggestion for a reciprocal agreement: 'Could you not say that you did not feel able to accept this fine offer which we make unless the United States matched it in some way?'[27]

Meanwhile, the War Cabinet's efforts to avoid Grecian entanglements met opposition from the British Ambassador, who declined to act on his instructions. Instead, he cabled the Foreign Office on the Saturday to ask if Britain could not offer more direct help, and Sir Michael stressed the damaging effect on British prestige if she failed to assist the only country to which she could actually supply the help promised in her guarantee. The Foreign Office asked that the War Cabinet should consider the Ambassador's plea when Ministers met the following week.[28] Finally, during this Saturday, General Irwin put on record his misgivings over the Dakar operation: the commander of the British troops believed his men were insufficiently trained and air cover would be inadequate.[29]

Göring was acutely conscious of slipping time: the Führer had given him a fortnight within which to defeat the RAF and only three days remained. On Saturday the weather cleared. Göring had ordered a round-the-clock offensive and, at about 12.30 p.m., the first wave came. Catching the protective fighters off balance while refuelling, the Germans so severely mauled Manston airfield that it had to be abandoned as a permanent base for Fighter Command. Three hours later the Germans were again fortunate with timing, and bombers reached their targets in the North Weald and at Hornchurch; further down the coast Portsmouth was hit, and a large number of civilians killed; and when daylight aircraft casualties were totalled, the Germans had lost 40, Fighter Command 20 – uncomfortably high for the RAF. German pilots carried out Göring's command for a 24-hour assault; during darkness 170 bombers came back, heading for air force installations in the south-east and industrial targets as wide apart as Cardiff, Swansea and South Shields. About 12 bombers were instructed to attack aircraft factories at Rochester and Kingston and oil refineries at Thames Haven; disobeying an express order, they hit the City of London and nine other London districts.[30] Next day, the 25th, while German aircraft again aimed at airfields, the decision was taken to undertake reprisal raids upon Berlin. 'The War Cabinet,' wrote Churchill in his memoirs, 'were much in the mood to hit back, to raise the stakes, and to defy the enemy.'[31] In fact, the War Cabinet never took this reprisal decision: Ministers had no meeting scheduled for this Sunday and were not summoned to any special session. The operation was only announced to them at the 12.30 p.m. meeting next day, 26 August, when Newall declared that 'we had despatched a large number of aircraft to bomb military targets in Berlin, but the weather had prevented a number of our machines from locating their targets'. He stressed that 'whereas German aircraft unloaded their bombs irrespective of whether they could locate military targets, our pilots had instructions to bring their bombs back if the targets could not be located'. This point, agreed Ministers, was worth emphasizing 'from the point of view of public opinion in the US'. Concern was expressed at possible public reaction to the next monthly return of civilians killed, which was likely to be 'fairly heavy', but the War Cabinet finally agreed that 'the figures of casualties were not high if expressed as a percentage of the normal death rate, or even of the peacetime road casualties.'

Ministers next discussed Greece and the Ambassador's request for a firm offer of help. Halifax suggested financial help, and also that Athens should be told Britain would increase bombing attacks on Italy. The War Cabinet agreed, and asked the COS to consider the feasibility of operating bomber squadrons from Greek airfields.[32] Ironically, later this same day the Greek Government, anxious to preserve neutrality, interned the crew of a British aircraft which had made a forced landing on Greek territory.

Churchill's attempt to have Middle East reinforcements sent through the Mediterranean had failed: he told the War Cabinet that the Commanders in Cairo had been asked their opinions; they had replied that an Italian attack upon Egypt was not believed impending, and reinforcements would be better brought round the long Cape route. Churchill thought that 'the War Cabinet ought not to take the responsibility of overruling the judgment of the commanders on the spot.... Nevertheless, he acquiesced in this decision with regret, since in his judgment the dangers of sending the tank units through the Mediterranean had been exaggerated.'

Luftwaffe raids again concentrated upon RAF sector stations during the 26th, after a night of scattered bombing on Midlands factories. The inclusion of night attacks in the German offensive had raised terrible new problems: night defences were still far from adequate, and Dowding had already informed the Air Ministry that the chances of Hurricanes being able to stop the enemy rested upon 'an occasional fortunate encounter'. Moreover, the RAF had been suffering heavily over the past three days: 69 aircraft had been lost, although the *Luftwaffe* had suffered 90 destroyed. Another brief lull came on the 27th, but Hitler was meanwhile considering whether the air war should be prolonged, even at the expense of putting back the invasion date. Plans for the land assault on Britain had still to be finalized, but a compromise between the navy and army views was reached on the 27th: the landing attempt in Lyme Bay would be excluded, thus narrowing the front, yet the front was extended in the other direction from Folkestone to Bognor. Increased emphasis was therefore given to the south coast – and British planners were still working on the assessment that the Germans would launch their main attacks upon the east.

On the 27th Churchill sent the letter to Roosevelt which he had drafted the previous Sunday and which made an 'unconditional' offer of the bases: the message had been approved by the War Cabinet at 12.30 p.m. Ministers also considered final plans for the expedition to Dakar, Operation 'Menace', and, despite General Irwin's misgivings and the possibility of an information leakage, they agreed that 'having regard to the value of its objects, the operation was one which we should be justified in undertaking'.[33] Free French moves were already being made in Africa, and perhaps influenced the War Cabinet decision: the Governor of Chad territory had declared his allegiance to de Gaulle on the 26th and Duala had been taken the same night. Brazzaville was to fall to the Free French next day, Wednesday, the 28th, after only two hours' fighting.

The *Luftwaffe* had once more resumed the attack. After raids on airfields during daylight on the 28th, 130 long-range bombers left the French coast just before dusk, heading for Liverpool. But so inaccurate and scattered were the attacks, that the Air Ministry believed the raid had been intended for the Midlands. During the same night the RAF struck at Berlin and, for the first time, killed civilians in the capital: officially the figures were 10 killed and 29 wounded. German newspapers displayed banner headlines: 'COWARDLY BRITISH ATTACK' ... 'BRITISH AIR PIRATES OVER BERLIN.' Newall told the War Cabinet next day, the 29th, that the Berlin bombing had been 'most successful', and Churchill said he proposed to send congratulations to Bomber Command: he would again refer to the restraint shown by RAF pilots in not dropping bombs if they were uncertain of hitting military targets, but he added: 'In view of the indiscriminate bombing practised by the Germans we might have to consider, in the near future, making a temporary but marked departure from our policy.' The Prime Minister also brought up the question of compensation for damage caused by German bombs; he was thinking especially of 'poorer classes.... The trouble was the inadequacy of the present legislative provision for compensating those who had lost their household effects, or the stock in trade of their small businesses,' and he believed 'considerably more would have to be done for persons of limited means.' The Chancellor of the Exchequer promised to examine the position.[34]

A second War Cabinet session started at 5 p.m. on the 29th, called to consider the latest Anglo-American development. Churchill's letter to Roosevelt had failed to settle the exchange problem, and his speech of the 20th had, according to the Americans, made the issue more involved rather than less. Lord Lothian had cabled the previous night, Ministers were told. The generosity of Churchill's public offer of the bases had complicated the position, since Britain had offered the facilities as a free gift and Roosevelt had no power to offer a gift of the destroyers. Cordell Hull now suggested that part of the facilities should be offered free and the rest as an exchange, and Roosevelt had further suggested that the assurance concerning the British fleet should be the subject of a separate letter exchange: the President would send a telegram asking if the 4 June and 20 August declarations were still valid, and Churchill would reply that they were. The War Cabinet decided to approve the latest American proposals.[35]

German bombers were again aimed at Merseyside on the night of 29-30 August; again the raids were ineffective. In Rome, Mussolini had apparently grown weary of waiting for the German invasion of Britain, and gave orders for the offensive against Egypt – which the British HQ in Cairo believed unlikely for the moment – to be launched irrespective of a German landing in England. Mussolini feared Hitler might come to an agreement with Britain, and wanted to have won 'at least one battle' to secure a better place at the peace table; Graziani reluctantly started his final preparations for the Italian advance. Ciano had travelled to Vienna, to be present at the final humiliation of Hungary and Roumania: on 30 August the Foreign Ministers of these two countries signed an agreement accepting the Axis settlement – with the Roumanian Minister, Manoilescu, slumping in a faint across the table when he saw the carve-up of his country. On the same day final instructions for the invasion of Britain were issued by the German Army Commander, Brauchitsch: 15 September remained the target date but,

Brauchitsch added: 'The order for execution depends on the political situation.'

The Battle of Britain had reached the critical, terrible stage. Hitler had decided the air offensive should continue: days of attacks upon Fighter Command airfields culminated in a long weekend of vicious onslaught; and it was during this weekend that victory or defeat hung in delicate balance. Weather reports of Friday, 30 August, accurately predicted a fine day with some cloud. By 9 a.m. British radar operators picked up first plots of enemy aircraft forming over Cap Griz Nez; by 10.30 a.m. the radar clusters indicated a heavy assault crossing the Channel. German bombers roared over the south coast, heading for Biggin Hill airfield, the Vauxhall factory at Luton and the Coastal Command airfield at Detling. In their attempt to block the bombers, Fighter Command for the first time flew over 1,000 sorties: many German aircraft nevertheless reached their targets. Biggin Hill suffered in the morning, and worse in the afternoon. Sticks of bombs shattered workshops, hangars and stores, ripped up runways and severed service mains; 65 of the station staff were killed. Luton received a fairly accurate attack and 50 civilians were killed. Detling was out of use for 15 hours. Thirty-six German aircraft were destroyed, but the strain on Fighter Command aircraft and pilots was reaching intolerable limits. And next day, Saturday, 31 August, the raiders returned. Targets were Debden, Hornchurch, Croydon, Duxford, Eastchurch – and Biggin Hill again. Duxford escaped after a successful interception, but other stations received almost deadly damage. Biggin Hill, where there had not been enough time to bury the previous day's dead, took a special beating: the Operations Room was completely demolished – WRAF personnel had continued to work unprotected until bombers were almost overhead; miraculously, when survivors crawled out from twisted girders and rubble in the choking dust and smoke, only one person had received fatal injuries – a boy bugler, borrowed from a local volunteer organization to help strained signals staff. By nightfall on this Saturday, Fighter Command had lost about 50 aircraft, in combat and on the ground; 41 *Luftwaffe* aircraft had been destroyed. And on Sunday morning, 1 September, the one remaining squadron at Biggin Hill had to take off to meet the fifth raid on the airfield since Friday morning. During the airfield raids, other attacks had continued on industrial targets in the Midlands and North; for the third night running another attempt had been made to reach Merseyside on the Friday, this time with considerably more success: 160 fires were started in Liverpool's commercial centre.

Fighter pilots, sick with weariness, climbed repeatedly into battered machines; physically, if not spiritually, they could not endure the strain for many more days. Many are the tales of heroism and sheer luck: the Polish pilot, on a training flight, who engaged a massive German bomber single-handed and sent it to the ground; the three pilots at Hornchurch, taking off when the airfield received a stick of bombs – one pilot emerged unscathed after his aircraft had been thrown upside down and had skidded across the runway at 100 m.p.h., the second pilot managed to crawl from his burning, shattered machine, the third, blown completely out of the airfield, walked in again two hours later. But luck, skill and brutal doggedness would soon be insufficient. Dowding wrote in his report: 'Fighter pilots were no longer being produced in numbers sufficient to fill the gaps in the fighting ranks.' Airfields had received such damage by the end of 1 September that the defence of London would soon be virtually impossible from air bases south of the capital; even more ominous, if the pressure were maintained the RAF would temporarily lose air superiority over the vital Kent and Sussex invasion beaches. And on this Sunday, shipping began to move from Germany's North Sea ports towards the embarkation harbours opposite England's south coast. Barges began to accumulate at Ostend: 18 on 1 September, 70 by the end of the following day, 150 on the 4th, 205 on the 6th.... Civilians continued their everyday affairs without fully appreciating the importance of the battle occasionally glimpsed high above their heads. Strangely, even War Cabinet discussions made no mention of the dwindling RAF reserves of aircraft and men; Ministers apparently had no appreciation of the proximity of defeat, and sessions had none of the sense of urgency of those, for example, during Dunkirk. No meetings were held on the Saturday and Sunday of this critical weekend, but Churchill, when the War Cabinet met at noon on Monday, did at least seem to realize the importance of recent fighting. The Prime Minister had spent Friday at Dowding's HQ. 'He was tempted to ask why the enemy should continue attacks on this heavy scale – which included some days as many as 700 aircraft – if it did not represent something like their maximum effort.' Churchill continued, with undue confidence: 'This might not, of course, be the explanation, but our own air force was stronger than ever and there was every reason to be optimistic about the 1940 air battle of Britain.'[36]

Air operations dwindled on 2 September, replaced by feverish British attempts to restore battered fighter airfields; and, during the day, Anglo-American notes were finally exchanged to complete the bases-destroyers deal. Long weeks of complicated negotiations were finished; America was to receive, 'freely and without consideration', the lease for bases and facilities, and America would also receive additional bases and facilities in exchange for 'naval and military equipment'., Further involved discussions later took place over details of the base allocations, complicated by the strength of local feeling in the areas concerned and also by the fact that the old American destroyers were found to be in acute need of extensive repairs. Despite the strident urgency of the original request for these warships, only 9 out of the 50 were able to enter service by the end of 1940.[37] Even when the agreement was signed on 2 September, Churchill was far from satisfied: three days later he sent a note to Lord Halifax suggesting a telegram should be sent to Lord Lothian to express War Cabinet appreciation of the Ambassador's handling of the issue; but Churchill's suggestion contained a sting: he asked: 'What is being done about getting our 20 motor torpedo-boats, the 5 PBY, the 150-200 aircraft and 250,000 rifles, also anything else that is going? I consider we were promised all the above and more too. Not an hour should be lost in raising these questions. "Beg while the iron is hot." '[38]

On 3 September, the first anniversary of Britain's entry into the war, the German High Command revised dates for the assault on the island. 'The earliest day for the sailing of the invasion fleet has been fixed as 20 September, and that of the landing for the 21st.' In London's Whitehall it was almost taken for granted that invasion was imminent, and most experts – including Churchill – believed it would be preceded by continued strong air attacks. The Prime Minister therefore wrote a series of urgent Minutes on 3 September, and the variety of topics reveals his resourcefulness and incredible energy. 'Prime Minister to Home Secretary: In spite of the shortage of materials, a great effort should be made to help people to drain their Anderson shelters.... Bricks on edge placed loosely together without mortar, covered with a piece of linoleum, would be quite good, but there must be a drain and a sump.' 'Memorandum by the Prime Minister: 1. The Navy can lose us the war, but only the Air Force can win it. Therefore our supreme effort must be to gain overwhelming mastery in the air.... We must therefore develop the power to carry an ever-increasing volume of explosive to Germany, so as to pulverize the entire industry....' Other Minutes were concerned with the economic blockade, with air raid warnings and with the rendezvous for War Cabinet meetings should a raid be in progress.[39] The latter subject was discussed by the War Cabinet during the day: Churchill suggested that if a 'red' warning was in operation before a meeting, Ministers should gather in the underground War Room. 'If a red warning was given after a meeting had begun at 10 Downing Street, he hoped that they would be able to continue their business without interruption.'[40]

Air raid warnings in general were discussed by the War Cabinet at a special meeting the following morning, 4 September – with the session held in the underground War Room. Considerable criticism had arisen over delays to production caused by these warnings, with Beaverbrook lamenting the drop in output and with Bevin strongly defending all possible precautions for work people. Churchill now pointed out that the red warning meant aircraft were flying over a certain area, and 'no one could tell whether the enemy aircraft intended to bomb that area or were on passage'. The War Cabinet decided more use should be made of lookouts posted at each factory, who would sound the alarm when enemy aircraft were detected or nearby fighting was in progress. 'It would then be everyone's duty to take cover.'[41]

While this War Cabinet meeting took place, Hitler addressed a hysterical audience of nurses and women social workers at Berlin's *Sportpalast*. 'In England they're filled with curiosity and keep asking, "Why doesn't he come?" Be calm. Be calm. He's coming! He's coming!' The Führer accused the RAF of indiscriminate bombing and, to shrill cheers, declared: 'When the British air force drops two or three or four thousand kilogrammes of bombs, then we will in one night drop 150 thousand, 230 thousand, 300 thousand or 400 thousand kilogrammes.' Count Ciano, listening to the broadcast in Rome, commented: 'Hitler must be nervous.' Just before midnight, RAF bombers arrived back over the German capital. In London, no special notice was taken of Hitler's warning: his words seemed merely a repetition of previous ravings and no mention of the speech was made at the War Cabinet meeting next day, 5 September. Instead, discussion dwelt on the statement Churchill intended to make in the House of Commons later in the afternoon, on the acquisition of American destroyers, and on the introduction of bomb damage compensation. On the latter topic, Churchill proposed to mention that 'out of some 12 million houses in this country only some 8,000 had been hit, of which very few had been totally destroyed. This was a far smaller percentage than that estimated before the war.'[42] Within a few hours Churchill's figures would be hopelessly outdated.

Evidence of approaching invasion steadily mounted, with reports of barges being concentrated, reports of new airfields being completed, together with heavy gun emplacements behind the French coast, rumours of bomber group redeployments and statements from captured spies. By dusk on 6 September the information seemed so conclusive that HQ Home Forces issued the preliminary alert: 'Attack probable within the next three days.'[43] The following morning details of all the evidence, including the estimate that moon and tide conditions would favour a landing between 8 and 10 September, were passed to the Chiefs of Staff. The COS, and General Brooke, Commander of Home Forces, met later to discuss whether Alert No. 1 – 'Invasion imminent and probable within 12 hours' – should now be issued. They agreed that 'the possibility of invasion had become imminent and that the defence forces should stand by at immediate notice'.[44]

By the time this COS meeting started, at 5.20 p.m., the first bombs were whistling down upon London's dockyard areas of Woolwich and the Isle of Dogs. And the terror of the Blitz had exploded.

The day following his *Sportpalast* tirade, Hitler had ordered 'harrassing attacks by day and night on the inhabitants and air defences of large British cities'. Now, on this Saturday afternoon, 7 September, Hermann Göring stood on the cliffs opposite the English coast and watched the 300 bombers and 600 fighters disappear over the sparkling sea. A few minutes later British fighter squadrons – expecting a further assault on airfields – were eluded and the enemy slipped through to reach the target. The first bombers appeared over London and made for Poplar and Canning Town to hit the Royal Victoria and West India docks. Bombs screamed down for almost 90 minutes, rending London from Rotherhithe to Barking on both sides of the Thames; Bugsby's Reach was completely devastated over an area nearly two miles long and half a mile wide. Bomb bursts spread to Kensington, Tottenham and Croydon.[45] And as the first bombers turned to leave, aircraft for the second wave were about to take off: the attack would now be in darkness – and Fighter Command had virtually nothing to offer in night defence. So 250 German bombers, guided by the immense billowing fires, reached London at 8.30 p.m. and by 4.30 on Sunday morning three main-line stations were out of action, hundreds more homes had been demolished and dockland blazed from end to end. Over 430 civilians died, 1,600 were seriously injured, thousands more were homeless. Over 600 tons of bombs had been dropped – the highest total during the Blitz was to be 1,026 tons and 4,252 incendiary containers on 19 April 1941. Londoners, in their sudden suffering, might have been comforted to know the Germans would be subjected to far worse: on the night of 14 October 1944, Duisberg received 4,547 tons.

Forty-one German bombers were destroyed during the Saturday night – but 44 British fighters were lost or badly damaged. Air Vice-Marshal Keith Park, Commander of 11 Group, Fighter Command, flew over the smoking capital next morning. He was, he recalled, 'very angry'. But he continued: 'I said "Thank God" because I realized that the methodical Germans had at last switched their attacks from my vital aerodromes on to cities.'[46] The most serious threat to Fighter Command, the destruction of bases from which they could operate south of London, was now likely to lessen; chances of the Germans gaining air superiority in the south of England were reduced. Sunday, 8 September, had already been designated a day of prayer: despite the suffering, it might well have been a day of thanksgiving. The Battle of Britain could now be fought to a victorious finish. But few realized this deliverance. A new war had been launched; and, amid confusion and fear of what the next day would bring, the invasion threat remained. Following the COS decision during the late afternoon of the 7th, Alert No. 1 was issued at 8 o'clock the same evening to Eastern and Southern Commands. Telephones and teleprinters passed on the codeword 'Cromwell', in some places leading to panic reaction when, forgetting 'Cromwell' meant imminent threat of invasion rather than actual landings, some Home Guard and army units rang church bells and blew up bridges. 'Cromwell' remained in force for 12 days, but on Sunday morning methods were devised to introduce intermediate stages on the alert sequence.[47]

Rumours long persisted that the Government had been thrown into complete confusion on the Saturday night and that 'Cromwell' was issued as a panic measure. Other rumours said the codeword had been put out without the knowledge of the Chiefs of Staff – Churchill, in his memoirs, makes this allegation.[48] Neither accusation is true. The COS came to their considered conclusion; General Brooke, who was present at the meeting – contrary to other claims – and who had responsibility for issuing the alert, did so himself. 'Cromwell' would have been declared whether or not the Blitz had started; moreover, Brooke checked the latest situation on the Sunday morning and 'found that all reports still point to the probability of an invasion starting between the 8th and 10th of this month' – in other words, in the next 48 hours.[49] Nor was the Government thrown into a panic; Ministers and officials continued to function as normal – indeed, unduly so: the War Cabinet did not meet on Sunday, 8 September, because it had now become the practice not to do so. Instead, Ministers met at their normal time, 12.30 p.m. on Monday at 10 Downing Street. Newall gave a comparatively brief statement: reports showed that, while considerable damage had been done, 'the intense bombing had had comparatively little effect on undertakings engaged in war production'.[50]

After a quiet night on the 8th, London suffered again on the 9th. From now on, until 3 November, the capital would be attacked each day in varying degrees. But on the 9th the Germans found they could not repeat the success of the 7th: this time Fighter Command was ready to swoop upon the laden *Luftwaffe* bombers. The first wave of about 100 aircraft, intending to hit London at about 5 p.m., was intercepted near Dover and failed to reach the capital; the second wave was engaged soon after crossing the coast at Beachy

Head and then again over south-west London; less than half the enemy aircraft reached their objective, and these scattered their bombs aimlessly. The cost to Fighter Command had been heavy, but less than the German toll: 28 *Luftwaffe* to 19 RAF.[51] More important, the RAF defence deflated the brief confidence gained by the Germans during the weekend; Admiral Raeder reported next day, 10 September: 'There is no sign of the defeat of the enemy's air force over southern England and in the Channel area.' Hitler once more hesitated to commit himself to 'Sealion'.

The British War Cabinet now began to consider a partial revision of the existing restricted policy of only bombing German military targets. The Chief of Air Staff commented at the meeting on Tuesday, the 10th, that German bombing of London had been 'quite indiscriminate'. Ministers believed that British bombers – 108 had been over enemy territory the previous night – 'ought to be instructed not to return home with their bombs if they failed to locate the targets'. Still only military targets, however, would be chosen as primary objectives. The War Cabinet asked the Air Secretary, Sinclair, to issue instructions.

By far the worst sufferers in the Blitz were the inhabitants of the East End of London, where almost 200,000 people lived at an average of 12 per dwelling, and where the gigantic U-shaped bend in the Thames shone in the moonlight to attract bombers like moths. Destruction and deprivation were concentrated in these narrow streets, close-lined with jerry-built houses; and it was here, more than anywhere, that local administration creaked and almost collapsed. 'Everybody is worried about the feeling in the East End,' commented Harold Nicolson. 'There is much bitterness.'[52] As early as the 10th, Sir John Anderson informed Ministers that 'a difficult situation was arising with regard to persons in the East End who had been rendered homeless'. The Minister of Home Security added that 'this matter had not, perhaps, been very well handled by all the local authorities, but arrangements had now been made for the matter to be taken over by the London County Council'. A special organization was also being set up in Whitehall, and the homeless from the East End of London would be transferred to districts further west: an appeal would be made to householders to find accommodation. Sir John said the Lord Mayor of London wished to start a fund for the relief of distress caused by the bombing. 'It would be difficult to refuse to allow this fund to be started, more especially as the American Ambassador and the Lord Mayor of Melbourne had opened similar funds.'[53]

Latest invasion information was discussed by the War Cabinet, and Ministers were told by Pound that 'a fair number' of small vessels were still entering the ports of Flushing, Ostend, Calais and

Boulogne.[54] General Brooke's diary entry for that day, the 10th, read: 'Still no invasion today. I wonder whether he will do anything during the next few days?' The following day the basic directive for 'Sealion' was in fact ready for issue at Hitler's HQ. In London, the War Cabinet considered the question of Britain's reaction to Germany's indiscriminate bombing; the suggestion was made that 'we should threaten Germany with reprisals by bombing any one of 20 German towns, to be named, if the indiscriminate bombing of London continued'. The War Cabinet finally asked the Air Secretary to consider such a measure, but not for immediate use.[55]

The previous night, the 10th, had been relatively quiet, but now the fair weather threatened another large assault; intercepted cypher messages and the continued movement of ships down the Channel added to the pile of invasion evidence; Churchill thought the time had come for a broadcast. 'The crux of the whole war has arrived,' declared the Prime Minister. The aircraft struggle had cost the enemy very dear, he claimed, but all preparations for invasion were steadily moving forward. 'We must regard the next week or so as a very important period in our history.... It ranks with the days when the Spanish Armada was approaching the Channel, and Drake was finishing his game of bowls; or when Nelson stood between us and Napoleon's Grand Army at Boulogne. ... What is happening now is on a far greater scale and of far more consequence to the life and future of the world and its civilization.' Bombers came as expected that evening, about 100 of them, and many reached the City. But by now anti-aircraft guns had been shifted back into the capital, and those already there were told to open fire – previously they had remained silent while the fighters attempted to provide protection and civilians, unaware of the frantic efforts being made by Fighter Command, had felt at the *Luftwaffe*'s mercy. Now, with dramatic suddenness, searchlights flared on and AA guns blasted up at the sky. Sir Archibald Sinclair described the effect, with some over-optimism, to the War Cabinet next day, Thursday, 12 September. Anti-aircraft defences were being more than doubled, he said, and on the previous night it had been decided to put up a 'pretty heavy barrage'; about 100 rounds per gun had been fired and 'as a result of the barrage one third of the raiders had turned back'. While aircraft which had penetrated the defences earlier in the night had flown at about 180 m.p.h. at a height of 12,000 to 16,000 feet, later in the night they had flown at about 240 m.p.h. at about 27,0000 feet. Sir John Anderson claimed that 'the morale effect on our people had been excellent'.[56]

Neville Chamberlain, pale and tired after an August operation and less often seen now in Whitehall, had chaired this War Cabinet meeting, while Churchill toured defensive positions in the Dungeness and North Foreland areas with Brooke and Dill. 'After lunch PM wanted to watch air-fight but there was none to see,' wrote Brooke. 'His popularity is astounding, everywhere crowds rush up to see him and cheer him wildly.'[57] The Prime Minister described this visit to the War Cabinet at 11 a.m. next day, the 13th, after which Ministers discussed the situation in the London area. A remarkable improvement in the morale of the people had taken place in the last 36 hours, said the Minister of Health; this change had, however, impeded evacuation. 'People who earlier had clamoured to be taken away were now reluctant to leave their homes.' The sewage situation was unsatisfactory, he added – a vital part of the pumping machinery had been damaged and the sewers were broken in a number of places. 'The population of certain parts of London were showing reluctance to use their Anderson shelters and to make use of street shelters. They preferred to congregate in other underground accommodation – for example under churches, schools and public buildings.... This overcrowding might well give rise to a health problem. Thus, inoculation against diphtheria and scarlet fever might be necessary.' Ministers discussed the possibility of using Underground stations for shelters: Sir John Reith, Minister of Transport, said he had examined this question, but still believed it more important to keep Tube trains running. Anderson pointed out that the Police Commissioner 'strongly deprecated the use of Tubes as shelters. The public had been educated to use shelters and there was broadly sufficient shelter accommodation available.' The War Cabinet agreed, and stressed the public should realize that the shelters provided, while not affording immunity from a direct hit, offered the best protection available. Despite this War Cabinet decision, crowds would still gather round the Underground stations and would loudly clamour to be allowed in; and, when doors remained locked, an ugly mood would sometimes be generated.

But, while the War Cabinet was in session, an incident occurred which boosted the morale of East Enders almost as much as the noise of the AA guns and which proved to some of them that all Londoners, rich and poor, were having to suffer. A lone German raider came low over central London, over the Thames and the elegant Whitehall buildings; Ministers heard the increasing roar as it passed above 10 Downing Street and over the green splash of St. James' Park. A message was hurriedly brought into the Cabinet Room: the dive-bomber had attacked Buckingham Palace. Six bombs had been dropped. The King and Queen, who had returned from Windsor moments before, were only 80 yards from the nearest explosion, but were uninjured. Queen Elizabeth said later: 'I'm glad we've been bombed. It makes me feel I can look the East End in the face.' Ministers immediately sent a message to the King. 'The War Cabinet offer their hearty congratulations to their Majesties on their providential escape from the barbarous attack made on their home and Royal persons.' Subject to the King's consent this message would be given full publicity.[58]

During the day the British warships *Nelson* and *Hood* moved south from Scapa to Rosyth to be in closer reach of a German invasion attempt; in London, bombs hit the Horse Guards, the House of Lords and War Office, and General Brooke wrote: 'Everything looks like an invasion starting tomorrow from the Thames to Plymouth. I wonder whether we shall be hard at it by this time tomorrow evening?'[59] But Hitler seemed impressed by Göring's onslaught upon London – 'above all praise', he declared: Britain might be defeated without an invasion. Moreover, British aircraft and light naval craft were causing severe damage to invasion barges. While Hitler continued to waver, his dubious ally decided to make his bid for victory – Mussolini ordered his forces in North Africa to advance and, when Graziani objected, the Duce told him to move by Monday or he would be replaced. So, on this Friday the 13th, an Italian artillery bombardment opened up on the frontier town of Sollum and six Italian infantry divisions and eight tank battalions lurched forward. The outnumbered British units began their fighting withdrawal. The offensive had arrived earlier than anticipated, but was nevertheless expected: the withdrawal had been long planned. 'I hope the Armoured Brigade will be in time,' minuted Churchill to Eden next day, 14 September. 'I have no doubt it could have been conducted safely through the Mediterranean and the present danger that it will be too late averted.'[60]

German bombing activity had slackened on the previous night, and General Brooke commented: 'Ominous quiet: German shipping moves greatly reduced and air action too.' The General wondered whether all the German activity had been a bluff to tie down British troops while Hitler helped Mussolini in Egypt.[61] A Berlin conference on this Saturday showed the Führer to be completely undecided whether to call off the invasion and rely upon the air force, or merely to postpone 'Sealion' while the *Luftwaffe* continued the attack. 'The enemy recovers again and again,' Hitler complained. 'In spite of all our successes the prerequisite conditions for Operation 'Sealion' have not yet been realized.' He was therefore obliged to trust Göring's pronouncement that the *Luftwaffe* would soon be victorious, and Göring was given three more days: Hitler would hold up his decision on the landings until 17 September. Göring hastened to make final preparations for his supreme effort.[62] 15 September was a Sunday and, as Churchill noted, the Battle of Waterloo was fought on this same day of the week. The Prime Minister had gone to Chequers for the weekend. Early in the morning he stood on the drive, turfed over to hinder recognition from the air, and noted the weather would probably favour a German attack – almost cloudless except for thin veils around the sun. He motored over to Air Vice-Marshal Park's 11 Group HQ at Uxbridge, where he arrived just after 10.30 a.m. Moments before, the first plots of German bombers had appeared on the huge operations table; the deep underground room was almost silent – even the large clock on the wall had a special quiet mechanism – and never during the day would the noise rise beyond a subdued hum. From this nerve centre stretched communications to a multitude of small, isolated, windy airfields scattered across the countryside south of London. Young pilots, most in their early twenties and most of them veterans of the air war, had been waiting at dispersal huts since dawn. Patrolling squadrons had long been airborne.

Field-Marshal Kesselring, commander of *Luftflotte* 2, had been honoured with the direction of the main assault. He planned to use all his bombers and fighters in a gigantic two-pronged attack upon London, while Sperrle, commander of *Luftflotte* 3, sent a diversionary raid to Portland. The first attack would be made in the morning and the second after lunch. *Luftwaffe* bombers and fighters took time to assemble on the far side of the Channel; meanwhile Park sent his first squadrons aloft. By 11.30 a.m., when the leading German aircraft reached the English coast, 11 squadrons from 11 Group were waiting. Fast approaching from further north was the amalgamation of squadrons from Duxford – the controversial 'Big Wing' led by Douglas Bader. Numbers 72 and 92 squadrons were first in action, immediately screaming down upon the lumbering enemy bombers when they located them near Canterbury – 'it was like rugger,' explained one pilot, 'if you hesitated because you thought you might get hurt, you probably would.' Another squadron, from Hornchurch, attacked almost at the same time, and these three Spitfire groups were still in action when Hurricanes darted down to join them. By now the German bombers had reached Maidstone and were losing cohesion and, as the first Fighter Command squadrons dropped away to refuel and re-arm, other RAF pilots arrived to harry the Germans for 15 miles up the Thames from the Medway towns. Four more Hurricane squadrons joined the struggle on the outskirts of London. German formations were ragged and riddled; bomber pilots desperately tried to keep together; London's blue sky became a glinting, seething mêlée; crazy vapour trails crossed and twirled as British and German units became intertwined. Hurricanes plunged and pierced and German bomber crews frantically released their loads. Bombs came whistling down at random from Beckenham to Westminster; residential areas around New Cross and Lewisham suffered most, and another bomb fell in Buckingham Palace grounds. *Luftwaffe* pilots battled back across Kent and Sussex, and Park ordered his last four squadrons to chase them across the Channel: for a while he had no aircraft completely uncommitted.

Fighter Command pilots returned to their bases, walked cramp-legged from their over-heated machines and, while the aircraft were readied again, snatched hurried lunches. Just sufficient time was available for some shot-down pilots to make their way back to bases by public transport. And then the second attack began. Even while German aircraft were over the Channel, Park boldly ordered his squadrons to intercept. Closing clouds favoured the enemy and Fighter Command precision therefore suffered, but the Germans were nevertheless engaged near Canterbury, over Maidstone and again London. This time more enemy bombers emerged unscathed, but German and British fighter pilots tangled in the most intense fighter aircraft engagement of the Battle of Britain. German pilots had longed for this moment when they could come to close grips with their Fighter Command counterparts; this, Göring declared, would send the RAF in flames to the ground while the *Luftwaffe* soared supreme. Göring's promise failed. When the buzzing groups broke apart, and the aircraft radios ceased their jumble of shouts, hysterical cheers and cold commands, the Germans were found to have held their own in the fighter pilot duel, and their bombers were thus given a clearer run at the target while the RAF were engaged. But this result was insufficient: the *Luftwaffe* needed much more – air superiority. The failure to obtain this vital advantage was the prime feature of the day's battle, not the aircraft casualty figures which were anyway suspect, nor the amount of bombs dropped on suffering London. The day's fighting had shown Fighter Command to be still unbeaten: Hurricanes and Spitfires had reappeared and Göring's previous boast that Dowding had only 100 machines left was shown as a lie to those weary, demoralized German pilots.[63] The day was heralded by the British as a tremendous victory when aircraft destruction figures became known. Sir Cyril Newall told the jubilant War Cabinet at noon next day that, during the 24 hours ending 7 a.m., 186 enemy aircraft had been shot down, 46 of them probables, and 72 had been damaged. British losses were 25 aircraft, with 13 pilots killed or still missing. 'As the figures of air casualties indicated, the fighting of the previous day had been most successful. The enemy had adopted bolder tactics; these had served only to increase his losses. The figures of enemy bombers destroyed were very striking.' Indeed they were – and also highly optimistic: the *Luftwaffe* probably lost about 60 aircraft, not 186 – but the implication of the result was still the same.

One unfortunate incident had occurred during the night bombing on the 15th, now discussed by the War Cabinet. East Enders, chaffing in their danger and acute misery, had reacted to the apparent easy living of their neighbours in the West. The Savoy Hotel had equipped its underground banqueting hall as a sumptuous restaurant-dormitory. So, just as alert sounded on the evening of the 15th, about 100 East Enders rushed into the hotel and insisted on occupying these comfortable quarters. The demonstration soon ended with the sounding of the all-clear. The Home Secretary agreed with the Prime Minister that 'it would be necessary to take strong action to prevent demonstrations of this kind, which, if allowed to grow, might easily lead to serious difficulties'. Only a few minutes before, Ministers had read a report by the Lord President of the Council on London's air raid damage: numbers of homeless people in Resettlement Centres had dropped from 17,000 to 10-11,000, and 'the centres were functioning much more satisfactorily'.

The War Cabinet then turned to a subject which had been simmering for the past few days: Operation 'Menace' – the expedition against Dakar. Prospects for success, always doubtful, had suddenly plummeted, and an urgent decision had now to be taken. The Dakar force had sailed on 31 August, despite continuing indications that information had leaked and despite last-minute reports of Dakar being considerably stronger than first believed. While the expedition was at sea, three French cruisers and three large destroyers had slipped through the Straits of Gibraltar; this news was delayed in transmission to London and in reaching anyone with responsibility for the secret Dakar operation. When, at about noon on 11 September, the First Sea Lord learnt of the French move, orders were urgently sent to Gibraltar for the French warships to be intercepted if they made for Dakar. Instructions arrived too late and the French fleet reached the port on the 14th, presumably with reinforcements. Only after the war was it learnt that these ships had, in fact, been *en route* for Libreville. Churchill now recounted the sad tale to the War Cabinet; he believed the information leakage – originating, he alleged, from Polish sources in Britain – had led the Vichy Government to show 'surprising resource' in despatching the warships so promptly. This had 'altered the whole situation.' To undertake the Operation Menace in this circumstances was, in his opinion, out of the question, and in view of the fact that the French warships might have troops on board, would, if attempted, end in bloodshed.... A fiasco had undoubtedly occurred and it was to be hoped it had not too much engaged public attention.' He described a COS meeting held the previous day, which had resulted in a recommendation that de Gaulle and his forces should proceed at once to Duala and advance into Chad, where the French leader would be welcomed. The British troops would be brought back. The War Cabinet agreed, and a telegram was drafted.

Ministers were also told at this meeting that the Italians, as expected, had now reached Sollum in their North African offensive. British troops, hopelessly thin on the ground, had long since abandoned the town as a base.[64] Managing to snatch a few words with Churchill after the meeting, Eden found him to be vehement against sending more reinforcements to the Middle East.[65] Churchill was, moreover, still uneasy about Wavell and the Commander's military dispositions; this anxiety was reflected in a War Cabinet decision reached next day, 17 September, when, after Sir John Dill reported that two enemy columns had occupied Sidi Barrani, Ministers invited the CIGS 'to obtain further information from the C-in-C Middle East as to the present dispositions of his forces and his immediate intentions'.[66]

The Prime Minister addressed a secret session of the House of Commons that afternoon: among his listeners was Neville Chamberlain, present in the Chamber for the first time since his operation and looking suddenly much older. 'The process of waiting keyed up to concert pitch day after day is apt in time to lose its charm of novelty,' declared Churchill. He warned MPs that they were in danger while they sat in session – the Houses of Parliament made excellent bomb targets and he added: 'I have very little doubt that they will need extensive repairs before very long.' As added safety measures, meetings would be unpublicized and would be brought forward so that business could be finished before bombers came. The Prime Minister sought support for War Cabinet Ministers. 'We are really doing our very best ... I ask the House to assist us.' Churchill had help from another quarter. Also on the 17th Hitler had all the reports in front of him dealing with the air battle of the 15th, and the British raids upon the invasion ports; the German Naval Staff had declared: 'The enemy Air Force is still by no means defeated.' And the Führer now decided to postpone 'Sealion' indefinitely without, for the moment, ordering complete cancellation.[67]

The Battle of Britain had been won, unknown to the British. But another operation was being lost – even before it had begun. In his Commons speech Churchill had admitted: 'Some things that ought to be done have not yet been done. Some things have been done that had better have been left undone.' He could well have been thinking about Dakar. A further complication had arisen, discussed by the War Cabinet that same Tuesday: a telegram had been received from Force 'Menace', suggesting that until it was known to what extent the arrival of the French cruisers had raised local morale, the presence of these warships did not alter the previous naval position. Churchill told Ministers he had therefore authorized the Force 'Menace' commanders to evaluate the situation themselves, in consultation with de Gaulle, and 'we would carefully consider any advice they might give'. Churchill's own view was that the operation should be cancelled; 'but there could be no harm in hearing what the officers in charge of the operation had to say.... The telegram in no way committed us to a new course of action.'[68] Unfortunately, Churchill was mistaken. Ministers met again in the Cabinet War Room at 9 p.m. while bombs burst just above in Whitehall, Burlington Arcade, Bond Street, Berkeley Square and Park Lane – and on the apparently safe Marble Arch subway, where the blast made the clean white tiles into deadly projectiles and 20 people died. 'The civil population was now in the front line,' Churchill said, and he asked the Home Secretary to submit recommendations for the immediate award of honours to selected civilians. One suggestion was to split this new award into two classes and call them, with the King's approval, the 'George Cross' and the 'George Medal'. The Colonial Secretary hoped the honour would be open to civilians in the Colonies, and he cited Malta as an example. The War Cabinet gave general approval. Dakar was again discussed: irate telegrams had been received during the day from de Gaulle and General Spears, already in Africa waiting for Force M, and with the former declaring: 'Having been informed of the new and negative decision reached by the British Government with regard to Operation "Menace", I wish to insist to you [Churchill] personally and formally that plan ... should be upheld and carried out.' De Gaulle's reasons were the blow to morale among the Free French if the operation were abandoned and the loss of prestige and valuable bases. If the British Government persisted in its 'new and negative' decision, he would go ahead alone – and he requested British naval and air cover. Equally categorically, Spears stated: 'If changes in policy are often puzzling in London they are heartbreaking here.' Only a few days before, he continued, the British had been prepared to face French warships on their way to Dakar, but now these warships were in harbour 'lying helpless', the Government had changed their mind; he stressed the loss of prestige de Gaulle would suffer and, if the General were left to go ahead alone, French opinion would swing totally against Britain.

The First Lord reminded the War Cabinet that the point at issue was not the strength of the French warships themselves, but the boost they may have given to local morale. But he revealed that Admiral Cunningham and General Irwin had now signalled their anxiety to go ahead with the direct operation. Churchill hinted at his own changed view. 'Although we did not desire a state of war with the Vichy Government, the War Cabinet had so far been prepared to take strong action against that Government's warships,' and, unlike the First Lord, he agreed with Spears' point concerning the willingness to attack French warships *en route* for Dakar, and added that 'it was clear, therefore, that the War Cabinet did not rate highly the danger of any hostile reactions from Vichy.... If our expedition came back with its tail between its legs, we could hardly hope the fact to escape notice.' Eden said that if the operation were not undertaken, de Gaulle would have 'no political future', and he believed the plan should definitely be carried out. Sinclair and Greenwood expressed similar views. Neville Chamberlain made his last recorded speech in a War Cabinet meeting: 'If the operation was abandoned it seemed to him that nothing could prevent the disintegration of the Free French forces in West Africa.' Attlee also believed, provisionally, that the operation should be continued. And the War Cabinet, while deferring a final decision until the following day, recorded the view that 'if the Commanders on the spot – Admiral Cunningham, General Irwin, General de Gaulle – who were in the best position to judge the situation – were, after full consideration, in favour of proceeding with Operation "Menace", in its original form (or in its original form subject to minor modifications) they were authorized by the War Cabinet to go ahead.'[69]

A telegram arrived from Force M, now in contact with de Gaulle, at 7.55 a.m. next day, 18 September. The commanders continued to insist that 'Menace' should be undertaken; the War Cabinet meeting at noon therefore confirmed the decision made the previous night, and authorized this Admiralty signal: 'We cannot judge relative advantage of alternative schemes from here. We give you full authority to go ahead and do what you think is best in order to give effect to the original purpose of the expedition. Keep us informed.' The telegram therefore differed slightly from the previous night's decision: the latter had referred to Operation 'Menace' 'in its original form', while this telegram gave the Force M commanders wide scope, authorizing whatever measures they thought necessary to achieve 'the original purpose'.

The War Cabinet – the last to be attended by Chamberlain – also heard the latest Middle East situation: Dill said two enemy columns had reached Sidi Barrani and were halted there.[70] Churchill and Eden were still in sharp conflict over the question of further help for Wavell, and later in the day the Prime Minister telephoned Eden to tell him he wanted to delay a convoy carrying the 6th Australian Division to Cairo. 'I called this "really maddening",' wrote Eden, 'all the arrangements had been made.'[71] Both Churchill and Eden were understandably but unduly worried: the Prime Minister by the invasion threat and the War Secretary by the heavy disproportion of strength between the Italians and British in North Africa; as far as the invasion was concerned, next day, 19 September, Hitler formally ordered the assembly of the 'Sealion' fleet to be stopped, and almost immediately afterwards British reports indicated a decreasing number of barges. And, to ease Eden's mind, the Italian offensive in North Africa had already come to a prolonged halt.

London had been bombed for eleven successive days. 'Already the Communists are getting people in shelters to sign a peace-petition to Churchill,' wrote Harold Nicolson on the 19th. 'One cannot expect the population of a great city to sit up all night in shelters week after week without losing their spirit. The only solution I can see at present is reprisals, which we are both unable and unwilling to exert.'[72] Nicolson was mistaken: the War Cabinet meeting on the 19th discussed this reprisal question. The raid on London the previous night had been exceptionally heavy; Ministers had had difficulty in travelling to the noon meeting, with most main streets in the West End closed, including Piccadilly, Regent Street, Bond Street, North Audley Street and Park Lane. The Home Secretary told the War Cabinet that about 200 people had been killed and 550 admitted to hospital. 'The most serious development had been the continued dropping of parachute mines, probably of the magnetic type.' These powerful 'land mines' had formed the subject of a Minute which Churchill had sent to Ismay earlier in the morning: 'My inclination is to say that we will drop a heavy parachute mine on German cities for every one he drops on ours; and it might be an intriguing idea to mention a list of cities that would be black-listed.'[73] The War Cabinet now agreed that 'we should retaliate by dropping mines over Berlin'.[74]

The policy of not allowing Underground stations to be used as shelters would clearly have to be revised: this restriction, imposed to prevent a 'shelter mentality' and to keep transport free for troops, was being circumvented by the public – people merely bought penny-halfpenny platform tickets and camped on the long stations. The Home Secretary told the War Cabinet on the 20th that 'he had visited some of the Tube railways to see how far they were being used as air raid shelters and the characters of the persons who took refuge in them'. Churchill believed the Tubes should now be thrown open to shelterers, at least at certain times, but other Ministers thought this 'most undesirable'. The War Cabinet asked the Home Secretary to circulate his recommendations.[75]

But next day, 21 September, the first Tube line was opened as a shelter, thus provoking an angry Minute from Churchill to the Home Secretary and Transport Minister because he had not been told beforehand. 'When I asked at the Cabinet the other day why the Tubes could not be used to some extent, even at the expense of transport facilities, as air raid shelters, I was assured that this was most undesirable.... I now see that the Aldwych Tube is to be used.... Pray let me have more information about this, and what has happened to supersede the former decisive arguments.'[76]

The Dakar fiasco reached its climax. 'Operation "Menace" began this morning,' Churchill told a 5 p.m. War Cabinet meeting on Monday, 23 September. He reported that 'at the outset it had appeared matters were progressing very favourably.... Later a message had been received indicating sporadic resistance was being shown and that our forces would have to interfere and open fire.' The Anglo-French force had approached Dakar in thick fog early in the morning; a bombardment had broken out between warships and shore batteries – hitherto thought to be weakly manned – and the warships had retired into the fog. De Gaulle had attempted a nearby landing in the afternoon, but this had been abandoned.[77] More details of the day's disaster reached London at 7.19 p.m. and, just after 10 p.m. and without further War Cabinet consultation, Churchill sent a personal message to the Force M Commander. 'Having begun, we must go on to the end. Stop at nothing.'[78]

Another offensive operation was being launched during this night of Monday, the 23rd. At the 5 p.m. meeting Churchill told Ministers that a number of indications had pointed to the possibility of an invasion attempt during the previous weekend. One of these had suggested that invasion would start at 3 p.m. on Sunday. 'In the light of the information,' continued Churchill, 'Ministers should consider whether British bombers should deliver a large-scale air attack on Berlin.' The Chief of Air Staff said the weather was suitable for the despatch of over 100 heavy bombers that night. Orders had already been given; the War Cabinet gave final approval. The 119 bombers therefore roared towards Berlin, and, with the War Cabinet's decision, tacit approval was given to lifting the restricted targeting policy: with so many bombers, not only military targets would be attacked. Thus began unrestricted bombing of Germany. Yet this grim decision, linked to the 'reprisal' discussion on the 19th, was based on a farcical mistake. President Roosevelt had been responsible for the warning to Churchill that invasion would be attempted at 3 p.m. the day before – Sunday – and Churchill had immediately telephoned Eden at his Kent home to tell him the news. The War Secretary walked to the nearby cliffs, saw the wind-tossed waves, and sent back a message to Churchill: if any Germans attempted the crossing they would be exceedingly sick. Only later was Roosevelt's mistake revealed; a code-word had been mixed up: instead of Britain the message should have read Indo-China and indeed, on 23 September the Japanese entered that country.[79]

On the same Monday a German High Command report stated: 'Even excluding the factor of enemy interference, the preparations for Operation 'Sealion' are not yet finished.'[80] British bombers droned over Berlin for four hours, ostensibly to deter an invasion which was no longer likely; factories in the north of the city were damaged, together with railway yards, and a gas works was destroyed. A splendid dinner was disrupted which had been laid on by Goebbels for Serrano Suñer, Franco's brother-in law, and Spanish Minister of Interior: the party had to retire in haste to the air raid shelter in the Hotel Adler, leaving their dessert and unable to emerge until 4 a.m. Seventy-five per cent of the bombers had reached their target, reported Newall to the War Cabinet on the 24th. During the previous five nights British bombers had flown 683 sorties, at a loss of only 4 machines. But the Germans had also been extremely active: bombing the previous day had been 'rather more intense' than on recent nights, said the Home Secretary; the attack had been directed on communications, and Liverpool Street Station and the Brighton line at Wandsworth Common were blocked. Direct hits had been sustained by several shelters.

A telegram had been received from Washington, reported Lord Halifax, in which President Roosevelt was shown to approve the Dakar operation: he would exercise his influence with Vichy to prevent the French declaring war.[81] Churchill had replied to this message: 'It looks as if there might be a stiff fight. Perhaps not, but anyhow orders have been given to ram it through.'[82] Any hopes of retrieving the Dakar situation collapsed that evening. Churchill described the situation to the War Cabinet next morning, Wednesday, 25 September: a telegram had been received late in the day showing the French forts had not been destroyed, despite close bombardment from British warships. Moreover, Churchill continued, 'the fire of the French warships had not been neutralized and the morale of the garrison had remained high. Fog had interfered considerably with operations.' A meeting had been held in London at 9.30 p.m. attended by Service Ministers and the Chiefs of Staff, and a telegram had been sent to the expedition commander seeking full details. The signal also suggested a landing might be made at nearby Rufisque under cover of night or fog. Since then another despatch had come from Force M reporting a landing was impracticable in the face of existing defences; 'the only alternatives were either an immediate withdrawal', continued the signal, 'or systematic bombardment'. Another telegram was brought into the War Cabinet: this, read out by the First Sea Lord, gave an answer to the request for more details: a French landing had been carried out at Rufisque, but troops had subsequently been withdrawn; HMS *Cumberland* had been damaged; air reconnaissance had been hampered by AA fire and fighters; Vichy French resistance remained unimpaired and morale high. The Force M Commanders said they intended to continue the bombardment. Still more information arrived: HMS *Resolution*, hit after the bombardment had resumed, was withdrawing. 'The situation is, therefore, obscure and unsatisfactory,' commented Admiral Pound. Churchill said two courses were open: to allow local commanders to go ahead with a landing if possible, or to order an end to the operation. He would have advocated the first choice before the news of the *Resolution* had arrived. As for the second alternative, Churchill now believed that 'there was no doubt the arrival of the French cruisers had changed the whole complexion of the situation. They had almost certainly brought to Dakar determined officers who had been put ashore to stiffen the forces there. The landing of a force at this juncture would be a serious step, for it might conceivably be cut off. Further, to keep our ships outside Dakar would be to expose them to the risk of attack from U-boats....' Attlee believed 'Menace' had been a 'justifiable gamble' but Vichy morale had been unexpectedly stiff. Halifax agreed. 'We had, perhaps, accepted too readily the rosy estimate of the operation which had been given by de Gaulle's supporters.' Greenwood agreed with Attlee and Halifax, and the First Lord of the Admiralty, Alexander, commented that 'although he had been against the operation from the beginning, yet having embarked upon it he would have advised its continued prosecution had not the *Resolution* been put out of the fight'.

Churchill left the Cabinet Room to draft a message, which was then approved: 'On all the information now before us, including damage to *Resolution*, we have decided that the enterprise against Dakar should be abandoned, the obvious evil consequences being faced. Unless something has happened which we do not know which makes you wish to attempt landing a force, you should forthwith break off. You should inform us most immediately whether you concur.'[83] The message left the Admiralty at 1.27 p.m.; in minimum time the reply came back: 'Concur in breaking off.'

October Ordeals

'This is worse than Norway,' wrote Harold Nicolson. 'What we need is a neat little triumph somewhere.' No favourable prospects seemed near. The Dakar failure had a depressing effect on Free French chances elsewhere, especially Syria; it increased tension and strain within the War Cabinet; above all, it had severely detrimental influence on Britain's prestige in America and in the Colonies and Dominions. Five days later Churchill received a message from Robert Menzies, Australian Prime Minister, containing one of the sharpest rebukes he was given during the war and complaining of lack of consultation. While Britain was in trouble with her friends, Germany improved her international relations: on 27 September a Tripartite Pact was signed in Berlin between Japan, Germany and Italy, and the substance of agreements between Japan and Vichy France was also made public. The Tripartite Pact was announced over the radio during the War Cabinet meeting on the 27th; Churchill immediately pointed out that, in the pact, Italy, Japan and Germany would help each other out if attacked by any power not taking part in this war or in the Sino-Japanese war. 'The Pact, therefore, seems to be directed against the United States.' Ministers agreed that 'the Pact, which would probably anger the United States, left matters very much as they were and did not affect the general situation. If anything, it was likely to accelerate the entry of the United States into the war.'[1]

German bombs continued their incessant destruction in Britain's capital. Heavy attacks on the night of the 23rd were repeated on the 24th. The West End had been the worst hit, especially the Tottenham Court Road area, and Waterloo Station had again been put out of action. The War Cabinet meeting on the 26th heard Sir Cyril Newall report on the successful enemy attack on the Bristol Aeroplane Company's works at Filton the previous day; the raid was repeated on the 27th, and Supermarine at Southampton was completely devastated. During this same day the Germans launched another massive daylight raid upon London, second only in size to that 'of the 15th, but most formations were broken up over Kent, and the *Luftwaffe* lost 55 aircraft to the RAF's 28. Three days later came the last major daylight raid on the capital.

October brought drenching rain and raw, rough winds; the terrors of the glorious, sun-soaked summer – 'Spitfire Summer' – had gone. Churchill cautiously told the Defence Committee on 3 October that although the risk of invasion had not greatly diminished, the prospect of broken weather did in fact make an attempt much less probable. Yet on this day the War Cabinet carried out a dress rehearsal in the event of having to flee from Central London: Ministers travelled out to top secret quarters near Hampstead, called 'Paddock', where they inspected apartments, had an excellent lunch, and sat down to a normal War Cabinet meeting. One item on the agenda concerned two telegrams, from Angora and Sofia, both reporting statements that the German Government did not expect to succeed in invading England and instead hoped by bombing the south and the Midlands, to bring about the collapse of the present Government. Ministers discussed possible German strategic aims for the next four months, on the assumption that these reports might be correct: certain indications pointed to a transfer of German troops through Italy to Libya, and this seemed more likely than an attempt to move through Spain or an advance into the Balkans. Ministers asked whether this meant more reinforcements should be sent to Malta or the Middle East; Churchill believed the question should be considered again in a few days.[2] In fact, with the ending of the peak invasion period Eden and Churchill had reached agreement over reinforcements for the Middle East: on 20 September the Prime Minister had finally settled that the next convoy should sail on 2 October, and on the latter day Eden had sent a further memorandum to Churchill suggesting additional help; this memorandum was approved by the Defence Committee on 3 October.

Also on 3 October came an announcement of War Cabinet changes. Neville Chamberlain had sought to resign before and had been persuaded to change his mind; by the end of September he was clearly in no state to continue. He was aware the cancer from which he suffered would soon kill him, and Churchill came, reluctantly, to the conclusion that he would have to find a new Lord President of the Council. On 24 September, after the troubled Chiefs of Staff meeting called to discuss Dakar, Churchill had told Eden that Chamberlain was dying and 'would have to give up soon'; he wanted to make Eden a full War Cabinet member. Eden wrote: 'He must bring another Tory into the War Cabinet and I was only one country would accept. If Edward [Halifax] were willing to become Lord President, he would like me to go to Foreign Office. If not, I should be Lord President and help him with matters of defence.' Eden said he preferred to stay where he was as War Secretary.[3] Churchill approached Oliver Lyttelton: 'Neville Chamberlain is dying. His loyalty and magnanimity have been wonderful: I understand his depth of character.... I cannot ask him to go into the shelters twice and three times a day, suffering as he does. Yes, he is dying. Now my plan is to move Anthony Eden from the War Office to the Foreign Office, and to move Edward Halifax ... to be Lord President.' The Prime Minister asked Lyttelton if he would be War Secretary: Lyttelton remembered feeling 'an exquisite thrill'.[4] Next day, 30 September, Churchill sent for Eden at 5 p.m. 'Edward clearly did not want to move to Lord President,' wrote Eden 'and he [Churchill] feared that if he suggested it Halifax would ask to go altogether, which Winston did not want at the moment Neville was leaving.' After dinner Eden saw Churchill again and told him 'I was ready to do everything I could, even to give up War Office, to be Lord President. I would then sit with Chiefs of Staff and him on Defence Committee.' However, late on Tuesday night, 1 October, Churchill told Eden he had unwillingly decided to turn down the Defence Committee idea, and Eden would remain where he was. 'He lamented that he could not give me Foreign Office and thus bring me into Cabinet.'[5] Lyttelton was therefore told Andrew Duncan was being moved to the Supply Ministry and he reluctantly agreed to accept the Board of Trade. The previous Supply Minister, Herbert Morrison, became an excellent Home Secretary and Minister of Home Security. Sir John Anderson became an equally valuable Lord President of the Council, and thus entered the War Cabinet. Sir John soon formed his Lord President's Committee: it became, in Churchill's words, 'almost a parallel Cabinet concerned with home affairs'. The Prime Minister stated in his brief to Sir John: 'It is essential that the larger issues of economic policy should be dealt with by your committee and primarily by you.... I wish you to take the lead prominently and vigorously.'[6] By the end of the year no home affairs or economic policy problems reached the War Cabinet without having first been sifted by the Committee; the War Cabinet was thus left free to concentrate on higher strategic issues and politics. And, if Fate had decreed, Sir John Anderson could have been Prime Minister: when Churchill and Eden flew to Yalta later in the war, Churchill advised the King that Sir John should succeed him at 10 Downing Street should he and Eden be killed.

So, at the start of October, Neville Chamberlain stepped into the dark, still upright, proper and lonely. One evening at the end of September Churchill had noticed workmen piling sandbags in 10 Downing Street, and was told Chamberlain had to have special treatment and, as he found it embarrassing to have this in the crowded shelter, a small private construction was being provided. 'Everyday he kept all his appointments, reserved, efficient, faultlessly attired,' wrote Churchill. 'But here was the background. It was too much. I used my authority.' Churchill had special messengers take all telegrams to Chamberlain's Worcestershire home so as to keep him fully informed, but the two men never saw each other again.[7] Chamberlain maintained his dignity and his convictions until the last: he wrote to Baldwin on 17 October: 'In September '38 we only had 60 fire pumps in London, which would have been burned out in a week. Some day these things will be known. My critics differed from me because they were ignorant.... I regret nothing in the past. I do regret that I should be cut off when I was capable of doing much more were it not for physical disability. But I accept what I can't help and hope I shan't cumber the earth too long.'[8] Chamberlain died three weeks later.

German bombers had now switched to mainly night raids: up to 13 November an average of 160 bombers dropped an average of 200 tons of high explosives and 182 canisters of incendiaries after the hours of daylight on London. Only six specialized RAF Blenheim night-fighter squadrons existed and these were unable to locate, track and fix, engage and hit bombers flying at speed above 12,000 feet. General Pile's anti-aircraft guns, at first forbidden to fire at targets not seen or specifically located, were hopelessly handicapped by outdated equipment. 'No defence exists against the bomber,' declared pre-war experts: no defence against the night bomber could have been more accurate. As a result of the failure to counter massed night raids in September, a committee was established under Sir John Salmond; another group, the Night Air Defence Committee, was convoked by Churchill, and he took the chair for the first meeting on 7 October. The search for night protection seemed a race against time, and yet development of necessary means had to be slow and tentative, by trial and error. And each day the War Cabinet meetings began with the death toll and bomber count for the night before.

Tensions inevitably led to conflict. The War Cabinet, working long hours in considerable danger, resented 'irresponsible' criticisms and, early in October, this led to the clash with certain newspapers. Churchill drew the attention of Ministers on 7 October to an article in the *Sunday Pictorial* of 29 September, which had 'contained a lot of false information, had characterized the Dakar affair as "another blunder", and had used language of an insulting character to the Government'. Only the previous day, Churchill continued, the same paper had published an article by Mr H. G. Wells from an obscure pamphlet, *The Bulletin of the Labour Book Service*, which contained a 'slashing' attack on Field-Marshal Sir Edmund Ironside and Lord Gort. 'The general tenor of Mr H. G. Wells's article ... had been that until the army was better led, we stood no chance of beating the Germans.' The same issue of the *Sunday Pictorial* had contained a leading article by the Editor amounting to 'a scurrilous attack on several members of the Government and obviously seeking to undermine confidence in the Government'. Much the same line had been taken in the leading article in that morning's *Daily Mirror*; Churchill declared that 'the immediate purpose of these articles seemed to be to affect the stability of the Government, and to make trouble between the Government and organized Labour'. Churchill believed there was far more behind these articles than 'disgruntled or frayed nerves ... they stood for something more dangerous and sinister, namely, an attempt to bring about a situation in which the country would be ready for a surrender peace'. The Attorney General outlined the legal position: the Government could undertake an 'executive act' and suppress these newspapers, but the proprietors could take the matter to Court. Ministers believed that 'although the articles in question were most objectionable, and scurrilous, to proceed against these newspapers, which made a wide popular appeal on account of their pictures, would do more harm than good'. However, the War Cabinet agreed with Churchill that 'the ulterior motive ... was certainly not the commercial motive of profit, and that the continuance of these malicious articles should not be tolerated'. The Home Secretary warned that if the Government attempted to suppress the newspapers, they would be told that the troubles in France had had their origin in the drastic suppression of all criticism by the French Government; he asked for more time to consider the matter.[9]

Discussion continued next day, 9 October, when the Home Secretary suggested a cautious approach: a 'friendly appeal' should be made to the Newspaper Proprietors' Association. Churchill angrily demanded sterner action. 'The articles in the *Sunday Pictorial* and the *Daily Mirror* constituted, in his view, a serious danger to this country.... It was intolerable that those bearing the burden of supreme responsibility at this time should be the subject of attacks of this kind.' The Prime Minister disagreed with Herbert Morrison's apparent suggestion that the Newspaper Proprietors' Association should be 'asked favours'; instead, the NPA representatives should be told that the War Cabinet was considering taking action, but before doing so had thought it right to tell them. Beaverbrook believed that the newspaper proprietors as a whole would wish action to be taken to restrain the *Mirror* and *Pictorial*, which were 'conducted in a manner which was damaging to the repute of newspapers generally'. The NPA, he added, had disciplinary powers. Churchill eventually said he was prepared to agree to Beaverbrook and the Lord Privy Seal, Attlee, sending for NPA representatives and speaking to them on the lines suggested, but he wished to make it clear that the Government must be prepared to take firm action to deal 'with this menace'.[10] The NPA deputation accordingly saw Attlee on the morning of the 11th. The *Daily Mirror* Chairman later told Cecil King of the Lord Privy Seal's message: 'He [Attlee] said that if criticism of the "irresponsible kind" inserted in our papers were to continue, the Government would introduce legislation making censorship of news *and* views compulsory. The NPA deputation ... said that compulsory censorship would wreck the Government.' Attlee was reported to have described the *Mirror* and *Pictorial* policy as 'subversive' and calculated to cause alarm and despondency at a very critical period. 'The Government had no objection to criticism,' said Attlee, 'but only to irresponsible criticism,' but according to the NPA, he had not defined what constituted the latter kind of comment.[11]

On Saturday, 12 October, Hitler formally declared 'Sealion' postponed. But the apparent threat would be maintained – and German bombers would be relied upon to batter the British into submission. Raids were immediately intensified: Newall reported to the War Cabinet on the 14th that 250 bombers had operated over Britain the previous night, mostly concentrating on London, but with Liverpool also receiving considerable damage.[12] The night of the 14th was even worse, almost as bad as the first raids on 7 September; Churchill, dining with Sinclair, Lyttelton and Moore-Brabazon at 10 Downing Street, had a narrow escape when a bomb hit the Treasury only 50 yards away, the blast shattering the windows of No 10. The Carlton Club, filled with about 250 people, received a direct hit – incredibly, no one was killed. The Prime Minister donned his tin hat and went to watch the spectacle from the Admiralty roof: most of Pall Mall seemed in flames, with at least five fierce fires burning in the area. St James's Street and Piccadilly were also alight.[13] Next morning, 15 October, members of the War Cabinet's Civil Defence Committee were told that only two railway stations, Paddington and King's Cross, were still in action, and that the Germans were now sending fighter-bombers in groups of three, flying comparatively low, and hence more difficult to engage with AA fire. People in the East End were apparently blaming the diminution of the barrage on shell shortages.[14] The War Cabinet, meeting at 5 p.m. that day, discussed the question of night bombing and civilian morale; the view was advanced that 'the civilian population in London were beginning to wonder whether we were hitting back hard enough at Germany.... If this feeling was allowed to grow it might have an unfortunate effect on our war effort.' Those concerned, claimed Churchill, were 'straining every nerve' to improve means of countering night bombing. 'There were good prospects that our defensive measures would be greatly improved within the next two or three months. In the meantime, we were retaliating as effectively as we could on Germany. But our bomber force was much smaller than that of the enemy and had to make far longer journeys. Meanwhile, the people of this country must stick it out.' Churchill added that he would consider making another broadcast.[15] Possible retaliatory measures were considered by the Defence Committee, also meeting on the 15th; the Committee put on record the desirability of delivering on Germany the maximum load of bombs, and stressed that some of these should be the heaviest type – 1,000 lbs.[16] This marked a further step towards area bombing of German territory.

London waited on that Tuesday night while a huge full moon hung heavy overhead. And the capital suffered the heaviest raid of the month, with nearly 450 German bombers dropping 538 tons of explosives; in addition, 70,000 incendiaries were let loose – for the first time on such a large scale. Over 400 civilians were killed and almost 1,000 fires were started. Herbert Morrison, Home Secretary, and a Cockney with intimate knowledge of Londoners, reported to the War Cabinet next afternoon. Public morale was good, but he warned 'we should look ahead, as morale might begin to suffer if the public felt that our reply to night bombing was ineffective. It was of the utmost importance that every effort should be made to press ahead as quickly as possible with the means of countering night bombing. During the last two or three nights two Tube stations had been pierced. The effect had been to make the public realize that practically no shelter was invulnerable.'

Attlee gave an account of his talks with the Newspapers Proprietors' Association and said that after he had seen the delegation Mr Esmond Harmsworth had telephoned to ask him to see representatives of the *Pictorial* and *Mirror*. On the advice of Lord Beaverbrook he had agreed to do so and Mr Bartholomew and Mr Cecil King had come to a meeting. 'Mr Bartholomew had been the more reasonable of the two. Mr King had at first tried to adopt the attitude that he did not see what harm these articles were doing.' The Lord Privy Seal told the War Cabinet that he had made it clear many people thought the articles 'were a deliberate fifth column activity'. Mr Bartholomew and Mr King had suggested an approach might have been made earlier but, the Lord Privy Seal primly concluded, 'at the end of the interview, however, they had both appeared somewhat chastened and had undertaken to exercise care in the future'.[17]

On 17 October, a week after Hitler's official postponement of 'Sea-lion', Göring issued full details of his plan for the continuation of the air war, in which he listed principal targets: the aircraft in-dustry, Fighter Command, London, the Birmingham-Coventry industrial complex and, to give the appearance that invasion was still likely, the principal south and west coast ports would be attacked. Also on the 17th, General Brooke noted in his diary: 'Evidence is amassing ... of an impending invasion of some kind or other.'[18]

London Transport had by now lost so many buses that an appeal had to be made on the 17th for reinforcements from outside the capital. On the same day, Churchill summoned a 'Shelter Meeting' at 10 Downing Street to demand full details of the provision of oil-stoves for heating and cooking facilities. And still the bombers came. The Chief of Air Staff gave his usual report to the War Cabinet on the 18th: 'During the previous night a total of about 250 enemy aircraft had been engaged, of which 200 had operated over London.'[19] On the 21st the Home Secretary reported: 'On the previous night about 70 people had been killed and 300 seriously injured in London.' Anxious reference was again made to the serious effect of the air raids on public morale: comment had arisen over the decrease in the AA barrage, and 'some disappointment' was evident over the failure to bring down more night bombers. 'Press statements to the effect that an antidote to the night bomber might be expected shortly had not been realized, with the result that Londoners were at the moment a little pessimistic.'[20] Next day, Churchill addressed a Minute to Sir Edward Bridges, War Cabinet Secretary, on the dangers of devastation in central London: it was 'probable indeed' that Whitehall and the centre of Government would be continuously demolished. 'Nearly all the Government buildings and shelters beneath them are either wholly unsafe or incapable of resisting a direct hit.... I have already asked for alter-native accommodation for Parliament, but no satisfactory plan has yet been made. The danger to both Houses during their sessions is serious, and it is only a question of time before these buildings and Chambers are struck.' Churchill urged all speed in finding other, stronger buildings and Lord Beaverbrook was eventually given the task of supervising the construction of bomb-proof Government centres – none of which were finished until the end of the Blitz. The Prime Minister, with much reluctance, now started to use and sleep in a converted office 70 feet below Piccadilly.[21]

Air Marshal Sir Charles Portal became Chief of Air Staff in succession to Newall, who left to become Governor-General of New Zealand. With his keen, heavy-lidded eyes, his rapier brain and his dislike of rhetoric, Portal soon became known for calm and apparently cold judgments. On 23 October, two days before he was welcomed to the War Cabinet by Churchill, Portal added another step up the ladder to area 'terror' bombing of Germany; he proposed that 'a primary target should be selected in a large populous area, and that a heavy concentrated attack should be delivered upon it. This would probably ensure the destruction of the target, e.g. a power station or gas works, and this in itself would have a considerable effect on those living near it, as well as on the industries situated in the town, by depriving them of power and demoralizing their workpeople.' He claimed the proposal followed the German example at Rotterdam.[22] The effect of bombing on the Rhine and Berlin was discussed by the War Cabinet on Tuesday, 29 October; according to a telegram from Belgrade, the 'cocksureness of German civilian population was disappearing,' and Lord Halifax commented that 'the German people seemed to have less power of resistance to air bombardment than the people of this country'. At the War Cabinet meeting the following noon, 30 October, after hearing that 200 enemy aircraft had been over London, Birmingham, Coventry and Liverpool the previous night, Churchill said that 'whilst we should adhere to the rule that our objectives should be military targets, at the same time the civil population around the target areas must be made to feel the weight of war'. He regarded this as a 'somewhat broad interpretation of our present policy and not as any fundamental change'. No public announcement on the subject should be made, he added. 'The Italians and, according to recent reports, the inhabitants of Berlin, would not stand up to bombing attacks with the same fortitude as the people of this country.' There, for six weeks, the question rested.

This same War Cabinet meeting on the 30th also discussed the possibility of a significant change in air raid shelter policy. Ideas until then, explained the Home Secretary, had been based on the assumption that raids would be comparatively short, and that shelters must be readily accessible. But prolonged night raiding had led 'certain sections' of the public to seek shelter, irrespective of warning, towards nightfall and to stay there until morning. Arguments against deep shelters were no longer entirely valid and Morrison therefore suggested that work should be put in hand for providing additional shelters by tunnelling: in London, this construction would be linked to the Tube system. The War Cabinet gave provisional agreement, but stressed that any statement should not indicate that there had been a reversal of existing policy.[23]

The change in policy was a tacit recognition that the air war was likely to be long, and that the danger remained of strain causing a breakdown in morale. And, next day, Churchill gave the Defence Committee a long and gloomy assessment of the war in general.

The last five months had shown Britain's ability to continue the war indefinitely, said the Prime Minister, but 'there seemed to be little possibility of any major offensive in 1940 or 1941'. By 1942 Britain should have overtaken the lag in munitions production; meantime, the country must be defended against invasion. It would have to be realized, he continued, that 'Germany was the master of Europe and the German army could move where it pleased. They would have ample forces for simultaneous campaigns in Spain and against Turkey and Russia and, at the same time, to help Italy with men and munitions. The Germans would inevitably turn their eyes to the Caspian and the prize Baku oilfields. In that event, Russia would have to fight.' Churchill added: 'The question might be asked "How are we to win the war?" ... For the moment all that we could do was to bank on the pressure of the blockade accompanied by remorseless bombing of Germany and Italy.' In discussion following this assessment, members of the Committee agreed that a German invasion could become a practical possibility if Britain were to relax. Sir Hugh Dowding said Britain had only managed to defeat German air attacks by day by a narrow margin, and 'it would be dangerous to assume that we could repeat this success in the face of sustained and determined German attacks unless the fighter force and the training organization behind it were both expanded.' Dill said it was doubtful whether we could afford to continue the flow abroad of the best trained units. 'We still had only an amateur army with an average of three pre-war officers per infantry battalion.'[24]

Londoners had now endured the Blitz for almost two months. They had suffered night raids for one month. And now, at the end of October, the War Cabinet had another preoccupation: a new enemy offensive started against one of Britain's few remaining friends. New commitments were arising, despite Churchill's statement to the Defence Committee that resources were still spread thin. The past month of bombing had also been one of intense and deadly diplomatic manoeuvring, involving most of the capitals of Europe.

On a blustery Friday, 4 October, Hitler and Mussolini met for talks high in bleak Brenner Pass. The effusive meeting dispelled the chilliness of surrounding air. 'Conversations were certainly most interesting of all that have taken place so far,' noted Ciano; he also observed: 'There is no longer talk about a landing in the British Isles.' Instead, Hitler expounded his policies of drawing France into the orbit of the anti-British coalition, and he again waxed anti-Bolshevist. Neither of the two leaders mentioned the Balkans or Roumania, although both men were busy making plans in that direction. But Hitler did stress the importance he was now about to give to the Mediterranean, and he tentatively took the step which the British HQ at Cairo had long feared: German units were provisionally offered for Mussolini's Egyptian campaign.

From early October the Middle East occupied increasing time at British War Cabinet discussions, and Churchill's uneasiness over Wavell continued. The Italians remained at Sidi Barrani and Dill told the War Cabinet on Monday, 7 October, that no indications had been received of an early enemy advance. The CIGS then gave details of Italian dispositions at Sollum and Sidi Barrani, at each of which two enemy divisions had been drawn up. Churchill immediately showed his irritation. 'This was the first occasion on which the War Cabinet had been informed that as many as four enemy divisions were in forward positions. It was important that they should be notified immediately of the arrival of any new divisions at the front.'

Despite the good humour displayed at Brenner Pass, German-Italian relations soon soured through rivalry for Roumania. 'A telephone call from the Duce,' commented Ciano in his diary on the 8th, 'requesting we take action in Roumania to elicit a request for Italian troops. He is very angry because only German forces are present in the Roumanian oil regions.'[25] Next day, Wednesday the 9th, assessments of the Axis talks at Brenner were discussed by the British War Cabinet; Sir Samuel Hoare had cabled from Madrid to say that according to the Spanish Foreign Minister, Hitler and Mussolini had decided a German offensive should be made on Egypt via Constantinople and Syria, and Ministers agreed the building of airfields and defences in the Roumanian oil fields by the Germans might prelude Turkish intimidation. If Germany decided to throw her weight into an eastward thrust, warned Churchill, the countries immediately in her path could do little more than delay her progress. 'We should take advantage of this delay to develop our army in the Middle East.'[26] Uneasy reports continued to filter back to London: next day Halifax referred to additional indications that German military authorities had been studying possible action in Greece and Yugoslavia, and that an attempt to invade Britain had been postponed until Spring. Churchill commented that evidence continued to accumulate of invasion preparation. 'Nevertheless, we should have to consider in the near future the extent to which we could afford to reinforce the Middle East at the expense of this country.'[27] Possibilities of a fact-finding mission by Eden to the Middle East had been discussed by the War Cabinet at the end of September and again on 9 October. Agreement with the idea resulted in the War Secretary's departure by flying boat from Plymouth on the 11th, with his arrival in Cairo scheduled for the 14th.

Map 2. *The Mediterranean, Near and Middle East*

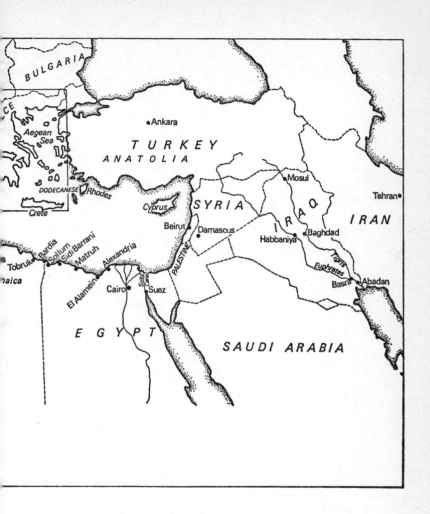

Meanwhile, on Saturday, 12 October, Hitler issued his formal postponement of 'Sealion', at least until Spring 1941. 'Preparations for "Sealion" shall be continued solely for the purpose of maintaining political and military pressure of England.' By now, Hitler's thoughts were concentrating on the East. His partner was enraged over German activities in Roumania, and Mussolini's pique was to have far-reaching repercussions. 'Hitler always faces me with a *fait accompli*,' stormed Mussolini to Ciano on this Saturday. 'This time I am going to pay him back in his own coin. He will find out from the papers that I occupied Greece.'[28]

Also on the 12th, the Chiefs of Staff discussed possible air reinforcements for Egypt, and concluded that additional squadrons could not be spared owing to the effect on home strengths.[29] On the same day, an assessment reached London from the British Ambassador in Turkey: about 2,500 German troops would arrive in Roumania towards the middle of the month, nominally as 'instructors', but these troops should be considered as the first instalment of a German force for the defence of Roumania against the USSR.[30] This report tied in well with a long cable from Sir Stafford Cripps, received on Sunday and discussed by the War Cabinet on Tuesday evening, 15 October. If forecasts of German plans were correct, said the British Ambassador to Moscow, Britain was probably faced with the last chance of moving Russian policy, since an increase in Axis activity or a success in the Balkans or Middle East would add to Russian fears and difficulties. Sir Stafford believed Russia did not want Germany to win the war and the Soviets would suffer some risk to prevent this coming about; in the short-term Germany could make Moscow more tempting offers, but in the long-term Britain had the advantage. The Ambassador therefore came to some surprising conclusions. Britain should promise to consult Russia on the post-war settlement of Europe and Asia, in association with other victorious powers, and should also pledge herself not to form or enter any anti-Russian alliance after the war; Russia's *de facto* sovereignty of the Baltic States should be recognized until the end of the war; extensive materials should be supplied; Britain should guarantee Russia against attack from Turkey or Persia and, especially, against an attack on Baku. Halifax told the War Cabinet that he had at first thought Britain should consult America over this possible, and drastic, approach to Russia, but he had then considered it sufficient to inform America of the action Britain was taking. Ministers agreed. Lord Halifax warned 'that it would be imprudent to build any hopes on the outcome of the new approach to Russia, which was mainly influenced by fear of Germany. Nevertheless, it was right that at the present juncture one more approach to Russia should be made, and that it should be on record that we made it.'[31] A cable left the Foreign Office later in the evening, authorizing Cripps to go ahead with his remarkable proposals.

Meanwhile, Anthony Eden's safe arrival in Cairo had been announced at the War Cabinet meeting on the 14th, and the War Secretary now began preliminary talks with Wavell, sending the first long report back to Churchill on the 16th: offensive operations against the Italians were being planned for January, Eden cabled, dependent on the arrival of equipment, and plans for an offensive in the Sudan were also being worked out; the Abyssinian revolt was going better than expected. 'Of course, Italy by some offensive of her own may upset any plans we make.'[32] Mussolini was, in fact, raging at his military commanders almost daily in an attempt to make them move forward, and he continued to demand an advance while Eden made his long tour of the desert.

Britain and Germany were anxiously watching which way Franco's Spain would move; and, on 17 October, British hopes were lowered by the appointment of Suñer as Foreign Minister, replacing Colonel Beigbeder, while Franco himself took over the Ministry of the Interior. The War Cabinet discussed the situation next day, the 18th, and Lord Halifax warned that the changes were 'bad from our point of view'. On the other hand, anti-German feeling in Spain remained strong, and the War Cabinet came to the conclusion that 'while ... it was wise to treat this change as a definite setback and make plans accordingly, we should still not assume that Spain was bound to come into the war against us, and we should make every effort to keep Spain out of the war'.[33] Optimism increased slightly next day when, at an interview with Sir Samuel Hoare, Franco maintained that the ministerial alterations did not mean a change of policy.

Sir Samuel Hoare, previously Home Secretary in Chamberlain's Cabinet, had a busy and complicated task in Madrid – notorious nest of spies, intrigues and diplomatic deviousness. Apart from listening to rumours, gathering intelligence and dealing with neutral Franco, the British Ambassador was also in the best position to have contact with the Vichy French. Conversations took place at frequent intervals between Sir Samuel and the French Ambassador and, on the 19th, Sir Samuel was instructed to make clear to his French colleague that Britain was still ready to co-operate with Vichy. But on the same day, alarming news reached the Foreign Office that Laval, recently appointed French Foreign Minister, had been informed of a German peace offer. This, following from Hitler's remarks to Mussolini at the Brenner Pass meeting, included French participation in the New Order, the use of French troops in Africa against the British and the co-operation of French naval and air forces. Laval, Darlan and Baudouin were believed in favour

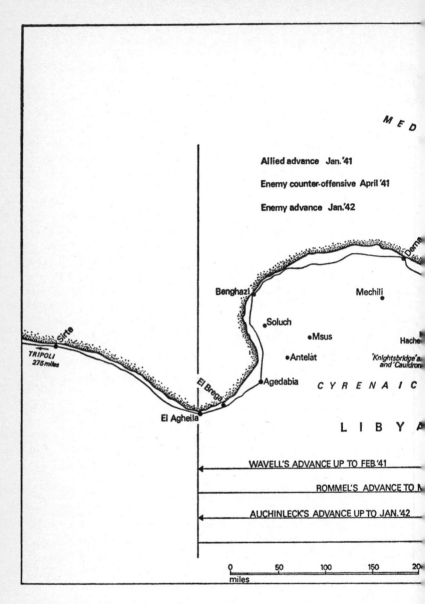

Map 3. *The Desert Struggle 1940-42*

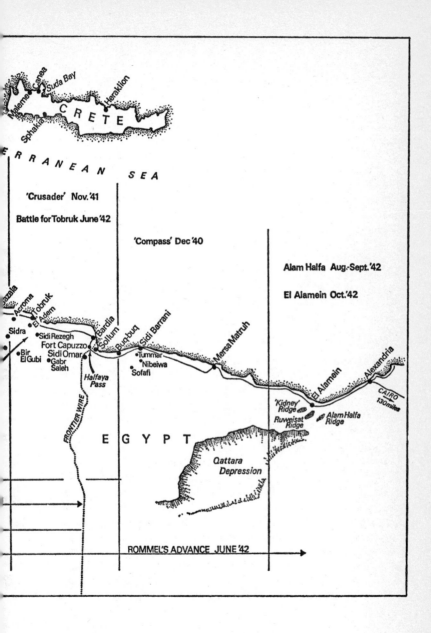

CRETE

Maleme • Canea • Suda Bay
Heraklion

Sphakia

MEDITERRANEAN SEA

'Crusader' Nov. '41

Battle for Tobruk June '42

'Compass' Dec '40

Alam Halfa Aug.-Sept. '42

El Alamein Oct. '42

Gazala
Acroma • El Adem
Tobruk
Sidra • Sidi Rezegh
Fort Capuzzo
Bardia
Sollum • Buqbuq
Sidi Omar • Sidi Barrani
Bir El Gubi • Gabr Saleh
Halfaya Pass
Tummar • Nibeiwa
Sofafi
Mersa Matruh
El Alamein
Alexandria
CAIRO 130miles

'Kidney' Ridge
Ruweisat Ridge
Alam Halfa Ridge

FRONTIER WIRE

EGYPT

Qattara Depression

ROMMEL'S ADVANCE JUNE '42

of these terms, but Pétain and Weygand were against.[34] The situation, which could have a disastrous effect on Britain, therefore hung in the balance, and the War Cabinet could see no way in which they could influence the French decision – until Churchill sitting alone in the Hawtrey Room at Chequers late at night with General Ismay, conceived one possible idea. He suddenly jumped up, according to Ismay, and exclaimed: 'I believe I can do it.' Ismay's account continued: 'Bells were rung; secretaries appeared; and he proceeded to dictate his first broadcast to France. He had no notes; but slowly and steadily, for a space of two hours, the words poured forth.' Dictation finished at 2 a.m.[35] In the midst of all this activity, Lord Lothian arrived home from Washington on 20 October, and he at least brought some encouraging news. Lord Halifax told the War Cabinet next day that the Ambassador had reported 'the almost miraculous change of opinion in the United States after it had become clear that this country was effectively resisting the German air attacks'.[36] But for the moment no positive international steps could be expected from America: the country was in a frenzy of Presidential campaigning for the 6 November election.

Winston Churchill's unmistakable voice crackled over the radio on Monday, 21 October. The Prime Minister, speaking from the War Cabinet's underground HQ in the midst of an air raid, proclaimed in his schoolboy French: 'Frenchmen! For more than 30 years in peace and war I have marched with you, and I am marching still along the same road...' The Prime Minister warned listeners of the treaty which might soon be signed on their behalf. 'It is not defeat that France will now be made to suffer at German hands, but the doom of complete obliteration.... Never will I believe that the soul of France is dead. Never will I believe that her place amongst the greatest nations of the world has been lost for ever!' And he ended: 'Good night then: sleep to gather strength for the morning. For the morning will come. Brightly will it shine on the brave and true, kindly upon all who suffer for the cause, glorious upon the tombs of heroes. Thus will shine the dawn. *Vive la France!*'[37] Churchill, despite his words to Ismay and the care lavished on this address, was well aware it would have no direct effect on Pétain and his Ministers; earlier in the day he had therefore taken another step and had sent a message to Roosevelt, in which he urged the President to warn the French Ambassador that the United States would 'disapprove very strongly' of anything like the surrender of the French fleet.[38] But tension increased: the Foreign Office learnt of a visit Laval was making to Hitler on 22 October at Montoire in occupied France; also on the 22nd, a telegram arrived from Cripps – he had sought an interview with Molotov, in order to present the far-ranging British proposals, but had received no answer; instead he was to see Andrei Vyshinsky, Deputy Foreign Minister, later in the day. At this meeting, the British proposals were described: in return for an agreement, Britain asked the Soviet Government to undertake a position of neutrality 'as benevolent as that adopted towards Germany'. Vyshinsky took the document for Soviet consideration.[39] Unknown to the British Foreign Office, Stalin was seeing the German Ambassador at about the same time Sir Stafford saw the Deputy Foreign Minister: the cordial Soviet leader told Count Schulenburg that Molotov would soon be visiting Berlin. And, also on the 22nd, Mussolini set the date for his surprise assault upon Greece – six days away.[40]

Hitler was busy seeing potential allies. Following his talks with Laval on the 22nd, he rushed in his special train to the Franco-Spanish border town of Hendaye to meet General Franco; but, after nine hours' discussion, he emerged disappointed: the Spanish dictator delivered long, monotonous and non-committal monologues in a tedious sing-song voice, and Hitler complained to Mussolini: 'Rather than go through that again, I would prefer to have three or four teeth yanked out.' The Führer hurried back to Montoire to see Pétain next day, the 24th, but the old and weary French leader also refused to go the whole way with Hitler – although he was nevertheless obliged to sign a repulsive, yet vague, agreement: 'The Axis Powers and France have an identical interest in seeing the defeat of England accomplished as soon as possible. Consequently, the French Government will support, within the limits of its ability, the measures which the Axis Powers may take to this end.' No details were agreed, and Hitler avoided pushing too hard for fear he might lose French North African territory, and even the French fleet.[41] While Pétain struggled with Hitler, British Ministers discussed the French situation at a War Cabinet meeting in Churchill's room at the House of Commons. Sir Samuel Hoare had sent an account of a conversation with the French Ambassador at Madrid: the latter had spoken of the 'deep cleavages of opinion in the Vichy Government and the growing resentment of the French people'.[42] Early next morning, Friday, the 25th, further pressure was put on the French: Sir Samuel Hoare cabled after midnight that the French Ambassador considered Churchill's broadcast would probably have an excellent effect, and suggested this should be followed by an appeal by the King or Churchill to Pétain. Lord Halifax and Churchill drafted a message for the King to send, mentioning Pétain's previous declaration that anything dishonourable would be rejected. Churchill described this note to the War Cabinet at 11.30 a.m.; at the same meeting Sir John Dill reported that 'no confirmation had been received of the rumours of an intended Italian attack on Greece. It seemed possible that the Italians thought that the visit of the Secretary of State for War to Egypt was connected with a coming offensive on our part.'[43]

As a result of Churchill's message to Roosevelt sent the previous Sunday, the President signalled on the 25th that 'very strong representations' had already been made to the French Ambassador at Washington, who had also been given a personal message for immediate communication to his Government: if the French now allowed the Germans to use their fleet in hostile operations against Britain, such action would constitute a flagrant and deliberate breach of faith with the US Government. This signal from Roosevelt crossed another appeal from Churchill; later in the day the President replied to this second appeal – he had now also decided the message to Pétain should be delivered personally by the US Chargé at Vichy. Churchill conveyed his thanks the following day, the 26th, and warned that 'everything was still in the balance'.[44]

While Washington, London and Berlin waited impatiently for the French, Cripps again saw Vyshinsky in Moscow, on the 26th, and was informed that the Soviet Government regarded the British proposals 'of the greatest importance'. Another meeting would be held later.[45] On Sunday, 27 October, the intense diplomatic activity temporarily faded. All possible appeals had been made to Pétain; only silence came from Vichy. But, to end this brief lull, Mussolini made another bold bid for military glory. The British War Cabinet Minutes for Monday, 28 October, began: 'The War Cabinet were informed that following an Italian ultimatum – delivered to Greece at 3 a.m. that morning and refused by the Greek Government – an attack on Greece had begun. Unconfirmed reports state that Athens has been bombed and that 10 Italian divisions, consisting of perhaps 200,000 men, were moving into Greece.'[46]

Mussolini bounced off his special train at Florence Station. Waiting to meet him was Adolf Hitler: the rendezvous had been arranged by the Italian leader. 'Führer, we are on the march!' exclaimed the beaming Duce. 'Victorious Italian troops crossed the Greco-Albanian frontier at dawn today!' Mussolini savoured revenge for all occasions when he, Hitler's friend and ally, had been last to know the Führer's intentions; Hitler barely managed to control his rage: the expedition had been launched at the wrong time of the year, would undoubtedly be inefficiently handled, and would upset all his careful plans for the Balkans.[47]

Eden was still in Cairo, and his first thoughts dwelt upon Britain's difficulties in giving help to the Greeks: 'We are not in a position to give effective help by land or air, and another guaranteed nation looks like falling to the Axis.'[48] If help were given the Middle

East would be forced to suffer; and aid was requested by the Greek Government within hours of the offensive opening. British Ministers meeting at 5 p.m., were told that General Ioannis Metaxas, Greek President of the Council, had asked for British naval and air assistance for the protection of Corfu and Athens, and the Greek Ambassador in London had contacted Lord Halifax with a similar appeal and with a reference to the British guarantee given by Chamberlain in April 1939. No land forces had been sought. Churchill told the War Cabinet that he had called a meeting of the Defence Committee, to be held later in the evening; meanwhile, the War Cabinet held a preliminary discussion, during which it was recalled that Greece had for some time been asking what assistance Britain could offer in the event of an attack. 'Up to now we had been extremely guarded in our replies.' Ministers believed it might be possible to increase bombing attacks upon Italy and especially to hit Rome, although 'it was of course most important to avoid bombs falling on the Vatican City'. It seemed likely that the Italians intended to occupy Corfu, but 'if they did, this would make very little difference to us strategically ... and it was out of the question to send our fleet to that area'. The War Cabinet agreed that the line to be taken to the Press would be that 'notwithstanding the defection of the French, we were doing all in our power to help the Greek Government'. The question was raised whether, as a result of the Italian attack, America would be more willing to make aircraft and other equipment immediately available, but Churchill commented that nothing which was available at short notice would be likely to affect the immediate situation.[48] More definite British help came from another direction: next day, 29 October, Air Chief Marshall Longmore, Middle East RAF Commander, signalled that on his own responsibility he had arranged to send a Blenheim squadron to Greece. Also on the 29th Churchill requested Eden to stay in Cairo, and he told the noon War Cabinet meeting that 'certain military measures in support of Greece were in preparation' as a result of the Defence Committee session the previous night. He added that for the moment it would be best not to discuss these measures, but 'the War Cabinet ought to be under no illusion as to the extent of the assistance we could give. We were severely limited by the size of our forces in the Middle Eastern theatre.'[49]

Amidst the flurry of anxiety over Greece remained the danger of a Vichy treaty with Germany. Churchill remarked at the War Cabinet meeting on the 28th that 'it was extraordinary that neither we nor the Americans should have received any information as to what had happened in the negotiations between the Germans and the Vichy Government'. The Prime Minister pointed out, almost accurately, that the Vichy Government might have agreed to join the German *bloc* without adopting a more hostile attitude towards Britain, but he added that 'the worst position from our point of view would be if the Vichy Government had agreed to hand over French bases to Germany and if General Weygand remained the servant of the Vichy Government. In that event our position at Gibraltar might become untenable.' Lord Halifax commented on de Gaulle's actions at Brazzaville: it was, he said, untrue that the General had established a rival Government, although he had decided to form a Defence Council for the French Empire. 'It was perhaps tiresome that he should have chosen this moment to set up a Council of Defence without prior consultation with us. But the correspondence which had passed with de Gaulle provided for the setting up of such a Council in due course.'[50] Britain had in fact been placed in an embarrassing position by de Gaulle: if strong support were given to his latest move, all appeals to Pétain would suffer decreased effect. Pétain himself made the situation even more uncertain in a broadcast two days later: he declared that although the principles of Franco-German collaboration had been accepted, their application had been left for a later date; the British Foreign Office considered it would have been better if Pétain had either accepted completely, or rejected entirely, the humiliating German terms – if he had decided upon the former, de Gaulle would have received more support from the French people, Britain could have given him all assistance, and the Vichy Government might have been overthrown. Sir Samuel Hoare was instructed on 1 November to find out all he could from the French Ambassador and to insist on Britain's right to ask Vichy to explain the position.[51]

Also on 1 November, the War Cabinet were at last given details of aid Britain could supply to Greece: Ministers were told of the Blenheim squadron being sent on Longmore's initiative; in addition, one British battalion would arrive in Crete that day, and two more battalions, completing a brigade, would be sent as soon as Wavell could make arrangements. Ministers believed that 'if, as appeared probable from the news already received, the Greeks put up a good resistance, we should have to be prepared to take some risks in order to send them help'. The possibility of transferring material due to be sent to Turkey was also discussed. 'It was urged that we should do everything we could to help Greece immediately. On the other hand, in the long run Turkey might be more important to us than Greece.'[52] Eden sent a telegram to Churchill: 'There is full agreement here as to the importance of preventing capture of Crete by Italians,' but, prophetically, he added: 'A further difficulty in basing aircraft in Crete is that Crete at present possesses only one aerodrome which can be made serviceable. Crete is very vulnerable to air attack....' And, equally a foretaste of the future: 'We cannot, from Middle East resources, send sufficient air or land reinforcements to have any decisive influence upon course of fighting in Greece.' To send such forces from Egypt, he maintained, would imperil Britain's whole Middle East position and 'jeopardize plans now being laid in more than one theatre'.[53] Yet, if Crete were taken, Britain's position in the east Mediterranean could rapidly deteriorate, and if Greece fell, Turkey would be threatened: Turkish territory lay across the land route from German-held central Europe, and to a large extent from Russia's route to the Middle East. Earlier on this Friday, 1 November, the COS had reported on a possible enemy advance in these directions; the report suggested the Germans might intend, after an occupation of Bulgaria and Greece, to move into Turkish Thrace and establish bridgeheads on the further side of the Straits, after which, probably in 1941, they might consolidate their position in Anatolia and advance into Syria and perhaps northern Iraq. Britain's hold on Egypt would be severely threatened: the alternative line of supply via Iraq and Palestine would be cut, and Britain's small army in Egypt would be forced to fight on two fronts.[54] The attitudes of Bulgaria, Greece, Syria and Iraq were of supreme importance. Mr Rendel, the British Ambassador at Sofia, learnt that the Bulgarian Government 'hoped' to remain neutral, but that the situation was considered 'delicate and difficult'. A statement by Inönü, the Turkish President, on 1 November, was also less definite than the Foreign Office had hoped: the Turks sought 'normal relationships with all the countries which show the same measure of goodwill towards us'.[55]

Meanwhile, Hoare continued his efforts in Madrid. On 2 November he was informed of Pétain's reply to the King's message: the French leader enunciated all wrongs Britain had done to the French fleet and her support to French rebels; however, the French Government would not make any unjustified attack, and they would know how 'honourably to respect the essential interests of the French nation'. Pétain's reply to Roosevelt's appeal had much the same content.[56]

President Roosevelt was now in the final frenzy of the election; the British War Cabinet anxiously awaited the outcome, fully aware of the close relationships which had been carefully nurtured between Churchill and Roosevelt. British Ministers also awaited developments from the other giant, Russia; on the 2nd, Cripps again saw Vyshinsky and the Ambassador anxiously sought a Soviet reply to the British proposals presented on 22 October. Once again the result was a disappointment – the Deputy Foreign

Minister merely asked Sir Stafford more questions and promised another meeting.[57]

Eden, still in sweltering Cairo, was anxious to return home to give the War Cabinet details of carefully considered offensive plans, which might now be hopelessly damaged by weakening the Middle East through aid to Greece. But, during the evening of the 2nd, he received another telegram from Churchill. 'Greek situation must be held to dominate others now. We are well aware of our slender resources.... I invite you to stay in Cairo for at least another week while these questions are being studied.'[58] Eden impatiently scribbled across this cable: 'Egypt more important than Greece.'[59] His wish to return to London led, wrote Eden later, to a 'somewhat tense argument'; telegrams flowed next day, 3 November, including a 'tirade' from Churchill asserting that Athens ranked higher than Khartoum and Kenya and, according to Eden, 'accusing us of pursuing safety-first tactics'. The argument was in fact based upon misunderstanding: Churchill failed to realize Wavell and Eden were strongly in favour of offensive action against the Italians in North Africa: the Prime Minister believed they were merely intending to remain on the defensive while Greece suffered. Eden, on the other hand, had all the information to refute these allegations – yet he was refused permission to fly home, and he felt that only in London could he reveal these top-secret schemes. The buzzing stalemate continued for another three days. And, while Eden was struggling to be allowed to return, the Chiefs of Staff recommended on 3 November that the previous policy of only limited aid to Greece should be eased, despite the consequent risk to strength in Egypt. Aid would still have to be restricted to aircraft and AA defences, but the COS proposed to despatch two more Blenheim squadrons, a Gladiator fighter squadron – to be followed by another later – and one heavy and one light AA battery. The Middle East would be compensated by sending out 34 Hurricanes and 32 Wellingtons, but the COS recognized Egypt would be left 'very thin'.[60]

No German bombers appeared over London during the night of 2-3 November – for the first night since 8 September. The silence was almost unnatural, but the main reason was correctly believed to be bad weather and no special note was taken by the War Cabinet: Portal merely reported at the next meeting that 'enemy attacks over the weekend had been on a low scale'. The Blitz soon resumed, with the War Cabinet being told two days later, 6 November, that 225 enemy aircraft had been over the country the previous night, most of them concentrating upon the capital.[61] Nevertheless, unsuspected by the War Cabinet, Göring was coming to the conclusion that different methods would soon have to be tried.

And Hitler was reaching the conclusion that he must also throw new offensive plans into operation. On 4 November he condemned the Italian campaign against Greece as a 'regrettable blunder', and, in a conference with his Generals, he discussed the possibility of attacking Italy's new enemy, even if this meant not helping in North Africa. He had anyway received a discouraging report of conditions in Libya from his emissary, General von Thoma: 'Every last man is scared of the British. The two opponents barely hurt each other.'[62] The War Cabinet meeting on the 4th approved the Chiefs of Staff recommendations for further aid to Greece; Churchill declared that 'the loss of Athens would be as serious a blow to us as the loss of Khartoum, and a more irreparable one'. Although the Prime Minister admitted that British public opinion was not anxious for British intervention, he said that 'if Greece was overwhelmed it would be said that in spite of our guarantee we had allowed one more small nation to be swallowed up'. Lord Halifax told Ministers that the Greek Ambassador had been to see him earlier in the day and had made requests for aircraft, AA guns, anti-tank guns and rifles.[63] The War Cabinet was therefore committing the country to steadily increasing involvement in the Grecian situation: the initial attitude, virtually amounting to more moral support, had gradually changed; but a British commitment to help the Greeks in their fight against the Italians, now going badly against Mussolini, would also drag the country into an infinitely more dangerous commitment to help the Greeks defend themselves against possible German intervention. Early on the 5th, less than 24 hours after Hitler had first discussed the idea of attacking Greece, the British COS completed a report based on such a possibility. Mussolini may have acted independently, said the report, but more likely his move was part of an Axis design to divert British land and air forces from Egypt; the Greeks might be able to hold out against the Italians, continued the paper, but the Germans would present a far different problem. No forces Britain could send in 1940 could long delay a German victory, and the Turks were unlikely to send assistance; Britain would therefore be making a mistake, believed the Chiefs of Staff, if forces needed for Egypt were locked up irrevocably in Greece. Help should remain restricted to air, sea and technical army units.[64] The report – which, in view of later events proved extremely wise – made discouraging reading.

Other items on the 5th also caused depression. Sir Samuel Hoare had seen the French Ambassador, and now reported that Laval might sign a peace treaty with Germany on the 11th;[65] the powerful German pocket-battleship *Admiral Scheer*, announced her fearful presence in the Atlantic by sinking the armed merchant cruiser *Jervis Bay*; shipping losses in recent days had soared threateningly, and Churchill now made his way to the Commons to reveal the gravity of these sinkings to anxious MPs. Harold Nicolson commented afterwards: 'If Chamberlain had spoken glum words such as these the impression would have been one of despair and lack of confidence. Churchill can say them and we all feel "Thank God we have a man like that!".... Thereafter he slouches into the smoking room and reads the *Evening News* intently, as if it were the only source of information available to him.'[66] Then, on the 6th, came news of Roosevelt's re-election. Churchill reacted with 'indescribable relief' and hastened to send congratulations: 'I feel you will not mind my saying that I prayed for your success.'[67] Churchill, in this message, made a remark which may have been prompted by War Cabinet discussions a few hours earlier: 'We are entering upon a sombre phase of what must evidently be a protracted and broadening war, and I look forward to being able to interchange my thoughts with you.' At their meeting, British Ministers had been told that the Assistant Naval Attaché in Washington had been given, in strict confidence, 'certain US naval defence plans' by the Plans Division of the Navy Department. These contained an appreciation of the policy which the US Navy should adopt in the event of America entering the war, and it was understood that this appreciation 'reflected generally' the view of Admiral Stark, American Chief of Naval Operations, and 'would be represented by him to higher authority'. The present situation was 'gloomy' said the report; ultimate completion of Axis control in the Mediterranean was anticipated, and this would largely nullify the British blockade. 'Very considerable direct naval, military and air assistance in European area must be given to the British to ensure victory,' and, if a fully offensive war was waged by America against Japan, the whole of American naval and industrial resources would be involved; with the adoption of such a forward plan against Japan, 'the US Navy would be unable to provide the minimum assistance in the Atlantic and Europe necessary to prevent a British defeat'. The report recommended that every political expediency should be adopted to preclude a conflict with Japan until the war had been won in the West. Should, however, war in the Far East be forced upon America, the appreciation proposed that 'they should conduct a strictly defensive war against Japan'. This might mean the acceptance of the loss of the Philippines and Borneo and even ultimately the Netherlands East Indies and Singapore.[68] Ministers took note of this American appreciation.

De Gaulle was still proving an embarrassment. The War Cabinet heard a telegram from General Spears at Duala, dated 29 October: the Free French leader proposed to return to London towards the end of November and re-establish his HQ there. Lord Halifax suggested a reply saying that while Britain would welcome de Gaulle's return for a visit, 'we doubted the wisdom of his establishing his HQ here.' Churchill thought it best to leave the situation for a day or two. The nature of the difficulty caused by de Gaulle was described in a Foreign Office signal to Sir Samuel Hoare next day, 7 November, which frankly recognized the 'certain duality' in Britain's relations with Vichy France; yet the Foreign Office claimed the Pétain Government displayed a similiar duality. Nevertheless, the French Ambassador at Madrid should be told that, although 'in the dark days which followed the armistice HM Government contracted certain obligations to General de Gaulle ... if the Vichy Government can satisfy us that they are resolved and are able to defend French overseas territory against the Germans and the Italians ... no conflict need arise between us'.[69] In London, rumours had arisen that the battleships *Jean Bart* and *Richelieu* might move to German controlled ports; if the attempt was made, decided the War Cabinet on the 8th, the warships must be sunk by submarines if necessary. Ministers also discussed what to do with General de Gaulle; Churchill preferred the General to come to London for 'consultation on the general situation rather than to stay indefinitely', and the War Cabinet agreed.[70]

Eden returned home on the 8th; he immediately saw Dill then hurried to Churchill's underground rooms near Piccadilly. He was given 'an affectionate greeting', after which he described Wavell's plans for a dramatic offensive – within minutes the Prime Minister 'purred like six cats'.[71] Britain was indeed going to be extremely active in the Middle East: the previous day, Thursday, the War Cabinet had been told details of the Chiefs of Staff assessment on possible German aims in the Balkans; the report had been considered by the Defence Committee, who had recommended a wide field of action, including the preparation of plans for giving help to Turkey, measures to prevent French authorities in Syria from menacing British interests, perfecting of plans for the destruction of the Iraqi oil wells and pipelines in Iraq, Syria and Palestine. The War Cabinet had approved these measures.[72] Now, therefore, in addition to help to Greece, Britain was preparing further help for Turkey and might become increasingly involved in Syria, Iraq, Palestine and Iran – all of which fell into the overworked Middle East command area and could possibly lead to complicated commitments. And Eden had arrived with detailed plans for a Middle East involvement in another direction: an offensive against the Italians which, if successful, could rout the entire enemy army in North Africa. Churchill, when he heard of Wavell's plans, wished he had been informed earlier. 'Nevertheless,' he wrote, 'no harm has been done.'[73] Perhaps not – but, on the other hand, news of the plans may have influenced the COS discussions, the Defence Committee considerations, and the War Cabinet talks held during the previous few days. The danger was rapidly increasing that Middle East Command might find itself called upon to undertake more than it could handle. Moreover, British resources were being spread forever thinner; and, on this same day, 8 November, the Minister of Shipping warned the War Cabinet that on the current rate of sinkings, British imports in the third year of war might fall to 32 million tons, compared with 43.5 million in the first year – and these figures made no allowance for increased military demands.[74]

Attending the underground meeting with Churchill and Eden were the Service chiefs, the other two Service Ministers and General Ismay. They heard the War Secretary explain that Graziani's army, over 80,000 strong, was spread along a 50-mile front in a number of fortified camps. Between these posts were large gaps, and one between Sofafi on the right flank and Mibeiwa extended for 20 miles; Wavell proposed that while light forces contained other camps, a force should be driven through this large gap, wheel to the sea, attack Mibeiwa and Tummar, and slash enemy communications. Detailed preparations had still to be made and Wavell was concerned over air strength – and the plan involved the considerable risk of sending Britain's best troops directly into the enemy's heart. Staff work would have to be superb: the advance would involve a 70-mile move over two successive nights in the open desert. But Churchill chuckled with joy; Ismay described him as 'rapturously happy'.[75] Wavell's plans had obvious approval; but so secret was this meeting and so secret the proposals, that the War Cabinet were never officially informed of either: no detailed discussion of the operation took place in the Cabinet Room until the offensive began. Eden had further talks with Sir John Dill next morning, 9 November, then travelled to Ditchley, Oxfordshire, where Churchill had been lent a house for weekends of full moon when Chequers might have been a target. The Prime Minister had journeyed down the previous night, still jubilant over North African plans and bringing with him, as usual, two detectives, valet, maid, two secretaries and 35 soldiers plus officers. Eden and Churchill closeted themselves in a quiet room and discussed the scheme again; and the Prime Minister agreed to the despatch of a telegram to Wavell to assure him of full support. The operation was now code-named 'Compass'.

Also on Saturday talks were held in London to find the best method of receiving American naval assistance – which might be the main means of bringing supplies to Britain for operations like 'Compass' to take place. Lord Lothian, due to return to his Embassy in Washington in two days' time, was asked by Alexander and the Naval Staff to do all he could to obtain US protection for British shipping. The Vice-Chief of Naval Staff pointed out that America might agree to convoy protection work, if this defended her own trade: Lothian said the way to get American assistance was to convince her that without such help Britain might be defeated.[76]

The Ambassador returned to Washington on the 11th. In Moscow, Cripps had the far less enviable duty of attempting to extract some Soviet response to the British proposals presented three weeks before, and his task was suddenly made even more difficult on the 10th when, to his consternation, the Russians announced a forthcoming trip to Berlin by the Foreign Minister. Sir Stafford immediately informed the Foreign Office in Whitehall of his suspicion that Molotov would reveal Britain's proposals; the Ambassador saw Vyshinsky on the evening of the 11th and complained strongly of Molotov's 'unprecedented' attitude and 'un-neutral' behaviour in accepting the Berlin invitation. Vyshinsky protested at Sir Stafford's interpretations, and said the proposals had caused a 'great stir' but thereafter his remarks were vague. The Foreign Office doubted whether Sir Stafford had used good tactics, since he might have given the impression Britain was 'very much frightened'.[77]

While Cripps was having his latest unproductive talk with Vyshinsky, the War Cabinet was meeting in the underground War Room, Whitehall. Churchill referred to Neville Chamberlain's death two days before, after the War Cabinet had last met: they had suffered a severe loss, he said. 'Mr Chamberlain's great grief in leaving life had perhaps been that he had not lived to see the end of the struggle.... But maybe he had lived long enough to feel confident as to the outcome.'

Churchill said a telegram had now been received from de Gaulle agreeing to come for consultation and adding he intended to return to French Equatorial Africa, where his presence was necessary.[78] The problem of de Gaulle therefore appeared settled for the moment; and, as for the Vichy Government, a telegram had been received from Sir Samuel Hoare offering some reassurance: the French Chargé had given him a note stating that Vichy had never taken the initiative in an attack against Britain and did not intend to do so. The Chargé appealed for British understanding. The Foreign Office concluded that the French had begun to realize they had some freedom of manoeuvre, due to British resistance and German difficulties with Italy and Spain, and Vichy had therefore rejected a firm interim settlement with Germany: Britain would have to be content with this situation.[79]

The War Cabinet were also informed on the 11th that enemy attacks during the previous week had averaged about 165 sorties

153

a night; during the last three nights British bombers had made on average 80 sorties a night and had lost a total of five aircraft. Portal added: 'Today, Monday, a number of Italian machines appeared over the Thames Estuary.' Casualties – later found to be exaggerated – were given as 12 Italian aircraft destroyed for certain, without RAF losses.[80] During this Monday night British aircraft inflicted infinitely more damage upon the Italians than those few Italian machines could accomplish in their Blitz participation. Shortly after Mediterranean dusk, Fleet Air Arm aircraft were released from the carrier *Illustrious*, lying 70 miles from the heel of Italy. Two waves of aircraft made for the heavily defended harbour of Taranto and plunged into thick flak – and when they departed 60 minutes later, with only two shot down, half the Italian battle fleet had been rendered useless for at least six months. The shorter sea-route to the crucial Middle East, carrying supplies to Malta, Cairo and Greece, had been made very much safer.

But next day Tuesday, 12 November, Hitler issued Directive No 18: 'Gibraltar will be taken and the Straits closed.' Included in this operation, 'Felix', would be the occupation of the Spanish Canary Islands and the Portuguese Cape Verde Islands; German naval planners were to study the possibility of capturing Portugal's Madeira and the Azores. Portugal herself might have to be occupied. German troops would not be sent to Libya until Italians had reached Mersa Matruh; meanwhile, plans were to be made to send dive bombers to attack the British fleet in Alexandria and mine the Suez Canal. And the German Army was ordered to prepare immediate plans to invade Greece through Bulgaria and Roumania.

'Off to See the Wizard'

'Political discussions for the purpose of clarifying Russia's attitude in the immediate future have already begun,' declared Hitler's 12 November Directive. 'Regardless of the outcome of these conversations, all preparations for the East for which verbal orders have already been given will be continued.' Even as Cripps saw Vyshinsky in Moscow and complained of Molotov's 'forthcoming' visit to Berlin, the Soviet Foreign Minister was secretly flying to confer with the Nazis. He arrived in Berlin on the 12th, a dark, drizzling day, and immediately began talks with Ribbentrop, who boasted: 'England is beaten.' Britain hoped for help from America but 'the entry of the United States into the war is of no consequence'. In Washington on the 12th, Admiral Stark submitted his Memorandum on National Defence Policy, substantially as revealed to the British War Cabinet on the 6th. Stark, with the full agreement of General Marshall, Chief of Army Staff, stated categorically: 'I... believe that Great Britain requires from us very great help in the Atlantic and possibly even on the Continents of Europe and Africa, if she is to be enabled to survive.' Stark's scheme known as 'Plan Dog' – Plan D – envisaged an offensive war in the West, should America be drawn into conflict, and a defensive war in the Far East; purely naval help would be insufficient – and he also intimated that Africa would be an acceptable approach to Europe. Stark recommended secret staff talks with Britain as a preliminary to possible US participation as a belligerent.[1]

In London on the same day Eden gave the War Cabinet his report on his Middle East mission. The Gibraltar defences had been greatly strengthened he began, but 'our people took a gloomy view of conditions in Spain and they did not believe that the Spaniards would resist a German attempt to advance'. The Malta garrison afforded reasonable assurance against an Italian landing; in the desert the military position was far more favourable than had seemed possible a few months previously, but Eden stressed that the chief British weakness was in the air. Portal gave figures of air reinforcements which were being sent, amounting to 116 aircraft by 7 December and about 390 by 25 January. Beaverbrook immediately declared that 'he wished to enter a serious protest' against these reinforcements, which he condemned as 'an open drain on our resources'. Britain had been saved by her Hurricanes and Spitfires and when the German air assault became formidable again, it would only be these aircraft which would stand between Britain and defeat. Churchill, who, unlike Beaverbrook, knew of plans for a North African offensive, hastily intervened: he was satisfied that 'the present reinforcements of the Middle East by Hurricane aircraft should not be interfered with'.[2] Eden's very secret information on Wavell's intentions, not even hinted at during the War Cabinet meeting, was discussed by the Defence Committee next day, 13 November. Already pressure was put on the Middle East Commander to start the offensive as soon as possible. Germany might soon intervene on Italy's behalf; now was the time to strike. Churchill made the same point, without going into details, at the War Cabinet meeting on the 13th. Taranto, he said, 'brought home the importance of hitting the Italians as hard as we could. If the Greeks could maintain themselves against Italy throughout the winter, the situation in this quarter might develop greatly in our favour. We should press this advantage all we could.'[3] Next day, the 14th, Churchill started applying his personal pressure: a telegram to Wavell listed a number of factors – the Italian check on the Greek front, 'poor showing of Italian airmen over Britain', low morale in Italy, Taranto, Wavell's own actions in the desert, and then he repeated the Defence Committee's conclusion of the previous day. 'It is unlikely that Germany will leave her flagging ally unsupported indefinitely. Consequently, it seems that now is the time to take risks and strike.'[4] In Cairo, Wavell refused to be hurried. Yet in a Memorandum on this Thursday, Admiral Raeder reminded Hitler that Mussolini's troops were actually retreating into Albania, Britain's prestige was being enhanced and her strategic position improved. And in North Africa the Italians were proving ineffective – 'Italy will never carry out the Egyptian offensive'. Germany must therefore step into North Africa. 'The fight for North Africa is the foremost strategic objective of German warfare as a whole.... It is of decisive importance for the outcome of the war.' But Hitler, unconvinced, replied: 'I am still inclined towards a demonstration with Russia.'[5]

Molotov had left Berlin earlier in the day. Talks had been disappointing; the shrewd Soviet Minister had replied cynically to Ribbentrop's protestations of friendliness. The night before, discussions had had to be held in an air raid shelter with Ribbentrop continuing his monotonous declarations that Britain was finished, to which Molotov replied: 'If that is so, why are we in this shelter and whose are these bombs which fall?'[6] Churchill, to whom Stalin later told this tale, claimed the British raid had been sent to impress Molotov; if so, the Germans gave a far more dreadful show of strength 24 hours later: on the night of Thursday, 14 November, a new word of warfare was invented – 'Coventration'. Small and compact, with a population of just over 213,000, Coventry was subjected to all the horrors of concentrated Blitz. Sprawling London could perhaps absorb the terror and damage; Göring hoped Coventry could not. So, for ten hours, German aircraft flung down HE and incendiary bombs, first setting fire to the ancient centre and the cathedral; and, when dawn struggled through the stinking clouds of sooty smoke, the whole city seemed destroyed. 'There were more open signs of hysteria, terror, neurosis, observed in one evening than during the whole of the past two months together in all areas,' said one report. 'Women were seen to faint in the street, to cry, to scream, to tremble all over, to attack a fireman...'[7] While refugees streamed into the clean, fresh countryside from the latest battlefield, the War Cabinet met in London to hear the official account; about 300 enemy bombers had taken part, said Portal, and he indicated that the raid had been expected – in an effort to reduce the offensive about 18 RAF aircraft had been sent 'to attack enemy aerodromes from which the bombers had been expected to take off. Fairly good results had been obtained. In addition, a continuous fighter patrol had been maintained over Coventry itself, but only one inconclusive engagement had taken place.' Sir John Anderson said that the raid had been the heaviest yet on a munitions centre; the damage had been very heavy, and the casualties, killed and wounded, were already believed to be around 600. Communications had been badly interrupted and water, gas and electricity supplies had failed. Reinforcements of police, firemen and fire appliances had been rushed to the city.[8]

German bombers returned to London that night, the 15th, but enemy aircraft also hit other cities; from now on raids would be directed on a succession of provincial centres in an attempt to shatter morale and destroy industrial production. The new policy was illustrated by the report given to the War Cabinet on Monday, the 18th: on Friday night, said Portal, 310 enemy aircraft had attacked targets in the Midlands and Bournemouth had also been seriously hit; on Saturday 120 German bombers had been over, but activity had been on a greatly reduced scale. The previous day 270 enemy aircraft had been over south-east England; by night 280 machines had attempted a concentrated attack on Southampton. Herbert Morrison, Home Secretary, described a visit he had made to Coventry on the day after the raid: on the whole the damage to munitions production was less than feared. Excellent work had been done during and after the raid, but between 800 and 1,000 people had been injured and the number killed totalled 290 so far. At first, Morrison continued, 'the local people had been shaken by their experience and had been bitter at what they regarded as the lack of active defences. Nevertheless, they had kept their heads.' The King's visit to the city on the 16th had been of the utmost value. Transport provision had been made for the evacuation of about 10,000 inhabitants, but only about 300 had taken up the offer. Eden criticized a BBC broadcast on the raid. 'This had been a most depressing broadcast and would have a deplorable effect on War-wickshire units.' Other Ministers agreed, and the War Cabinet asked the Chancellor of the Exchequer, the Home Secretary and the Minister of Information to examine what changes might be necessary in the constitution and management of the BBC 'in order to ensure its effective control by HM Government'.[9]

Count Ciano was taking tea with Hitler at the latter's mountain retreat. 'There is a heavy atmosphere,' mourned Ciano. Italian forces were being pushed back in Albania. 'Hitler is pessimistic and considers the situation much compromised by what has happened in the Balkans. His criticism is open, definite and final. I try to talk to him, but he does not allow me to proceed.'[10] Yet despite their successes the Greeks were urgently seeking more help; like the British, they feared German intervention and, that evening, the Defence Committee met in London to consider latest requests for air reinforcements. Only a few days had passed since restrictions on aid had been partially lifted; now however, Wavell's plans were known and the resulting change in attitude was illustrated in Churchill's report to the War Cabinet next day. The Prime Minister still gave no details of 'Compass' but said the Defence Committee had been faced with the dilemma of conflicting claims, and had decided to stick to the promise of sending five squadrons but no more.[11]

The Defence Committee session described by Churchill had met with no bombs bursting in the streets around them. London had been quiet; the normal casualty report to the War Cabinet next morning, the 19th, had unusual significance. 'By day – London, none killed, three injured.... By night – London, none killed or injured.' The capital was now to be only one target among many, and the long, concentrated period of Blitz was over: between 18 November and 19 January 1941, London was to experience only six major raids and two lighter ones.

Churchill's comment to Ministers concerning the 'dilemma of conflicting claims' and the shortage of resources, may also have been linked with discussions at a COS meeting held immediately prior to the War Cabinet. Provisional COS approval was given to a new offensive plan – a particular favourite of the Prime Minister: Operation 'Workshop'. This had first been suggested to the COS on 30 October by Sir Roger Keyes, Director of Combined Operations, and involved the capture of Pantelleria, a small Italian island off Sicily and about 120 miles from Malta. Sir Roger believed the island would offer an aircraft staging base, an alternative to Malta, and would be a thorn in the side of Italy and Vichyite Tunis. A strength of four commandos was estimated to be the total required for a landing force. Admiral Sir Andrew Cunningham, C-in-C Mediterranean Fleet, was vehemently against the idea: the island, once taken, would have to be held and the strain on resources would be intolerable; Britain would have a second Malta to supply and defend. The COS, at a meeting on 16 November, had seemed to appreciate these objections, but now, on the 19th, they considered the operation feasible, providing the enemy garrison was no larger than estimated and provided the operation would not interfere with the other possibility, Operation 'Brisk', for the capture of the Azores if Spain entered the war on the Axis side. On the same day, the 19th, the COS also submitted to the Prime Minister a long memorandum on the defence of Singapore, which stressed it was no longer possible to secure the base by merely holding the island. All Malaya would have to be held. Moreover, reinforcements would have to be sent; local commanders had recommended a total garrison of 26 battalions, of which only 17 were provided for at the moment.[12]

Greece, the Mediterranean, North Africa, Singapore and Home Defence – Britain's resources were becoming seriously overstretched. Churchill therefore told the War Cabinet on the 20th that he was considering sending a further letter to Roosevelt, to point out the added strain and to ask if America could spare more destroyers.[13] The Prime Minister was also increasingly fretting over the apparent inactivity in Cairo; he had been excited by Wavell's plans, and now the waiting, which Eden found 'uneasy', was to Churchill becoming intolerable. Eden wrote in his diary on the 20th: 'Found telegram that Winston wanted to send to Wavell, which is partly repetition of what I have already sent, with his approval. Telephoned and tried to persuade him to let me handle the business. Some acrimony, not much success.'[14] Hitler was also impatient. He had told the Spanish Foreign Minister two days before: 'I have decided to attack Gibraltar and my operation is prepared in the utmost detail.' But Spain still refused to commit herself to the Axis; the Führer wrote to Mussolini on the 20th that Spain must be brought into the war as soon as possible; moreover he also disclosed plans to march on

Greece through Bulgaria, but this move could not be made before mid-March.

Much uncertainty surrounded Bulgarian intentions, Lord Halifax told the War Cabinet on Friday, 22 November. King Boris was believed to have taken his Foreign Minister with him on a recent visit to Berlin, and they had travelled in a German aeroplane. Halifax reminded Ministers that 'we had repeatedly warned Bulgaria against allowing herself to fall into the hands of Germany', and that the Turks had given a private assurance that they would go to war if the Bulgarian Government allowed the Germans to enter their country, or if Germany attacked Bulgaria. Two courses were open to Britain. First, as suggested by Cripps, the Turks should call upon Bulgaria to demobilize and threaten a declaration of war; it was, however, not certain whether Bulgaria was mobilized in this sense, nor were the Turks likely to agree to this idea. The second course fell into two stages: the first would be for Britain to press the Turks and Yugoslavia to make a joint declaration to Bulgaria that they would make war on her if she allowed the Germans to enter her territory and, if the Turks and Yugoslavia agreed, Britain could then advance to the second stage, in which Turkey and Yugoslavia would invite Bulgaria to join a tripartite undertaking to resist German attack. Halifax preferred not to put strong pressure on Turkey: her reaction would probably be a request for large additional munition consignments which Britain would not be able to meet, and he therefore favoured the second course. Ministers agreed and asked Halifax to start negotiations.[15]

Bulgaria was therefore under pressure from Berlin, London and Moscow; but Berlin received Sofia's favours: the day after this War Cabinet discussion, 23 November, the Bulgarian Government assured Hitler that their sympathies lay with him.

Among all the strains of the Blitz, high-level diplomatic developments and strategic planning, Sir John Dill, the hard-working and intensely loyal CIGS, was bearing an almost impossible private burden: his wife had had a paralytic stroke, and each time he snatched a few hours to go home to Windsor he could see she was slowly dying. 'She could not make herself understood,' wrote his colleague, General Brooke. 'He kept guessing what she could mean, usually unsuccessfully, and finally, with a disappointed look in her eyes, she would throw her head back on her pillow.' Brooke's diary entry for 22 November read: 'It is pathetic. He is urgently in need of rest, cannot, I think, face going home for a week's leave.'[16] Dill had never managed to achieve a good relationship with the ebullient, impulsive Churchill; arguments became more frequent and bitter, as both men became tired and strained in this hectic, uncertain period. And now the unfortunate CIGS had also to stand between the chafing Churchill and the stubborn Wavell, who still refused to go faster than he thought feasible. The Prime Minister strongly criticized the Cairo Commander at a Defence Committee meeting on 25 November, following a telegram from HQ Middle East on the 23rd saying that General Sir Alan Cunningham, commander in Kenya, had decided it was not possible to carry out 'bold' operations in Kenya during the winter. Churchill was anxious for action against the Italian-held port of Kismayu, and General Smuts, who had recently visited Kenya, urged a similar operation. Dill said he had received a further telegram from Wavell, reporting he would soon hold a conference of commanders. Churchill was far from satisfied, and immediately after the meeting sent a peevish Minute to Sir John and Eden. 'I understand we are to receive from you a full account of the reasons now alleged to prevent operations against Kismayu before May, and that you will make a strenuous effort not to succumb to these reasons.'[17] Churchill had overcome his irritation sufficiently to share a champagne and oyster dinner with Eden in the Prime Minister's bedroom that night, and the two men discussed steps to be taken should 'Compass' be a success: Churchill believed the offensive might have wide influence. Next day, 26 November, he sent another prodding signal to Wavell, in which he clearly bore in mind his talk with Eden. 'News from every quarter must have impressed on you the importance of "Compass" in relation to the whole Middle East position, including Balkans and Turkey, to French attitude in North Africa, to Spanish attitude, now trembling on the brink, to Italy, in grievous straits, and generally to the whole war.'[18]

On the same day, Marshal Pietro Badoglio, Italian Chief of General Staff, handed in his resignation to Mussolini. The General Staff had been thrown into complete crisis by the débâcle in Greece and by the failure to push forward in Egypt. Ushers at the Palazzo Venezia were told to show Italian Ministers into different rooms to prevent brawls; Badoglio went off to shoot pheasants.[19]

Meanwhile, German bombing of British cities had continued. Greenwood, Minister without Portfolio, told the War Cabinet on the 25th that Birmingham, where about 407 people had been killed in raids over the past week, had probably suffered more damage than Coventry. The War Cabinet asked Anderson to study the feasibility of a 'mobile column' of experts and workers, ready to rush to areas of heavy bombing. Ministers also discussed a cartoon which had appeared in the *Daily Mirror* on the 18th, and which implied the Minister of Labour had taken capitalist bribes. The Attorney-General believed proceedings could be instituted for criminal libel; an alternative would be to suppress the newspaper and Ministers were reminded this had been considered some weeks before. Bevin now said he would prefer to start legal action but the War Cabinet deferred discussion for the moment.

Turning to Foreign Affairs, Halifax told the War Cabinet that 'the upshot of a good deal of information from different quarters was that probably not very much had been settled at the discussions between Hitler and Molotov in Berlin'. He also said Germany and Italy seemed equally surprised at effective Greek resistance. 'There were also some grounds for the view that Germany did not want to spread over the whole of the Balkans at the present time, that Germany had not yet made up her mind how to act, and that her timetable might have been disarranged.' Churchill, wearing a grey romper suit, much to dour Halifax's amusement, now said, rightly, that Mussolini might have been afraid Hitler was going to do a deal with France at his expense, and had given the order for the Italian ultimatum to Greece contrary to Hitler's wishes. 'If this was so, it might be that Germany had no counter move ready to redress the position. But it would be rash to draw any conclusion favourable to ourselves. Germany might well be meditating a stroke on the lines that would be most embarrassing to us, namely through Bulgaria to Salonica.'[20] But next day, the 26th, the Foreign Secretary read two telegrams to the War Cabinet, one from Budapest and one from Sofia, both of which contained reports that 'no military initiative in south-east Europe was contemplated by Germany at present'.[21]

On the 27th Ministers resumed discussion on the *Mirror* cartoon and Churchill was now against taking further measures. 'In his considered view, no Minister was under an obligation to expose himself to the trouble of taking action in regard to a cartoon of this nature, more especially in wartime. In essence, the cartoon really amounted to no more than a vulgar insult.' Bevin said he was prepared to accept Churchill's advice.[22]

Wavell pushed on with plans for 'Compass', now almost ready; German staff officers finalized plans for 'Felix' against Gibraltar – main details were ready on the 27th; and, in London, General Brooke continued preparations to meet and defeat 'Sealion'. Eden lunched with Brooke on the 29th; 'he believes in likelihood of German attempt at invasion in spring,' wrote Eden, 'and so do I.'[23] But at least the winter months gave some respite: Churchill minuted to Brooke next day, the 30th – the Prime Minister's 66th birthday – 'I have authorized the ringing of church bells on Christmas Day, as the imminence of invasion has greatly receded'. Also on Saturday the 30th, the Chiefs of Staff were informed that Roosevelt had agreed to secret staff talks being held in Washington, following the suggestion made by Admiral Stark in his Plan D memorandum.[24]

Wavell held his commanders' conference on 2 December and, as desired by Churchill, Middle East HQ decided to attack the Italians in Kassala. The Abyssinian rebellion was to be stimulated by all possible means; but the attempt to take Kismayu port was still to be left until spring. Churchill showed his anger at a meeting of the Defence Committee on the 4th and criticized Eden for not having asked Wavell for the date on which 'Compass' would start, extending his irritation to the general and the Army as a whole. Eden replied that he did not believe in fussing Wavell with questions. 'I knew his plan, he knew our view, he had best be left to get on with it.' Eden wrote: 'This did not suit W [Churchill]. Dill was very angry at his attitude.'[25] The overworked Prime Minister, together with other Ministers, was showing the strain of successive disappointments, of the incessant bombing and of the long hours and many meetings. Churchill's favourite scheme, Operation 'Workshop', came up for discussion again at the Defence Committee meeting next evening, 5 December, and he received an added disappointment: the Committee was reluctant to give full approval to this idea for capturing Pantelleria. Sir Dudley Pound said the COS had given further consideration to the operation and it was 'their duty to report frankly their opinion of the unlikelihood of success of the operation'. Pound said this success would be ruled out by lack of surprise and insufficiency of destroyers. Churchill said he regretted the COS verdict. 'There was, of course, no absolute guarantee of success in war, nor was it ever possible during a campaign to provide what could be regarded as fully adequate resources for any particular battle or operation. Many of the greatest battles of history had been won with forces which, before the event, would have been considered hopelessly inadequate.' Eden agreed with Portal that the operation would only have a 'four-to-one chance', and the Committee decided that 'in the face of the arguments put forward by the Chiefs of Staff, the present plan for Workshop cannot be accepted'. The Chiefs were asked to see whether the idea could be improved to an extent that would justify them in recommending its adoption to the Committee.[26] Churchill took Eden to one side after the meeting. 'Winston unhappy at plan being turned down,' wrote Eden. 'Proposed I should go out to command in Middle East.... I declined very firmly.'[27]

Also on the 5th, the first echelon of a German 'military mission' of about one division completed its move to Roumania and, in Berlin, Hitler held a top-level conference to discuss future strategy. An awesome programme resulted: after 15 December – air war against British forces in the Eastern Mediterranean; early February – attack on Gibraltar lasting four weeks and enabling troops to be deployed 'elsewhere' by May; early March – invasion of Greece, again lasting about four weeks; mid-May – the attack on Russia by about 130 or 140 divisions.

Churchill had also been assessing the future in a long, gloomy letter to President Roosevelt first mentioned to the War Cabinet on 20 November. The document was given to Cordell Hull in Washington on Sunday, 8 December; on the same day Lord Lothian arrived back in America after his long consultations in London and, in an arrival comment to the Press he perhaps summed up Churchill's message: 'Well boys, Britain's broke. It's your money we want.' In his letter, which reached Roosevelt on a cruise in the Caribbean, Churchill warned that Britain now faced the 'mortal danger' of the steady and increasing diminution of sea tonnage. 'Our shipping losses ... have been on a scale almost comparable to that of the worst year of the last war.' The Royal Navy was desperately short of convoy escort vessels; the danger of the French navy joining Germany still remained. In the Far East the Japanese were reported preparing 'five good divisions' for possible use as an overseas expeditionary force; 'we have today no forces in the Far East capable of dealing with this situation should it develop.' Churchill therefore suggested America should reassert the doctrine of freedom of the seas, and should afford protection to her lawful maritime trading – 'a decisive act of constructive non-belligerency' which would more than any other 'make it certain that British resistance could be effectively prolonged'. Failing this, the Prime Minister sought 'the gift, loan, or supply of a large number of American vessels of war, above all destroyers, and for US influence on Eire for British use of bases. Churchill also requested merchant ships and asked the President to give earnest consideration to the supply of 2,000 combat aircraft a month. He warned that the greater the help, the sooner Britain's dollar credits would be exhausted. 'The moment approaches when we shall no longer be able to pay cash.' The Prime Minister was sure the President would agree Britain should not be divested of all saleable assets; 'after the victory was won with our blood, civilization saved, and the time gained for the United States to be fully armed against all eventualities, we should stand stripped to the bone'. If this happened, he warned, Britain would be unable to pay for imports from America after the war, with resulting high unemployment in the United States. But Churchill left the President to think of a possible solution.[28]

German bombers returned in force to attack London on the night of 8 December. Herbert Morrison told Ministers on the 9th of extensive damage by HE bombs and incendiaries on communications, houses, public and commercial buildings and oil installations. At least 85 people had been killed. The Palace of Westminster had also been hit and the House of Commons would meet that day in the Annexe. Ministers were informed of a meeting held earlier in the day to review progress in night defence measures. 'While we should not look for any immediate and spectacular results,' said Morrison, 'many promising developments were being resolutely driven forward.'

But, to take the edge off depression, excited and surprised Ministers were told by Churchill that, early in the morning, British forces in North Africa had launched a major offensive upon the Italian army. 'Compass' had at last begun. Eden declared that 'we might hope to inflict a decisive defeat on the 1st and 2nd Libyan Divisions'.[29] Preliminary moves had in fact started three days before, when British troops under the command of General Sir Henry Maitland Wilson had sneaked forward 40 miles on the 6th and had then stayed silent in the scorching desert. A further leap had been made on the 8th; complete secrecy was still maintained – Ciano's diary entry for this day merely recorded: 'Nothing new.' At dawn on Monday the 9th, the first assault stabbed into the soft and unsuspecting Italian lines. First reports reaching London from Cairo were scrappy and confused and Eden, Churchill and Dill anxiously awaited fresh signals. Scarcely any firm information was available for the War Cabinet meeting at noon on the 10th, but the battle for the critical town of Sidi Barrani was fast developing, with clashes occurring at Tummar, Nibeiwa and Sofafi. British and Australian advance elements were preparing to reach forward for Buq Buq and Halfaya. Early on the 10th a second push had been made by the Coldstream Guards, advancing from Mersa Matruh and, by evening, a signal was received declaring large numbers of prisoners had been taken, too many to count but amounting to 'about five acres of officers and two hundred acres of other ranks'. Churchill, pacing his room at 10 Downing Street and fretting for fresh news, snatched at every telegram brought in and constantly consulted maps strewn about him. He beamed at one message from a young tank officer: 'Have arrived at the second B in Buq Buq.'[30]

Churchill had also received satisfaction from a Defence Committee meeting held late in the previous night, 9 December, when Operation 'Workshop' had again been discussed. Pound had said the COS still believed the operation had doubtful chance of success. 'Nevertheless, if the political risks of failure could be accepted, they felt that the operation should go ahead, provided the C-in-C, Mediterranean, was satisfied that he could accept the commitment involved in the subsequent maintenance of the garrison.' Beaverbrook thought the force for the operation should sail, on the understanding that the execution of the attack could be reconsidered at a later stage, and Eden agreed with this compromise. Attlee believed much would depend on the outcome of the Libyan battle. Churchill said he would be the first to call off the operation if it was found that it would not fit harmoniously into the development of strategic plans, but he believed that merely because the COS thought the operation had only a three to one chance of success – odds which he personally did not accept – this did not mean the operation should not be undertaken. The Defence Committee therefore changed the previous decision and agreed the force should sail to take the island, although the Committee retained the option to cancel this new decision.[31]

Hitler was also rearranging his programme. France was still un-co-operative, and 'Felix', the attack on Gibraltar, was consequently abandoned on the 10th – 'the necessary political situation no longer exists'. Relations with Vichy France were considered deplorable, and Pétain was proving dangerously stubborn: Hitler therefore issued Directive No 19, Operation 'Attila'. 'In case those parts of the French colonial empire now controlled by General Weygand should show signs of revolt, preparation will be made for the rapid *occupation of the still unoccupied territory* of continental France. At the same time it will be necessary to lay hands on the *French home fleet*.'[32]

Just after lunch on the 11th two more telegrams reached White-hall from Cairo: uncertainty continued about Sidi Barrani, but the British were closing in; by the previous evening 6,000 Italian pri-soners had been taken. Churchill went to give the House of Com-mons a short, very cautious statement: he told MPs that about 500 prisoners had been captured and an Italian general killed, add-ing that British troops had reached the coast. 'It is too soon to attempt to forecast either the scope or the results.... But we can at any rate say that the preliminary phase has been successful.' An-other telegram had arrived: the British were still closer to the important objective of Sidi Barrani. Then General Haining, Vice-CIGS, came rushing into Eden's office: another signal had been flashed from Cairo; Eden telephoned Churchill and commented: 'It seems too good to be true.' Dill reported the triumphant news to a delighted War Cabinet at 11.30 next morning, 12 December. 'Sidi Barrani has been captured. Pockets of the enemy were still holding out at Point 50, some nine miles to the south-east. The 4th Armoured Brigade were making for Sollum and were now east of Buq Buq.... Over 7,000 prisoners had reached Matruh, and there were large numbers still in the forward area. Large fires had been started at Sollum and Halfaya, some 5 miles to the south.' Ministers heard more good news, on a different subject: Sir Samuel Hoare had signalled that M. Dupuy, Canadian Chargé at Vichy, had been told by Darlan that the French would resist German pressure to attack the de Gaulle Colonies, at least until February, and there was now no question of the Germans being granted the use of French bases.[33]

British and Australian troops were driving the Italians across the desert. 'A catastrophic telegram has arrived from Graziani,' wrote Ciano. 'A mixture of excitement, rhetoric and concern. He is thinking of withdrawing to Tripoli.... I visit Mussolini and find him very much shaken.'[34] Already, early this Thursday, as the BBC played the Australian marching song now becoming popular in London – 'Off to see the wizard, the wonderful wizard of Oz' – Churchill had started to press Eden for faster pursuit. 'After an angry riposte from me,' wrote Eden, 'it emerged that he had not seen telegram that appeared during the night giving details of further plans. But this is all symptomatic of his distrust of local leaders.... Our talk was less cordial than usual.'[35]

Lord Lothian, in the few days since his return to Washington, had continued his campaign to arouse American support – a campaign considered of utmost importance in London, despite Foreign Office disapproval of the Ambassador's blunt words to newspapermen on his arrival. On the night of 12 December, he was to have delivered a speech at Baltimore but, feeling unwell, he handed it over to his second in command. Within a few hours he was dead. This tragic and untimely news threw the Foreign Office into consternation and was to have important repercussions in the War Cabinet: Churchill immediately sought a replacement from a multitude of possible candidates, including Lloyd George, Vansittart, Pound, Rob Hudson, Sir Ronald Lindsay, Oliver Lyttelton and Beaverbrook.

Meanwhile, also on the night of the 12th, the War Cabinet held their second session of the day, chaired by Attlee. He opened by saying that Churchill, unable to attend the meeting, was in favour of a modification of British bombing policy; Portal added that Churchill had given instructions for retaliatory plans to be prepared. 'Up to the present we had never sent more than 80 bombers to attack one town, and we had never concentrated on the destruction of a town as such. We had been faithful to our policy of picking out military targets.' The Germans, on the other hand, had clearly altered their bombing policy and did not observe such restrictions. 'The political question for decision by the War Cabinet,' he continued, 'was whether we were to concentrate as formidable a force of aircraft as we could command, with the object of causing the greatest possible havoc in a built-up area.' If this 'crash concentration' was decided upon, suitable towns would have to be selected, and he listed a number of military considerations which would have to be taken into account in making the fearful choice of which centre of population to destroy. The target should be a town of some industrial importance; 'we should rely largely on fires, and should choose a closely built-up town, where bomb craters in the streets would impede firefighters'; the town should be one which had

not been 'visited' frequently by the RAF and 'where the ARP organization was unlikely to be in good trim'; the target should be as
near to Britain as possible ; and 'since we aimed at affecting the
enemy's morale, we should attempt to destroy a greater part of a
particular town. The town chosen should therefore not be too
large.' With these considerations in mind, the Air Staff had drawn
up a list of possible targets: Hanover came first and Mannheim
second, followed by Frankfurt; Duisberg was a suitable target, but
had already been heavily bombed, as had Dusseldorf. Münster was
a town of suitable size; Emden was too small, Cologne too big.
Ministers then discussed the question and some fears were expressed that if Britain adopted this reprisal policy, the Germans
might step up their effort, but Portal said the enemy was probably
doing all in its power. The selection of Hanover met with considerable criticism. 'Hanover was the centre of the old German
aristocracy, was strongly anti-Nazis and had long associations with
this country.' The War Cabinet finally decided 'crash concentration'
should be tried as an experiment one night in the near future, with
a town chosen from Mannheim, Duisberg, Dusseldorf and perhaps
Hamburg.[36]

While British Ministers had been taking this grim decision,
Hitler had reacted to the British advances in Libya and the Greek
successes in Albania and, next day, Friday the 13th, his Directive
No 20 was issued. 'My intention is ... (a) to establish in the coming
months a constantly increasing force in Southern Roumania. (b) On
the arrival of favourable weather – probably in March – to move
this force across Bulgaria to occupy the north coast of the Aegean
and, should this be necessary, the entire mainland of Greece. We
can rely upon Bulgarian support.'[37]

'Hitler's next move is a matter of speculation,' said Churchill at
the next War Cabinet meeting on Monday, 16 December. 'It looks
as if he does not mean to make any effort in the Balkans where
things are quiet. It might be that he will take charge of Italy, but
that would not be a victory for him.' The most menacing outlook
was Spain, the Prime Minister continued, and there had been some
indications of a German push in that direction aimed perhaps at
occupying the North African coast. Churchill said he had discussed the situation with the Foreign Secretary and the COS, and
it had been decided to delay 'certain operations' to keep reserves
in hand. The main operation referred to by Churchill was, in fact,
'Workshop' – the decision to delay departure of the Pantelleria
force for at least a month had been taken the previous Saturday, in
view of the fears, actually outdated, of a German thrust through
Spain, and Churchill had acquiesced quietly to the postponement;
plans for 'Workshop' would however remain prominent in Top

Secret War Office files. Halfaya had been cleared, Dill told the War Cabinet, although Sollum and Fort Capuzzo were still held by the enemy. The weather in the desert had turned from sandstorm to rain, he continued, and this made the supply situation especially dangerous; difficulty had been experienced in the disposal of prisoners – who might amount to over 30,000. British casualties, excluding those suffered by the Armoured Division, amounted to 500.[38]

Sollum and Capuzzo were taken by the British later on the 16th. And that night 134 RAF bombers took off for Germany: Mannheim had been the town selected for indiscriminate attack. The spiral of slaughter twisted higher. Churchill was meanwhile dining with Anthony Eden, and told him he had approached Lloyd George to ask him if he would be Ambassador in Washington. The old war leader, although flattered, had declined on medical grounds. Next morning, the 17th, Churchill called Kingsley Wood, Sinclair and Eden to his room after a late sitting of the Defence Committee, and he now suggested Lord Halifax should succeed Lord Lothian, with Eden taking over the Foreign Office. Eden wrote: 'I went home sad at the thought of leaving the soldiers.'[39] But another slight complication was to arise.

Roosevelt had returned from his Caribbean cruise, having had ample time to study Churchill's long letter of 8 December; he had given especial thought to the problem of Britain's inability to pay for American help – a problem which Churchill had left him to solve. On the 17th, the day after his return, the President held a press conference and suggested his possible solution: if your neighbour's house was on fire, said Roosevelt, and you had a hose, you did not bargain about a selling-price but immediately lent the hose. 'There is absolutely no doubt in the minds of a very overwhelming number of Americans that the best immediate defence of the United States is the success of Great Britain.' So, he suggested, America might build up war production for goods which both Britain and America might need: these goods would be more valuable in British use than 'kept in storage' in America. Thus, the idea of Lend-Lease originated. 'What I am trying to do is to eliminate the dollar sign. That is something brand new in the thoughts of practically everybody in this room, I think – get rid of the silly, foolish dollar sign.' The British Foreign Office at first, lamentably, failed to realize the importance of Roosevelt's remarks. Nor was any mention of the press conference made at the War Cabinet meeting next day, the 18th, and not until that night did the embassy in Washington suggest to the Foreign Office that Churchill might make public acknowledgement; but the Foreign Office did not apparently think such a move was needed and besides, the

Treasury would have to be consulted. The Treasury, in turn, thought Churchill should wait longer before making a speech – he had made no arrangements to do so and by then Parliament had adjourned until 21 January. The Prime Minister was still involved with settling a successor for Lord Lothian; during that evening, the 18th, Lord Halifax called to see Eden and confessed he did not really want to go to Washington – he would prefer to retire to his native Yorkshire. Eden replied with a general remark that 'in wartime all must go where sent'.[40]

On this day came Hitler's Directive No 21. The document was headed by a name soon to become a synonym for terror and destruction: Barbarossa. 'The German Armed Forces must be prepared to *crush Soviet Russia in a quick compaign* before the end of the war against England.... Preparations ... are to be completed by 15 May 1941.'[41]

The British War Cabinet were highly satisfied with their latest escalation of violence: the meeting on the 19th heard a report that 'the large scale operation against Mannheim on the night of 16 December was thought to have given excellent results. About 100 tons of high explosives had been dropped and 14,000 incendiary bombs. Extensive fires had been caused, some of which were still burning when a second operation had been undertaken on the night of the 17 December.' There had been a further small attack on the previous night. Recent fighting in Libya had been 'extremely satisfactory', Ministers were informed; the position at Bardia was developing slowly but favourably, and at Sidi Omar about 800 prisoners and a battery had been taken. The total British and Imperial casualties reported up to 16 December amounted to 72 killed and 738 wounded; about 31,500 enemy prisoners had been received into camps.[42]

Churchill gave a long statement to the Commons on the war situation before Members rose for the Christmas recess: the Libyan campaign was still developing well, but the Prime Minister warned of continued air attacks at home, and sinkings in the Atlantic were increasing at a dangerous rate. 'We must regard the keeping open of this channel to the world against submarines and the long distance aircraft which are now attacking as the first of all our military tasks.' Churchill then saw Eden and asked the War Secretary to dine with him: a complication had arisen over the Washington appointment. Halifax had apparently told the Prime Minister he did not want the Washington post and had hinted Eden might like to go; this was strongly denied by Eden. Halifax lunched with the War Secretary next day, and when the latter reprimanded him for saying he (Eden) would like the Washington post, Halifax retorted: 'I only said that I thought you might hate it a little less than myself.' Eden spent that night at Chequers with Churchill and was told a letter had been sent to Halifax to finalize the appointment. The two men discussed a successor at the War Office, and Eden again recommended Oliver Lyttelton. This time, however, Churchill favoured Captain David Margesson, Chief Whip to the National Government, and with whom Churchill had frequently clashed during his pre-war period as a Tory rebel. Lord and Lady Halifax saw Churchill on the 20th, after Lord Lothian's Memorial Service in Westminster Abbey, but were unable to persuade the Prime Minister to change his mind. Rumours of the new appointments appeared in the *Daily Mail* next day, 21 December, and Roosevelt was hurriedly asked for his consideration of Halifax as the new Ambassador. And, two days later, Eden appeared at the War Cabinet meeting as Foreign Secretary, while Halifax was described as HM Ambassador (Designate) to the United States.

While the remnants of the Italian Army tottered back in North Africa and British forces scooped up thousands more prisoners, Churchill prepared to spend a few Christmas hours at Chequers; Hitler went to celebrate the holidays with troops and *Luftwaffe* units along the English Channel; Mussolini stayed in sleety, bitter Rome – Ciano noted: 'Christmas. The Duce is sombre.'

Still no mention of the tentative Lend-Lease proposals had appeared in the War Cabinet Minutes; instead, at the meeting on Friday, 27 December, Ministers were informed that 'of the 50 destroyers which we had obtained from the United States, only 9 were at present in action' and a telegram was being sent to the Americans describing the defects.[43] Cadogan jotted in his diary: 'Americans are being *very* tiresome about financial matters.'[44] A telegram then arrived from the Washington Embassy, disclosing that Roosevelt intended to make a broadcast to say US interests required her to ensure the victory of the Democracies; but, the signal added, the 'real battle' would be engaged when Roosevelt's proposals were under Congressional discussion. Ministers therefore waited with interest and some apprehension for Roosevelt's statement on the 29th.

In the hours before the text came through, German bombers lit the Second Fire of London. The 29th was a Sunday; most of the offices and warehouses in the City were locked up for the weekend, and many had no fire-watchers. For two hours, picked to coincide with the Thames low-water period, incendiaries showered down upon the helpless capital. Water mains were shattered by parachute mines and the Fire Services were almost overwhelmed. Almost 1,500 fires were started, all but 100 in the City itself. Air Marshall 'Bomber' Harris, Deputy Chief of Air Staff, was among the witness. 'Although I have often been accused of being vengeful during our subsequent destruction of German cities,' he wrote later, 'this was the one occasion and the only one when I did feel vengeful.'[45] Yet more civilians had been killed in other raids – and as many had been killed in the deliberately indiscriminate RAF attack on Mannheim on the 16th. The War Cabinet nevertheless condemned the barbarity of the latest German assault when Ministers met at noon next day; Churchill pointed out that 'no military objectives had been aimed at, and the enemy must have known what he was attacking'. Herbert Morrison reported the raid to have been comparable in severity to that on the night of 7-8 September; he also commented that the attack, and recent raids on Manchester, had shown inadequacies in fire-watching – at the War Cabinet meeting next day it was agreed compulsory fire-watching must be introduced. Ministers also heard a report from Budapest, giving a 'depressing' account by the American Naval Attaché in Berlin of 'the lack of success of our bombing raids on Berlin'. Another telegram from Berne recommended that 'we should adopt a different technique when bombing Italy, where, owing to the emotional temperament, pinprick raids on several towns simultaneously would have a greater morale effect, whereas raids of the Coventry type were needed in Germany'.

The War Cabinet had now received a full text of Roosevelt's 'fireside chat' over the radio the previous night. The President had declared : 'The British people are conducting an active war against [the] unholy alliance.... Our own future security is greatly dependent on the outcome.... I make the direct statement to the American people that there is a far less chance of the United States getting into [the war] if we do all we can now to support the nations defending themselves against attack.' Britain must be supplied with the implements of war 'in sufficient volume and quickly enough so that we and our children will be saved the agony and suffering of war'. Churchill told the War Cabinet on the 30th that 'although President Roosevelt's speech of the previous day had been in general terms, it had been satisfactory from our point of view, and he had been encouraged by it. It committed the US to implacable hostility and resistance.'[46] Other Ministers agreed, and the Prime Minister wrote to Roosevelt on the 31st thanking him, yet raising points which were causing him anxiety : how long would Congress debate the proposals? And how could Britain pay for goods in the meantime?[47]

A long, stern New Year message was passing from Hitler to Mussolini. 'The War in the West is won. A final violent effort is still necessary to crush England. Spain : profoundly troubled by the situation.... I am very saddened by this decision of Franco, which is so little in accord with the aid which we – you, Duce, and myself –

172

gave him.' The Führer hinted at action in the Balkans, but avoided details and added: 'It is simply necessary, Duce, that you stabilize your front in Albania.' As regards Russia, Hitler considered it essential for Germany to have an army sufficiently strong 'to deal with any eventuality'. The Führer turned to North Africa. 'Duce, I do not think that in this theatre any counter-attack on a large scale can be launched at the moment.'

Neither Hitler nor Mussolini could find much to comfort them at the end of 1940. Hitler had lost the Battle of Britain and, by ending successive night raids on the capital, had admitted the loss of the Battle of London. Spain and Franco unco-operative; Roosevelt increasingly hostile; Russia lurking to the East; Mussolini's armies scattered in the Libyan sand and lost in Albanian forests. Nor could the British War Cabinet find any hope for good New Year prospects; Britain had survived 1940, but resources were still over-stretched: Egypt was now secure, but clouds were gathering in the Far East. Bombing pressure on London might have eased, but the country was still subjected to terrible nightly suffering; and, after three months of night raiding, the British defences had done no better than destroy one aircraft out of every 326 German bombers. Invasion might still come; indeed, at the end of December Admiral Raeder urged Hitler: 'It is absolutely essential to recognize that the greatest task of the hour is to concentrate all our resources against England.'[48] The COS estimated in early 1941 that Germany could muster a total army strength of 250 divisions, of which 90 were ready for immediate service in any theatre; the Allies could only gather just under 60 divisions, and these would not be at full strength until late 1942. Above all, the Battle of the Atlantic loomed ahead, and Britain's shipping strength had already been severely sapped: at the start of 1941 the Allied cargo fleet was up to 2.5 million tons smaller than it had been in autumn 1939.[49] Churchill summed up the position in his letter to Roosevelt on 8 December: 'The danger of Great Britain being destroyed by a swift, overwhelming blow, has for the time being very greatly receded. In its place, there is a long, gradually maturing danger, less sudden and less spectacular, but equally deadly.' The British War Cabinet could be thankful for past deliverances, but feared the future.

Indecision

Churchill's closest colleagues independently supply a composite picture of the Prime Minister during this period: 'tired', 'strained', 'irritable', 'angry'; and at least one of his colleagues was increasing his burden, rather than helping him carry it: on 2 January 1941, Beaverbrook was asked to become Chairman of the new Import Executive, while still remaining Minister of Aircraft Production. Beaverbrook replied by sending in his resignation from the MAP – among his undeclared reasons for refusing the Import Executive and wanting to go completely was the appointment of Bevin to be Chairman of the sister body, the Production Executive. Churchill angrily answered on 3 January: 'Your resignation would be quite unjustified and would be regarded as a desertion.' Beaverbrook acquiesced.[1] The Prime Minister had more than enough to saturate his mind without Beaverbrook's tantrums: 'Looking back upon the increasing tumult of the war,' he wrote later, 'I cannot recall any period when its stresses and the onset of so many problems all at once or in rapid succession bore more directly on me and my colleagues than in the first half of 1941.'[2] Minutes of the War Cabinet, Defence Committee and Chiefs of Staff meetings are woven with wandering discussions on how Britain could both block enemy moves and make moves of her own with existing limited resources. An essential factor in Churchill's brilliant ability as a war leader was his restless prodding for action when none was taking place, and his equal prodding for more of it when operations were in progress, very often to the consternation of his military advisers. And these first weeks of 1941 saw British planners and Ministers in considerable confusion – hesitating and changing their minds over priorities and policies in North Africa, the Balkans and Home Defence. As so often in these first years of war, the Germans were just ahead – perhaps only by a week – in planning and reaching decisions along a parallel line to the British.

Early in January, Churchill gave a general review of the situation to the Defence Committee. The 'ceaseless stream' of reinforcements to the Middle East had deprived the country of 'half of our best tanks and much of our artillery', but risks had been well run. 'It was now necessary to decide how much further we should advance in Libya. The fine port of Benghazi was a tempting objective. We might, however, have to rest content with Tobruk.' Churchill continued: 'There was little doubt that the Germans were collecting a considerable force in Roumania and would be ready to move an army on any date after 20 January.... We must, therefore, do our utmost to assist the Greeks ... even at the expense of further advance into Libya.' Aid to Greece would not prevent Britain from taking action in Abyssinia where the Italians were in a 'forlorn position'. He added: 'The Italian position in the Dodecanese was wilting, and profitable action could no doubt be fitted into our plans.' A German advance through Spain at that time of year would be 'a most dubious enterprise' and it seemed as if General Franco would not grant permission or yield to force. French opinion had swung over to Britain and the Libyan victories had had an invigorating effect; as far as the Far East was concerned, 'the naval defeats which we had inflicted upon the Italians would strongly influence the Japanese. The mistake of taking warships at their paper-value had been brought home to them.' Attempted invasion of Britain could still not be ruled out. 'It would be a harder task for the Germans now than in the previous summer, but the need for them to do it was greater. It was difficult to see how Hitler could get what he wanted without defeating us, and it would be the height of folly to neglect our precautions. A sense of alarm was necessary to keep our troops keyed up to ceaseless vigilance.' Shipping sinkings had been extremely heavy recently, Churchill warned, and this would be the limiting factor for future operations. The reaction of desert victories on US opinion had been 'extremely favourable', concluded Churchill. 'President Roosevelt was thinking of aid to us in the largest terms. We did not, at present, need US troops. It would be a mistake to use shipping to transport them.'[3] American developments were also the subject of the first War Cabinet meeting of the year, on Thursday, 2 January, at 11.30 a.m. Roosevelt had warned that his Lend-Lease plan needed legislation, and he had given 16 February as the approximate date on which a Bill would become law; Ministers were told 'it ought to be possible, however, to make appropriations under the existing law, in order to enable us to make day to day payments under our contracts in the interim period. This was our main difficulty. The President was inclined to deal with the matter on broader and more general lines, but he showed no disposition to be alarmed at the size of our financial demands.' Ministers were told it had been decided to give particulars of the defects in the destroyers discreetly to the US Naval Attaché, rather than direct to Roosevelt as decided upon at 27 December War Cabinet meeting.[4]

During these days of uncertainty, of sinkings in the dark Atlantic, German moves in the Balkans, ominous stirrings in the Far East, the effect of the desert victories was of supreme psychological importance, not least upon Churchill and other War Cabinet members. Bardia, held by almost four Italian divisions, was the next objective, and on Friday, 3 January, the Australian offensive began. Troops clung to perimeter defences while engineers hurriedly filled in anti-tank ditches, and armoured units swept into Italian positions; by the time the War Cabinet met on Monday, 6 January, the great stronghold had fallen and Tobruk was isolated. Ministers were told 25,000 enemy prisoners had so far been taken; Churchill commented on the low allied casualty total of only 400, then referred to a BBC broadcast earlier in the morning which had stressed the 'pitiful' condition of the Italian defenders and he added that 'it was undesirable to belittle what the Australians had done by putting too much emphasis on the fact that there had not been much fighting. The line to take was that the Italians, normally excellent soldiers, had not on this occasion fought with their accustomed bravery, owing to their being out of sympathy with the cause for which they were fighting.' Ministers agreed. News from Bulgaria was disquieting, warned Eden: 'There were a number of indications that Bulgaria was under strong pressure.' Sir Michael Palairet, Ambassador at Athens, reported anxiety over the slowing down of the Greek advance in Albania.[5] The two main international subjects, North Africa and the Balkans, were brought together at the War Cabinet meeting next day, 7 January. Allied advance elements were already westward of Tobruk: operations in the last month had accounted for a third of the total Italian strength in Libya and Churchill said he had invited the COS to consider 'whether we could now afford some further assistance to Greece, more particularly reinforcing our air detachment'. Eden mentioned that the Greek Ambassador was calling on him during the afternoon.[6] At this interview the Ambassador complained that practically nothing had been done to meet a Greek list of the most urgent requirements submitted two months before; concern continued to mount in Athens over German moves and the lack of progress in Albania. Pressure for strong British support was therefore increasing, and in turn for sacrifices from the North African theatre. Meanwhile, also on the 7th, Churchill criticized Wavell for apparent over-strength in rear sections of his army and asked that 'you have less fat and more muscle, that you have a smaller tail and larger teeth.'[7]

Eden, after seeing the Greek Ambassador, presided over a Foreign

Office meeting to discuss Russia; Cadogan noted: 'Glad to find A [Anthony Eden] not "ideological" and quite alive to uselessness of expecting anything from these cynical bloodstained murderers.'[8] Russian concern was mounting over German troops in the Balkans; Ribbentrop therefore instructed the German Ambassador at Moscow to stress 'troop movements result from the fact that the necessity must be seriously contemplated of ejecting the English completely from the whole of Greece'. This assurance would, the Nazi Foreign Minister thought, soothe the sensitive Soviets, and yet for the next two days, 8 and 9 January, Hitler held a top-level military conference at the snowy Berghof, at which he condemned Stalin as 'a cold-blooded blackmailer' and told his commanders that Russia would have to be brought to her knees 'as soon as possible'. Meanwhile, North Africa must be held: Hitler was now determined to send support to the Italians: Wavell's worst fears for Libya would soon be confirmed. Yet while Hitler's conference was continuing on Wednesday evening, 8 January, the Defence Committee met in Whitehall and Churchill commented: 'The prosecution of the campaign in Libya must now take second place.' All information pointed to an early German advance into Greece via Bulgaria. 'The Greek army, which was fully engaged in Albania, would find itself in a hopeless position. The Russian attitude was unknown, but a German advance would be against her interests.... It might be that the help which we could bring the Greeks in the time available would not be enough to save them.' Eden stressed the importance of British help to Greece as a means of winning over the Turks. 'Furthermore, the Greeks were a temperamental race and we must do something to maintain their morale.' The Defence Committee therefore decided 'it was of the utmost importance, from the political point of view, that we should do everything possible, by hook or by crook, to send at once to Greece the fullest support within our power' and 'a decision on the form and extent of our assistance should be taken within the next 48 hours at the latest'. The COS were asked to submit recommendations to a further meeting next day, 9 January.[9] The Defence Committee therefore met on the 9th at 9.45 p.m., and decided first priority should be the capture of Tobruk, after which Libyan operations should be severely limited and assistance to Greece would assume top priority. Decisions as to the form of aid would await advice from the Commanders at Cairo, after they had conferred with General Metaxas, President of the Greek Council.[10] The COS told Cairo that the Government were prepared to authorize the despatch to Greece of mechanized and specialized units, plus air forces, to the limits of one infantry tank squadron, one cruiser tank regiment, 10 artillery regiments and 5 aircraft squadrons. On 10 January a worried reply came from Wavell, who feared the Germans might be attempting to draw British strength from North Africa, and he hoped the COS would 'consider most urgently whether enemy's move is not bluff'. Churchill immediately sent a stiff signal: 'Our information contradicts idea that a German concentration in Roumania is merely a "move in war of nerves" or a "bluff to cause dispersion of force...." We expect and require prompt and active compliance with our decisions.' Wavell had said he proposed to fly to Athens early next week; Churchill stated this visit 'will enable you to contrive the best method of giving effect to the above decisions. It should not be delayed.'[11]

During this Friday, 10 January, the Lend-Lease Bill was introduced into the US Congress. The day before a slight, emaciated figure had arrived at an airfield in Dorset, exhausted by his flight from America. Harry Hopkins was soon to be as great a friend to Churchill and Britain as President Roosevelt, to whom he acted as special adviser. Hopkins, constantly ill, was too tired to dine at 10 Downing Street that night and went straight to Claridges Hotel; the following morning he saw Eden and Cadogan, then went for a three-hour lunch with Churchill and reported back to Roosevelt: 'Number 10 Downing Street is a bit down at heel. Most of the windows are out.... Churchill told me it wouldn't stand a healthy bomb.' He described his first meeting with the Prime Minister. 'A rotund-smiling-red-faced gentleman appeared – extended a fat but none the less convincing hand and wished me welcome to England. A short black coat – striped trousers – a clear eye and a mushy voice....' The two men established an immediate and intimate relationship. 'His was a soul that flamed out of a frail and failing body,' enthused Churchill.[12] Germany was also active in her international affairs: despite Hitler's obsessive planning for 'Barbarossa', the Russo-German agreement of 1939 was renewed on 10 January and a trade agreement signed in Moscow. Italy was given important military help: German aircraft from Sicilian airfields began to operate against British shipping, dramatically announcing their presence on the 10th when the *Illustrious* received severe damage. Back in London the Defence Committee were considering a warning from Brooke that a German invasion attempt on Britain was by no means unlikely. 'The series of reverses suffered by Italy at sea, on land and in the air, had reduced the scope of enemy offensive operations in Africa and in the Mediterranean; the danger of invasion had therefore increased.' The C-in-C Home Forces expressed his concern over the withdrawal of naval forces from an anti-invasion role to convoy escorting, and over the despatch of overseas reinforcements: he urged a review of the army manpower situation and said the allotment of equipment to Home Forces should be increased from the existing 40 per cent. Air Marshall Sholto Douglas, Dowd-

178

ing's successor as C-in-C Fighter Command, also regarded an attempt at invasion as highly probable. 'Up to the present there had been no appreciable movement of German air forces away from North-West Europe,' and he hoped 'our fighter defences would not be depleted by the despatch of squadrons overseas'. A supremely optimistic view was taken by Admiral Sir Charles Forbes, C-in-C Plymouth, who thought 'the chances of invasion being successful were so remote and the consequences of failure were likely to be so serious for Hitler, that we should do all we could to persuade the Germans to attempt invasion'. He suggested the Prime Minister should 'try to give the impression that we were living in a fool's paradise'. Churchill commented: 'An attitude of undue confidence might court disaster.'[13]

Considerable divergence of view therefore existed: Churchill believed the next German move would come through the Balkans; Wavell urged for British successes in North Africa to be consolidated before the Germans intervened in the desert; General Brooke considered further reinforcements to the Middle East would be highly dangerous. Both Churchill and Wavell were unfortunately correct: next day, 11 January, Hitler stated in Directive No 22: 'The situation in the Mediterranean area, where England is employing superior forces against our allies, requires that Germany should assist.' German forces would be moved to Libya from about 20 February and X Air Corps would continue to operate from Sicily; German air units would also fly from airfields in Tripoli in direct support of Italian land forces. But Hitler added: 'German formations in the approximate strength of one Corps, including 1st Mountain Division and armoured units, will be detailed and made ready to move to Albania,' and one of the tasks assigned to them would be the opening of passes west of Salonica, thereby supporting a frontal attack by a German army advancing from Bulgaria.[14] The War Cabinet discussions on the Balkans were resumed two days later, Monday 13 January – the same day that Wavell flew to Athens. Eden reported: 'The main danger was a German move in Bulgaria, possibly at first by the same method as had been used in Roumania, without directly infringing the neutrality of Yugoslavia or Turkey.' Russia's attitude was of interest, continued the Foreign Secretary; Russian policy would continue to be dominated by fear, but the Soviets had issued an official statement that they had not been consulted about German troops going through Bulgaria.[15] Meanwhile, the Foreign Office also learnt that Prince Paul of Yugoslavia was apprehensive over British aid to Greece which, he maintained, would merely bring the Germans down upon the Balkans; Churchill minuted: 'The evidence in our possession of the Germans' movements seems overwhelming. In the face of it Prince Paul's attitude' looks like that of an unfortunate man in a cage with a tiger, hoping not to provoke him while steadily dinner-time approaches.'[16] The Prime Minister signalled to Smuts: North African operations would be eased after Tobruk's fall, although the offensive would 'go on while the going is good so as to make as far-thrown a western flank for Egypt as possible, meanwhile shifting all useful elements to impending war front Bulgarian-Greek frontier.'[17] Greece and North Africa – forces for each were therefore required from Britain's slender resources. Churchill's message to Smuts contained a certain contradiction: to go on while the going was good in North Africa, while taking 'all useful elements' for Greece. Dangers of a dispersal and weakening of effort were thereby increased; and Churchill's thoughts returned to yet another operation – 'Workshop', the capture of Pantelleria island. 'The effective arrival of German aviation in Sicily', Churchill told the COS on 13 January, 'may be the beginning of evil developments in the Central Mediterranean.... I am very apprehensive of the Germans establishing themselves in Pantelleria.... It is necessary now that "Workshop" should be reviewed.'[18] The subject was raised at a Defence Committee meeting at 9.30 that night, with Churchill stressing the Germans might occupy Pantelleria first. But according to Vice-Admiral Phillips, Vice-Chief of Naval Staff, 'even if we had fighters in Malta and Pantelleria we still could not protect our convoys. The only method of gaining complete control in the central Mediterranean would be to take Sicily.' Portal agreed; Churchill refused to give way. 'We were open to very grave reproach for not having taken Pantelleria when we still had an opportunity. This would be classed as one of the capital errors of the war.... We had missed the chance, and now we would find that the Germans would occupy the island and probably a position on the African coast, and we should find the Mediterranean closed to us. The fate of Malta itself might be sealed.' Churchill urged: 'We ought now to see whether we could still take the island.' After the Prime Minister's gloomy assessment, members of the Committee could hardly fail to agree to further consideration: the COS were therefore asked to review 'Workshop' and report in a week's time.[19]

Lord and Lady Halifax left London on 14 January on the first stage of their journey to Washington, and Churchill travelled to Scapa Flow to bid them farewell – the Ambassador would sail in Britain's newest battleship, *King George V*. With·Churchill went Harry Hopkins, whom the Prime Minister had found to have as deep a hatred of Nazis as he himself, although expressed less flamboyantly. Churchill had flourished his oratory at a dinner a few nights before: 'We seek no treasure, we seek no territorial gains, we seek only the right of man to be free.... As the humble labourer

180

returns from his work when day is done, and sees the smoke curling upwards from his cottage home in the serene evening sky, we wish him to know that no *rat-a-tat-tat*' – the Prime Minister's knuckles pounded the table – 'of the secret police will disturb his leisure or interrupt his rest.... What will the President say to all this?' After considerable pause, Hopkins drawled: 'Well, Mr Prime Minister, I don't think the President will give a damn for all that.' Churchill scowled; then the American added: 'We're only interested in seeing that Goddam sonofabitch gets licked.'[20] 'The people here are amazing from Churchill down,' declared one of Hopkins' first reports to Roosevelt, 'and if courage alone can win – the result will be inevitable. But they need our help desperately.... *Churchill* is the gov't *in* every sense of the word – he controls the grand strategy and often the details....'[21] Yet despite reports sent back by Hopkins and despite Roosevelt's own inclinations, Halifax had a difficult task ahead. Many Americans still considered they had won the last war and had hardly been thanked for it, let alone repaid the money lent: the United States had been caught once and were not going to be caught again; a *New York Times* article two days before Halifax's departure had described Americans as having 'not yet apparently abandoned their resolution either to be pushed nor descend into it [war], if they can safely keep their footing on the rim.'

Hopkins stressed to Roosevelt: 'The most important single observation I have to make is that most of the Cabinet and all of the military leaders here believe that invasion is imminent.' And this expectation by some Ministers was one reason for argument within the Cabinet: the so-called bombing controversy. The bomber was the only weapon which could strike direct at Germany. Should it be used for this purpose, or should raids be concentrated upon German forces just across the Channel and hence damage the enemy's invasion potential? Or should bombers be used against U-boat pens, or communications? The controversy was to continue. Now, in early January, it centred on the question whether an all-out attempt should be made to destroy Germany's synthetic oil production. At the end of December Portal had presented a paper based on a report by the Lloyd Committee: apparently the next six months offered a unique opportunity of striking at Germany's oil resources; supplies from Roumania should therefore be sabotaged if possible, and Germany's 17 synthetic oil plants should be devastated – this would require at least 3,400 bomber sorties every four months. The COS approved Portal's paper on 7 January and the matter was brought before the Defence Committee on Monday, 13 January. The important point, Portal declared, was to lay down a firm policy: this would stop the many temptations to disperse bomber effort on to various targets. Dalton and Hankey agreed, but Eden and

Churchill displayed doubts. Synthetic plants were not normally near population centres, and Eden pointed out that 'we should not overlook the importance of attacking the German people. The reason the Germans were attacking our people was probably because it was this kind of attack that they themselves most feared.' Churchill was sceptical of 'cut and dried calculations which showed infallibly how the war could be won,' and added that 'the proposal would mortgage the greater part of our air effort for several months ahead, on plants, generally speaking, removed from the large centres of population. Against the proposal would have to be weighed up the loss of attacks against naval targets, German cities, the German aircraft industry, upon which we had recently been urged to devote our efforts, and the bombing of Italy, which many people thought so essential.' He thought 'there was a good cause for scattering our bombs over a large area on some occasions'. Portal strongly disagreed, as did most Ministers present, and Churchill admitted 'there would be no harm in trying the policy advocated by the Chiefs of Staff, although he doubted whether it would be possible to stick to it. The strength of the defences around the oil plants would increase, and the pressure of events would force us to divert efforts.'[22] A new directive was therefore issued to Bomber Command two days later, 15 January, to the consternation of those, including General Brooke, who believed German invasion forces would be allowed greater freedom to grow in strength. In the event, Churchill proved correct: the directive was theoretically in effect for two months, but so uncertain was the weather that the oil targets only received exclusive attention on three nights in the period up to 27 February: naval targets, on the other hand, were attacked on 19 nights.[23]

General Wavell flew to Athens on 15 January; and he soon found that despite the hours of discussion in Chiefs of Staff, Defence Committee and War Cabinet sessions, the official Greek position differed completely to the British. General Metaxas believed British troops offered for the defence of Salonica would be insufficient and would merely provoke German attack; the army chief, General Papagos, declined the artillery and tanks offered for the Albanian front and sought transport and clothing instead. Metaxas believed the best course would be for materials to be consigned to Greece ready for the landing of a strong expeditionary force. In general, the Greeks believed the limited British help would do more harm than good, and Papagos later pointed out that 'the commencement of British operations in Africa practically at the same time as the Greek operations in the Balkans ... made any serious and timely strengthening of Greece impossible'.[24] The Defence Committee considered the surprising Greek reaction at a meeting on the evening of the 16th: Ministers agreed help could not be forced on the Greeks, but the COS were asked to signal Wavell repeating the British arguments: 'It may be that the Greeks have information which is not available to us, and which causes them to view the German preparations in a different light. If you are satisfied with the Greek refusal of recent assistance as being given in the full knowledge of our information, then we must submit to their judgment.' The Committee decided that if refusal was maintained, British emphasis should once again shift back to North Africa. 'We should be entitled to revise our decision that after the capture of Tobruk, first priority should be given to assistance to Greece.' Churchill also believed Prince Paul of Yugoslavia had told the Greeks that if they allowed British land forces to enter their country, the Yugoslav Government would allow the Germans to attack Greece through Yugoslavia. 'No doubt he had then tried to curry favour with the Germans by telling them that he had kept British forces out of Greece.'[25] The telegram to Wavell was despatched next Friday, 17 January. On the same day, Russia expressed her fears of a German move in the Balkans and issued a sharp protest to Berlin: the Soviet Union could not be 'indifferent to events which threaten the security of the USSR'. Churchill's assessment of Prince Paul's policy seemed correct: a Greek note delivered to the British Ambassador on the 18th revealed that Yugoslavia would withdraw her pledge to resist a German demand for passage if a German attack was provoked by the despatch of British troops to Macedonia. The Greeks criticized the proposed dispersal of British forces between North Africa and in the Balkans: they felt obliged to 'draw attention of HM Government most particularly to the fact that the problem of South-East Europe cannot be faced with forces now at their [British] disposal in the Near East'.[26] The British COS did at least succeed in having another potential strain on resources removed: at a Chequers meeting this Saturday morning Churchill very reluctantly agreed to the postponement of 'Workshop' for one month. The operation was abandoned a few days later.

On Sunday, 19 January, British forces re-occupied Kassala; on the Monday morning the War Cabinet were informed that plans for the attack on Tobruk had been delayed owing to sandstorms.[27] Eden dined with Churchill at 10 Downing Street that evening, then both walked down the passage to a Defence Committee meeting, held to sort out some of the muddled Middle East schemes. Following the sudden and stubborn Greek attitude, Sir Dudley Pound said the COS believed Britain should ensure her hold on the Eastern Mediterranean to protect the safety of the main fleet base at Alexandria and to enable forces to be sent to Greece or Turkey later, if necessary. To carry this policy out, Cyrenaica should first be cleared and Benghazi secured and, to diminish the threat to lines of communication with Greece or Smyrna, the Dodecanese should be occupied. As far as the central and western Mediterranean were concerned, the COS were against an operation to take Sardinia – involving conditions 'very similar to those which had led to failure in Norway. It would be impossible for us to provide any depth to our air support.' Sicily was ruled out for the same reasons. Churchill reacted bitterly: the COS statement seemed to lead to the minimum of aggressive action.... All that the COS could recommend was the capture of Benghazi and the Dodecanese. 'While he was entirely in favour of both, he was not prepared to agree that they were a satisfying objective for the great forces now gathered in the Middle East.' According to Eden, 'the key to the whole situation was Turkey', and all operations should be directed to facilitate support to her: if the line of communication to Turkey was threatened by the Dodecanese, the capture of these islands was even more important than securing Benghazi. Churchill restlessly complained he wanted 'to give the war more active scope'. Malta must remain one of the first charges on British resources; attack on Greece must be countered by aggressive British action elsewhere; he wanted further study of plans for the capture of Sardinia and Sicily, in case unforeseen circumstances arose, such as dissension between the Italians and Germans. 'There was general agreement,' concluded Churchill, 'that Benghazi and the Dodecanese must be cleared up as soon as possible and that the army of the Nile should be immediately set to work to constitute a mobile reserve which would be ready to proceed as required, either to Greece or Turkey or for other operations in the Mediterranean.' Some Committee members suggested the Germans might be building up in the Balkans to divert British attention and forces away from Britain herself; other Ministers, including Churchill, believed the Germans would not risk invasion – chances of success were difficult for the enemy to calculate and failure would be disastrous. Instead, threat of invasion would be maintained while German forces occupied Bulgaria, thus isolating Yugoslavia and dominating Greece, after which the enemy would advance through the Ukraine to the Caucasus.[28] While the Defence Committee held this Monday evening meeting, Hitler and Mussolini were concluding a two-day conference at the Führer's Berghof HQ: main topics were Russia and North Africa. German help would soon be given to the Italians in the latter area under Operation 'Sunflower': the 5th Light (Motorized) Division would start for Tripolitania about 15 February. 'I don't see great danger coming from America,' Hitler declared, 'even if she should enter the war. The much greater danger is the gigantic Russian bloc.' Following the Defence Committee decision, the COS cabled Wavell next day, Tuesday, 21 January, authorizing an attack on Benghazi. Within a day after receiving this signal, Wavell informed the COS that the other main objective, Tobruk, was in British hands. This valuable port, isolated since 6 January, was attacked by Australian troops piercing the southern perimeter wire; resistance had ceased by the 22nd with nearly 30,000 enemy prisoners taken. The Italian Army in North Africa had almost been finished as a fighting force; and Hitler pondered whether his offer of help should be reversed – or whether assistance should be substantially increased.

In London, General Alan Brooke was working on the assumption the Germans had invaded the Canary Isles, Iceland, Ireland and Scotland: a gigantic Home Defence Exercise began on the 22nd and lasted until the 25th.[29] The War Cabinet was in fact informed on the 23rd that Continental weather made invasion attempts unlikely during the next few weeks, and it might be possible to grant more extensive army home leave. London's bomb-battered streets were sodden with stained slush after the break in the recent intensive cold spell; the capital was soon to experience a resumption of concentrated bombing, and a raid on the 30th was described to the War Cabinet as causing the highest number of daylight casualties since 25 October. Meanwhile, Ministers were told on the 27th that the unfavourable weather had resulted in some 20 per cent of German first line aircraft being moved from bases facing Britain's coast.[30] Churchill told this meeting that Harry Hopkins had received a telegram from President Roosevelt, 'requesting him to cable to America at once a list of our most immediate demands which could be met during the next few months'. The President, added Churchill, hoped the Lend-Lease Bill would pass into law at the end of February.[31] Prospects for useful Anglo-American co-operation indeed seemed brighter. A War Cabinet session on the 20th had been adjourned while Ministers listened to a broadcast of Roosevelt's inaugural address – 'We do not retreat. We are not content to stand still'; on 16 January Roosevelt had issued an historic directive, based on Admiral Stark's Plan D, submitted on 12 November, which specified the main US effort in the event of war would be made in the west, not in the Pacific. Also as a result of Roosevelt's acceptance of Plan D, four British war plans representatives had left for America on 12 January for secret staff talks; discussions began on Wednesday, 29 January.

'Churchill is an obstinate and senile liar,' screeched the head of the German Labour Front in a Berlin newspaper article on the 29th. 'He is a fraud, predisposed to cruelty and brutality....' Closeted in close conference in Berlin were Admiral Raeder and

Generals Halder and Brauchitsch, acutely apprehensive over British desert successes and Hitler's preoccupation with Russia. 'Objectives are not clear,' complained Halder. 'We do not strike at England. . . . Our infantry will be tied down [in Russia] at a time when England disposes of growing forces in every theatre.'[32] Halder's pessimism was premature: British objectives had also still to be clarified, and further contradictions were soon to arise. Meanwhile the Prime Minister was prodding Wavell: two telegrams went to Cairo on the 26th, one containing Churchill's criticisms of inactivity in Kenya, the other warning that the Germans were already using Bulgarian airfields. 'We must expect a series of very heavy, disastrous blows in the Balkans. . . . The stronger the strategic reserve which you can build up in the Delta and the more advanced your preparations to transfer it to European shores the better.'[33] Next day, the 27th, Wavell stressed the dangers of overstretch: 'Hitherto the war [has] been conducted on an irreducible minimum of force, which [has] in fact been well over the danger line;' this risk might have been justified when dealing with the Italians; the Germans presented an infinitely different problem.[34] But Churchill's eyes remained fixed upon the Balkans and now more especially upon Turkey: Eden's remarks at the 20 January Defence Committee meeting – 'the key to the whole situation is Turkey' – began to have more impact as the realization grew that German pressure upon that country might be decisive. If the Greeks continued to refuse British aid, the Turks might not, and on 29 January the COS recommended the despatch of three fighter and seven bomber squadrons to Turkey, plus about 100 AA guns. The Chiefs recognized that if Turkey accepted this assistance, Britain could offer little or no additional help to Greece.[35] But an added difficulty arrived later on this Wednesday. News was received of the death of General Metaxas, the Greek leader who had won respect and confidence despite early widespread opposition. The British War Cabinet meeting at 5.30 p.m. agreed his death was a serious loss and a heavy blow to confidence and unity within Greece.[36] No mention of the recommendation for aid to Turkey was made at this meeting, yet the idea was still under consideration by Churchill, despite possible changes in Athens policy resulting from the Greek President's death. A further COS session, attended by Churchill, Eden and Service Ministers started at 9.30 p.m. The meeting lasted until midnight, and ended with approval for the COS recommendation: Churchill should send a telegram to the Turkish President. The possibility of a visit by Eden was also discussed and the Foreign Secretary noted in his diary: 'Winston . . . anxious that I should see Wavell who he feels is insufficiently aware of Balkan dangers.'[37] The Turkey offer was accordingly made in a letter from Churchill

186

to President Inönü on 31 January; full War Cabinet approval was not apparently considered necessary. Also on the 31st Churchill addressed a minute to the COS which seemed to contradict previous War Cabinet and Defence Committee conclusions. 'We must not overlook the decision we conveyed to General Wavell, that once Tobruk was taken the Greek-Turkish situation must have priority. The advance to Benghazi is most desirable, and has been emphasized in later telegrams. Nevertheless, only forces which do not conflict with European needs can be employed.' The COS therefore cabled Wavell: 'Steps to counter German infiltration into Bulgaria must now have the highest priority.'[38] Yet Greece alone had been considered most important at the beginning of January, specified for example in the Defence Committee decision on the 9th: 'After Tobruk has been dealt with, assistance to Greece would assume first priority.' Turkey had been barely mentioned at this stage; and after the Greek refusal of aid, priority had shifted back to North Africa not, as claimed by Churchill, merely because it had been 'emphasized in later telegrams', but as a result of a definite Defence Committee decision on the 20th that Wavell was to regard the capture of Benghazi as of the 'highest importance'. The C-in-C Middle East had every reason for feeling disgruntled at this rapid rearrangement – Greece, back to North Africa, and now Turkey, all within three weeks. And, despite the recommendation for aid to Turkey, a considerable number of senior officers were concerned over British involvement in the Balkans. Major-General Kennedy, Director of Military Operations, considered Home Defence and North Africa should receive most attention. 'We can hardly be too strong in the British Isles,' he wrote in a Memorandum on 2 February. 'In the Middle East we must not throw away our power of offensive action by adopting an unsound strategy in Greece.'[39] Churchill was now discounting the invasion threat; also on the 2nd, a Sunday, General Brooke spent the night at Chequers, where he gave Churchill a long description of the recent Home Defence exercise. 'Winston's reactions were very typical,' wrote Brooke. 'He criticized the scale of the German attack.... He even implied that this had been done in order to influence him into considering the threat greater than it really was.'[40]

Next day, 3 February, Ministers heard of and belatedly approved the offer made to Turkey three days before. They also heard the offer was likely to be rejected. Churchill said that 'evidence in our possession showed that the Bulgarian Government were conniving at the German infiltration ... it was only a question of short time before Germany would be in a position to compel Turkey to fall in with her wishes under the threat of bombing'. Britain had therefore offered air help; Churchill's message had been handed

187

to the Foreign Minister, 'who however had viewed our offer with some dismay and had said that he could give no final answer without consulting the Turkish President and the Prime Minister. He affected to regard as exaggerated reports of the German penetration into Bulgaria.' Churchill warned: 'There was every prospect that south-eastern Europe would witness this spring a repetition of last spring's events in Scandinavia and the Low Countries.'[41] While this War Cabinet meeting was being held in London, a six-hour Army High Command conference was taking place in Berlin: Hitler was anxious to pounce upon Russia once the southern flank had been made secure. 'When "Barbarossa" commences, the world will hold its breath!' But Admiral Raeder continued to believe the defeat of Britain was crucial; next day, 4 February, he told Hitler: 'Working in close co-operation, our aircraft and submarines are capable of exerting a decisive influence in the struggle against Britain and America.' The Führer was prepared to accept some of the advice offered to him despite his Russian obsession and, two days later, he issued a directive which was to have profound and almost fatal effect. 'The aim of further operations against the British homeland must be to concentrate all means of naval and air warfare against the enemy's supplies.... These missions must be carried out by the forces remaining in this area even if strong units of the Air Force are withdrawn to other theatres.'[42] Nor did Hitler refuse to heed those who urged Italian setbacks in the desert should result in withdrawal of German help; on 5 February, Hitler wrote to Mussolini to say that a complete *Panzer* division would now be sent to North Africa, as well as the Light Division, but he added the insulting stipulation that the Italians must promise to resist a further British advance. Also on 5 February, British troops suddenly upset this plan for bolstering the Italians before they suffered further defeats. One of Churchill's reasons for changing first priority back from the desert to the Balkans had been the forecast that Benghazi would not be taken for about another month; this, implied Churchill, was too long. But on 5 February, the 7th British Armoured Division battled forward to Msus, inland from Benghazi, stabbed north and slashed the crucial coastal road. The CIGS reported to the War Cabinet at 12.15 p.m. on Thursday, 6 February that 'there were signs of Italian movement out of Benghazi, and General Wavell had ordered forces to press on rapidly'.[43] By nightfall the enemy were in complete confusion; next morning the Italians surrendered and brought the total number of prisoners taken to 130,000 in only two months. The British conquest of Cyrenaica was complete; Wavell's triumph was supreme and the way open for clearing the Italians out of entire North

Africa, if first priority were returned to this operational area.

A special Defence Committee meeting would be summoned on 10 February to discuss this priority issue, but meanwhile Ministers had been given another urgent preoccupation – Japan. At the War Cabinet meeting on the 6th the Foreign Secretary revealed that 'on the previous day' Japan had warned her Embassy staff in London to reduce their contacts with the British authorities to a minimum, and 'to be prepared to leave the country at short notice'.[44] The Foreign Office had grown increasingly apprehensive since 31 January, when the Japanese had negotiated an armistice between Vichy French and Thailand in their frontier dispute, and rumours had spread that this might mean an imminent Japanese attack on Malaya. The Japanese Ambassador Mamoru Sigemitsu, gave an unconvincing explanation of his country's policy in an interview with R. A. Butler on 1 February; reports reached London from Tokyo, Bangkok and Hanoi of a possible Japanese advance into Thailand and southern Indo-China; the Joint Intelligence Sub-Committee warned on 5 February that a Japanese assault against the Dutch East Indies was probable in the near future.[45] When the situation was discussed at the War Cabinet meeting on the 6th, Churchill believed recent German mining of the Suez Canal might be an attempt to show Japan that British supplies to the Far East could be stopped. The COS warned there was no military action Britain could take further than reinforcements already sent, and Britain and America should rely on a firm diplomatic line; Churchill discussed this recommendation with the COS that night and it was agreed that Eden should speak in strong terms to the Japanese Ambassador: this he did in a one hour, 40 minute meeting next morning. Eden, speaking slowly to allow the Ambassador to jot down his words, said Britain would not give way to Japanese claims and would defend herself to the utmost – and, with the increasing amount of American aid now being received, he bluffed, Britain was certain to win.[46] This meeting was discussed by Eden and Churchill during the Friday night; next day, the 8th, the Foreign Secretary lunched with Hopkins, who agreed Roosevelt would be well advised to warn the Japanese Ambassador 'in words of one syllable' of America's interest in Far East affairs.[47] Two days later the Chiefs of Staff approved a warning signal to C-in-Cs overseas, and the following day, the 11th, agreed that Malaya should have priority over the Middle East for troops and stores from India. Also on the 11th, Eden instructed Halifax to urge Roosevelt to warn the Japanese; this was done on the 14th. On the 15th Roosevelt himself received a warning from Churchill: 'The weight of the Japanese Navy, if thrown against us, would confront us with situations beyond the scope of our naval resources.'[48]

But the Prime Minister also said in this message 'I am not myself convinced that this is not a war of nerves.' And on this same day the Japanese informed the Foreign Office that they were prepared to act as mediators 'anywhere the world over'; an offer which the Foreign Office received sceptically and indeed the Japanese Foreign Minister retracted it on 27 February. But the War Cabinet nevertheless concluded on the 17th that Far East tension was once more relaxing.[49] Churchill cabled Roosevelt on the 20th: 'I have better news about Japan. Apparently Matsouka [Foreign Minister] is visiting Berlin, Rome and Moscow in the near future. This may well be a diplomatic sop to cover absence of action against Great Britain.'[50] The Japanese scare had however shown the speed with which a Far East crisis could erupt; Churchill's warning over Britain's inability to confront Japan's Navy still applied. And the scare had further complicated consideration of the North African and Balkan situations.

After the brilliant capture of Benghazi on the 6th and the decimation of the entire Italian 10th Army, Wavell acted on previous instructions and did not attempt to advance into Tripolitania: his troops occupied Agheila on 8 February, then halted while Wavell waited for the COS and War Cabinet to settle priorities. Also on Saturday, 8 February, the first German troops started for North Africa – and a secret agreement was reached between the German and Bulgarian General Staffs concerning the transfer of Hitler's troops through Bulgaria to attack Greece. And the confused Anglo-Greek relationship was made even worse as a result of an Athens meeting between the British Ambassador and the new Council President, Koryzis; Sir Michael Palairet asked whether the statements by General Metaxas of 18 January, declaring proposed British help to be insufficient, still held good. The Ambassador was astonished to hear Koryzis had never even seen these statements. Next day the British were asked whether their offer of help remained open.[51] Since this aid had been offered priority had switched from Greece to Turkey, and then had come the desert victories, much earlier than expected, which offered the chance of a sweep into Tripolitania before the Germans arrived – or, with Cyrenaica now safely cleared, enabled more troops to be sent to the Balkans. Eden, who wrote 'Turkey still loomed larger in my mind than Greece', sent a Minute to Churchill early on Monday, 10 February, containing 'more question marks in it than was my habit'. What added chances of aid to Greece did the desert victories afford? Would even additional aid be sufficient? 'Greek forces are inadequate to make any effective defence of the Macedonian front. Is it conceivable that we could send and maintain sufficient forces

190

to fill the gap? I should fear not.' Eden implied that Britain would be better helping Turkey.[52] Preliminary discussions began at a War Cabinet meeting at 5 p.m. on this Monday, when Churchill pointed out that 'the position in the Eastern Mediterranean was altered by the capture of Benghazi at a much earlier date than had been expected. In what way could our forces in the Middle East now be employed?' Ministers left detailed examination to a Defence Committee meeting to be held later that night.[53] At 9.30 p.m. Committee members therefore gathered at 10 Downing Street; fateful decisions were to emerge.

Consideration was first given to arguments in favour of a further advance in North Africa: the capture of Tripoli would have great effect on Italian will to fight elsewhere; it might be possible to take the territory 'with quite a small force'. Any effective counter-attack upon the British would be prevented except by sea-borne expedition; 'we should also find ourselves side by side with the French, which might be very valuable later on.' 'If we did not take Tripoli now the Germans and Italians would be able to reinforce the place ... it might be impossible to capture it later on.' Then came arguments against: 'The C-in-Cs had been told after the capture of Tobruk that the European situation must take priority over future African operations, although they might go for Benghazi if the going was good. It would be wrong to alter this decision'; 'the uncertainties of the Balkan situation made it very desirable that the Army of the Nile should concentrate'; fighters from Tripoli would still be unable to provide full cover for Mediterranean convoys. Ministers unanimously agreed 'we should adhere to our existing policy of stopping when a secure flank had been gained by the capture of Benghazi'. Discussion then turned to whether aid should be offered to Greece or to Turkey – as Eden pointed out 'we could not do both'. Ministers agreed account had to be taken of the guarantee given to Greece on 13 April 1939: if another country to which Britain had given such a pledge were conquered without strong British effort to defend it, the effect would be deplorable, especially in America. The Committee unanimously agreed to concentrate on Greece. Another consideration, according to Churchill, was the need to settle Mediterranean plans quickly in view of Japan's menacing attitude. And at another meeting of the Defence Committee held next day, 11 February, Ministers agreed Anthony Eden and General Sir John Dill should fly out to the Middle East immediately to co-ordinate action.[54] The decision was to prove disastrous.

Wavell's orders, drafted by Churchill, were despatched early on Wednesday the 12th: 'If Greece, with British aid, can hold up for some months German advance, chances of Turkish intervention will be favoured. Therefore it would seem that we should try to get in a position to offer ... transfer to Greece of the fighting portion of the Army which has hitherto defended Egypt and make every plan for sending and reinforcing it to the limit.'[55] Also on this Wednesday a senior German officer, to be described by a British Intelligence summary the following month as 'obscure', stepped foot on Tripolitanian soil to command the growing number of German troops – Lieutenant-General Erwin Rommel. His task seemed desperate: to organize some kind of defence against the headlong British advance; but orders were already being prepared in Cairo to reform divisions, replace large units with smaller units, cut down supply bases – all the massive administrative details involved in the switch from North Africa to the Balkans: in Wavell's understatement: 'We must get tidied up.'[56] Also on 12 February, Eden and Dill travelled to Plymouth and their waiting Sunderland flying boat. Eden had been given an extremely impressive brief by the Prime Minister: he would represent HMG in all matters diplomatic and military; he had power to act on his own initiative in an emergency without reference to the War Cabinet; the principal object of his mission was to organize the despatch of speedy succour to Greece, but an operation to occupy Rhodes – Operation 'Mandibles' – was also to be executed as soon as possible and the campaign in Eritrea should be completed. Eden should also 'address himself to the problem of securing the highest form of war economy in all armies and air forces of the Middle East for all the above purposes, and to making sure that the many valuable military units in that theatre all fit into a coherent scheme and are immediately pulling their weight', and he would advise on the selection of commanders. Clearly, Anthony Eden had duties far wider than those of Foreign Secretary; similarly, drastic decisions which he was to take spanned far wider fields than diplomacy. Churchill wrote in his memoirs: 'I drafted and obtained formal Cabinet approval for the Instructions to the Foreign Secretary on his mission'; in fact, the official Minutes now reveal that not until 20 February, when Eden was already in Cairo, were the War Cabinet informed of these instructions.[57] Meanwhile, Eden and his party were obliged to wait at Plymouth while bad weather raged across the Continent, until just before midnight on the 14th when their dangerous flight began.

During the 14th the Yugoslav Prime Minister and Foreign Minister made a hazardous journey to see Hitler at Obersalzberg, where they were informed that if Yugoslavia joined the Tripartite Pact she would be spared German armies tramping across her soil in the event of operations against Greece. Next morning, after reaching Gibraltar with barely sufficient fuel for a further 10 minutes' flying time, Eden sent a message to his old friend Prince Paul, Yugoslav Regent, suggesting a meeting in southern Serbia; Prince Paul was soon to send his refusal. The Foreign Secretary remained stranded at Gibraltar on the 16th and 17th, attempting to ease his mind by reading *War and Peace*. Back in London on the 17th the War Cabinet were informed by the COS that 'German air force concentration in Roumania was probably nearly complete.... The Greek army had again taken the offensive in Albania, apparently with success.'[58] Eden and Dill flew from Gibraltar to Malta next day, Tuesday, 18 February; in Berlin, Hitler announced that troops under General Rommel would henceforth be known as the German *Afrika Korps*. The Führer issued further orders on the 19th: troop crossing into Bulgaria for advance on Greece would commence on 2 March. Just before midnight, Eden and Dill finally arrived in Cairo. 'You've been a long time coming,' commented the brusque Wavell. A three-hour session with the three C-in-Cs took place next morning and full agreement was reached that all help should be given to Greece at the earliest possible moment. Back in London Ministers were receiving their first information on Eden's mission at a noon War Cabinet meeting, at which the instructions given to Eden by Churchill were 'generally endorsed'. Yet Churchill now began to show reluctance over a Greek expedition. 'If the Greeks decided to oppose a German advance,' he declared, 'we should have to help them to the full extent of our power ... It might be well that a German thrust towards Salonica would be irresistible; but if the Greeks decided to fight, we should do what we could. It was possible, of course, that before making the advance the Germans would offer the Greeks such attractive terms that they would feel bound to make peace. In that case we could not very well blame them ... We should have done our duty and should then have to content ourselves by making our position in the Greek Islands as strong as possible.' In this event, continued Churchill, 'the question of advancing into Tripoli would again arise'. He hoped Britain would not have to put a large part of her army into Greece, and he gave the sombre warning 'it was unlikely that it would be possible for a large British force to get there before the Germans'. The Prime Minister said one account of the recent Yugoslav talks was that the Nazis had been 'studiously polite', pressing the Yugoslavs to adhere to the New Order but not demanding the right of troop passage. Churchill also commented 'there were signs of German infiltration into North Africa'.[59]

Soon after this War Cabinet meeting on the 20th Churchill cabled to Eden and Dill, and again he displayed reluctance over a Greek commitment: 'Do not consider yourselves obligated to a

Greek enterprise if in your hearts you feel it will only be another Norwegian fiasco.' But Eden's first cable was already on its way: 'We are agreed we should do everything in our power to bring the fullest measures of help to Greeks at earliest possible moment.' Eden showed strong optimism which contradicted Churchill's warning to the War Cabinet concerning lack of time: 'If the help we can offer is accepted by the Greeks, we believe that there is a fair chance of halting a German advance.' Clearly, Greece had eclipsed the prominent position previously held by Turkey in Eden's mind. 'My own conclusion, which General Dill and C-in-C share, is that in the immediate future assistance to Greeks, who are fighting and are threatened, must have first call on resources.'[60] Moreover, in a signal to the Vice-CIGS on the 21st, Dill confirmed his change of mind over expectations of a successful enterprise. 'I came out here with firm ideas that forces sent to Greece would inevitably be lost and that we should concentrate on help to Turkey. I have now heard views of three C-in-Cs, Marshall Cornwall [recent member of staff mission to Turkey] and Heywood [army member of Military Mission in Greece]. It has been made clear to me by them: (a) That Turkey will not fight at our bidding; (b) that she may fight if we show that by helping Greece we can stem a German advance; (c) that there is a fair military chance of successfully holding a line in northern Greece if we act at once....'[61] Eden's mission flew to Athens on the 22nd. The Foreign Secretary motored to Tatoi, the King's country palace, and was immediately read a declaration by Koryzis, repeating Greece's determination to fight despite all odds. The King had wished this to be emphasized *before* he heard what Eden had to offer; yet Eden had made up his mind that the Greeks must be helped *before* he heard this gallant declaration of defiance. Nevertheless, when 10-hour discussions began, Koryzis repeated misgivings that insufficient British help would merely precipitate German attack. Military talks between Generals Dill and Wavell, and Longmore, Air Officer C-in-C Middle East, on the one hand and General Papagos on the other, came to the critical conclusion that in view of Yugoslavia's doubtful attitude the only defensive line that could be held, giving time for troop withdrawals from Albania, was the 70-mile 'Aliakhmon position', running from the sea west of the Vardar River, north-west to the Yugoslav border. Salonika would have to be sacrificed unless Yugoslavia could be brought in – and Eden said he would make another attempt to do so. Meanwhile, the Greeks would immediately make preparations to withdraw to the Aliakhmon line; work would start on communications; British troops would move from Egypt, commanded by General Maitland Wilson. Details were conveyed to the Prime Minister on the 24th; soon afterwards Eden sent another

194

message: 'We are all convinced that we have chosen the right course, and as the eleventh hour has already struck felt sure you would not wish us to delay for detailed reference home.'[62] Eden was already making full use of his generous instructions. He flew back to Cairo on the 24th prior to a journey to Ankara. In London the War Cabinet were summoned for a special meeting at 5 p.m. on this Monday. First, Ministers heard a grim report on the war in British skies; Portal stressed the vulnerability of Whitehall – although 146 HE bombs had already fallen within a thousand yards of the Cenotaph, 'we must be prepared for a considerably heavier attack'. The War Cabinet nevertheless agreed 'we should fight the battle from Whitehall, unless and until we were bombed out or our communications broke down'. In fact, during the 12 weeks from 19 February to 12 May, only 7 out of 61 raids involving more than 50 aircraft would be directed against London – but no less than 39 would be directed at Britain's western ports, terminal points for the Atlantic supply lines.

Spread on the Cabinet table were copies of optimistic signals from Wavell and Dill, together with a COS assessment. The latter seemed to present the gloomiest possible evidence, yet still advised approval for the Greek operation: only by going to Greece could a Balkan front be formed, said the COS, and Germany would be forced to fight at the end of a long communications line. But a Greek commitment would be endless and exhausting, using up Britain's strategic reserve in the Middle East and perhaps leaving none for Turkey or Egypt. 'The possible military advantages ... are considerable, though their achievement is doubtful and the risks of failure are serious. The disadvantages of leaving Greece to her fate will be certain and far reaching. Even the complete failure of an honourable attempt to help Greece need not be disastrous to our future ability to defeat Germany. A weighty consideration in favour of going to Greece is to make the Germans fight for what they want....' The COS boldly concluded: 'On balance we think the enterprise should go forward' but added: 'Every possible effort should be made to get the Turks and the Yugoslavs to join in the struggle on our side. Without the support of one or other our help to Greece is unlikely in the long run to have a favourable effect on the war situation as a whole.' And yet the Eden mission was firmly convinced that Turkish or Yugoslav help would not be forthcoming. The War Cabinet had therefore to make an extremely difficult and dangerous decision. Churchill prepared the way. First he covered himself by drawing 'particular attention' to his remark to Eden about avoiding 'another Norwegian fiasco'. In spite of this telegram, Churchill continued, Eden had recommended the enterprise – 'the telegrams received ... were impressive'. Churchill especially emphasized Wavell's opinion: 'Wavell was in favour of the operation, although he was inclined to understatement, and so far had always promised less than he had performed and was a man who wished to be better than his word.' He then turned to Dill's statement; the CIGS had 'always doubted whether Germany could be successfully resisted.... He had now sent a remarkable telegram to the Vice-CIGS.' Churchill reminded Ministers that the COS had, on balance, considered the enterprise should go forward and he added that pending a decision of the War Cabinet, he had given instructions for preparations to proceed. Churchill's hesitation had vanished with the arrival of Eden's telegram; he declared himself 'in favour of going to the rescue of Greece, the results of which might be to bring Turkey and Yugoslavia in, and to force the Germans to bring more troops from Germany. The reaction of the United States would also be favourable. On the other hand, the difficulties of maintaining an army on land must not be over-rated.' He felt, however, that 'if the Greeks were to fight the Germans we must fight and suffer with them. If any of his colleagues had misgivings about the enterprise they should express them now.' First to reply was Mr Robert Menzies, Australian Prime Minister, who attended War Cabinet meetings while visiting London. Before an Australian force could be employed in a new area of war he would have to communicate with his colleagues and he would like to be reassured on one or two points. 'How long, for instance, would it take to put our troops into Greece in order to take up defensive positions? Could our shipping maintain the strain of the operation?' Menzies was also 'a little uneasy' about the equipment for the 7th Australian Division, which was to be employed in the operation and which he said was at present equipped on a training scale. Churchill did not anticipate the German advance taking place until about 12-15 March, and British troops should arrive at their positions 'at about the same time'; the Vice-CIGS said 'Mr Menzies could rest assured that no Australian forces would be put into the line without the full establishment of the necessary weapons'. In answer to a question Portal said the RAF would have about 250 aircraft in Greece during March; the Germans had between 400 and 450 aircraft in Roumania, but not all of these were operational. Menzies pointed out that 'the justification for the enterprise rested upon the prospect of our being able to put up a good fight. If the enterprise was only a forlorn hope, it had better not be undertaken.' Could he say to his colleagues in Australia that 'the venture had a substantial chance of success'. Churchill evaded a direct answer. 'In the last resort this was a question which the Australian Cabinet must assess for themselves on Mr Menzies's advice. In my opinion the enterprise was a risk which we must undertake. At the worst I think that the bulk of the men could be got back to Egypt. Churchill added that he believed the war turned on 'firstly, holding England, secondly, holding Egypt, thirdly, retaining command of the sea, fourthly, obtaining command of the air, and lastly, keeping open the American arsenals. The enterprise in Greece was an advance position which we could try to hold, without jeopardizing our main position.' In answer to another question, Sir Alexander Cadogan said Turkey was more likely to come into the war if the operation took place, but the Yugoslav position was obscure 'and I do not put high the prospects of her making a stand against Germany'. Churchill pointed out that 'the courage of the Serb race must not be forgotten. The Yugoslav Government was trembling, but the effect of our helping the Greeks might stiffen the resistance of the Balkan people.' Beaverbrook feared the enterprise would involve serious strain on shipping, 'particularly if it should prove necessary to withdraw our forces'. Churchill then asked Ministers to state individually whether they agreed with the Greek operation; all were in favour of sending the troops. The War Cabinet therefore asked Churchill to inform Eden of this approval, subject to similar approval from the Australian and New Zealand Governments. 'No need anticipate difficulties in either quarter,' cabled Churchill to Eden in the evening of the 24th. 'Therefore, while being under no illusions, we all send you the order "Full steam ahead".'[63] Symbolically, Monday, 24 February also saw the first small engagement between British and *Afrika Korps* troops in the North African desert, and the British suffered most.

Daily the Balkan situation slid from bad to disastrous. Eden reported from Ankara on the 26th that the Turks approved Britain's decision to help Greece, but refused to commit themselves to entering the war unless directly attacked. Next day, Eden heard Yugoslavia would defend her territory and would not allow passage to foreign troops, but she refused to say what her attitude would be if German armies marched through Bulgaria, *en route* for Greece. Ministers were informed on the 27th that New Zealand and Australia gave consent to their troops being used, although with considerable anxiety: Mr Menzies said his colleagues had made plain that had more time been available they would have 'sought advice' on the small size of the proposed force, and they could not agree to Australian troops taking part unless fully equipped and backed by detailed evacuation plans. The New Zealand Government had almost identical reservations. Churchill was nevertheless 'deeply moved by the messages from the Commonwealth and New Zealand Governments. They had responded magnificently to what was perhaps the most severe proposal ever put before the Dominion Governments.' The War Cabinet thereupon confirmed their decision of the 24th.[64] Also on the 27th the War Office asked General Wavell for an appreciation of the position in North Africa following the arrival of the German armoured formations; in his reply Wavell declared there was no evidence that more than one armoured brigade group had landed, and the distance to Benghazi, plus the poverty of communications and water, made it unlikely the enemy could maintain a large enough force to advance against Benghazi in the near future. A larger offensive was extremely unlikely before the end of the summer.[65] The War Office was apparently reassured; but two factors had to be taken into account, one of which had already been stressed by Cairo – the almost complete absence of intelligence sources in Italy's North African possessions, due to the Government's desire to avoid incidents before Italy entered the war. The second factor was Rommel.

Eden spent one more day in Ankara on the 28th, but the Turks still refused to commit themselves; the Foreign Secretary reported this lack of co-operation to London. 'Telegram from "A" at Angora, which puzzles me,' wrote Cadogan. 'It is couched in jaunty and self-satisfied terms talking of the "frankness" and "realism" of the Turks. The "reality" is that they won't do a damned thing.... What's bitten him?'[66] The Prime Minister also seemed concerned by Eden's non-reaction; he hastened to draft a telegram in reply: 'Obvious German move is to overrun Bulgaria, further to intimidate Turkey by threat of air attacks, force Greece out of the war and then turn on Yugoslavia, compelling her to obey; after which Turkey can be attacked or not.' Churchill, perhaps mindful of the COS assessment on the 24th that Turkish or Yugoslav support was essential, urged Eden to appeal again to Belgrade; he also stressed a possible escape route from a British commitment: if Eden felt no reasonable hope of a Balkan collapse being prevented, 'you should still retain power to liberate Greeks from any bargains and at the same time to liberate ourselves'.[67] On this last day of February, final orders were issued for the German offensive and, during the night, small advanced formations crept from Roumania across newly prepared Danube bridges into Bulgaria. The preliminary move upon Greece, 'Marita', had begun. Piloff, President of the Bulgarian Ministerial Council, left for Vienna on Saturday, 1 March, and signed the Tripartite Pact; Bulgaria's army now mobilized and began to take up positions along the Greek frontier, while the Yugoslav army remained inactive to avoid provocation. In London, the COS worried about another aspect of British aid to Greece: a report completed on 1 March estimated that the despatch and maintenance of an expeditionary force on the scale proposed would entail a total loss of 910,000 tons of imports over a 12-month period.[68] Fears expressed by Beaverbrook to the War Cabinet on the 24th were apparently correct, and unknown to the British the Battle of the Atlantic had already quietly begun; less than 24 hours before, Hitler had issued a further directive on the war against British shipping, finalizing respective navy and *Luftwaffe* roles. Main elements of the German 12th Army rumbled from Roumania across the frozen Danube on Sunday, 2 March, and roared through Bulgaria towards Greece. Eden and Dill hurried from Ankara to Athens during the afternoon and found, to their shocked dismay, that the Greek attitude had disastrously changed and the military situation been radically affected.

Then, for a space of almost three critical days, came a complete absence of reports from Eden. While 'long and painful' meetings were held in Athens from the night of 2 March to the night of 4 March, the Prime Minister and War Cabinet in London were kept totally uninformed both of the new situation and Eden's consequent decisions. Ministers meeting at 5 p.m. on the 3rd merely had Eden's telegram of 28 February describing his futile talks at Ankara, which had caused Cadogan so much bewilderment and which had so far not been read by Ministers. The official minutes do not record the War Cabinet's response, but according to Cadogan's diary: 'Everyone's reaction is the same – how *can* one account for the jaunty tone of a recital of *complete* failure? The Germans have swarmed over Bulgaria, and there we are.' Ministers were also informed that Atlantic shipping losses were now increasing at an alarming rate.[69] General Wavell had travelled back to Cairo to supervise the despatch of troops for Greece, and the first detachment sailed from Egypt on the 4th – Operation 'Lustre'. Also on the 4th, the Naval C-in-C Mediterranean, Admiral Sir Andrew Cunningham, warned London that transport of the 'Lustre' force would absorb the whole Fleet activity for two months and resources would be 'taxed to the limit' if not beyond; other offensive operations, including the occupation of Rhodes – 'Mandibles' – would be impossible.[70] While Eden struggled with the Greeks and still failed to inform London, Hitler hastened to bolster his position: the German Ambassador at Ankara assured President Inönü that no harm would come to the Turks unless the Turks took steps necessitating a change in German attitude; on the same day Prince Paul of Yugoslavia visited Hitler at Berchtesgaden and verbally committed his country to following Bulgaria's co-operative example. 'Prospects in the Balkans were not promising,' Churchill told the War Cabinet at 6.15 p.m. on this Tuesday. 'Bulgaria was now under German control. It looked as thought Greece would have to fight for her life, and as though Yugoslavia intended to take no action before she was surrounded.'

The Prime Minister's doubts had returned: he said 'no further telegram had yet been received from the Foreign Secretary.... No doubt he would report again as soon as he had returned to Egypt.' No British troops could arrive in Greece for another four days; 'if General Dill and General Wilson wished the movement to proceed, I would be most disinclined to issue countermanding orders. Nevertheless, I still think the Cabinet might wish to take a final view of the whole situation.'[71] This final view would however have to await more news, and adequate discussion would not be possible for another 24 hours.

'Speed is the thing that matters here,' wrote Rommel to his wife on 5 March; in London the War Office remained unaware of the efforts and activities of this 'obscure' General in the North African desert. Attention remained riveted on the Balkans and on soaring shipping losses in the Atlantic. At the Foreign Office a cable came from the Ambassador at Sofia to say he had broken relations with Bulgaria; and, also on the 5th, a long, startling signal at last arrived from Eden. His words caused immediate astonishment. 'I think his head is turned a little,' exclaimed Cadogan. The cable described the altered Greek attitude revealed to Eden on 2 March. 'On arrival here [Athens] we found a changed and disturbing situation and the atmosphere quite different.... General Papagos had on the last occasion insisted strongly that the withdrawal of all troops in Macedonia to the Aliakhmon line was the only sound military solution. We had expected that this withdrawal to the Aliakhmon line had already begun. Instead we found that no movement had in fact commenced.' Papagos claimed the previous decision had been dependent upon the receipt of an answer from the Yugoslavs as to their attitude, and now stated that in view of the German entry into Bulgaria, withdrawal was no longer possible since his troops would risk being caught on the move; withdrawal from Macedonia would moreover have serious political consequences inside Greece, while retirement from Albania would be impossible since Greek troops there were exhausted and outnumbered by the Italians. Papagos therefore wanted a complete switch from the previous decision to hold the Aliakhmon line: despite previous insistence that only this position was militarily feasible, he wanted to hold a line further forward near the Macedonian frontier – regardless of the risk of Germans arriving first. Adequate preparations would anyway be impossible and Papagos himself admitted this line could not be held for long. Eden had urged Wavell to come to Athens and discussions had taken place for the next 'indescribably anxious' two days, as the result of which Eden used the discretionary powers which Churchill's instructions had given him 'to act as he thinks best' in an emergency, and had made decisions revealed by Churchill to the War

Cabinet at 5.30 p.m. – and which Cadogan believed to have been beyond the scope of Eden's brief. Churchill began by telling Ministers that 'deprived of the guidance of General Metaxas, General Papagos seemed to have lost confidence'. Eden and his advisers had been faced with three alternatives: First, 'to attempt to dribble up our forces piecemeal to the Macedonian frontier. This was the course that General Papagos had wished to see pursued. We had refused to consider it.' Second: 'To accept the Greek offer of 16 to 23 battalions for the Aliakhmon line instead of the 35 battalions which we had been led to expect and to build up our concentration behind this.' Third: 'to withdraw our offer of military support altogether.' Churchill added that 'after some misgiving', Eden and his advisers had reached agreement with the Greeks on the second solution, with the proviso that the command and organization of the Aliakhmon line should be entrusted to General Wilson. Eden had declared: 'Military advisers ... did not consider it by any means a hopeless proposition to check and hold the German advance on this line.' British forces would nonetheless be obliged to fight with less Greek support, with inadequate preparations and with a deficient communications system. The First Sea Lord read the latest COS appreciation to the anxious War Cabinet. 'We were to have had 35 Greek battalions to help us hold the line. We are now told that we are to have 3 Greek divisions and 7 battalions from Western Thrace, but that these only amount to 23 battalions at the most. With the exception of the 12th Division these are all newly formed and have not yet fought. One of the divisions can hardly have any guns, and the remainder can only have captured Italian material. But, in addition to the 35 battalions for which we had hoped, we had contemplated that the Greeks would be able to draw some of their divisions from the Albanian front. General Papagos now says that this cannot be done as they are "exhausted and outnumbered". We have always contemplated that "Mandibles" [Rhodes] would be captured before – or at least simultaneously with – the move to Greece. But it now appears that "Mandibles" cannot be undertaken until the movement to Greece has been completed. This means that instead of being able to concentrate all available air forces against the German advance, considerable air operations will have to be conducted against "Mandibles" in order to protect our line of communications to Greece. The mining of the Suez Canal has become a more acute handicap. It was to have been opened on 3 March, but the Germans put in 10 more mines that day. The canal is now completely closed. ... We have no means of knowing how much delay will be imposed on a German advance.... If the delay is short, we should at the best have one armoured brigade and one New Zealand brigade to oppose the first two German divisions on the Aliakhmon line.' The Chiefs

of Staff gave their verdict: 'Our conclusion is that the hazards of
the enterprise have considerably increased. Nevertheless, despite
our misgivings and our recognition of the worsening of the situation,
we are not as yet in a position to question the military advice of
those on the spot.' Pound reminded Ministers of the COS report of
24 February, which had declared that: 'The possible military
advantages to be derived from going to the help of Greece are considerable, though their achievement is doubtful and the risks of
failure are serious.... On balance we think that the enterprise
should go forward,' and he said the COS did not wish to alter this
previous decision. Churchill recalled the written instructions given
to Eden, which had authorized him not to hesisate to act on his
own authority if matters were too urgent to allow time for referring
back to London, and he then read a further personal telegram from
Eden in which he said he saw no alternative between encouraging
Greece 'to the best of her power to resist', and 'standing by and
allowing her to collapse before the German threats'. While the proposition was a taut one, 'neither he nor his advisers saw any alternative to doing our best to see it through'.

Churchill made another attempt to retain freedom of action. If
the Greeks had taken any steps or entered into any commitments
on the strength of undertakings received from Britain, then 'we
should have no alternative but to go through with the plan'. However, Churchill continued: 'As far as we could see, they had taken
no such action. Indeed, they had not taken the steps which we had
expected'; he added: 'It was still open to us, if on consideration
this seemed the wisest course, to tell the Greeks that we would
liberate them from any undertaking which they had given to us. It
would follow of course that the Greeks would be free to make terms
with Germany.' Cadogan feared that if Greece were abandoned it
might have bad effect in Spain and in North Africa. Churchill
replied that the effect in these areas would be worse 'if we landed
in Greece and were driven out'. The War Cabinet finally agreed
that no immediate decision was necessary and 'the position should
be kept fluid and no further commitments entered into'. Churchill
was invited to draft and despatch a telegram to Eden setting out
doubts expressed in the meeting.[72] The Prime Minister was clearly
hesitating. Members of the Defence Committee, meeting at 10 p.m.,
heard him declare that 'in the face of a German ultimatum the
Greeks would find it impossible to carry on the struggle. There was
little or nothing which we could do to assist them in time.' He had
drafted the telegram to Eden and believed this should be accompanied by the COS assessment; Pound asked for further time to
prepare this commentary for despatch, and the meeting adjourned
for 30 minutes, after which Churchill's telegram and the assessment

were approved. Ministers agreed 'there must have been some factor unknown in this country which influenced the Foreign Secretary and the CIGS to consider that there was still a chance of holding up the German advance.'[73] Churchill's signal therefore sought further information, failing which he warned the War Cabinet would probably seek to change Eden's decision. Information so far supplied, cabled Churchill, made it difficult for the War Cabinet to believe 'we now have any power to avert fate of Greece unless Turkey and/or Yugoslavia come in, which seems improbable.... We must be careful not to urge Greece against her better judgment into a hopeless resistance alone when we have only a handful of troops which can reach scene in time.... We must liberate Greeks from feeling bound to reject a German ultimatum. If on their own they resolve to fight, we must to some extent share their ordeal. But rapid German advance will probably prevent any appreciable British Imperial forces from being engaged.' Churchill concluded: 'I send you this to prepare your mind for what, in the absence of facts very different from those now before us, will probably be expressed in Cabinet decision tomorrow.'[74]

In his memoirs Churchill claimed he sent this message 'after reflecting alone at Chequers on the Sunday night upon the Chiefs of Staff paper and the trend of discussion in the War Cabinet that morning'.[75] In fact, Churchill was not alone but was attending a Defence Committee meeting; he was at 10 Downing Street, not Chequers; the time was Wednesday night, not Sunday; the War Cabinet had been held in the evening, not in the morning. The inaccuracies perhaps help reveal the strain of those anxious days, caused not only by the Balkan situation, but by Atlantic sinkings, by Malta, and even by the manpower problem: a directive by the Prime Minister next day, 6 March, warned that to achieve the programme of 60 Field Force divisions, British manpower would be at full stretch and further expansion impossible except at the expense of one of the other services or of essential industries. This meant the army would not be large enough to play a primary role in defeating the enemy, except by resisting invasion. 'That task can only be done by the staying power of the navy and above all, by the effect of air predominance.'[76] Yet the navy's staying power and most other factors in Britain's ability to wage war were in turn affected by essential imports and, also, on 6 March, Churchill issued a directive which declared: 'We must assume that the Battle of the Atlantic has begun.' The paper listed means to be employed in defeating Germany's attempt 'to strangle our food supplies and our connection with the United States'.[77] Latest losses in shipping were soon to become a regular War Cabinet feature, and from 19 March to 8 May a new group formed by Churchill, the Battle of the

Atlantic Committee, would hold weekly meetings. Tonnage losses, rising sharply in March, were to become critical in April; in the words of the official war historian: 'No offensive operations by land or air, in Europe or elsewhere, could save us from defeat if we lost, even for a few weeks, the power to bring in the food and raw materials and armaments without which we could not fight or live.'[78] Germany's ability to wage this deadly struggle was rapidly increasing: whereas only 32 U-boats were operational in March – although these accounted for 42 ships totalling 817,877 tons – by July the U-boat fleet would comprise almost twice this number; and German aircraft sank 157 ships in March, April and May, totalling 583,070 tons.[79] Also on the day of Churchill's orders for the Battle of the Atlantic, Hitler issued a further directive: despite plans for the attack on Russia, the principal navy target would be Britain, and pressure must be maintained against her supply routes – the *Luftwaffe* would continue raids against Britain and especially against her Atlantic ports. 'This mortal danger to our lifelines gnawed to my bowels,' wrote Churchill.[80]

Meanwhile, the problem of the Balkans remained unsolved and Ministers met again at 6 p.m. on this Thursday, 6 March. First Portal said particulars had just been received of 'a very heavy air attack on Malta the previous day'. Renewed enemy interest in Malta seemed ominous: only 48 hours before Admiral Cunningham had warned that aid to Greece would leave no naval resources for other commitments. Ministers had before them a jumble of telegrams and messages, including an assesment sent from Athens on the German military position, copies of two telegrams from the British Ambassador at Athens, Sir Michael Palairet, to Eden at Cairo and a signal from Eden containing the text of the agreement signed by Generals Dill and Papagos: through this signature, aimed no doubt at preventing further change in the Greek attitude, Britain was formally committed to the expedition as decided upon by Eden, unless Greece agreed to relieve her ally from these obligations. Cadogan commented: 'A has evidently committed us up to the hilt,' and he wrote to Halifax a few days later: 'When this was revealed to them [the War Cabinet], it gave rise to mixed emotions in some of the members – annoyance they should have been rushed in this way, secret satisfaction that if the thing went wrong there was a good scapegoat handy!'[81] But the long list of telegrams before the War Cabinet had one glaring gap: Eden's reply to Churchill's urgent telegram seeking more information. The Prime Minister's message had evidently reached the Middle East some time before: a copy of one of Sir Michael Palairet's telegrams to Eden revealed the Ambassador's anxiety at Churchill's hint of a new War Cabinet decision – 'I have just read the Prime Minister's message to you.

I need not emphasize to you the effect of our now withdrawing from the agreement actually signed by CIGS and Greek C-in-C and now in process of execution here by General Wilson.... There is no question of "liberating the Greeks from feeling bound to reject the [German] ultimatum". They have decided to fight Germany alone if necessary. The question is whether we help or abandon them.' Palairet, like Cadogan, apparently believed Britain already committed by Eden's and Dill's actions. Churchill however maintained his attempt to preserve War Cabinet initiative, albeit in an indirect manner. 'The aspect of the situation which had caused me most anxiety,' he told Ministers, 'was lest the Greeks might feel that we had put undue pressure on them, and persuaded them to put up a hopeless resistance against their better judgment.' Whereas Palairet had implied the world would condemn Britain for going back on her word and abandoning yet another small country, Churchill now claimed that if Britain went ahead she might be condemned because 'we had caused another small nation to be sacrificed without being able to afford effective help'. But he was forced to recognize that all now depended on the Greeks: 'If ... the Greeks were really determined to fight, knowing the limitations of the help we could give them, we had no choice but to carry out the agreement reached at Athens.' No decision could be taken until a reply had come from Eden to 'the very searching questions', continued Churchill, but he felt Eden would take the same line as Palairet. He also felt the chances of military success must be greater than so far indicated: 'It was inconceivable that the CIGS could have signed the military agreement with General Papagos if he regarded the chances of success in the operation as hopeless.' After Churchill's somewhat desperate discourse came a frank, realistic – and accurate – statement to the War Cabinet by Menzies, the Australian Prime Minister. The problem had been presented in a way that made it unduly difficult, he complained. When the War Cabinet had arrived at their earlier decision to send military aid to Greece, the military advisers in the Middle East had stated the operation, though hazardous, offered a reasonable chance of resisting the German advance. 'All new factors brought out in recent telegrams added to the difficulties of the operation and no reason was offered why the operation should succeed.' The War Cabinet had not been kept well-informed, Menzies complained, and 'the action of the Foreign Secretary regarding the military agreement between General Dill and General Papagos was embarrassing'. The situation might be presented in one of two ways to the Dominions, he continued; the first was to tell them that the proposition did not look as good as it had done before, but as the Greeks had decided to fight on they could not be left in the lurch, and some chance of success remained.

If the proposition was presented in this fashion, Menzies felt confident of the reception it would receive in the Dominions. The second way was to say 'the proposition was a bad one, but it must be proceeded with because we had been committed by an agreement signed in Athens, which had not been referred home'. Menzies reminded the War Cabinet that the Dominions were providing three-fifths of the force to be used. 'If they were told that they were now committed to the use of their forces in a situation which had definitely worsened, without further effective consultation ... there would be a great deal of resentment.' After hearing this depressingly truthful assessment, the War Cabinet 'deferred decision until the following day, when it was expected the Foreign Secretary's reply would have been received'.[82] They could do nothing else.

A short, interim and uninformative reply to Churchill's 'searching questions' reached London from Cairo at 10.10 p.m. 'Begins. CIGS and I in consultation with three C-in-Cs have this afternoon re-examined the question. Unanimously agree that despite heavy commitments and grave risks which are undoubtedly involved, especially in view of our limited naval and air resources, the right decision was taken in Athens. Ends.' At 2.15 a.m. on the 7th came one more sentence from Eden: 'We have had further discussion this evening with General Smuts and C-in-Cs and further detailed appreciation follows tomorrow morning.' Forty minutes later Churchill sent a long cable to Eden which began: 'I am deeply impressed by steadfast attitude maintained by you and your military advisers.' But Churchill added that two points were dominant: 'We must not take on our shoulders responsibility of urging the Greeks against their better judgment to fight a hopeless battle.... If however, knowing how little we can send at particular dates, they resolve to fight to the death, obviously we must, as I have already said, share their ordeal'; second – and Churchill's words reflected Menzies' statement to the War Cabinet – 'it happens that most of the troops to be devoted to this solemn duty are the New Zealand Division and, after March, the Australians. We must be able to tell the Australian and New Zealand Governments faithfully that this hazard from which they will not shrink, is undertaken, not because of any commitment entered into by a British Cabinet Minister and signed by the CIGS, but because Dill, Wavell and other C-in-Cs are convinced that there is a reasonable fighting chance.... Please remember in your stresses that so far you have given us few facts or reasons on their authority which can be presented to the Dominions as justifying the operation on any grounds but *noblesse oblige*.' Another brief item from Cairo arrived at 3.45 a.m.: 'General Wavell has explained to Generals Blamey and Freyberg [Australian and New Zealand commanders] additional risks involved in venture in

Greece under existing situation. Both have expressed their willingness to undertake operations under new conditions.' The War Cabinet were handed these telegrams at noon on the 7th, plus a telegram from Palairet describing a 'marked improvement' in Papagos's attitude. Pound said information had also been received from the C-in-Cs, Middle East, who believed the COS had underestimated by 'from one to four days the time which it would take the Germans to reach the Alaikhmon line.... Our military advisers on the spot were convinced that the Greek campaign would not be a hopeless venture. The Chiefs of Staff are prepared to accept their judgment ... that the campaign should go forward.' Bevin commented that the advice from the C-in-Cs was given added value from not having been proffered under political pressure. 'Indeed, the political pressure had been in the opposite direction.' Churchill listed a number of considerations, most of them exceedingly frail, which seemed to him important. 'We had a fair chance of reaching the Aliakhmon line in time to check the German advance. If so, there might be a pause while the enemy brought up new forces. The Yugoslavs were adopting a cryptic attitude, but we need not despair entirely of their entry into the war on our side. If the Anglo-Greek force were compelled to retire from the Aliakhmon line they would be retiring down a narrowing peninsula, which contained a number of strong defensive positions. We should shortly have strong air forces in Greece. They would be outnumbered by the enemy's air forces, but the odds would not be greater than they had been on many occasions in the last few months.' Churchill added that British policy could not be presented as having forced the Greeks into making hopeless resistance and he concluded 'his view was that we should go forward with a good heart'. Churchill had therefore managed to convince himself. Menzies, although saying he 'found himself in agreement with the Prime Minister', added 'it was curious that, while a decision was being taken in virtue of the trust which we reposed in the judgment of our advisers in the Middle East ... the arguments with which they had supplied us told against, rather than in favour of, their advice.' Churchill said a military appreciation was on the way from Cairo to supply detailed arguments, 'but we know the conclusions already. The time had now come for taking decisions. In his view it was our duty to go forward.' The War Cabinet agreed and invited the New Zealand and Australian Governments to give their assent.[83] After the meeting Churchill therefore signalled to Eden: 'Cabinet decided to authorize you to proceed with the operation and by doing so Cabinet accepted for itself the fullest responsibility.'[84]

A telegram arrived from Smuts at Cairo. 'We should not leave

Greece alone at this grave juncture and the consequences of such a step now might be worse in their effects on the Balkans and on our cause generally than even a possible setback in action. But the risk of such a setback is very real.' And during the late afternoon of the 7th answers to Churchill's questions of 5 March finally arrived from Eden, now totally irrelevant. Eden repeated there was no question of urging Greece against her better judgment, and he rejected any charge that his decision had pushed Britain into a new commitment – 'We have already undertaken commitments towards Greece. Eight squadrons of the RAF ground defence and anti-aircraft personnel have been operating there for months past.' Eden apparently saw no difference between this small presence and the despatch of over 50,000 troops. He stressed the effects on the Balkans if British help was not forthcoming: 'Collapse of Greece without further effort on our part to save her by intervention on land, after the Libyan victories had, as the world knows, made forces available, would be the greatest calamity. Yugoslavia would then certainly be lost; nor can we feel confident that even Turkey would have the strength to remain steadfast.' A further telegram reached London from Eden at 8.35 p.m. 'We are all convinced not only that there is a reasonable fighting chance, but that we have here an opportunity, if fortune favours, of perhaps seriously upsetting the German plans. It very much depends on the air.' Once again, no firm reasons were put forward to explain Eden's conviction.[85] An uneasy lull now fell upon the diplomatic front. In Belgrade, the Yugoslav Government still attempted to protect themselves by finding some accommodation with the Nazis; in Cairo, Eden remained helpless but hopeful. The New Zealand and Australian Governments signalled their assent to their troops being used. Militarily the Greeks were further extended and weakened in Albania after repulsing a new Italian offensive on 9 March. The British 1st Armoured Brigade landed and began to move north, but these troops would not reach the forward area until 27 March. British air strength in Greece only totalled about 80 operational aircraft; the Germans were able to employ over 800 operational aircraft and yet, as Eden had commented: 'It very much depends on the air.' The War Cabinet were informed on Monday, 10 March, that 'there had been no definite diplomatic developments in the Balkans. The Yugoslav Government had sent an officer to Athens to consult with General Wavell's Chief of Staff, but had made it clear that this step did not mean any definite commitment.'

Another unwelcome subject now returned to the War Cabinet agenda: night bombing on London had been resumed. Ministers at this 10 March meeting heard details of attacks made on the 8th and 9th: damage had resulted in about 50 London boroughs, said the Home Secretary, especially in Westminster, Lambeth, Southwark and the docks area, with about 184 people killed. Portal claimed that the C-in-C, Fighter Command, was satisfied that 'definite, although slow, progress was being made with night interception of aircraft. Improvement was also being shown in AA defence.'[86] This meeting, held in the emergency HQ in North London, was chaired by Attlee: Churchill was suffering from bronchitis. But his recent depression had been eased by invigorating news from Washington two days before; exactly a month after Churchill had made a public appeal to the Americans – 'Give us the tools and we will finish the job' – Hopkins had cabled to say the Lend-Lease Bill would soon become law. 'Thank God for your news,' replied Churchill on the 9th. 'Strain is serious.' He cabled Roosevelt the same day: 'Our blessings from the whole British Empire go out to you and the American nation.'[87] The Lend-Lease Bill received Roosevelt's assent on Tuesday, 11 March, and the President was thereby authorized to 'sell, transfer title to, exchange, lease, lend or otherwise dispose of ... any defence article' to any nation whose defence he deemed vital to US security. American production was, for the moment, restricted, and it would take time for money to be allocated to procurement agencies and for expansion to turn into deliveries. Nevertheless, in London discussions on an import programme were immediately held with the new American Ambassador, John G. Winant. But the availability of aid from America made it all the more important the Battle of the Atlantic should be won, and frightening information was given to the War Cabinet on Monday afternoon, 17 March. Shipping losses during the previous four days amounted to 27,000 tons and the actual total could be much higher – seven ships totalling about 25,000 tons had been attacked the previous day, 'although it was not yet known if all seven had been sunk'. Churchill warned: 'The position resulting from the present shipping losses presented a most formidable problem and one which must be tackled by every means in our power. We were at the moment completely on the defensive at sea and the Admiralty had had to disperse many important units from the Home Fleet for convoy duties and to hunt the raiders on the Atlantic routes ... A very heavy toll had been taken of our merchant shipping.' Churchill added that 'at the present time our naval resources were at a fuller stretch than they had been at any time during the last war'. Churchill had been considering means whereby US assistance could be obtained and had had a highly interesting – and dangerous – conversation with the new US Ambassador and Averell Harriman, now acting as Hopkins' representative in London. 'One method of relieving our difficulties,' Churchill now told the War Cabinet, 'would be if the US would convoy ships west of the

30th Meridian. Another way would be if the US would allow some of their warships to cruise in the Atlantic and to pass on to us information obtained by them as to the whereabouts of German raiders. Such an act would be less un-neutral than the convoying of ships.' He added that he had been 'greatly encouraged' by the attitude shown by Harriman and Winant. 'These two gentlemen were apparently longing for Germany to commit some overt act that would relieve the President of his election and pre-election declaration regarding keeping out of the war. Mr Harriman had said that the US ships would take over the long hauls, leaving us the short hauls.' The Prime Minister concluded: 'Our shipping loss difficulties were the blackest cloud that we had to face. But we must remember that we had dealt with and overcome equal perils in the past.'[88] Ironically, the German naval chief was attempting to pursue the very policy which Winant and Harriman wished the Germans to adopt: Admiral Raeder saw Hitler next day, 18 March, reported that American warships were escorting US convoys bound for Britain as far as Iceland and demanded authority to attack them without warning.[89] But the Führer had sufficient cares without America being brought into the war; like Churchill, he was having to consider too many aspects in too many areas at the same time. Fears were growing of a British attack on the North French Coast or upon Norway – with the latter German apprehension had increased after the successful British raid on the Lofoten Islands on 4 March. And, at a staff conference on 17 March, Hitler reluctantly agreed that certain elements intended for 'Barbarossa' would have to be diverted to the offensive on Greece in view of the movement of British troops to bolster Greek forces. Meanwhile, Hitler increased attempts to press the Yugoslavs into the war on the Axis side.

Eden had received new instructions from Churchill on 14 March: 'It is better for you to stay in Middle East until opening phase of this crisis has matured.'[90] Campbell, British Ambassador in Belgrade, reported the Yugoslavs were weakening and might join the Axis, and Eden therefore sent another appeal to the Prince Regent on 17 March suggesting Sir John Dill should visit Belgrade for talks. Prince Paul politely refused. 'Indications of the position in Yugoslavia were somewhat conflicting,' said Churchill at the War Cabinet meeting on the 17th. The Vice-CIGS admitted he had no recent news on the progress of British troop moves to Greece: he thought the reason why the Germans had not yet moved over the Bulgaria-Greece border was probably due to doubts over Yugoslavia's attitude, weather conditions, and perhaps the wish to wait for the result of the Italian offensive in Albania.[91] At their next meeting, at noon on Thursday the 20th, Ministers were informed that Eden had had 'a satisfactory discussion in Cyprus on the Tuesday with Sarajoglu,

Turkish Foreign Minister: the latter had considered it vital Yugo-slavia should hold out against German pressure and he doubted whether Hitler would risk an attack on Greece if they did so; he had agreed to send a message to the Yugoslav Government, and Churchill commented on the "encouraging attitude displayed".[92] Ministers at this meeting also heard that a German raid on London the previous night had been one of the heaviest so far. About 200 enemy aircraft had taken part, and at one time about 50 had pene-trated to the inner artillery zone – 'the highest at any time in the war'. Yet at a War Cabinet meeting on the 13th, only one week before, Portal had claimed increasingly effective measures against enemy night bombing: 'In December we had destroyed one bomber in every 326 which had come over. In January one in every 110. In February one in every 95. In the first 12 days of March, one in 63.'[93] Cadogan wrote in his diary a comment Churchill had made after the War Cabinet meeting on the 20th. 'I'm not afraid of the air,' he had apparently said. 'I'm not afraid of invasion. I'm less afraid of the Balkans, but – I am anxious about the Atlantic.'[94] Within hours another worry was added to Churchill's list – and the Balkan situa-tion had severely slipped.

Rommel had flown to Hitler's HQ the previous day to report his North African preparations: he was disappointed to hear 'there was no intention of striking a decisive blow in Africa in the near future'. He himself intended to exploit British weaknesses. While Rommel conferred with Hitler, Wavell toured forward positions commanded by General Philip Neame, and was appalled by the dispositions and by the state of the Cruiser tanks. 'There was nothing much I could do about it,' wrote Wavell later. 'The movement to Greece was in full swing and I had nothing left in the bag.'[95] Next day, 20 March, Wavell reported to London that an enemy attack on a limited scale seemed to be in preparation and that the situation on the Cyrenaica front was causing him anxiety: if British advance positions were taken no good blocking points existed south of Benghazi.[96] German military preparations in Bulgaria were nearing completion and Hitler presented an ultimatum to Yugoslavia on Saturday, 22 March: Belgrade had until the 25th to sign the Tripar-tite Pact. Also on the 22nd, Churchill appealed to Dr Cvetkovic, Yugoslav Premier: 'If Yugoslavia were at this time to stoop to the fate of Roumania, or commit the crime of Bulgaria and become accomplice in an attempted assassination of Greece, her ruin will be certain and irreparable.'[97] But at a secret session on the 21st the Yugoslav Government had already decided upon their fate – a decision which was revealed to British Ministers in the course of a War Cabinet meeting on Monday, 24 March. This meeting opened at 10 Downing Street at 5 p.m. with gloomy information on sinkings in the Atlantic, on the over-stretch of the Royal Navy and on recent terrible bombing damage. Since 20 March about 10,000 tons of shipping had been lost and 35,000 tons damaged. The German battle-cruisers *Scharnhorst* and *Gneisenau*, constant threats to British merchantmen when at sea, had been sighted on the 20th by an aircraft from *Ark Royal*, 600 miles off Cape Finisterre, and the Prime Minister warned: 'While the *Scharnhorst* and *Gneisenau* were at large in the Atlantic, every important convoy had to be escorted by a big ship.... Our naval resources were stretched to their fullest limit. The Home Fleet was now dispersed and no attempt was being made to assert our command of the North Sea. Fortunately, at the moment there were no indications of imminent invasion and the dispersed naval units could be concentrated within about a week.' A note was hurried into the Cabinet Room; Ministers were informed that 'according to a message just received from Belgrade, the Yugoslav Prime Minister and Foreign Minister were leaving that night for Vienna to sign a pact with Germany'. Nothing more could be done; even discussion seemed useless. Eden prepared to fly home.[98]

Rommel had returned to the desert the previous day, 23 March. Before his visits to Berlin and Rome, he had instructed his 5th Light Division to plan a limited assault on the British detachment at Agheila on the Tripoli border; now, on the 24th, the attack went in and British deficiencies were revealed. Rommel prepared for a further advance. As Eden and Dill were taking off from the Nile on Tuesday, 25 March, heading for Malta, the ceremony of Yugo-slavia's signing the Tripartite Pact was being broadcast over German and Belgrade radios. Almost immediately unrest began to grow in the Yugoslav capital. Churchill's hope revived and he sent urgent instructions to Campbell, Ambassador at Belgrade, on the 26th: 'Do not let any gap grow up between you and Prince Paul or Minis-ters. Don't take NO for an answer.... This is no time for reproaches or dignified farewells.' Also on the 26th, Churchill sent an anxious cable to Wavell: 'We are naturally concerned at rapid German advance to Agheila. It is their habit to push on whenever they are not resisted.'[99] Wavell believed administrative problems would pre-vent a large-scale enemy offensive, but in his reply to Churchill on the 27th he warned: 'I have to admit to having taken considerable risk in Cyrenaica after capture of Benghazi in order to provide maximum support for Greece.'

This Thursday, 27 March, was hectic and eventful. In Washing-ton, the American and British staff talks ended with the completion of the ABC-1 report, which laid down the first declaration of com-mon strategic principles between the United States and the British Commonwealth, including the recognition that the Atlantic-

European area would be decisive, involving the principal US military effort, while a war against Japan would be fought on defensive lines. An additional report, ABC-2, recommended an increase in heavy bomber production to support a sustained air offensive against Germany. In London, Robert Menzies was warned at a special meeting that Britain would incur great danger in a war against Japan, without American support, and he was also told that air reinforcements to Singapore could not be sent immediately.[100] In Berlin, the Japanese Foreign Minister was being entertained by Ribbentrop; Matsuoka was urged to press for Japan to launch a 'quick attack upon Singapore.... The capture of Singapore would perhaps be most likely to keep America out of the war because the United States could scarcely risk sending its fleet into Japanese waters.'

Belgrade was by now in turmoil. Delighted British Ministers were told at the War Cabinet meeting this Thursday that 'a military *coup d'état* had taken place in Yugoslavia in the small hours of that morning'. The President of the Council and a number of Ministers, including the War Minister, had been placed under arrest; young King Peter had taken the Royal authority out of the hands of the Regent and had entrusted the Government to General Simovitch; Churchill commented: 'The repudiation of the Government which had signed the three-power Pact was a clear rebuff to our enemies,' and said he had asked Eden and Dill to return at once to Cairo; he had also authorized the Ambassador at Belgrade to inform the new Government that, on the basis they were determined to denounce the pact with Germany and to help in the defence of peace, Britain was prepared to give recognition. Churchill had sent a message to the Turkish President urging action, and he had telegraphed Roosevelt, informing him of measures taken. Finally, he had given instructions to Portal to bring to higher strength RAF bomber squadrons in Greece. The War Cabinet approved.[101] Hitler had also been active. Thrown into one of the most frenzied rages of his life, the frantic Führer ordered his military chiefs 'to destroy Yugoslavia militarily as a nation', without warning and with 'unmerciless harshness'. The *Luftwaffe* would obliterate Belgrade. Yugoslav remains would be tossed to Hungary, Roumania and Italy. But, he declared: 'The beginning of the "Barbarossa" operation will have to be postponed up to four weeks.' Keitel wrote: 'The decision to attack Yugoslavia meant completely upsetting all military movements and arrangements made up to that time. "Marita" (the move on Greece) had to be completely readjusted.' Only a few hours before, the first British troops had reached the weak and inadequate Aliakhmon line. Temporarily, the tide continued to surge in Britain's favour. Forces in Eritrea, held up for some weeks by Italian mountain defences at Keren, broke through on the 27th and pushed for the

Red Sea coast; Abyssinia operations were also proving successful – General Cunningham's forces were making for Addis Ababa. And, to complete Italian discomfort, warships under Admiral Cunningham, brother of the commander in Abyssinia, won the brilliant victory of Cape Matapan on the 28th in which the enemy battleship *Vittorio Veneto* was damaged and three 8-inch cruisers were destroyed. In Belgrade, crowds cheered King Peter and spat at the German Ambassador, while in London the Joint Intelligence Committee reported that if the Yugoslav army attacked the Italians in co-operation with Greek units, Mussolini's forces might be eliminated within three weeks; the report added that a German attack on Yugoslavia would be delayed by bad terrain and weak communications.[102] This assessment was apparently given credence by a message from Simovitch to the British Air Attaché in Belgrade: the army was being fully mobilized and an attack on the Italians in Albania was imminent.[103] Eden returned to Athens and managed to secure an invitation for Dill to visit Belgrade: the CIGS would leave on the 31st.

But next day, 29 March, warmth had begun to disperse from the new situation. Eden realized the implications of Simovitch's message to the British Attaché; the Yugoslav army was in the process of being mobilized, but why had this not been done already? On the 29th the British Ambassador managed to see the Yugoslav Prime Minister, and was told the new Government intended to seek time: the Tripartite Pact would not be ratified, but neither would it be denounced; the Yugoslav army would not move until the Germans attacked Salonica, and Simovitch asked Britain not to force him to undertake any action likely to provoke Hitler.[104] Despite the cooling atmosphere, some optimism remained when the War Cabinet met on Monday, 31 March. Good news had been received concerning the *Scharnhorst* and *Gneisenau*: these two massive raiders had not been sailing for another sortie in the Atlantic, as feared on the 24th, but had made for Brest where they had been attacked by 95 RAF bombers the previous night. 'A number of bombs straddled the ships,' reported Portal. Ministers then discussed the Balkan situation, with Churchill expressing admiration for Eden's 'vigorous handling' of affairs. Turkey's short-sighted policy had placed her in a precarious position, he continued, and Eden had instructed the British Ambassador to warn the Turks of the dangers in continuing to stand alone and aloof. With the approval of Menzies, Churchill had cabled the Australian Cabinet, pointing out how greatly events had moved in Britain's favour since the decision to send British Imperial troops to Greece. 'Enough has already happened,' added Churchill, 'to remove any doubts about the rightness of our decision.'[105]

The previous day Wavell had signalled to Neame in Cyrenaica:
'I do not believe that he [Rommel] can make any big effort for
another month.' Now, on the 31st, Rommel proceeded to prove him
very wrong: *Afrika Korps* units moved against British forward
positions at Mers el Brega and after fierce fighting swept onwards;
Rommel was acting against orders, but he wrote: '*Luftwaffe* reports
clearly showed that the enemy was tending to draw back.... It was
a chance I could not resist.'[106]

Dill arrived at Belgrade that evening; the statements made by
Simovitch to the British Ambassador on the 29th were repeated
with great emphasis, but the CIGS managed to secure agreement
for staff talks at Florina, just over the Greek border, and for Yugoslav signature to a brief statement declaring that if the Germans
attacked Greece, the Yugoslav Government would join with Britain
in giving Greece all possible aid. In return Britain would give all
possible aid to help Yugoslavia if the latter were attacked by Germany. But next morning, 1 April, the Yugoslav Premier refused to
sign the statement and now said staff talks could only comprise an
exchange of ideas; a visit by Eden was out of the question.[107] A
disappointed Dill returned to Athens on 2 April, where he
attended discussions with Eden and Papagos; the three agreed to go
to the Florina talks the following day, but Eden and Dill would
stay in the background. Also on the 2nd, Eden was 'mystified' by a
telegram from Wavell, 'which, when referring to reluctance to send
staff officers to our talks, speaks of enemy attack in Western Desert.
We know nothing of this from any other sources.' Eden was reassured by General Maitland Wilson who believed that if the enemy
attacked in the desert 'we should have them where we want them'.[108]
Wavell however was becoming increasingly concerned and now even
faced the possibility of having to evacuate Benghazi, taken so
triumphantly less than two months before. 'Some forward posts
were overrun yesterday,' he reported to the COS on 2 April, and
he said the mechanical conditions of the Armoured Brigade were
causing Neame much anxiety. 'As I can produce no more armoured
units for at least three or four weeks, I have warned him to keep
three bridges in being, even it if involves considerable withdrawal,
possibly from Benghazi.'[109] Churchill, still buoyed up by Wavell's
previous optimistic assessment of limited enemy strength, was not
unduly concerned, although he cabled to Wavell: 'It seems most
desirable to chop the German advance.... Any rebuff to the
Germans would have far-reaching prestige effects ... any serious
withdrawal from Benghazi would appear most melancholy.' During
the day, German units consolidated around Agedabia, British troops
pulled back to Antelat, and Rommel moved his HQ into the battle
line. Wavell also decided to go up to the front. As he prepared

to fly to one end of his vast command area, a black trouble cloud was forming in Iraq: the pro-Axis Rashid Ali seized power during the day, forcing the Regent to seek safety on a British gunboat at Basra. Through Iraq passed the land route to the Persian Gulf and the oil pipelines to the Mediterranean; only a few days before Basra had first been considered as a possible port for the trans-shipment of US supplies to the Middle East. Hitler now decided to sell Rashid Ali 'arms of the best quality'.[110]

While British Foreign Office officials studied the implications of the Iraqi developments, steps were also attempted to prevent another country from falling further into Hitler's control. The Hungarian Ambassador at London sent an urgent signal to Budapest: the Foreign Office had stated formally that if Hungary took part in any German move against Yugoslavia she must expect a British declaration of war. Soon after receiving this warning during the evening of the 2nd, the Hungarian Premier also received news that German forces had already crossed the frontier: Count Teleki thereupon shot himself. Churchill was meanwhile attempting to give another warning, this time to the Japanese. He sent a courteous message during the day to Matsuoka, the Japanese Foreign Minister, now visiting Moscow on his European travels: Japan, advised Churchill, should think twice before provoking a war against Britain and America. A telegram arrived from Halifax during the night: Mr Welles had given him a report of Hitler's statement to Prince Paul of Yugoslavia the previous month, in which the Führer had declared his intentions to attack Russia. Welles also said that Göring had told Matsuoka that Germany intended to launch this offensive immediately after an attack on Britain. As a result of this and other reports, Churchill decided on 3 April to send a personal warning to Stalin; this he transmitted to Sir Stafford Cripps with instructions that it should be delivered to Stalin personally. Not until 19 April was this message actually handed over: Sir Stafford raised repeated objections, on the need for the warning, the timing, and the means. Heated exchanges were to take place between Churchill, the Foreign Office and the stubborn Ambassador.

Thursday, 3 April, saw continuing and depressing developments in Yugoslavia, Cyrenaica and Iraq. Hitler issued his Directive No 26, detailing his Balkan campaign and military tasks allotted to Hungary, Bulgaria and Roumania. Reports reached London from the Ambassador at Belgrade showing the Yugoslavs still hesitating.[111] Eden was travelling north to Florina where Yugoslav-Greek staff talks would start during the evening; in transmission to Eden were fresh instructions from Churchill, sent as a result of a further sharp deterioration in North Africa. Wavell's visit to the front had confirmed his fears that Neame had lost control of the situation and that Benghazi must be evacuated; in London the Chiefs of Staff agreed that 'the re-establishment of a front in Cyrenaica should have priority in the resources of all three services in the Middle East', and approval was given to a proposal by Wavell that 'Mandibles', the occupation of Rhodes, should be postponed, and that the 7th Australian Division should delay departure for Greece.[112] Churchill, presiding at this COS meeting, gave latest information to the War Cabinet at noon. 'The Germans were believed to have suffered considerable losses (in Cyrenaica),' but 'forces against us were believed to consist of one German armoured division, certain elements of two other German armoured divisions and four Italian divisions.' Ministers heard one brighter item: 12 Hurricanes had been successfully flown into hard-pressed Malta. But the War Cabinet were also told that 'air attacks against our shipping had been more intense during March than in any previous month', and a new threat had arisen from a different direction: Churchill said that 'secret information had been received that Admiral Darlan had obtained permission from the German Armistice Commission to take the *Dunkerque* across to Toulon. Once at Toulon the ship would be for all practical purposes in German hands.' This, reminded Churchill, was the exact opposite of the course urged on the French by Britain and America; the question now was whether two Royal Navy submarines in the area should be ordered to attack the *Dunkerque* on her way across. Churchill favoured this submarine action and had cabled Roosevelt the previous day to ask if he agreed. Pound warned that 'the navy had its hands so full that they would be most reluctant to take any action which might bring the French fleet into the war'. Ministers agreed to await Roosevelt's reply.[113]

After difficulty contacting the Yugoslav representatives, staff talks began at Florina at 10.30 p.m. 'Conference patchy and no definite plans laid,' commented Eden.[114] Also at 10.30 p.m. the Defence Committee met at 10 Downing Street. A reply had come from Roosevelt: the President would 'understand' an attack on the *Dunkerque*. Pound continued to argue strongly against the idea, as did Cadogan and to a lesser degree Attlee, but Alexander, First Lord of the Admiralty, supported Churchill. The operation was given tentative approval. The Committee then considered recent telegrams concerning North Africa, including details of the evacuation of Benghazi; surprise was expressed at the German ability to transport and maintain such powerful forces at the end of a long line of communication. Ministers approved a draft telegram from Churchill to Eden, despatched immediately after the meeting finished at midnight: 'Evacuation Benghazi serious, as Germans once established in aerodromes thereabouts, will probably deny us use of Tobruk. Find out what is strategic and tactical plan to chop the enemy.... Far more important than the loss of ground is the idea that we cannot face the Germans and that their appearance is enough to drive us back many scores of miles. This may react most evilly throughout Balkans and Turkey. Pray go back to Cairo....'[115] Priority was therefore once again shifting back to North African sands: yet the New Zealand Division was following the British 1st Armoured Brigade into threatened Greece; staff talks at Florina were no more fruitful on the 4th than they had been the previous evening. Eden now heard rumours of an attack to be launched on Greece next day, 5 April, but 'since nothing could be done further', he flew back from Florina to Athens. There he found Churchill's instructions to go to Cairo; reluctant to obey, he signalled Churchill to tell him so and stayed in Athens intending to await the reply. Meanwhile, Churchill sent a warning to the Yugoslav Prime Minister: 'From every quarter my information shows rapid heavy concentration and advance towards your country.'[116] Wavell, on the other hand, sent repeated warnings to Athens and London concerning the deteriorating desert situation, in which British forces were desperately trying to withdraw faster than Rommel could advance. So anxious did Wavell sound that Eden worried most of the night and woke Dill early on the 5th to say that they had best return to Cairo, as Churchill had instructed. British withdrawal turned into headlong retreat; Rommel had now received full approval for his offensive and pressed on with terrifying speed and brilliant assurance, sending out curt orders to his forward elements on the 5th: 'Mechili clear of enemy. Make for it. Drive fast. Rommel.'[117] Hitler told Mussolini more German troops were *en route* to North Africa. Eden, now in Cairo, reported: 'General conclusion to which we have all come is that the Italian-German effort in Cyrenaica is a major diversion well timed to precede the German attack in the Balkans.'[118] Also on the 5th a promising item of information came from Moscow: the Soviets signed a pact of non-aggression and friendship with the new Yugoslav Government. And, from Washington, came information that the *Dunkerque* would not sail for at least 10 days, hence easing Admiralty fears for the moment, and as it happened, indefinitely.

Throughout the 5th, reports had filtered into the Foreign Office of imminent German action in the Balkans. Rumours increased as night fell. And at 5.30 a.m. on Sunday, 6 April, Hitler declared war on Yugoslavia and Greece. Only 95 minutes later mass German bomber formations appeared over the largely undefended Yugoslav capital; orders were simple: 'Destroy Belgrade in attacks by waves.' Operation 'Punishment' had begun.

Aegean Agony

German bombers battered Belgrade for 72 hours and slaughtered 17,000 civilians; forces prodded down into Greece on the 6th and the *Luftwaffe* struck at Piraeus. Rommel's advance forces were nearing Mechili and Generals Neame and O'Connor were captured. Only in far away Abyssinia were skies brighter: General Cunningham's units entered Addis Ababa during the day. Despite the immense events, no War Cabinet meetings took place on the 6th, a Sunday. Ministers could have done little. Clearly no reinforcements for Greece could be sliced from the reeling North African army; for the moment Ministers could only hope the Greek forces and their allied assistance – about 62,000 British Imperial personnel were eventually sent – would be able to hold the German attacks from Bulgaria and possibly Yugoslavia. Odds were even more unbalanced than believed at that time: 10 German divisions would be employed in the assault on Greece of which five, including three armoured, would be thrown against two divisions of British, Australian and New Zealand troops.

Britain severed diplomatic relations with Hungary on Monday, 7 April; Eden started home from Cairo; the COS agreed to send six Hurricane squadrons to the Mediterranean – according to Portal the need there was even greater than at home. The COS then turned to a completely different area of future conflict: Malaya. A proposal by the C-in-C, Far East, was approved, laying down that in the event of a Japanese threat to Malaya through southern Thailand, British troops should advance into the Thai isthmus north of Singora, despite Britain's non-aggression treaty with Thailand. Churchill warned of the dangers of a continued diversion of strength to the Far East, an area which, he said, was unlikely to become active unless Britain were heavily beaten elsewhere.[1] The Joint Intelligence Committee completed a report which judged Germany unlikely to wage war on Russia for the moment; in Berlin Brauchitsch ordered that Yugoslavian developments must delay 'Barbarossa': all preliminary plans must be completed on the basis that the attack would now be launched about 22 June. The War Cabinet met at 5 p.m. after Ministers had heard Wood present his budget to the Commons – income tax, despite objections from Churchill, was boosted to 10s in the pound, and the exemption limit lowered to £110 a year, with a portion of increased taxation to be paid back later as 'post-war credits'. Ministers now heard latest details of the continuing bombing of Belgrade and were also given latest shipping losses: since the War Cabinet had last met 18,300 tons had been lost through U-boat and 43,700 through air attack. The Iraq situation had deteriorated and 'it looked as though a show of force ... might be necessary before the position could be redressed'. A telegram from Wavell stated the Regent might recover his position with the support of a firm British declaration, if this were backed by the largest air demonstration which could be carried out by aircraft already in Iraq; Wavell warned this show of force must be made sufficient, since British resources did not allow actual armed intervention. Two hours before the War Cabinet met, another cable had arrived from Wavell, this time on the Cyrenaica situation. 'Position in Western Desert greatly deteriorated yesterday, due to enemy moving on Mechili by desert route and further vehicle losses of 2nd Armoured Division by mechanical breakdown and air bombing. Third Armoured Brigade has little or no fighting value and losses and state of Indian motor brigade are not known.' Churchill told the War Cabinet that a telegram had also been received from Eden saying the Germans were advancing in greater strength and more rapidly than had been anticipated. Churchill added that 'Tobruk was a strongly fortified place and the German force which had advanced so rapidly could hardly possess the necessary artillery to reduce it. If we could hold the advance at Tobruk we would be well satisfied. But we must recognize that this might not be possible.' The Prime Minister then re-read a cable sent by Wavell five weeks previously which had given 'a hopeful appreciation of the situation in Cyrenaica and the scale of attack likely to be expected from the enemy'; Churchill continued: 'The War Cabinet decision regarding assistance to Greece had largely been founded on this appreciation' and he laid stress on Wavell's statement that: 'Eventually two German divisions might be employed in a large-scale attack. This with one or two infantry divisions would be the maximum maintainable via Tripoli. Shipping risks, difficulties of communications and the approach of hot weather make it unlikely that such an attack could develop before the end of the summer.' Menzies said his Australian colleagues were anxious about the situation and their cable stated 'quite clearly' Menzies had said the military advisers discounted the likelihood of a Cyrenaica attack. Menzies therefore considered himself placed in an embarrassing position by Wavell's underestimation; he believed it had been 'perhaps unwise' to hold Benghazi with half-trained troops, and commented that the German advance would upset plans for sending further troops to Greece. Churchill agreed and added 'it was also unfortunate that it would be impossible to proceed in the near future with plans for operations in the Dodecanese, which would continue to be a threat against our sea communications with Greece.'[2] Churchill left the War Cabinet meeting described by Cadogan as 'altogether very gloomy', and sent a stiff signal to Wavell: 'You should surely be able to hold Tobruk with its permanent Italian defences, at least until or unless the enemy brings up strong artillery forces. It seems difficult to believe that he can do this for some weeks.... Tobruk therefore seems to be a place to be held to the death....'[3] The telegram reached Cairo at 0305 hours on 8 April, when Wavell was already flying to Tobruk in a battered and unreliable Hudson aircraft; he landed amidst sand squalls and told the British commanders of course Tobruk was to be held: he had merely come to settle details.[4]

In London the Joint Planning Staff concluded that the enemy's Balkan and Libyan operations were co-ordinated – an inaccurate opinion previously expressed by Eden. Contrary to an appreciation by Joint Intelligence on 28 March, the Joint Planners believed Yugoslav resistance was unlikely to be prolonged. The report also recommended all possible steps should be taken to overthrow Rashid Ali's Government before Iraq became completely German-controlled, and urged India should be asked to send a small force to Basra. This latter step was soon taken.[5] Within hours the warning concerning Yugoslav resistance had been proved correct. Meanwhile Wavell had disappeared in the desert. The C-in-C had left Tobruk late in the afternoon, in deteriorating weather, after one false start when the Hudson's wheel brake had seized; oil pressure failure had resulted in a detour to abandoned El Adem, likely to be overrun at any moment, but the aircraft had managed to take off at nightfall. Since then there had been complete silence.[6]

News of this possible catastrophe had still to reach London when the War Cabinet met at 9.30 p.m. and Churchill's account of the North African position was even optimistic: 'There were signs that the rush of the enemy's advance was exhausting itself and that the situation gave less cause for anxiety.' Greek troops were holding out at Roupel Pass and on the Nestos line in Macedonia.[7] But grim news flashed to London during the night: resistance had collapsed in South Serbia, opening the way into Macedonia and on to Salonica; and General Wilson, whose troops had had insufficient time to settle into the inadequate Aliakhmon line, ordered the first withdrawal next day, 9 April, to begin on the night of the 11th.

Wavell had re-emerged from the desert. Anxious officers at Cairo received a message in the early hours of the 9th: the C-in-Cs Hudson had had to make a forced landing; Wavell and his party had emerged unscathed and were fortunately found by a Sudanese patrol. On reaching Cairo the weary Wavell immediately sent a cautious reply to Churchill's signal concerning Tobruk. 'Although first enemy effort seems to have exhausted itself, I do not feel we shall have long respite and am still very anxious. Tobruk is not good defensive position.'[8] While this message was on its way, Churchill was making a sad statement to the Commons: his announcement had originally been planned as a congratulation for recent British desert victories. Only the capture of Massawa, chief port of Eritrea, which had fallen to the British the previous day, lightened his news. The Germans, he declared, had entered Salonica at four o'clock that morning. Eden and Dill arrived back in London early next morning, Thursday, 10 April. Wavell's latest telegram was believed by Churchill to leave in doubt the question of defending Tobruk; the Prime Minister drafted another signal to the Middle East: 'It seems unthinkable that the fortress of Tobruk should be abandoned.' Dill secured Eden's agreement that the telegram would be unwise, and Eden persuaded Churchill to allow Wavell a free hand, but another telegram came from Cairo: 'I propose to hold Tobruk.... My resources are very limited, especially of mobile and armoured troops and of anti-tank and anti-aircraft weapons. It will be a race against time.' Churchill immediately signalled: 'We all cordially endorse your decision to hold Tobruk and will do all in our power to bring you aid.'[9] The Prime Minister had nevertheless been left in a sour mood; he apparently grumbled to Eden about the situation in general and claimed, not entirely incorrectly, that he had never wanted to help Greece.[10]

The British Ambassador in Baghdad believed it would be expedient, despite loss of prestige, to agree to some form of recognition of Rashid Ali's Government if Britain could thereby get troops into the country. The Foreign Office undertook to study this suggestion.[11] During the day, American merchantmen took over British tasks in the Red Sea following the declaration of the area as no longer a combat zone after the defeat of the Italians in Eritrea; and also on the 10th came the first recorded clash between American and German warships, when the US destroyer *Niblack* dropped depth charges on a menacing U-boat in the Atlantic. Next day Roosevelt secretly extended the US Fleet patrol area to cover all North Atlantic waters up to 25 degrees West, soon altered to 26 degrees, and the British were invited to take advantage of this extra protection with the US Navy being informed of convoy routes: a major step forward in the Battle of the Atlantic.[12] April 11 was Good Friday;

Churchill had minuted to Sir Edward Bridges, the War Cabinet Secretary: 'It is very important not to have a serious break in the work at Easter.... I am told that Easter is a very good time for invasion.'[13] Ministers therefore assembled at 11.30 a.m. and heard a lengthy report from Eden on his prolonged Middle East adventures. Hitler's plan in the early spring, he said, had been to overrun the Balkans by peaceful methods; thereafter, Hitler would have attacked the British positions in the Eastern Mediterranean, neutralized Turkey and threatened Russia. 'This plan had to some extent been retarded and thrown out of gear by the Greek resistance and the Yugoslav *coup d'état*, which would not have taken place but for the help which we had given to Greece. The Germans would now try to carry out by force the plan that they had intended to effect by intimidation. They would accompany this with as strong an attack on our positions in Cyrenaica as they could.' Dill read an appreciation from Wavell: 'It is essential to hold enemy as far west as is possible to reduce air threat to naval base at Alexandria and other bases in Egypt, also because of morale effect in Egypt.' Wavell stressed the weaknesses of Tobruk: not naturally strong, vulnerable water supply, limited opportunity for air support, vulnerability of harbour to mining or heavy air attack. Attlee commented he 'had been somewhat surprised at the rigidity and force with which the attack developed in Libya, in face of the telegrams which had been received'. Dill admitted there had been considerable underestimation of enemy strength; Menzies said previous incorrect assessments made him 'very uncomfortable about the position of our forces in Tobruk'.[14]

German bombers roared over the West country and raided Bristol that Good Friday night, while Churchill waited in his special train outside the city; next morning he conferred an honorary degree upon Winant, US Ambassador, with the building next to the University still burning and with many of his audience soiled from the night's horror. In the North African desert, Bardia fell to the enemy and Wavell reported on defensive plans. 'If I get time to put the organization into effect we shall be back to something resembling situation of last autumn with additional excrescence of Tobruk.... The next few months will be very difficult, quite apart from what happens in Greece.'[15] British troops were withdrawing from the Aliakhmon position, acutely threatened on their left flank and with the allied line strung far too thin. German motorized units filtered into Belgrade's rubble-strewn streets on Easter Sunday and Hitler issued Directive No 27: 'Yugoslavia – the aim of the operation is to destroy the remaining Yugoslav forces.... Greece – as soon as adequate forces have been concentrated ... the *decisive* attack against Anglo-Greek forces in northern Greece will be launched.'

Churchill sent a brave telegram to Roosevelt: 'We are of course

223

going all out to fight for the Nile valley. No other conclusion is physically possible.... Even if Tobruk has to be evacuated from the sea, which we command, there are other strong fighting positions already organized. I personally feel that this situation is not only manageable, but hopeful. Dill and Eden, who have just come back, concur.'[16] The Prime Minister presented a different picture to the Defence Committee, meeting at Chequers that Sunday: he referred to 'the gravity of the situation' in Cyrenaica, and declared that 'the enemy's armoured forces were advancing on Egypt without meeting any serious resistance' although 'they had little or nothing behind them at present'. If immediate and drastic steps were not taken to cut enemy communications and block the port of Tripoli, 'we should find ourselves driven out of Egypt'. The navy must 'at all or any cost' interrupt communications: the honour of the Navy was involved. Pound said that 'the loss of one or two capital ships would be a very serious matter at the present time when the attitude of Japan was in the balance', to which Churchill replied that Japan was more likely to come into the war if the Germans overran Egypt and managed to 'kill or capture the whole of our vast army there'. Pound suggested no decision should be taken until a reply had been received from Admiral Cunningham, C-in-C Mediterranean. The Committee agreed. Churchill thought a telegram should be sent to Palairet for communication to General Wilson, instructing him 'to impress on General Papagos in the strongest possible terms the necessity for closing the gap between the Greek western army and the BEF'. This was also agreed.[17]

Wavell's fears of precious troops being sent to Iraq suddenly seemed justified. The Defence Committee meeting at 3.30 p.m. next day, Easter Monday, agreed the Ambassador should negotiate with Rashid Ali for the opening of the overland route from Basra and for the landing of the troops from India, in return for recognition of his Government: but if Rashid Ali refused to allow HMG to exercise their treaty rights, 'force should be used'.[18] Ministers had barely finished this meeting when the War Cabinet met at 5 p.m.: latest situation reports on fighting in Greece and North Africa were immediately read; the CIGS said the most serious news concerned an enemy thrust to cut off the Greek army in Albania: 'There was a risk that a wedge would be driven between the main Greek army in Albania and the forces holding the Aliakhmon line, and our left flank would be left in the air.' Ministers were reminded of the effort made to persuade the Greeks to bring back part of their main army in Albania, or to withdraw the right flank of their main forces, to avoid this very danger; Churchill commented that 'we should be in no way responsible for the consequences'. Dill said the Greeks were trying to carry out this move, but it would take at least 10 days for completion. 'In the meantime there were only three Greek divisions and our own two divisions in a position to oppose the main German thrust into Greece.' Telegrams from Cairo were slightly more optimistic: Wavell believed the situation in Egypt to be serious but not desperate, and there was no cause for the alarm 'which has already shown itself in certain elements in the United States'. Churchill stressed that as long as the enemy communications could be cut, by land and sea, the situation could be restored, and he had embodied his ideas in a Directive, read to the War Cabinet: the paper repeated that Tobruk should be 'an invaluable bridgehead or sally-port'.[19] The Defence Committee assembled again in the Cabinet War Room at 9.45 p.m. to consider this directive; during discussion news came in of the successful defeat of an attack on Tobruk – 'Between 200 and 300 German p.o.w. captured at Tobruk morning 14 April stated they were badly shaken by our artillery fire and were very short of food and water. These troops wept when their attack was driven off, and their morale is definitely low.' Churchill's hopes of German over-stretch and of the value of Tobruk as an offensive base seemed confirmed. A telegram was immediately approved. 'Bravo, Tobruk! We feel it vital that Tobruk should be regarded as sally-port and not, please, as an "excrescence".'[20] Churchill's call for Tripoli to be put out of action by the Royal Navy led to heated exchanges next day, 15 April, between the Admiralty and Admiral Cunningham. The latter vehemently opposed risking his fleet by a bombardment in a highly dangerous stretch of water, especially as the results would be uncertain; the Admiralty therefore suggested an alternative – the use of the battleship *Barham* as a blockship. Cunningham angrily replied that 'it seems to me doubtful if there is one chance in ten of getting this large ship into the right position', and he deplored the sacrifice of the ship and possibly of men – and he reluctantly agreed to a bombardment. This would take place in a week's time.[21]

The end had clearly been reached in Greece: evacuation or elimination were now the only choices left for the BEF. The Defence Committee met at 9.30 p.m. on the 16th, with Ministers making their way through a massive air raid known afterwards as 'The Wednesday'. Discussions were still continuing at 10.50 when a message was received from Wavell: the gallant Greeks now apparently wished the British to leave them. 'Have received following from Wilson timed 1700 hours today. Begins: "Just had conversation with Papagos who described Greek army as being severely pressed and getting into administrative difficulties owing to air action.... Agrees to withdrawal to Thermopylae position.... Papagos also suggested that as things may become critical in future we should re-embark British troops and save Greece from devastation. Consider this course should commence with occupation new position."' Wavell said his instructions to Wilson had been as follows: 'We must continue fighting in co-operation with Greeks so long as they resisted but authorized any further withdrawal necessary.' Wavell requested instructions over action to be taken on Papagos' suggestion about re-embarkation. 'Presume definite request to this effect from Greek Government should be obtained before any actual re-embarkation is begun. Propose however to make all arrangements with this in view. Am assuming Crete would be held.' Ministers now agreed this Greek offer should be accepted. 'While it would be wrong in any way to prejudice the safety of the Greek army, no good purpose would be served by our remaining in the country under present conditions.' A telegram was approved for immediate despatch to Wavell: 'We cannot remain in Greece against wishes of Greek C-in-C and thus expose country to devastation. Wilson or Palairet should obtain endorsement by Greek Government of Papagos' request. Consequent on this assent evacuation should proceed without however prejudicing any withdrawal to Thermopylae.... We shall aid and maintain the defence of Crete to the utmost.'[22] When Ministers emerged from the Cabinet War Room bombs were still blasting around them – over 1,000 people died in London that night.

The capital still smouldered and smoked, with buildings collapsing and rescuers digging in the rubble, when the War Cabinet met at noon next day, 17 April. Churchill sat at his usual place at the Cabinet table and ruefully remarked he now had a better view of Nelson's Column in Trafalgar Square: part of the Admiralty had been demolished. Ministers were told of the Defence Committee's decision the previous night; the War Cabinet approved. The clear implication of Papagos' statement, commented Churchill, was that the Greek army was unable to continue the struggle. 'We had always taken the view that we should not go to help the Greeks unless they wanted us to do so. If the Greeks now decided that they did not wish to continue the struggle on the mainland, we should fall in with their views.' Discussion followed on prospects for withdrawal. 'We had 59,000 men in Greece,' warned Churchill, and he feared artillery and tanks would be lost. A telegram from Wavell on the North African situation had reached the War Office at 3.20 a.m., and was now read to the War Cabinet: the Germans seemed to be aiming at containing the British forces at Tobruk to enable a mobile force under Rommel to penetrate as deeply as possible into Egypt. 'Rommel evidently hopes to exploit soft spot so far as his transport situation and our resistance will allow him. His belief that he has defeated the enemy in front of him may lead him into difficulties.' Churchill thought that 'the German thrust seemed to be of manageable proportions, and there was a good chance that it might be liquidated'.[23]

Yugoslavia capitulated during the day, releasing more German forces for Greece. General Wilson drove to the Greek Palace where he met the King, Papagos and the British Ambassador. Discussion centred on the means and timing of evacuation, but Wilson felt confident he could hold the Thermopylae line a while longer. Koryzis, the Greek Prime Minister, told Palairet the Greek Government were ready to prejudice their own troops to benefit the British, since they regarded themselves as hosts. Next day, 18 April, Koryzis killed himself.[24] At a Defence Committee meeting on the 18th the Prime Minister sought approval for a public statement that 'if Athens and Cairo were bombed we should proceed with the systematic bombing of Rome'. This was agreed.[25]

German troops were mopping up in Yugoslavia; guerrillas were taking to the mountains, King Peter was flown out by RAF flying-boat, but Ronald Campbell, the British Ambassador, was captured by the Italians, eventually to be repatriated in June. Also on the 18th the first Indian troops landed at Basra: Rashid Ali had proved surprisingly accommodating over the question of 'transferring' troops across Iraq in return for British recognition of his Government.[26] The COS at their meeting on the 18th confirmed that priority had once again switched back to North Africa; Air Marshall Longmore had appealed for guidance on the use of his inadequate air strength, and the COS replied: 'Following directive has been issued by the Prime Minister and Minister of Defence. . . . You must divide between protecting evacuation and sustaining battle in Libya. But if these clash, which may be avoidable, emphasis must be given to victory in Libya. . . . Victory in Libya counts first, evacuation of troops from Greece second.'[27] But no mere directive could ease Wavell's colossal burden, dealing as he had to with operations in Greece, Libya, Crete, Iraq – officially still in the Indian command area – Kenya, Somaliland, the Sudan, Abyssinia and Syria, and he and the other two C-in-Cs now appealed for administrative assistance. Their difficulties were increased by having to consult the local representatives of so many British Governmental departments on political and financial matters; Eden's visit had shown the benefits of being able to channel matters through one man, and they therefore signalled: 'We consider it necessary for some authority to be established here to deal, inside the broad lines of policy laid down by HMG, with the political aspects of issues affecting more than one department or territory. This will of course entail his being directly responsible to the War Cabinet and not to any one department.'[28]

London received its heaviest *Luftwaffe* onslaught of the war on Saturday night, 19 April, with another 1,000 people killed, and 1,026 tons and 4,252 incendiary containers dropped. As a result of this Saturday and the previous Wednesday, 148,000 houses were destroyed or damaged: during the Blitz in September and October, damage had averaged about 40,000 homes a week.[29] Churchill spent the weekend at Ditchley, Gloucestershire, where he heard on Sunday that the Greek armies on the Albanian frontier had surrendered. Yet the Prime Minister now wondered whether British evacuation would perhaps be premature. 'I am increasingly of the opinion,' he minuted to Eden, 'that if the generals on the spot think they can hold on in the Thermopylae position for a fortnight or three weeks, and can keep the Greek Army fighting, or enough of it, we should certainly support them.... Every day the German air force is detained in Greece enables the Libyan situation to be stabilized.'[30] While this note was on its way to Eden on Sunday evening, he received a telephone call from Churchill, who wanted him to go to London and 'take command of the situation'. The Prime Minister had been handed worrying signals sent by Wavell to the CIGS: 'Future outlook will cause anxiety for some time, owing to my weakness in tanks.... Stop Press. I have just received disquieting intelligence. I was expecting another German colonial division.... I have just been informed that latest evidence indicates this is not a colonial but an *armoured* division.' Wavell had pleaded: 'CIGS, please give your personal assistance.'[31] Eden immediately set off for London. Churchill had already sent Ismay to call the COS together: the Prime Minister wanted approval for 307 of Britain's best tanks to be sent immediately direct through the dangerous Mediterranean. The COS 'did not seem too well pleased at having their one day of rest disturbed', remembered Ismay, and they were also strongly against the tank proposal – British strength at home would be dangerously weakened and the Mediterranean route involved unwarrantable risks. The COS were still arguing against the idea at dinner-time but by the time Eden arrived later they were reluctantly reaching the conclusion that the proposal would have to be accepted.[32]

COS fears were expressed to the Defence Committee next day, 21 April, but approval was given: the convoy, 'Tiger', would leave on the 26th. The Royal Navy would therefore receive an additional burden, although the Mediterranean Fleet would be strengthened by one battleship. And yet at dawn the Mediterranean Fleet had begun the Tripoli bombardment, an operation which Cunningham feared might result in excessive losses. Later in the day, after the Defence Committee had met, the Admiralty learnt with extreme relief all had gone well. 'To my astonishment,' reported Cunningham, 'surprise was achieved.' Another signal from the Admiral complained: 'It has taken the whole Mediterranean fleet five days to accomplish what a heavy bomber squadron working from Egypt could probably carry out in a few hours.... We are finding our present commitments rather more than we can deal with efficiently.' Burdens were soon to be increased; and the effect of the Tripoli bombardment had been marginal.[33]

Ministers at this Defence Committee meeting on the 21st also heard Churchill confess hesitation over British evacuation from Greece. 'There was a lamentable lack of information ... which made it difficult to get a clear picture.' But, Churchill added: 'If the Greek Government wished to continue the struggle and the Greek Army stood firm, and the generals on the spot thought that we could put up an effective defence ... the right course was to stand. If, however, Greek resistance crumbled or the Greek Government asked us to withdraw, we should evacuate as soon as possible.' Air cover could only be carried out at the expense of Libyan operations, warned Portal; Menzies read a discouraging appreciation sent by General Blamey, commander of the Australian troops: forces were being extremely hard pressed especially through German air attacks. Churchill said it was not possible, on information available, to decide whether to hold or evacuate, and added that more news might result from a meeting reportedly taking place in Athens, attended by Wavell. The Committee therefore deferred a decision until the War Cabinet meeting that evening.[34]

By then the decision had in effect already been taken. A telegram reached the War Office from Wavell at 1.04 p.m. 'New Zealand division had one battalion cut off in Vale of Tempe, otherwise practically intact ... 6th Australian Division lost two battalions north of Larissa in earlier fighting and are reduced to 50 per cent or less. Large proportion of anti-tank guns lost.... Position of enemy uncertain at present.... Enemy air bombing has been very heavy and continuous throughout retreat and although it has done comparatively little material damage, it has had some morale effect.' Wavell had explained the Greek Government's suggestion of a withdrawal to General Blamey: 'He was quite clear ... that only policy was early re-embarkation.' Wavell concluded: 'Wilson and I are going to see Palairet now to discuss what is to be said to King and Greek Government.' An hour before the War Cabinet met, a cable from Palairet reached the Foreign Office. 'General Wavell asked His Majesty the state of the Greek Army and whether it could give immediate and effective aid to the left flank of the Thermopylae position, as without this the British forces could not hold the position indefinitely.... HM said that the General he had sent to the front to report ... had not yet returned, but he agreed that the time factor rendered it impossible for any organized Greek force to support the British left flank.... General Wavell said that in that case he felt it was his duty to take immediate steps for re-embarkation of such portion of his army as he could. The King entirely agreed and seemed to have expected this. He spoke with deep regret at having been the means of placing the British forces in such a position.' These telegrams were waiting for Ministers at 5 p.m. If the War Cabinet had been asked, said the Prime Minister, he thought that they would certainly have decided that the British Imperial Force must be evacuated. The War Cabinet agreed the decision taken in Athens must stand. Churchill hoped there would be no need for an immediate announcement, and 'public discussion in Parliament was to be deprecated at this stage.... We should keep it clearly before the public mind that it would have been impossible for us to have deserted Greece.'[35] The King of the Hellenes re-treated with his Government to Crete next day, 22 April; on the same day reports were received in London of activity indicating a German attack on the island. The COS met this Tuesday to discuss Germany's probable next move: a difference of opinion emerged between the War Office and Foreign Office, with the former believing a German attack on Russia unlikely until after an attempted invasion of Britain, and the Foreign Office representative declaring the threat to Russia might well develop as soon as the Greek campaign was completed.[36]

Greek forces, exhausted, decimated, outnumbered, were incap-able of further fighting. Resistance ended on Thursday, 24 April. The British War Cabinet, meeting at noon, had still to hear of Greece's surrender, but concern for the Imperial troops was especi-ally voiced by Robert Menzies – 'uneasy as to whether our forces in Greece ... would be given sufficient protection from the air'.[37] His fears seemed confirmed by a signal received from Cairo later in the day: all Hurricanes in Greece had been lost.[38] Also on the 24th the Australian Government asked the COS for a candid general appreciation, with an 'accurate statement of assistance we could definitely rely on rather than hope for': among threats which the Australians judged possible were German control of Turkey and Iran, the closing of the Straits of Gibraltar and the Suez Canal, Japanese attacks on Singapore, the Dutch East Indies and even Australia. They thought it unwise to assume immediate American entry into the war if these came about.[39]

Dunkirk, Brest, Cherbourg, St Nazaire, and now small ports and beaches in Southern Greece – all within a year. British troops were once again being pulled from the advancing Germans, and, unlike Belgium and Northern France, the Germans now had complete command of the air. Evacuations, termed Operation 'Demon', began during the night of 24 April and would continue for almost a week. Only 15,361 of the troops were taken direct to Egypt – the rest went to Crete. Next day, Hitler issued Directive No 28, describing Operation 'Mercury': 'As a base for air warfare against Great Britain in the Eastern Mediterranean we must prepare to *occupy the island of Crete*.' Airborne forces would constitute the primary weapon. The Joint Intelligence Committee, in a report completed on 27 April, warned that German airborne attacks on the island were imminent, and Churchill told the War Cabinet at 5 p.m. next day that he had sent a telegram to warn Wavell; he added that he was 'somewhat doubtful of our ability to hold Crete against a prolonged attack'. Ministers were told some 27,000 troops had so far been saved from Greece, of whom 13,000 had landed in Crete; Churchill believed 'we could congratulate ourselves on the number of troops evacuated.... It might well be that our total losses, killed, wounded and prisoners, would be between five to ten thousand. The concluding stages of the Greek campaign had been a glorious episode in the history of British arms. The losses we had inflicted on the German troops had almost certainly exceeded our own, notwithstanding the fact that the withdrawal had been effected almost without air support.' He felt no regrets over the decision to send troops. 'Had we not done so, Yugoslavia would not now be an open enemy of Germany. Further, the Greek war had caused a marked change in the attitude of the United States.' But the Prime Minister warned that 'we must now expect a period of great enemy activity in the Mediterranean. Attacks would be made on Crete and Malta, and probably West Africa and Gibraltar. The enemy's plan was, no doubt, to base strong air forces on Crete and Rhodes.'

Egypt was threatened from another direction: Vichy-controlled Syria. German air forces operating from this strategically situated country could strike at Egypt, the Canal Zone and the oil refineries at Abadan, and, Eden now told the War Cabinet, 'the position of Syria was serious'. An attempt was being made to find out what action the French High Commissioner, General Dentz, would take if German airborne troops landed in the country. Eden also favoured an approach to the Vichy authorities to deal with two other contingencies: German occupation of Morocco and the passage of German troops through unoccupied France. 'We should make it clear that if the Vichy Government allowed any of these things to happen, we should hold ourselves free to take action as military necessities might require, for example bombing German lines of communications in France, and should no longer be bound by our undertaking to restore the independence and greatness of France.' Other Ministers agreed.[40] Even before this War Cabinet discussion on Syria, Churchill had asked Wavell what help he could supply to the Free French if a struggle were to develop in this Vichy area; Wavell replied later on the 28th: he could only manage a single brigade group.[41] In Iraq on the 28th the British Ambassador had a difficult interview with Rashid Ali, and was told it was out of the question for more British troops to land, as requested. Rashid Ali refused to accept Britain's right under their treaty to have troops in the country; his attitude became so threatening that the Ambassador decided to send British women and children from Baghdad to the RAF base at Habbaniyah.[42]

The Defence Committee met at 9.30 p.m. to discuss the North African situation – and to hear a vigorous explosion from Churchill, described by Cadogan as extremely tired. The previous night at Chequers, General Kennedy had incensed him by suggesting 'there might be worse things to lose than Egypt',[43] and Menzies had seemed to hint at the same conclusion during the War Cabinet meeting that evening. Churchill now declared Egypt must be fought for 'every inch of the way'. He had 'formed the impression that our comparatively easy successes against the Italians, followed as they had been by our sudden reverse at the hands of the Germans, had not been a good preparation for the army for what was now confronting them.... Nothing would be more ignominious than to be driven out of Egypt by an inferior army operating at the end of a long, precarious line of communications.... The Tobruk garrison seemed to be allowing itself to be hemmed in.' Sir John Dill interrupted: raids were being carried out from Tobruk, and 'our soldiers were in no way inferior to the Germans, but they were at present suffering from an inferiority of equipment'. Churchill turned his baleful attention on the RAF: Longmore had apparently removed his fighters from Tobruk, but 'Tobruk should be used as an advanced landing ground', and Churchill was 'amazed to hear ... the RAF had only 14 serviceable Hurricanes'. Portal replied that 'the fighters would use Tobruk for refuelling and rearming.... On 18 April there had been 90 serviceable Hurricanes in Egypt and the Sudan ... it should be remembered that it was not possible to repair on the spot aircraft damaged in the desert.'

Churchill repeated his fears of an imminent airborne attack on Crete, and Portal said that 'it seemed quite possible the Germans could operate about 300 transport aircraft from aerodromes at Athens and Larissa. Their technique would probably be to start with a heavy air attack on the defences at dawn, followed by a large number of parachutists to seize aerodromes.' He would examine more closely the time which the Germans would need to prepare an attack, but he thought it could not come for about a week.[44] The Defence Committee ended just before 1 a.m. London was quiet and dark: *Luftwaffe* attention had been switched to Plymouth. Last troops were leaving southern Greece; about 12,000 were left behind, dead or missing, and much valuable equipment. Troops came ashore on the beautiful island of Crete, thankful for its safety. 'Crete was warned of possibility of airborne attack on 18 April,' reported Wavell next day, the 29th. 'Crete now contains at least 30,000 personnel evacuated from Greece.... Morale reported good. Arms mainly rifles, with low proportion light machine-guns.'[45] Also on the 29th, the COS replied to the Commonwealth Government's 24 April request for a frank appreciation of the situation as a whole: the Chiefs refused to accept the number of possible German moves as listed in the Australian statement, and insisted the war would be won or lost in or around the UK. Menzies attended a Defence Committee meeting later this Tuesday, where he was told by Churchill that Japan would probably not enter the war until after a successful invasion of Britain, and would anyway be unlikely to declare war if America would be brought in. Menzies was clearly unconvinced and asked for a further meeting with the COS; this was arranged for 1 May.[46] A difficult question came from America during the 29th: 'What did we think would be the result,' asked Colonel Knox, Secretary of the US Navy, 'if the US now moved almost the whole of the Pacific Fleet into the Atlantic?' The question stemmed from Roosevelt's recent authorization for three battleships and a carrier to be transferred to the Atlantic; the authorization had since been cancelled, but some of his advisers were now pressing for an even more daring measure.[47] The subject was added to the Defence Committee agenda for the following night, 30 April.

A reply came from the approach to the French High Commissioner in Syria: General Dentz ambiguously informed the British that his orders were to resist all aggression. In Iraq, 240 women and children reached the RAF base at Habbaniyah during the evening of the 29th, planning to fly on to Basra. But, during this Tuesday night, Iraqi forces surrounded the base. Defending forces numbered about 2,200, civilians 9,000, while the besieging troops totalled 9,000 with 50 guns. Early in the morning of the 30th the British were told that the treaty with Iraq had been violated: fire would be brought down upon the camp and airstrip if aircraft attempted to take off or armoured cars tried to leave. The Prime Minister authorized 'such measures being taken as were necessary to restore the position, including, if need be, the use of our air forces against the Iraq army'.[48] Should this fail, the British Middle East forces, hard pressed in North Africa, about to suffer a German onslaught upon Crete, with the Syrian situation ominous, would find themselves with a further commitment.

* * *

Talks delayed Anglo-Iraqi hostilities for a few more hours. Meanwhile, also on 30 April, Wavell visited Crete and immediately told the War Office that defence of the island was 'a difficult and dangerous commitment'. At Churchill's suggestion command of this hazardous operation had been given to Major-General Bernard Freyberg, VC, who, with his New Zealand Division, had only just arrived from the mainland. Freyberg, brave and indomitable, rapidly came to the same conclusion as the equally unflappable Wavell. In London, Churchill renewed his attack on Middle East Command. He was 'not happy with the situation in Libya', the Defence Committee were informed at 10 p.m. that Wednesday. 'Sufficiently vigorous steps were not being taken by any of the three services to strike the Germans before they became stronger, and to prevent the arrival of reinforcements and stores.' Churchill recognized the navy had been fully engaged with the Greek evacuation, but ships making for Cyrenaica ports should be stopped. The official Minutes continued: 'The Prime Minister inquired whether it was known what General Wavell proposed to do. The Army appeared to be adopting a supine attitude and he would like to be reassured that this would only continue while forces were being gathered together.' General Dill merely replied that a telegram had been sent to Wavell asking for his proposals. Both Beaverbrook and Churchill expressed concern over the apparent inability of the RAF to cope with aircraft repairs.

The Defence Committee then considered the question of the deployment of the US Pacific Fleet. Admiral V. H. Danckwerts, of the British naval mission in Washington, had discouraged the suggestion that these warships should all move to the Atlantic; Churchill was indignant that the Admiral had not welcomed the idea – the move would be of great psychological importance, as well as dealing German naval forces in the Atlantic a decisive blow in the event of hostilities. The Committee supported Churchill, despite strong objections from the First Sea Lord, who believed such a large fleet would not help win the Battle of the Atlantic and would be better kept as a deterrent against the Japanese.[49] Almost immediately a protest over the Committee's conclusion came from Menzies, who had not been present at the meeting, and who stressed the matter was one vitally affecting Australian defence. A special meeting of the Defence Committee was therefore arranged for the next afternoon, 1 May: Menzies did not disagree with the decision to ask the Americans to move a strong naval force into the Atlantic, but objected that the Dominions had not been consulted. Discussions with the Dominions led to a reply being sent to America on 8 May: Britain would welcome a larger US naval presence in the Atlantic, but hoped at least six capital ships and two carriers would remain in the Pacific; as a result, three American battleships and a carrier passed into the Atlantic in June, leaving a fleet of nine battleships and three carriers based at ill-fated Pearl Harbour.[50]

'Evacuation now complete,' signalled Wavell to the CIGS at 00.30 hours, 1 May. 'Only small number picked up by destroyer last night at Kalamata which is in enemy hands. Majority cut off at Kala believed to be labour and non-combatant units.... Troops in good heart.... No doubt that our troops were completely on top whenever they met Germans under reasonable conditions.' War Cabinet ministers were informed at noon that about 43,000 front-line soldiers had been evacuated, out of between 55,000 and 56,000. The latest Iraqi situation was that fighting had so far not broken out and negotiations were continuing. Churchill told the meeting that this was the last session which would be attended by Menzies, and Ministers expressed their thanks for his constructive presence at War Cabinet sessions during his stay.[51]

Earlier that morning the COS had repeated their judgment that 'we have no grounds for believing an attack on Russia is imminent'.[52] Only the previous day Germany's Ambassador to Moscow had been shocked to hear of Hitler's 'Barbarossa' plans, and the date for the offensive was now confirmed as 22 June.

Late on 1 May Freyberg signalled Wavell: 'Forces at my disposal are totally inadequate to meet attack envisaged. Unless fighter aircraft are greatly increased and naval forces made available to deal with seaborne attack I cannot hope to hold out with land forces alone.... If for other reasons these cannot be made available at once, urge that question of holding Crete should be reconsidered. I feel that under terms of my charter it is my duty to inform New Zealand Government of situation.'[53] As a result the New Zealand Government urged London that either their troops should be supplied with sufficient means to defend the island or the decision to hold it at all costs should be reviewed.

At dawn on 2 May first sporadic firing began around the Habbaniyah base, Iraq; also on the 2nd the Defence Committee officially returned Iraq from the Indian to Middle East Command. During the day Wavell gave details of his North African intentions, as requested by the Prime Minister on 30 April, and Churchill in turn expressed himself discontented by this reply: Wavell had ordered plans to be prepared for early offensive action against Rommel, but this would depend on the arrival of strong reinforcements. Also on 2 May, Rommel realized he had insufficient strength to take Tobruk, and Halder wrote in his diary: 'Rommel is in no way equal to his task.' The German Chief of Staff sent von Paulus out to report.[54] Two more depressing signals came from Wavell.

'Defence of Crete will present difficult problem,' warned the first, 'mainly on account of enemy air superiority.' Churchill nevertheless hastened to reassure the New Zealand Government: every effort would be made to re-equip the New Zealand Division, especially with artillery 'in which General Wavell is already strong'; an airborne attack on Crete would suit New Zealanders 'down to the ground' – fighting would be man to man and the British could reinforce the island quicker than the Germans.[55] This comforting cable was sent to the New Zealand Prime Minister, then at Cairo, early on Saturday, 3 May. Wavell's second alarming signal reached the War Office, repeating arguments against sending troops from Egypt to Iraq. 'Nothing short of immediate action by at least a brigade group with strong support of artillery and armoured fighting vehicles could restore situation. There are no guns or AFVs in Palestine and to send forward weak and unsupported forces of cavalry or infantry seems merely asking for further trouble. My forces are stretched to limit everywhere and I simply cannot afford to risk a part of forces on what cannot produce any effect. I do not see how I could possibly accept the responsibility for force at Basra of whose dispositions and strength I am unaware, and consider that this must be controlled from India.' The Defence Committee was already meeting: Ministers agreed the COS should consider an urgent draft reply.[56] Also on this Saturday, the German Embassy at Paris was told to obtain Vichy permission for transit of aircraft and supplies across Syria to Iraq. 'A commitment to Iraq was inevitable,' cabled the COS to Wavell next day, 4 May. 'We had to establish a base at Basra, and control that port to safeguard Persian oil.... The line of communication to Turkey through Iraq has also assumed greater importance owing to German air superiority in the Aegean sea.' The signal, No 88, added: 'There can be no question of accepting the Turkish offer of mediation. We can make no concessions.'[57] Reports from von Paulus to the German High Command had been intercepted; Churchill was therefore able to prod Wavell with the information that almost half a million men were now under the Cairo command whereas it seemed Rommel had no more than 25,000.[58]

'He is the most bloodthirsty or amateurish strategist in history,' roared Hitler in a Reichstag condemnation of Churchill that night. 'This man has been chasing around Europe like a madman in search of something that he could set on fire.' *Luftwaffe* bombers were pounding Liverpool in attacks described to the British War Cabinet next morning, Monday, 5 May: Merseyside had suffered on the previous four nights, said the Home Secretary. Repeated raids on towns of moderate size presented many difficult problems, he continued: at Plymouth for example, which had been bombed for

236

five successive nights during the last week, many people had to evacuate the town at night because no quarters were available, but they found that most billets outside the town were already filled with evacuees from London.[59]

General Freyberg in Crete now seemed more optimistic. 'Cannot understand nervousness,' he cabled later in the day, 'am not in the least anxious about airborne attack', but he added: 'Combination of seaborne and airborne attack is quite different. If that comes before I can get the guns and transport here the situation will be difficult.'[60] Churchill continued to pester Wavell over North African inactivity. 'Have you read my telegram of 4th inst? Presume you realize the highly secret and authoritative character of this information?' 'I saw the secret message yesterday,' cabled an irritated Wavell, and he repeated he would attack as soon as reinforcements arrived.[61] This signal, which arrived later on the 5th, was rapidly followed by Wavell's reply to the COS cable justifying the Iraq operation. 'Your 88 takes little account of realities. You must face facts'; Wavell then listed meagre forces he was preparing for operations against the Iraqis, but stressed these would be unable to reach Habbaniyah until 10 May at the earliest. 'I feel it my duty to warn you in gravest possible terms that I consider prolongation of fighting in Iraq will seriously endanger defence of Palestine and Egypt.' Wavell's uncompromising statement was discussed by the Defence Committee next day, 6 May. Two serious military points were raised, commented Churchill. 'First, General Wavell seemed doubtful whether the mobile column which he was assembling would prove strong enough.... Secondly, General Wavell expressed doubts as to whether Habbaniyah could hold out.' The Prime Minister had therefore asked the COS to give their opinions – his Minute to the Chiefs had included acid criticism of Wavell: 'Fancy having kept the Cavalry Division in Palestine all this time without having the rudiments of a mobile column organized!', and, neglecting the fact that Iraq had only been officially transferred from the Indian to Middle East Command area four days before, he had added: 'He seems to have been taken as much by surprise on his eastern as he was on his western flank.... He gives me the impression of being tired out.' General Dill now said that 'if mere numbers and equipment were taken into account, the force would not be sufficient to take on the Iraqi army, which was over one division in strength in the Habbaniyah area', but the CIGS continued: 'The Iraqis should not be rated too highly, however, and our forces would have good air support.' The COS therefore considered the risk of sending 'this small column a long distance across the desert' should be accepted, and 'there appeared to be no good reason why Habbaniyah should not be able to hold out'. The Defence

Committee accepted this assessment; Wavell was told: 'There is an excellent chance of restoring the situation by bold action, if it is not delayed.' Ismay wrote: 'This was the first occasion in the war on which the COS overruled the commander on the spot.'[62]

This Defence Committee had met at noon in the House of Commons, for Ministers to be in time and on hand for the start of a two-day Vote of Confidence debate. Almost a year had passed since the momentous debate on the disastrous Norwegian campaign which had thrown Chamberlain from power; the threat to Churchill was by no means on the same scale, but critics were nevertheless vocal: MPs spoke of the need for clear-cut war aims, failures in war production, over-concentration of troops in Britain, and a detailed attack came from Leslie Hore-Belisha, ex-War Minister in Chamberlain's Cabinet: 'The army must have more mobility and more armour.' Churchill reserved his main defence for the end of the debate next day. Meanwhile, he had been astonished by criticism from another quarter – in the form of a long, detailed Memorandum by General Sir John Dill, dated the same day, 6 May; if accepted, this powerful paper from the CIGS would have meant revising almost all existing strategic plans. Dill, like Brooke, believed insufficient attention was being paid to possible invasion attempts. 'If need be, we must cut our losses in places that are not vital before it is too late. I believe that we have gone to the limit, if not beyond it, in respect of the security of Great Britain.' Dill claimed the armoured forces in Britain in June would be the equivalent of three fully effective armoured divisions, which, in the event of invasion, would have to face double this number of German; it would take up to a week to concentrate adequate naval strength; 'our bombers cannot deal with more than six invasion ports effectively. . . .' Dill continued: 'A successful invasion alone spells defeat. It is the United Kingdom therefore and not Egypt that is vital. . . . Egypt is not even second in order of priority, for it has been an accepted principle in our strategy that in the last resort the security of Singapore comes before that of Egypt. Yet the defences of Singapore are still considerably below standard.'[63] Churchill would take a week to draft a reply. One decision which had prompted Dill's Memorandum had been the recent acceptance of Churchill's proposal to send much-needed tanks direct to Egypt. The dangers were indeed considerable; now, on 6 May, the 'Tiger' convoy passed Gibraltar and entered the menacing Mediterranean. The next 48 hours were a period of acute anxiety at the Admiralty and 10 Downing Street. But on the 17th another pressure point was at least partially eased: the siege of Habbaniyah ended with the retirement of Iraqi forces from the nearby plateau, rapidly pursued by British forces from the base.

The Prime Minister went to the Commons for the close of the Vote of Confidence. Lloyd George blamed Churchill for trying to do too much: 'No one man, however able he is, can pull us through. I invite the Prime Minister to see that he has a small War Cabinet who will help him – help him in advice, and help him in action.' This speech was perhaps the most powerful of the debate, yet, as Harold Nicolson observed, when Lloyd George criticized Churchill 'his little eyes twinkled with admiration and (I am not in the least exaggerating) with love'. Churchill stood to reply, sombre faced and dressed in black suit embellished with huge watch-chain. He expressed strong confidence in the Egyptian and Mediterranean situation; he attacked Hore-Belisha with considerable scorn, and spent care in replying to Lloyd George, detailing the composition of the War Cabinet and the functions of the COS and Defence Committees: 'This is the body, this is the machinery; it works easily and flexibly at the present time, and I do not propose to make any changes in it until further advised.'[64] When the House divided the Government's motion received 477 votes in favour, including Hore-Belisha's, and only 3 against. Churchill may not have had plans for altering the War Cabinet itself, but he nevertheless made a Ministerial revision only the next day, 8 May: the Ministries of Shipping and Transport were merged into the Ministry of War Transport, with the non-party Lord Leathers placed at the head, where he would remain for the rest of the war.

Also on 8 May the War Cabinet were informed, for the first time, of the 'Tiger' convoy, carrying 306 tanks and 50 Hurricanes. 'This valuable cargo was being carried in five ships which steamed at the rate of 14½ knots,' said Churchill. 'The convoy was at the present moment in the danger zone.... Should the whole of these reinforcements succeed in reaching General Wavell he would have over 400 heavy tanks at his disposal. With this force the military situation in North Africa might be turned to our advantage.' Dill warned that the tanks would not be able to move straight into battle after they had arrived: time would be needed to run them in.[65] Reports from Iraq showed the situation to be easing; on the other hand, the Syrian threat was increasing. Secret negotiations had taken place in Paris on 5 and 6 May, following the German request to the Vichy Government for transit facilities, and suitable agreement had now been reached. Some indication of this had reached London: the Defence Committee agreed at their meeting on the evening of the 8th that General Dentz in Syria was unlikely to resist German pressure. The only British mobile force in Palestine had been detailed for Iraq operations. The Free French had however a force of six battalions, with some artillery and tanks, commanded by General Catroux who was anxious to move Syria from Vichy

239

control. The Defence Committee therefore decided all available help and encouragement should be given Catroux for him to enter Syria as soon as Germans arrived – if he went in earlier, Ministers claimed, he would be unlikely to receive much local support.[66] This decision to use Catroux's force clashed with the policy urged by Wavell – previously supported by Churchill – that the Free French should be kept in check to avoid resentment among the French population.[67] The Defence Committee also considered another telegram from Wavell, concerning Iraq: the General still insisted his forces were inadequate for a full-scale operation against Rashid Ali's troops. 'I still recommend that a political solution be sought.' Churchill took it upon himself to transmit the Defence Committee's reaction next day, 9 May: 'Our information is that Rashid Ali and his partisans are in desperate straits. However this may be, you are to fight hard against them.' Negotiations, added the Prime Minister, would merely lead to delay 'during which the German Air Force will arrive'.

Churchill also informed Wavell of the Defence Committee decision concerning Free French troops in Syria: these would not be used until Dentz had proved unwilling to resist the arrival of German aircraft. Unknown to the British, German and Italian aircraft had already started to build up in Syria.

Reports had reached London on rapid German progress in preparing for the Cretan offensive, called by the British 'Scorcher'; the COS cabled Wavell: 'It appears to present heaven-sent opportunity of dealing enemy heavy blow.'[68] Wavell was himself planning a limited attack; he told London on the 9th: 'I have ordered all available tanks to be placed at disposal of Gott's force for Sollum area. This is now in active preparation and should take place soon. I shall only cancel it if complete disaster overtakes "Tiger".'[69] 'Tiger' was in fact progressing well: enemy air attacks had been beaten off on the 8th, and although one ship had sunk after hitting a mine during the night, the remainder had steamed through the most dangerous stretch by the evening of the 9th. Late that night Churchill gathered Eden, Beaverbrook, Attlee and David Margesson in his study, and declared he was in favour of changing General Auchinleck and Wavell about – Auchinleck, C-in-C India, had shown himself generous with the offer of troops for Iraq. Amery agreed, so did Beaverbrook; Attlee and Margesson hesitated; Eden believed Wavell to have the better mind, but 'one does not know how he is bearing the strain and one cannot tell, though some of his recent reactions seem to indicate that he is flagging' – he advised a delay until the Cretan campaign had closed. Churchill agreed.[70]

Saturday, 10 May, saw the last and possibly the worst night of the London Blitz. A huge 'Bomber's Moon' illuminated the ravaged capital as the *Luftwaffe* droned amongst the searchlights; as on 29 December, water in the Thames was unusually low; 2,200 fires raged. More Londoners were killed than in any other raid – 1,436 – and 1,792 were seriously injured. Sixteen enemy aircraft were brought down, the maximum yet in night fighting. While *Luftwaffe* bombers preyed upon London, a single *Messerschmidt* had been heading for Scotland. Rudolf Hess, Hitler's closest confidant, Nazi Party Deputy leader, next in line after Göring to succeed Hitler, had left Augsburg, Germany, at 5.45 p.m. to make his personal bid for peace. Churchill was informed next afternoon that Hess had dropped by parachute near the Duke of Hamilton's home, and at first refused to believe it. The official documents now support Churchill's later statement that 'I never attached any serious importance to this episode'; nor, apparently, did many others in the Government or Foreign Office – Cadogan complained next day, 12 May, that Hess had 'taken up *all* my time and I am 48 hours in arrears with work,' and the arrival of this strange character was not considered worthy of a War Cabinet meeting until Thursday, 15 May.

On Monday, 12 May, Ministers heard 'Tiger' had been completed with the loss of only one ship. Churchill now believed Wavell had all the tools he required, and the Middle East Commander himself appeared to be acting more vigorously; a cable arrived on the 13th: 'Without waiting for "Tiger" I ordered available tanks to join Gott's force to attack enemy.... We will try to liquidate this tiresome Iraq business quickly.... I am doing my best to strengthen Crete.... I discussed the question of Syria with Catroux this afternoon.'[71] But, as always, it had become a race against time: information had now reached London of the presence of German aircraft in Syria, and reports were received of French arms and ammunition being sent by rail from Syria to Iraq. British counter-action was discussed by the Defence Committee next day, 14 May, when Ministers agreed the RAF should bomb Syrian airfields, irrespective of the effect on relations with the Vichy French.[72] Meanwhile, Churchill found time to complete an argumentative reply to Dill's memorandum on invasion, presented on 6 May. 'I gather you would be prepared to face the loss of Egypt and the Nile Valley, together with the surrender or ruin of the Army of half a million we we have concentrated there, rather than lose Singapore.' Churchill wrote in his memoirs: 'Many governments I have seen would have wilted before so grave a pronouncement by the highest professional authority.' The CIGS did not directly pursue the matter, but the general conflict of views and temperament between Dill and Churchill continued.[73]

Hess finally achieved a place on the War Cabinet agenda. He had been extensively interviewed, and his arrival had been mentioned in the Press the previous day following a German statement on the 12th that he was the victim of 'obsessions' and 'progressive illness'. Churchill had had a violent argument with Cadogan, Eden and Beaverbrook: he wanted to make a statement, but met with strong opposition because the wording of his announcement corresponded to a second German broadcast that Hess had flown with a peace offer. 'Hitler would heave a sigh of relief,' declared Cadogan. Churchill, in a violent temper, had finally given way; now, at the War Cabinet meeting on the 15th, he said he 'thought it best to wait a litle longer. There was no pressure for an early statement.'[74]

Eden made an announcement to the Commons blaming the French for the Syrian situation; Pétain declared in a broadcast that evening, the 19th, that recent negotiations with the Germans were 'lightening the path of the future' and he appealed to French people to follow him 'without any mental reservations'. RAF aircraft prepared to attack Damascus airfield. General Wavell warned the CIGS that the Germans probably intended an early attack on Crete, as a preliminary to an attack on Egypt on the west through Libya and from the north through Syria.[75] In the Western Desert the limited British attack, Operation 'Brevity' was launched in the Sollum area but fighting soon faded. 'Enemy proved rather stronger than we thought,' reported Wavell, 'and has forced us back on defensive till "Tiger Cubs" come into action.'[76] Renewed controversy was now to arise over the delay in bringing these 'Cubs' – tanks carried by the recent 'Tiger' convoy – into more immediate use. Churchill had condemned Dill's invasion memorandum on the grounds that forces must be sent to hold Egypt; he condemned Wavell for inaction and pointed out sacrifices made in sending reinforcements urgently needed at home. A balance had to be found, and this seemed to be contained in an appreciation considered by the COS on 16 May: 'The infantry available (in Britain) is in our opinion the bare minimum, but the weakness is in armoured forces.... It will be March 1942 before we have 6 armoured divisions and 4 army tank brigades fully trained and equipped, which are the minimum requirements for the security of the UK.' The RAF situation was equally serious. 'The number of squadrons in Fighter Command will be the absolute minimum considered necessary for security.' But balanced against these depressing figures were two factors: the unlikelihood of imminent invasion and the critical position in the Middle East. One sentence in the report summed up the overall situation: 'In view, however, of the grave weakness in the Middle East and the improbability of invasion in the next few weeks, a temporary reduction in the aircraft and crew strength of our bomber force might be accepted.'[77]

Wavell's days as Middle East Commander were coming to an end; his colleagues felt as he did, and, on 18 May one of them was abruptly replaced – Air Marshal Longmore, still in Britain for consultations, was succeeded by his deputy, Air Marshal A. W. Tedder. Also on Sunday the 18th, the British brigade group from Palestine, 'Habforce', reached Falluja near Habbaniyah and engaged Iraqi troops; fighting, not on a large scale, took place during the next few days. The RAF attacked German aircraft in Syria, and the Ambassador cabled on the 19th that these strikes had been welcomed by Free French sympathizers. Eden believed this now gave opportunity for Free French action, and raised the matter at a War Cabinet meeting during this Monday afternoon. Churchill believed the Vichy French should be given one last chance of stopping the passage of German aircraft, failing which 'we should proclaim Syria to be an independent Arab State'. Pound said the COS had sent a telegram to Cairo, asking for preparations to be made for 'the largest force which could be managed without prejudice to the security of the Western Desert, with a view to a move into Syria at the earliest posible date'. 'PM still hankering after his stupid statement about Hess,' wrote Cadogan in his diary. 'Insisted on reading it with great gusto to the Cabinet.' Churchill, after this reading, asked whether the statement should be made in Parliament the following day, and Cadogan was relieved Ministers were against the idea; according to the Minutes: 'Hess had already received so much attention in the Press that public opinion would favour giving the topic a rest. The absence of a statement was also calculated to maintain anxiety of the Nazi leaders.'[78]

For the past six days German aircraft had been attacking Crete, mainly striking at the three airfields. The Germans now believed the defences had been sufficiently softened. An optimistic message had arrived from Freyberg via Wavell: 'Everywhere all ranks are fit and morale is high.... I do not wish to be over-confident, but I feel that at least we will give excellent account of ourselves. With help of Royal Navy I trust Crete will be held.' Churchill had signalled Wavell: 'May you have God's blessing in this memorable and fateful operation, which will react in every theatre of the war.' And to Freyberg: 'All our thoughts are with you in these fateful days. We are sure that you and your brave men will perform a deed of lasting fame....'[79]

Two hours before dawn on Tuesday, 20 May, more German aircraft came over, more bombs flung down. And hissing towards Crete came glider after glider, swooping in west of the vital Maleme airfield and around the town of Canae. Dawn had broken; thick dust and plumes of smoke from the earlier bombing hung high in the air. More aircraft; and this time came the paratroops, thousand upon thousand dropping down through the dust and smoke into the thundering maelstrom of quickening battle.

More Germans were killed on this Tuesday than the total so far after 20 months of war. Men of the elite *Fliegerkorps* XI were slaughtered in scores, and more were constantly thrown in to be sacrificed. But ground was gained, first in feet, then in yards; individual enemy groups coagulated and vital territory consolidated, while defenders were lashed from the air by repeated low-level machine-gunning and screaming dive-bombers.

First reports reached London while the COS were meeting. Nothing could be done but anxiously await further news; the Chiefs therefore discussed Syria and decided Free French troops should be moved to the border as soon as possible, despite strong reservations already expressed by Wavell. The Defence Committee confirmed the decision during the afternoon, and a signal was immediately despatched.[80] Wavell was already under terrifying strain, and on this same day reported the *Afrika Korps* had been reinforced: a renewed offensive was therefore possibly imminent. Crete appeared to be holding out, and a cautious note came from Freyberg at 10 p.m.: 'We have been hard pressed. So far, I believe, we hold aerodromes ... and the two harbours. Margin by which we hold them is a bare one, and it would be wrong of me to paint optimistic picture.'[81] Casualties were causing concern at the German HQ, Athens; General Student, commander of *Fliegerkorps* XI, decided all remaining strength should be hurled at Maleme airfield, and just before first light on the 21st whole clusters of paratroopers again plummeted upon the island; more gliders whispered in. By the time the Defence Committee met at 10 Downing Street at 3 p.m. the Germans had established a fatal foothold at Maleme airfield, but Ministers retained some optimism, unaware of latest developments. Crete was a key Mediterranean position, said Churchill; not only would its capture be looked upon as a severe loss in prestige, 'but it would bring the German air force within effective range of our fleet at Alexandria with all that this entailed'. Yet the Prime Minister saw 'no reason why we should not retain our hold on the island, providing that General Wavell was able to land reinforcements on the southern side and that the navy could prevent anything in the way of a German seaborne landing'. Ministers agreed that 'with such reinforcements as could be rushed in, General Freyberg should be able to hold his own against airborne attack'.

An extremely disquieting signal had arrived from Wavell concerning Syria, in which he accused the Defence Committee of ignoring his advice in favour of Free French opinion. 'Effect of action by Free French alone likely to be failure.... You must trust my judgment in this matter or relieve me of my command. I am not willing to accept that Catroux, de Gaulle or Spears should dictate action that is bound seriously to affect military situation in Middle East.' General Dill saw Wavell's point of view; he told Ministers that Wavell should either be allowed to carry out the policy he believed sound, or indeed be relieved of his command. The Defence Committee adopted a harder attitude and pointed out the contradiction in Wavell's telegram: he had wished to avoid operations in Iraq and Syria because of troop shortages, and this had been one of the reasons why the Defence Committee had favoured using Free French troops, now, however, Wavell had apparently sufficient resources for a mixed Anglo-French operation. The Committee therefore agreed to a draft reply, despatched by Churchill: 'There is no objection to your mingling British troops with the Free French ... but, as you have clearly shown, you have not the means to mount a regular military operation.' All that could be done, therefore, was 'a kind of armed political inroad'. The telegram refuted Wavell's allegation that Free French representation had influenced the decision: the latter arose 'entirely from the view taken here by those who have supreme direction of war.... For this decision we, of course, take full responsibility, and should you find yourself unwilling to give effect to it, arrangements will be made to meet any wish you may express to be relieved of your Command.'[82] Soon after the meeting an unhappy Dill sent two letters, one to Auchinleck warning him to be ready to relieve Wavell, the other to Wavell himself which declared: 'What a time you are having.... I do not know whether or not you will pack up on receiving the telegram from the Defence Committee – or rather the PM.... From your own personal point of view you will be sorely tempted to hand in your portfolio – you could hardly go on a better wicket – but from a national point of view it would I feel be a disaster.'[83]

German troops were extending their control at Maleme. As night fell on the 21st the sea skyline to the west was suddenly lit with vivid orange and yellow flashes and a second later came the mighty roar of naval guns, as a German troop-convoy was intercepted and, until 2 a.m., the crammed German ships were pursued and destroyed: about 4,000 enemy troops drowned. Royal Naval vessels were also involved in a different type of hunt. Early on the 21st information had reached the Admiralty that two large enemy warships had been seen leaving the Kattegat; later these warships had been identified as the gigantic *Bismarck* and the *Prinz Eugen*. All available Royal Navy vessels were ordered to concentrate on these massive raiders, now in Bergen Fjord, and the battle-cruiser *Hood* and the new battleship *Prince of Wales* steamed from Scapa just after midnight, together with six destroyers, to join the cruisers *Norfolk* and *Suffolk* already in the Denmark Straits.

As British warships headed towards the *Bismarck* on Thursday, 22 May, in Berlin Hitler instructed Admiral Raeder that the German navy's main task must now be the disruption of British sea links; in France Kesselring began to shift his *Luftwaffe* HQ to Posen, ready for 'Barbarossa'; the bloody battle around Maleme continued. 'The enemy had made lodgements at different points,' Ministers were told at the 12.30 p.m. War Cabinet meeting, 'it was believed, they had not obtained control over any large areas.... Little definite news was available owing to the destruction of cyphers.' Ministers were informed that latest reports from Wavell indicated 'the prospects of a Free French success in Syria were much less favourable than previous estimates'.[84] Yet Wavell had now apparently acquiesced to the Defence Committee decision. 'I am moving reinforcements to Palestine,' he cabled, 'because we feel we must be prepared for action against Syria, and weak action is useless.' Describing the general situation, the General added: 'The object of the Army must be to force the enemy in Cyrenaica as far west as possible ... and to hang on to Crete and Cyprus. It will not be easy, with our resources.... We have some difficult months ahead, but will not lose heart.'[85]

While the War Cabinet had been having its 22 May meeting, another German troop convoy had been approaching Crete, and was now forced back. An urgent signal flashed from Admiral Cunningham to the naval commander in Cretan waters: 'Stick it out.... Must not let the army down.' But Cunningham warned the COS that if the Mediterranean fleet continued to sustain heavy losses it would be unable to prevent a landing.[86] And before the day closed the Royal Navy received another serious setback: a naval aircraft braved grim weather over the North Sea, penetrated heavy enemy fire at Bergen Fjord, and found the *Bismarck* and *Prinz Eugen* had disappeared. This worrying news reached Admiral Tovey, C-in-C, Home Fleet, at 8 p.m.; he immediately left Scapa in the battleship *King George V* with a powerful fleet in an attempt to block the exit from the Denmark Straits into the Atlantic. Pound told his COS colleagues next morning, Friday, 23 May, that he would be spending all his time in the Admiralty War Room to direct operations against the *Bismarck*, and he would therefore be unable to attend COS for the next few days. The same day Tedder warned Portal that it appeared no longer possible for the Royal Navy to operate in the vicinity of Crete by daylight, owing to enemy air strength, and RAF Blenheim bombers from the Western Desert could not hope to stop German troop convoys protected by Messerschmidt 110s. And Admiral Cunningham now signalled the Admiralty that he was forced to a 'melancholy conclusion' – British air weakness must mean defeat in the seas around Crete. By now two cruisers and three destroyers had been sunk and one battleship immobilized – among the cruisers was the *Kelly*, commanded by Captain Lord Louis Mountbatten, rescued with 278 other officers and men. The Admiralty told Cunningham the battle must continue. 'It is vitally important ... to prevent a seaborne expedition reaching the island.... Their Lordships most fully appreciate the heavy strain.'[87]

Some optimism nevertheless remained, reflected in the Defence Committee discussion at noon. Churchill commented that 'the situation appeared to be in hand except for the Maleme area, where the Germans had forced a lodgement and airborne landings were taking place. It was unfortunate that the defenders had not been able to stamp out the parachutists in this area, and it was essential that the German lodgement west of Canae should be obliterated by vigorous counter-attacks.' The Prime Minister warned that 'the fleet could not protect the island indefinitely from seaborne landings' but if the situation could be restored while the power of the Fleet was active, the enemy 'would be faced with the prospect of beginning all over again'. Ministers agreed that 'General Freyberg should throw in all the available reserves, including, if necessary, reinforcements to be landed that night, in an effort to restore the situation'.[88] Churchill sent an appeasing cable to Wavell: 'These are very hard times, and we must all do our best to help each other.... It is your views that weigh with us, and not those of Free French.... We cannot have Crete battle spoiled for the sake of Syria. Therefore inferior methods may be the only ones open at the moment.... We hope "Habforce" will soon enter Baghdad.'[89] On the same day Hitler declared in Directive No 30: 'I have ... decided to hasten developments in the Middle East by supporting Iraq.'

German engineers had now restored the battered Maleme airstrip and troop carriers were bumping down through heavy fire at the rate of over one every three minutes; a counter-attack attempted by exhausted New Zealand troops had failed. Out in the freezing squalls of the Atlantic, the cruisers *Suffolk* and *Norfolk* sighted two warships approaching from the north: the *Bismarck* and *Eugen*. Churchill left London to spend the Saturday and Sunday at Chequers – 'it was likely to be an anxious weekend'.

At 7 a.m. on the 23rd Churchill was told the Royal Navy's largest and fastest capital ship, *Hood*, had blown up and sunk; at 8.30 a.m. he learnt the *Prince of Wales* had been forced to break off action with the *Bismarck*. Later reports revealed all the *Hood*'s company, over 1,500 men, had drowned, and the *Prince of Wales* – only passed 'fit for battle' one week before – had been severely damaged. She had however inflicted wounds on the *Bismarck*, slowing her down, and was still in contact. Churchill tried to occupy his mind by reading the masses of War Office and Foreign Office cables. A report had been sent by Wavell's Chief of Staff: the Germans were now estimated to have upwards of 10,000 men around Canae and Suda; Freyberg's force numbered about the same, but his men were very tired – and the Germans had the overwhelming advantage of air supremacy. The defenders were suffering from shortages of food, ammunition and medical supplies; reinforcements were having supreme difficulty in forcing through. The COS replied: 'Our difficulties in Crete are great, but ... so are those of the enemy ... reinforcements in greatest strength should be sent as soon as possible.'[90] At 6.40 p.m. on this Saturday the *Bismarck* suddenly turned upon her pursuers to let the *Eugen* slip away. The *King George V* and the *Illustrious* were hurrying from the north-east; aircraft from the *Illustrious* attacked the enemy at 8 p.m. Then, at 3 a.m. on the 25th, contact broke. Throughout the Sunday desperate attempts were made to regain touch, and, on the assumption that the German warship would be making for St Nazaire or Brest, forces were sent in that direction, but by evening the Royal Navy hunters were beginning to suffer fuel shortages.

Further reports had come from Cairo, stressing naval difficulties and the problems of reinforcing Crete. Churchill believed insufficient attempts were being made, and a special COS meeting on the Sunday afternoon agreed the battle might yet be won, if all Services threw themselves into greater effort. The Prime Minister approved a stiff telegram: 'If the situation is allowed to drag on, the enemy will have the advantage because, unless more drastic naval action is taken ... the enemy will be able to reinforce the island.... The Fleet and the RAF must accept whatever risk is entailed.'[91] Meanwhile, Wavell had been considering the controversial Syrian operation; despite his other pressures he had made a rapid visit to Palestine and to Basra, where he had met Auchinleck, returning to Cairo early this Sunday, 25 May; discussions were held with Generals de Gaulle, Spears and Catroux, after which Wavell drafted a plan, Operation 'Exporter', for a Syrian expedition, but he stressed that the Anglo-French forces would not be able to move until the first week in June, and he believed the total strength would be inadequate. The expedition would be commanded by Wilson.[92]

Monday, 26 May, was a day of anger, suspense and tragedy. In Cairo the COS signal urging more drastic action over Crete, led to a C-in-Cs conference, after which a caustic cable was sent by Cunningham to the Admiralty. 'Their Lordships may rest assured that determining factor ... is not fear of sustaining losses, but need to avoid loss which, without commensurate advantage to ourselves, will cripple the fleet.... So far as I am aware, enemy has not yet succeeded in getting any considerable reinforcements to Crete by sea.' He warned: 'It is inadvisable to drive men beyond a certain point.'[93]

The *Bismarck* had been sighted but was still escaping; German troops were now beginning to outnumber exhausted defenders in Crete; Rommel's forward units advanced in the Western Desert and captured the important position of Halfaya: the War Cabinet, meeting at 10 Downing Street at 5 p.m., were confronted with gloomy news from all areas. Pound described the hunt for the *Bismarck*. 'It was hoped to carry out a torpedo bombing attack on her that afternoon. If she was not intercepted she might make St Nazaire next day.... When the last report had been received *Rodney* had been about 35 miles from *Bismarck* and *King George V* about 100 miles.' A message came into the Cabinet Room: carrier aircraft had been airborne from 3 until 5 o'clock without sighting the warships and chances of a torpedo bombing attack were therefore fading. Ministers heard latest news of the Crete battle, and were told only a third of the Mediterranean Fleet remained undamaged. 'A very unpleasant Cabinet,' wrote Cadogan. 'Tonight [Winston] was almost throwing his hand in. But there is a bit of the histrionic in *that*.'[94] Far worse news was on its way to Whitehall. Wavell had received a despairing signal from Freyberg: 'I regret to have to report ... limit of endurance has been reached by troops under my command here at Suda Bay.... Our situation here is hopeless.' And Freyberg warned: 'I feel I should tell you that from an administrative point of view difficulties of extricating this force in full are now insuperable. Provided a decision is taken at once a certain proportion of force might be embarked.' Despite this appeal for speed, Wavell pressed Freyberg to make one more attempt to drive back the enemy, and even if this failed, not to evacuate immediately but to retire to new positions. 'It should thus be possible to hold enemy for some time.' Wavell despatched an urgent warning signal to London: 'Matter is in balance and doubtful whether we can retain permanent hold.' Churchill replied in the early hours of the 27th: 'Victory in Crete essential at this turning point in the war. Keep hurling in all aid you can.'[95]

Churchill spent most of the night in the dimly-lit Admiralty War Room, and, as news from the Crete quarter darkened, the *Bismarck* situation suddenly brightened. The wounded warship slowed and became almost unmanoeuvrable; hunters closed in; at daybreak the battle began, and Churchill informed the War Cabinet at 10.30 a.m. that *Bismarck* 'had received four hits from torpedoes and was virtually stationary.... There was every hope that we should soon receive information that this enemy ship had been destroyed.' But the mood in the War Cabinet room abruptly changed; Churchill declared that 'all chances of winning the battle in Crete now appeared to have gone and we should have to face the prospect of the loss of most of our forces there. There was no action that we in this country could take.' The problem was now presented of how to explain this dreadful news to the British public, and Churchill proposed a delay: Ministers agreed that he should merely say in a Commons statement that hard fighting was continuing; he would emphasize the enemy advantage of air superiority.[96] This announcement was made immediately after the War Cabinet meeting: the situation in Crete was not too good, he said, but he expressed confidence over Libya and Iraq. Churchill concentrated on the *Bismarck* story and described the latest clash. 'It is thought that this is now proceeding, and it is thought that there cannot be any lengthy delay in disposing of this vessel.' Churchill sat down; almost immediately a secretary in the official gallery began waving a small sheet of paper. Brendan Bracken took it and passed it to the Prime Minister. 'I crave your indulgence, Mr Speaker. I have just received news that the *Bismarck* has been sunk.' Wild cheers broke out in the Commons; the scene and dramatic intervention were reminiscent of the time when Chamberlain received Hitler's invitation to Munich.

Dill received another signal from Cairo at 3 p.m. 'Have ordered evacuation troops from Crete as opportunity offers.' And at 5.26 p.m.: 'It has become quite obvious that attempt to prolong defence will not only be useless but is likely to exhaust navy, army and air resources as to compromise defence positions in Middle East even more gravely.' Wavell also warned: 'Fear that troops at Heraklion may have considerable difficulty in holding out and evacuation of remainder will not be easy.' The Defence Committee met in the Cabinet War Room at 9.45 p.m.; Churchill immediately declared that 'events now necessitated the evacuation of our forces from Crete, and an order to this effect had been sent to General Wavell'. The Committee spared no time for discussion of the disaster itself; consideration was given instead to the wider Middle East situation, and Churchill showed his incredible post-disaster resilience, perhaps his greatest source of strength. 'The first essential was to defeat the German army in Libya. Our second task would be to try to peg claims in Syria with the small forces which could be made available without disrupting our effort in Libya.' Pound stressed the vital importance of this recapture of Cyrenaica. 'Unless this could be done it would be difficult for the Mediterranean Fleet to keep open the line of communications to Malta or to interrupt the German lines of communications from Crete to Cyrenaica.' Not surprisingly, the COS 'were not in favour of attempting to defend Cyprus.... Retention of Cyprus would be of little value if the Germans got into Syria.... We would have to fight the Germans in Syria sooner or later, and it would be better to go in now.' The Admiral added that once in Syria 'we could do to the Germans in Cyprus what they had done to us in Crete'. Ministers agreed with Wavell's plan for Operation 'Exporter', and also approved a suggestion by Eden that the Turks should be offered to assist in the operation, despite possible Arab estrangement. The Turks would thereby possibly be won further into the British side, said the Foreign Secretary, who admitted his idea was 'rather devious', in that the Turks were unlikely to accept the offer but would be pleased to receive it. Churchill complained he was 'unable to understand what was happening in Iraq': he had expected 'for days now to hear that we were in Baghdad'.[97] In fact, almost as the Defence Committee ended late on the 27th, the advance on Baghdad was beginning.

Evacuation from Crete would start next night, 28-29 May. At their meeting on the morning of the 28th the COS resumed discussion on the immediate need of a desert offensive, now to be code-named 'Battleaxe' and Wavell was told: 'Our first object must be to gain a decisive military success in the Western Desert and to destroy the enemy armoured forces.' Churchill insisted on adding a private message, considered by the CIGS to be unnecessary and unwise: Wavell now had a definite numerical superiority, signalled the Prime Minister, and he asked if Wilson could be given command, despite his appointment to lead 'Exporter'. An extremely cautious reply came from Cairo late that Wednesday, causing Churchill renewed irritation: the earliest date for the beginning of the forward move would be 7 June, and 'I think it right to inform you that the measure of success which will attend this operation is in my opinion doubtful'. Wavell listed various 'disquietening features' disclosed in recent operations: British armoured cars were too lightly protected; infantry tanks were too slow and vulnerable; cruiser tanks had little advantage over German medium tanks; technical breakdowns were still too numerous. 'We shall not be able to accept battle with perfect confidence in spite of numerical superiority.'[98]

Over 32,000 troops were cooped on Crete; only two ports were usable and only for a few hours each night: Heraklion, on the north coast, already under heavy air attack, and Sphakia on the south, only approachable by rough mountain track described by Freyberg as the *via dolorosa*. Three cruisers and six destroyers were sent to Heraklion during the 28th, but half their AA ammunition had been fired before the destination was reached. About 4,000 troops were embarked between midnight and 3 a.m. on the 29th before these warships had to leave; air attack continued, and one destroyer had to be beached. Another received three direct hits, killing 260 soldiers, another also received a direct hit, killing 103. The fleet limped into Alexandria the next night, and the decision was taken to abandon Heraklion. The hard road to Sphakia, where 6,000 had been embarked on the night of the 28th, was the sole route to survival. Even this exit would have been closed if the War Cabinet had taken a different decision at noon on the 29th. The choice had been offered: to go on with evacuation despite possible crippling losses to the Mediterranean Fleet, or to abandon the troops. Ministers unanimously agreed the operation should proceed. The Prime Minister ended the meeting by hoping that 'those whose duties permitted would take the opportunity to be away for a few days during the Whitsuntide recess'.[99]

A brief item was entered in the German Naval War Diary for this day, 29 May: 'The preparatory movement of warships for "Barbarossa" has begun.' British warships were again heading for Crete, and more men were snatched to safety, despite increasing Royal Navy and RAF losses. Admiral Cunningham, disturbed and exhausted by the whole affair, including the previous implications that the navy had been insufficiently active, sent a personal letter to the First Sea Lord: if the Prime Minister or the Admiralty wished a change in command he would not feel annoyed, especially as events might have shaken the Fleet's faith in his handling of the affairs. Pound wisely ignored the suggestion.[100] Wavell was meanwhile edging closer to departure; also on 30 May he sent a cryptic signal listing defects which had been discovered in tanks brought by Churchill's 'Tiger' convoy, and next day, he sent a further message: the earliest date on which he could now launch 'Battleaxe' was 15 June.[101] Freyberg had left Crete, at Wavell's explicit order, and on the morning of 31 May, Wavell, the New Zealand Prime Minister and General Blamey agreed the Royal Navy could not be asked to do more; Wavell flew to Alexandria to see Cunningham. 'I gave him our decision and absolution from further effort.' The Admiral replied that 'the navy had never yet failed the army in such a situation ... he was going in again that night.'[102]

Welcome information had reached the Middle East from London; the COS had decided at their meeting earlier on the 31st to endorse a Joint Intelligence Committee report on possible German intentions. 'Although many good reasons could be adduced why Hitler should decide, after the capture of Crete, to exploit his success by action towards Egypt, all the evidence points to Germany's next move being an attempt to enforce her demands on the Soviets.' Cairo HQ might have chance to strike before further reinforcements reached Rommel. And Hitler had already missed his

Iraq opportunity: Baghdad had been entered and Rashid Ali had fled. The COS agreed upon armistice terms to be offered: British forces were to occupy strategic points and German and Italian service personnel were to be interned.

Another 4,000 men were taken from Crete on this last, extra night. Next day, 1 June, Churchill claimed to Eden he had wanted the rescue attempts to be continued for another night, but he had found Wavell had already issued orders for remaining troops to capitulate.[103] About 18,000 had been rescued, out of the 32,000 on the island; army dead numbered 1,800 – slightly less than the naval total. Nine warships had been sunk, 17 seriously damaged; 46 aircraft had been lost. German casualties were almost 4,000 men killed excluding terrible casualties suffered by sea-borne units; over 200 aircraft had been lost. While Göring might claim Crete had shown there were 'no impregnable islands', the campaign had deterrent effect on German plans for Malta. Not knowing *Fliegerkorps* XI to have been the only one of its kind, British planners worked on the assumption that similar offensives might be launched upon Britain, and already, on 28 May, the COS had appointed a special committee to report on measures to guard against airborne attack. 'The tragic sequence of events in Crete had reached their conclusion,' Churchill declared at the War Cabinet meeting on Monday, 2 June. A number of questions arose, he continued. 'Why had not long range guns been fixed where they could fire on the aerodromes? Why had not the aerodromes been mined and more tanks landed? Again, the public would ask why, if we had taken 17,000 men off, we could not have sent adequate reinforcements to hold the island?' Churchill answered himself. 'Once we had lost the aerodromes, we no longer had it in our power to bring in reinforcements and supplies except at excessive cost to the Fleet.' The Prime Minister expressed dissatisfaction with Cunningham. 'After 5,000 men had been embarked on the first night, the Commander-in-Chief Mediterranean had telegraphed home emphasizing the serious losses the fleet might suffer if further troops were removed. We had insisted, however, on the evacuation proceeding and a further 12,000 had been got away without any further serious naval losses.' Pound intervened. 'The Commander-in-Chief had made it clear that he was prepared to carry on with the evacuation until the last ship, but he had thought it his duty to inform the Government of the large naval losses which the operation might entail in view of its repercussion on our position in the Mediterranean.' Churchill switched his criticism to Wavell: on the Saturday night he (Churchill) had heard of preparations to abandon evacuation – presumably on the Sunday – and he and the First Sea Lord had believed further efforts should be made to rescue 5,000 men still on the beaches, but before the order could be given the commander on Crete had reported the remaining men were incapable of further resistance and that 'in accordance with directions previously received from General Wavell, he had ordered them to capitulate'. Ministers joined in the attack: insufficient aerodromes had been prepared, and 'a comparison was drawn between the speed with which the Germans made aerodromes available', although the Minutes added: 'It was pointed out that the Germans used what was, in effect, slave labour.'

No Minister is recorded as having spoken in defence of Wavell or Cunningham; no one apparently referred to Wavell's repeated warnings of the dangers from airborne attack, no mention was made of equipment shortage; 5,000 men were not in fact left waiting on the beaches – most of them were scattered wide and could not be gathered in time. Churchill could not have known of the decision taken by Wavell, and agreed by the New Zealand Prime Minister, to relieve Cunningham of all further attempts to evacuate troops – an absolution which the Admiral flatly refused to consider, much to Wavell's relief. Granted the lack of information, the War Cabinet Minutes for this 56th meeting of 1941 seem nevertheless shabby. Unlike the Minutes after Dunkirk or after the fighting on the Greek mainland, there is no reference to the heroism of the troops or the courage of the Royal Navy and RAF – and yet the Minutes also declared that '25 per cent of the German air force had been employed against Crete and more than 25 per cent of her transport aircraft. The enemy might have lost 400 aircraft.' Battling against these odds was no mean feat. Ministers turned to other topics. Eden said he proposed to see the Soviet Ambassador later in the evening, and intended to say that 'If Russia was attacked by Germany, we would take action elsewhere to relieve the pressure.' A telegram had been sent to Cripps recalling him for consultation.[104]

'There is a storm of criticism about Crete,' cabled Churchill to Wavell on the 3rd, 'and I am being pressed for explanations on many points. Do not worry about this at all now. Simply keep your eye on Syria and above all "Battleaxe". These alone can supply the answers to criticism, just or unjust.'[105] And these alone could prevent Wavell's ousting from Cairo – yet the General still had serious doubts over the timing of 'Battleaxe' and over the strength of 'Exporter'. Meanwhile, the British Expeditionary Force – BEF – was being ridiculed as the 'Back Every Fortnight'; the *Daily Herald* declared on 4 June: 'Our first reaction to the bloody fiasco of Crete was bewilderment. Our second was anger,' and the *Daily Mail* pointed out that British troops had been in the island for 7 months, and had lost it after only 12 days. On 5 June Churchill told the

254

War Cabinet of pressure for a debate on Crete, warning that the debate must be held; he added he was satisfied that 'there had been overwhelming justification on military grounds for the course which had been adopted'.

Eden reported a conversation with the Russian Ambassador earlier that Thursday: Maisky had been 'by no means shocked' when Eden had said Germany had plans for attacking Russia. But Eden told Ministers that 'the Foreign Office view was still that Russia would make substantial concession rather than fight Germany'. Discussion turned to Syria, where Operation 'Exporter' was scheduled to start in three days' time; Churchill warned that 'the Vichy Government might take warlike action against us', but he did not think they would actually declare war. The COS were asked to consider the possibility of counter-attacks by air raids on Vichy and Toulon and unlimited submarine warfare against French shipping in certain zones.[106] Wavell reported later on the 5th that fighting in Syria would be avoided as far as possible; he repeated his warning that he had always estimated the strength required as two divisions and one armoured division, whereas Wilson would only have most of one division, an Indian Brigade, plus six Free French battalions and only part of an armoured division. He therefore regarded success dependent on Vichy attitude. The General wrote to a friend this Thursday: 'It's all a matter of equipment, and that is still desperately slow to come out.'[107] Next day, 6 June, Wavell sent his 'Battleaxe' appreciation: the offensive would be in three stages, first an attack on enemy forces in the Sollum-Capuzzo area, second an advance to the Tobruk area and raids by the Tobruk garrison, third, exploitation. He warned that reduced strength at the end of the first stage might rule out the second and third.[108]

'Exporter' began on Sunday, 8 June, exactly a week before 'Battleaxe' was planned to start. The joint force aimed to reach Damascus and Beirut on the first day, but opposition hardened, especially against the Free French units as Wavell had predicted. In London, Churchill was annoyed by lack of information; General Dill sent an admonishing request to Cairo for more news just before midnight – all the COS had to go on, he complained, were Press flashes. The request brought no response: Wavell flew to the Western Desert next morning, 9 June, discussed plans for 'Battleaxe' and stayed the night at the front. The War Cabinet had therefore no information on 'Exporter' when Ministers met at 5 p.m. on the 9th and Churchill was by now extremely angry – the Commons debate on the Government's handling of recent affairs was to start next day and Churchill had to make a general statement. 'It's damned bad manners,' he growled.[109] Reports had meanwhile been multiplying of German preparations for an attack on Russia, and earlier on the 9th the Joint Intelligence Committee produced a paper declaring the Germans might reach Moscow within six weeks; military effects of the war would include a postponement of an invasion attempt on Britain, dispersal of forces, reduction in air attacks on Britain and on shipping, and a temporary removal of the German threat in the Middle East. Eden raised the subject at the War Cabinet meeting: nothing more could be done in the diplomatic field to encourage Russian resistance, but he added that if Maisky gave him the opportunity, he would say that 'if Russia became involved in war with Germany, we would do all that we could, for example by air action in the West, to draw off German air forces'. Ministers agreed.[110] When Eden made this statement to the Ambassador next day. Maisky 'nodded, but made no comment'.[111]

Late on the 9th the CIGS had sent an urgent signal to Wavell: 'Essential that PM should have fuller report Syrian operation for his statement to House at noon tomorrow.' Wavell, in the desert, was unable to oblige; Churchill could therefore only make a vague announcement that the Syrian operations in no way meant British territorial designs on the country or anywhere else in French territory, but were to ensure that Syria gave as little possible trouble. Most detailed criticism in the debate came as usual from the ex-War Minister, Hore-Belisha. 'It would be helpful for the future if we were to ask ourselves whether at Dakar, in Cyrenaica, in Greece, and now in Crete the forfeits which we have incurred have not been at least in part due to an imperfect assessment of possibilities, and indeed of probabilities, and consequently to ineffective preparation.' As usual Churchill replied by involving Hore-Belisha in responsibility: 'The state in which our army was left when the Right Hon. Gentleman had ended his two years and seven months' tenure at the War Office ... was lamentable.' Churchill stalked up to Hore-Belisha in the Smoking-Room: 'If you fight me I shall fight back.'[112] No division followed the debate; as Churchill had commented to War Cabinet Ministers the day before: 'People criticize this Government, but its great strength – and I dare say it in this company – is that there's no alternative!'[113]

'Sorry about lack of information from Syria,' Wavell wired next morning. 'My almost hourly requests produce nothing.... Communications are poor and forward troops especially Free French are apparently not reporting.'[114] News which had arrived was depressing. General Dentz had 35,000 troops, the best – about 8,000 – being Frenchmen. Vichy supporters had reacted vigorously to the Free French advance and by 12 June Damascus was still 10 miles away – and these last miles would take another 9 days to cover.

Meanwhile, other disturbing news reached London concerning the Middle East. Attention of Ministers was drawn on the 12th to a telegram received from the Military Mission in Washington: the US Ambassador at Cairo had reported 'considerable dissatisfaction' among Australian and New Zealand troops and 'the morale of the RAF in Egypt was low'. This, on the eve of 'Battleaxe', was considered disquieting, and the War Cabinet asked the CIGS and Chief of Air Staff to report. Ministers then discussed Russia. Earlier in the day the Joint Intelligence Committee (JIC) had reported the situation might 'come to a head' in the second half of June, and the COS had decided Britain might have to put drastic pressure on Russia not to concede – with this pressure possibly including RAF attacks on the Baku oil refineries.[115] Ministers at the War Cabinet meeting agreed that 'Germany might wish to destroy the USSR military forces now, when they might hope to do so easily. A German ultimatum might take the form of demanding complete control of the ... Ukraine and of the Caucasus oilfield. Germany might hope in this way to outflank Turkey.' Eden said Germany probably intended to deliver her ultimatum when military concentrations were complete – the JIC had reported over one-third of the German army was now disposed on the Soviet frontier.[116] Eden saw Maisky the following evening, 13 June, and warned that 'in the past 48 hours the information reaching us had become more significant'. He told the Ambassador that Churchill had agreed Britain would be prepared to send a service mission to Moscow in the event of German aggression, and Britain would give 'urgent consideration' to Russia's economic needs. Maisky maintained German troop concentrations had been exaggerated: Germany was not intending to attack Russia. 'The atmosphere was stiff,' wrote Eden.[117] Maisky was sticking to the rigid Soviet line; that same evening a Tass communiqué declared: 'Even before the return of the English Ambassador Cripps to London, but especially since his return, there have been widespread rumours of an impending war between the USSR and Germany.... Despite the obvious absurdity of these rumours, responsible circles in Moscow have thought it necessary to state that they are a clumsy propaganda manoeuvre.' Next day, Saturday, 14 June, Hitler held an 8-hour conference to settle final 'Barbarossa' details; in London the JIC completed a revised version of their report produced on the 9th, cutting the estimated time it would take the Germans to reach Moscow from 6 to 3 or 4 weeks.[118]

General Wavell was enjoying a game of golf with General Blamey, his Australian deputy. Earlier on this Saturday he had sent a final message to General Beresford-Peirse, GOC, Western Desert: ' "Battleaxe" is the most important operation yet undertaken in

Middle East.... First decisive defeat of German troops on land will be outstanding event.' Late in the afternoon of this 14 June, British forces began their forward move from Sofafi and Buq Buq, hoping to achieve surprise. Rommel's 15 *Panzer* Division was waiting for them, armed with half his total tank strength and positioned across any approach along the coast. Rommel had anticipated a British move, now, at 9 p.m., he alerted his reserve force for an advance forward from south of Tobruk. After an early morning air offensive on Sunday, 15 June, ground forces clashed around Halfaya and Capuzzo; in these early stages British progress seemed satisfactory: although Halfaya held out, Capuzzo fell to the Guards Brigade in the afternoon.

'It looks as if a vast German onslaught on Russia is imminent,' wrote Churchill to Roosevelt during the day. 'Should this new war break out we shall of course give all encouragement and any help we can spare to the Russians, following the principle that Hitler is the foe we have to beat.'[119] Halifax opened discussions with Welles on this Sunday over possible US help to Russia; Welles said there would be no objections in principle, but practical difficulties might arise. Also on the 15th Ribbentrop warned the Hungarians: 'The Führer will probably be compelled, by the beginning of July at the latest, to clarify German-Russian relations.'

'Today – it's 2.30 a.m. – will see the decision,' wrote Rommel to his wife on the 16th. 'It's going to be a hard fight, so you'll understand that I can't sleep.'[120] 'We are sending you all information as it comes in,' signalled Wavell to the CIGS at 12.30 p.m. 'General impression heavy fighting and close-run battle.' Dill gave details to the War Cabinet at 5 p.m. on the 16th: the enemy were surrounded at Halfaya, but still resisting. 'There is no reason to be dissatisfied with the progress made, although we have had a number of tanks put out of action by mines.' The Turks seemed about to sign an agreement with Germany, warned Eden, which he described as 'unfortunate', but the terms could have been worse – and 'there was nothing we could do'. Ministers were also told that the German concentration against Russia was proceeding and 'should by now be nearly complete'. Attending this meeting was Cripps, in London for consultations, and he now gave a statement on Soviet-German relations: fundamentally, he declared, the Soviets were hostile 'to both the Germans and ourselves. Probably they regarded us as the more stable of the two, but Germany as the more dangerous from a short-term point of view.' The facts of recent German troop concentrations were well known in Moscow, the Ambassador claimed. 'The general belief in well-informed circles in Moscow was that Hitler would pitch his demands so high that it would be impossible for the Soviet Government to accept them. His reasons for this might be as follows: (a) In a year's time his own military position was likely to be weaker and the Soviet's stronger; (b) If he made war on Russia now he could count on considerable sympathy in certain quarters in the United States; (c) He might argue that his Russian campaign would be over in time to allow him to stage an invasion of the United Kingdom.' Sir Stafford believed the Soviets 'would go to considerable lengths' to appease Hitler; if they failed and war broke out, 'the prevailing view in diplomatic circles in Moscow was that Russia could not hold out against Germany for more than three or four weeks. By the end of that time the enemy might be in Leningrad, Moscow and Kiev.' Eden said he had just seen the US Chargé who had told him that the American Ambassador in Moscow viewed the situation in very similar fashion to Cripps.[121]

The decisive moment of 'Battleaxe' had been reached while the War Cabinet had been sitting. A fierce engagement between the British 7th Armoured Brigade and the 5th Light Division took place near Sidi Omar: the German tanks managed to fight through and made for Sidi Suleiman. This was Rommel's opportunity; the battle was following his favourite pattern – first, let the enemy wear himself down, and by now the British had suffered considerable tank losses, then, 'I planned to concentrate both armoured divisions suddenly into one focus and thus deal the enemy an unexpected blow in his most sensitive spot.' Rommel forged the second arm of his pincer movement: 15th *Panzer* was ordered to disengage and strike to the north of the 5th Light Division, also towards Sidi Suleiman, even though this left the area north of Capuzzo largely undefended.[122] The two arms advanced throughout the night of the 16th; by dawn they had started to converge behind Capuzzo and within striking distance of Halfaya, cutting communications to British forward troops. Early on the 17th the Germans intercepted a British signal requesting Beresford-Peirse to come forward to take an urgent decision: Rommel deduced the British were bewildered and losing cohesion, and he ordered his pincer moves to make for Halfaya, thus closing the net around Capuzzo and the bulk of the British forces. Wavell flew up with Beresford-Peirse, but the order to withdraw had already been given to the 4th Indian Division. The British forces began to pull back; just past noon Wavell flew back to Cairo. Tanks, armoured cars and other precious equipment were now littering the scarred desert. The Defence Committee had met at noon to hear Churchill give details of 'the great effort which we had made, and the serious risks which we had taken, to give C-in-Cs adequate reinforcements (in Libya).... By these means we had given C-in-Cs in the Middle East a superiority in numbers of weapons, tanks and aircraft, which were so essential.

...For the first time we were in a position to face the Germans in a position of level footing.' The present battle, he continued, was aimed at wiping out the enemy force in Libya.

The Prime Minister then gave his views of the position in other areas. The situation in Iraq was 'very good', but resistance in Syria had been greater than expected. 'We had assembled the best possible force in the circumstances ... but it was unfortunately deficient in armoured fighting vehicles.' On the Home Front, 'an investigation was being made regarding the defence of our aerodromes which should take account of the lessons learnt from the Crete battle'. The Battle of the Atlantic continued to cause anxiety: 'With American assistance we could sustain shipping losses of up to 400,000 tons a month' – yet the War Cabinet had been informed only the previous day that shipping losses for April totalled 585,000 tons, including the heavy losses in the Mediterranean, and the figure so far for May was 461,000.[123]

No news came from Cairo during the afternoon. Churchill could stand the waiting strain no longer; he took the unusual step of going to Chequers this Tuesday evening, where the astonished house-keeper had to remove shutters and dust-sheets. And there Wavell's signal was handed to the Prime Minister: 'I regret to report failure of "Battleaxe"....' Churchill shuffled out into the garden. Both sides had suffered heavy losses: 29 British Cruiser tanks and 58 Infantry tanks; many of the latter from mechanical breakdown; 100 German tanks were claimed destroyed. Both could do little more than consolidate positions.

Hitler's other, infinitely larger offensive claimed priority over reinforcements to Rommel. On the night of the 18th a further report of German intentions towards Russia reached the Foreign Office from Birger Dahlerus – the ubiquitous and unsuccessful Swedish peace-maker during the last months before war. Next day Hitler revealed he was already thinking beyond a Russian conquest: Directive No 32 declared: 'The siege of England must be resumed with the utmost intensity by the Navy and Air Force after the conclusion of the campaign in the East.' Also on the 19th Churchill told the War Cabinet that steps were being taken to guard against another possible German offensive. 'The United States were sending a force of Marines to Iceland. Later they proposed to send about 25,000 soldiers, who would relieve the British garrison ... when the news comes out it is bound to create a great impression.'

This meeting had opened with the 'Battleaxe' result. 'In the early stages this operation had developed favourably. Later the enemy had counter-attacked with very large forces, and it had been decided to break off the operation. Both sides were now back where they had started.'[124] The Syrian campaign was reaching a climax. Wavell had sent reinforcements, such as could be spared, and part of the Iraq 'Habforce' had been ordered to advance from the south while Indian troops from Iraq moved up the Euphrates. Damascus fell to the Australians on 21 June. General Dentz would persist in the struggle for another 21 days, but the end was already clear; Syria and Iraq had been removed from possible German penetration; Turkish fears were reduced, although too late to stop the treaty with Germany on the 18th.

Late in the afternoon of the 20th Churchill had sent over to War Office copies of two signals he wanted despatched, one to the Viceroy of India to be passed to General Auchinleck and the other to Wavell. 'I have come to the conclusion,' began the latter, 'that public interest will best be served by appointment of General Auchinleck to relieve you.... I have greatly admired your command and conduct of these armies both in success and adversity.... I feel however that after the long strain you have borne a new eye and a new hand are required in this most seriously menaced theatre. ... You should proceed at your earliest convenience to India.'[125] General Dill immediately crossed over to 10 Downing Street to protest, although more against the decision to send Wavell direct to India, without home leave, rather than against the transfer itself. The telegrams left next day, Saturday, 21 June. The move had been made without reference to the War Cabinet, unlike most of the other senior personnel changes, but there is no evidence Churchill would have met with Ministerial opposition. Wavell received his telegram early on the 22nd, and replied with dignity the same day: 'I think you are wise to make change and get new ideas and action on the many problems in the Middle East and am sure Auchinleck will be successful choice.' A request by Wavell for a short home leave was refused. Churchill was reported to have commented: 'I can't have him hanging about in London living in his club' – other possible reasons were the need for speed and the need to avoid an unsettled vacuum in either Cairo or India. And by then, momentous events had erupted.

Churchill had travelled down to Chequers on the Friday night, 20 June. Eden and Dill were among the house-guests; after-dinner discussion on Saturday centred on the possible date for the German attack on Russia and the likely length of the campaign: Dill thought the Soviet army would be unable to hold out longer than six or seven weeks. At 2 a.m. on the 22nd, the Russian Ambassador in Berlin was told that Ribbentrop wished to see him at 4 a.m. Schulenburg was told to see Molotov at the same hour. Both dawn interviews took place: war was declared; just 30 minutes before, Hitler's artillery had begun its mighty, murderous bombardment.

10

Barbarossa

Churchill's man-servant entered Eden's bedroom at 7.30 a.m. on Sunday, 22 June, carrying a large fat cigar on a silver salver. 'The Prime Minister's compliments, Sir, and the German armies have invaded Russia.' Down the corridor Dill commented: 'I suppose they'll be rounded up in hordes'; Cripps soon reported from Moscow: 'The Germans will go through Russia like a hot knife through butter.' Churchill had declared the previous night: 'If Hitler invaded Hell I would make at least a favourable reference to the Devil in the House of Commons,' and he therefore announced he would make a broadcast that evening at 9 o'clock. His speech was ready a mere 20 minutes before the scheduled time: 'No one has been a more consistent opponent of Communism than I have for the last 25 years.... But all this fades away before the spectacle which is now unfolding.... Any man or state who fights on against Nazidom will have our aid.... We shall give whatever help we can to Russia and the Russian people.'[1]

Hitler planned three drives deep into Russia: 29 divisions under von Leeb advancing from East Prussia in the north; 50 divisions under von Bock to the south on either side of the Minsk-Smolensk-Moscow line; 42 divisions under von Runstedt driving from the Lublin area towards Kiev. On this first day tactical surprise was achieved along the entire front: over 10,000 prisoners were taken; 800 aircraft were destroyed, mainly on the ground; Russian units had been deployed too far forward and were pulverized by massive artillery bombardment, and the crude communications network did not permit sufficient re-grouping. Russia, that 'brainless clay colossus', would apparently be destroyed within the four or five months which Hitler had allotted to the campaign.[2] Dill had given the Soviets seven weeks at the most; Harold Nicolson noted: 'Eighty per cent of the War Office experts think that Russia will be knocked out in 10 days'; the Foreign Office gave a longer estimate, but Cripps expected no more than four weeks. The US War

Secretary, Stimson, informed Roosevelt that he and the US Joint Chiefs of Staff believed 'Germany will be fully occupied in beating Russia for a minimum of one month and a possible maximum of three months'.[3] And the German offensive opened new fears: Hitler, triumphant from his Soviet victory, would be spurred on to fall upon Britain – and the German army, never yet defeated on land, would have even greater confidence. Moreover, the full, fearful force of the mighty German war machine was now revealed to an even greater degree than during the invasion of the Low Countries and the fall of France.

Nevertheless, a period of stock-taking could take place in London. Pressures eased, for the moment. War Cabinet meetings became less intense and less frequent, indeed, this had already become evident: while 28 sessions had been held in March, this dropped to 11 in April, 12 in May, and only 8 in June, 12 in July and 9 in August. This resulted from the removal of imminent threat to the British homeland, and from the excellent work of the Lord President's Committee, which lifted much of the domestic burden from the War Cabinet. In addition, there had been a gradual shift in favour of the Defence Committee: Churchill had found it easier to refer strategic matters to his smaller group, only obtaining War Cabinet approval after the main discussions – sometimes even after the event. A further shift was now taking place, from the Defence Committee to the COS: Churchill, acting as Defence Minister, involved the COS in detailed discussion, after which subjects were referred to the Defence Committee; later, even the Defence Committee sank from sight; planning and discussion took place at COS level and matters were then taken direct to the War Cabinet, who were however merely informed and not consulted. This procedure, conferring heavy responsibility on the COS, enabled rapid decisions – and also allowed Churchill greater control. He had fashioned a small group around himself, including Eden, Beaverbrook, Ismay and the COS; and yet Churchill was by no means seeking to acquire dictatorial power: the system was one of convenience rather than corruption. War Cabinet Ministers had their own responsibilities and the more flexible system allowed them greater freedom to see to their respective tasks. Some decisions should no doubt have been referred to the Cabinet but were taken by Churchill and the COS, but the Prime Minister took care to abide by the COS judgments, and the COS were fully prepared to stand up to him. Nor should the shift in emphasis be exaggerated: War Cabinet meetings were still far from sparse, still averaging about three a week, and the drop in frequency indicates rather the intense rapidity with which they had been held during 1940. Moreover, all too soon pressures would increase again and with them disasters of nightmare proportions.

On Monday, 23 June, the War Cabinet heard Churchill's explanation of his moves following news of the offensive against Russia the previous day; the Prime Minister apologized for not having consulted his colleagues but quick action had been necessary. The meeting discussed the correct attitude towards Communism, now Britain and Russia were on the same side, and Churchill said 'it was important that the Labour members of the Cabinet ... should continue to draw a line of demarcation between the tenets of the Labour Party and those of Communism'. Attlee replied he was proposing to emphasize this in a broadcast the following night.[4] Eden, in a Commons statement next day, Tuesday, repeated Britain's offer to help Russia in every way possible. Already, in a meeting with Maisky on the Sunday, Eden had found the Soviets were suspicious that Britain would treat them as they had treated Britain in 1939. Maisky feared Germany might combine the offensive against Russia with a peace move towards Britain: would the British war effort continue unaltered? The effort would, in fact, be increased, Eden had replied. Cripps returned to the Moscow Embassy with a small British Military Mission on 27 June, and on the same night was seen by Molotov who asked the British to 'clarify' their position – what degree of co-operation was proposed? Eden told the War Cabinet on the 30th that the same question had been put to him by Maisky earlier in the day; he had assured the Soviet Ambassador 'we were with them up to the hilt in all military and economic measures' and an exchange of political views could probably be arranged.

'Authentic news from Russia was scarce,' this meeting on the 30th was told, 'but it looked as though the Russian forces had been concentrated too far forward and had been taken by surprise.' The Germans had apparently broken through on a wide front both in north-east Poland and in Lithuania; another German drive was developing on a front Vilna-Dvinsk; south of the Pripet Marshes the Germans seemed to have achieved a breakthrough after hard fighting in the Luck-Lwow sector. The COS considered the Russian position to be 'very grave, although German air and land losses had been considerable'.[5] The COS reported to the War Cabinet on 4 July that 'the Russians did not seem to have lost confidence' and the latest Soviet fighter aircraft had been doing well; the main German thrust, astride the Minsk-Smolensk railway towards Moscow, was however causing a serious threat.[6] But at the end of the first week in July the COS began to present faint evidence of unsuspected Soviet ability, informing the 10 a.m. War Cabinet meeting: 'The

German attacks have resulted in considerable advances, but the Red Army is still fighting better than we might have hoped.... Much would depend on the next few days, and it is uncertain whether the German forces have been halted by the stout Russian resistance or have paused for maintenance purposes.'[7] 'We are all very glad,' wired Churchill to Stalin, 'that Russian armies are making such strong and spirited resistance to the utterly unprovoked and merciless invasion.... The longer the war lasts the more help we can give.... We welcome arrival of Russian military mission in order to concert future plans. We have only got to go on fighting to beat the life out of these villains.' This message, despatched at 4.30 p.m. on the 7th, was delivered by Cripps next day, and the Ambassador's report of the interview was read to the War Cabinet on the 9th: Stalin had raised the possibility of an agreement between the two countries, in which mutual help would be mentioned without details as to quantity, and each would agree not to conclude a separate peace. Ministers decided Britain's initial response should take the form of another message from Churchill to the Soviet leader: this, despatched at 1 a.m. on 10 July, said it would be necessary to consult the Dominions, but that Churchill himself was wholly in favour of the idea.[8] A diplomatic agreement on lines suggested by Stalin was signed two days later, 12 July.

The degree of Russian resistance seemed almost too good to be true, and the COS therefore warned the War Cabinet on Monday, 14 July: 'The situation might well be more serious than the Russians were prepared to admit, although the Germans were experiencing considerable difficulties over maintenance. The events of the following week would be of great importance.' But an eventual Soviet defeat was still taken for granted, and, as Eden told this meeting, 'much friendly opinion in America was concerned with the dangers that might result if Hitler started a peace offensive after crushing Russia'.[9] Hitler was indeed confidently planning ahead; also on 14 July he issued a new directive: 'Our military mastery of the European continent after the overthrow of Russia will make it possible considerably to reduce the strength of the *army*.... The manning and equipment of the *navy* will be limited to what is essential for the direct prosecution of the war against England and, should the occasion arise, against America.' By 17 July a reasonably accurate assessment could be made of the German-Soviet military situation, despite continued Russian reluctance to reveal information. The daily Cabinet War Room Record, left on the table for Ministers to inspect, declared: 'The German drive towards Leningrad has made slow progress.... In the south, German troops are north and south of Kiev, but have not yet managed to enter the town.' Ministers were told that the most serious threat seemed to be in the centre, where two German drives had been made and where the enemy were claiming to have entered Smolensk.[10] Hitler showed first signs of hesitation in another directive issued on the 19th: considerable time would be needed for Army Group Centre to mop up strong enemy forces and, in the south, the German thrust was 'restricted in its freedom of movement and effectiveness by the fortress of Kiev and the Russian 5th Army in its rear'.

Also on the 19th Maisky handed Churchill the first direct communication from Stalin to the Prime Minister; from the start Stalin appealed for a Second Front. 'The position of the Soviet forces at the front remains tense.... The military situation of the Soviet Union, as well as of Great Britain, would be considerably improved if there could be established a front against Hitler in the West – Northern France, and in the North – the Arctic.' The latter would be a joint Anglo-Soviet operation, with Britain providing naval and air forces.[11] The Defence Committee meeting on 10 July had already discussed possible help to Russia: General Golikof, head of the Russian Military Mission, had requested assistance in the Murmansk area and 'an operation to be undertaken to draw forces away from the Russian front'. The former would involve British naval and air help; the COS proposed to send an admiral and a senior air officer to the area to obtain more information. Churchill told the Defence Committee that he would 'very much like to see small naval forces operating with the Russians' at Murmansk, and he hoped there would be no delay in sending such a force when further information had been obtained. As for the Russian request for an operation to draw German forces from the east, Pound told the Defence Committee that the COS were examining a scheme to send naval forces towards the Belgian coast, with strong fighter aircraft escort, in the hope that German bombers would be sent to attack and a large air battle would result. The COS had come to the conclusion that raids against the enemy-occupied coast were unlikely to help the Russians, and a raid on Norway was especially unfeasible at that time of year. The Defence Committee agreed, but asked for further investigations.[12] Studies had however not given grounds for optimism by the time Churchill received Stalin's appeal on the 19th. The Prime Minister, after consulting the COS, replied on the 20th: he begged Stalin to appreciate Britain's limited resources and disadvantageous geographical position; an offensive against France seemed unlikely – 'the Chiefs of Staff do not see any way of doing anything on a scale likely to be of the slightest use to you', and, with a Northern operation 'it would be impossible to land troops, either British or Russian, on German occupied territory in perpetual daylight without having first obtained reasonable fighter air cover'. Britain could only offer to increase naval operations against the German navy in northern waters, and 'we are also studying as a further development the basing of some British fighter air squadrons on Murmansk'.[13] On the same day, 20 July, rumours reached London that plans were being prepared for the evacuation of Moscow.[14] Next day Eden revealed to the War Cabinet that Maisky had already expressed fears that Stalin would be disappointed with Churchill's reply 'and would suggest that we should do more to help them than supply war materials'. Ministers were also told Maisky had presented large demands for aircraft to the Air Secretary, 'who had told him that they could not be met'. Sinclair now informed Ministers, however, that a limited number of aircraft might be offered, some of US manufacture, without damage to essential British needs.[15]

Harry Hopkins was on his second mission to London for Roosevelt. He had attended War Cabinet meetings on the 17th and 21st, and late on the 24th took part in discussions at 10 Downing Street on general strategic problems; also attending were the COS, and high-ranking US officers in London ostensibly to discuss Lend-Lease business. Hopkins warned that American production was still limited, and supplies might not be available for both British and Russians. Four days later Hopkins left London for Moscow, where talks began with Stalin on 30 July, the day that Hitler issued a new, and fateful, directive. Russian opposition was being found increasingly obstinate, especially in front of Moscow, and a serious difference of opinion had surfaced between von Brauchitsch, C-in-C of the German Army, and the Führer. The former wanted all available German strength to be given to Army Group Centre to smash through Timoshenko's forces and reach the Russian capital. Hitler wanted easier and sweeping victories in the north around Leningrad and in the south towards the Caucasus. Moscow, he maintained, could wait. Directive No 34, dated 30 July, therefore declared: 'Army Group Centre will go over to the defensive, taking advantage of suitable terrain.' Stalin, in his talks with Hopkins, claimed the Germans were already going over to the defensive and a renewed major offensive was unlikely before winter. His confidence made a deep impression on Hopkins: the war would be continued into 1942 when the German armies might find themselves more evenly matched – provided supplies reached the Soviets. Hopkins, at a second meeting with Stalin on the 31st, suggested a three-power Conference should be held to discuss the aid issue.[16] Stalin's optimistic report to Hopkins was reflected in the COS statement to the War Cabinet on 4 August. 'The Russians were still fighting hard and there were no signs of collapse, but the Germans still held the initiative. The Russians remained optimistic about the course of the war, and claimed that the heavy German attacks, starting at the end of July, had been repulsed with heavy losses, and considered that these marked the end of the second phase of the German operation.'[17] Ministers were told on the 7th that the Russians were fighting 'extremely well' and the Germans had made little progress during the previous week except around Odessa.[18]

A miracle had happened. The German-Russian campaign had been underway for over six weeks, the maximum time which the CIGS had believed possible, longer than other experts had considered credible. The Red Army had settled down from hasty retreat to fighting withdrawal; German hordes were becoming exhausted; Russia might survive the winter. Implications were immense: Britain would have longer breathing space; even if Germany were eventually victorious she might be bled too weak to attempt invasion of Britain. But, simply because Russia had survived so long, the call to help her must become increasingly insistent: a short, deadly campaign would have given insufficient time. Now came more reason and more need for a Second Front, and future British operations would have to take into account the Russian factor. Further complications and pressures were being injected into British strategic planning, and British resources might be further limited both by the need to send aid and by cuts in the US Lend-Lease programme as America also supplied the Soviets. Russia's success in surviving clearly called for discussion at topmost level: at the end of the first week in August, Attlee had taken over the chair at War Cabinet meetings and Winston Churchill was on board the ill-fated *Prince of Wales*, heading for Placentia Bay, Newfoundland, to meet President Roosevelt.

Six weeks' respite had meanwhile given time for various housekeeping tasks: the new commander had taken over in Cairo – and already difficulties had arisen with relations with London; relations with de Gaulle had also soured; at home, the bomber controversy had flared again, and plans for increased Home Defence preparedness had been repulsed ...

General Sir Claude Auchinleck arrived in Cairo on 30 June: a dignified, commanding figure, outwardly self-confident, secretly shy and sensitive; an introvert when contrasted with Churchill. General Sir John Dill had already warned the new C-in-C, Middle East, of what to expect from the Prime Minister; in a 'personal and secret' letter dated 26 June he had admitted that great pressure had been put on Wavell, who as a result had advanced into Syria with much less strength than desirable and had attacked in the Western Desert before fully prepared. 'The fault was not Wavell's, except in so far as he did not resist the pressure from Whitehall with sufficient vigour.' The CIGS had added: 'You may be quite sure that I will back your military opinion in your local problems, but here the pressure often comes from very broad political considerations; these are sometimes so powerful as to make it necessary to take risks which from the purely military points of view may seem inadvisable.... *You* should make it quite clear what risks are involved if a course of action is forced upon you which, from the military point of view, is undesirable. You may even find it necessary, in the extreme case, to dissociate yourself from the consequences.' On this day, 26 June, Dill had been feeling especially disgruntled with the Prime Minister, who had insisted more tanks should be sent to Egypt through the Mediterranean and the CIGS had strenuously opposed the idea, threatening to resign, and, if Churchill refused to accept his resignation, to appeal to the War Cabinet: Churchill had abandoned his scheme for the moment.[19]

Two moves had been made in an attempt to improve the Administrative situation in Cairo and to ease Auchinleck's burden. Churchill had decided to appoint a senior officer to take charge of the Middle East army's entire rear services. General Haining, until then Vice-CIGS, therefore arrived in Cairo, with the title of Intendant-General, and he sent his first report on 24 June, just before Auchinleck's arrival. 'The root of the administrative problem is not within the Army or peculiar to it. It lies in the relationship between the Royal Navy, the Army and the RAF and representative Government Departments.' Haining therefore cleared Wavell of charges which Churchill had levelled that he had had 'too much fat and not enough muscle,' and Haining asked for powers to co-ordinate and control all basic administration, to replace present individual systems leaving day-to-day administration to respective C-in-Cs: a system which had already been urged by Wavell and his two colleagues on 18 April, although Wavell had sought a civilian in charge of this central grouping, answerable to the War Cabinet. Randolph Churchill, serving in the Middle East, had suggested a similar idea to his father on 7 June. As a result Oliver Lyttelton, then President of the Board of Trade, was appointed Minister of State and sent to Cairo as War Cabinet representative. 'I may be sending you to your death,' warned Churchill. His duties were to relieve C-in-Cs of 'extraneous responsibilities', to provide political guidance, and to settle matters 'involving several local authorities', for example in relations with the Free French and other groups. Lyttelton would preside over a Middle East Defence Committee. This bold experiment – a section of the War Cabinet in an operational area far from home – was eminently successful, largely due to the personalities of Lyttelton and Auchinleck and to lack of division within the War Cabinet itself.[20]

Lyttelton reached Cairo on 5 July, the same day Auchinleck officially replaced Wavell. Soon afterwards the latter departed for even more onerous duties in India and the Far East. He left behind a remarkable achievement: British control had been extended and hardened from Kenya to the Turkish frontier, from the Iranian Gulf to the far Western Desert. He had battled with limited resources, handicapped by tremendous problems of supply – the bulk of equipment and stores had to come from Britain, and distances within the command area itself were vast. Wavell's success had meant sacrifices: apart from the loss of nearly 30,000 men and valuable equipment in Greece and Crete, the battle order of Middle East forces had been rendered chaotic by often simultaneous operations in Abyssinia, Kenya, Syria, Iraq, the Western Desert, Greece and Crete. Units had been separated and command chains severed. Regrouping had started but cohesion and hence efficiency would take time to acquire. But now Wavell's achievements had to be defended, and if Churchill was to be believed, time was limited. Even before 5 July, the pressure had begun: a telegram on the 1st urged action in the Western Desert as soon as possible, to which Auchinleck replied on the 4th that Syria must first be cleared up, and a desert offensive would need two and probably three armoured divisions, plus a motor division. Churchill hastily pointed out on the 6th that by the end of July Auchinleck would have 500 tanks, and this strength could not immediately be improved upon. 'Our Intelligence shows considerable Italian reinforcements of Libya, but little or no German. However, a Russian collapse might soon alter this.... It is difficult to see how your situation is going to be better after the middle of September than it is now, and it may well worsen. I have no doubt you will maturely but swiftly consider the whole problem.'[21] Auchinleck took until 15 July to reply; his careful cable countered Churchill's arguments point by point, and the Prime Minister's anxiety and disappointment in Auchinleck multiplied. Auchinleck acknowledged he would have 500 tanks, but, after allowance for reserves and repairs, no more than 350 could be expected operational; the General inferred that the offensive value of Tobruk had been overstressed in London and declared: 'I cannot be confident that Tobruk can be maintained after September'; Auchinleck expressed fears of a German advance from the north, through Turkey, hence rendering a premature offensive in the Western Desert even more unwise.[22]

The Defence Committee met to consider the Middle East on 17 July: the minutes show that Churchill's pressure for action, for which he alone has since largely been blamed, was fully shared by his colleagues. The Prime Minister said he proposed to send a short telegram to Auchinleck stating that if a strong offensive could be delivered in the Western Desert before the end of September, 'we should be prepared to send out 150 of our latest Cruiser tanks, leaving the UK in the first week of August'. Dill stressed the risks of reducing tank strength in Britain: 'There was still time for the Germans to finish off the Russian campaign and to stage an autumn invasion.' But Attlee emphasized the importance of re-occupying Cyrenaica while the Germans were still engaged in Russia, and he thought Auchinleck 'had overstressed the imminence of the threat from the north which would take some months to develop. We could not meanwhile afford to wait on the defensive throughout the Middle East.' Alexander, First Lord of the Admiralty, said: 'We should strike our blow in Cyrenaica within the next four weeks. We could not afford to postpone the offensive until our forces were perfectly trained and equipped; we should take the initiative before the enemy wrested it from us.' Eden drew attention to 'the magnitude of the forces at present locked up in the Middle East without apparent prospect of engaging the enemy in battle and thus encouraging the Russian effort'.[23] Another telegram urging action was therefore sent by the COS on the 19th; this referred to Auchinleck's doubts over maintaining Tobruk after September and stated: 'We therefore assume that any offensive to regain Cyrenaica cannot be postponed beyond that month.... It looks from here that the best, if not the only, chance of retaking Cyrenaica is to launch an offensive by the end of September at the latest. Would you feel like doing this if we were to send you an additional 150 cruiser tanks at once?'[24] With this telegram went a personal message from Churchill, in which he stressed the Defence Committee's belief that a German offensive from the north was unlikely before the end of September at the earliest; he added: 'The Defence Committee were concerned to see the 50th Division, your one complete, fresh, British division, locked up in Cyprus.' Auchinleck reacted vigorously on 23 July: this division had been sent to Cyprus after most careful consideration and 'I hope you will leave me complete discretion concerning dispositions of this kind'. He added: 'We think here that German offensive against Syria through Anatolia might develop in first half September.... I entirely agree as to desirability of using present German preoccupation in Russia to hit enemy in Libya, but I must repeat that to launch an offensive with the inadequate means at present at our disposal is not in my opinion a justifiable operation.'[25]

Deadlock had been reached. Churchill had been dealt 'sharp disappointment', and complained of the 'stiffness in General Auchinleck's attitude, which would not be helpful to the interests we all served'. Russia was 'in the crisis of her agony' while Britain allowed forces in Egypt to stand inactive. Churchill therefore told the War

Cabinet on 24 July that 'recent telegrams from General Auchinleck revealed a certain difference in outlook on the situation. General Auchinleck had mentioned the possibility of a German attack through Anatolia early in September. This was most unlikely.' Churchill had 'invited General Auchinleck to pay a short visit for consultation'.[26] Auchinleck therefore reached London on 29 July with Air Marshal Tedder, and gave his situation report to the War Cabinet on the 31st. The situation in Abyssinia and Somaliland had been practically cleared up, he began, and this part of the command had virtually ceased to be operational. Syria was being consolidated as rapidly as possible; Cyprus would soon be capable of resisting any large scale attack likely to be brought against it. In Libya a stalemate had arisen. 'We had not enough armoured forces to attack. While the enemy was better off in this respect, it did not appear that he intended to make any early attack. His supply situation was precarious, thanks to the attacks on his bases and communications by the Royal Navy and RAF. The enemy was nervous and feared that we were staging an attack at the end of the present month.' Tobruk was safe for the moment.[27] Argument was left until the following day, when Auchinleck and Tedder were confronted morning and afternoon by the Defence Committee. The next three months seemed to present a great chance in the Western Desert, said Churchill in his opening remarks. 'Very great efforts had been made and were being made to pour troops and equipment into the Middle East, and yet we were now told that nothing could be done until 1 November.... It would be a very great reflection on us if, in this vital period when the Russians were bearing the full brunt of the attack, and when conditions were so favourable, we took no action of any kind.' Auchinleck retorted that 'the necessity for action was obvious but the means were not so easy'. Pressure was being kept up on the enemy, but to stage a major offensive might mean the destruction of the Middle East army's only brigade of cruiser tanks. Defence Committee members were told that Britain had about 230 tanks available for desert operations, and the Germans had about the same number, comparable to the British cruisers. All experience showed, said Auchinleck, that a major offensive could hardly succeed without about a two to one superiority, which Britain would not have before 1 November, and the British infantry tank was not suitable for a desert battle. Eden stressed the political aspect. 'If the Russians held the Germans, they would be in a position to say that they had won the war for us.... If the Russians failed, then not only would our chance of a successful offensive pass, but we should be accused of having done nothing to save them.' Alexander drew attention to the constant naval losses caused through maintaining Tobruk by sea. Churchill

272

pressed for tanks arriving in the Middle East to be brought into action sooner. 'It seemed incredible that it should take a month for a brigade of the 1st Armoured Division to be fit for action.' Auchinleck refused to agree to a cut in this period: tanks had to be unloaded, checked, and possibly repaired, and formations had to be trained for desert warfare.

The Committee then adjourned until 3 p.m., when Churchill stressed the enemy's supply difficulties. 'The Royal Navy and RAF would have to intensify their efforts to cut the enemy's communications, but it would be wrong to ask them to take even greater risks if the army was not prepared to take advantage of this situation by fighting a battle.' The next two months were vital, declared Attlee. 'If we waited until November the Germans would be able to switch back their forces and our chances would be gone.' Auchinleck refused to give ground. 'The last offensive had failed because it had been launched before the army was ready. If the same kind of thing were repeated we should not only jeopardize our tank forces, but also the whole of Egypt.' Attlee disagreed: 'The failure should be attributed to the fact that everything was not thrown into the battle. In any case, how could Egypt be saved if we waited to strike until the Germans had ample time to be reinforced?' The Middle East commander repeated that he would attack as soon as he thought a 'reasonable chance' of success might result. War could not be waged on the basis of waiting until everything was ready, declared Churchill; but Eden showed signs of agreeing with Auchinleck: although politically he wanted a battle, he did not want another like the last, which had failed 'because we had insufficient armoured forces and the co-operation between the army and air force was not sufficiently good'. This brought a retort from Tedder: 'There were no grounds for saying that there was a lack of co-operation between the air force and the army.' The intervention, the first recorded in the Minutes from Tedder, resulted in Churchill switching his attention to the RAF. 'There were nearly 50,000 airmen in the Middle East or on the way; there were 2,000 aircraft and 15,000 pilots – and yet only 450 machines could be put into battle. This appeared to be much too small an effort.' Tedder refuted the figures: at present he had a front-line strength of 560 aircraft of modern types, and he stressed that 200 pilots were constantly employed on the Takoradi supply route across from the West African coast, others were employed as instructors in Kenya, Egypt and the Sudan. He was, in fact, short of operational pilots. Churchill warned that 'during the next day or two' he would 'set down the general conclusions which had emerged from the discussions'.[28] The clearest conclusion was however Auchinleck's refusal to change his mind; Churchill wrote later: 'He certainly shook my military advisers with all the detailed arguments he produced. I was myself unconvinced. But General Auchinleck's unquestioned abilities, his powers of exposition, his high, dignified, and commanding personality, gave me the feeling that he might after all be right, and that even if wrong he was still the best man.'²⁹ Auchinleck's date of 1 November for the offensive was therefore accepted.

Syria, a complication to over-stretched Middle East Command from the start, had meanwhile continued to be so and had caused Lyttelton, newly-arrived Minister of State in Cairo, a number of dangerous moments. On 11 July, six days after Lyttelton's arrival, Dentz had sought an armistice but General Maitland Wilson, C-in-C Syria, cabled Lyttelton that the Vichy French had 'boggled at certain clauses and refused to sign'. The Minister of State immediately drafted instructions to Wilson: he 'could tell them we should accordingly resume hostilities at 10 a.m. the following morning'. As this message was being coded for despatch to Wilson, a cable arrived at Cairo from Churchill: on no account were Syrian hostilities to be resumed. Lyttelton courageously decided to send the orders; fortunately the Vichy French agreed to the terms and an armistice was signed on 14 July.³⁰ But new troubles came to a head between the British and Free French in the Middle East: de Gaulle had already expressed annoyance at the British Government's desire to see Syria granted independence as soon as possible. Other difficulties emerged, and on 21 July after having given an anti-British interview to an American newspaperman, de Gaulle marched into Lyttelton's office 'white with suppressed passion', and thrust a paper into the Minister's hand announcing the withdrawal of all Free French troops in the Levant from the command of the British C-in-C. Lyttelton tore the document up. Bitter arguments gradually quietened into some semblance of discussion and by 25 July an agreed interpretation of the armistice convention had been reached. Yet difficulties remained; Eden warned the War Cabinet on Monday, 4 August, that 'the situation in Syria was disturbing. General de Gaulle had adopted a very difficult attitude, and there had been signs of collusion between him and the Vichy French. Efforts were now being made to induce General de Gaulle to return to England.'³¹ Not until September would he oblige.

Attention shifted to Iran, important both for its oil and for its geographical position. The Iranian Government had welcomed German interest, partially as an off-set to Russian and to a lesser degree British influence. Britain had been unable to act, both through troop shortages and through opposition which would have resulted from the Soviet Union. 'Barbarossa' had changed this situation, and on 8 July the idea of a joint approach to Tehran had been approved by Stalin at his first meeting with Cripps. Three days later the War Cabinet asked the COS to consider Anglo-Russian military action if the Iranian Government refused to expel the German community; Wavell cabled on the 17th: 'It is essential to the defence of India that Germans should be cleared out of Iran now.'[32] But the COS reported on the 18th that action should be confined to south Iran, and that at least one division would be required to secure the oilfields; forces would have to come from Iraq where troops were already insufficient for internal security duties. Nevertheless the British and Russian Ambassadors made requests to the Iranian Government next day, 19 July, stating Iranian independence could only be achieved if Iran preserved freedom from foreign control and certain specified Germans should therefore be expelled. The Iranian Government took virtually no action.[33] Eden told the War Cabinet on 28 July: 'The Soviet Government had now informed us that they were willing to take part with us in any military plans that might be necessary.' The Russians agreed that an Anglo-Soviet troop concentration should be combined with the presentation of joint demands, but, continued Eden, the Russians also proposed to add a further demand for the free transit of troops and materials across the country – 'there might be some difficulty in linking up the second demand with the first'.[34] The situation was causing Churchill concern. He minuted after a COS meeting on the 31st: 'I cannot feel that this operation, involving war with Iran in the event of non-compliance, has been studied with the attention which its far-reaching character requires', and he therefore established a special co-ordinating committee, chaired by the Lord President.[35]

The Western Desert and Iran – these were two subjects for uncertain military planning on the eve of Churchill's voyage to see Roosevelt. Moreover, prospects of a Spanish entry into the war on the Axis side had dangerously increased: General Franco, in a speech on 17 July, attacked America and declared the Axis had won the war. The War Cabinet decided on 21 July that it would be inadvisable to take any positive action, but the Defence Committee meeting later this Monday decided plans should be prepared for the occupation of the Canary Islands, Operation 'Puma', in mid-August, should Spain enter the war, or even appear likely to do so. Sir Alexander Cadogan described this session in his diary: 'I then put up A [Anthony Eden] to ask how far the objective was from the mainland. None of the Cs of S could answer! (Ye Heavens! After Namsos and Crete!).... Pound measured it roughly on a Mercator's projection of the world hanging up on the wall.... This is really shattering.'[36] Churchill informed the War Cabinet of the 'Puma' decision on the 24th: about 20,000 troops would leave about 10 August, not reaching the destination until 10 days later.

'The actual decision as to whether the operation should be carried out must, of course, depend upon the situation at the time.' But he added: 'We must now take General Franco's speech as an indication of hostility to us ... we should be well advised to make certain of securing the Canaries before we were anticipated.' The Prime Minister warned that 'there were considerable Spanish forces in the islands, and there would probably be hard fighting'.[37]

Meanwhile General Brooke, for one, was refusing to discount the possibility of a German invasion attempt on Britain. Back on 17 June Brooke had given a grim warning to the Defence Committee that 'the increase in his commitments was outstripping the increase in his forces'. He was unable to protect all the fighter airfields in the country, and he had added: 'Comparing our position now with that of a year ago, the main difference was that the Germans had had time to improve their arrangements and to make the necessary special aircraft for invasion.'[38] Since this warning on 17 June inadequate British resources had been spread still thinner and the call had come for the Second Front. On 2 July Brooke was summoned to a COS meeting to discuss possible raids on the Continent aimed at easing pressure on Russia.[39] But Brooke continued to advise against sapping undue strength from the Home Front and stressed the constant threat to Britain. The C-in-C, Home Forces, had an increasingly difficult struggle, shown by his attempt to have a large-scale, realistic exercise to test plans for London's defence against airborne attack. The War Cabinet were informed of this scheme on 23 June; Ministers were warned that road traffic would be stopped and 'many workers might be prevented from reaching their place of work and business would be seriously impaired'. Ministers therefore deferred a decision 'until the implications could be more clearly envisaged'.[40] The matter was discussed again on 7 July, when Ministers decided that 'in view of the considerable volume of opposition against the scheme voiced in the War Cabinet', the idea should be examined by the Defence Committee.[41] Brooke accordingly appeared on 10 July, but failed to convince Ministers of the need for the exercise, which was postponed on the grounds that it would increase fears among the public and would cause undue dislocation. The prevalent attitude was revealed at a War Cabinet meeting on 7 August, when Ministers were informed that the COS had reported to the Prime Minister on the unlikelihood of invasion in the near future. 'The COS had therefore recommended that the defence and other services should be informed that they might expect, from now on, to receive one month's notice of impending invasion.' The War Cabinet approved.[42]

Behind all these discussions – the Middle East, Iran, Home Defence, Russia – was the old problem of shortage of equipment.

British production formed the subject of a Commons debate on 9 July, when some Ministers urged the creation of a Ministry of Production to cover the needs of the Services, and to link existing Ministries concerned with production – Aircraft Production, Admiralty and Supply. The energetic Beaverbrook had taken over the latter on 1 July, with Andrew Duncan returning to the Board of Trade, but despite Beaverbrook's vigour, the demand for an overall Production Minister would continue and Churchill would be obliged to pay increasing attention to it; meanwhile the various departments continued to clamour for their particular demands to be met, and the 'tank' and 'air' lobbyists remained vocal. Brooke and Auchinleck constantly cried for more tanks; yet the only immediate method of striking direct at Germany, and thus the only means of showing some possible direct help for Russia, remained the air offensive. But which bombing targets should be chosen? By now it had become evident to economic experts that the policy of striking at Germany's oil resources, adopted in January, should be reconsidered: results had fallen well below expectations. Moreover, in May Churchill had received a powerful private paper from Lord Trenchard, urging a massive onslaught on German morale by mass-bombing of population centres. Acting on this paper and on new advice from economic experts that the German transportation system should be attacked, the COS submitted fresh recommendations to the Defence Committee on 25 June. 'Subject to the requirements of security,' Britain should have separate short- and long-term policies: with the former 'we should attack transportation targets so as to achieve dislocation, coupled with the maximum direct effect on morale,' and as a long-term policy the RAF should, when sufficient force was available, 'undertake the direct attack on the morale of the German people'.[43] These recommendations were embodied in a new directive on 9 July. Some 10,000 sorties were flown during July, August and September, but although up to 12,000 tons of bombs were dropped the effect was not spectacular.[44]

When Churchill set sail for Placentia Bay he could at least be comforted by one factor: Anglo-American relations were closer than ever before. American forces had started to land in Iceland on 7 July, announced by Roosevelt two days later. In Berlin, Admiral Raeder immediately demanded permission to sink US freighters in the convoy area and US warships if required; Hitler refused – he was 'most anxious to postpone the US entry into the war for another one or two months'. American convoys began to travel the Atlantic with increasing frequency and British vessels sailed with them; the extension of the US patrol zone in April, and now the convoys to Iceland, were more valuable than any other measures in winning the Battle of the Atlantic. Collaboration on other matters also increased; Hopkins was a regular visitor to War Cabinet meetings during his second stay in London, and he gave Ministers an optimistic report at their meeting on 17 July. The American political situation had greatly improved, he claimed, 'thus the people of the United States had warmly supported the President's decision to send troops to Iceland. While it would not be true to say that the American people as a whole were anxious to enter the war, if the President decided that the time had come to make war on Germany, the vast majority of the population, of all parties, would endorse his action and accord him their full support.'[45]

The physically weak though indefatigable Hopkins had flown to his talks with Stalin and had returned in time to reach Scapa Flow to accompany Churchill on the *Prince of Wales*. By then he was so exhausted that he had to be ordered to bed for the two days before the warship sailed. 'We shall get him in fine trim on the voyage,' cabled Churchill to Roosevelt on the evening of 4 August. 'We are just off. It is 27 years ago today that Huns began their last war. We must make a good job of it this time....'[46]

Even if a battleship had not been chosen for prestige and protection, such a massive vessel would almost have been required to accommodate Churchill and his host: with the Prime Minister went the First Sea Lord, the CIGS, the Vice-Chief of Air Staff, Sir Alexander Cadogan, Lord Cherwell, Colonel Hollis and Colonel Jacob of the Defence Minister's office, doctors and personal staff, senior officers of the technical and administrative branches and planning departments, secretaries and a large ciphering staff. Ismay and Portal had been left behind to work with Attlee. Lord Beaverbrook, the new Minister of Supply, would fly out direct. Churchill spent the time reading telegrams, brooding over the future battle in the far-away desert and enjoying the novel *Captain Hornblower RN* which Lyttelton had lent him. 'I find *Hornblower* admirable,' cabled Churchill to Lyttelton at Cairo, causing consternation among staff officers who initially believed this to be the name of some unknown operation. The Prime Minister also asked Hopkins if he played backgammon: 'Yes,' Hopkins answered, 'but I play high,' to which Churchill replied: 'That's all right, I play low.' Churchill had lost seven guineas by the time a short signal reached London on Saturday, 9 August: 'Prime Minister to His Majesty the King: With humble duty, I have arrived safely.'[47]

Roosevelt was waiting on board the cruiser *Augusta*, and talks began that first evening, Churchill with the President, Sir Alexander Cadogan with Sumner Welles, the British staff officers with their

US equivalents. Initial discussion centred on the idea of a Joint Declaration, suggested by Roosevelt the first night; Churchill offered a draft outline the following day based on notes by Cadogan. This contained five points, to which Roosevelt added two more and the War Cabinet another. Talks led to a tussle over Point 4: Britain and America would 'strive to bring about a fair and equitable distribution of essential produce, not only within their territorial boundaries, but between the nations of the world'. Roosevelt wished to insert 'without discrimination and on equal terms' but Churchill insisted this would affect the 1932 Ottawa Agreements, by which inter-Commonwealth trade received preferential tariffs. At this stage the American delegation had their way. Agreement was also reached on Naval Plan IV – the scheme for the US Navy to patrol the America-Iceland stretch. Churchill revealed British plans for occupying the Spanish Canaries – Operation 'Puma'; Roosevelt said he was holding strong forces ready for 'coming to the aid of Portugal' in the Azores.

Also on 10 August, discussion took place on the rapidly growing Japanese menace. Tokyo had squeezed permission from Vichy France during July to station troops in southern Indo-China and occupy bases. Similar demands were being presented to Thailand. In a bid to curb Tokyo, America had frozen Japanese assets on 25 July, stopping all trade between the two countries except by special licence. The British Foreign Office had feared this might offer Japan the abrupt choice of a complete policy reversal, or, more likely, an immediate aggressive advance, but Britain had nevertheless followed America's action, and, with still greater hesitation, so had the Dutch East Indies – who had still to receive a firm promise of support in the event of war. It seemed for a while this blockade policy might work: on 6 August, while Churchill had been at sea, the Japanese Ambassador at Washington, Admiral Nomura, had advanced new proposals in the desultory American-Japanese negotiations for a general Far East settlement: if normal trade relations were resumed Japan would undertake not to advance further in south-east Asia; she would withdraw from Indo-China at the finish of the China 'incident' on condition her special status in Indo-China was recognized; Japan would recognize the neutrality of the Philippines. But the proposals meant Japan would not have to abandon territory already gained, moreover, a number of other conditions were attached: America must agree to foster direct negotiations between Japan and China and to procure Japanese access to the natural resources of the south-west Pacific; finally, America and 'her associates' must refrain from any further Far East military preparations. In London fears had meanwhile increased that Japan's next move would be to occupy the Kra

Isthmus in Thailand, immediately to the north of the Malayan border, thereby threatening Singapore from the port of Singora. The COS had discussed the issue on 5 August and believed Japan should be forestalled by an immediate British occupation of Singora, despite the risk of war and the severe deficiencies in British Far East strength: in June the Defence Committee had been told that the forces required to defend the Far East amounted to 'two equivalent divisions from the Field Force' plus two divisions of local forces and 22 aircraft squadrons, but, this report had added: 'The army garrison, though nearly up to strength, is seriously deficient in important items of equipment, notably anti-tank, anti-aircraft and field guns. The present Air Force comprises 12 and one-third squadrons.' Following the COS discussion on the 5th concerning a move into the Kra Isthmus, the C-in-C Far East advised caution: although previously in favour of such a forestalling operation, he now apparently felt his forces would be insufficient to face possible consequences.[48]

This uncertain situation surrounded the Churchill-Roosevelt talks. Roosevelt wanted negotiations with Japan to continue, despite the recent one-sided offer, in order to gain more time; Churchill had long wanted America and Britain to join in a strong deterrent warning to Japan, believing war to be inevitable without such a warning. The Defence Committee had discussed the situation during his absence, and cabled: 'Situation would be best met by parallel warnings by United States privately to the Japanese Government through the diplomatic channel, to the effect that any incursion by the Japanese forces into Thailand would produce a situation in which we should be compelled to take counter-measures likely to lead to war.'[49] Armed with this telegram Churchill apparently succeeded in securing Roosevelt's agreement to an American Note being handed to the Japanese Ambassador, with the wording based closely on the Defence Committee suggestion: 'Any further encroachment by Japan in the South-West Pacific would produce a situation in which the United States Government would be compelled to take counter-measures, even though these might lead to war between the United States and Japan.'[50]

Just after 2 p.m. on the 11 August telegrams describing discussions so far were despatched from the *Prince of Wales* to London. Included was a long message to Attlee summarizing the main items and giving the proposal for a Joint Declaration. 'You should summon the full War Cabinet, with any others you may think necessary, to meet tonight, and please let me have your views without the slightest delay.... I fear the President will be very much upset if no Joint Statement can be issued, and grave and vital interests might be affected.' This cable failed to reach London until after midnight; Attlee nevertheless obeyed instructions and War Cabinet ministers were roused from their beds. The meeting began at 1.45 a.m. and was also attended by Fraser, the New Zealand Prime Minister. The official Minutes state: 'In discussion, the view was expressed that, while the Declaration in certain respects fell short of what the War Cabinet would themselves like to have seen issued, the right course was to accept it in its present form, subject to modification of a limited number of points.'[51] A telegram to Churchill suggested a different version of the difficult Point 4 and asked for the inclusion of an additional point dealing with social security. This reached Churchill by 4 a.m. on the 12th, local time. The War Cabinet met again at 10 a.m. and gave the declaration further consideration, after which a second telegram was sent repeating arguments against Point 4.[52] Meanwhile, Beaverbrook had also insisted a modification should be made to protect the Ottawa Agreements, and as a result the words 'with due respect for their existing obligations' were inserted. 'Please thank Cabinet for amazing swift reply,' cabled Churchill to Attlee later in the afternoon. 'Your promptness has enabled me to start home today.'[53] Before departing, Roosevelt and Churchill discussed aid to Russia and drew up a joint message to Stalin: 'We suggest that we prepare for a meeting to be held at Moscow, to which we would send high representatives who could discuss ... matters directly with you.'[54]

At 3 p.m. two days later, while Churchill was on his return sea voyage, Attlee broadcast the Joint Declaration, thereafter known as the Atlantic Charter: Britain and America announced they sought 'no aggrandizement' and 'no territorial changes that do not accord with the freely expressed wishes of the peoples concerned'; they respected the right of all peoples to choose their own forms of government; they would 'endeavour, with due respect to their existing obligations, to further the enjoyment by all States, great or small, victor or vanquished, of access, on equal terms, to the trade and to the raw materials of the world'; they wished to bring about the fullest possible collaboration in the economic field, 'with the object of securing for all improved labour standards, economic advancement, and social security'; they called for the abandonment of the use of force; 'after the final destruction of the Nazi tyranny they hope to see established a peace which will afford to all nations the means of dwelling in safety'. The Charter, as with news of the Churchill-Roosevelt meeting, was received with initial enthusiasm in Britain and free Europe, but this soon faded. No dramatic events followed; America had still not entered the war. This disappointment clouded the full implication of the Charter; in Churchill's words: 'The fact alone of the United States, still technically neutral, joining with a belligerent Power in making such a Declaration was

281

astonishing. The inclusion in it of a reference to "the final destruction of Nazi tyranny" ... amounted to a challenge which in ordinary times would have implied warlike action.'[55] As for other results of the conference, staff talks had led to wider understanding of respective policies and plans, and the British COS had given their American counterparts a comprehensive written statement for further American study; naval plans had been co-ordinated; but the other major item, a warning to Japan, was soon to lead to disappointment for Churchill. Definite, tangible developments from the Atlantic Conference were therefore negligible. One American verdict of the event contains some truth: 'The Prime Minister's theatrical superiority over his predecessor is obvious in every respect.... He was a master of arranging what appeared to be war to the hilt. Neville Chamberlain had been both too ingenuous and too limited to recognize the need for seeming to do something at a time when nothing effective could be done.'[56] Churchill's ability had a positive value at this uncertain stage of conflict. And so did another limited, yet by no means insignificant, result of the conference – the British War Cabinet was shown to be an efficient, effective and invaluable instrument for the British war leader. But by far the most dramatic content of the talks concerned highly sensitive information which Churchill had obtained about Roosevelt's attitude to war with Germany, information so secret that Churchill waited until his return before passing it to the War Cabinet.

Churchill reached London in the early hours of Tuesday, 19 August, and reported to the War Cabinet at 11.30 a.m. His account contained a certain amount of self-satisfaction. And he revealed the astonishing depth of Roosevelt's intense desire for war. If the American people, and especially Congress, were still determined to keep out of conflict, Roosevelt hoped to manoeuvre the Germans into giving the Americans no choice. The Prime Minister began by saying he had established intimate friendship with Roosevelt – 'of the six meals they had had together, five had been on the President's ship'. The American leader was 'obviously determined that they should come in' but 'clearly he was skating on very thin ice in his relations with Congress, which, however, he did not regard as truly representative of the country'. Churchill continued: 'If he [Roosevelt] were to put the issue of peace and war to Congress, they would debate it for three months. The President had said that he would wage war, but not declare it, and that he would become more and more provocative. If the Germans did not like it, they could attack American forces.' Full agreement had now been reached on the scheme whereby the American navy would have their convoy system in full operation between their country and Iceland by 1

September. This would release 52 British destroyers and corvettes based on Halifax for convoy duty on other routes. Each Atlantic convoy would be escorted by five US destroyers, together with a capital ship or a cruiser. And Churchill added: 'The President's orders to these escorts were to attack any U-boat which showed itself, even if it were 200 or 300 miles away from the convoy. Admiral Stark intended to carry out this order literally, and any commander who sank a U-boat would have his action approved. Everything was to be done to force an "incident". This would put the enemy in a dilemma that either he could attack the convoys, in which case his U-boats would be attacked by American naval forces, or, if he refrained from attack, this would be tantamount to giving us victory in the Battle of the Atlantic. It might suit us, in 6 or 8 weeks time, to provoke Hitler by taunting him with this difficult choice.' Churchill said he had thought it right to give Roosevelt a warning that he, Churchill, 'would not answer for the consequences if Russia was compelled to sue for peace, and, say, by the spring of next year, hope died in Britain that the United States were coming into the war. The President had taken this very well, and had made it clear that he would look for an "incident" which would justify him in opening hostilities'. Dealing with supplies for Russia, Churchill said Britain might have to make some sacrifices, but these would be well worthwhile if the Russian front remained in being; he announced that Beaverbrook would go to Moscow soon after returning to London – at that moment he was attending discussions in Washington.[57]

The Chiefs of Staff, in their assessment of the Atlantic talks, commented: 'We neither expected nor achieved startling results. The American COS are quite clearly thinking in terms of the defence of the Western Hemisphere and have so far not formulated any joint strategy for the defeat of Germany.'[58] Even before Churchill's return to London the main joint plan, a warning to Japan based on the Defence Committee's suggestion, had been altered. Cordell Hull believed the agreed text to be 'dangerously strong' and liable to excite Japanese extremists. Roosevelt therefore changed the wording, without notifying Churchill; the message handed to Nomura on the 17th had been blunted and the word 'war' carefully avoided: if Japan continued to follow an aggressive policy, America would be compelled 'to take any and all steps necessary towards safeguarding the legitimate rights and interests of the United States and American nationals and towards ensuring the safety and security of the United States'.[59]

Operation 'Puma', the move against the Canaries, was postponed since Germany showed no definite signs of moving into Spain; British forces would however remain ready. But on the day of his return Churchill finally committed Britain to military action in Iran. A joint Note had been agreed upon, in which the Soviets made no mention of free transit rights, and this was delivered on the 17th; the Iranians cluttered apparent compliance with conditions and qualifications, and Maisky therefore told Eden that Russia wished to take military action in conjunction with Britain. Churchill minuted on 19 August: 'I think the Russian view is reasonable, and we ought to move with them while there is time.'[60] The operation was planned to start on 25 August; Churchill warned the COS on the 24th that if Iranian resistance proved stronger than anticipated, reinforcements might have to be sent from Egypt, despite Auchinleck's plea that he was already under-strength.[61] Meanwhile, on the 20th, the COS received grim warning of inadequate British forces in the threatened Far East. In August 1940 it had been decided that the primary Malayan defence should be entrusted to the RAF, with a front-line strength of 336 aircraft. Now, a year later, only 180 aircraft were available, and most of these were obsolete. Air Chief Marshal Brooke-Popham, RAF C-in-C Far East, pointed out that the absence of a strong fleet had been the reason for the COS decision to rely mainly on aircraft, yet 'we have no reserve air crews and few reserve aircraft.... This means bluntly that at present not only is our ability to attack shipping deplorably weak, but we have not the staying power to sustain even what we could now do. As our air effort dwindles (as it would, if war came now) so will the enemy's chances of landing increase. Long stretches of beach cannot be defended everywhere, and fighting inland is certain to occur. In these conditions our troops might expect to receive little support from the air.'[62]

This warning revealed the full danger behind Churchill's attempt to deter the Japanese through threat of war: should the bluff be called, Britain's Far East position would be extremely precarious. And existing weapons deficiencies gave added relevance to a report to the War Cabinet on 25 August by the Minister of Supply after his discussions in America. Beaverbrook declared US production to be in need of 'very considerable development before any great increase could take place'. He added: 'One point which required constant watching was the tendency of the United States authorities to divert elsewhere supplies and munitions resulting from orders which we had ourselves placed before the Lend-Lease Act had been passed.' Russia and China were receiving some of these goods, and he warned there was no prospect of obtaining any appreciable supplies under the Lend-Lease procedure in the near future because of the demands from these two countries. But also attending this War Cabinet meeting was Halifax, on a brief visit to London, and he now confirmed Churchill's excellent news given to the War

Cabinet on the 19th: 'The President and all the principal members of the Administration were anxious to come into the war, and would be relieved if some incident, such as the torpedoing of an American ship, aided this event.'[63]

Beaverbrook had therefore warned that supplies to Britain might suffer from the need to help Russia – yet Beaverbrook was almost immediately to become the most fervent British advocate of support for the Soviets. An added problem now began to become prominent: how were these supplies to reach the USSR? Difficulties were outlined on 25 August by Lord Hankey's Committee for the Co-ordination of Allied Supplies in a Memorandum submitted to the COS. 'At the present time the only route of access to Russia being used on any considerable scale is that to Vladivostock, but this route may be closed at any moment by the Japanese. The northern routes are exposed to enemy action and to seasonal limitation.... The Iranian routes alone hold out a certain prospect.'[64] Iranian roads would have to be improved for this southern route to be feasible, and this, under existing circumstances, meant Anglo-Soviet control over the country. The joint expedition had in fact begun at dawn this Monday. Unlike the operations in Iraq and Syria, the operation was accomplished without delays or complications: the Iranians, hopelessly outnumbered, sued for a cease-fire on the 28th. The question of sending materials to Russia via the Iranian Gulf and Iran was raised at a meeting of the Defence Committee on 3 September and again at the War Cabinet session the following day. Churchill insisted a firm line should be taken and all effort should be made to increase the country's railway potential. On 10 September, the same day that the Iranian Government closed the German and Italian Legations, a further Anglo-Russian note was therefore delivered, demanding the handing over of communications. Five days later British and Russian troops began to move on Tehran; on the 16th the Shah announced his abdication and his son agreed to the Anglo-Soviet terms. British and Russian troops began to take over key points on the railway during October, and, at the end of January 1942, an alliance was signed between the three countries for the duration of the war.

On 28 August, three days after the joint operation against Iran began, Churchill officially sought War Cabinet approval for Beaverbrook to head a British mission to Moscow, scheduled to leave with Harriman's delegation in late September. The War Cabinet agreed; Beaverbrook did not. 'I shall have nothing to give or promise the Russians,' he complained to Churchill on the 29th. 'And so it seems to me that Eden should lead it. For he will be able to make speeches and to encourage the martial and national spirit of the Russians.'

He also claimed Hopkins should be included in the party – 'our own shortage in supplies is largely due to the failure of American deliveries under British contracts'.[65] But a Minute headed 'Action This Day' was delivered to Beaverbrook on the 30th. 'I wish you to go to Moscow with Mr Harriman in order to arrange the long-term supply of the Russian armies.' Churchill was fully aware of the difficulties of Beaverbrook's task; his Minute continued 'This can only be achieved almost entirely from American resources, though we have rubber, boots etc. . . . Your function will be not only to aid in the forming of the plans to help Russia, but to make sure we are not bled white in the process; and even if you find yourself affected by the Russian atmosphere I shall be quite stiff about it here.'[66] The hazards, and the need, of the mission suddenly increased at the beginning of September, when optimism over Russian resistance was suddenly shaken by a gloomy message from Stalin, hinting at imminent Soviet collapse. With these hints came renewed calls for help. The Prime Minister had written to Stalin on 29 August, confirming an offer of 200 Tomahawk aircraft made on 25 July and offering a further 200 Hurricanes. Maisky called at 10 Downing Street at 10 p.m. on 4 September with Stalin's reply: the Soviet leader claimed relative military stability had been broken during the previous week, owing to a vast increase in German strength, and the country was faced with 'a mortal menace'. Stalin continued: 'I think there is only one means of egress from this situation – to establish in the present year a Second Front somewhere in the Balkans or France, capable of drawing away from the Eastern Front 30-40 divisions.' Stalin also asked for 30,000 tons of aluminium and a monthly minimum of 400 aircraft and 500 tanks. 'I realize that this present message will cause dismay to Your Excellency. But what is one to do?' Maisky stayed with Churchill and Eden for 90 minutes after handing over this desperate appeal; the Ambassador's words were even grimmer than his leader's: this might be a turning point in history, and if Russia were defeated, he warned, how could Britain win the war? Churchill detected a note of blackmail and his temper began to rise. 'Remember that only four months ago we in this island did not know whether you were coming in against us on the German side. Indeed, we thought it quite likely.' Churchill, his voice louder, declared Britain had still felt she would win even with both Russia and Germany against her. 'Whatever happens, and whatever you do, you of all people have no right to make reproaches to us.' 'More calm, please, my dear Mr Churchill,' pleaded a startled Maisky. Churchill's temper had already been ill-served by a cable from Sir Stafford Cripps, who believed Stalin's message to be a true and even moderate assessment, and who had commented: 'It demonstrates the result of our not

286

being able to do anything to create a diversion, and shows that unless we can now at the last moment make a superhuman effort we shall lose the whole value of the Russian Front.' Churchill angrily replied: 'When you speak ... of "a superhuman effort" you mean I presume, an effort rising superior to space, time and geography. Unfortunately, such attributes are denied us.' He added: 'I sympathize keenly with your feelings as you watch the agony of Russia at close quarters, but neither sympathy nor emotion will overcome the kind of facts we have to face.'[67]

An attempt was made to face these facts at a War Cabinet meeting at 12.30 p.m. next day, 5 September, when Churchill described the Maisky meeting. 'Although there was nothing in the actual words which Maisky had used,' Churchill said he had 'the feeling that the possibility of a separate peace could not altogether be excluded'. Eden agreed and added that Maisky had stressed the necessity of the forthcoming Moscow talks being enlarged to cover joint strategy. The Ambassador had also suggested greater pressure should be put on Finland to cease fighting – Finnish forces had renewed operations in the Karelian area in July; Eden hesitated over a British declaration of war on Finland 'in view of certain shipping arrangements with the Finns which were now in force'. Churchill told Ministers he had emphasized to Maisky that 'we would not hesitate to sacrifice 50,000 men if we thought that by doing so we would relieve the pressure' but 'all the military advisers ... were agreed that there was nothing effective which could be done this year.' Maisky had been invited to hear the COS view at a meeting earlier in the morning; the First Sea Lord told the War Cabinet that Maisky 'had made great play on the fact that we controlled the sea and could land anywhere we liked. He suggested we should land a force of 15-20 divisions [in France] so as to draw off 30-40 from Russia.' The Chiefs had explained that in narrow waters sea power and air power must be considered together, and that 'even if we managed to land fairly considerable forces, the Germans could concentrate their divisions, of which they still had 20-30 in France, much quicker by rail than we could by sea'. Pound continued: 'The Chiefs of Staff had tried not to harp too much on the difficulties ... as they realized that considerable sacrifices would be justified if any good objective could be achieved. They had emphasized, however, that nothing we could do could possibly cause the Germans to draw off appreciable land forces from the eastern front this autumn. Maisky had suggested that the best way in which we could ensure against invasion would be to engage the Germans in France. The COS had pointed out the fallacy of this argument. The best opportunity the Germans had had of successfully invading this country was when a feeble front was established

287

on the River Somme. If the Germans had allowed that front to remain, our strength would have been drawn away into France and we should have fallen an easy prey.'

Churchill then read a draft reply to Stalin, commenting that he felt Stalin was 'worthy of being told the truth and was capable of facing the facts of the situation'. The draft therefore stated bluntly that military operations on the scale proposed by Stalin were out of the question, and although Britain would do her best, there was little likelihood of substantial supplies reaching Russia in time to influence current operations. Bevin agreed with this draft: 'It would be wrong to mislead the Russians by promising to do things which were beyond our power.' But Beaverbrook thought the content 'too harsh and depressing'; he believed Britain should offer half the Russian request for 500 tanks and 400 aircraft a month, with this being sent from Britain's own resources when the Arctic route was reopened. 'We would then press the Americans to supply the other half from their own resources without diminishing our appropriations.' He admitted this would mean great sacrifices, 'but to keep the Russian army in the field would be an objective worthy of every ounce of energy'. Sinclair, Secretary of State for Air, warned that 'we could hardly spare that number of aircraft if the whole weight of the German attack were shifted back to the West', but Eden pointed out that Maisky had stressed 'if the German weight were transferred to the West, then the Russians would do what they could to assist us'. Beaverbrook pressed again for an early offensive in the Western Desert: 'A big success in that theatre would have great morale effect even though it might not have directly assisted the Russians.' Churchill replied he was anxious as Beaverbrook to see an early offensive, but 'it would be unwise' to override Auchinleck's judgment. The Prime Minister said he would re-draft his reply to Stalin on the lines of Beaverbrook's proposal, which, he said, was 'a course I am inclined to favour'.[68] The revised signal therefore declared: 'I am cabling President Roosevelt to expedite the arrival here of Mr Harriman's mission and we shall try even before the Moscow Conference to tell you the numbers of aircraft and tanks we can jointly promise to send each month, together with supplies of aluminium, cloth etc.... For our part we are now prepared to send you, from British production, one half of the monthly total for which you ask in aircraft and tanks. We hope the United States will supply the other half.'[69] Maisky was summoned after the War Cabinet meeting, and, while the reply to Stalin was being typed, was admonished by Churchill for the propaganda which had started in Britain for a Second Front. Churchill, Beaverbrook and Eden then went to celebrate with an oyster and partridge dinner at the Ritz.

In Berlin, the Hitler-Brauchitsch argument had continued over the correct 'Barbarossa' strategy; Hitler had refused to change his mind that the main effort must be directed at the Crimea, the industrial and coal region on the Donetz, and the Russian oil supplies in the Caucasus. In the north, Leningrad must be isolated and German forces must link with the Finns fighting to regain territory lost to Russia in the 1939-40 winter. On 6 September, the day after the despatch of Churchill's reply to Stalin, Hitler's plans were incorporated into Directive No 35. Army Group Centre would not resume the advance on Moscow for the moment, but its right flank would join in a move by Army Group South to push the Russian 5th Army back across the Dnieper, while its left flank would join the right wing of Army Group North. Offensive plans were also being made in Tokyo: the Imperial Conference secretly decided on this Saturday that if in a month's time Japan's minimum demands had not been accepted in Washington, the decision for war would be taken. In London, Churchill was once again impatient over Britain's lack of offensive operations: Stalin's insistence on British action had intensified his irritation over the apparent inactivity of Auchinleck's army. To help push the Middle East Commander on to the offensive, two more regular British divisions would be sent; on 1 September Churchill had appealed for American help in carrying them to Egypt, now, on the 6th, a reply was received from Roosevelt: 'I am loaning you our best transport ships.'[70] Auchinleck's opponent was also being prodded unwillingly into action, and transport was of similar importance. Mussolini was anxious for Tobruk to be taken, but at the end of the first week in September Rommel warned that unless the transport position to Tripoli improved considerably, the Tobruk operation would not be possible until the end of the year, and he would be unable to take advantage of British fears of the threatened German move down through the Caucasus. The advantage would instead swing in Britain's favour. But Auchinleck was now faced with a new complication, caused by the Australian Government – which, following the ousting of Robert Menzies on 25 August, was now led by A. W. Fadden, with a fragile majority of one. Under strong pressure from their opposition, the Australian Government now sought to improve the conditions of their gallant, battle-hardened troops in North Africa. Churchill revealed disturbing news to the War Cabinet on 8 September: Fadden had asked for the relief of the Australian garrison at besieged Tobruk, and was anxious to make a statement in the Commonwealth Parliament on 15 September. Churchill had told Fadden that the views of the COS and the C-in-C Middle East must first be obtained, but, Churchill told the War Cabinet: 'If Mr Fadden still demanded the removal of the Australian garrison ...

'they would have to be relieved, irrespective of military considerations.'[71] However, in a cable to Auchinleck, Churchill declared: 'I am pretty sure the Australians will play the game if the facts are put before them squarely.... Australia would not tolerate anything shabby.'[72]

The Prime Minister now had another worry: Cripps reported that when he had presented the Prime Minister's letter to Stalin the Soviet leader had seemed 'very depressed and tired', with 'some return of the old attitude of suspicion and distrust', and seemed unsure whether Russia could hold out until the following spring.[73] The latest British offer seemed insufficient. While waiting for the official Soviet reply, the British COS continued their attempt to plan some kind of military diversion; on 8 September General Brooke was asked to consider 'a feint attack on the Cherbourg Peninsula' – 'a mad scheme', he commented.[74] Yet despite pressures and complications, Churchill could still manage an optimistic review of the general situation given to the Commons on the 9th, during which he became so moved by his oratory and by words quoted from Kipling that he choked and was unable to continue.

Auchinleck now supplied the CIGS with reasons why the relief of the Australians at Tobruk would be a severe mistake. His cable, received on 10 September, insisted 'the health and morale of the Tobruk garrison is very good', but admitted that 'the power of endurance of the troops is noticeably reduced and this is likely to be further reduced as time goes on, and I detect signs of tiredness among those of responsible positions'. He continued: 'An alternative solution to relief would be to strengthen the powers of resistance of garrison.' Auchinleck felt confident of Tobruk's power to withstand attack once reinforcements had arrived; relief of the garrison would throw an additional burden on the navy and RAF to the detriment of the offensive so cherished by Churchill. Relief could only be carried out during a moonless period, and would therefore have to be split into two operations, in September and in the third week of October – on the eve of the planned offensive. Auchinleck claimed it would be difficult to find replacements for the 9th Division without jeopardizing his attack; his views were shared by the other two C-in-Cs and Oliver Lyttelton. Auchinleck clearly thought once this conclusion had been conveyed the idea would be abandoned: he, as military commander, had stated his point of view and this should be sufficient. 'Subject to your approval I propose therefore to abandon idea of further large-scale relief of Australian personnel.'[75] Auchinleck's cable was read to the War Cabinet at noon on 11 September; Churchill proposed to send the message to Fadden with a covering letter pointing out 'the grave consequences which might ensue, not only to the Australian forces but to our future plans, if the Australian Government insisted on this relief'. Cranborne, the Dominions Secretary, claimed the agitation for the relief was largely political: 'The Australian Labour Party had always been mildly isolationist and was out to argue that Australian troops should be kept for the defence of Australian soil', and owing to the attitude of the Press many Australians imagined their troops were bearing the brunt of the Middle East fighting; he suggested 'some emphasis might be laid on the activities of British troops'. General Dill told this meeting that 'the Germans were trying to reinforce their troops in Libya'.[76] Next day Churchill turned from one troubled ally to another. General de Gaulle had finally returned to London, and called to see the Prime Minister; he spoke of the humiliations endured by his representatives from British military authorities who appeared to be trying to diminish the Free French role, and he criticized the British attitude towards Syria's future, but discussion cleared some of the suspicions. Churchill, reporting the confrontation to the War Cabinet on the 15th, said 'there could now be some relaxation in the attitude of caution which had been enjoined upon departments in their relations with the Free French'.[77]

Beaverbrook was preparing for his mission to Moscow, now scheduled to leave on the 22nd, and for the preliminary Anglo-American talks starting on the 15th. He outlined his campaign plan at a meeting of Service and Supply Ministry representatives on the 13th; his first intention was to press the Americans to fulfil allocations already promised; he agreed firmly with the COS view that the Americans should clearly understand nothing they intended to offer the Russians should come from supplies already promised to Britain. Beaverbrook also concerned himself with advice on the military question of the Second Front; next day, 14 September, he urged Churchill to sanction an operation against a North French port. 'A raid is feasible at any time before the end of October. The nights are long enough for the expedition to cross the Channel undetected.... And the weather conditions are sufficiently stable.... Motor and tank landing craft are available.' Beaverbrook favoured Cherbourg as a target. But the plan, similar to that Brooke had been asked to consider on the 8th, was unlikely to find COS support.[78] The COS believed the RAF would not be able to provide sufficient cover and questioned the availability of adequate numbers of landing craft; forces would be difficult to find when the strength in the Far East was already dangerously low, and when efforts were being made to build up for the Middle East offensive; any British troops managing to land in France would soon be hopelessly outnumbered. But if a limited scheme such as Beaverbrook's had to be considered unrealistic, proposals now made by Stalin were ludicrous by comparison: the Soviet leader, in reply to Churchill's last offer, declared on the 15th: 'It seems to me that Great Britain could without risk land in Archangel 25-30 divisions, or transport them across Iran to the southern regions of the USSR.' Churchill read this letter to a stunned War Cabinet at 5 p.m. on the 15th, without comment. Stalin was asking Britain to transfer troops equal to the number based in Britain, twice as many as deployed in the Middle East, three times as many as Britain had managed to deploy in France by spring, 1940. The fantastic appeal may have stemmed from sheer unthinking desperation: Hitler's latest offensive was having effect; Kiev was about to fall; Soviet units were retreating in the eastern Ukraine and across the Donetz basin and a renewed drive on Moscow was expected at any moment. Churchill now tackled the difficult task of drafting a reply.

Also on 15 September, Anglo-American talks began in London on the question of supplies; almost immediately British Ministers received another profound shock. Lord Beaverbrook's attempt to settle the subject of American supplies to Britain separate from those to Russia was very firmly rebuffed by Averell Harriman. The Americans refused to accept Britain had any right for first consideration. Harriman declared his delegation would state the total quantity of US aid available for export over the next nine months, and the sole purpose of the meeting was to proportion this allocation between Russia and Britain; the British found to their consternation that they would receive much less than they had confidently expected: 2,096 medium tanks and 1,800 light tanks instead of up to 2,718 of the most valuable medium – and, as the total Russian share of US tanks over the nine months would be only 1,524, Beaverbrook felt obliged to suggest a further 726 light tanks should be taken from the British share, to bring supplies up to the 250 a month and match the offer Britain was already making. As the official historian pointed out, 'the final effect of these allocations, taking our own promises to Russia into account, was to leave us 1,613 tanks short of our minimum requirements'. The aircraft situation was equally disturbing: 8,234 aircraft instead of up to 9,500 as expected, including less than 200 heavy bombers instead of a much needed 700 – yet Anglo-American staff discussions had already decided the bombing of Germany was an indispensable prelude to victory.[79] But as British Ministers emerged disappointed and even disgusted from these joint talks, news came of Anglo-American co-operation in another sphere, no less essential.

Early in the month a US destroyer had been unsuccessfully attacked by a U-boat, and Roosevelt had declared on the 11th: 'From now on, if German or Italian vessels of war enter the waters the protection of which is necessary for American defence, they do so at their own peril.' Now, on the 15th, Ministers were told at the 5 p.m. War Cabinet meeting that a slow British convoy of 69 vessels had been attacked on three successive days by U-boats in Greenland waters, and 17 vessels had been torpedoed. The Chief of Naval Staff declared: 'The United States Navy has sent three destroyers to the assistance of the convoy.'[80] This help, rendered on the 13th, marked the first direct protection given by US warships to a British convoy; the Americans, officially neutral, had gone searching for the enemy. By chance, the U-boats had slipped away before the destroyers arrived; if they had not done so, the 'incident' eagerly sought by Roosevelt may have occurred, in reverse. As it was, Hitler told Admiral Raeder on the 17th that great care should be taken 'to avoid any incident in the war on merchant shipping before about the middle of October'.

Despite Auchinleck's statement, the Australians still insisted on the relief of Tobruk. War Cabinet Ministers heard on the evening of the 16th that Fadden had cabled to say his Government had considered the subject from two main points: the concentration of the Australia Imperial Corps into one Corps, under its own commander directly responsible to the Commonwealth Government, and the necessity of relieving the garrison in view of the decline in its power to resist. Fadden reminded Churchill that the first point had already been promised, in March 1940. The Australian Prime Minister then dealt with items in Auchinleck's statement. 'Naval risks: These are noted but in the absence of effective naval opposition in the Mediterranean, or of any contemplated naval operations, this does not appear to be a sufficiently weighty reason'; Fadden refused to accept that air protection would be inadequate, in view of the aircraft reinforcements sent; 'it would appear possible to complete relief and install new garrison by assumed date of proposed offensive even if anticipated date is realized'. Fadden continued: 'It is observed that the C-in-C states that although health and morale is very good, power of endurance is notably reduced. If garrison cannot be relieved, it will be required to stand up to a total period of 8-10 months' continuous front-line service under conditions of great hardship and trying climate. At the end of this time they are to carry out an offensive operation. The proposal to reinforce the garrison with one battalion of heavy tanks appears to acknowledge decreasing power of garrison.' At 1.30 a.m. on the 15th a short telegram had been despatched to Fadden from Churchill: 'Orders will at once be given in accordance with your decision.' Ministers now agreed that the decision was 'lamentable' but that 'the sooner the operation of withdrawing the Australian troops at Tobruk was carried out the better'.[81] Two days later, on 18 September, a cable arrived from Oliver Lyttelton in Cairo. 'I think you should know that the results of exchanges with Australian Government ... have greatly perturbed Auchinleck. He showed me a telegram last night in which he asked to be relieved of his command, and stated that he had made this request only after 24 hours' reflection. I persuaded him not to send it because I feel strongly as you do that in him we have an excellent commander and I feel sure that the battle will prove you right. Auchinleck stated that if the Australian Government had based their request on political grounds he would have had nothing to say. But to reject his advice on purely military grounds when separated from the theatre of war by 10,000 miles strikes at roots of his military authority.' Auchinleck, continued the Minister of State, had been strongly influenced in his decision to resign by the actions of General Blamey, the senior Australian officer in the Middle East, who was Auchinleck's Deputy and immediate subordinate. 'Blamey admits that telegram of Australian Government largely follows the one which he himself sent but which he will not show to Auchinleck. . . . Blamey has really produced no sound military reasons for taking up this attitude.' Lyttelton added: 'It crosses Auchinleck's mind that HMG endorses opposite view to his own. . . . I would suggest that if you feel able to do so you should send Auchinleck a telegram saying that you personally regard his military reasons as sound but that HMG had no alternative but to accept the Australian Government's request. . . . I would feel inclined to suggest informal message should be made to Australian Government suggesting the replacement of Blamey whose conduct I regard as weak and disingenuous.' Just over an hour after receiving this disturbing news, Churchill hastened to reassure Auchinleck. 'Minister of State tells me that you are distressed by Australian attitude and Blamey's conduct. I therefore assure you that the COS entirely endorse the military views expressed in your [signal], so do Cabinet and I. We telegraphed this to Australia feeling confident they would accept it as decisive.' Allowance should be made to the political situation in Australia, continued Churchill, and added: 'Whatever your and our personal feelings may be, it is our duty at all costs to prevent an open dispute. . . . Everything must be borne with patience, and in the end all will come right. You have all our sympathy and confidence.' Explaining the situation to the War Cabinet, Churchill said that 'at the proper time' it would be necessary to inform the Australian Government of 'this difficulty' with Auchinleck. 'It might also be desirable to find a relief for General Blamey.'[82] The Australian General did in fact stay in the Middle East for a considerable time longer; he eventually left to become C-in-C Allied Land Forces in the South-West Pacific under MacArthur. Moreover, he had acted within his rights: he was entitled and even

294

bound to correspond directly with his Government on matters affecting the welfare of Australian troops.

In addition to this delicate problem, Churchill was also trying to deal with the equally sensitive Stalin. He had decided to ignore Stalin's preposterous proposal for up to 30 British divisions to be sent to help the Russians; instead, in his reply to the Soviet leader on 17 September, he had declared: 'All possible theatres in which we might effect military co-operation with you have been examined by the Staffs. The two flanks, north and south, certainly present the most favourable opportunities. If we could act successfully in Norway the attitude of Sweden would be powerfully affected, but at the moment we have neither the forces nor the shipping available.' He had added that he hoped the Moscow talks would be able to start on the 25th. This reply was read to the War Cabinet on the 18th, when Ministers were also told that German forces by-passing Kiev had joined and were attacking from the east and south to push encircled Russians back towards the city. General Anders, Polish Commander in Russia, had stated the Ukraine situation was very serious.[83] Next day Kiev fell, and German units had already penetrated 150 miles beyond.

In London the Defence Committee met at 6 p.m. and Ministers agreed the American aid proposals would have to be accepted, as revealed in the Harriman-Beaverbrook discussions, despite their adverse and even dangerous effect on British programmes. Beaverbrook said he was convinced the Russians would abandon the struggle unless Britain herself could make 'exact and substantial offers'. The course of the war or limitations of transport might prevent Britain 'fulfilling these offers in entirety', but he did not think he could do anything useful in Russia unless he was equipped with an offer 'on a really attractive scale'. Beaverbrook was moreover convinced 'we could, if we bent our energies to it, very greatly increase our present plan of production, and that it would be well worth our doing so, even at some expense to the size of our own forces'. Churchill hastened to curb Beaverbrook's enthusiasm: he realized the Supply Minister would have a very difficult task, but added that 'it would be unwise to be too specific in offers for the distant future, when the position would be so speculative, and knowing as we did that the war might easily swing back in our direction'. If the Russians had a breathing space, 'that would be the very time when they would press for us to fulfil our obligations'. Anything Britain could offer 'would appear like a drop in the ocean, though it might mean a great sacrifice on our part.... America, not us, would have to be the arsenal.' Churchill decided he would draft a directive for Beaverbrook; the meeting adjourned and resumed at 10.30 p.m. when this draft was approved.[84] 'We must consider ourselves pledged,' declared the directive, 'to fulfil our share of the tanks and aircraft which had been promised to Russia, and Lord Beaverbrook must have a considerable measure of discretion as to what quantities of other equipment and of material should be offered.' Assurance must be given of increased quotas from 1 July 1942, to 30 June 1943, when British and American war production would have reached new heights, but 'it would be wiser not to be committed to precise figures' and attention should be drawn to shipping limitations. As for a Second Front: 'All ideas of 20 or 30 divisions being launched by Great Britain ... have no foundation.' Britain would only be able to provide an expeditionary force of six or seven divisions; nevertheless, Britain had every intention of intervening by land in spring '42, and three projects were being considered: an operation in Northern Norway, an operation in French North Africa in the event of further German encroachment which the French were prepared to resist, and further operations in the Middle East after the Western flank had been secured, either in direct support of the Russians in the Caucasus or east of the Caspian, or in support of Turkey should she join the war.[85] On 22 September Beaverbrook, Harriman and the other five American and five British team members set sail from Scapa Flow in *HMS London* on their seven-day voyage. Included in the party was Ismay, on the assumption that the conference would also discuss strategic matters. Beaverbrook was armed with a letter from Churchill to Stalin: 'You will realize that the quotas up to the end of June 1942 are supplied almost entirely out of British production, or production which the United States would have given us under our old purchases or under the Lend-Lease Bill.'[86]

Also on the 22nd Ministers were informed at their 6.15 p.m. meeting of indications that the enemy 'were endeavouring to force the siege of Tobruk' – a 'reconnaissance in force' had recently been launched. Two days later Oliver Lyttelton attended a War Cabinet meeting and presented a full report: providing the enemy made no attempt to reduce Tobruk, 'it might be possible to stage a bigger offensive in the Western Desert than was at present contemplated'. The Minister of State described the difficulties which were having to be overcome: General HQ Cairo had grown from a small operational staff into a large and highly centralized organization; in the past year the army had fought campaigns in eight different countries – as a result the C-in-C had few complete units in his command. 'This fact, almost as much as the shortage of armoured vehicles, was the reason why the C-in-C had not been in a position to undertake the offensive.' But 'it should be possible to strike a heavy blow in the Western Desert and still leave ourselves time to transfer troops to the Near East before the enemy had time to develop an offensive there in the spring'.[87] Rumours persisted that Rommel was about to steal the initiative. Next day, 25 September, the War Cabinet were informed: 'There was nothing to report on Tobruk, although an enemy attack was expected'; and on the 29th: 'There were signs that an enemy attack on Tobruk might take place at any moment.'[88] Nothing happened and the scare subsided; not until 26 October would Rommel in fact issue orders for an offensive, scheduled to start between 15 and 20 November. Nevertheless, the 'reconnaissance in force', made on 14 September, had important results: the Operation, 'Midsummer Night's Dream', intended as a practical exercise to conclude 21 *Panzer* Division training, confirmed Rommel's opinion that the British were unready to attack and he was lulled into a false sense of security.[89] The September rumours of an attack on Tobruk also heightened British tension over the withdrawal of the Australian troops from the besieged garrison. The War Cabinet were informed on the 29th that one Australian brigade had been removed and the other two brigades plus divisional HQ would be evacuated in the next dark period. Churchill said he intended to ask Fadden to reconsider the Australian decision; this attempt to halt the withdrawal met with no success.[90]

Lord Beaverbrook and Harriman reached drab and menaced Moscow on 28 September. On the same day the first of the 'PQ' convoys carrying supplies to Russia left Iceland: the 10 merchant vessels in this PQ 1 arrived safely at Archangel on 11 October. The Battle of Kiev had finished on 25 September with 665,000 Russian prisoners taken, according to German claims; on 29 September, as Beaverbrook and Harriman struggled with an 'unmannerly and apparently disinterested Stalin'[91] Hitler issued orders for 'the future of Leningrad' – *no* future was in fact intended: the Führer had decided 'to have Leningrad wiped from the face of the earth'. The same fate was planned for Moscow.

Stalin's attitude suddenly altered. Although the Russians refused to discuss strategic subjects and hence wasted Ismay's presence, Beaverbrook and Harriman obtained agreement on the supply question. Churchill signalled on 3 October: 'Now come home and make the ⸺ stuff.'[92] Full details arrived from Moscow at 4.40 a.m. on the 4th and were discussed at a meeting of the Defence Committee (Supply) that afternoon, chaired by Attlee. The document covering the agreement provided for almost everything previously agreed in London, the most significant changes being the monthly addition of 250 Bren-gun carriers, and the Russians agreed to a proportion of 300 fighters to 100 bombers instead of the reverse for which they had originally asked. The document clearly specified that 'Great Britain and the United States will give aid to transportation of these materials to the Soviet Union and will help with delivery' – an important point in view of Stalin's later insulting reproaches over alleged lack of British and American delivery efforts, with Stalin claiming Britain and America had sole responsibility for this supply task. 'The effect of this agreement,' cabled Beaverbrook, 'has been the immense strengthening of morale in Moscow. Maintenance of this morale will depend upon delivery. If there is a heavy failure in October then the situation will in our opinion deteriorate.' He concluded: 'Arrival is the only test. Despatch means nothing to Russians.... I do not regard the military situation here as safe for the winter months. I do think that morale might make it safe.' The Defence Committee (Supply) gladly endorsed the agreement and Churchill wired Stalin: 'We intend to run a continuous cycle of convoys, leaving every 10 days.' The War Cabinet approved actions taken at a meeting on the 6th, with Churchill describing results as 'highly satisfactory'.[93]

Winter nights were drawing in. Bombers might soon return to rip London's black-out and scatter seething fire. Arctic pack-ice began to spread crackling and creaking down towards the bleak Norwegian and Russian coasts, ready to push small supply convoys closer to German aircraft and prowling U-boat packs. Far away in sultry Singapore, fears multiplied of approaching Japanese aggression. In the sweltering North African deserts, preparations were being made for the next great offensive: 'Crusader.' Japan and Libya – these were two major preoccupations of the British War Cabinet during these early autumn days. But Russia remained paramount; and, as the clean white autumn crocuses burst open in London's parks, German tanks crashed forward on the road to Moscow. Hitler had at last ordered the resumption of the offensive; on 2 October, as Beaverbrook's satisfied signal of the supply agreement was on its way to Whitehall, Operation 'Typhoon' had been launched. 'The enemy in the East has been struck down,' cried the Führer on the 3rd, 'and will never rise again.' Many in London's Whitehall now believed him.

'Three thrusts are now being launched,' declared the Cabinet War Room record on the 9th. 'The first is east or north-east of Smolensk, the second east of Roslavl, each being directed against Moscow, and the third towards Orel.'[94] Orel, a key city south of the capital, had in fact fallen a few hours before. Four days later Ministers were warned that 'the Germans are now advancing steadily on most sectors of the front from Smolensk to the Black Sea and it seems that the next few days might decide the fate of Moscow'.[95]

Beaverbrook returned to London and reported to the War Cabinet on the 13th. Earlier Cabinet Minutes show that the Minister of Supply had become an extreme advocate of maximum supplies to Russia and of the urgency of a Second Front, even before he left for Moscow. His Moscow mission did not therefore create Beaverbrook's Second Front zeal, but it certainly increased it: his feelings flared at a Defence Committee meeting on Wednesday night, 15 October. Military help could be delayed no longer, he warned. 'There has been nothing but procrastination and idleness on our part throughout the time that the Russians have been engaged in a desperate struggle; not a single blow has been struck by our army, although it is clear that the Germans could not possibly be strong on the enormous front which they are holding from Norway to Libya while their armies are fully engaged in Russia.... Every proposal which has been put forward has been negatived by the Chiefs of Staff and there does not seem to be among the Services any sense of the urgency of the situation.' In fact, while Beaverbrook had been away, a new scheme had been proposed – and, in order to give better chance of success, the Defence Committee had taken the drastic step of authorizing a study of gas as a possible weapon. This operation, 'Ajax', involved the capture of Trondheim; the Defence Committee had considered possibilities at a meeting on 2 October, and had agreed that 'the use of mustard gas against key airfields as part of the plans for Operation "Ajax" should be considered, firstly, by the C-in-C, Home Forces, as to its value in facilitating the success of the operation, and secondly, by the COS'.[96] This fearful decision led to a special messenger arriving at General Brooke's home at midnight on the 2nd, with orders for him to carry out the examination and report by the next Friday – only one week away. Discussions had started at Chequers on the 3rd, with Brooke already trying to persuade Churchill against the operation as a whole. Long hours of deliberation always brought Brooke back to the same conclusion – the plan was completely impracticable, with or without the use of gas. General Paget, military commander of the 1940 'Sickleforce' attempt in Norway, agreed, and the COS had already turned down the basic idea, although not a scheme using mustard gas, for the same reason: lack of air support. At 6.30 p.m. on Sunday, 12 October, Brooke had had to endure a two-hour cross-examination from an angry, obstinate and unreasonable Churchill at 10 Downing Street; Brooke, equally stubborn, had refused to alter his opinion.[97]

Now, at the Defence Committee meeting on the 15th, Churchill replied to the irate Beaverbrook, and maintained he had been equally anxious to take advantage of the Russian situation, by getting a foot in Norway; hence the instructions to Brooke and

Paget to make a plan. 'But instead of a plan, a paper had been produced showing all the insuperable objections to any action.' Churchill said he had been disappointed, but 'in face of the disinclination of General Paget, who had practical experience of the country and who had proved his metal in difficult circumstances, to undertake the operation,' he had not felt he could press the idea. Operation 'Ajax' was therefore scrapped, and with it the proposal that Britain should initiate the terror of gas warfare.

Attlee clearly felt some sympathy with the COS; he told the meeting that three arguments were being used to urge operations by British forces: the diversion of German forces from the Russian front – 'but this was an objective which we could not achieve'; the encouragement of Russian morale – 'this we might achieve, if the operation was successful'; the use of the opportunity presented by German preoccupation with Russia – 'this we could achieve only if we could find an operation which was effective'. He continued: 'Time was short and we clearly could not stage anything in Norway or elsewhere which could take place before the forthcoming operations in Cyrenaica. The right policy would therefore be to be ready to exploit a success in that theatre.' Eden believed an advance on Tripoli might provide the psychological moment for attack on Sicily; Churchill agreed, and, still clutching at a Norwegian operation, said the latter might provide good cover. The Defence Committee decided a Sicily scheme should be studied.[98] Two days later, 17 October, the Defence Committee heard that this latter plan, Operation 'Whipcord', was unlikely to progress very far. The COS reported that the earliest date upon which a force could sail from Britain would be 23 November – after the planned date for the desert offensive. Unless this date could be improved on the 'psychological moment' would be missed; the CIGS pointed out that the most serious limiting factor was shortage of shipping, and he drew attention 'to the complicated processes which the staging of an operation of this magnitude, involving a long sea voyage, must inevitably represent'. Churchill insisted that every possible step should be taken to cut down the time of preparation.[99]

An ominous report had arrived from Cripps on the 15th: the Soviet Government and the diplomatic corps were leaving Moscow for Kuibyshev, 500 miles to the east.[100] Four days later Stalin issued an Order of the Day: 'Moscow will be defended to the last,' and a state of siege was proclaimed. Beaverbrook resumed his attack, thrusting a searing Memorandum before the Defence Committee on the 20th. 'Since the start of the German campaign against Russia,' declared this paper, 'our military leaders have shown themselves consistently averse to taking any offensive action.... There is today only one military problem – how to help Russia. Yet on that issue the COS content themselves with saying that nothing can be done. They point out the difficulties but make no suggestions for overcoming them. It is nonsense to say that we can do nothing for Russia. We can, as soon as we decide to sacrifice long-term projects and a general view of the war which, though still cherished, became completely obsolete on the day on which Russia was attacked.... The COS would have us wait until the last button has been sewn on the last gaiter before we launch an attack. They ignore the present opportunity. But they forget that the attack on Russia has brought us a new peril as well as a new opportunity. If we do not help them now the Russians may collapse. And, freed at last from anxiety about the East, Hitler will concentrate all his forces against us in the West.'[101] Beaverbrook demanded at this Defence Committee meeting on the 20th that his points should be answered; Churchill said the paper 'expressed the impulse which the whole Cabinet felt', but added he had not taken it 'as meant to be an attack requiring a reply in detail'. Beaverbrook immediately retorted that 'it was intended to be an attack'; he found himself 'in disagreement with colleagues on the Russian issue'. The official Minutes continued: 'He wished to take advantage of the rising temper in the country for helping Russia. Others didn't. He wanted to make a supreme effort so as to raise production to help Russia. Others didn't. He wanted to fulfil in every particular the agreement made in Moscow. Others didn't. He wished the Army to act in support of Russia. The Chiefs of Staff didn't. The line of cleavage between himself and his colleagues and the COS was complete.' Churchill said he was sorry to hear this statement, which he must of course regard as an attack on himself: what plan did Lord Beaverbrook wish the Chiefs of Staff to adopt? The Norwegian plan, replied Beaverbrook. Churchill said this had been found impossible, at least until December, by which time the crisis in Russia would be passed one way or the other. The arguments in favour of an operation in Norway were convincing to him, retorted Beaverbrook. The Prime Minister, for all his previous criticisms of the COS, now showed himself fully prepared to stand up for them in the face of Beaverbrook's onslaught. 'Nothing we could do now would influence the battle in Russia, which might not turn out badly. He would go further and say that even if we had started to act on the first day that Germany had attacked Russia we could not have appreciably affected the issue.' He added that the COS would be at Beaverbrook's disposal 'to go fully with him into details of any project which he would like to put forward'.

Beaverbrook shifted his attack. 'We were not fulfilling what had been decided upon for supplies to Russia under the Moscow agreement.' Churchill replied that he had deliberately arranged for

Beaverbrook to be chairman of the Executive to deal with such matters: 'If there was any shortcoming, it was open to him to report the matter immediately to the War Cabinet', and he asked in what respect supplies were failing. Aircraft and spares for tanks, answered the Supply Minister. 'The Air Ministry were trying to give the Russians an American type of fighter inferior to the type promised. ... The proposal made in Moscow was that we should supply Hurricanes, Tomahawks, or Kittihawks, and Spitfires. ... The Air Ministry were now preparing to substitute for Spitfires the Airacobras.' Sinclair, the Air Secretary, said the Russian request for Spitfires was understood to have been withdrawn, and the reason for sending the Airacobra was that the latter had the same engine as the Kittihawk and Mustang, being supplied to Russia by the Americans, and this aircraft was a cannon fighter, which he understood the Russians required. Beaverbrook then accused the CIGS of not releasing tank spares for Russia. Sir John Dill denied knowledge of this refusal; what he had said was that he did not want any tanks to be taken from the hands of the troops, and he thought the requirements both for tanks and spares were being met from production. He would immediately look into the question.[102]

The Defence Committee showed itself united against Beaverbrook; dangers of a split could therefore be contained, although after this meeting Ismay minuted to Churchill that in view 'of the importance of the Minutes of the meeting they should be considered highly secret and not circulated'. Meanwhile, reports from Russia continued to show a rapidly deteriorating situation. German forces were said to be at Mozhaisk, 65 miles from Moscow. Also on the 20th, Churchill sent Roosevelt an euphemistic warning: as soon as Hitler 'stabilized' the Soviet front he would begin 'to gather perhaps 50 or 60 divisions in the West for the invasion of the British Isles'.[103] The Russians suddenly repeated Stalin's suggestion of 15 September that Britain should send up to 30 divisions to fight on Russian soil: Molotov complained to Cripps on 23 October that no reply had been received. The Ambassador answered as best he could and requested help from London; Churchill cabled on the 25th: 'You were right of course to say that the idea of sending "25 to 30 divisions" ... is a physical absurdity. It took eight months to build up 10 divisions in France. ... The margin by which we live and make munitions of war has only narrowly been maintained.'[104] The situation was discussed by the War Cabinet on the 27th, when Ministers were also informed Cripps had warned of deteriorating Anglo-Soviet relations and had declared: 'If we could not open a Second Front the only way in which we could improve matters was to send troops to Russia', suggesting at least a Corps. Even Lord Beaverbrook hesitated, and said the records of his conversations with Stalin showed the latter had 'not strongly pressed either for the despatch of troops to Russia, nor for the creation of the Western Front.... Stalin's outstanding purpose had been to get supplies.' Ministers also had before them a report by the Joint Intelligence Committee, warning the Germans might be about to launch an offensive towards the Baku oilfields, and Ministers therefore agreed the C-in-Cs India and Middle East should consider whether the 50th Division, then in Cyprus, and the 18th Division, *en route* for the Middle East, should be based on Baku in late January with adequate air support. This conclusion was reached despite opposition from Churchill – 'these formations would form a small body on a large front; they would be armed with different arms to the Russians, and would be certain in the end to be overwhelmed'.[105] Partly as a result of this Defence Committee decision, but mostly in view of renewed opposition from COS and Middle East Command, the Defence Committee agreed that evening to shelve Operation 'Whipcord' against Sicily, causing Churchill added depression.

By 1 November Churchill's opposition to the Baku scheme seemed correct; Wavell warned that even two divisions would block the Trans-Iranian railway. On the same day the Prime Minister expressed irritation over the Soviet attitude towards military talks: signals from Cripps indicated Britain was being blamed for non-co-operation, and Churchill minuted to Eden: 'Did we not tell them definitely we would consult on military matters? Certainly I wrote a paper for Lord Beaverbrook's guidance.'[106] At a War Cabinet meeting on the 3rd, Churchill suggested he should offer to send General Wavell, a fluent Russian speaker, to Moscow; Ministers agreed, and Churchill's offer of Wavell and General Paget, C-in-C designate, Far East, was made to Stalin next day. When informed by Eden, Maisky persisted in asking whether the General would be able to discuss the despatch of 25-30 divisions to Russia; the Foreign Secretary repeated 'this was quite outside our powers'.[107] Churchill continued to fret over the Baku scheme. 'It is quite certain,' he warned the COS on the 5th, 'that if the Germans press hard neither the 18th nor the 50th British divisions could be on the spot in time.' A far better idea, he said, would be four or five heavy bomber squadrons based in north Iran, and he ordered a plan prepared. 'Pray let this be done during the week.'[108] Next day the Cabinet War Room record declared: 'Reports have been received that the Germans are about to launch a new offensive.'[109]

Stalin's frigid and insulting reply to Churchill's latest offer was handed over by Maisky on Saturday, 8 November: 'I fully agree with you that clarity should be established in the relations between the USSR and Great Britain on mutual military assistance.' But Stalin warned: 'As long as the present situation exists there will be difficulty in securing mutual confidence.' If Generals Wavell and Paget were able to discuss war aims, plans for post-war Europe and mutual military assistance, Stalin would be happy to meet them; otherwise he would be unable to spare the time. He complained about Britain's reluctance to declare war on Finland, Hungary and Roumania, and added: 'Tanks, planes and artillery are arriving inefficiently packed ... sometimes parts of the same vehicle are loaded in different ships ... planes, because of imperfect packing, reach us broken.' This letter was discussed by the War Cabinet at 5 p.m. on the 11th; Churchill revealed he had told Maisky that 'a telegram of this type could not be answered', and he told Ministers there had been 'some frank speaking': he had explained to the Ambassador that 'if Russia had only let us know that they were coming into the war on our side, matters might have been less difficult'. Maisky had been told that as far as war aims were concerned Britain could not go beyond the wording of the Atlantic Charter. Eden thought the Russians feared 'that we and the United States would get together and leave them out of the [peace] settlement'. Beaverbrook blamed Stalin's lack of English – 'no doubt the telegram had suffered in translation' – and he also reminded Ministers of the great stress Stalin was having to endure. Churchill thought no reply should be sent, but Beaverbrook argued that 'if there was a delay there was a danger that the Russians would suffer from a feeling of isolation'. The War Cabinet agreed that Maisky should be told a reply could not be sent for the moment, since the telegram raised very large issues.[110] Eden therefore saw the Ambassador next day, 12 November, and informed him of the War Cabinet's reaction; Maisky insisted Stalin was under great stress, an apology which was repeated on the 20th after Maisky had clearly received instructions from Moscow to warm the atmosphere. Churchill accordingly contacted Stalin on the 21st, suggesting a visit to Moscow by Eden and indicating Britain had finally decided to declare war on Finland if that country did not cease hostilities against Russia within a fortnight.[111] This brought a far friendlier message from Stalin two days later, agreeing to Eden's visit and revealing renewed optimism. 'The resistance of our forces grows and will grow. Our will to victory over the enemy is unbending.'[112]

Eight days later the final assault on Moscow would begin. But already the general situation was veering back in Russia's favour. The Germans had entered Rostov on the 21st; five days later they were thrown out again – the first time Hitler's army had received a major reversal, and, as the German *Panzer* ace Guderian observed: 'That was the writing on the wall.' At the same time Timoshenko opened his offensive against newly-won German posi-

304

tions in the Donetz area. Leningrad still survived. Above all, Hitler had left his assault on Moscow too late: November was closing with blizzards and sub-zero temperatures. As early as the 17th the War Cabinet had been told: 'On the Murmansk front the Germans appeared to have withdrawn to a winter line.... Winter had arrived abnormally early on the central sector and in the Crimea.'[113] On the 21st Halder had noted in his diary that the tough and perceptive Guderian had telephoned to say his troops 'had reached their end'. Fears for Russia would continue, but by now, in late November, anxiety had accelerated from another development: Japan's blood-colour sun was fast rising in the East.

'Japan is approaching a serious decision,' wrote Eden to Hankey on 1 October. 'In my opinion the most likely way to keep her quiet is to convince her that any further adventure on her part will meet with formidable and combined opposition.'[114] Also on 1 October a signal reached London from the C-in-C Far East and the C-in-C China Station which seemed to contradict the Foreign Secretary's warning. 'It must now have become apparent to Japan that war with the United States, Dutch or ourselves probably means war with all three' and the C-in-Cs believed Britain and her western allies were safe for the moment. 'Japan is now concentrating her forces against the Russians and cannot suddenly change this into a concentration in the south.'[115] Eden's Minute and this signal, one pessimistic, the other hopeful, contained a common factor: Japan could still be deterred – a belief strongly held by Churchill and the COS. Yet what forces could be used as a deterrent? And what forces were available, should war erupt?

On 16 October news was received in London of a drastic reshuffle in Tokyo. The Prime Minister, Prince Konoye, resigned in opposition to the Imperial Conference's decision for war if negotiations with America failed, and was succeeded by ex-War Minister Hideki Tojo. 'The fall of Prince Konoye's Government is an ominous sign,' minuted Eden to Churchill. 'Although the complexion of the new Cabinet is not yet announced, we must expect the constitution of one more under the influence of extreme elements.... There is nothing yet to show in which direction Japan will move, if in any.' But, Eden added, the stronger the front presented to her, the less likely she would be to take aggressive action. 'In this connection you will recall that we discussed some little time ago the possibility of capital ship reinforcements to the Far East. The matter has now become more urgent, and I should be glad if it could be discussed at the Defence Committee tomorrow afternoon.'[116] The previous discussion referred to by Eden concerned the despatch of more battleships to the Far East: Churchill urged a fleet of modern battleships but the Admiralty preferred the old R-class. The argument, now more urgent, was continued at the Defence Committee meeting on the 17th, with Churchill declaring that: 'It seemed wrong to send a squadron of capital ships that were neither strong enough to engage the weight of the Japanese navy, nor yet fast enough to avoid action except in circumstances of their own choosing. The presence of one modern capital ship in Far Eastern waters could be calculated to have a [deterrent] effect on the Japanese naval authorities, and thereby on Japanese Foreign policy.' The Prime Minister reminded the Defence Committee that the battleship *Repulse* had already reached the Indian Ocean. 'No time should now be lost in sending the *Prince of Wales* to join up with her at Singapore.' Eden agreed, and added: 'If the *Prince of Wales* were to call at Cape Town on her way to the Far East, news of her movements would quickly reach Japan and the deterrent effect would begin.' Churchill invited the First Lord to consider this idea. 'In view of the strong feeling in the Committee in favour of the proposal,' he hoped 'the Admiralty would not oppose the suggestion.'[117] Discussion was resumed at the Defence Committee meeting on 20 October. Pound feared this transfer of Britain's most powerful warships would weaken Atlantic defences, and he stressed: 'If we detached the *Prince of Wales* to the Far East, we should then lay ourselves open to incurring additional losses as a result of unsound dispositions.' He noted the Committee were prepared to accept this responsibility, but continued: 'The deterrent which would prevent the Japanese from moving southwards would not be the presence of one fast battleship. They could easily afford to put four modern battleships with any convoy destined for an attack in southern waters. What would deter them would be the presence at Singapore of a force, such as the *Nelson*, *Rodney* and the R-class battleships, of such strength that to overcome it they would have to detach the greater part of their fleet and thus uncover Japan.' Churchill did not believe the Japanese would attack Malaya in any great strength. 'The main danger would be to our trade from Japanese battle cruisers or cruisers. The former would be sufficiently powerful to sink an R-class battleship,' and he repeated he did not believe the Japanese would go to war with America and Britain. Pound, outnumbered, decided to play for time, admitting the value of a report from Cape Town of the arrival of the *Prince of Wales* and suggesting she should be sailed to that port: a decision for her onward journey could be taken later. The Defence Committee accepted this compromise.[118] The *Prince of Wales* accordingly left for Cape Town on Saturday, 25 October, flying the flag of Admiral Sir Tom Phillips, late Vice-Chief of Naval Staff. Four days later a worrying report was received from Duff Cooper, previously Minister of Information and now Chancellor of the Duchy of Lancaster, who had been sent on a mission of inquiry to the Far East in August. He now revealed Britain's Far East possessions were even less well prepared for war in the political and administrative senses than they were in the military sphere; a widening gap existed between the framers of policy in London and the executives in the Far East; the number of individual and competing authorities had multiplied alarmingly. Policy-making and administrative links were dangerously slow, and Duff Cooper urged the appointment of a Commissioner-General.[119]

Also on the 29th Britain's Ambassador at Tokyo, Sir Robert Craigie, was told that the Americans were deliberately dragging out negotiations and that the Japanese would not tolerate the situation much longer.[120] But two days later fresh information was taken as showing the Japanese were not, as yet, planning to move against British possessions; the Prime Minister referred the War Cabinet to a telegram reporting that General Chiang Kai-Shek believed the Japanese would attack the Yunnan. Such an attack, aimed at cutting the Burma Road and hence closing the last land supply route to China, would at least indicate Japan was once more concentrating her energies on defeating China rather than turning to the south. A similar conclusion was reached in a Joint Intelligence Committee report submitted on this Wednesday. Churchill nevertheless believed firmer Anglo-American action should be taken, and he read the War Cabinet a draft telegram to Roosevelt: 'What we need now is a deterrent of the most general and formidable character.... The Chinese have appealed to us, as I believe they have to you, to warn the Japanese against an attack in Yunnan. I hope you might think fit to remind them that such an attack ... would be in open disregard of the clearly indicated attitude of the United States Government. We should of course be ready to make a similar communication.' Churchill's telegram concluded: 'No independent action by ourselves will deter Japan, because we are so much tied up elsewhere. But of course we will stand by you.... I think myself that Japan is more likely to drift into war than to plunge in.' Attending this War Cabinet meeting on 5 November was Sir Earle Page, special Australian envoy, who warned his country was especially concerned over the lack of air strength at Singapore: nine months ago, he said, it had been estimated that the minimum air strength required in Singapore was 336 aircraft. 'We now had 130 in the front line.' Churchill replied that the development of the air force had been slower than had been hoped: aircraft had to be sent to Russia, to the Middle East, and had to be kept at home to be ready for a possible invasion attempt the following spring. Sinclair disagreed with the figures given by Page. 'We had 250 aircraft in Singapore, which were serviceable now or within 14 days. The figure of 336 aircraft which the COS had estimated as our minimum requirement had been arrived at before the decision to reinforce our naval forces.' Churchill added that 'we had taken some risk in detaching the *Prince of Wales* from the Home Fleet. The *Prince of Wales* was now on her way to Cape Town and likely to proceed to Singapore'.[121] Roosevelt's reply to Churchill's appeal reached London on the 9th, described by Churchill to the War Cabinet as 'somewhat negative'. The President believed any 'new formalized verbal warning or remonstrance' might inflame rather than deter.

Churchill declared at the annual Guildhall banquet on the 10th that if America became involved in war with Japan 'it is my duty to say that the British declaration will follow within the hour.' And, on the 11th, five days before reaching Cape Town, the *Prince of Wales* was ordered to proceed on to Ceylon and then to Singapore with the *Repulse*. Strangely, there is no mention in any of the Defence Committee, War Cabinet or COS Minutes of the drastic decision to these important – and ultimately tragic – orders to Admiral Phillips, despite the lengthy record of the previous debate. The decision was now even more hazardous: the aircraft carrier *Indomitable*, which was to have accompanied the battleships to the Far East to give essential air protection, ran aground in Jamaica on the 3rd, and could not be with them. But the despatch of the *Prince of Wales* onwards from Cape Town had been made virtually inevitable after the War Cabinet discussion on the 5th, when Page had voiced Australian apprehensions over Singapore's air strength: the reinforcement of the Far East fleet had been used by Churchill as a balance against the lack of aircraft. On the other hand, the danger of a disaster was rapidly increasing: should the Royal Navy be unable to stop a Japanese landing in Malaya, the RAF would have doubtful strength with which to strike at the invaders; and back in August the RAF C-in-C Far East had warned: 'Long stretches of beach cannot be defended everywhere, and fighting inland is certain to occur. In these conditions our troops might expect to receive little support from the air.'[122] The Australians apparently saw the danger far more clearly than the British War Cabinet and Defence Committee; despite the naval reinforcement for the Far East, Page repeated these fears at the Defence Committee meeting at 5.30 p.m. on the 12th: this session revealed the complacency and inaccurate thinking prevalent among British Ministers and service chiefs in connection with the Far East. Australia recognized the paramount importance of the defence of the UK, said Page, and also of the necessities of the situation in the Middle East. 'Nevertheless, Australia felt that up till now the importance of the situation in the Far East had not been sufficiently recognized.' He did not overlook the despatch of the *Prince of Wales*, 'an action which Australia greatly appreciated', but Australia thought, however, that 'we might also increase our air strength at Singapore, even at the expense of other theatres.' Dill tried to reassure Page by describing the strength of the Singapore garrison, totalling over 63,000 men with 14,000 volunteers. 'In addition to the heavy fixed defences of the fortress, there were over 200 anti-aircraft guns.... There were, however, shortages in field and anti-tank guns.' Eden, like Churchill, believed an attack on Malaya to be unlikely: and he described the four forms which Japanese aggression was likely to take: '(1) An attack on Russia. We had no commitment to come to Russia's assistance in that eventuality nor had they pressed us in the matter in any way.... (2) An attack on Thailand. Here our main interest was in the Kra Peninsula. We had no commitment to Thailand. (3) An attack northwards from Indo-China against the Burma Road.... (4) An attack against the Dutch East Indies. This was nearer to a direct threat against us.' Churchill also tried to sooth Australian fears; he was 'not one of those who believed that it was in Japan's power to invade Australia'. Nevertheless, he would renew his assurance that 'if Australia were gravely threatened, we should cut our losses in the Middle East and move in great strength to Australia's assistance.' Churchill also hinted that America would enter the conflict if Japan turned towards Australia. 'It was ... in the President's power to make war without declaring it. Roosevelt was a great leader. In the last 12 months American opinion had moved under his leadership to an extent which nobody could have anticipated.'[123]

American-Japanese negotiations in Washington had meanwhile dropped into dangerous deadlock, revealed to Halifax by Welles on 18 November: the Japanese had said an 'explosion' might occur if an agreement were not reached, to which the Americans had replied they could not abandon certain principles: settlement could not be linked with the Axis powers, and Japan must withdraw troops from China. Kurusu, special Japanese envoy, had declared opinion in his country would not allow this immediate withdrawal; without a withdrawal there could be no agreement, the Americans had countered. Yet on 5 November, the same day that Roosevelt had received Churchill's request for a general warning to Japan, the US Joint Board had pointed out that the US Pacific Fleet was inferior to the Japanese fleet and could not undertake a major offensive unless all warships were withdrawn from the Atlantic. The paper had added that although American naval and air strength was gradually increasing in the Philippines, and by mid-December

309

would have become a positive threat to any Japanese move south of Formosa, not until March 1942 would it be a decisive deterrent.[124]

Both Britain and America were relying on a deterrent which could not be backed by adequate strength should the bluff be called. Meanwhile, on Tuesday, 18 November, British attention was switched to another area of combat: the Western Desert. 'Crusader' had at last been launched.

These past eight weeks had been a period of intense pressure for the cool, controlled General Auchinleck: troubles with the Australians over Tobruk, grumbles from Churchill, detailed planning and frantic efforts to reach peak readiness for the great offensive.

On 8 October Churchill received a disconcerting telegram from Peter Fraser, the New Zealand Prime Minister, who, in extremely courteous fashion, requested answers to embarrassing questions. 'In the light of our experience in Greece and particularly in Crete, you will understand that we are naturally apprehensive lest our troops should again and for the third time be committed to battle without adequate air support.' The New Zealand Government would be obliged if they could be supplied with 'the best appreciation possible of prospective air, tank and AFV strengths of the enemy and ourselves in the Middle East'.[125] Detailed answers were made doubly difficult by a telegram arriving this same day from Tedder, RAF C-in-C Middle East, implying he would be outnumbered in the air. Portal immediately disagreed with Tedder's figures. While attempts were made to sort out the difference, necessary in order to send a full reply to Fraser, Churchill received a signal from Auchinleck asking if the second half of the Australian relief from Tobruk could be cancelled. Fadden's brief period as Australian Prime Minister had ended at the start of October, when his Government was defeated in a Budget division; the Labour Party came to power under Curtin, again with a majority of only one. Churchill therefore appealed to Curtin on the 13th, but the new Australian leader refused to alter his predecessor's decision. Meanwhile the problem over air strengths was satisfactorily solved: Air Chief Marshal Freeman was rushed to Cairo to check figures, and his findings, while substantially the same as Tedder's, took new reinforcements and improvements into account and judged the British would have clear numerical superiority: a reassuring telegram was accordingly sent to New Zealand.

More and more seemed to hang upon 'Crusader'. Churchill's attitude was clearly shown in an emotional signal sent to Auchinleck on the eve of Freeman's departure for Cairo, with the message revealing the pressure of events on the Prime Minister – and which, in turn, resulted in pressure on Auchinleck. 'Upon "Crusader", and the use made of it, issues affecting the whole immediate future of the war depend.... Feeling here has risen very high against what is thought to be our supine incapacity for action. I am however fully in control of public opinion and of the House of Commons. Nevertheless, it seems to me, on military grounds alone, that everything should be thrown into this battle.... God has granted us this long breathing space and I feel sure that if all is risked all may be won.'[126] No breathing space had been granted to Auchinleck: time available had been too short, and he now dealt Churchill a severe blow. In cables to Cairo on 17 September and 5 October, the Prime Minister had expressed the hope that the relief of Tobruk would not delay 'Crusader'; now on 17 October, Auchinleck replied that the relief would not affect the date because he had decided the offensive must be postponed, from 1 to 15 November, for other critical reasons. Churchill's reaction exploded in a telegram next day. 'Date (1 November) was mentioned by you to Defence Committee, and though we felt the delay most dangerous we accepted it.... It is impossible to explain to Parliament and the nation how it is our Middle East armies have had to stand for 4½ months without engaging the enemy while all the time Russia is being battered to pieces.... No warning has been given to me of your further delay, and no reasons.' Churchill declared Attlee was to travel to America the following Monday, and was to have taken a letter revealing the date of the offensive as 'early November', and the Prime Minister complained: 'It is not ... possible for me to concert the general movement of the war if important changes are made in plans agreed upon without warning or reason.'[127]

Churchill brought the issue and contents of further signals to the attention of the Defence Committee on Monday, 20 October, the same day that the Committee discussed Beaverbrook's stern memorandum about the lack of British offensive activity to help the Russians. Auchinleck was clearly determined not to give way to pressure, and he was supported by Oliver Lyttelton, Minister of State at Cairo: the latter had signalled that the C-in-Cs were perturbed at the idea that 'HMG did not believe their assurances that they would act at the earliest date possible', and, continued Churchill, Lyttelton had said it was essential to wait while certain modifications had been completed to the axle arms of tanks. Churchill commented: 'As to the first point, it of course depended on what one considered to be the earliest date possible. Of course, if it was necessary to wait until every conceivable thing was ready, the date would be much later than if one accepted certain disadvantages in order to strike quickly, observing that all the time the enemy would also be building up his strength.' As to the axle arm modifications, this was the first Churchill had heard of the problem. Another cable had been received from Auchinleck, continued Churchill, in which he claimed he had not departed from his previous undertaking that he might act on 1 November – if the 150 cruiser tanks, together with trained personnel, arrived in the Middle East between 13 September and the 20th. The tanks had not arrived until 4 October and needed modifications taking three weeks; Auchinleck had repeated his conviction that 2 or 3 armoured divisions would be needed to assure the recapture of the whole of Cyrenaica. Churchill told the Committee he thought 'it was most misleading to talk in terms of divisions'. He calculated that whereas 'we had 616 Cruisers or Infantry tanks, the enemy had only 168 comparable tanks in his 3 armoured divisions. The preponderance in tanks was therefore very nearly four to one.' Churchill added, however, that there was no choice but to accept Auchinleck's later date, 'though the Defence Committee might feel that they had been ill-used and that the delay might complicate the whole of our affairs. There did not seem to be anything gained by recrimination.' The Committee agreed.[128] Churchill read two telegrams to the War Cabinet on the 27th dealing with the removal of Australian troops from Tobruk. At midnight on the 25th he had signalled to the Australian Prime Minister: 'Relief is being carried out in accordance with your decision, which I greatly regret.' At 11.59 a.m. on the 26th, Curtin was informed: 'Our new fast minelayer Latona was sunk and the destroyer Hero damaged by air attack last night in going to fetch the last 1,200 Australians.... Providentially, your men were not on board.... Cunningham reports that it will not be possible to move these 1,200 men till the next dark period, in November. Everything in human power has been done to comply with your wishes.'[129]

Churchill's restless mind was already ranging far ahead beyond 'Crusader', as was revealed in a long telegram to Lyttleton on 25 October; this signal, dealing with the then proposed plan for the capture of Sicily, 'Whipcord', examined general possibilities of a successful follow-up to 'Crusader', including 'Acrobat' – the British conquest of Tripolitania. 'If we can before January secure the combination of airfields – Tripoli, Malta, Sicily and Sardinia – and can establish ourselves upon them, a heavy and possibly decisive (air) attack can be made on Italy.' Churchill continued: 'The reaction upon France and French North Africa following such achievements, including the arrival of British forces on the Tunisian border, might bring Weygand into action.... The foundation of the above is of course a victorious "Crusader".[130] Churchill told the COS on the 28th that he considered 'Whipcord' was at an end following opposition to the idea, but he added that a force should stand ready to exploit 'Crusader'. 'There is no reason, unless hope be a reason, to expect that General Weygand will invite us into Bizerta or Casablanca.... Should he do so, we must be ready to profit by so great a turn of fortune.' He therefore called for studies of a possible entry into French North Africa. 'The name of this operation will be "Gymnast".' And, Churchill added: 'I have received advice from America that our friends there are much attracted by the idea of American intervention in Morocco.'[131] Seeds were therefore being sown for the mighty operation which was to take place in almost exactly a year's time, but, as Churchill told the COS on 2 November, 'we have definitely decided to play the sequence, "Crusader", "Acrobat", "Gymnast".' And the problem of ticking them off in order was to prove agonizingly slow to solve.

'I am not nervous about "Crusader",' confided Auchinleck in a private letter to Ismay on 6 November, 'but I wonder if you and those others who sit at a council table with you realize ... how everything hangs on the tactical issue of one day's fighting, and on one man's tactical ability on that one day.... Rather a terrifying thought?'[132] The thought was made even more frightening when one realized that upon the one day, on the one man, rested hopes for North Africa, for developments with Turkey, Spain and above all Russia: Churchill told the War Cabinet on 17 November that successful Cyrenaica operations 'would have a profound effect on our relationships with other countries. With regard to Russia, we should no longer be in a position that they were fighting and we were not, except in the air.'

Conspicuously absent from this 17 November War Cabinet meeting was Dill. Churchill now informed Ministers 'of certain changes proposed in army appointments.... General Sir John Dill, Chief of the Imperial General Staff, would be retiring towards the end of December, when he reached the age of 60. He had been offered and had accepted the post of Governor of Bombay.' Brooke was proposed as his successor, and Lieut.-General Paget would take over from Brooke as C-in-C, Home Forces. Major-General Montgomery would be appointed Commander, Southern Command, and it was also proposed that Major-General Nye should be appointed Vice-CIGS in succession to Sir Henry Pownall, who would probably become C-in-C, Far East. The War Cabinet approved the changes; the announcements would be made during the week, but the new appointments would not become officially effective until the end of the year.[133] Churchill had been actively considering Dill's replacement for at least a fortnight, and Brooke had been offered the post after a dinner at Chequers on the 16th. 'It took me some time to reply,' wrote Brooke, 'as I was torn by many feelings. I hated the thought of old Dill going.... I hated the thought of what this would mean to him.' 'It is sad to leave the Army that one loves in the middle of a war,' commented Dill to Eden, 'particularly at a time when one knows one has its complete confidence and even affection. I leave in great sadness but with no bitterness.'[134] Brooke, when offered the post by Churchill, was 'temporarily staggered' by the magnitude of his new task: invasion possibilities remained; Middle East difficulties were increasing; the Mediterranean was almost closed to British shipping; Russia was fighting for survival at the very gates of Moscow; American-Japanese talks seemed at the point of final severance. Churchill left Brooke alone with his thoughts. 'I am not an exceptionally religious person,' admitted Brooke, 'but I am not ashamed to confess that as soon as he was out of the room my first impulse was to kneel down and pray to God for guidance.'[135] Within 48 hours of this desperate prayer by the lonely and apprehensive CIGS-designate, on his knees in the quiet of Churchill's Chequers' study, lightning cracked vivid from North African skies and rains sluiced cold upon hot desert sand – and tanks of the British 8th Army squealed forward amidst the sullen thunder.

Auchinleck's basic aim was simple. 30 Corps would establish a strong position at Gabr Saleh, where battle would be offered to the main enemy armoured force. Meanwhile 13 Corps, to the right of 30 Corps, would outflank the enemy and contain the German frontier posts. Auchinleck planned that the armoured battle, fought on British terms, would result in the destruction of *Afrika Korps*; only then would the attempt be made to relieve Tobruk, synchronized by a break-out by the besieged garrison. 'Crusader' began only five days before the German attempt to re-take Tobruk was scheduled to start. Rommel was concentrating upon his own plans; initially the British achieved complete surprise, with 30 Corps sweeping silently westwards while 13 Corps pushed forward and refuelled at dumps secretly established beyond the frontier. First reports were dismissed by Rommel as a British 'reconnaissance in force', and the British advance continued largely unopposed throughout the 18th. But lack of strong opposition led to a serious British mistake: over-confident yet puzzled by the absence of the enemy, the commander of 8th Army, General Sir Alan Cunningham, allowed his forces to become fragmented next day, Wednesday the 19th. 22 Armoured Brigade thrust forward to Bir el Gubi and 7 Armoured Brigade to Sidi Rezegh: 30 Corps thereby lost some of its solidity and strength with which to oppose the main German armour. And, by midday, Rommel was awakening to the threat; although he still delayed drawing his *Panzer* divisions together, German tanks struck back at

Gabr Saleh and caused extensive casualties to two regiments of 4 Armoured Brigade.

'It now seems certain that the enemy was surprised,' reported Auchinleck that Wednesday night, and he added: 'I myself am happy about the situation.'[136] But by now the original British plan, so simple in conception, had become confused. German and British armoured units milled round in the desert, both failing to bring a decisive engagement. And, while British strength gradually became dispersed, the *Panzer* units were concentrating, chiefly as a result of the hold by elements of 30 Corps on the Sidi Rezegh ridge southwest of Tobruk: Crüwell, *Afrika Corps* commander, reacted vigorously to this threat and swung his *Panzers* back to the west. By late afternoon on the 20th, German tanks had severely mauled 4 Armoured Brigade, positioned at Gabr Saleh and attempting to keep contact with 30 Corps's left flank. Rommel's full energy had returned, and at 4 a.m. on the 21st he ordered the *Afrika Korps* to unite in an all-out attack. Meanwhile Cunningham had been persuaded the offensive by Tobruk garrison should be launched early on the 21st, sooner than planned; Friday, 21 November, therefore promised the full British-German clash. In London, news from Cairo was received with optimism. Churchill told the Commons on the 20th that this was the first time British and German forces had met on equal terms, and, while warning against premature exultation, he exuded considerable optimism. Also on the 20th the Prime Minister cabled Roosevelt: 'The approach and deployment of our forces ... has been most successful, and the enemy was taken by surprise.... The chances do not seem to be unfavourable.'[137] The President was heavily involved with other matters: during this day, the 20th, the Japanese delegation at the struggling negotiations had presented Tokyo's 'final' proposals.

Eighth Army and *Afrika Korps* tanks met on the 21st in the fiercest armoured battle of all the North African campaign. British units at Sidi Rezegh attempted a pincer movement into the German formations; Crüwell's *Panzers* attempted to drive deep wedges into the British lines; a push from Tobruk was launched, with Rommel personally taking command of tanks trying to block this sally; 13 Corps attempted a subsidiary advance towards the coast. German and British formations were layered in shifting convulsion – to continue for two hellish days. The RAF had air mastery, but the German-British stranglehold on the ground had become so tight that the two armies could barely be distinguished. Burnt and twisted tanks piled up on the blackened sand. Auchinleck reported on the 22nd: 'Prospects of achieving our immediate object, namely, the destruction of the German armoured forces, seem good.' The British still held Sidi Rezegh and the New Zealand Division under the

315

famous Freyberg was gradually moving round to give support. But 30 Corps was becoming weaker; the link between Cunningham and Auchinleck never achieved the almost instinctive cohesion enjoyed by Rommel and Crüwell, and, after midday on the 22nd, Rommel ordered the remains of 21 *Panzer* to make a wide turning movement and stab at Sidi Rezegh ridge from the west. Heavy artillery intended for the Tobruk bombardment was used in support. The unexpected switch achieved complete success: the *Panzers* drove in through swirling dust and thickening smoke, forcing General Gott's units to fall from the ridge to positions defended by 5 South African Infantry Brigade. 'It looks as if the battle is moving to its climax,' signalled Auchinleck on the 23rd. This Sunday dawned with thick mist shrouding the battlefield: soon after first light the New Zealand Division plunged forward at Sidi Rezegh ridge and surprised the *Afrika Korps* HQ. Crüwell was elsewhere, directing a bold manoeuvre by 5 *Panzer* Regiment and 15 *Panzer* Division southwest behind the South African Brigade and General Gott's 22 Armoured Brigade. His aim was to press these 30 Corps remains on to 21 *Panzer*'s infantry astride the high ground south of Sidi Rezegh. The south-west move had been completed by midday; early afternoon the massive charge forward began. Casualties were terrible for both sides; but by nightfall the South African Brigade was finished, having lost 3,394 men. Crüwell now commanded this section of the battlefield; Rommel believed the British about to collapse and forged ahead towards Egypt to cut off 30 Corps's retreat and drive 13 Corps back on to the Sollum minefield.

General Cunningham saw the situation in a similar fashion to Rommel, although from the opposite viewpoint. He estimated on the 23rd that 30 Corps had only 44 tanks left; he believed the two *Panzer* divisions to have about 120. Armour superiority had been lost and soon no serviceable tanks would remain, his retreat would therefore be threatened and nothing would be saved with which to defend Egypt. Cunningham failed to take sufficient account of enemy disorganization or of advantages from a last desperate gamble. Such a decision had to be taken by his C-in-C: Auchinleck flew to Cunningham's HQ during the afternoon of the 23rd, and when Cunningham felt obliged to raise the question of calling off the offensive, Auchinleck used his authority to order remaining strength into renewed attack. The C-in-C believed the enemy also to be fully extended – as shown by the ability of the New Zealand Division to work round and attack the Sidi Rezegh front. Auchinleck was correct; both Cunningham and Rommel were premature in their assessments. Owing to Auchinleck's handling of the situation at this critical point, the 8th Army did not lose the ability to maintain the offensive; Rommel on the other hand was asking his weakened and exhausted *Panzer* units to accomplish more than they could in thrusting forward for Egypt; moreover, this move meant ignoring the 8th Army's vital supply dumps. He lost his opportunity of scattering the British remnants on the battlefield – and he had to leave the hold on Tobruk dangerously weak.

War Cabinet Ministers were informed at 5.30 p.m. on the 24th: 'The Germans are fighting with great tenacity and casualties on both sides are heavy. South of Tobruk the position is very confused, but we have gone a long way towards rolling up the enemy's frontier positions.'[138] Churchill received another message from Auchinleck, now back in Cairo. 'I have decided to replace General Cunningham temporarily by General Ritchie, my present Deputy Chief of Staff. . . . I have reluctantly concluded that General Cunningham, admirable as he has been up to date, has now begun to think defensively, mainly because of our large tank losses.' Auchinleck had secured Lyttleton's agreement; Churchill sent his approval early on the 25th and the War Cabinet were informed at 12.15 p.m.[139] Rommel's raid crossed the Egyptian frontier wire on the 25th and his armour made abortive attempts to smash positions held by 4 Indian Division. His forward assault would have been classed as a masterpiece, if it had been successful; it failed, largely due to Auchinleck's determination to continue the British offensive south of Tobruk. The absence of the bulk of enemy armour on the 25th and 26th allowed 8th Army to regroup, and Rommel was obliged to return to deal with this threat in his rear, with weaker forces than before. 25 March was perhaps the decisive day of the stubborn battle. It also saw the loss of the *Barham* in the Mediterranean, sunk by torpedoes within five minutes with the loss of over 500 men – a foretaste of British difficulties soon to come.

This Tuesday was also critical in the slide towards war with Japan. Roosevelt cabled Churchill to say the Japanese final proposals of the 20th pledged an evacuation of southern Indo-China while a general settlement was reached with China or peace restored in the Pacific as a whole, after which the Japanese would leave Indo-China completely. In return, the United States was to supply petroleum to Japan, was to refrain from interfering with her efforts to 'restore peace' in China, and was to help Japan to trade with the Dutch East Indies. Commercial relations between Japan and America were to be returned to a normal basis. Roosevelt said he intended to counter this Note with a '*modus vivendi*': this outlined specific conditions to be attached to the Japanese withdrawal from southern Indo-China, while agreeing to Japan's demands for commercial improvements on a limited basis. 'I am not very hopeful,' concluded Roosevelt, 'and we must all be prepared for real trouble, possibly soon.'[140] Churchill condemned this attempt to reconcile American and

Japanese positions. 'Of course it is for you to handle this business, and we certainly do not want an additional war. There is only one point that disquiets us. What about Chiang Kai-Shek? Is he not having a very thin diet?'[141] Also on the 25th Cordell Hull, US Secretary of State, warned the US War Council of dangers of surprise attacks; the Americans had broken Japanese cypher codes and therefore had been able to read this message from Foreign Minister Tojo to the Japanese Ambassador three days before: 'There are reasons beyond your ability to guess why we wanted to settle Japanese-American relations by the 25th. But if the signings can be completed by the 29th ... we have decided to wait until that date.... After that things are automatically going to happen.' And also during the 25th the Japanese carrier task force sailed towards Pearl Harbour.[142]

Churchill's objections and strong opposition from the Chinese reinforced opinions already held by Hull, who came to the conclusion that the counter-proposal should be scrapped for far stiffer demands. Hull, knowing full well that the Japanese meant war, almost come what may, and alarmed by reports of Japanese naval movements possibly towards Thailand, placed his suggestions before Roosevelt on the morning of the 26th, and new American terms were presented to the Japanese during the afternoon. They stood no chance of acceptance. Ten points were listed, three of which were bound to be rejected by the Japanese: 'Japan to withdraw all her forces both from China and Indo-China'; 'The United States and Japan to recognize no other Government in China than that of Generalissimo Chiang Kai-Shek'; 'The United States and Japan to agree that no Pact with any third Power should be so interpreted as to conflict with the main object of the present agreement; that is, the preservation of peace in the Pacific.'[143] The British were not informed of these points, merely described by Hull to Halifax as 'a general statement'. The British Ambassador reported during the night of 26th-27th that while Hull ought not to have acted without showing the new document to the British Government, no harm had been done.[144] Next night the Foreign Office instructed Halifax to discover the details of this statement as soon as possible.

Meanwhile, the 8th Army had been making frantic use of time made available by Rommel's 'dash to the wire'; the New Zealand Division, supported by 1st Army Tank Brigade, had recaptured Sidi Rezegh and forced through to link with the Tobruk garrison on the 27th. The British threatened Rommel's communications. But the cost had been enormous: the brave New Zealand Division was almost completely exhausted; 13 Corps had no reserves; 30 Corps, now concentrated in the area south and west of Gabr Saleh,

318

had only about 70 tanks left, and was unable to prevent the move back towards Tobruk by the *Afrika Korps*. The New Zealand Division was therefore exposed to terrible suffering on the 29th and 30th, and Rommel regained all former ground except El Duda – which merely gave the Tobruk garrison, once more isolated, a large extra salient to defend. But Rommel's two *Panzer* divisions had only about 40 tanks between them; artillery, signals equipment and vehicles were urgently required. Moreover, the supply route across the Mediterranean was almost completely blocked by the Royal Navy and RAF, and reinforcements would therefore be slow to arrive and meagre in quantity. Rommel would soon have to pull back to safer lines. Auchinleck had been urged by Churchill on the 27th to take command of 8th Army himself, but had declined, wishing to remain at GHQ to 'see the whole battle and retain a proper sense of proportion'; however, on 1 December he flew to the Advanced HQ, where he remained with General Ritchie for 10 days closely supervising the further reorganization and reinforcement of the British army. The War Cabinet had been kept fully informed of the desert situation through the daily COS assessments and Cabinet War Room reports, but Ministers had taken no part in decision-making. Auchinleck had reserved complete freedom of action for himself, making full use of Oliver Lyttleton as the War Cabinet's representative in Cairo; the C-in-C's replacement of Cunningham, for example, was mentioned at the War Cabinet meeting on 1 December when the Prime Minister admitted: 'It was doubtful whether this action was within General Auchinleck's competence. ... The Minister of State, however, had endorsed his action.'[145]

Nor was the War Cabinet directly involved with the other pressing topic during these days. The Japanese situation was barely discussed; decisions were taken elsewhere. And, with this topic, discussion was anyway inhibited by lack of information: instructions from the Foreign Office to Halifax on the 27th, to discover the substance of the 'general statement' given to the Japanese on the 26th, met with inadequate response; the Foreign Office again asked Halifax to obtain a copy, and the Ambassador saw Hull on the 29th, when he was informed the situation was unchanged but early Japanese action was expected. Hull searched on his desk for a copy of the American document but said he was unable to find one. Following a written request, the Ambassador finally succeeded on 2 December.[146] War Cabinet discussion on 1 December was therefore outdated and inaccurate. Churchill began by describing the *modus vivendi* and his unfavourable reaction to it. 'The Dutch had felt doubts too, and the Chinese had reacted strongly against the proposals, which had been abandoned by the US Government.' Churchill continued: 'In the end, the US Government had submitted to the Japanese a note setting out the broad lines on which they would wish to see a wider settlement.... The impression had been that this document had been badly received.... Thereafter the tension had increased and there had been reports that Japan was moving forces southwards.' The Prime Minister commented that the latest statement by the Japanese Cabinet, as reported in the press, was that the Washington talks would continue although great differences remained between the American and Japanese standpoints. Churchill thought that 'we were entitled to regard this as a favourable development'. Ministers were told that the reported Japanese move southwards, possibly against Thailand, had led to an exchange of telegrams with the Dominion Governments. The C-in-C Far East had asked for permission to move into the Kra Isthmus if Japanese warships were found to be approaching this strategically important section of Thailand; the COS feared the operation would precipitate war and should be avoided so long as uncertainty remained over American support. Churchill had sought Canadian, Australian and New Zealand views. The Canadians had replied at 7.45 a.m. on 1 December, stressing strongly that 'so long as there is any uncertainty about the degree and immediacy of US support it would be a terrible mistake to commit any course of action which might result in a war between Japan and the British Commonwealth of Nations'. At 6.10 p.m. on 30 November, the Australian Prime Minister had cabled to say that if Thailand were attacked the Commonwealth should intervene with or without American participation, even though Curtin added that 'our latest advices from Washington are that in the event of Japanese attack on Thailand no definite understandings on armed support from the United States can be anticipated.' Thirty minutes after this signal the New Zealand Government wired that an attempt should be made to forestall a Japanese occupation of Thailand – 'if the United States Government are in general agreement and are willing to proffer such assurances of assistance as the American Constitutional situation will allow'. Also on the evening of the 30th Smuts cabled to say great weight should be attached to the opinion of the C-in-C on the spot; he added: 'The United States cannot fail to support us.' Churchill now told the War Cabinet that after considering these replies the COS still maintained no action should be taken which would be likely to precipitate war with Japan, unless American military support could be assured. The exception would be action to protect Britain's vital interests, and although 'an occupation by Japan of the Kra Isthmus could only be with the object of attacking Singapore ... it would not be itself an attack on our vital interests'. Churchill added he still believed that 'we ought not to assume that the outbreak of war between England and Japan would necessarily precipitate the United States into the war. There was a strong party in the United States who would work up prejudice against being drawn into Britain's war.' The Prime Minister read a message to Roosevelt sent the previous day: 'It seems to me that one important method remains unsaid for averting war between Japan and our two countries, namely a plain declaration, secret or public as may be thought best, that any further act of aggression by Japan will lead immediately to the gravest consequences.' This message was therefore similar to the warning Churchill had wished Roosevelt to make after the Atlantic Conference at the beginning of August. Churchill summed up the position: he believed 'we should not resist or attempt to forestall a Japanese attack on the Kra Isthmus unless we had a satisfactory assurance from the United States that they would join us should our attack cause us to become involved in war with Japan'. Ministers agreed.[147]

At 8 o'clock that Monday morning, 1 December, General Brooke had driven to the War Office to take over as CIGS, although not officially intended to do so until about the end of the month. Inevitably, he had already discussed with Dill the possibility of Japan entering the war; and, he wrote later, 'he told me frankly that he had done practically nothing to meet this threat. He said that we were already so weak on all fronts that it was impossible to denude them any further.' Brooke agreed, 'but it left us in a lamentably dangerous position'.[148] Also on 1 December the Japanese Imperial Conference ratified the decision already taken by the Liaison Conference that, as no change was likely in America's attitude, the only course was to fight. December 8, one week ahead, had been selected as the day of attack.

Hitler's assault on Moscow started its final phase soon after dawn, using the greatest tank force ever concentrated on one front. By evening of this 1 December, von Bock, commander of Army Group Centre, had telephoned Halder to say he could no longer operate with his weakened forces, but next day a reconnaissance battalion of the 258th Infantry Division had filtered through to the Khimki suburb, within sight of the Kremlin spires. Halder noted: 'Enemy resistance has reached its peak.' In London the COS Committee discussed aid to the struggling Soviets; Brooke feared the offer of two divisions to help defend the Baku oilfields 'would probably mean having to close down the Libyan offensive', and insisted 'our policy ... should be to direct both military and political efforts towards the early conquest of North Africa. From there we shall be able to reopen the Mediterannean and to stage offensive operations against Italy.'[149] Rommel was stubbornly refusing to give ground around Tobruk. He had so far lost 142 out of 249 tanks, his men were nearing total exhaustion, units were decimated and short of ammunition, British reinforcements were known to be arriving while he could expect few fresh supplies. Yet on 2 December, Rommel gave his orders: counter-attack. Vicious fighting was to continue for the next five days, although the odds against the *Afrika Korps* were hopeless: Auchinleck, while also suffering from deficiencies, had the massive advantage of air superiority. But also on the 2nd the German military Attaché in Rome reported: 'The situation in North Africa demands the utmost efforts to supply the German forces' and on the same day Hitler turned aside from the gigantic Battle of Moscow to issue Directive No 38; a complete Air Corps would be transferred from the Eastern front to Sicily, to be commanded by Kesselring. The decision had drastic consequences.

Also on 2 December the *Prince of Wales* and *Repulse* reached Singapore. War Cabinet and Defence Committee discussions had mainly been centred on the value of these warships as a deterrent measure: deterrence was now too late; final Japanese plans were being completed. And, although obviously unaware of just how close Britain and Japan stood to war, Admiralty anxiety had increased. A last minute attempt was now made to remove the warships from danger: a signal was made late on the 2nd to Admiral Phillips, commander of the fleet, suggesting he should order the *Prince of Wales* and *Repulse* to leave Singapore. On 3 December a further signal, endorsed by Churchill, suggested the Admiral should attempt to obtain American agreement for the transfer of some US destroyers to Singapore, after which the two capital ships should be taken from the danger area; on the same day Phillips reported his intention to send *Repulse* and two destroyers to Port Darwin, and preparations were made for the vessels to sail on the 5th.

Eden was preparing for his visit to Moscow, and his mission was discussed at a long meeting of the Defence Committee on the evening of the 3rd. Churchill warned that Eden would have to explain 'the reasons why it was quite impossible for a large army to be sent either to the north or the south of the Russian front'; the question remained whether Eden should make a definite pledge for two divisions and 10 RAF squadrons to be sent to the Baku area. The COS were strongly in favour of keeping everything for Libya, but Churchill was 'inclined to doubt ... whether by the time the 18th Division arrived in January it could possibly be required in the desert.' Pound said the Russians had constantly pressed for a Second Front to be opened, and 'this we had now done in Libya, and already very considerable [enemy] air forces were being drawn away from the Russian front'. He added that the German position in the desert might collapse at any moment; 'we must prepare to replace tired troops with fresh so as to take advantage of a favourable turn in the situation'. Brooke agreed. 'In Libya we had the only offensive front on which we could engage the Germans. It was essential to keep it going.' Ministers decided that 'in view of the advantages to be gained by pressing on with the offensive in North Africa, and in view of the change in the Russian situation caused by the successful battle at Rostov, it would be unwise to send British forces to the Don'. Eden believed it would be best to tell Stalin the British position 'with complete frankness'.[150] Britain was approaching a decision, which can only be described as shoddy, judged necessary for harmonious Anglo-Soviet relations. Stalin had long urged Britain to declare war on Finland, Roumania and Hungary. Diplomatic relations had already been broken with the latter, but Ministers had been especially reluctant to treat the Finns as enemies: British sympathies had been strongly in support of Finland during her desperate attempts to face Russian aggression in the fighting of winter 1939-40. But in the face of Stalin's insistence, the War Cabinet had decided on 1 December that the Finns should be given an ultimatum to cease fighting and agree to a return to the 1939 frontiers. The ultimatum would expire on 5 December; by 2 December it was already clear the Finns would not oblige. Churchill had sent a personal appeal to the Finnish leader, Field-Marshal Mannerheim: 'I am deeply grieved at what I see coming, namely, that we shall be forced in a few days out of loyalty to our ally Russia to declare war.' Mannerheim replied on the 2nd: 'I am sure you will realize that it is impossible for me to cease my present military operations before my troops have reached positions which in my opinion would give us the security required.... It was very kind of you to send me a personal message in these trying days.'[151] Now, on 3 December, Churchill told the War Cabinet he wished it to be on record that he believed 'this declaration of war on Finland, and also on Hungary and Roumania would not assist either our cause or that of the Russians. The sole justification for it was that it was necessary in order to satisfy the Russian Government.' Churchill referred to the statement made by the Hungarian Foreign Minister to the American Ambassador at Budapest when informed of Britain's intended action. 'Now we no longer have two roads,' the Hungarian had said, 'but only one we do not want to follow.'[152]

Eden prepared a memorandum for Stalin, considered by the War Cabinet at 6 p.m. the following day, proposing an Anglo-Soviet declaration to collaborate in making and maintaining a peace settlement. He told Ministers the document was intended to remove Stalin's suspicions; the War Cabinet, while approving his memorandum, stressed Eden should 'avoid being drawn into any precise discussions as regards territorial changes or boundaries'. Churchill then revealed the Defence Committee decision made the previous night that the Libyan offensive should be maintained and troops would not be sent to help the Russians on the Don. The Prime Minister said the COS had been asked to consider whether a further 500 tanks and 500 aircraft could be sent to Russia to compensate for the lack of troops. Brooke commented the COS had done so earlier in the day: 'It would be inadvisable to withdraw tanks already earmarked for the Middle East and India. This meant that any extra supplies to Russia must be taken from tanks allocated to Home Defence'; the COS had nevertheless suggested 50 'Churchill' tanks should be sent each month until June, making 300. 'It must be remembered that three of our tank brigades in the country would, as a result, be short of tanks,' and if the Germans succeeded in landing in Britain the same number of tanks as Britain possessed, 'complete chaos must result for some time'. Portal said British aircraft could not be spared, but it might be possible to send 300 aircraft from America. 'It must be remembered,' he continued, 'that we had only about 100 more fighters of the Hurricane and Spitfire types ... in this country, than at the time of the Battle of Britain.' Churchill pointed out that 'while we had fulfilled our deliveries to Russia,' American deliveries were lagging, and the United States 'now proposed to divert to Russia shipping which had previously been allocated to sustain the import programme to this country'. The suggestion was made that Eden 'might postpone his visit, giving as a reason the difficulties of the international situation, particularly in the Far East'. Churchill vehemently disagreed – 'a postponement would be disastrous'.

Eden then handed round latest telegrams received from Halifax; these included details of the Ten Points given to the Japanese envoys by Hull on the 26th and finally revealed to the British Ambassador on 2 December. Ministers agreed the points went even further than the strong attitude Britain had urged America to adopt and were 'very satisfactory'. The War Cabinet were also informed of Roosevelt's approval to a statement that 'in the event of any direct attack on ourselves or the Dutch, we should obviously all be in it together'. Churchill commented that 'in the light of this assurance, we could now say to the Dutch that if any attack was made on them by Japan, we should at once come to their aid, and that we had every confidence that the United States would do so also'. The Prime Minister also believed instructions could now be given to the C-in-C Far East, to put Operation 'Matador' into effect if necessary – the move into the Kra Isthmus.[153] The words 'if necessary' were to bring unfortunate complications: the Far East Commander, Sir Robert Brooke-Popham, was uncertain how far he was free to act and 'Matador' was delayed for three fatal days from 5 to 8 December.

Soon after this War Cabinet meeting on the 4th, the COS met to resume discussion on aid to Russia. Brooke had his first experience of the Prime Minister's temper, when the COS tried to persuade Churchill not to agree to an irrevocable promise that 10 RAF squadrons should be transferred to South Russia from Libya. Churchill reacted violently: the COS did nothing but obstruct his intentions, he exclaimed, and they had no ideas of their own and merely blocked schemes he put forward. Attlee and Eden tried to pacify him but failed; Churchill sat in sulky silence, then suddenly slammed his papers together and slouched from the room without another word. 'It was pathetic and entirely unnecessary,' wrote Brooke. 'It is all the result of over-working himself and keeping too late hours.... God knows where we should be without him, but God knows where we shall go with him!'[154] Next day, 5 December, Churchill behaved as if nothing had happened and agreed to the COS stipulation that the squadrons should only be sent when North African circumstances permitted, and only if Turkey had not meantime been attacked.

Britain declared war on Finland, Hungary and Roumania on the 5th. In the Battle for Moscow all German assaults had been stopped along a 200-mile semi-circular front; next day, Saturday, the Soviets struck back. An unknown general, Georgi Zhukov, launched forces totalling 100 well-equipped divisions, completely under-estimated by the Germans. The Third Reich had been dealt a blow from which it would never recover; and next day would come another from the far side of the world, eventually to be equally disastrous for Hitler. As Zhukov's tanks crept from Moscow's swirling blizzards, and as Rommel came to the reluctant conclusion that the *Afrika Korps* must pull back over the North Africa deserts, reports reached Singapore that Japanese convoys had sailed from Saigon and Camranh Bay. Just after noon on the 6th, air reconnaissance reported two, or possibly three, Japanese convoys about 80 miles south-east of Cambodia Point. Contact was lost in the tropical rainstorms; it was therefore difficult to assess whether the warships were merely carrying out manoeuvres, or, if intending aggressive action, where the attack would be directed – Thailand, Malaya or the Dutch East Indies. GHQ Far East delayed action, apart from ordering general alert: it was unclear whether the situation necessitated Operation 'Matador', the move into the Kra Isthmus. *Repulse* and two destroyers had set sail for Port Darwin the previous day, 5 December.

News of the convoys reached London at about 5 p.m. British time, just as Brooke was preparing to leave his office for home. Pound immediately called a COS meeting, attended by Cadogan, but after three hours of discussion the session agreed no action could be taken without more information.[155] The COS stayed near their offices throughout the night. In Singapore, about eight hours' time difference ahead, daylight had already come on Sunday, 7 December, and all available aircraft were aloft in the attempt to regain contact with the Japanese warships. Not until late afternoon would this be established; meanwhile the doubts persisted and all plans hung in suspense. One definite decision was taken: the *Repulse* would turn back from her voyage south. In London the COS met early and sat in almost continuous session throughout the day. Even now doubts persisted over whether America would enter the war if Malaya or the Dutch East Indies were attacked, despite recent statements by Roosevelt. Eden and Cadogan left Euston in the afternoon, making for Scapa Flow at the start of their mission to Russia. Churchill stayed at Chequers, where his house guests included the American Ambassador and Averell Harriman. Hitler was at his HQ at Wolfsschanze, East Prussia, studying latest dismal reports from the Moscow front.

Just after midnight on 7-8 December, local time, a short signal was flashed to Singapore HQ from 8 Brigade, Kota Bharu. Three Japanese warships were anchored off the dark beaches and troops were already wading ashore. Other signals reported Japanese landings were proceeding unhindered at the Thai ports of Singora and Patani, the very points at which they had been expected and which would have been covered if 'Matador' had been launched. London time was about 6 p.m., Sunday, 7 December. And even before first reports arrived from Singapore, even more momentous news had arrived from across the Atlantic. The COS had dispersed. Ismay was dining at the Carlton Hotel; an excited waiter hurried up: the BBC had just declared the Japanese had attacked the American fleet at Pearl Harbour. No member of the COS Committee had ever considered such a move. Ismay felt like shouting for joy. 'How I wished I could have been with the Prime Minister at that moment!' Churchill had just finished dinner at Chequers with Ambassador Winant and Harriman; he switched on the radio and half-listened – Harriman caught a few words about the Japanese attacking the Americans. Churchill's butler confirmed the news. The Prime Minister walked to the telephone and called Roosevelt and was told: 'We are all in the same boat now.'[156] Telephone calls were immediately made to all War Cabinet Ministers, the COS, Service Ministers, the Speaker of the House of Commons and the political party Whips, arranging for Parliament to be assembled next day, 8 December, and for the War Cabinet to meet. Another call was put through to Eden, then at Invergordon; Churchill told him to continue his journey to Russia, and revealed he himself proposed to cross the Atlantic to meet with Roosevelt. 'I could not conceal my relief and did not have to try,' wrote Eden. 'I felt that whatever happened now, it was merely a question of time.'[157] Churchill felt 'the greatest joy.... We had won the war. England would live; Britain would live; the Commonwealth of Nations and the Empire would live.'[158] Adolf Hitler hurried back to Berlin from his East Prussian forest lair, and made ready to declare war on the United States of America.

Allies

Relief over America's imminent entry into the war would have been severely reduced if Churchill and Ministers had known that the new turn in the conflict would bring setbacks and a long line of disasters: almost the worst was still to come. And elation was soon tempered by news of the catastrophic losses inflicted on the US fleet at Pearl Harbour, even by the meagre details available when the War Cabinet met at 12.30 p.m. on 8 December: 'The United States authorities had been taken by surprise. American losses include the battleship *Oklahoma*, which had been capsized, and a destroyer in dock which been blown up. The battleship *Tennessee*, a destroyer and a minelayer had been set on fire.' Further information would reveal four of the eight battleships in harbour sunk outright and only two escaping serious damage, plus the sinking of three cruisers and three destroyers, and 219 aircraft destroyed or damaged. Meanwhile, Ministers were told that 18 Japanese aircraft had attacked Singapore the previous evening, but no damage had been suffered at the naval base. The Colonial Secretary, Lord Moyne, had received a report of an air raid that morning on Hong Kong and Kowloon. Pound said the first Japanese attack on Malaya, at Kota Bharu, had been repulsed but a subsequent landing had succeeded and troops were reported infiltrating towards Kota Bharu airfield.

Churchill described his call to Roosevelt the previous night: the President had told him he would go to Congress with a message declaring the opening of hostilities, and Churchill had replied Britain would declare war immediately after America. Later however a message had been received from Tokyo that Japan had already declared war on America and Britain, and Churchill hoped the War Cabinet would authorize him to tell Parliament that Britain had declared war on Japan. The War Cabinet agreed and approved the immediate delivery of a communication to the Japanese Chargé. This, signed by Churchill and despatched from the

Cabinet Room, was expressed in courteous terms: 'Sir.... HM Ambassador at Tokyo has been instructed to inform the Imperial Japanese Government in the name of His Majesty's Government in the United Kingdom that a state of war exists between our two countries. I have the honour to be, with high consideration, Sir, Your Obedient Servant...' As Churchill later commented: 'When you have to kill a man it costs nothing to be polite.'[1] The Prime Minister told the War Cabinet he had long believed Japanese conflict with America would only be part of an arrangement whereby Germany and Italy would also open hostilities with the United States. 'This was a development which must be expected in the near future.' Churchill then disclosed his plan for travelling to America: 'There were already indications that the US naval authorities proposed to make certain re-dispositions ... which would vitally affect us. There was also a risk that they would wish to retain, for their own forces, munitions of war which they had promised to allocate to us.' The war 'should be concerted at the highest level. There were also important issues involved affecting co-operation with Russia and the attitude towards Vichy France.' Earlier in the day Eden had telephoned Attlee and the American Ambassador, urging them to oppose Churchill's suggestion of a voyage to America, and Attlee had said he would raise objections at the War Cabinet meeting, apparently agreeing with Eden that the Prime Minister and Foreign Secretary should not be out of the country simultaneously; but if Attlee declared his opposition at the War Cabinet meeting, no mention is made in the official Minutes: approval was given to Churchill's plan.[2]

The Prime Minister entered the House of Commons soon after 3 p.m., his shoulders bowed, his face grim. Hidden was the private jubilation over America's early entry into the war; he now thought it expedient to warn of future hardships. 'It is of the highest importance that there should be no underrating of the gravity of the new dangers we have to meet, either here or in the United States. The enemy has attacked us with an audacity which may spring from recklessness, but which may also spring from a conviction of strength.' Churchill only allowed optimism to creep in at the close of his statement. 'In the past we had had a light which flickered, in the present we have a light which flames, and in the future there will be a light which shines over all the land and sea.' As the Prime Minister was speaking, the battleships *Prince of Wales* and *Repulse* and four destroyers were forging northwards through the South China Sea; Admiral Phillips had sailed at 5.35 p.m. local time to raid Japanese shipping off Singora, relying on surprise to offset the weakness of his force against air attack. Shortly after midnight Phillips received a signal from Singapore: powerful Japanese bomber forces were operating from southern Indo-China; the northern front in Malaya seemed to be crumbling; RAF fighter protection over Singora would be impossible. Phillips decided to press on, provided he could remain undetected the following day, 9 December. But, late afternoon on the 9th the *Prince of Wales* reported sighting a Japanese reconnaissance aircraft, and with surprise lost the fleet turned back for Singapore.[3]

No more than token resistance had been offered by Thai forces and by 9 December the enemy were able to operate over 150 aircraft from newly acquired bases. Previous hesitation in London and Singapore over violating the Thai frontier had disastrous effects. 'Matador' had not been undertaken and the British 11th Division, commanded by General Percival, was ordered to take up defensive positions instead. But the plan for a defensive deployment had also involved a movement over the Thai border and was again fatally delayed; the British troops were, moreover, geared for 'Matador' and took too long to switch. Above all, although the first air raid on Singapore, early on the 8th, had inflicted only a small amount of damage, alarming weaknesses in the air defences had been revealed. By 9 December the RAF had lost 60 of the 110 aircraft in northern Malaya – over one-third of the total force available for the defence of the country. The Japanese had acquired complete and decisive air superiority over the battle area. The warning given by the RAF C-in-C in August, that lack of aircraft might mean little air support for ground forces, had come true; the RAF had remained below strength, with the main excuse for the failure to send more aircraft being the reinforcements given to the fleet through *Prince of Wales* and *Repulse*, but, despite the presence of these capital ships, the Japanese invasion forces had been successful. Ground units would now be called upon to pay the price.

Churchill cabled instructions to Duff Cooper, still in Singapore. 'You are appointed Resident Cabinet Minister.... You will serve under, and report directly to, the War Cabinet.... You are authorized to form a War Council.'[4] This desperate decision was taken too late. Another decision had also to be made; again, events would move too fast. During the evening of the 9th Churchill called a meeting of the Defence Committee to review the naval situation. Ministers, assembling in the Cabinet War Room at 10 p.m., heard that the position was indeed serious: Japanese forces had crossed the Kra Isthmus to the Indian Ocean coast; further details of the Pearl Harbour losses had been received; the naval balance in the Indian Ocean and Pacific had been entirely upset. Britain had one key weapon left: the strength provided by the *Prince of Wales* and *Repulse*. The COS had examined the possibility of these powerful battleships being sent into the Indian Ocean to restore the position, but this scheme was considered too dangerous. The meeting agreed instead the battleships must leave Singapore and head either for Australia, as Admiral Phillips had already suggested, or join the remnants of the US Pacific Fleet at Hawaii. Churchill urged the latter course. 'It would indeed be a proud gesture at this moment, and would knit the English-speaking world together.' The Prime Minister was also attracted to the idea of the battleships vanishing into the Pacific Islands and operating a vague menace 'like rogue elephants'. Discussions continued until after midnight, but a final decision was deferred for a further meeting next day.[5]

The meeting broke up about 1 a.m. London time, or about 8.30 a.m. Singapore time, Wednesday, 10 December. The *Prince of Wales* and *Repulse* were off Kuantan: Admiral Phillips had been returning to Singapore when news had been received of a supposed Japanese landing in this area, and he had altered course to investigate. No enemy were found. At 10.20 a.m. the enemy found the British. A reconnaissance aircraft reported the presence of the British fleet, and 40 minutes later the bombers arrived. The first wave concentrated upon the *Prince of Wales*, and both her port propellors were put out of action by torpedoes; the second wave closed in on the *Repulse*, but she escaped damage and turned back towards her ailing sister-ship. At 12.22 the bombers returned: *Repulse* was now shattered amidships and 11 minutes after this second attack had started she turned over and sank. The *Prince of Wales* only survived until 1.20 p.m. A total of 840 men were lost, including Admiral Tom Phillips and his Flag Captain, John Leach; 2,081 men were picked out of the water by the escort destroyers. The news reached London early on Wednesday, 10 December, British time; the First Sea Lord immediately telephoned the Prime Minister. Churchill claimed this the most direct shock he suffered throughout the war: Japanese warships sailed supreme throughout the Far East. Ismay, who had dreamt two nights before of such a catastrophe, commented: 'Nature is merciful. She sets a limit to the amount of pain.... When that limit is reached, numbness sets in.' Churchill hurried to the House of Commons and reported the appalling news, and other dismal reports arrived during the day: the Japanese had occupied Guam; the Philippines, subjected to a devastating air offensive on the 8th which had destroyed half General MacArthur's heavy bomber force and almost a third of his fighters, received renewed deadly attention, with Cavite naval base destroyed; two landings were made in northern Luzon. Churchill received a disappointing response to his suggestion for a meeting with Roosevelt: the President seemed unenthusiastic and stressed the dangers.

But also on the 10th excellent news came from Cairo. 'Enemy is apparently in full retreat,' reported Auchinleck. 'El Adem is taken. ...I think it is now permissible to claim that the siege of Tobruk has been raised. We are pursuing vigorously in fullest co-operation with the RAF.'[6] And Churchill had recovered his incredible resilience by the time the War Cabinet met at 6 p.m. on this Wednesday. He began by describing the changed balance of naval power in the Pacific. 'Until the position could be brought round, we should have to suffer considerable inconveniences; our shipping would be exposed to enemy attack, and we might have to take a lot of punishment.' He said the Americans were now moving their Atlantic fleet to the Pacific, but even this would not result in as strong a force as the Japanese. 'For the moment we could not send more ships to the Pacific, and we should have to develop a different kind of warfare.' Sir Earle Page suggested Russia should be asked to come into the war against Japan, but Churchill replied that 'in view of the enormous hammering which Russia was giving the German Army,' he did not think she should be asked to declare war on Tokyo. The Prime Minister then reviewed the general situation, and managed to find grounds for optimism. 'First, the United States were now in the war with us. Second, there was no doubt that the German armies had suffered serious defeat on the Russian front.... Third, so far as the battle in Libya was concerned, we could now say that the tide had definitely turned in our favour.... These developments far outweighed the immediate consequences of the position in the Far East, serious as they were.' Churchill said he had received a reply from Roosevelt about his proposed visit to America, suggesting that he should go in January and possibly that the meeting should be held in the West Indies. Churchill added he 'was not satisfied' and thought it important that the visit shoud take place much sooner, although the *rendezvous* was immaterial. He had sent a message in this sense.[7]

Next day, 11 December, Churchill gave a Commons statement; Hitler addressed the *Reichstag*. The Prime Minister spoke sombrely to a silent House, which 'seemed to hold its judgment in suspense';[8] the Führer declared war upon America amidst the shrieks of his hysterical henchmen. Japanese pressure was meanwhile being exerted upon Hong Kong. Three battalions from the garrison had been deployed on the mainland to delay the expected attack, now, during the 11th, orders were given for the withdrawal on to the island. The general military situation was discussed at 10 Downing Street that evening at a meeting of the Defence Committee and COS: although news from the Far East was bad and likely to worsen, the situation was considered not yet desperate. Brooke feared forces would be drawn from North Africa to the Far East – Ismay had warned him during the day that Churchill wanted the 18th Division transferred – and the meeting agreed with Churchill's suggestion. But the meeting also decided a major diversion of forces from other areas would be strategically unsound, and Churchill himself stressed that 'Germany was still the primary enemy' – Japan would best help Germany by drawing British strength to the Far East, a move which must be resisted. Admiral Layton, successor to Phillips, was warned that no immediate naval reinforcements would be sent except the carrier *Indomitable*, due at Cape Town on 1 January.[9] The decision underlined the pitifully meagre arsenal at Britain's disposal. As the COS stressed next day, 12 December, the Japanese occupation of Thailand now threatened Burma, previously neglected and almost without troops; Brooke maintained Burma must be helped, yet he himself was the foremost opponent of weakening the Middle East or the Home Front. The COS as a whole agreed that while the defences in Burma must be strengthened, it was of extreme importance to sustain as far as possible the defence of Malaya.[10] Inadequate forces had therefore to be juggled between one area and another. Churchill cabled Wavell, C-in-C India, on the 12th: 'You must now look East. Burma is placed under your command. You must resist the Japanese advance towards Burma and India.... I shall endeavour to feed you with armour, aircraft and British personnel to the utmost possible, having regard to the great strain we are under.'[11] Churchill also signalled Eden, still at sea on HMS *Kent*; two days before the Prime Minister had told him that in view of latest events the 10 RAF squadrons should not be offered to the Russians, and Eden was now informed 'we cannot make any promises beyond our agreed quota of supplies'.[12]

Churchill told the War Cabinet at 12.30 p.m. on the 12th that Roosevelt had telegraphed the previous day: while the President could not leave America at the moment, he would now be glad to receive the Prime Minister at the White House. Churchill told Ministers he had therefore decided to leave that night. With him would go the First Sea Lord, the Chief of Air Staff and Lord Beaverbrook. Also in the party would be Sir John Dill – whose inclusion resulted from a meeting between Brooke and Churchill the previous afternoon: Brooke had urged that Dill should be head of the Military Mission in Washington instead of becoming Governor of Bombay; Churchill had agreed after some hesitation. The Prime Minister now gave the War Cabinet a summary of the situation as he saw it, apparently intended as guidance for Ministers in his absence. Information from the Russian front indicated the German forces before Moscow were being 'cut to pieces and might well suffer a catastrophe'. As regards the Far East, Churchill continued, the Chief of Naval Staff believed Britain should fight a 'carrier war' until a fleet could be re-established; he, Churchill, thought it also important to fight the Japanese so hard on the ground that 'in place of, say, 6 divisions ... they would have to put on shore a force of 12 or 14 divisions. The maintenance of so large a force would involve them in difficulties and might well prove too big a strain for their resources.' Referring to the loss of the *Prince of Wales* and *Repulse*, Churchill revealed the Admiralty had known it was intended to use these battleships to attack Japanese forces landing on the Malayan coast 'but the Admiralty had not intervened to stop the operation. Possibly, however, the Admiralty had not been aware of the fact that fighter cover would not be available.' Churchill stressed that any criticism in Parliament 'should be resolutely dealt with, and arrangements should be made that a Labour critic should be answered by a Labour member and so forth'. Churchill said the time might shortly come when Britain should say to the Vichy Government that 'if they would stand with us in maintaining the independence and integrity of North Africa, we should do our best to restore their Empire. But if they failed us at this point, we would have nothing more to do with them.' He proposed to take up this matter with the Americans; a crisis might arise during his absence and a decision might have to be taken whether to launch the operation against French North Africa – 'Gymnast'. In this event Churchill hoped the Americans would agree to put a force into Casablanca.[13]

Earlier that morning the Japanese had opened their main attack on the 11th Division at Jitra in north-west Malaya near the Thai border. By evening one British brigade had been reduced to quarter strength and the two others had suffered heavily. The Divisional commander obtained permission to withdraw 30 miles south to unprepared positions at Gurun, where a prolonged stand would be extremely unlikely. On the west coast in the Kota Bharu area, the Japanese advance had continued and airfields had been abandoned, and, also on 12 December, General Percival gave permission for a general withdrawal to start on the 15th, initially to the railhead at Kuala Krai.

Eden arrived off Murmansk in thick fog; Churchill travelled to the Clyde to board the *Duke of York*, and he sailed that night on his first war-time voyage to Washington. Attlee, Ismay and Brooke were left in London to deal with the multitude of political, diplomatic and military affairs needing urgent attention; officially Brooke had still to take over as CIGS, and yet he now had to act as chairman of the caretaker COS committee, attended by the Vice-Chiefs of Naval and Air Staffs, in the absence of the First Sea Lord and Chief of Air Staff, who were with Churchill, and the Vice-CIGS who was with Eden. A triangular flow of signals now began between the *Duke of York*, Eden's party, and Whitehall. Churchill's powerful presence was no less evident despite his absence in mid-Atlantic. 'Pray do all in your power,' he urged Attlee, Ismay and Brooke on the 13th, 'to get men and materials moving into India, and reinforce with aircraft from the Middle East as soon as the battle in Libya is decided in our favour.'[14] By now, after a delay while stocks were built up, the 8th Army was in front of a German line running south from Gazala and Auchinleck prepared to attack. In Malaya, British forces were withdrawing to Gurun and Kuala Krai; troops on mainland China completed their withdrawal to Hong Kong island on the 13th, and the following day a Japanese summons to surrender was refused. Intensive air and artillery bombardment opened up on Hong Kong during the 15th; on the same day orders were given for the evacuation of Penang on Malaya's north-west coast. Auchinleck's offensive against Rommel's Gazala position was launched. Eden reached Moscow. And from all fronts: Burma, Malaya, Libya and Russia, came cries for assistance. Virtually no answer could be given. On this Monday Churchill gave his first warning about Singapore: 'Beware lest troops required for ultimate defence Singapore Island and fortress are used up or cut off in Malay peninsula.' This signal to the COS continued: 'Nothing compares in importance with the fortress. Are you sure we shall have enough troops for prolonged defence?'[15] Ministers at the War Cabinet meeting held at 5 p.m. were told: 'The Japanese intentions appeared to be: (a) A major attack on Singapore, with a simultaneous, but less powerful attack on Luzon. (b) An attack on Hong Kong. (c) An advance on Rangoon and/or Lashio with a view to stopping our supplies to China.'[16] To this list had to be added another offensive launched next day, 16 December: the invasion of North Borneo, soon to be overrun. And on the 17th the Japanese reached Penang, where despite demolitions during the evacuation of the previous 48 hours the enemy found barges, yachts and junks, soon to enable them to launch repeated amphibious attacks on the flanks of withdrawing British forces. General Percival visited the front on the 18th and ordered 3 Corps to stand west of the Perak river to hold the enemy as far north as possible.

British attacks on the Gazala line had only met with moderate success: Rommel was obliged to continue his withdrawal, but could do so in good order. He had lost the honours of the campaign; the allies could now re-occupy the whole of Cyrenaica. But the 8th Army was now completely stretched and Ritchie had difficulty in even keeping his forward armour in contact with the German rear-guard. Rain poured down upon the rough desert tracks, vehicles were operating far from the new forward base at Tobruk, and supplies, always deficient, could only arrive in paltry amounts. On the 19th British naval strength in the Mediterranean was severely sapped when Italian frogmen slipped into the port of Alexandria and fixed time-bombs to the battleships *Queen Elizabeth* and *Valiant*: both were heavily damaged. On the same day news reached naval Force K, based at Malta, that an important enemy convoy was heading for Tripoli with supplies for Rommel: three cruisers and four destroyers sailed to intercept but ran into a new minefield off Tripoli, and one cruiser, *Neptune*, exploded and sank, the two others were damaged, plus one destroyer. The convoy arrived unscathed. According to a German staff assessment: 'The sinking of the *Neptune* may be of decisive importance for holding Tripolitania. Without this the British force would probably have destroyed the Italian convoy. There is no doubt that the loss of these supplies at the peak of the crisis would have had the severest consequences.'[17] Rommel was therefore by no means beaten; the battle for supplies had still to be won; German air strength in the Mediterranean was rapidly increasing. And the Royal Navy had suffered a succession of terrible losses: *Ark Royal, Barham, Prince of Wales, Repulse, Queen Elizabeth, Valiant.* Not until 23 April 1942, would Churchill dare to reveal to the House of Commons in Secret Session that: 'In November and December last year in a few weeks we lost or had put out of action for a long time, seven great ships and more than one-third of our battleships and battle-cruisers, and ... this happened at a time when we were fully extended and had to meet the attack of a new, fresh and tremendous enemy and while our great ally was temporarily entirely crippled at sea.'

Churchill was now looking beyond temporary setbacks to future plans. The Prime Minister worked during his eight-day voyage on three papers on the future course of the war. These, and the subsequent COS contributions, were to form the basis for the coming talks in Washington; they also established a British viewpoint which was to be closely and stubbornly adhered to during intense allied discussions in 1942. Churchill's first paper declared: 'We ought ... to try hard to win over French North Africa, and now is the moment to use every inducement and form of pressure at our disposal upon the Government of Vichy and the French authorities.' Forces should be ready to take advantage of a Vichy invitation: Britain would supply about 55,000 men under this operation, 'Gymnast', apart from anything Auchinleck could bring in from the east through 'Acrobat', and, Churchill continued: 'It is desired that the United States should at the same time promise to bring in, via Casablanca and other African Atlantic ports, not less than

150,000 men during the next six months.' The plan must be undertaken with or without Vichy co-operation. Churchill also believed US bomber squadrons should come into action from the British Isles. 'Our own bomber programme has fallen short of our hopes. It is formidable and is increasing, but its full development has been delayed.' Churchill's second paper, not in fact completed until after his arrival in America, dealt with the Pacific: Japan's strength must deteriorate, he maintained, and her maximum power had been displayed at the time of Pearl Harbour. Thereafter resources would run short, and the Japanese must be kept 'as busy as possible'. Naval superiority must be regained at the earliest moment; carriers would have to be improvised. Finally, Churchill looked to 1943, when naval superiority would be reasserted in the Pacific and territories regained, Britain would be better able to resist invasion, and the whole West and North African shores would be in Anglo-American hands. The time would have come to turn upon Europe. 'We have therefore to prepare for the liberation of the captive countries of Western and Southern Europe by the landing at suitable points, successively or simultaneously, of British and American armies strong enough to enable the conquered populations to revolt.' Churchill added: 'We might hope, even if no German collapse occurs beforehand, to win the war at the end of 1943 or 1944.'[18]

One step led to another in Churchill's mind. Clear North Africa in 1942, and the base would be prepared for the assault on Europe. Churchill emphasized that his plans for 1942 'fall short of bringing the war to an end.... The war can only be ended through the defeat in Europe of the German armies, or through internal convulsions in Germany produced by the unfavourable course of the war, economic privations, and the Allied bombing offensive.' The Prime Minister's ideas were straightforward: he could indulge in a dramatic simplification which his professional advisers, concerned with the problems involved, could not enjoy.

The COS on the *Duke of York* were working on their own paper while Churchill pondered his, and the Directors of Plans had produced an assessment of the present military position which provided an independent background to Churchill's schemes. An attempted German invasion of Britain next spring could still not entirely be ruled out, said the Planners, and forces must therefore be kept for 'at least the minimum of protection', especially through naval strength. Account must also be taken of three possible German moves: an advance into Spain; naval expansion in the Atlantic through the acquisition of submarine bases at the Vichy West African ports of Casablanca and Dakar; naval expansion in the Indian Ocean through bases in Vichy Madagascar. Current

337

British operations in Cyrenaica would greatly improve the western flank in the Middle East, but the Planners, unlike Churchill, feared a German advance from the north via the Caucasus and into Turkey. Naval supremacy must be regained in the Far East, but the paper warned this could only be accomplished at the expense of the Middle East. The Planners could not therefore see scope for offensive operations in the near future, apart from action against the Canary Islands and Madagascar; instead they envisaged the old long-term strategies of 'bombing, blockade and subversion', added to which would be assistance to Russia to enable her to wear down the German war machine. This section would therefore seem to confirm Churchill's continual criticism of his professional advisers that they put forward no constructive ideas of their own and merely obstructed those he suggested. But the Planners came near to Churchill's broad outline of future strategy when they allowed themselves to stand back and view the more distant future. 'We hope that the offensive against Germany will take the form of large-scale land operations on the Russian front, large-scale bombing operations supplemented by amphibious raids of increasing weight from the United Kingdom and a gradual tightening of the ring around Axis-controlled Europe by the occupation of strategic positions in the Atlantic Islands, North and West Africa, Tripoli and Turkey.... These operations will be followed in the final phase by simultaneous land operations against Germany herself from the West by the British, from the South by the United States and from the East by the Russians.' Like Churchill, the Planners therefore envisaged American weight being directed from the south rather than across the Channel. 'Our study of the problem of the final assault on the Continent has brought out very clearly the limitations imposed on the size of the forces by the difficulties of providing special landing-craft in sufficient quantity. For example, even for the short cross-Channel passage from England to the Continent, we do not foresee such forces exceeding 17 divisions, half of which will be armoured.'

At COS meetings on the 18th and 19th, attended by Churchill and Beaverbrook, agreement had been reached on a merger of views expressed by the Planners, the Prime Minister and the COS, and the COS were able to produce a document intended as a basis of discussion with their US counterparts. The Memorandum, although a merger, swayed more towards Churchill's papers: more immediate, detailed problems were put to one side to allow the clear, longer view taken by Churchill and the Planners in their final section on future strategy. The agreement already reached in Anglo-American talks was re-stated: 'Germany was the predominant member of the Axis powers, and consequently the Atlantic and European area

338

was considered to be the decisive theatre.' Essential features of Grand Strategy were listed: the realization of the 'victory programme' of armaments; maintenance of essential communications; 'closing and tightening the ring around Germany'; wearing down and undermining German resistance by air bombardment, blockade, subversive activities and propaganda; the continuous development of offensive action against Germany; maintaining only such positions in the Eastern theatre as will safeguard vital interests 'while we are concentrating on the defeat of Germany'. As far as closing and tightening the ring was concerned, this would be achieved 'by sustaining the Russian front, by arming and supporting Turkey, and by gaining possession of the whole North African coast'. The document also declared: 'In 1943 the way may be clear for a return to the Continent, either across the Mediterranean or from Turkey into the Balkans, or by simultaneous landings in several of the occupied countries of North-Western Europe. Such operations will be the prelude to the final assault on Germany itself.' With a slightly different degree of emphasis the COS and Churchill therefore saw North Africa, and hence 'Gymnast', as offering most scope for operations. Both saw North Africa as the most suitable for American intervention. Neither envisaged a single large-scale assault across the Channel against Europe, even in 1943.[19]

Stalin, described by Eden as 'a quiet dictator', was thinking even further ahead. He had surprised the British Foreign Secretary by insisting on discussing post-war Europe, yet Eden had agreed at a War Cabinet meeting on 4 December, three days before departing for Moscow, that he would 'avoid being drawn into any precise discussions as regards territorial changes or boundaries'. Now, at his Kremlin talks, Eden found 'Russian ideas were already starkly definite'.[20] The War Cabinet, meeting at 10.15 a.m., on the 19th, were read a telegram received from Eden at 10.15 the previous night. 'I was summoned to meet Stalin at midnight.... At the outset Stalin said ... what interested him was the question of the frontiers of the USSR after the war. He would agree that the Polish frontier might be left an open question, but he wanted our immediate endorsement of his territorial claims in Finland, Baltic States and Roumania. In vain I argued that I had not come for this.... He hinted more than once that if he was not satisfied it might be better to have no agreement.' Eden had another meeting with Stalin, reported in a telegram to London which arrived at 1.15 a.m. that day, 19 December. Stalin had produced a formula whereby Russia and Britain would 'work for the reconstruction of Europe after the war with full recognition to the interests of the USSR in the restoration of its frontiers violated by Hitlerite aggression'. Eden commented: 'I pointed out that this, if it meant anything, meant a recognition by us now of the Soviet 1941 frontiers as the frontiers of the peace settlement', and he had said Britain could not possibly agree to such a document. His cable continued: 'This of course, is deplorable, but I do not see how HMG can here and now by treaty agree to post-war Soviet frontiers without American agreement. I should be glad of immediate views of War Cabinet.... My present intention is to leave Saturday evening.' Ministers agreed Britain could not sign such an agreement: at the time of the Atlantic Charter an assurance had been given to the Americans that Britain would make no secret commitments regarding post-war settlements, and if Britain acquiesced to Soviet demands in this respect 'we should inevitably be forced to enter into similar commitments in other cases'.

'The situation in Hong Kong is very serious,' Ministers were informed. 'The Japanese have effected a landing on the north-east corner of the island and have made a deep penetration. It looks as though the island cannot hold out much longer.'[21] Also on the 19th, Churchill expressed further fears for Singapore in a signal to the COS in London. 'After naval disasters to British and American sea-power in Pacific and Indian Ocean we have no means of preventing continuous landings by Japanese.... The C-in-C (Far East) should now be told to confine himself to defence of Johore and Singapore, and that nothing must compete with maximum defence of Singapore.'[22] The Defence Committee met that evening to discuss the rapidly deteriorating situation; approval was given to a staff report on Far East strategy which stressed that carriers must be relied upon to meet the Japanese naval threat. Yet, at that time Britain only had four modern carriers – *Formidable*, *Illustrious*, *Indomitable* and *Victorious* – plus the 24-year-old *Furious* and the smaller *Eagle* and *Hermes*, built in 1924. Unified allied direction of the war was urgently required, the report also declared, and it was hoped this would result from the Washington discussions; the paper then made the unreasonable statement that it was 'very necessary that the United States forces should act offensively on sea, land and in the air and at once'. Yet Pearl Harbour had only been attacked 13 days before. The report listed 'vital' points which must be held: Burma, especially Rangoon and the Irrawaddy basin, Ceylon, Singapore Island and Southern Malaya, Sumatra, Java and Timor.[23]

Japanese forces in Luzon had gradually pressed forward; on 21 December the main invasion force for the Philippines landed in Lingayen Gulf, threatening Manila itself. Hong Kong continued to survive, battered, short of water, but determined – even though the end could only be a few days away. Attlee read latest telegrams to the War Cabinet at 5 p.m. on Monday, 22 December. The Governor of Hong Kong had cabled at 09.33 hours on the 21st: 'GOC advises that we are very rapidly approaching a point at which only remaining resistance open to us will be to hold for a short time only a small pocket in centre of city.... I feel it will be my duty to ask terms before this position is reached.' But this appeal had crossed a message from Churchill to Hong Kong: 'The eyes of the world are upon you. We expect you to resist to the end. The honour of the Empire is in your hands.' A signal from the Admiralty had added: 'In spite of conditions you [the Governor] and GOC are facing, the difficulties of which are clearly understood, HMG's desire is that you should fight it out.' 'Instructions of HMG are understood,' replied the Governor early on the 22nd. 'You may be quite confident that we have, and always have had, every intention of fighting it out. Please understand that what I have in mind, with the unanimous concurrence of my Defence Council, was no more than a last minute endeavour to save civilians.' This cable had concluded: 'Enemy's next break will probably leave our ball in the end pocket, where we shall follow your instructions. We are all very cheerful.' The War Cabinet were also informed on the 22nd that British forces in Malaya were in 'a difficult tactical situation, owing to the length of the Malayan coastline'. They could be constantly outflanked by new Japanese landings in the rear.[24]

Churchill reached Washington this Monday evening. Roosevelt was waiting: 'I clasped his strong hand with comfort and pleasure,' wrote Churchill. Talks began the same night, and the Prime Minister later cabled the War Cabinet: 'There was general agreement that it was vital to forestall the Germans in North-West Africa and the Atlantic Islands,' with or without French invitation to their territory, and Roosevelt 'favoured the idea of a plan to move into North Africa being prepared for either event'. This report reached London on Tuesday, 23 December; all seemed to be going well at the Washington conference – codenamed 'Arcadia' – even though Roosevelt almost immediately adopted a less definite stand on a North African operation. Talks would last for almost a fortnight, meanwhile, apart from matters arising in Washington which needed immediate attention, the War Cabinet and the caretaker COS were allowed to concentrate on day-to-day problems. A report arrived from Wavell, dated 22 December, expressing concern over Burma – described as 'far from secure'; the great weakness, Wavell warned, was the dependence on Rangoon as the only port of entry. The C-in-C India then made the hazardous flight to Chungking with the American General Brett, for 'rather futile' talks with Chiang Kai-Shek.[25] Wake Island fell to the Japanese on the 23rd; on Christmas Eve the Japanese waded unopposed across the Perak River in Malaya, despite General Percival's hope that the enemy would be held for some time west of this line. War Cabinet Ministers were informed at 11.30 a.m. on the 24th that 'the garrison at Hong Kong was still holding out, although in a grave position'. The Defence Committee, meeting at 5 p.m., discussed details of a 'scorched earth policy' for Malaya – 'no arms, foodstocks or other valuable material must be left intact for the enemy'.[26] Two hours later the War Cabinet met again: a telegram had been received from Churchill giving drafts of a Joint Declaration and requesting urgent Ministerial consideration; one draft merely covered a declaration by Churchill and the President, the other envisaged a document signed by all allies. The War Cabinet preferred the latter.[27] Discussion was continued at a further War Cabinet meeting next morning, Christmas Day, and Ministers agreed a telegram should be sent from Attlee to Churchill giving approval. Ministers were told that other signals from Washington had caused the COS some concern: it seemed the Americans were considering a system of areas of strategic responsibility for the conduct of the war and the COS believed this system, 'arbitrarily laid down on a geographical basis', would be 'dangerous and wrong.... The strategy of the war must be looked at as a whole, and predominant roles in the fields of operation allocated in accordance with the general strategic situation and the resources of the allies.' This opinion would be conveyed to Washington.

General Brooke then revealed: 'We have received no report from Hong Kong since early yesterday, and the Japanese claim to have captured the island might well be true.' Singapore seemed next to be threatened; War Cabinet attention was drawn to various rumours concerning lack of defensive equipment at Singapore, and Ministers agreed immediate steps should be taken to inquire into these allegations.[28] The tragic but expected confirmation of the fall of Hong Kong reached General Brooke during late evening. Brooke had spent an exhausting Christmas Day – officially his first day as CIGS. He had sat with the caretaker COS committee from 11.30 a.m. to 6 p.m., discussing the relative priorities of the Far East and Middle East, and considering signals received from Churchill concerning 'Gymnast'. The COS in London were perturbed by the Prime Minister's apparent desire to push on with this operation against French North Africa, with or without a Vichy invitation; Brooke, preferring the clearing of Tripoli by Auchinleck's forces – 'Acrobat' – feared 'Gymnast' would over-commit British strength; the Vice-Chief of Naval Staff confirmed that shipping available would not permit an occupation of North Africa if sufficient reinforcements were to be sent to secure Singapore, Burma and the Indian Ocean communications.[29]

Generals Wavell and Brett flew back from Chungking on Christmas Day and landed at Rangoon seconds before a heavy Japanese air raid: Wavell counted 17 bombs falling within 50 yards of his trench, the nearest 30 feet away. Brett reported to Washington: 'Aircraft defence ineffective. Air defence extremely weak.... Conditions very critical.... Continued bombing by Japs will completely immobilize port of Rangoon within three weeks.' Wavell condemned this report as alarmist, but he himself had described Burma's position as 'far from secure'.[30] General Brooke spent much of Boxing Day discussing reinforcements to the Far East. He saw Bruce, the Australian High Commissioner, during the afternoon and attempted to reassure him that Singapore would not be abandoned; Bruce 'went away satisfied', Brooke believed.[31] Singapore had long been held the key to Australian safety. Curtin, the Australian Prime Minister, had been subjecting Churchill to a flow of telegrams throughout the Washington conference, suggesting, among other schemes, that an Anglo-American fleet should be formed forthwith to bring the Japanese fleet into decisive action. Churchill had cabled on the 25th: 'We do not share the view expressed in your telegram to Mr Casey (Australian representative in Washington) that there is the danger of early reduction of Singapore fortress, which we are determined to defend with the utmost tenacity.'[32] But the Australian Prime Minister telegraphed Roosevelt on Boxing Day: 'Reinforcements earmarked by the UK for despatch to Malaya seem to us to be utterly inadequate, especially in relation to aircraft.'[33] The Australians continued to be anxious and had every reason to be: reports from the Commonwealth Commissioner in Singapore showed air cover for the island was dwindling fast. 'As things stand at present, the fall of Singapore is to my mind only a matter of weeks.' On 27 December an article by Curtin appeared in the *Melbourne Herald* which appeared to repudiate links with Britain and to rest all hopes on America. 'The Australian Government ... regards the Pacific struggle as primarily one in which the United States and Australia must have the fullest say.... Australia looks to America, free of any pangs as to our traditional links with the United Kingdom.' The article was immediately seized upon by Goebbels as excellent propaganda; Churchill cabled the War Cabinet: 'I hope there will be no pandering to this, while at the same time we do all in human power to come to their aid.' He added: 'I hope you will endeavour to let all issues stand over until I return.'[34]

Churchill had already asked Attlee if approval could be given for his mission to be prolonged; Attlee apparently gave this permission without reference to the War Cabinet, and Churchill cabled on the 27th: 'Thank you so much for agreeing to lengthen my stay.

On Tuesday, 30 December, I am addressing the Canadian House of Commons.'[35] As far as General Brooke was concerned the Prime Minister's return was becoming dangerously overdue. 'PM and his COS Committee in USA brewing up a series of discrepancies with what we are preparing here,' he wrote in his diary on the 27th. These 'discrepancies' were mainly concerned with 'Gymnast'; Brooke explained his point of view to a 2½-hour meeting of the Defence Committee starting at 5 p.m. on this Saturday: 'Crusader' should be exploited to the fullest extent, bearing in mind the need to reinforce the Far East, and shipping would seriously limit chances of 'Gymnast'. 'On the face of it it seemed beyond our power to do "Gymnast" without sacrificing both the Middle and Far East. To meet the fighter commitment we might have to curtail the supply of Hurricanes to Russia.... It did not appear, therefore, that the prospects of being able to launch Operation "Gymnast" were very favourable.' The CIGS added that a telegram had been despatched to the COS in Washington 'asking for confirmation of our immediate policy. The COS here took our policy to be first: security of Singapore and Burma, second: the completion of "Acrobat", and third: "Gymnast", in which the United States would play the major part.' Attlee suggested it would be better if US bombers were sent to the Far East, rather than brought to Britain to operate against Germany.[36] Further disquiet, bordering on consternation, resulted from a cable next day, Sunday the 28th, in which Churchill described American proposals for a united Anglo-American command area in the Far East, to include Burma – the so-called ABDA command. 'The whole scheme wild and half-baked', exclaimed Brooke in his diary.[37] The idea had been first raised by General Marshall, US Chief of Staff, in discussions on Christmas Day, and had been elaborated by Roosevelt next morning at plenary session. British reaction had been unenthusiastic; Churchill had said the distances involved in the Pacific were immense and each local commander had his instructions and knew his duty, and the main problem was disposition of available reinforcements – a matter for Governments rather than a C-in-C. Admiral King had made reservations on behalf of the US Navy. But Marshall had persisted, supported by Roosevelt and Hopkins. Churchill had begun to sway towards approval: he had told the British mission during the evening of the 26th that advantages would be obtained from general direction of Pacific operations stemming from Washington, with London dealing with the Atlantic area. Next day Pound had stated that the unified command scheme might smooth naval co-operation in the area, and, by the evening of the 27th the COS in Washington were ready to accept Marshall's scheme in principle. They recommended an

344

American officer as supreme commander; Churchill replied the Americans wanted Wavell and he dismissed the COS objections that the Americans 'were attempting to shift disaster on to our shoulders'.[38]

War Cabinet Ministers meeting at 10 Downing Street on Monday morning, 29 December, therefore had a long telegram from Churchill for consideration, dealing with the ABDA proposal and with Wavell's appointment to the command. Ministers agreed to meet again at 2.30 p.m. after the scheme had been studied by Brooke and his colleagues. The Minutes for the second session later on the Monday declared that 'doubts were expressed about various aspects of the scheme, but the Cabinet had only had an outline of the scheme and were without knowledge of discussions which had led to it. Further, the Prime Minister and his advisers clearly strongly favoured the scheme, discussions on which had already gone a long way. In the circumstances, the War Cabinet decided that the right course was to accept the plan in principle, whilst making certain comments in detail.' Fears were felt that if a plan for unified command were confined to the Pacific, 'the claims of other vital theatres of war might therefore be endangered. It was emphasized that Germany was our main enemy, and that the Pacific was not the main theatre of war. It was essential that some machinery or system should be established to plan the strategy of the war as a whole.'[39] As Brooke commented: 'Cabinet was forced to accept PM's new scheme owing to the fact that it was almost a *fait accompli*.' The CIGS was especially concerned with the return of Burma to the Far East area, rather than the country's inclusion in neighbouring India Command.[40] Also on the 29th, Churchill sent a message to Wavell, via Attlee, informing him of his new appointment. 'You are the only man who has the experience of handling so many different theatres at once, and you know we shall back you up and see you have fair play. Everyone knows how dark and difficult the situation is.' Churchill wrote in his memoirs: 'The offer which I had to make to General Wavell was certainly one which only the highest sense of duty could induce him to accept. It was almost certain that he would have to bear a load of defeat in a scene of confusion.'[41]

Wavell would now command British, American, British Empire and Dutch land, sea and air forces in an area covering Malaya, Burma, across to the Philippines and south to Australian supply bases. Wavell's reaction was typical. 'A pretty tall order. I accepted it of course.'[42]

The Japanese flames licking across this huge sheet of Wavell's Atlas could not be stamped out by any decisions resulting from the

'Arcadia' conference; talks in Washington had to be concerned with the future – with recovery and eventual reconquest. Despite the disasters in the Far East, Churchill and his professional advisers concentrated strategic thoughts more upon Europe and the Middle East; Germany was the main enemy; the Far East was anyway fluid and nothing long-term could be decided until some of the present confusion had been cleared – and this could only be done by steps already put in motion with the limited means available. Strategic decisions might be possible, but not, for the moment, those of grand strategy. The Americans on the other hand were primarily preoccupied with the Pacific: Pearl Harbour had only recently been attacked. In a sense Roosevelt had been right in his reluctance for Churchill to come so soon, and Harry Hopkins had passed a pertinent warning to Churchill while the Prime Minister had been *en route*: the British would be unwise to bring forward too many cut and dried plans, because the US Chiefs of Staff were concerned with immediate Pacific matters and could not give their minds to wider strategic problems.

Yet Churchill and his delegation persisted in presenting long-term ideas for the Middle East and Europe. The COS document, based on the *Duke of Kent* discussions, was considered at Anglo-American staff talks on 24, 27 and 31 December. Only minor alterations were made and this document, known thereafter as WW 1, became the first formal declaration of an agreed allied strategy. Confirmation was thereby given to the recognition of Germany as the principal enemy, and the plan outlined the 'tightening the ring' policy with the return to the Continent in 1943 'across the Mediterranean, from Turkey into the Balkans, or by landings in Western Europe'. WW 1 was useful as a general line of approach. But few details were specified by the British COS and the Americans were too preoccupied with the Pacific to seek them. A wide gap was therefore left between the strategic principles and their practical application, and both Britain and America could read their own ideas in the wording, but these ideas might differ considerably. At the end of December the Anglo-American staff discussions turned to the more practical question of 'Gymnast'. Almost immediately Hopkins' warning was apparently proved justified: an American War Department paper declared: 'Our acceptance of a commitment in North West Africa at this time would prove to be a mistake of the first magnitude.' Difficulties were indeed considerable; General Weygand, known to be anti-German, had been dismissed as French Delegate General in North Africa the previous month; Pétain had started further negotiations with the Germans; allied landings might be opposed. The uncertain political background led to uncertain military planning: the Anglo-American staffs asked the Joint Planning Committee, formed during the conference, to study 'Gymnast', but this committee was unable to agree on the size of force required for the operation. How much French co-operation could be expected? What would be the speed of German reaction? What size of area did the expedition hope to control? American experts even feared as many as 300,000 men might be needed; the British hoped a small, mobile, rapid operation might be sufficient. Differing estimates affected the number of transport vessels required. Eventually a compromise plan emerged, in which three American and three British divisions would be employed during the first three months, plus 348 aircraft, mostly American, with the US force directed at Casablanca and the British at Algiers.

Underlying the whole discussion was the need for speed if the operation was to be undertaken. Britain's 8th Army had achieved success and use must be made of it; moreover, the 8th Army advance might lead to increased German pressure on Vichy France for permission to use North African bases. But allied planners now struck the main obstacle – shipping. Attempts were made to find sufficient transport. Yet on 1 January the staffs had provisionally to accept a proposal by General Marshall that the convoy would have to use shipping already planned for the first movement of US troops to Northern Ireland. The Battle of the Atlantic had taken its toll. British import levels had been maintained and some stocks had even increased by domestic readjustments, yet shipping was still extremely scarce. Autumn and winter of 1941 had seen a decline in sinkings, but these would soon rise again: 48 ships, totalling 276,795 tons, would be lost in January in the North Atlantic, compared with 10 vessels totalling 50,682 tons in December. America's entry into the war had positive disadvantages: U-boats now roamed throughout the Atlantic, no longer under orders to avoid an 'incident', and US warships in the Atlantic were being thinned in order to re-build strength in the Pacific. Moreover, U-boat production was increasing; 249 enemy submarines would be in commission in January, 91 of them operational, compared with 158 in July 1941. Meanwhile, General Brooke feared that resources urgently needed for Auchinleck's 'Crusader' and 'Acrobat' would be diverted to the Far East or to 'Gymnast' and that Rommel's strength would steadily increase again. The CIGS had every justification for his fears. Royal Navy losses in the Mediterranean coincided with the arrival of still more U-boats, and *Fliegerkorps* II was now operating from Sicily. In November barely 30,000 tons of enemy military stores had been landed in North Africa, only 40 per cent of the total shipped; in January this would change to 60,000 tons at negligible loss. Moreover, British supplies had still to be sent to Russia, with consequent drain on shipping and resources. By the end of the year 53 loaded ships had been escorted to north Russia; no losses had yet resulted, but it had been found impossible to maintain the 10-day cycle promised by Churchill: the average interval between convoys had worked out at 15 days. And soon the winter darkness would change to almost permanent daylight. The Russians had so far not given any assistance in convoy protection, despite the Moscow agreement that Britain and America would merely 'give aid' to the transportation of materials. And, while America's entry into the war might help with shipping in the long run, the United States war production had increasingly to take into account her own needs and those of the Soviets: Churchill's fears increased that American aid allocations to Britain would be diverted to the Soviet Union. The lack of resources and the lack of shipping which were now found to hinder plans for 'Gymnast' would clearly remain to complicate future offensive schemes.

Churchill's mission would not end until 14 January, but clearly closer and continuing contact would have to be maintained. One important step was now taken to establish this permanent link: the creation of the Combined Chiefs of Staff committee. The CCS would hold its first meeting on Friday, 23 January, in the Federal Reserve Building, Washington, attended by General George Marshall, described by Ismay as 'a big man in every sense of the word and utterly selfless', stern and formal and a brilliant organizer, 'a very great gentleman', according to Brooke, 'who inspired trust but did not impress me by the ability of his brain';[43] Admiral Ernest King, tough, stiff, suspicious and blunt; General Arnold, the air force chief who, since there was no independent Air Force in America, came under Marshall's command – cheerful and smiling and well-suited to his nickname 'Hap'; Admiral H. R. Stark, US Chief of Naval Operations; Admiral Sir Charles Little, RN; Lieutenant-General Sir Colville Wemyss and Group Captain S. C. Stafford. And as chief British representative would be Field-Marshal Sir John Dill, left behind when Churchill departed for home, and almost immediately a close friend of Marshall.

The CCS was perhaps the most valuable practical result of the 'Arcadia' Conference, charged with 'determining and recommending the broad programme of requirements based on strategic policy, submitting general directives as to the policy governing the distribution of available weapons of war, and settling the broad lines of priority of overseas movement'. The CCS did not therefore originate strategy, but advised and acted upon strategy already agreed by the individual American and British Governments. They acted as a balance, complement and focal point for schemes originating in Washington and London – or, specifically, from Roosevelt and Churchill, both of whom had strong ideas and both of whom needed an occasional tug on the reins; as Henry Stimson, US War Secretary, commented, the leaders required 'the balancing restraint of carefully organized staff advice'.[44] Only America and Britain were included on the CCS committee, thus excluding, in Hopkins' words, 'everybody and his grandmother'; moreover, the system was created at a time when America and Britain were almost equal – American war production and manpower would ultimately make her predominant, but meanwhile Britain had greater war experience and organizational cohesion. An imbalance might have resulted from the CCS meeting in Washington, attended by the American Chiefs and only British Deputy-Chiefs of Staff, but this extra US influence was avoided by the fortuitous presence of Field-Marshal Dill.[45] Through the frequent sessions – 54 in 1942 – the CCS established continuity, and they were backed by other joint committees, including the Joint Planning Staff. Churchill commented on the CCS: 'There was never a failure to reach effective agreement for action, or to send clear instructions to the commanders in every theatre'; the plea made by the War Cabinet on 29 December – 'It is essential that some machinery or system should be established to plan the strategy of the war as a whole' – had been largely answered.[46]

'Here's to a year of toil,' Churchill toasted American newspapermen on New Year's Eve. 'A year of struggle and peril and a long step towards victory!' Twelve months before the Prime Minister had been at his peak of popular power; his performance in the dark days of 1940 had carried him through the flagrant mistakes and setbacks of 1941. Only 'Crusader' now seemed to mark a credit. The Battle of the Atlantic had still to be won. And although the British public did not know the full extent of the various defeats and were fed far fuller information on the successes, criticism was nevertheless rapidly mounting. Churchill had to re-establish himself. Yet as with 1941, 1942 opened with a confusion of plans and over-stretched resources. The one specific operational scheme discussed at 'Arcadia', 'Gymnast', was fated to be temporarily shelved, leaving the grandoise and vague expression of future hopes, WW I, as a potential source of misunderstanding. Meanwhile the jumble of events in the Mediterranean, Middle East and Far East all clamoured for attention. Confusion would continue through long painful weeks until the pressure of events themselves forced resources to find their own shallow level. Churchill and the COS, and now the Americans, had still to regain the initiative; only the Russians had clear aims.

349

Eden had returned to London on 30 December and gave a report on his Moscow discussions to the War Cabinet on Thursday, 1 January. 'From our point of view, the greatest difficulty would arise as regards the Baltic States, which Stalin wished us to recognize as falling within Russia's strategic frontier.' Eden warned that this question of frontiers would have to be considered by the War Cabinet before long. 'It must be remembered that, if we won the war, Russian forces would probably penetrate into Germany and that at a later date she might well want more than her 1941 frontiers.' Eden reported optimistic assessments of the present military situation; he also said that 'the time had now been reached when they should assent to Sir Stafford Cripps's desire to be recalled from Moscow'. Ministers were informed that supply difficulties were preventing large-scale operations by the 8th Army against Rommel's positions, but an assault on Bardia had begun; the situation at Manila 'appeared to be grave'; little change was reported in the Malayan situation.[47]

Signals sent to overseas commanders on 1 January, based on decisions taken in Washington, attempted to maintain a balance in the allocation of resources between Far and Middle East. The security of Singapore was classed as second only to the security of Britain, but 'the defeat of Germany must remain our primary object. Consequently for the present we should not divert more of our resources than necessary to hold the Japanese.' 'Crusader' should be exploited to maximum possible extent.[48] A clear danger therefore existed of spinning the thread so thin that it snapped at a number of critical points. On 2 January the Defence Committee heard of considerable confusion surrounding Wavell's new command. Wavell had sent a bewildered signal which had been referred to the Committee by the COS. 'Grateful if you could elucidate very early following points.... Is it intended that I should absorb whole or part of existing C-in-C Far East Staff.... On whom shall I rely for intelligence?... Shall I collect fresh nucleus staff?... What are my relations with Duff Cooper?' Ismay commented in a minute to the Defence Committee: 'The COS find some difficulty in replying to General Wavell's questions, since they do not know exactly what our delegation, who are responsible for making the arrangements, have in mind.' Neither did the Defence Committee; Wavell's queries were therefore referred to Washington.[49] 'Speed was ... essential in settling letter of instructions to Wavell,' apologized Churchill in a signal to Attlee on the 3rd. 'It was necessary to defer to American views, observing we are no longer single, but married.' The Prime Minister supplied further details of the ABDA system, and at least one of Brooke's criticisms seemed partly unfounded: administratively Burma would remain in the Indian command. Churchill also declared: 'We live here as a big family, in the greatest intimacy and informality.... There is not the slightest sign here of excitement or worry about the opening misfortunes which are being taken as a matter of course.'[50] But Dill wrote to Brooke on the same day: 'At present this country has not – repeat not – the slightest conception of what the war means, and their armed forces are more unready for war than it is possible to imagine.'[51]

Churchill was still trying to smooth relations with New Zealand and especially Australia, both directly affected by the ABDA decision, even though they did not fall within the command area – Brooke, for one, thought this another serious mistake. Both increased their pressure for greater participation in decision-making. 'Night and day,' cabled Churchill to Curtin on the 3rd, 'I am labouring here to make the best arrangements possible in your interests and for your safety.'[52] The fruits of this labour would not be offered until 19 January, and Curtin was to find them sour to his taste. Not until that date would Churchill reveal to the Australian Prime Minister the 'deadly secret' of the damage done to the *Queen Elizabeth* and *Valiant* at Alexandria on 19 December and the sinking of the *Barham* in the Mediterranean on 25 November. And Britain might soon suffer another infinitely more serious loss in the Mediterranean. The COS warned on the 3rd that Malta might be 'next on the list. Air attacks ... have already begun, and the increasing scale of this offensive will reduce the island's ammunition and stores, and will make reinforcement progressively difficult.' British intelligence believed the Germans would try to eliminate Maltese resistance through air attack alone; combined operations would be launched if these failed.[53] Next day an Italian convoy began to cross the Mediterranean, reaching Tripoli unhindered on the 5th: this success, according to Admiral Cunningham, showed existing surface forces were now powerless to intercept enemy seaborne supplies, and maritime aircraft were inadequate even for reconnaissance purposes; unless strong reinforcements could be sent, Cunningham continued, Malta could not be maintained and enemy supplies to Tripoli would continue at full spate.[54]

Churchill flew south on Sunday, 4 January, for 5 days' rest in the Palm Beach sun. In London next day the *Daily Express* began its powerful campaign for the launching of a Second Front to help the Russians. 'The Tower of Evil stands there, just over the way, casting its darkness over the Continent....' The War Cabinet meeting this Monday heard depressing news from all fronts – except the Russian. 'On the west coast of Malaya we have withdrawn to meet seaborne threats to our communication.... In the Philippines, Manila has been occupied by the enemy.... At Agedabia our forces, which are operating some 400-500 miles in front of their railheads, are severely limited by the supply problems. The ports of Tobruk, Derna and Benghazi are now being operated, but so far only on a limited scale.'[55]

Wavell flew from Delhi to Singapore to take up his stern task; Duff Cooper received a signal from Churchill to say his mission had ended with Wavell's appointment. On the day of the ABDA commander's arrival, 7 January, Japanese tanks thrust forward through British positions by the Slim River, and Wavell hurried to 9 and 11 Divisions in the front line. Also on the 7th, Rommel withdrew to his final position at El Agheila on the western border of Cyrenaica: 'Crusader' could at last be called finished. Rommel had retreated over 500 miles and had lost almost a third of his force; German casualties were about twice as many as the British. But Rommel's army was still intact and the western flank remained uncleared. The 8th Army was vastly over-extended, while German and Italian supplies were increasing rapidly. Auchinleck maintained that British gains must be consolidated through a further offensive effort, or the previous year's events would be repeated – 'when Rommel hustled us back to Tobruk and the frontier'. But to accomplish another offensive, British reinforcements would have to be sent and supplies built up, needing time and resources. And also on 7 January, further discussions on 'Gymnast' took place in Washington; it soon emerged that forces could not be assembled until at least mid-February, and American ability to find necessary cargo ships and naval escorts seemed extremely doubtful.

'Formations and units of 9 and 11 Divisions with very few exceptions are no longer fit to withstand attack,' signalled Wavell on the 8th.[56] The General planned extensive withdrawals to allow time for re-grouping and all possible reinforcements: the main British line would now be drawn 150 miles further back along the river Muar. On 9 January Churchill sent a signal to Wavell revealing renewed fears for Singapore, while in London on this Friday the COS discussed remaining possibilities of carrying out 'Acrobat' – the occupation of Tripolitania – despite the 'Crusader' delays, the problem of supplies and the Far East situation. 'I am beginning to wonder whether the operation is on,' wrote the CIGS.[57]

Churchill started by train from Florida to Washington on the night of the 9th, and would arrive back at the White House on the 11th. 'I have availed myself of a few days' quiet and seclusion,' he wired the COS and Defence Committee while *en route*, 'to review the salients of the war as they appear after my discussions here.' The signal showed Brooke had been correct in doubting whether 'Acrobat' was still 'on'. The Prime Minister declared: 'The stubborn resistance of the enemy in Cyrenaica, the possibilities of

General Rommel withdrawing, or of being able to escape with a portion of his troops, the reinforcements which have probably reached Tripoli and others which must be expected during the delay, and above all the difficulties of supply for our advancing troops – all will retard, or may even prevent, the full completion of "Acrobat".' He added: 'We are therefore in a position to study "Super-Gymnast" more thoroughly (allied landings in Vichy Africa) and to proceed with "Magnet" (movement of US troops to Northern Ireland) with the utmost speed.' Turning to the Far East, Churchill revealed an attitude very similar to that shown after the Fall of France in 1940: he condemned defensive thinking and called for as many small raids as possible.[58] Next day, 11 January, Churchill cabled Auchinleck from Washington: 'I am sure you and your armies did all in human power, but we must face the facts as they are.'[59] On 12 January Churchill showed the President a copy of his signal to the COS, and he also told the 'Arcadia' conference that 'the arrival of General Auchinleck's armies on the Tunisian border could not be expected as early as at one time it was thought possible'. Moreover, the urgency for intervention in Vichy North Africa had eased, paradoxically partly because of Rommel's success: while his ability to preserve his forces reasonably intact had blunted the decision of 'Crusader', this in turn had removed the need for German intervention in Vichy North Africa to acquire more bases. Hence Anglo-American intervention could be delayed. Discussions on 'Super-Gymnast' and on 'Gymnast', now the name for a more limited operation to give aid to Weygand, would continue awhile, but without any hope of immediate execution. For a few days Auchinleck refused to abandon his pressure for 'Acrobat'; signalling Churchill on the 12th: 'I am convinced that we should press forward ... for many reasons, not the least in order that Germany may continue to be attacked on two fronts, Russia and Libya', but three days later he had to accept an assessment by General Ritchie, 8th Army commander, that an offensive could not be resumed before 11-15 February and that meanwhile Benghazi must be built up as a supply base.[60]

Churchill left Washington for Bermuda on the 14th on his first stage of the journey home. 'I shall soon be silent for a while,' he cabled Attlee, 'though I trust not for ever.' The Prime Minister decided to fly from Bermuda: an extremely hazardous, 3,500 mile journey. He left on the 16th. 'I must confess that I felt rather frightened,' wrote Churchill, and he had need to be: the aircraft barely managed to avoid flying over German batteries at Brest, then was identified as a hostile aircraft as it approached Britain – fortunately six Hurricanes failed to intercept. The decision to fly brought the Prime Minister home a week earlier than expected:

he stepped off his Paddington train into a frosty, biting wind, and an icy reception from critics. 'Bungling and mismanagement are on a scale that cannot be concealed,' had declared Cassandra in the *Daily Mirror* five days before. A 'disgusted' Harold Nicolson had noted in his diary on the 14th: 'Meeting of the National Labour Executive.... Frank Markham says that ... we must get rid of Churchill who will never win the war. Others say that Winston is not an organizer and is no judge of men.... Kenneth Lindsay says that Shinwell is the only man in the House prepared to make a stand against Winston, and Cripps is the only possible alternative Prime Minister.'[61] Cripps had started his voyage from Moscow on the 9th; the problem of what to do with him now began to grow.

Churchill had read latest criticisms in the morning papers on the train from Plymouth; he had put the last one down and commented in a tired voice: 'There seems to be plenty of snarling.' Daily more news came to feed this discontent: 'Crusader' had not achieved a dramatic, morale-boosting climax; only the Russians seemed to be showing Hitler how to fight; the Cabinet War Room situation report for the 12th declared: 'It is thought that Kuala Lumpur has now been evacuated.' First Japanese troops had in fact entered Malaya's capital the day before, and next day Wavell warned that reinforcements might have to be thrown piecemeal at points of greatest danger as soon as they arrived, despite inadequate training or acclimatization.[62] Australian disquiet had grown, and Churchill had reacted sharply in a cable to Curtin on the 14th: 'We are doing our utmost in the Mother Country to meet living perils and onslaughts. We have sunk all party differences and have imposed universal compulsory service, not only upon men, but women. ... We have successfully disengaged Tobruk, after previously relieving your men who so gallantly held it for so long. I hope therefore you will be considerate in the judgment which you pass.' But the cable had contained an ominous warning: 'I do not see how any one could expect Malaya to be defended once the Japanese obtained the command of the sea and while we are fighting for our lives against Germany and Italy. The only vital point is Singapore fortress and its essential hinterland. Personally, my anxiety has been lest in fighting rearguard actions down the peninsula to gain time we should dissipate our forces.'[63] A totally different anxiety arose on the 15th: the newly commissioned *Tirpitz*, 40,000 tons, sister-ship of the sunk *Bismarck* and more powerful than any British warship, slipped from the Baltic to Trondheim ready to prey on the northern convoys. Also on the 15th Wavell officially took over his ABDA command and sent a long general appreciation, warning that with his present resources he saw no possibility of affording General

354

MacArthur the support in the Philippines which he seemed to expect. The Japanese onslaught on British lines by the Muar river began during the day, and Churchill sent another signal concerning Singapore. 'Please let me know your idea of what would happen in the event of your being forced to withdraw into the island?... What are defences and obstructions on landward side?'[64] Wavell's woeful reply, dated the 16th but not available to Churchill until the 19th, was to cause the Prime Minister perhaps the greatest alarm since he stepped into 10 Downing Street.

Meanwhile Japanese air raids on Rangoon had been intensified and on 16 January the move into Burma began. General Brooke read the latest gloomy assessment of the overall situation to the Defence Committee at 5.30 p.m.: General Auchinleck had told Wavell that the earliest date of departure from the Middle East of two Australian divisions scheduled for the Far East would be 5 February. Wavell had replied that 'the Japanese advance had been more rapid than had been expected, and that every day which could be gained ... was of importance....' Brooke also told the Defence Committee that: 'There were indications that an attack on Malta seemed likely in the near future,' but the Germans might be restricted by shortages of transport aircraft and gliders.[65] 'The situation is developing to our advantage,' wrote Rommel to his wife on the 17th, 'and I'm full of plans that I daren't say anything about round here. They'd think me crazy. But I'm not.'[66] Brooke wrote to Auchinleck on the same day to sympathize over the weakening of the Middle East. 'I realize that your plans for regaining Cyrenaica might have to be abandoned.... It is a question of reinforcing where we are most immediately threatened.[67]

Churchill reported to the War Cabinet this Saturday on his American visit. The President's last words to him had been 'Trust me to the bitter end' and the Prime Minister continued: 'An Olympian calm had obtained at the White House. It was perhaps rather isolated.... They [the Americans] were not above learning from us, providing we did not set out to teach them. The State Department was apt to be somewhat jumpy.... The Americans were setting about the war with great vigour.... The disaster at Pearl Harbour had had a great effect in the United States. They were resolved to settle matters finally with Japan. But they realized that the main pressure must be kept on Germany. As a means to this end they were keen on the project of occupying the north and west coast of Africa.' Churchill had explained that 'our aim should be to marshal our forces on a line Iceland-British Isles-North Africa, ready for an offensive in 1943. But it was clear that shipping was the limiting factor in any plans that were made.'[68]

On 18 January Curtin replied to Churchill's signal sent four days before: Australia had long warned that a stronger naval force was required in the Far East and had stressed the need to make Singapore impregnable, but for years the recognized needs of Malayan defence had been neglected and governments in London had shown unjustified complacency. Churchill's reply, despatched the following day, 19 January, might have been expected to display Churchillian anger; instead the contents were mild. He revealed the severe damage caused to the *Queen Elizabeth* and *Valiant* at Alexandria the previous month. 'These evil conditions will pass,' soothed the Prime Minister. 'By May the United States will have a superior fleet at Hawaii.' On the same day the Prime Minister attempted to remove Commonwealth criticisms over lack of adequate representation in decision-making; he cabled the Australian and New Zealand Prime Ministers to say it was proposed to establish a Far Eastern Council at Ministerial level, based in London and presided over by Churchill, attended by representatives of Australia, New Zealand and the Netherlands.[69] Churchill was soon to find this proposal completely unacceptable to the New Zealand and Australian Governments, who believed that as America would inevitably have the preponderant voice in Pacific war discussions, major decisions should be taken in Washington; thus, accredited representatives should attend War Cabinet meetings in London and a Pacific War Council should be established in America. A compromise was eventually reached, with Pacific War Councils in both London and Washington, the former having its opening meeting on 10 February. The London branch did not however play an important part in the direction of the war; a greater role, still stopping short of direct policy-making, was performed by the Washington Council, meeting for the first time on 1 April.[70]

In his surprisingly mild reply to Curtin on the 19th, Churchill made no mention of Singapore, despite urgent British and Australian preoccupation with its defence and despite Curtin's claim that it should have been made impregnable long before. The absence of reference stemmed from Churchill's shocked discovery on this same day that the island was in fact virtually indefensible. Churchill had constantly called Singapore a 'fortress'; now, with Japanese troops thrusting down Malaya and virtually no mainland defences left with which to stop them, Churchill had learnt the island had never been a fortress and could not possibly be made into one before the enemy arrived. Existing defences had been laid down to protect the island from a naval offensive, on the assumption that mainland Malaya would still be in British hands and the RAF would still be providing air cover. Churchill had also spoken of the 'prolonged defence' of the island; this was also impossible: the civil population of almost a million – crowded on to

356

an island no larger than the Isle of Wight – would have to be maintained and supplied; the naval base in the north of the island was close to mainland Malaya; the narrow straits between the mainland and the island were bordered by overgrown creeks and mangrove swamps providing excellent cover for amphibious assault. The appalling truth was revealed to Churchill on the 19th in Wavell's reply to his telegram of the 15th: 'Until quite recently all plans were based on repulsing seaborne attacks on island and holding land attack in Johore or farther north, and little or nothing was done to construct defences on north side of island to prevent crossing Johore Straits.... The fortress cannon of heaviest nature have all-round traverse, but their flat trajectory makes them unsuitable for counter-battery work.' Churchill later described his stunned reaction: 'I saw before me the hideous spectacle of the almost naked island and of the wearied, if not exhausted, troops retreating upon it.' The impact on the Prime Minister must have been formidable: 'Crusader' not the success he had hoped; 'Acrobat' shelved; 'Gymnast' put to one side; the terrible naval losses; the invasion of Burma and Borneo; defeats already suffered in Malaya; rising criticism at home. And now this. 'I ought to have known. My advisers ought to have known and I ought to have been told, and I ought to have asked.'[71] Churchill's first response was anger: he summoned Ismay in 'a towering rage', thrust Wavell's telegram into his hand and shouted at him to read it. 'I could scarcely believe my eyes,' wrote the equally unsuspecting Ismay.[72] Churchill dictated a vicious Minute to the COS, blazoned 'Action This Day'. 'What is the use of having an island for a fortress if it is not to be made into a citadel? ... How is it that not one of you pointed this out to me? ... I warn you this will be one of the greatest scandals that could possibly be exposed.... The city of Singapore must be converted into a citadel and defended to the death. No surrender can be contemplated.'[73]

Churchill revealed Wavell's telegram to horrified Ministers at a War Cabinet meeting that evening and declared that 'it should be made clear that it is the duty of the Singapore garrison to hold out to the last, should military resistance in Johore collapse'. He said he was prepared to take upon himself the full responsibility for the political decisions governing the size of forces in Malaya at the outbreak of hostilities. 'There were, however, certain matters connected with the defence of Malaya which called for inquiry. (1) On several occasions our forces had been outflanked by Japanese landings on the west coast. Our naval forces had failed to stop this.... (2) [Churchill] wished to be assured that the defence plans for the naval base of Singapore and for Singapore Island, made adequate provision for the following: (a) obtaining control of all

357

small craft ... (b) the destruction of any small craft attempting to cross the Straits.' The Prime Minister fired a list of questions: 'What steps were being taken to extend the ground defences to the landward side? Had a complete scheme of demolitions, covering all the objects of military importance, been drawn up? How far had the preparations for carrying out the scheme, if need arose, advanced? Was the water supply secure?...' The COS were asked to submit a report.[74]

Major-General Hutton, Commander in Burma, warned Wavell on the 20th that the enemy might 'launch at anytime an attack greater than we can withstand.... There are signs that this may have already started and I cannot guarantee safety of Burma with forces now available.'[75] Wavell was desperately trying to organize defence measures at Singapore; early on the 21st he sent Churchill another foreboding signal: 'I doubt whether island can be held for long once Johore is lost.' A second signal came from Wavell later in the day: 'I did not realize myself until lately how entirely defences were planned against seaward attack only.' All therefore depended on the mainland resistance being kept up as long as possible, yet the COS also received a message from Wavell: 'Situation in Malaya greatly deteriorated.'[76] The COS meeting at 11.30 a.m. this Wednesday had to give urgent consideration to a Memorandum from the Prime Minister outlining a grave choice which must now be made: should reinforcements now *en route* for threatened Singapore be allowed to continue, even though they might be merely caught in the final collapse, or should they go to Burma? In Churchill's words, reinforcements could be 'doomed or diverted'. 'Forces which might have made a solid front in Johore,' declared his paper, 'or at any rate along the Singapore waterfront, have been broken up piecemeal. No defensive line had been constructed on the landward side. No defence had been made by the Navy to the enemy's turning movements on the west coast of the peninsula. General Wavell has expressed the opinion that it will take more troops to defend Singapore Island than to win the battle in Johore. The battle in Johore is almost certainly lost.' Discussions were resumed in the early evening, when Churchill said he was in favour of sending reinforcements to Singapore if a reasonable chance remained of the fortress holding out – a chance which Wavell seemed to indicate was non-existent. Brooke insisted Wavell must be consulted before any decision was taken. Painful discussion continued at a Defence Committee meeting starting at 10 p.m. 'It was now apparent that we could not consider Singapore as a fortress,' repeated Churchill. 'If the battle in Johore went against us it was possible that a prolonged defence of Singapore island could not be made.... Taking the widest view, Burma was more important than Singapore. It was the terminus of our communications to China which it was essential to keep open. The Americans had laid the greatest stress on the importance of keeping the Chinese fighting on our side. Burma was badly in need of reinforcements.' And he added that 'if it looked as though Singapore could only hold out for a few weeks it might be that some of the reinforcements which were destined for Malaya ought rather to be sent to Burma. We did not want to throw good money after bad.'[77] A definite decision had still to be taken; as Churchill put it, 'a similar hesitation to commit ourselves to so grave a step prevailed'. The Prime Minister had in fact made his view plain enough: reinforcements should not be sacrificed in the hopeless defence of Singapore, but should be spared for Burma. But this was a military verdict and Ministers – including Churchill – clearly had other considerations in mind: the loss of prestige in the apparent abandonment of Singapore, the effect on the doomed garrison if reinforcements on the way to the island were diverted, and above all the attitudes of Australia and New Zealand. Curtin in his signal of the 18th had stressed that 'in the last resort the whole internal defence system of Australia was based on the integrity of Singapore and the presence of a capital fleet there'. The capital fleet had been sunk, but Churchill had assured Curtin on the 14th: 'Everything is being done to reinforce Singapore and the hinterland.' The Defence Committee feared Australian reaction to the realization this pledge was worthless. Yet the damage had already been done: present at this Defence Committee meeting was Sir Earle Page, the Australian representative, and he immediately judged it his duty to send a warning cable to Melbourne. Unaware of this last development, Churchill, Eden, Beaverbrook and Alexander discussed the tragic situation over drinks after the meeting. 'Winston was tired and depressed, for him,' wrote Eden. 'His cold is heavy on him. He was inclined to be fatalistic about the House, maintained that the bulk of Tories hated him, that he had done all he could and would be only too happy to yield to another, that Malaya, Australian Government's intransigence, and "nagging" in House was more than any man could be expected to endure.'[78]

As Eden and Beaverbrook tried to boost Churchill's flagging confidence, further disquieting news was being transmitted to London from a different area of war. 'On 21 January,' reported Auchinleck in his later despatch, 'the improbable occurred, and without warning the Axis forces began to advance.' Early that Wednesday Rommel had scribbled a note to his wife: 'Army launches its counter-attack in two hours' time.... I've decided to take the risk.'[79] His move surprised both his superiors, whom he had only informed of barest details, and the British; General Ritchie

359

was in Cairo and the 8th Army was caught unprepared. Retreat began immediately. Rommel put himself at the front of his tank units and urged them forward over the desert, determined to reach Agedabia before the British could recover. Reports reaching London underestimated the threat; the War Cabinet were informed at 6 p.m. next day, 22 January, that 'General Rommel has delivered a counter-stroke on Agedabia which might be no more than a reconnaissance in force, which has driven our outposts in about 10 miles'.[80] Ritchie reached the fighting in the afternoon of the 23rd and still reported the enemy appeared to be attempting a reconnaissance in force; soon would come 'a God-sent opportunity to hit him really hard when he puts his neck out as it seems possible he may be already doing'.[81] Ritchie's optimism was reflected in a reassuring cable from Auchinleck to Churchill: 'If Rommel persists he is likely to expose his eastward flank to attack.... I realize the public at home may be upset by enemy reoccupying Agedabia but it may well be that Rommel may be drawn on into a situation unfavourable to him.'[82]

The 'public at home' included an increasing number of Churchill's critics. 'The question is beginning to arise in the minds of many,' declared the left-wing *Tribune* on this Friday, 'is he as good a war maker as he is a speech maker?... People will expect to hear from him the outline of a plan which will use all our resources on a world scale.... Churchill obviously has no plan.... But a plan we must have.' Aneurin Bevan, once an admirer of Churchill, had recently acquired most of the control of *Tribune*, and he now launched a major campaign against him – 'my declaration of war'. Also on the 23rd Cripps arrived back in London, anxious to resume Parliamentary life, a fervent supporter of the Second Front, and seen by some as an alternative to Churchill at 10 Downing Street. The Prime Minister was extremely anxious to bring him safely into his Government.

The British 8th Army continued to withdraw, confused and misreading the situation, throughout Saturday, 24 January. During the afternoon a further signal came from Auchinleck revealing rising concern: 'Enemy has been able to maintain unexpected strength forward apparently, and his initial advance seems to have disconcerted temporarily at any rate our forward troops.... But his supply position this time is in no way comparable with last year.'[83] Then, in the early hours of Sunday, 25 January, a Service signal from the Naval Liaison Officer, 8th Army, to the C-in-C Mediterranean, was passed to the COS: preparations were being made to evacuate Benghazi, previously judged an essential base port for the British position in western Cyrenaica and for the further advance into Tripolitania, and the signal warned: 'Should Benghazi fall Derna will follow.' Churchill was shown a copy of this signal early on the Sunday morning and immediately sent an angry message to Auchinleck. 'I am much disturbed by the report from 8th Army, which speaks of evacuation of Benghazi and Derna. I had certainly never been led to suppose that such a situation could arise.'[84] Auchinleck immediately flew forward from Cairo, reaching the desert front early in the evening. Rommel's tanks were streaking forward and, according to the diary of 15 *Panzer*, 'broke into the enemy at tearing speed and threw him into complete confusion'. Auchinleck managed to stop a premature withdrawal from Benghazi, but the German advance formations reached Msus, the strategic point in the centre of the Cyrenaica bulge which had played such an important part in the British army's own capture of Benghazi from the Italians almost exactly a year before. Rommel prepared for his next surprise, to be launched in 72 hours' time.

Churchill had invited Cripps to lunch at Chequers this Sunday, and he offered the former Ambassador the post of Minister of Supply; Churchill intended to make Beaverbrook Minister of Production. Cripps said he would consider the idea. On the same day the perceptive Goebbels jotted in his diary: 'The Australians are extremely angry.... I am issuing orders to continue to probe this open wound and to rub salt in it.' During this heavy weekend Churchill received a long and irate telegram from Curtin. 'Page has reported that the Defence Committee has been considering the evacuation of Malaya and Singapore. After all the assurances we have been given the evacuation of Singapore would be regarded here and elsewhere as an inexcusable betrayal. Singapore is a central fortress in the system of the Empire and local defence.... We understood that it was to be made impregnable.' The Australian leader added that even in an emergency, reinforcements must not be diverted to Burma but to the Dutch East Indies. 'Anything else would be deeply resented.' Churchill confronted Page with this telegram at the War Cabinet meeting at 6 p.m. on Monday, 26 January. Churchill thought that the Australian representative had 'unintentionally misled' his Government, and he reminded him that Wavell had been given firm instructions that the garrison at Singapore should fight it out, 'if need be in the ruins of Singapore'. The island would not therefore be abandoned, and Page had given an incomplete account. 'Clearly no decision could have been taken on such a grave matter without full consultation with the Dominions. Proceedings of the Defence Committee would be gravely hampered if an incomplete discussion, which formed no part of the conclusion of the meeting, was to be reported to the Dominion Governments.' Page replied that his telegram had been 'a factual statement of the decision disclosed to the Defence Committee, together with his own observations'. He insisted he had been within his rights, and he reminded the War Cabinet that although Australia had never been unwilling to send her forces overseas, 'in doing so she had denuded herself to a dangerous extent'. Churchill commented that 'it went without saying that the Australian troops and air squadrons serving overseas must move homewards to the defence of their own country, now that danger threatened it. But effect could only be given to this progress very gradually. All available shipping was mortgaged for essential military movements.'[85] No more was to be heard of diverting the troops to Burma; reinforcements sailed on to Singapore. Yet, Wavell had been visiting Rangoon and cabled during the day that the initial Japanese move into Burma could be held – all should be well, provided reinforcements arrived.[86]

Next day, 27 January, Parliament started a three-day debate on the Government's handling of the war. 'I have come to the conclusion,' declared Churchill at the start of proceedings, 'that I must ask to be sustained by a Vote of Confidence.' He made no attempt to gloss the general situation. 'It is because things have gone badly and worse is to come that I demand a Vote of Confidence.' He warned: 'Cyrenaica has been regained. It has still to be held.... I cannot tell what the position at the present moment is on the western front in Cyrenaica. We have a very daring and skilful opponent against us, and, may I say across the havoc of war, a great general.... Another battle is even now in progress.' The Prime Minister also warned: 'There never has been a moment, there never could have been a moment, when Great Britain or the British Empire, single-handed, could fight Germany and Italy, could wage the Battle of Britain, the Battle of the Atlantic, and the Battle of the Middle East, and at the same time stand thoroughly prepared in Burma, the Malay peninsula and generally in the Far East.' He concluded: 'I stand by my original programme, blood, toil, tears and sweat, which is all I have ever offered.' Next day, 28 January, as the debate continued and critics rose to attack Churchill – mainly on the grounds that the posts of Defence and Prime Minister should not be combined – General Percival gave orders for the troops in Johore to prepare for the withdrawal to Singapore Island. And the Germans thrust forward again in Cyrenaica: exploiting British indecision, Rommel feinted towards Derna while his real spearhead struck unexpectedly through rough terrain south-east of Benghazi. By the evening of the 28th *Afrika Korps* units were closing on the port. Cripps declined Churchill's invitation to be Supply Minister unless he could have a seat on the War Cabinet itself. He also disliked the idea of working under Beaverbrook. The Prime Minister refused Cripps' request to sit on the War Cabinet; Cripps was therefore left free to express his ideas in public, while Churchill hastily tried to think of another post he could offer. Meanwhile he went to the Commons to make the final speech for the Government. 'I offer no apologies. I offer no excuses. I make no promises.... But at the same time I avow my confidence, never stronger than at this moment, that we shall bring this conflict to an end agreeable to the interests of our country and the future of the world. I have finished. Let every man act now in accordance with what he thinks is his duty in harmony with his heart and conscience.'

Votes were counted: 464 to 1. Outside in the Commons lobby the news agency tapes began chattering reports from Berlin and Tokyo. The Germans claimed to have entered Benghazi; the Japanese claimed to be only 18 miles from Singapore Island. Both claims were correct. 'A black day for a Vote of Confidence,' commented Harold Nicolson's diary entry for the 29th: [87] 'One of the dark days of the war,' wrote Brooke in his diary next day. 'News bad on all sides. Benghazi has been lost again, and Singapore is in a bad way.... I doubt whether the island can hold out very long.'[88] Hitler declared in a broadcast: 'That twaddler, that drunkard, Churchill, what has he achieved in all his lifetime?' *Tribune* resumed its attack: 'This is no National Government and Churchill is no National Leader. He struts in that guise.' Auchinleck cabled that the loss of Benghazi was only temporary, but added: 'It must be admitted that enemy has succeeded beyond his expectations and mine, and that his tactics have been skilful and bold.' Next day, 31 January, Auchinleck warned: 'I am reluctantly compelled to conclusion that to meet German armoured forces with any reasonable hope of decisive success our armoured forces as at present equipped, organized and led must have at least two to one superiority.'[89] Also on the 31st the COS finally put on record that 'Gymnast' was not feasible at the moment; 'Acrobat' had clearly been ruled out by Rommel's counter-stroke. All reinforcements should be earmarked for the Far East.[90]

With characteristic understatement Wavell reported from Singapore: 'We have rather a thin time ahead.' Withdrawal from Johore had been completed, with heavy losses in the closing stages: early that morning the last two pipers of the Argyll and Sutherland Highlanders had led their weary, decimated battalion across the narrow causeway separating Singapore from the mainland; the notes of 'Hielan' Laddie' faded down the dusty road, and sultry silence fell heavy, to be shattered seconds later by the roar of an explosion as the causeway was blown.

Search for a Solution

Ministers were informed at 5 p.m., Monday, 2 February, that all possible mainland forces had been pulled back to Singapore, and the Royal Navy had evacuated some 2,000 men from the west coast of Johore. 'The garrison of Singapore amounts to the equivalent of about four divisions. Food supplies, the water supply and ammunition stocks are considered sufficient.' The Germans seemed to have halted their advance in Cyrenaica for the moment.[1] Singapore was discussed at a long COS meeting at 10 p.m. Churchill wanted the naval base 'completely wrecked' and extensive demolitions undertaken elsewhere; positions must be improvised in surrounding islands, relief supplies organized, Ceylon and India strengthened. 'How is it that we were only told last week that two out of three aerodromes on the island are commanded by artillery from the mainland? Why were no others constructed?' The Prime Minister, according to Cadogan, 'hectors most brutally', following his success in the previous week's debate.[2] General Wavell, as resilient as Churchill in his taciturn way, signalled on 3 February: 'There is every intention and hope of holding.' Reinforcements had now arrived; but these, mainly men of the 18th (Territorial) Division, would have to be pushed into action after months of dulling sea-voyage and with inappropriate training.[3] General Percival disagreed with the policy of extensive demolitions as urged by the Prime Minister: 'To put extensive scorched earth policy into effect immediately would be to so undermine the morale both of the troops and public as to prejudice seriously our ability to hold Singapore.'[4]

Churchill had to attend to domestic matters. Conflict between Beaverbrook and Bevin had continued, especially over the working of Bevin's Production Executive; Beaverbrook-Churchill relations had continued to fluctuate. Now the Prime Minister proposed to appoint his old yet troublesome friend to the new post of Minister of Production. Beaverbrook agreed, and the appointment was announced on 4 February; Sir Andrew Duncan became the new Supply Minister. But complications arose over the White Paper defining powers of the new Minister: Churchill had specified Beaverbrook would carry out all duties exercised by the Production Executive, but after pressure from Attlee and Bevin, excluded 'those relating to manpower and labour'. This, and other problems, were to lead to a week of sharp exchanges.[5]

'The situation as regards shipping is most disturbing,' wrote the CIGS on the 4th. 'It is the one situation which will affect our whole strategy during the coming year.' The giant battleship *Tirpitz* remained at Trondheim as a potential threat; the battle-cruisers *Scharnhorst* and *Gneisenau* and the cruiser *Prinz Eugen* remained blockaded at Brest – but an Admiralty paper dated 2 February had warned they could attempt to break out and the Germans would know 'full well that we have no heavy ships with which to oppose them in the Channel'.[6] 'It would be as well to make sure,' Churchill cabled to Hopkins on the 6th, 'that the President's attention has been drawn to the very heavy sinkings by U-boats in the Western North Atlantic. Since 12 January confirmed losses are 158,209 and probable losses 83,740 [tons].'[7] PQ convoys to Russia remained a drain on Britain's naval resources. Yet a growing and influential section claimed Russia was receiving inadequate help, and the Second Front lobby had now been joined by Cripps, who wrote in *Tribune* on 6 February: 'This is indeed a total war [in Russia], total in its suffering and total in its effort. Has it been total in the same intense degree so far as we in England are concerned?' On the same day, Anglo-Soviet relations were discussed at a noon War Cabinet meeting, specifically connected with Stalin's insistence to Eden that Britain should recognize the 1941 Russian frontiers. Ministers showed themselves deeply divided. Britain should accept Stalin's request, declared Beaverbrook. 'Our relations with Russia were deteriorating; we could not afford to wait.... It was worth remembering that so far Russia had contributed more to the war effort than the United States to whom we had made such frequent concessions.' Unless a treaty was signed, warned Eden, Britain would not obtain 'any real co-operation', and 'no treaty could be signed except on the basis of Russia's June 1941 frontiers with Finland, the Baltic States and Roumania'. Attlee strongly disagreed. 'The action proposed was only too reminiscent of what had been done in the last war.... Further, as soon as one claim had been agreed to, we should be faced with others.' Sir Archibald Sinclair believed Russia would anyway be in occupation of the Baltic States at the end of the war, 'and it would not be in our power to get them to leave. By agreeing to accept these frontiers now, we should go a long way to removing the risk of bad feeling.' Bevin wanted to make quite sure that 'Stalin's claim ... represented his ultimate aims in this direction'; Eden reassured him that 'Stalin's statement was quite specific on this point'. Churchill proposed a compromise, although he believed 'the right plan was that all these matters should be settled at the Peace Conference' and he referred to 'the uncertainty as to what the position would be at the end of the war'. He added: 'The immediate point at issue was how this matter should be presented to the United States' and he preferred 'a balanced representation'. The War Cabinet agreed Eden should draft a telegram to Halifax, instructing the Ambassador to explain the position.[8] But when Eden informed Maisky of this approach to America, the Russian Ambassador warned it was with Britain, not the United States, that his government wished to conclude a treaty.[9] The British attempt to sort out their own minds by seeking American reaction ran into embarrassing difficulties: Roosevelt told Halifax that he was confident he could reach agreement with Stalin direct. Attempts by Churchill to revert negotiations to a tripartite basis failed, but in early March the President also failed to change the Russian attitude after talks with Litvinov, the Soviet Ambassador at Washington. The situation would remain stagnant until the War Cabinet took the matter up again in early April. Meanwhile the Second Front movement in Britain continued to grow in strength; on 8 February Cripps addressed a large crowd in Bristol. 'There seems to be a lack of urgency in the atmosphere of this country.... If we give to Russia all the support we can, then, in my view, there is every chance of Germany being defeated by this time next year.' He hinted that Churchill was unwilling to have him in the Government.

Soon after noon on 8 February heavy artillery fire opened up on Singapore's landward defences; at 11 p.m. the barrage gained added intensity, severing communications to forward troops. An hour later 4,000 Japanese climbed into small motor boats and collapsible launches and the first attack wave spread across the dark channel. Defending the front opposite this section of the Straits were only 2,500 Australians. The War Cabinet were informed at 6 p.m. on the 9th: 'The Japanese have penetrated about five miles inland. Tengah aerodrome is in enemy occupation.' Brooke told Ministers that although this was serious news, Britain had large numbers of troops on the island. Depressing reports had also come from Cairo: 'Increased enemy pressure has caused a further withdrawal.' Even news from Russia had deteriorated: 'Heavy snowfalls have hampered Russian moves.' Eden referred to telegrams from Washington, suggesting 'we were letting others, and particularly Australian troops, do all the fighting for us, and that the material assistance sent was largely of American origin'. Brooke noted in his diary: 'Nothing but abuse for the Army.'[10] The CIGS was summoned by Churchill at 10.45 p.m. to help draft a telegram to Wavell, despite Brooke's reluctance to interfere with a commander at a distance. 'It was reported to the Cabinet by the CIGS that Percival has over 100,000 men,' Churchill told Wavell. 'In these circumstances the defenders must greatly outnumber Japanese forces who have crossed the Straits.... There must at this stage be no thought of saving troops or sparing the population.... Commanders and senior officers should die with the troops. The honour of the British Empire and of the British Army is at stake ... the whole reputation of our country and our race is involved.'[11]

Churchill had written to Cripps on the 9th, criticizing points made in his Bristol speech; at the same time he realized Cripps would have to be brought into the War Cabinet. On the 10th he turned to Beaverbrook, and, understandably in the circumstances, showed no patience with his cantankerous colleague: Beaverbrook was informed details of the new Production Ministry would be published, whether he liked them or not. 'I send you a proof of the White Paper.... So far as I'm concerned, it is in its final form. I have lavished my time and strength during the last week in trying to make arrangements which are satisfactory to you and to the public interests.... I can do no more.' Churchill hinted another resignation offer by Beaverbrook would not be refused; Beaverbrook accepted the White Paper, and Churchill announced details in the Commons that afternoon.[12]

Wavell landed at Singapore at dawn on the 10th at the same moment as the Japanese commander, Yamashita, crossed the repaired causeway to the Island. Wavell met groups of bewildered, leaderless troops; commanders had been separated from units, units from artillery support; orders were lost in the tangle of retreat and approaching defeat. Incredibly, Wavell looked through this humid, stultifying smoke of disaster to future victory in the Far East. 'I should like to be informed as soon as possible,' he had signalled the CCS, 'of general outline of Allied plan for defeat of Japan ... my lay-out and organization may be affected by plan for eventual advance.'[13] Wavell reluctantly decided he must leave Singapore and return to Java. Waiting at the quayside at midnight on the 10th for his flying boat to be prepared, he slipped six feet on to rocks and barbed wire, lacerating his back and breaking two bones. His aircraft took off at dawn, leaving Singapore covered with thickening smoke. 'Battle for Singapore is not going well,' he warned on the 11th. 'Japanese with usual infiltration tactics are getting on much more rapidly than they should in the west of island. I ordered Percival to stage counter-attack with all troops possible.' Wavell disputed the number of troops Churchill claimed at Percival's disposal. 'I do not think he has more than 60,000 to 70,000 at the most.'[14] During the 11th the Japanese asked the British to surrender; no reply was sent, and another massive enemy assault was launched at dawn on Thursday, 12 February, with close air support. In Burma, Japanese forces established themselves west of the Salween river. Goebbels wrote in his diary: 'The Führer regards the [imminent] fall of Singapore as a very serious thing for the English.... Churchill's position may be badly shaken.... This distrust has been especially fed by the silly declarations of Cripps.'

Ministers were discussing latest pessimistic reports from the Far East at the noon War Cabinet meeting on the 12th when a message was brought in by the First Lord of the Admiralty: *Scharnhorst* and *Gneisenau* had left Brest and were 'steaming up the Channel, surrounded by a number of vessels believed to be E-boats and destroyers'. Portal immediately confirmed the news of this breakout.[15] The warships, together with the *Prinz Eugen*, had begun their impudent run up the English Channel late the previous night; if successful, the move would not only mean a more active threat to British shipping, but would also be a body blow to remaining British prestige. This Thursday had dawned misty; enemy jamming of British radar was successful, and not until 11.25 a.m. did the Admiralty receive the news. Hugging the coast for maximum shorebased air support, the warships survived RAF and destroyer attacks to reach port in Germany early on the 13th. The Germans had sailed past Britain's front door. As Churchill commented: 'National wrath was vehement.' Few knew that the Admiralty had warned of such a possibility only 10 days before. Cadogan confided to his diary: 'So far I have been unable to hear that we have been able to knock any paint off them. We are nothing but failure and inefficiency everywhere and the Japs are murdering our men and raping our women in Hong Kong.... I am running out of whisky.'[16] Not until later could it be revealed that the British attacks had severely damaged the *Scharnhorst* and the *Gneisenau* never appeared again.

Some technical and specialist personnel and nurses had already been told to leave Singapore: about 80 vessels left during the 13th and the following day – almost all were sunk or captured by the enemy. 'Enemy now within 5,000 yards of sea front,' signalled Percival to Wavell on the 13th. 'In opinion of commanders troops already committed are too exhausted either to withstand strong attack or to launch counter-attack.... It is unlikely that resistance can last more than a day or two.' Percival added: 'There must come a stage when in the interests of the troops and civil population further bloodshed will serve no useful purpose.... Would you consider giving me wider discretionary power?' Wavell dictated his reply

368

from his hospital bed that same day. 'You must continue to inflict maximum damage on enemy for as long as possible.... Your action in tying down enemy and inflicting casualties may have vital influence in other theatres.' A telegram from Wavell reporting Percival's signal and his reply reached London that day, 14 February; Wavell added: 'Fear however that resistance not likely to be very prolonged.' Main concern centred on the Japanese threat to the water supply to the teeming population. The Australian Commander reported to Melbourne: 'Wavell has ordered all troops to fight to last. If enemy enters city behind us, will take suitable action to avoid unnecessary sacrifice.' A cable from the Governor, Sir Shenton Thomas, reached the Colonial Office: one million people were crowding into a diminishing area. 'Water supplies very badly damaged and unlikely to last more than 24 hours. Many dead in streets and burial impossible.' Wavell replied to another signal from Percival: 'Your gallant stand is serving purpose and must be continued.'[17]

But Churchill, at Chequers during this Saturday afternoon, 14 February, had made up his mind – without calling the Defence Committee, War Cabinet or a full COS meeting. 'Prime Minister to A. P. Wavell: You are of course sole judge of moment when no further results can be gained in Singapore and should instruct Percival accordingly. CIGS concurs.' The signal reached Java just after 4 a.m. on Sunday, the 15th; at 8 a.m. Wavell signalled Percival 'I give you discretion to cease resistance.' Just after 3 p.m. Percival sent the expected answer: 'Owing to losses from enemy action water, petrol, food and ammunition practically finished. Unable therefore continue the fight any longer.'[18] The signal link to Singapore fell silent. Hostilities ceased at 8.30 p.m., and about 80,000 troops were herded into terrible captivity: Britain's army had suffered the severest reversal in its long history. Churchill sat alone with his thoughts at Chequers. 'It was his darkest hour,' wrote Beaverbrook. 'The weight of his burden would have crushed any other man.'[19]

Churchill had now to avoid being crushed by his critics. Later that evening, 15 February, he made a broadcast calling for national unity; Harold Nicolson feared this appeal would recall Chamberlain's fatal tactics in the Parliamentary debate which had thrown him from power, and Cadogan and Eden shared similar apprehension. Next day Churchill met Eden for lunch and admitted he would soon have to make governmental changes.

The COS met in almost continuous session during the 16th to discuss effects of the disaster. Debate similar to that before the fall of Singapore took place: should territory be left unreinforced – this time Dutch Java – in order to send troops to Burma? By the time the War Cabinet met at 5 p.m. news had been received of the fall of Palembang, the important base in southern Sumatra; Sumatra and Java would clearly be the next Japanese stepping stones. Ministers had before them a cable from the Australian Prime Minister, dated 15 February, stressing dangers to Australia and calling for Australian troops in the Middle East to be moved to the Pacific. Despite these urgent topics, Churchill opened by mentioning the *Scharnhorst* and *Gneisenau* break-out; the Prime Minister, who according to Cadogan was 'truculent and angry', declared 'the picture of the incident as presented by the British press showed complete ignorance of the position. If at any time during the last 10½ months these vessels could have been repaired they would have been able to break out directly on to the Atlantic trade routes. But, owing to the efforts of the RAF, it had not been possible to render these ships ready for sea.... On balance, the position was eased by their removal from Brest to German ports.'

Churchill said that as only a fortnight had passed since the last Commons debate on the general war situation and as a full report of events at Singapore had still to be received, 'a debate on the matter on the following day would not serve any useful purpose'. Ministers were told that it was unlikely any troops had escaped from Singapore; the War Cabinet agreed 'it was clear now that Japan was a most formidable and dangerous antagonist.... Our military performance in Malaya had left much to be desired.' It seemed 'a pity' that the reinforcements had gone to Singapore instead of to Burma, but Ministers were reminded that the Australian Prime Minister had declared that failure to defend Singapore to the utmost would be 'an inexcusable betrayal'. Clearly, however, 'these troops would have been better employed elsewhere'. Ministers agreed the same question had now to be faced as regards Sumatra and Java. 'The maintenance of our line of communication with China by the Burma Road was of utmost importance. We should have to consider whether we ought not to divert to Burma and to Australia reinforcements now on their way.'[20] Detailed consideration was given to this question at a Defence Committee meeting later this Monday evening; the Committee agreed that 'lacking command of the seas, we could hardly expect to hold Java for long.... There was great danger that if we attempted to reinforce Java we should merely be allowing our forces to be destroyed piecemeal.' Essential bases were considered to be Burma, Ceylon, India and Australia. 'Strategically the sound policy to pursue would be to concentrate everything on the defence of these.... Although it would be a hard blow to the Dutch it would be better to withhold reinforcements from Java and to concentrate on holding Australia.' It would be necessary 'to let the Dutch have their say' at the Pacific War Council next afternoon; the Defence Committee agreed to defer further discussion but decided provisional arrangements should be made for the leading Australian division from the Middle East to proceed to Australia and for the brigades of the British 70th Division to move to Burma and Ceylon.[21]

Discussion was taken up again at a COS meeting next morning, 17 February, attended by a Dutch representative; a cable from Wavell indicated the Australian reinforcements were anyway unlikely to reach Java before the island fell. 'I recommend that at least one division should go to Burma and both if they can be administratively received and maintained.' The COS also had a Minute from Churchill: 'I am sure it would be impossible to act contrary to General Wavell's main opinion.' The COS agreed and decided to pass their recommendation to the Pacific War Council: one Australian division should go to Burma, the other to Australia.[22] But another cable arrived from Curtin during the day, insisting both divisions in the Australian Corps, the 6th and 7th, should return home. The Council met at 6.30 p.m. Considerable sympathy was expressed for the Dutch, but agreement was reached that Canberra should be asked to allow the 7th Division to proceed to Burma, despite Curtin's latest telegram, as these troops were the nearest fighting units to Rangoon. Java would not be reinforced.[23] Meanwhile, the ABDA command system was fast becoming obsolete with the Japanese advance; Roosevelt cabled Churchill on the 18th, suggesting the Americans should assume primary responsibility for the right flank in the Pacific, based on Australia, while the British should concentrate on the left, covering Burma, India and China.[24] The Japanese crept closer to Java, taking Bali on the 18th; on the same day Wavell was appalled to hear from Hutton, commander in Burma, that Rangoon might be impossible to hold; Brooke wrote in his diary: 'Burma news bad. If the Army cannot fight better than it is doing at present we shall deserve to lose our Empire.'[25] Lord Linlithgow, Viceroy of India, cabled Churchill: 'Our troops in Burma are not fighting with proper spirit, I have not the least doubt that this is in great part due to lack of drive and inspiration from the top.'[26] The Prime Minister sent this signal to Wavell, who replied late on the 18th: 'I am very disturbed altogether at lack of real fighting spirit.... Neither British, Australians nor Indians have shown real toughness.' Churchill had suggested Hutton's replacement by Alexander, at present holding Southern Command in England; next day, 19 February, arrangements were made for his immediate departure. Hutton would be his Chief of Staff.

Churchill had completed plans for War Cabinet changes: one

at least had been forced upon him. Beaverbrook had resigned on the 18th, this time accepted; according to Churchill, his friend was tired and ill from asthma. The new War Cabinet was announced on the afternoon of the 19th, with 7 members instead of 9. Churchill retained the Defence Ministry but gave the leadership of the House of Commons to Cripps, who also became Lord Privy Seal. Attlee became Deputy Prime Minister and Dominions Secretary. Lyttelton took over from Beaverbrook as Minister of Production – Beaverbrook had therefore only held this office for a fortnight. Bevin remained Minister of Labour, Sir John Anderson remained Lord President of the Council, and Eden stayed at the Foreign Office. Churchill, Attlee, Cripps, Eden, Lyttelton, Bevin and Anderson therefore formed the War Cabinet. Kingsley Wood remained Chancellor of the Exchequer, but no longer in the War Cabinet, and Greenwood, previously Minister without Portfolio, resigned. Other changes, not of War Cabinet Ministers, included the appointment of Lord Cranborne, previously Dominions Secretary, to be Leader of the House of Lords; Captain David Margesson was replaced as War Secretary by his Permanent Under-Secretary, Sir James Grigg; Llewellen took over from Moore-Brabazon at the Ministry of Aircraft Production; R. G. Casey, the Australian representative at Washington, replaced Lyttelton as Minister of State at Cairo.

Having attempted to deal with some of the domestic criticism, Churchill was now faced with another, tragic, tussle with the Australians. Fears in Australia naturally soared with the Japanese advance, and especially after the devastating sea and air bombardment of Darwin on the 19th, and the invasion of Timor on the 20th. Wavell had signalled Canberra asking for the Australian 7th Division to be diverted to Rangoon; Churchill and Roosevelt made the same request on the 20th, with the Prime Minister declaring: 'There is nothing else in the world that can fill the gap,' and with Roosevelt promising Australia an extra 27,000 men; both stressed Australia was not in immediate danger. On the other hand, the British COS completed a report on the 21st which gave a frightening assessment of the Japanese threat both in the direction of Burma, where the Australian reinforcements were so urgently required, and also towards Australia, which was 'insecure at present' and should be reinforced by troops from America and by Australian troops returning home.[27] First indications of the Australian Government's response came in a short signal from Dill to Churchill early on the 22nd: 'Hopkins has just told me that Curtin has refused President's appeal.' Later on this Sunday a long cable reached Churchill from Curtin: the British request broke promises given by Churchill that the Australian troops would be transferred to the Pacific, and if granted, it would seem likely more demands would be made for the diversion of remaining Australian troops *en route*.[28]

But Churchill was now in a highly embarrassing position. Without reference to the Defence Committee or War Cabinet he had already – on the 21st – ordered the Australian troop convoy to turn north towards Rangoon. Late on the 22nd he had to inform Curtin of this premature decision: 'We knew that if our ships proceeded on their course to Australia while we were waiting for your formal approval they would either arrive too late at Rangoon or even be without enough fuel to go there at all.' Churchill revealed an even more plausible motive in a signal to Wavell. 'Convoy has now got so far north that it will have to refuel (at Colombo) before going to Australia. So what about it? This gives three or four days for the Australian Government, with its majority of one, to think matters over....'[29] An angry, acid reply came from Curtin on the 23rd: 'You have established a physical situation which adds to the dangers of the convoy, and the responsibility for the consequences of such diversion rests upon you.' 'Your convoy is now proceeding to refuel at Colombo,' huffed Churchill. 'It will then proceed to Australia in accordance with your wishes.'[30] Churchill revealed the whole sad saga to the War Cabinet at 6 p.m. The Prime Minister said he took full responsibility for his action in changing the course of the convoy. 'As soon as the convoy had turned north, its escort had been increased, and this increased escort would continue to accompany the convoy. It so happened that some of the transports would now not have sufficient fuel to proceed to Australia without a further call at Colombo to re-fuel.' Churchill added that he regretted Sir Earle Page had not been informed, 'owing to a misunderstanding', when the convoy had been ordered to turn north. Page said he for his part regretted the failure of the efforts made to persuade his Government to send the troops to Rangoon; he felt sure that the letter he had now received from Churchill 'would dissipate any possible misunderstanding on the part of the Australian Government in regard to the Prime Minister's action'. He noted that the transports would re-fuel at Colombo, and he was sure that 'the greatest importance attached to a strong force being available in Ceylon in order to make sure that the whole of the island and its facilities were denied to the Japanese'. He therefore thought the Australian Government should be asked if the troops could be disembarked at Colombo and used to reinforce the garrison, at least temporarily, and if Churchill 'felt any reluctance in putting this proposition' Page would be very ready to make the suggestion on his own responsibility. The First Sea Lord described the idea as 'valuable', but Brooke warned it would not be possible to hold the shipping at Colombo, and it would not be worthwhile for the troops to disembark unless they could stay for at least a month or six weeks.[31] Page achieved success: two brigades of 6 Division were disembarked at Colombo as temporary reinforcements.

Wavell closed down his Java HQ at noon on the 25th, handing over to the Dutch. ABDA command was in effect quietly allowed to dissolve; Wavell signalled the CCS with his regrets for the failure: 'It was a race against time and enemy was too quick for us.' Equally heart-breaking tasks lay ahead: Wavell would now revert to being C-in C India, and threatened Burma remained with him.

Churchill's Ministerial changes were announced to the House of Commons on 24 February. 'It was right and necessary,' declared the Prime Minister, 'that a Government called into being in the crisis of the Battle of France should undergo both change and reinvigoration,' and he believed the result was 'a more tensely-braced and compact administration'. He gave a long description of 'the method by which the war has been and will be conducted' – hence making clear that he would not consider changes in this system. He insisted there was nothing which he did as Defence Minister which he could not do as Prime Minister, but the dual role enabled him to better supervise the general conduct of the war, 'which I do under the authority of the War Cabinet and the Defence Committee'. Day-to-day direction of the war was left to the COS, he continued, who, in addition, 'advise me, they advise the Defence Committee and the War Cabinet, on large questions of war strategy and supply'. He refuted suggestions that he had undue control over the COS: out of 462 COS Committee meetings in 1941, he had presided at only 44. Powerful voices were still raised to demand changes in the structure, including Lord Swinton, Lord Chatfield, former Minister for Co-ordination of Defence, and Professor Hill, who were among those who called for a Great or Combined General Staff. Attacks on Churchill's administration would inevitably continue: recent setbacks combined to give the impression something was radically wrong at the top. Even some of those in the highest governmental circles believed some kind of injection should be made to stimulate decision-making – Eden was apparently worried, although more because he felt Churchill's health and hence energy were declining. 'A. spoke to me of the general situation,' wrote Cadogan on 2nd March. 'He feels – as I do – that for the last fortnight there has been no direction of the war. War Cabinet doesn't function – there hasn't been a meeting of Defence Committee. There's no hand on the wheel. (Probably due to PM's health.) Brendan and Cripps urge that A. should be Deputy Defence Minister.'[32] But Churchill was determined to run it his way, and his way was good enough – providing Churchill himself could stand the strain during these grim weeks.

374

The Governmental changes were generally well-received, insofar as they went, especially the inclusion of Cripps. But Cripps himself showed he did not intend to be a docile War Cabinet member: on 25 February the new Leader of the Commons criticized bombing policy, questioning whether concentration on Germany was worthwhile. The bombing controversy was soon to rise again: three days before, Air Marshal Sir Arthur 'Bomber' Harris had succeeded Peirse as Chief of Bomber Command, and his almost fanatical belief in strategic bombing possibilities, combined with his tremendous energy, was to have powerful impact; meanwhile Churchill told the Commons of the need to take the weight off Russia 'by the heaviest air offensive against Germany which can be produced'. Taking the weight off Russia was to be Beaverbrook's main preoccupation; the former Production Minister was soon to tour America to urge for greater help for the Soviets, to the embarrassment and annoyance of many in Whitehall. Already, on 25 February, the CIGS complained in his diary about sending so many weapons to Russia: 'Personally, I consider it madness.'[33]

Admiral Raeder had long been urging intensified German action in the central Mediterranean; now, on 25 February, the German Naval Staff increased the pressure. 'A successful operation in the near future against the main artery of the British Empire ... would prove of vital importance to the war as a whole.' Hitler was however still preoccupied with halting the Russian winter offensive and preparing for his spring campaign against the Caucasus oilfields. The Führer's determination to slaughter the Soviets remained undiminished, despite the retreat of his forces from Moscow – by the end of February they had been pushed back up to 200 miles – and despite terrible losses: Halder noted on the 28th that 202,251 German troops had so far been killed, and total casualties, 1,005,636, represented 31 per cent of the entire German force. 112,687 men had suffered from frost-bite. Hitler, in addition to Russia, was also engaged in new defensive plans for north and west Europe; his apprehension over a possible allied invasion attempt was steadily increasing. The Führer was therefore too busy to pay over-much attention to the Mediterranean, for the moment. But even if German activity in the area remained at the existing level, Malta remained in great danger. Brooke warned the War Cabinet on the 25th that 'the situation in Malta would be critical unless we could recapture Benghazi before May at the very latest', in order to secure advance airfields for added air cover.[34] Churchill therefore cabled Auchinleck next day: 'According to our figures you have substantial superiority in the air, in armour and in other forces.... The supply of Malta is causing us increasing anxiety.... Pray let me hear from you.' The COS also signalled to the Middle East Commander: 'We feel that we must aim to be so placed in Cyrenaica by April dark period that we can pass substantial convoy to Malta.'[35]

A 1,500 word appreciation by Auchinleck was already on its way to London; this, dated 27 February, caused immediate dismay and anger – in the official historian's words, it 'raised a storm in Downing Street; the waters were not calm again until the end of March'.[36] The Middle East situation was placed on the agenda for the Defence Committee meeting scheduled on 2 March; Churchill drafted a stinging signal, described by Brooke as 'offensive'. Ministers assembled at 10 p.m. on the 2nd and were read Auchinleck's cable. Despite the need for early action in the desert – mid-March or April according to the COS – Auchinleck did not propose a major offensive before June. While fully understanding Malta's critical situation, he claimed he would not have reasonable numerical superiority in tanks before 1 June and added: 'To launch a major offensive before then would be to risk defeat in detail and possibly endanger safety of Egypt.' Churchill told the Defence Committee that Auchinleck's appreciation 'had come as a shock' and he had set down in his draft reply 'the thoughts which had come into my mind'. Pound hurriedly intervened: 'The COS were in agreement with the Prime Minister and were greatly disturbed.... They felt, however, that the first step should be the despatch from the COS of a telegram setting forth all the military arguments of the case.' Attending this meeting was Lyttelton, new Minister of Production and ex-Minister of State at Cairo, who had only returned from Egypt that day. He immediately spoke up for Auchinleck, and suffered a severe grilling; the confrontation showed how detailed factors, seen as minor items in London and possibly overlooked, could affect wide considerations of strategy with which Churchill was primarily involved. The reason for the 'cautious note' struck by Auchinleck, claimed Lyttelton, was that at Agedabia and again at Agheila two of the British armoured brigades had been defeated by inferior enemy forces who had themselves suffered little loss. 'This was mainly due to mechanical defects in their [the British] tanks and particularly to a failure in the cooling system.... The effect of this had been a loss of faith in equipment and this in turn had reacted on tactics.' Churchill wanted to know why the defect had not been noticed before; Lyttelton replied that up to and during the early part of the battle the tanks had used distilled water, and the defect had developed when impure water from desert wells had had to be used. He continued: 'On top of this mechanical failure must be reckoned the superior gun power of the German tanks.... The Germans had developed a better form of tactic ... their tanks moved slowly from position to position waiting till they had discovered the location of our artillery and anti-tank weapons. They kept out of

376

the range of the latter and suffered little damage from the former.' Attlee asked how it was that Rommel, defeated and driven back, could mount so successful a come-back after so short an interval. 'Rommel had realized,' replied Lyttelton, 'as we did, that there were only two places in which to stand and fight in Cyrenaica, either right forward or right back.' The Germans had pulled back, taken advantage of superior gunpower and better mechanical efficiency, and forced the British to withdraw. Brooke said two defects had developed in the cruiser tanks: one in the fan-belt drive and one in the lubrication system. Modifications were possible and spares and experts were being flown out to Egypt. Attlee thought that unless a successful offensive could be launched, 'our whole strategy would be upset. Would it not be better to adopt the strict defensive and take such troops as could be spared to places where they could be better employed?' Lyttelton said that on internal security grounds alone at least eight divisions would be needed in the Middle East. Churchill then returned to his original query: he still could not understand why the defects had not been noticed in the tanks at an earlier stage. 'Surely every step should be taken to test out material before a battle, particularly as the fate of the whole campaign depended upon the reliability of tanks.' The Prime Minister, ignoring the fact that he had constantly criticized Middle East HQ for taking too long in testing and preparing newly-arrived tanks for battle, said an inquiry would be necessary. Attlee pointed out that air superiority was normally considered the vital factor in any battle, yet in spite of the RAF's complete superiority, Rommel had apparently found no difficulty in advancing; to which Lyttelton replied that full effect from bombing in the desert could not be expected; convoys of lorries moved very widely dispersed and in the course of fluid operations it was very difficult to distinguish friend from foe.

The Defence Committee approved a cable to Auchinleck already drafted by the COS, and invited Attlee to lead an inquiry into the situation surrounding the tank defects.[37] The COS cable, dated the 3rd, re-emphasized fears for Malta – 'it may not have been known to you when you wrote your review that, if we do not succeed in running a substantial convoy into Malta by May, the position there will be critical' – and the COS criticized Auchinleck's assessment of relative strengths.[38] Attlee was to take almost three months to complete the requested report; this, dated 2 June, would confirm many of the points made by Lyttelton – the crusader tank had been pressed into production before the pilot model had been adequately tested, and before defects had been detected and corrected.

Urgent discussions continued on the perilous Far East situation. Air Vice-Marshal Maltby had been left in command of British forces in Java, and Churchill had signalled on 26 February: 'Every day gained is precious, and I know that you will do everything humanly possible to prolong the battle.'[39] In Burma, Japanese patrols crossed the Sittang river on 27 February, thus removing the last serious obstacle before Rangoon. 'I cannot see how we are going to go on holding Rangoon much longer,' warned Brooke on this day. Churchill's depression increased. 'Poor old PM in a sour mood and a bad way,' observed Cadogan on 4 March. 'I don't think he's well and I fear he's played out,' and next day: 'Poor old Winston, feeling deeply the present situation and the attacks on him, is losing his grip. The outlook is pretty bloody.'[40] Also on the 5th, General Alexander arrived in Burma; within 24 hours he had decided Rangoon must be abandoned. And fears were growing for Ceylon: Admiral Layton, appointed C-in-C on 5 March, was told by the Admiralty on the 6th that the risk of losing two R-class battleships would be justified if the sacrifice would 'appreciably interfere' with an enemy invasion; Wavell claimed a 'Pearl Harbour' type of raid was the most likely enemy intention, and he opposed locking up troops on the island who were urgently needed elsewhere.

Churchill appealed for Roosevelt's help: a cable on 4 March recognized 'Gymnast' was now out of the question for several months and continued: 'Taking this factor into account, can you lend us the shipping to convoy to the Indian Ocean ... a further two complete divisions?' A cable on the 5th revealed Churchill's despair. 'When I reflect how I have longed and prayed for the entry of the United States into the war, I find it difficult to realize how gravely our British affairs have deteriorated by what has happened since 7 December.' The Prime Minister asked for the despatch of two American divisions, one to New Zealand and the other to Australia, to enable troops from these countries to remain in the Middle East. In Washington the temporary abandonment of 'Gymnast' was seen by many as giving added opportunity for the Second Front to be launched across the English Channel in 1942; and the grand strategic debate now re-opened.

Staff officers on both sides of the Atlantic would soon make monotonous use of the code-names 'Sledgehammer' and 'Round-Up', with the former referring to a cross-Channel operation in 1942 and the latter to a large-scale invasion attempt across the Channel in 1943. Both were favoured by the American chiefs – with the exception of Admiral King whose eyes remained fixed upon the Pacific – by Stimson, US Secretary of War and initially by Hopkins. All, on both sides of the Atlantic, were agreed that an invasion of Europe must eventually be attempted, but differences now became fully apparent over the questions of method and timing. The vagueness of WW I, agreed upon at the 'Arcadia' conference, hindered rather than helped the search for a developed common strategy.

General Arnold put the US air force view when he declared the way to win the war was simply to hit Germany 'where it hurts most, where she is strongest – right across the Channel from England, using the shortest and most direct road to Berlin'. General Marshall, his superior, applied the same reasoning to the deployment of ground forces, and Stimson argued the case at a meeting called by Roosevelt on 5 March to discuss Churchill's requests for transport and for American divisions to move to Australia and New Zealand. The War Secretary urged the despatch of overwhelming strength to Britain; this 'would now have the effect of giving Hitler two fronts to fight on if it could be done in time while the Russians were still in. It would also heavily stimulate sagging British morale.'[41]

The original ABC-1 report in spring 1941 had specified that the war against Japan should be fought defensively, and Germany should be dealt with first; the 'Arcadia' conference had confirmed this decision and had emphasized Germany was the primary enemy – all efforts should therefore be made to defeat her. But Churchill, in his cables to Roosevelt on the 4th and 5th, had laid stress on offensive operations against Japan, implying that for the moment at least a defensive position should be adopted against Germany. In reply to a Joint Staff Mission signal following Roosevelt's conference, Churchill said the COS concurred with him in stating the 'essentials' as 'the assumption of offensive operations against Japan', secondly, 'taking the weight off Russia during the summer by the heaviest air offensive against Germany which can be produced', and thirdly, 'British mastery of the Indian Ocean'. Apart from the air offensive against Germany, Churchill would therefore seem to be departing from the ABC-1 and Arcadia conclusions. The reason was basically the unexpected pressure of events in the Far East; no one had previously been able to see that Japan would have so much success.

But despite the setbacks in the Far East, Stimson, Marshall, Arnold and others in Washington were stressing that an early cross-Channel assault should have main priority, and the American War Plans Division was given the task of detailed planning for such an offensive. This department, soon called the Operations Division, or OPD, was later headed by Eisenhower, who was therefore given the unusual experience of eventually carrying out the strategic concept which he planned; Eisenhower had already stated his view in a Memorandum on 28 February: 'We should at once develop, in conjunction with the British, a definite plan for operations against North-West Europe.' These operations, he had added, must be 'sufficiently extensive in scale as to engage, from the middle of May

379

onwards, an increasing portion of the German Air Force, and by late Autumn an increasing amount of ground forces'.[42]

The Combined Chiefs of Staff met on 7 March to consider a reply from Roosevelt to Churchill – a procedure meaning in effect that British and American service chiefs in Washington would draft a reply from the US President to the British Prime Minister. The signal, despatched on 8 March, agreed to the loan of shipping, despite the fact that this 'seriously reduces present possibilities of offensive action in other regions', and the cable agreed to the American reinforcements for Australia and New Zealand. The loan of ships was conditional on 'Gymnast' not being undertaken for the moment, movements of US troops to Britain being limited and direct movements to Iceland stopped.[43] 'I was well content,' wrote Churchill. The cable fitted Churchill's scheme, rather than that advocated by Stimson and Marshall whose arguments presented at the meeting with Roosevelt on the 5th seemed to have been put to one side. But Roosevelt also cabled a personal message to Churchill, dated the 9th: 'I am becoming more and more interested in the establishment of a new front this summer on the European continent, certainly for air and raids.'[44]

Roosevelt therefore showed himself sympathetic towards Stimson's scheme, although viewing potentialities on a small scale. The way was opening for misunderstanding and argument, and not only between one side of the Atlantic and the other. In London, more shocking news had been received from the Far East: Alexander had been forced to abandon Rangoon, and was now leading his forces through terrible terrain in an attempt to reach the safety of India. Burma was left free for the enemy; and on 8 March the Japanese entered Rangoon; Java fell the same day. Yet despite anxieties caused by the Far East situation the COS turned on the 10th to discuss European strategy, and the debate showed the lack of unanimity even among the British over early cross-Channel operations. The COS were now chaired by Brooke, following his takeover from Pound the previous day: Pound continued to be First Sea Lord and therefore a committee member. This meeting on the 10th was also attended by Lord Louis Mountbatten, in his capacity as Adviser on Combined Operations: six days later he was officially appointed Chief of Combined Operations with a seat on the COS committee. The meeting was primarily concerned with aid to Russia; the previous day Churchill had cabled Stalin: 'We are continuing to study other measures for taking some of the weight off you.'[45] With this pledge in mind, the COS discussed a bold report by their planning staff strongly advocating 'Sledgehammer': 'Apart from the supply of material, we are giving no direct help to Russia, though our Middle East operations and our air-offensive are, to a limited extent, making Germany divert forces.... This is not enough.... Our greatest contribution to a German defeat would be the creation of a major diversion in the West designed to upset German plans and divert German forces from the East. Lack of shipping precludes the strategy of such a diversion anywhere except across the Channel.' The planners envisaged the seizure and retention of a bridgehead on the Continent. Previous discussion had always been based on the assumption that such an expedition would only be feasible when Germany had already been weakened by other means – bombing, the Russian campaign, uprisings in occupied territories. But the planners now envisaged early help even if troops had to be sacrificed against a still-strong Germany.

Argument broke out between the COS and their advisers. The Directors of Intelligence maintained an operation would be unlikely to divert enemy land forces unless accompanied by a popular rising; the Foreign Office representative said this was unlikely unless the allied forces had clearly come to stay. The Directors of Planning, on the other hand, continued to argue that 'the summer of 1942 was likely to be decisive on the Russian front, and it was vitally important that we should do our utmost to influence the course of operations'. Mountbatten pointed out that the required number of landing-craft were unlikely to be available before July; he favoured Cherbourg as a target but most others urged the Pas de Calais area. Brooke voiced opposition to the whole idea : Britain could not afford to lose six or eight best divisions in a diversion of this nature. The COS did however agree to further studies; at a later meeting on 21 March detailed examination was referred to General Bernard Paget, Air Marshal Sir Sholto Douglas and Mountbatten.[46]

Meanwhile the 'Sledgehammer' lobby in America received support from Hopkins, who wrote to Roosevelt on the 14th to say he agreed with General Arnold's proposal to concentrate all forces originally scheduled for 'Magnet' – the movement of US troops to Northern Ireland – and 'Gymnast' in Britain to support a cross-Channel assault as soon as possible in 1942.[47] Two days later the US Joint Chiefs of Staff accepted the possibility that if top priority were given to a cross-Channel operation in 1942, the South-West Pacific might severely suffer. Already, on 10 March, the Combined Chiefs of Staff had linked the Far East with the Middle East in an attempt to establish world-wide priorities, and Admiral Stark, US Chief of Naval Operations and CCS Chairman had shown himself a powerful supporter of operations in North Africa. He believed that 'the loss of the Middle East would be much more serious to the United Nations than the loss of the Far East.... The Middle East was the one place Germany could be fought.' Stark had asked Dill how the British people felt on this subject, 'as there were people in the US who held the opinion that the Far East was of greater importance'. Dill had replied that with Singapore lost, 'the importance of the Middle East had enormously increased'.[48]

Halting the Japanese advance in the Pacific and Indian Oceans; plans for Europe; the North African situation – tangled and sometimes cross-threaded debate on these three areas continued at the White House, at 10 Downing Street, the offices of the US and British Chiefs of Staff, and at the temporary HQ of the CCS in the Public Health Building, Washington. The British COS on 11 March gave general approval to Roosevelt's scheme, detailed in his message to Churchill on the 9th, for a clear division of Anglo-US responsibilities in the Indian and Pacific Ocean areas. In Burma, General Alexander's withdrawal was proceeding satisfactorily – but the operation would take two long months. In Egypt, General Auchinleck continued to display his stubborness. In reply to the COS cable urging an early offensive in view of Malta's precarious situation, Auchinleck insisted the issue involved the question of whether, in the effort to save Malta, the whole British position in the Middle East would be jeopardized. Churchill immediately cabled: 'I should be glad if you would come home for consultation at your earliest convenience.'[49] Auchinleck declined: in the present 'fluid' state of affairs he thought it his duty to remain on the spot. His refusal was discussed at a COS meeting on Friday morning, 13 March, with the Prime Minister yet to hear. Brooke and his colleagues drafted a Memorandum intended to tone down Auchinleck's obstinacy; unfortunately Churchill telephoned from Chequers and Brooke had to inform him of the General's reply. An irate Churchill immediately threatened a change of command in Cairo and refused to consider Auchinleck's suggestion that Brooke and the Chief of Air Staff should fly out for talks. Churchill telephoned again in the afternoon: he himself would send a telegram. 'I shudder at what he may put in it,' wrote Brooke.[50] In fact, the content was comparatively calm. 'I have done everything in my power to give you continuous support at heavy cost.... It would give me the greatest pain to feel that mutual understanding had ceased.' Churchill told Auchinleck that Cripps was about to leave on a mission to India and would stop in Cairo for discussions on the 19th or 20th, where he would also be joined by General Nye, the Vice-CIGS.[51]

On 18 March, three days after Churchill's cable to Auchinleck, Rommel was attending top-level discussions in Rome, and apparently agreed the attack on Tobruk could not take place till after an assault on Malta, a decision confirmed by Kesselring on the 21st. At that moment a British convoy was sailing for the threatened island, and its fate clearly demonstrated Malta's dangerous isolation. Four merchant ships had left Alexandria on the 20th carrying 26,000 tons of urgent supplies. Despite Admiral Vian's brilliant action in throwing his escort force against a vastly superior Italian fleet, only meagre protection could be given against air attack; only two merchantmen reached harbour at Malta, and one was sunk while being unloaded. Only about 5,000 tons of supplies were landed. Churchill's conviction of the need for an early North African offensive increased: forward airfields must be secured. But the Prime Minister suffered a further disappointment; Cripps supported Auchinleck. 'I am very satisfied with the atmosphere at Cairo,' cabled Cripps on the 20th. 'When I first arrived I felt a rather prickly atmosphere.... That has now completely disappeared.' The Lord Privy Seal declared: 'I have no doubts as to Auchinleck's offensive [spirit], but I think his Scottish caution and his desire not to mislead by optimism cause him to overstress in statement the difficulties and uncertainties.' Cripps sent a long telegram on technical details, despatched with the approval of the C-in-Cs and Sir Walter Monckton, Acting Minister of State: British strength was not sufficient to give reasonable chance of a success; an attack before mid-May would lead to unwarrantable risk; Auchinleck feared an enemy attack developing in the north via the Caucasus or Turkey, or upon Cyprus.[52]

Cripps left for India and escaped Churchill's wrath, but by now General Nye had reached Cairo. 'I have heard from the Lord Privy Seal,' cabled Churchill to him on the 22nd. 'I do not wonder everything was so pleasant, considering you seem to have accepted everything they said, and all *we* have got to accept is the probable loss of Malta and the Army standing idle, while the Russians are resisting the German counter-stroke desperately, and while the enemy is reinforcing himself in Libya faster than we are.'[53] Also on the 22nd came Nye's long, detailed report; the Vice-CIGS supported Cripps and Auchinleck. 'First:... If formations are to have 50 per cent reserve tanks it will only be possible by 15 May to equip two armoured brigades and two army tank battalions in addition to those now equipped.... Fifth: Considerations of training, both of armoured personnel and other arms ... arise and limit the date by which these formations will be operationally ready even if tanks available.... Seventh: C-in-C estimates that 50 per cent numerical superiority over German tanks and equality with Italian tanks necessary to give reasonable prospects of success.... Eighth: Probable number of tanks in possession of enemy by 15 May is admittedly a guess, but at worse may be 360 German and 312 Italians, which would require on C-in-C's estimate, 850 tanks of ours to give reasonable prospect of success. Ninth: It appears that at the very best we are not likely to have more than 500 tanks with formations in the forward area exclusive of reserves and I [Infantry] tanks by 15 May.

Tenth: The deduction is that no offensive operations are justified before 15 May and only then if enemy tank strength is less than that given in Eight.'[54]

The various signals were discussed by the Defence Committee on Thursday, 26 March; Churchill had to admit that 'in view of the opinions expressed by Cripps and of the estimates of relative tank strengths given by Lieutenant-General Nye's telegrams, there seemed no alternative but to accept the date given by General Auchinleck'. But another jab was thrown at Cairo. 'Reports which had now been received of the relative tank strength in the middle of March, showed that General Auchinleck had probably missed an opportunity of taking the offensive at a time when he had a considerable superiority.' Alexander, First Lord of the Admiralty, warned the Royal Navy would probably be unable to prevent enemy convoys crossing the Mediterranean and he 'deplored the necessity for postponing the offensive'. But Brooke said the interval 'would make a great deal of difference in the state of our tanks and the training of our armoured formations. In addition the railhead would have advanced to El Adem and this would ease the subsequent maintenance problem.' Churchill warned that 'there was always a possibility that the scale of enemy reinforcements would exceed General Auchinleck's estimates and would thus cause him to postpone his operation'.[55] A cable left the War Office, accepting the 15 May date; almost immediately a signal bounced back from the Middle East Defence Committee, stressing the date had been conditional on enemy tank strength being less than that at present estimated for 15 May. 'C-in-Cs cannot bind themselves in anyway to launch an offensive on 15 May in spite of the very obvious and urgent need to take the offensive as soon as possible.'[56]

'The coastline of Europe will, in the coming months, be exposed to the danger of an enemy landing in force,' declared Hitler's Directive No 40 dated 23 March. Operational considerations would not be the only factors determining the time and place, continued the Führer. 'Failure in other theatres of war, obligations to allies, and political considerations may persuade him to take decisions which appear unlikely from a purely military point of view.' Next day, 24 March, the CCS sought to examine British and American studies for a European offensive: planners were to answer these questions: '(a) Is it possible to put ground forces on the Continent during 1942 with sufficient support to give reasonable assurance that they can be maintained there? (b) Is an invasion of the Continent early in 1943 a possibility? If so, the estimates as to materials required should be reconciled. (c) If the answer to (a) above is in the negative, how does this affect US participation in or assistance to the British defence of the Middle East in 1942?'[57] These pertinent questions were put in an attempt to clear growing confusion over 'Sledgehammer' for' 1942 and 'Round-Up' for 1943; the British delegates reported more hope of progress. The hope soon faded: the creditable CCS attempt failed, largely through the impetus of respective American and British discussions.

The American OPD under Eisenhower had now completed a detailed report for a major assault across the Channel, scheduled for 1 April, 1943, and Eisenhower warned on the 25th: 'Unless this plan is adopted as the eventual aim of all our efforts, we must turn our *backs* upon the Eastern Atlantic and go, full out, as quickly as possible, against Japan.' And the American planners believed that in order to concentrate forces, attention and resources on this 1943 ('Round-Up') scheme, 'Sledgehammer' must be an essential preliminary. Also on the 25th a White House meeting took place between Roosevelt, Stimson, the American Joint Chiefs of Staff and Hopkins. Initially, Roosevelt seemed to favour operations in the Mediterranean basin, condemned by Stimson as the wildest kind of 'dispersion debauch'; Roosevelt felt the matter should be discussed by the CCS, but Hopkins feared this would result in American ideas for a Channel operation being blocked and suggested the plan be taken direct to the highest British authorities. Two days later, the day the OPD plan was formally submitted to Roosevelt, Stimson sent the President a letter urging him to take a firm stand on the OPD scheme. A further meeting was held at the White House on 1 April, and Roosevelt was persuaded to agree to an early Second Front attempt in Europe: the President wanted early action against Germany, to help Russia and to help his domestic political affairs. On 18 March, before these discussions on the OPD plan, Roosevelt had cabled Churchill: 'I expect to send you in a few days a more definite plan for a joint attack in Europe itself.' Now, on 2 April, he cabled the Prime Minister: 'I have come to certain conclusions which are so vital that I want you to know the whole picture. . . . The whole is so dependent on complete co-operation by the United Kingdom and United States that Harry [Hopkins] and Marshall will leave for London'; this was followed by a personal letter dated 3 April: 'What Harry and Geo. Marshall will tell you all about has my heart and *mind* in it.'[58] Hopkins and Marshall left America on the 4th with the OPD scheme, known now as the Marshall Memorandum. The report requested from their planners by the CCS on 24 March had been superseded.

Meanwhile, the British COS had also continued discussions on operations across the Channel. They fully realized the importance of a Second Front in 1942 to aid the Soviets, declaring in a signal to the Mission in Washington on 6 April: 'We consider that importance of helping Russia in 1942 is so great that consideration of offensive in 1943 should not prevent us from doing anything we can, however small, this summer [1942].'[59] But two factors were involved, one political – help to Russia – and the other military. The COS concerned themselves with the latter, and depressing conclusions emerged. On 28 March the COS considered the report prepared by Paget, Douglas and Mountbatten: re-entry into France with present British resources was likely to fail, and a bridgehead was unlikely to be held; German strength against the Russians, especially the *Luftwaffe*, would be more likely drawn through RAF actions alone. Portal contended however that air-operations were unlikely to create the wastage of German fighters necessary to help the Russian, and Brooke stressed that an operation would only be worthwhile if it succeeded in easing this German pressure on the Russian front.[60] A slightly more optimistic report was presented to the COS on 8 April: the occupation of a bridgehead was practicable, but only if a number of conditions were met – 'enemy reinforcements, of the order of 2-3 divisions, or considerable strengthening of the coast defences prior to the assault would render operation impossible.'[61]

The Americans concentrated their thoughts on 1943, and emerged optimistic. A 1942 operation, although considered essential, had not at this stage received the same amount of detailed examination. The British concentrated on 1942, and emerged pessimistic: shortage of landing craft, unlikelihood of large-scale American reinforcements in 1942, the difficulties – of which Brooke and Paget had painful practical experience – involved with re-embarkation in the face of a stronger enemy; Brooke, as C-in-C, Home Forces, had also had the task of building defences against an enemy invasion attempt, and this gave him an awareness of the need to keep sufficient forces in Britain – conversely, it also gave him an insight into opposition the British forces might themselves encounter in an invasion against the Germans. The COS had also to consider the position in North Africa, where, since the earliest days, hopes had been concentrated of bringing German forces in the field to a decisive, although not ultimate, defeat. The 8th Army must be sustained. At the same time, Churchill began to push his scheme for an operation in Norway – stimulated, in turn, by raids undertaken by Mountbatten's Combined Operations units, and especially by the daring demolition of the St Nazaire dry dock on 28 March.

Yet the Prime Minister, for all his enthusiasm for spectacular operations which might lead him to support 'Sledgehammer', realized the implications of Japan's highly-successful sweep. Churchill, in his call for offensive operations against the Japanese which seemed to contradict the 'Arcadia' decisions, was stating a recognized but otherwise undeclared fact: for a while the Far East must have priority. From January to March the main American troop movements, totalling over 70,000 men, had been to the Pacific; American warships had had to quit the Atlantic for the Far East. The need to at least halt the Japanese offensive therefore affected Western plans proposed for 1942. 'Sledgehammer' could not be isolated from overall strategic considerations; resources had still to be balanced. And the publication of Minutes of meetings reveals clearly the harassed state of mind of the British COS immediately prior to the Hopkins-Marshall visit with their cross-Channel proposals. On 31 March the COS approved a report on Middle East and Mediterranean strategy which stressed the essential importance of Iranian and Iraqi oil supplies – vital both for the continuation of the war in the west, and also for Australia owing to the shortage of tankers to bring supplies from America. 1942 was the critical year, said the report: if Germany secured the Caucasian oilfields, Russia might be defeated, with great danger to Britain's own oil supplies in the Persian Gulf. Russia must therefore be bolstered by pressure on the Axis in as direct a form as possible and as soon as possible. Yet the report declared this pressure could only be placed in Libya.

Next day and on 2 April the COS discussed another report, dealing with the Japanese threat to India and the Indian Ocean; the paper warned that present British weaknesses, coupled with American inability to give immediate help, could enable Japan to cause 'irreparable damage' in the area. 'An invasion of Bengal, an assault on Ceylon, or an attack on our Eastern fleet, would each if successful prove a devastating blow to us.... We are in danger of losing our Indian Empire – with incalculable consequences to the future conduct of the war.' Immediately after this report came another, on the inter-relation of strategy in the Middle East and in India. Both depended on Indian Ocean security, and with present British weaknesses the Japanese threat to India was even greater than the German threat to Malta. All available warships should be sent to the Indian Ocean; local defence of Ceylon should be built up as fast as possible; next in the list of priorities should be the early assumption of the Libyan offensive.'[62]

At the end of March, Admiral Somerville, commander of the Eastern fleet, received information of an imminent Japanese naval attack on Ceylon. On 4 April, the day Hopkins and Marshall started for London, a large enemy task force was sighted approaching Ceylon; just before dawn on Easter Sunday, 5 April, Colombo was attacked by 80 enemy dive-bombers and later in the day Japanese aircraft sunk two British cruisers. Somerville, learning he was opposed by a far superior force, retired westward following previous instructions. Ceylon again suffered air raids on the 9th; already, on the 7th, Churchill had requested Roosevelt to order the US Pacific Fleet to make some diversion to relieve the Indian Ocean pressure. The Japanese had control of the Bay of Bengal and could obtain local command of the waters around Ceylon whenever they wished.[63] Wavell appealed for reinforcements on the 12th: 'Unless effort is made to supply our essential needs, which I have not over-stated, I must warn you that we shall never regain control of Indian Ocean and Bay of Bengal and run risk of losing India.'[64] The British COS had no way of knowing that this Easter foray marked the limits of Japan's westward naval expansion. The COS could only consider the acute threat to Britain's communications. And this threat had to be added to all other dangers: to Malta, to the Persian Gulf through a German move south, to Burma, to Egypt. It was therefore hardly surprising that the COS were reluctant to devote time to long-range plans for an offensive against fortress Europe in 1943; day-to-day problems seemed far too urgent. Nor was it surprising the COS had doubts over the resources to be used for the creation of a Second Front on the Continent in 1942, apart from RAF bombers striking at Germany herself.

The strategic bombing offensive, placed in this overall context, had obvious attractions. These were emphasized in a Memorandum from Professor Lindemann – now Lord Cherwell – addressed to Churchill and dated 30 March. The paper, circulated to the Defence Committee on 9 April, examined the effects of bombing on Britain, then declared: 'In 1938 over 22 million Germans lived in 58 towns of over 100,000 inhabitants which, with modern equipment, should be easy to find and hit. Our forecast output of heavy bombers, including Wellingtons, between now and the middle of 1943 is about 10,000. If even half the total load of 10,000 bombers were dropped on the built-up areas of these 58 German towns the great majority of the inhabitants (about one-third of the German population) would be turned out of house and home.' Cherwell reminded Churchill that 'having one's house demolished is most damaging to morale. People seem to mind it more than having one's friends or even relatives killed.' The spirit of the German people would be shattered, Cherwell concluded. Sinclair, the Air Secretary, told the Prime Minister on 13 April that he and Portal found the calculations 'simple, clear and convincing'.[65] Others disagreed, notably Sir Henry Tizard, but mainly on the grounds that the estimated heavy bomber force available was far too high.[66] Churchill eventually took up a suggestion by Portal that bombing policy should be referred to an independent authority, and a rather non-committal report was presented by Mr Justice Sinclair. Meanwhile, high hopes rested on the strategic bombing offensive against Germany; but Wavell complained: 'It certainly gives us furiously to think, when, after trying with less than 20 light bombers to meet attack which has cost us three important warships and several others and nearly 100,000 tons of merchant shipping, we see that over 200 heavy bombers attacked one town in Germany.'[67]

Anglo-American talks in London took place against this tense, tight and tug-of-war background. The Americans were also having to endure terrible suffering and losses; on 3 April, after a six week lull, the Japanese renewed the offensive on Bataan peninsula, Luzon, and at midnight on 8th-9th about 78,000 Philippine and allied troops were forced to surrender. Pearl Harbour had still to be avenged. The Americans wanted to hit back hard at the primary enemy, Germany, and they rushed to put this retaliation into practice. The British COS agreed with the sentiment but questioned the practicalities. The Americans were rightly worried about British war-weariness. 'During the last fortnight,' wrote Brooke on 31 March, 'I have had for the first time since the war started a growing conviction that we are going to lose this war unless we control it very differently and fight it with more determination.... I wonder if we shall muddle through this time like we have in the past?'[68] Although Brooke's spirits may have risen again by the time he drove to meet Marshall and Hopkins at Hendon on Wednesday, 8 April, the symptoms of his 'liverish' condition remained.

13

Misunderstanding

Talks in London during the Hopkins-Marshall visit were an essential follow-up to the Washington conference the previous winter. But respective American and British attitudes at 'Arcadia' were now reversed in London. The British had presented a plan at Washington, WW I, which had been accepted with very few modifications by the Americans, mainly because the scheme was concerned with future allied strategy, written in unspecific language, and because the Americans were preoccupied with immediate events in the aftermath of Pearl Harbour. The paper had been sufficiently vague to fit ideas held by both nations. Now, however, the Americans were presenting a momentous set of proposals which could be seen by them as a logical step-forward from the unspecific WW I. But the British, like the Americans during 'Arcadia', were concerned with more immediate affairs and were too preoccupied to look far ahead, as the American proposals required them to do.

While Brooke was at Hendon airfield, meeting General Marshall for the first time, the War Cabinet were in session at 10 Downing Street. Ministers had now finally agreed Stalin's request for recognition of the 1941 frontier should be granted, except for the Russo-Polish border. Eden was instructed to inform Maisky of Britain's willingness to negotiate and that a visit by Molotov to sign a treaty would be welcomed. Roosevelt, despite his dislike of this British recognition of Russia's 1941 borders, next week invited Stalin to send Molotov and a general to Washington to discuss 'a very important proposal involving the utilization of our armed forces in a manner to relieve your critical Western Front'. The two invitations would lead to further Anglo-American complications.[1]

The American Second-Front plan was revealed to Churchill in a private meeting during the afternoon of 8 April, according to the account later written by Hopkins. The Prime Minister made no mention of this meeting in his memoirs; Brooke's diary certainly showed he, the CIGS, had to wait until next morning.[2] The importance of the time difference lies in the fact that, again according to Hopkins, Churchill immediately indicated he was in favour – before the COS and Defence Committee had been consulted. 'Western Europe,' declared the plan, 'is favoured as the theatre in which to stage the first major offensive by the United States and Great Britain.' This opening statement clearly referred to the main invasion of Europe, 'Round-Up', but almost immediately the paper added: 'Another, and most significant consideration is the unique opportunity to establish an active sector on this front this summer, through steadily increasing air-operations and by raids or forays all along the coasts.' The paper continued: 'Decision as to the main effort must be made now. This is true even if the invasion ["Round-Up"] cannot be launched during this year.... Decision now will stop continued dispersion of means.... Our proposal provides for an attack, by combined forces of approximately 5,800 combat airplanes and 48 divisions, against Western Europe as soon as the necessary means can be accumulated in England – estimated at 1 April 1943, provided decision is made *now* and men, material and shipping are conserved for this purpose.' The plan for the 1943 operation included the 'establishment of preliminary active front this coming summer – for training, demonstration, deception and destruction', and the Americans considered that an advantage of their plan lay in the fact that 'during the preparatory period, it provides means to act promptly under either of the following eventualities: (a) If the imminence of Russian collapse requires desperate action, a sacrifice attack could be made immediately. (b) If German forces are almost completely absorbed on the Russian front, or a deterioration of the German military power is evident, a prompt movement to the Continent could be undertaken.'[3]

General Marshall revealed the plan to the COS next morning, 9 April: he said he wanted to reach a decision as to what form the main Anglo-American effort was to take, and when and where it was to be made. In the interval before the main operation Russian resistance must be maintained and American personnel must gain war experience, hence his ideas for raids. Substantial American troops would not however be able to arrive before mid-September, hence an 'emergency operation' would have to be undertaken by mainly British forces should Russia or Germany collapse in 1942. The British COS, preoccupied as they were with immediate considerations, devoted most of their comments to these 'raids' and the 'emergency operation' in 1942. Emphasis was given to the seriousness of the Indian Ocean situation and the Middle East.[4] Privately, Brooke believed the Americans 'had not begun to realize what all the implications of their proposed plan were'.[5] Ironically, Churchill told Eden during the early afternoon that he feared the COS would agree with Marshall's scheme as 'a pretext for doing less elsewhere'.[6] The COS started to draft their reply next day, Friday, but other business kept crowding in: much of the time at the COS meeting on the 10th had been spent discussing plans to help India; enemy air attacks on Malta had intensified; increasing casualties were being suffered by the PQ convoys to Russia: Ministers were informed at the War Cabinet meeting on the 13th, attended by Hopkins and Harriman, that one ship returning from Russia had been sunk by aircraft and two by U-boat, and Churchill declared at the meeting that 'it was important we should make the Russian Government realize the extent of the risks that were being run, and the efforts being made'.[7] Another preoccupation resulted from breakdown of talks with India: Cripps had presented the Indian Congress with a British pledge to grant full independence to India if demanded by a Constituent Assembly after the war, but Cripps cabled on the 11th to say this proposal had been rejected: 'In view of Congress there should be immediately a National Government.' Cripps intended to return to London.

Churchill cabled Roosevelt on the 12th: 'I have read with earnest attention your masterly document about the future of the war.... I am in entire agreement in principle with all you proposed, and so are the COS.' The COS were in fact still considering their reply and would continue to do so for another 24 hours. Churchill did however warn the President: 'We must of course meet day-to-day emergencies in the East and Far East while preparing for the main stroke,' although he continued: 'I thought the proposals made for an interim operation in certain contingencies this year met the difficulties and uncertainties in an absolutely sound manner.'[8] General Marshall reported to Washington on the 13th that 'great firmness' would be needed to prevent 'further dispersions' of military effort.[9] His fears were apparently confirmed when he received the COS reply next morning: while the COS entirely agreed plans should be prepared for major operations on the Continent in 1943, 'Round-Up', doubts were expressed for 1942, a possible 'Sledgehammer'. The COS agreed that if Russia was being defeated supreme sacrifices might have to be made to draw off German forces, but even a limited operation could not be launched later than August if a port was to be captured by the third week of September, after which deteriorating weather would cause disastrous difficulties. The COS stressed pressure from other areas of war – action envisaged against Germany in 1942 might be made useless if the Japanese were not held in the meantime. General Marshall countered by saying that once a project was firmly fixed, problems became greatly eased: forces must not be so dispersed in 1942 that the main project for an operation in Europe in 1943 was lowered to the status of a residuary legatee for whom nothing was left. Brooke insisted complete agreement existed over plans for 1943, but he repeated that cross-Channel operations in 1942 might have to be on a small scale, and their slight military value must be weighed against the danger of Germany and Japan joining forces in the Indian Ocean. One agreement emerged from this meeting: an American planning staff, soon to be headed by Eisenhower, would come to London to work with the British.[10] Discussion would be resumed at a meeting of the Defence Committee that Tuesday night, but Marshall apparently already considered his visit a failure: British officers gathered that 'in spite of our [the British] efforts and intentions to the contrary the Americans thought ... we did not mean to do real business on their plan – this because of our insistence on the seriousness of the situation developing in the Middle East and Indian Ocean.'[11]

The War Cabinet met at noon to discuss another aspect of allied co-operation. Eden said he had sought the views of Hopkins and Marshall over supplies to Russia after June 1942, and had suggested another three-power conference in Moscow. The Americans did not favour the idea, continued Eden, and thought that 'if one was held we should be strongly pressed to increase supplies. They suggested that the right plan would be that the American and British authorities should make a quick survey, on the basis of which they should determine what supplies we could afford to send to Russia, and that we should then tell the USSR what we proposed to do.' Eden thought such a conference should take place as soon as possible in London. Lyttelton, Minister of Production, suggested the best line of approach should be to consider how many ships could be sent to Russia each month; Pound said that on present experience 25 ships was the top limit for a convoy, and two convoys of 25 ships per month represented the absolute maximum; the First Lord of the Admiralty emphasized 'the serious losses which were likely to be incurred if we continued the effort to sail convoys to Russia on the present scale throughout the summer months'.[12] Outside events continued to clamour for attention. Wavell and his Navy and RAF colleagues in Bombay demanded immediate air reinforcements. Churchill cabled to Cripps, now at Cairo: 'I hope you will not let it be thought that we here are not deeply concerned with the prolonged inaction of the Libya Army. ... Rommel will grow stronger at a greater rate than our people.' Fighter aircraft were being successfully flown into Malta from the US carrier *Wasp*, but Churchill told Cripps that enemy air attacks prevented bombers being stationed on the island, thus allowing greater freedom for enemy convoys to Tripoli, and he added: 'The Middle East air will be increasingly drawn upon for the Indian emergency.'[13] Brooke had to attend a meeting at 5 p.m. with Oliver Lyttelton, then rushed back to the War Office for talks on latest reports with General Nye, then had discussions with General de Gaulle, and finally hurried to 10 Downing Street for the Defence Committee meeting starting at 10 p.m.

Churchill opened this session by declaring he had 'no hesitation in cordially accepting' the American plan. 'The conception underlying it accorded with the classic principles of war – namely, concentration against the main enemy.' But the Prime Minister added: 'One broad reservation must however be made – it was essential to tie on defence of India and the Middle East. We could not possibly face the loss of an army of 600,000 men and the whole manpower of India. Furthermore, Australia and the island bases connecting that country with the United States must not be allowed to fall. . . . This meant that we could not entirely lay aside everything in furtherance of the main object proposed by General Marshall.' Marshall said that 'it was a great relief to him to know that there was a basic agreement on general principle. All were in complete agreement as to what should be done in 1943. All were in complete agreement as to the necessity for developing the strongest air offensive against Germany.' But the American continued: 'There were two points of doubts. . . . The first was whether sufficient material would be available from the United States for the support of the Middle East and India; the second was on the practicability of making a landing on the Continent, other than a large-scale raid, in 1942. We might be compelled to do this, and we must, in any case, prepare for it.' He admitted there had been insufficient time before he left America to study the problem of operations in 1942, and 'on the data available', he had concluded that they could not be undertaken before September'. Brooke stressed the 'entire agreement' for the 1943 project but 'operations on the Continent in 1942 were governed by the measure of success achieved by the Germans in their campaign against Russia. If they were successful we could clearly act less boldly. If however the Russians held the Germans or had an even greater measure of success, our object should be to force the Germans to detach air forces from the Russian front. This would be done either by air operations or else by the landing of troops.' Brooke warned that 'we had felt that matters would come to a head before September and that we might have to act before then: in that event we should, of course, welcome the participation of whatever US forces were available in the country.' The CIGS then referred to the dangers in the Far East and of a possible junction between the Japanese and Germans. 'These considerations led the COS to the view that, although they welcomed the idea of an offensive in Europe, it was absolutely necessary to take measures to prevent a collapse in the Indian Ocean.' Hopkins gave his interpretation of the American view. 'If public opinion in America had its way, the weight of American effort would be directed against Japan. Nevertheless, after anxious discussion the President and the American military leaders had decided that it would be right to direct the force of American arms against Germany. It should not be thought, however, that there was any mis-understanding in the minds of the American Government as to the position in the Middle East and the Pacific.' The American decision had been governed by two main reasons. 'First, the United States wished to fight not only on the sea, but on land and in the air. Second, they wished to fight in the most useful place, and in the place where they could attain superiority, and they were desirous above all of joining in an enterprise with the British.'

Hopkins commented: 'The decision which had to be taken was one of the most momentous which had ever been faced. On it depended the preservation of all that democracy held dear. The decision once taken could not be reversed.' Attlee believed 'a new phase of the war' was about to begin: 'hitherto we had been hanging on to the best of our ability.... Now the time had arrived for us to wrest the initiative.' Eden described the American plan as 'a great picture of two English-speaking countries setting out for the redemption of Europe'. Complete unanimity on the frame-work of the plan clearly existed, said Churchill, although details had still to be worked out. 'The two nations would march ahead together in a noble brotherhood of arms.... All preparations could now start and we could go ahead with the utmost resolution. It would gradually become known that the English-speaking peoples were resolved on a great campaign for the liberation of Europe.'[14] With this fine rhetoric the meeting closed in the early hours of 15 April. The session had indeed shown complete unanimity for the 1943 plan, but the meeting had not shown the considerable disagreement felt by the British COS towards the 1942 'emergency' operation – the official Minutes do not record Brooke as specifically mentioning British criticism.

And not only did Brooke have grave reservations about a 1942 operation, but he now believed serious deficiencies existed in the 1943 scheme. 'Round-Up' formed the main subject of talks between Brooke and Marshall during the afternoon of the 15th, described by Brooke later as 'an eye-opener'. He wrote: 'I discovered that he [Marshall] had not studied any of the strategic implications of a cross-Channel operation,' and the CIGS's diary entry for the 15th read: 'I asked him this afternoon – Do we go west, south or east after landing? He had not begun to think of it.' Brooke maintained that if Russia collapsed, the Germans would concentrate in France and would therefore make an invasion impossible. 'Under these circumstances our only hope would be to operate in Africa.'[15] Also on the 15th Churchill renewed his appeal to Roosevelt for help in relieving Indian Ocean pressure; Japanese domination in the Indian Ocean 'would result in the collapse of our whole position in the Middle East' through the interruption to convoys and to oil supplies.[16]

The American proposals were discussed again by the British COS on the 16th, and the committee were unanimous in considering the 1942 scheme surrounded by problems and dangers. Much would need to be done to settle logistical and tactical questions for the larger, 1943, operation.[17] Yet when Hopkins and Marshall left on the 17th, Churchill reported to Roosevelt: 'We whole-heartedly agree with your conception of concentration against the main enemy, and we cordially accept your plan.' But Churchill added 'one broad qualification'; he referred to his telegram of 15 April and emphasized: 'It is essential that we should prevent a junction of the Japanese and the Germans.' However Churchill continued: 'The campaign of 1943 is straightforward.... Broadly speaking, our agreed programme is a crescendo of activity on the Continent, starting with an ever-increasing air offensive both by night and day and more frequent and large-scale raids.'[18] This cable illustrates Churchill's attitude throughout the London discussions: high hopes are emphasized in stirring language, but with underlying hesitations and qualifications. A 'crescendo of activity on the Continent', and yet the 'broad qualification' and no mention of detailed problems still to be solved. Roosevelt's reply on the 22nd illustrates the principal American reaction to the discussions: 'I am delighted with the agreement which was reached between you and your military advisers and Marshall and Hopkins. They have reported to me on the unanimity of opinion relative to the proposal.' Roosevelt, on the 17th, had already promised US air help in response to Churchill's appeal for assistance in the Indian Ocean area; now, on the 22nd, he declared: 'I believe that any junction between Japanese and Germans is going to take a great deal of doing, but realize that the remote prospect of this is something that must be watched.'[19] Churchill's qualification was therefore dismissed as being based on a 'remote prospect' and as far as the President was concerned 'unanimity of opinion' had been achieved in London.

The Americans considered their plan as one complete unit: 1942 operations would prepare the way for the 1943 offensive, and an 'emergency' operation might have to be attempted in the event of Russian or German collapse. US attention was therefore concentrated on the main 'Round-Up' campaign; Marshall had admitted at the Defence Committee meeting on the 14th that 'there had not been much time before he left the US to study the problem of operations in 1942'. The 1943 offensive had claimed his time. The British, on the other hand, tended to separate the 1942 plans from the larger scale schemes for the following year: they were more concerned with immediate problems. Nothing had happened to change the views of the COS from those which had emerged during the March consideration of a 1942 cross-Channel operation. As for 1943, 'complete unanimity' on the general principle was easily obtained: the 'concept of concentration against the main enemy' for which Roosevelt had been praised by Churchill was in fact the essence of the Prime Minister's own plans prepared before the 'Arcadia' conference, and embodied in WW I. Germany had always been considered the primary enemy; the conquest of fortress Europe had always been considered necessary. Anglo-American agreement was already in existence on the principle of this strategy; the London conference had merely confirmed this previous decision. The COS clearly considered that discussion had only just begun.

Churchill also had his doubts over the 1942 'Sledgehammer' scheme, but he wrote later: 'I was however very ready to give "Sledgehammer" ... a fair run with other suggestions before the Planning Committees. I was almost certain the more it was looked at the less it would be liked.'[20] Very soon Churchill would begin to press for two alternatives for the current year: he would regain enthusiasm for operations against Norway, 'Jupiter', and for operations against French North Africa, 'Gymnast', or as later developed, 'Torch'. Ironically, an American first resurrected the idea of operations against French North Africa. Admiral Stark, outlining his views at the Combined Chiefs of Staff meeting on Tuesday, 21 April, declared he had always stressed the importance of the Middle East theatre. 'If it fell, the blockade of Germany would be broken, and it was, in addition, the one place, other than Russia, where the German army had been actively engaged.'[21]

Results of the London talks were therefore vague, ambiguous and dangerous for future Anglo-American understanding. Symbolically, a note was attached to the Minutes of the important Defence Committee meeting on the 14th: 'It should be noted that there has been no opportunity for those who attended the meeting to check the statements attributed to them. The Minutes should therefore not be quoted, but they should be regarded merely as giving a general indication of the course of discussion.'[22] The Americans had come away generally optimistic, just as the British had done from the Washington talks. The 1942 plans were, the Americans believed, firmly linked with the 1943 schemes – the document containing the US proposals was not split into two parts, one dealing with 1942 and the other for 1943. British agreement in principle for the 1943 offensive was taken to mean agreement for the document as a whole. The Americans were mistaken now, as the British had been after the Washington talks. Both times Churchill had used his oratory and his emotion and had seen a broad panoramic view of the future. But the Prime Minister's ability to cut through the tangle of everyday concerns in order to see the high peaks of Grand Strategy had to be matched by painstaking work by the COS, considering immediate realities. The partnership of far-seeing, colourful, inspiring War Leader and sober, professional COS worked well; but this time the balance had been upset by the arrival of Hopkins and Marshall. The Americans had presented an impressive vision of the future, and Churchill's exuberance had cloaked even his own hesitations.

Nevertheless, despite British doubts over 1942 plans, staff work would continue in London, first by the British alone, then with the Americans under Eisenhower. Immediately after the departure of the American delegation, the British COS approved a paper outlining next stages: consideration would be given to 'the conversion of the UK into an advanced base for operations in western Europe', to 'a series of raiding operations to be carried out during the summer of 1942' combined with an active air offensive over north-west Europe, to prospects for the capture of a bridgehead, and to a large-scale descent on western Europe in the spring of 1943. These points were listed in a report given to the War Cabinet on the 29th. But the Prime Minister emphasized at this meeting that 'while preparations should proceed on the basis that we should make a resolute effort to capture a bridgehead on the Continent in the late summer [of 1942], we were not committed to carrying out such an operation'. The War Cabinet agreed.[23] Planning did not mean agreement. General Marshall told the Combined Chiefs of Staff on 21 April that 'he had found the views of the British Chiefs of Staff were, almost, in complete accord with his own'. This sentence in the Minutes was given an addition, authorized by a corrigendum dated 22 April – 'regarding operations proposed for 1943'. The extra five words made a great deal of difference.[24]

Outside pressure had continued to mount. Disturbing news reached London on 20 April from General Dobbie, Governor of Malta. Back in March, Dobbie had reported the situation in the island as critical; now he declared: 'It has ... gone beyond that point, and it is obvious that the very worst may happen if we cannot replenish our vital needs, especially flour and ammunition and that very soon.... It is a question of survival.'[25] Further desperate attempts would have to be made to sail convoys through; meanwhile Ministers were becoming concerned about the effect of the strain on the 63-year-old Dobbie. On 21 April Churchill referred the War Cabinet to a telegram from the Middle East Defence Committee suggesting that 'Sir William Dobbie was in need of a rest, and proposing that a young and energetic civil Governor should be sent out to take his place,'[26] and a Defence Committee meeting on the 22nd agreed with the COS suggestion that Dobbie should be replaced by Lord Gort, commander of the BEF in France in 1939-40 and now Governor of Gibraltar.[27] Gort was informed of his new appointment in a cable from Churchill on the 25th; on the same day Roosevelt told Churchill that the US carrier *Wasp* would be able to make a second trip with Spitfires for Malta. And, on 9 and 10 May these newly arrived aircraft took to the air against enemy bombers with highly effective results: daylight raids on the island ceased. But the struggle to bring food and other essential supplies was to continue, and the Defence Committee had concluded on 22 April that the island was unlikely to be able to hold out beyond the end of June.[28]

Desperate attempts were being made to build up naval forces in the Indian Ocean; meanwhile Alexander's forces continued to withdraw through Burma, and Wavell continued to call for help. The COS told him on 16 April that they were doing all they could, but on 29 April he was informed that the two Australian brigades then temporarily in Ceylon would probably have to return to their country 'fairly soon' and two British and one East African brigade intended for the defence of the island might not be immediately available. Wavell retorted: 'The War Cabinet must really make up their minds whether or not they propose to defend India and Ceylon seriously.'[29] Churchill promised Wavell that the Australians would not be moved until the British reinforcements arrived – a presumptuous decision in view of the Australian Government's agreement for a 'temporary' loan of their units.[30]

This complication over troops for Ceylon resulted from a decision by the War Cabinet on 24 April for the launching of a new offensive operation, in turn stemming from the Japanese threat to the Cape-Middle East sea route. Plans had long been discussed for the seizure of Diego Suarez at the northern end of Vichy-controlled Madagascar to prevent the possibility of French permission for a Japanese submarine base. An expeditionary force had sailed from Britain on 23 March, on the understanding the operation could still be called off. On 20 April the War Cabinet had discussed recent changes in the Vichy Government, including the restoration of Laval, and fears had been expressed over taking provocative action, but four days later Churchill informed the War Cabinet that the convoy for the operation, 'Ironclad', had turned the Cape and all arrangements had been made for the plan to be carried out early in May by a force of two, or if necessary three brigades. These included men intended to replace the Australians at Ceylon. Churchill believed the change in the Vichy Government did not mean the operation should be cancelled, and Eden agreed. The Prime Minister added Roosevelt had been informed but 'preferred not to be openly associated'; Eden hoped the Americans would later make it clear 'they heartily concurred'. Ministers agreed the expedition should go forward.[31] Landings were scheduled for 5 May. The operation meant a further strain on shipping resources, and only two days before, when discussing Malta, the Defence Committee had had to take a drastic decision over naval dispositions, partly as a result of 'Ironclad'. Only six capital ships remained in the Home Fleet at Scapa Flow: the Defence Committee agreed these must stay in home waters, thus accepting the Admiralty view that this was 'the only area where the war can immediately be lost'. In view of other existing commitments, including 'Ironclad' and the Russian convoys, the next Malta convoy would have to be postponed until June – and the same Defence Committee meeting had also concluded that Malta was unlikely to survive beyond June at the latest.[32]

The situation concerning the PQ convoys to Russia was deteriorating: War Cabinet Ministers were told on Monday, 20 April that only eight ships of the outgoing convoy to Russia had arrived in Murmansk. One ship had been sunk, but 15 had turned back suffering ice damage. Those not badly damaged would be included in the next convoy, but the Vice-Chief of Naval Staff warned serious congestion was likely to occur if the Americans continued to send ships destined for Russia 'without regard to our capacity to convey them to their destination.... Further, the Americans were reported to be sending ships loaded with cargoes not of the first priority.'[33]

On Thursday afternoon, 23 April, Churchill delivered his fourth major speech to the Commons sitting in secret session; his address, almost 10,000 words, was one of the longest, most revealing and gloomiest given by the Prime Minister during the war. He described the fall of Singapore, and he revealed the startling news that in seven weeks a third of Britain's battleships and battle cruisers had been lost or crippled; he made no attempt to minimize the Japanese victories, nor the desperate position in the Indian Ocean area. 'No one will accuse me of glossing over with a smooth and thin veneer the ugly realities of our situation.' Harold Nicolson wrote: 'It is a long and utterly remorseless catalogue of disasters and misfortune. And as he tells us one thing after another, gradually the feeling rises in the packed House. "No man," Members begin to feel in their hearts, "no man but he could tell us of such disasters and increase rather than diminish confidence."'³⁴ Churchill put emphasis on the difficulties of aid to Russia: 'Our northern convoys are a task of enormous difficulty and hazard.... We convoy not only our own contribution but that of the United States, which to a large extent, is taken from what the United States would otherwise have given us.' And he warned: 'There is a further serious complication – the *Tirpitz*, the *Scheer* and the *Hipper* lie in Trondheim Fjord. Every British-American convoy to Russia is liable to attack by swift, heavy, modern German surface ships.' Across the Atlantic, Lord Beaverbrook also made a speech this Thursday. All help should be given to Russia, he now thundered. A Second Front in Western Europe would provide an opportunity 'to bring the war to an end here and now.... Strike out to help Russia! Strike out violently – strike even recklessly.' Beaverbrook, who had lunched with Roosevelt and Hopkins the previous day, continued his exortation for immediate operations to help the Soviets and added: 'Communism under Stalin had produced the most valiant fighting army in Europe.... Communism under Stalin has produced the best generals.'

The triangular relationship between Washington, London and Moscow was passing through a sensitive period. Next day, 24 April, Eden reported to the War Cabinet on discussions with the Ministers of Production and War Transport and the First Lord of the Admiralty, concerning an approach to America over supplies to Russia. The Americans would be asked to regulate sailings and to ensure ships only carried high priority supplies for the moment. Eden warned that 'the present cycle of convoys would have to be reduced, and the utmost which could be managed was six convoys in two months. The number of ships in each convoy must be restricted to 25.... A request should be made, at the very highest level, for increased Russian assistance in the defence of the convoys.' Parallel with discussions on convoys were negotiations for an Anglo-Soviet treaty and for the visit of Molotov to London and Washington. Churchill revealed latest embarrassing developments to the War Cabinet at this 24 April meeting. Roosevelt had received a cordial message from Stalin, who was sending Molotov and a general to visit Washington, and the President had suggested on 22 April that they should visit America before coming to England. Roosevelt wanted to discuss the American proposals for operations against Europe as a Second Front effort. But Churchill referred to a telegram, also dated 22 April, containing a personal message from Stalin to himself, and agreeing to Molotov's visit to London; Churchill commented that it was clear Stalin intended Molotov to visit Britain before going to America. 'It was important to ensure that we so handled matters as to avoid giving offence either to the United States or to Russia.' Churchill therefore thought that 'the right line would be to say to the United States that as Stalin was proposing to send Molotov to visit us, we could not refuse, but that it was important that Molotov should go to the United States before any irrevocable decisions had been taken here'. Eden and Cripps suggested the negotiations for the treaty should be taken to a point at which substantial agreement had been reached, after which Molotov would travel to America and return to London on his way home. The War Cabinet agreed.[35] This, substantially, was the procedure which eventually took place, but it failed to prevent further complications.

Churchill cabled Hopkins on the 26th to warn him of PQ convoy restrictions. On the same day PQ 15 sailed from Iceland, comprising 25 merchantmen; two days later the homeward convoy, QP 11, left Russia. Also on the 28th, Churchill received a cable from Roosevelt concerning the proposed convoy reductions. 'I am greatly disturbed by your cable to Harry [Hopkins], because I fear not only the political repercussions in Russia, but even more the fact that our supplies will not reach them promptly. We have made such a tremendous effort ... to have them blocked except for most compelling reasons seems to be a serious mistake.' Three days later Roosevelt signalled: 'Admiral King is communicating with Pound today about the urgent necessity of getting one more convoy in May in order to break the log jam of ships already loaded or being loaded.' On 1 May the battleship *King George V*, one of the precious capital ships remaining in the Home Fleet, rammed the destroyer *Punjabi* in thick fog, and the destroyer's depth-charges exploded as she sank, damaging the battleship. Churchill replied to Roosevelt on 2 May: 'With very great respect, what you suggest is beyond our power to fulfil.... I beg you not to press us beyond our judgment in this operation.... I can assure you, Mr President, we are absolutely extended, and I could not press the Admiralty further.' A terse answer came from Roosevelt next day: 'It is now essential for us to acquiesce in your views regarding Russian convoys, but I continue to hope that you will be able to keep convoys of strength of 35 ships.'[36] As the War Cabinet had been informed a week before, the Admiralty had already decided on a 25-ship maximum; nevertheless Churchill felt able to tell Ministers next day, Monday 4 May: 'Our position has been fully explained and the President has now agreed to our proposals.'[37] Anxious signals now started to come from the other direction: Stalin asked on the 6th for the sailing in May of the '90 steamers loaded with various important war materials' which were 'bottled up at present'. Churchill told the

War Cabinet on the 11th he had cabled a reply emphasizing the heavy risks involved; this signal, despatched on the 9th, had added: 'I am sure that you will not mind my being quite frank and emphasizing the need for increasing the assistance given by the USSR naval and air forces.' The appeal would meet with limited response, and Ministers were also informed on the 11th that 'there were indications that our difficulties in protecting convoys to Russia were likely to increase'.[38]

Further complications had arisen in the Anglo-Russian treaty negotiations. The British draft, handed to Maisky on 13 April, had shown willingness to grant Stalin's request for recognition of the 1941 frontiers, but had specified there should be a joint statement safeguarding the Polish frontier question. Russian counter-proposals were received from Maisky on 1 May: these sought a secret protocol concerning Russo-Finnish and Russo-Roumanian pacts of 'mutual assistance', and they made no mention of the safeguard for the Polish frontier issue. Eden complained to Maisky on the 5th that the Russians 'invariably raised their price at every meeting'.[39] Negotiations shuddered to a standstill. But on the 5th the Ambassador had raised another Anglo-Soviet question which had been causing considerable difficulty in War Cabinet discussions – and which had once again increased the possibility of gas warfare.

As early as 18 March Churchill had reported to the Defence Committee of rumours of possible German intentions to use gas in Russia, and he had revealed a suggestion by Eden that he, Churchill, might send a message to Stalin saying 'if the Germans initiated the use of gas against the Russians we would immediately retaliate on the civilian population of Germany'. Churchill had added that 'we could also offer publicly to state this fact in advance if Stalin thought it advisable'. Portal had told the meeting that 'our dropping capacity was a good deal greater than that of the Germans', and the Defence Committee had agreed with Eden's suggestion; Stalin was informed.[40] But one aspect of the situation had been overlooked and was brought to the Committee's attention on 17 April: a COS report showed Britain might be at a considerable disadvantage if gas warfare began – Japan might begin to use gas against India. The Committee agreed that 'we could clearly not escape from the commitment already made, although it might be possible to withdraw from the intention to make a public announcement. In view of the fact that the Japanese were now in a position to use gas on advantageous terms against India, where no serious preparations were possible, it was thought that the matter might be reopened with the Russians.'[41] This embarrassing situation was explained to the War Cabinet on the 31st, and another factor had now to be taken into account: the disadvantage of gas warfare if British troops were engaged on the Continent under the new American proposals.[42] Eden told the War Cabinet on the 7th that Maisky had asked him on the 5th for the date when the British were going to make their promised declaration; Eden had replied that 'the position had, on investigation, proved to be more complicated than it had seemed when the Prime Minister had spoken to the Ambassador'. Ministers were told that 'the Ambassador had been considerably distressed'. In discussion, Ministers believed 'the Japanese were unlikely to be influenced in a decision whether or not to use gas by events in Europe ... if they thought that the use of gas was in their interests, they would use it'. The Minutes continued: 'As regards this country, while gas warfare would probably result in difficulties for a few days, our anti-gas precautions could be regarded as satisfactory.' The War Cabinet therefore decided the balance was in favour of a public declaration.[43] Churchill accordingly announced that if the Germans used gas on the Russian front the RAF would take immediate reprisals.

The Second Front movement gained momentum and stridency: the *Daily Express* began organizing mass meetings; a Second Front demonstration in Trafalgar Square was attended by over 50,000 people. Churchill bravely welcomed the agitation as an indication of 'the militant, aggressive spirit of the British nation'. In turn, pressure on the COS and planners steadily increased, and on Friday, 1 May, Churchill had presented the COS with an updated version of his own mini-Second Front scheme – landings in Norway. 'High strategic and political importance must be attached thereto. It may be all that we have to offer to the Russians.' Target for 'Jupiter' would be the two airfields used by the enemy in northern Norway. 'If we could gain possession of these airfields and establish an equal force there not only would the Northern sea route to Russia be kept open, but we should have set up a Second Front.... If the going was good we could advance gradually southward, unrolling the Nazi map of Europe from the top.'[44] Churchill was to find the COS extremely unresponsive.

The COS were meanwhile devoting many hours to the American proposals for cross-Channel operations in 1942; as Portal stated in a paper dated 2 May: 'No one can say now whether or not we shall be able to undertake "Sledgehammer" this summer,' but a clear directive and target date had nevertheless to be issued to Force Commanders in case it became 'strategically and politically essential to land on the Continent', i.e. as a sacrifice.[45] The COS were also increasingly involved with the Middle East. The scheduled date for the offensive was still 15 May; a cool reception was therefore given to a signal from the Cairo commanders, dated 3 May, which suggested that in view of dangers to India the right policy might be to stand on the defensive in the Middle East until the summer. This cable was discussed on the 4th, when Churchill seemed disinclined to give it undue attention – according to Brooke: 'He was in good form and said he felt elated, I think probably mainly with excitement at thought of attack on Madagascar.'[46] Also on the 4th, Hitler issued new orders for the Mediterranean operations: the attack on Malta was to be postponed until mid-July; priority would be given to an offensive against Tobruk – which was to be completed by 20 June.

The Madagascar operation began at 4.30 a.m., 5 May, and reports reaching London during the day described excellent progress: the Vichy French, although resisting, had been taken by surprise. Churchill cabled Cairo: 'We hope today to occupy Diego Suarez,' and he said that although the next two months would no doubt be very dangerous in the Indian and Pacific Oceans, the Japanese 'cannot do everything at once.... We know of no special grounds for assuming that a heavy invasion of India is at this moment imminent or certain.' The Prime Minister's optimism had therefore returned, and he concluded: 'All our directions ... remain unaltered in their purpose and validity, and we trust you will find it possible to give full effect to them about the date which you mentioned to the Lord Privy Seal [15 May].'[47]

'The Americans seem to be taking a long time to get into their swing,' complained Brooke in a private letter to Wavell on this Tuesday, 'and their share of the war at sea is not very conspicuous yet. This is what worries me most.' The CIGS added: 'The process of trying to control the Prime Minister's actions is fraught with difficulties and uncertainties.'[48] The CIGS presumably had in mind Churchill's 'Jupiter' plan for Norwegian landings; and a German report completed this same day warned sufficient Allied forces were available for creating a 'Second Front' in Norway, France or elsewhere, but insufficient shipping would probably restrict planning.[49] In Washington, possible German intentions were being discussed by the Combined Chiefs of Staff: Eisenhower outlined a report by Colonel Ratte, recently US Military Attaché in Bucharest and Lisbon and an expert on German military affairs; Ratte estimated that the strength of the German forces was now greater than ever, and he was convinced that 'the Germans would attack England this spring. They would not attack either in Russia or the Middle East and would use only from 100 to 125 divisions to hold the Russian front. The Germans had trained vast numbers of airborne troops and he (Ratte) estimated that in a maximum of 3-5 days between 200,000 and 250,000 German airborne troops could be landed in England.... This would be followed by a strong air attack and a seaborne landing.'[50] Eisenhower apparently failed to mention that if this estimate were correct, the British would need all the troops they could muster at home, and the Germans would presumably be able to deploy a similar kind of strength to meet an allied cross-Channel attempt. But next day, 6 May, General Marshall recognized the need for full American assistance to Britain if the agreements reached in London were to be honoured: 'We must remember that this operation for 1942 depends primarily upon British forces and not our own. They have far more at stake than we and are accepting very grave hazards to which our own risks are not comparable.'[51]

Churchill's elation, noticed in recent days by Brooke, suddenly vanished. A cable arrived from Auchinleck on the 7th. The date settled so laboriously for the start of the desert offensive had been thrown back again, from 15 May to at least 15 June. The Cairo C-in-Cs claimed that to start before would incur risk of heavy tank losses and might bring only partial success; a reversal would have disastrous consequences. Moreover, even the 15 June date might have to be put back to August, should a fresh Italian armoured division arrive in the battle zone before the target date. And if aircraft had to be diverted to Turkey or to the Northern front, plans for an offensive might have to be scrapped completely.[52] Brooke was summoned to Churchill's bedside and found the Prime Minister 'in one of his dangerous moods': Auchinleck must be recalled, stormed Churchill, and General Alexander sent to Cairo from Burma. Brooke feared that in Churchill's upset state 'he might well take some wild decision which it would then be very hard to wean him from', yet the CIGS had himself been severely disturbed by Auchinleck's signal, especially by the apparent disregard for Malta, and almost two months before Brooke had noted: 'It is very exhausting, this continual protecting of Auchinleck.'[53] Churchill demanded that the matter should be considered by the COS and War Cabinet next day, 8 May, and he was only slightly restored to good humour by continuing reports of progress in the Madagascar operation: by 11 a.m. on the 7th all fighting had ceased and the base was secure against Japanese encroachment; Churchill claimed Operation 'Iron-clad' was valuable as a boost to morale: 'It was in fact for long months the only sign of good and efficient war direction of which the British public were conscious.'[54] But by now the Japanese considered the Indian Ocean as a backwater; furthest limits of expansion had already been reached. And while the last stages of the British capture of Diego Suarez were taking place on 7 May, an infinitely more significant and dramatic operation was beginning in the Pacific; Corregidor fell on the 6th and a Japanese invasion force entered the Coral Sea from the east, aiming at Port Moresby in New Guinea. American vessels under Admiral Fletcher moved to intercept, and US-Japanese carriers clashed in the Battle of the

Coral Sea on 7 and 8 May. The Americans rightly claimed victory. For the first time the Japanese had been met head-on and had been defeated, and the effect was invigorating – although not until after the Battle of Midway Island would the loss of the US carrier *Lexington* be revealed. Relief felt in Australia did not however end the requests for reinforcements: Dr Evatt, Australian Foreign Minister, pleaded with the COS on the 12th for all possible help to spare his country from the terrors of invasion.[55]

Apart from 'Ironclad' the British had still to reveal their merits, and Auchinleck seemed determined to keep them hidden. Churchill read his signal to the astonished War Cabinet at 3 p.m. on the 8th, and the Prime Minister said he had sent an interim reply ordering preparations to be continued for an offensive on or about 15 May, pending War Cabinet consideration of the General's message. Brooke then revealed his own impatience with the Middle East Commander. The telegram did not deal with two very important factors, said the CIGS; first, 'the bearing which operations in Cyrenaica would have on the Malta situation, secondly, the possibility of German offensive action, which by all indications might take place at the end of May'. The CIGS handed round a paper setting out the present order of battle in Libya: 'on the best estimates available' the British army in North Africa would have 566 tanks on 1 June, excluding infantry tanks, whereas the enemy would have 521; on 15 June the figures would be 748 and 590 respectively. Brooke said that the COS did not think Auchinleck should be given a direct order to attack on 15 May; 'at the same time the COS thought it would be right to tell General Auchinleck that his attack should be carried out in such a way as to provide the maximum support for the convoy to Malta in the June dark period'. Ministers were asked to give their views, and all agreed the attack would be better launched in late May. Churchill showed himself surprisingly mild. 'Battles were not won by arithmetical calculations of the strength of the opposing forces. From this point of view, the telegram of 6 May was somewhat disappointing and difficult to understand.' He thought the C-in-Cs, Cairo, should be told that the War Cabinet wanted an attack to take place in the latter half of May, but the telegram should not give Auchinleck a positive order. Brooke suggested that the telegram might also give the War Cabinet's agreement to a counter-stroke in the event of a German offensive in early June. A telegram was drafted by Churchill and immediately despatched.[56]

An answer came next day from the Middle East Defence Committee, now chaired by Casey. Malta had already been 'neutralized', claimed the Committee, and the fall of the island would therefore have little effect on the enemy's position in North Africa, nor would it necessarily be fatal to the security of Egypt. Moreover, even if a desert offensive were launched in May, problems of supply would probably delay the operation of aircraft to assist Malta from landing grounds near Benghazi until July. 'To launch an offensive with inadequate armoured forces', continued the signal, might well 'result in the almost complete destruction of these troops,' hence endangering Egypt. An early enemy offensive might well favour the British in their present position. Cairo was still determined to delay the offensive until at least 15 June; clearly the stubborn Auchinleck would either have to be replaced or given way to, or a compromise reached. His replacement had been made more difficult by the backing given from the Middle East Defence Committee. The COS, meeting during the afternoon of the 10th, attempted a compromise, described by Brooke to the War Cabinet meeting at 6 p.m. 'It was true that in the last offensive it had been five and a half weeks before we had reached Benghazi. But if we started an offensive this in itself would prove a diversion which would be of material help to the June convoy to Malta.' The COS had decided the conclusion to be drawn from the latest Cairo telegram 'was that the C-in-C, Middle East, did not realize the importance of Malta'. Brooke added that 'the security of Malta was vital and the latest date which our attack should be launched, unless it was launched earlier as a counter offensive, should be whatever date was suitable to provide a diversion or distraction which would assist the passage of a convoy to Malta in the June dark period.' The War Cabinet agreed and a telegram sent.[57] Auchinleck would take nine days to reply.

Rumours began to reach London of a new German campaign about to open in Russia: War Cabinet Ministers were informed next afternoon, 11 May, that 'a German attack launched in the Crimea on 8 May might be the prelude to an offensive in the south. It had been thought that the main drive would be in that sector, and there were some indications of troop movements to the south.'[58] A major offensive would increase Stalin's demands for supplies, and, if launched in the south, would increase apprehension in the Middle East over German moves down through the Caucausus. And increasing pressure from the Soviets would accelerate the demand for a Second Front. Churchill was still casting his mind for possible diversionary operations; also on 11 May he presided over a COS meeting called to discuss a suggestion he had made for a landing in Alderney. The Chiefs were unresponsive.[59]

Next day, according to the prime proponent of the Second Front, Beaverbrook, Churchill cabled Hopkins with a request to submit Beaverbrook's name to the President as British Ambassador in Washington, an appointment which the former Minister of Production had long sought. This request, also described by Hopkins in his memoirs but not by Churchill, involved Halifax's return to London to become Leader of the House of Lords. No reference to the idea is to be found in the War Cabinet files, nor was the scheme carried through, but Hopkins had an idea of Churchill's motives: 'The naming of Beaverbrook as Britain's Ambassador following his statements would be in effect another form of commitment to the Second Front.'[60] If Churchill's aim was to link his Government more firmly with the Second Front doctrine, definite military plans were all the more urgent. The Prime Minister's idea of an attack on Alderney was found unacceptable by the COS, but instead they gave approval on 13 May to another, more ambitious scheme carefully worked out by Combined Operations: an assault on Dieppe, Operation 'Rutter', involving a force of 10,000. Execution date was fixed for the end of June.[61] This COS approval was welcome news to the Prime Minister, but Churchill continued to chaff over inactivity in Egypt: the Middle East Defence Committee's intervention on Auchinleck's behalf had clearly caused displeasure; Churchill reminded Cairo on the 13th that the Committee had been set up as a means of bringing all parties together – 'it is not recognized as an entity having executive responsibility in operational questions'.[62]

On 13 May Stalin replied to Churchill's message of the 9th, which had promised as many merchantmen as possible would be taken to Russia but which had sought increased Soviet help. Stalin declared all possible measures would be taken to give this assistance, but added: 'It is necessary however to take into consideration the fact that our naval forces are very limited, and that our air forces in their vast majority are engaged at the battle-front.'[63] The last convoy, PQ 15, had lost three vessels in one heavy attack on the 3rd; two cruisers had also been lost. The next convoy was scheduled to leave on 18 May, but recent losses convinced the Admiralty that PQ 16 would suffer disastrous casualties and it was urged that sailings should be suspended. The COS agreed, but Churchill argued in a Minute dated 17 May: 'Not only Premier Stalin but President Roosevelt will object very much to our desisting from running the convoys now. The Russians are in heavy action, and will expect us to run the risk and pay the price.... The US ships are queuing up. My own feeling, mingled with much anxiety, is that the convoy ought to sail on the 18th. The operation is justified if a half gets through.'[64] Also on the 17th, Churchill sent a short signal to Auchinleck, who had still to reply to the cable ordering an offensive in time to distract enemy attention during the June dark-period convoy to Malta. The silence from Cairo was disconcerting; as Churchill wrote: 'We did not know whether he would accept or resign.' The

Prime Minister therefore cabled: 'It is necessary for me to have some account of your general intentions.'[65]

The War Cabinet discussed the PQ situation at 5.30 p.m. next day, 18 May; ships of PQ 16 were riding at anchor waiting to sail that night. Churchill began by putting the views expressed by the COS. 'With the ice barrier in its present position the convoy must sail for six or seven days within range of enemy bombers based in Norway. The Germans had about 100 bombers in this area.... The scale and duration of the air attack on the next two convoys would be likely to be greater than any yet experienced.' The COS therefore believed 'it would be expedient to cancel the convoys due to sail in May and June and increase the size of the convoys sailing after the beginning of July, when it would be possible to take a more northerly route'. The Admiralty would be prepared to take the risk of increasing the size of these postponed convoys to 50 ships. Some Ministers thought this number of ships would be too much for the Russian ports to handle. The suggestion was made that Stalin should be asked if the supplies now expected were in fact urgent, but the meeting felt that he would merely reply that the attempt should be made to force the convoys through. Churchill then declared that 'it was our duty to fight these convoys through, whatever the cost. The Russians were engaged in a life and death struggle against our common enemy.... In the last convoy, 22 out of 25 ships had got through, in spite of our apprehensions; this time we might again do better than we feared.' The War Cabinet decided the convoy should sail as arranged, and added that Stalin should be urged to provide additional air help.[66]

Ministers at this meeting were also told that General Alexander had now completed his brilliant withdrawal of up to 8,000 British and 30,000 Indian troops over the Burmese border into Assam. 'The road to India was barred,' commented Churchill, and the monsoon had broken out, ending land operations in Burma and north-east India for several months. Ministers heard other good news: intelligence reports now indicated the Germans were not after all intending to launch an offensive in the Crimea; indeed, the Russians had launched their own attack six days before in the Kharkov area.[67] Optimism was premature; next day, 19 May, the Germans counter-attacked, and the Germans were about to open their massive assault on Sebastopol, capital of the Crimea.

Another German offensive seemed imminent: Auchinleck replied to Churchill on the 19th and reported: 'There are strong signs that the enemy intends to attack us in the immediate future. If he does attack, our future action must be governed by the results of the battle and cannot be forecast now.' But the General also declared: 'My intention is to carry out the instructions of your message of

10 May.'[68] Churchill had now to face another barrage of criticisms in the House of Commons; on 19 and 20 May another debate took place on the Government's handling of the war. Members complained about the apparent inactivity of British forces, and the usual opponents remained prominent. 'Who decided to defend Crete?' asked Hore-Belisha. 'Who decided that Crete was defensible when the mainland had gone? Who decided that Singapore should be defended?' All the credit Churchill had managed to build up through his secret session speech on 23 April now seemed gone. Goebbels commented: 'Churchill's conduct of the war was attacked with exceptional vehemence.... It is nothing short of an enigma how this man can still be so popular.' The New York Times provided the answer: 'Without leadership of the kind he has given there would be no debate today in the Commons – certainly not the clamour of a militant England impatient to invade Europe.'

On 20 May Auchinleck sent a long despatch to Ritchie, commander of 8th Army, giving his assessment of Rommel's likely moves: he believed the German leader would attempt to smash through the central defence minefields while feinting south towards Bir Hacheim, and Auchinleck therefore urged Ritchie to keep the British armour massed in the centre. Ritchie on the other hand believed an enemy sweep south of Bir Hacheim to be more probable; General Willoughby Norrie, commander of 30 Corps, believed the main German attack would come in the north towards the coast. Also on the 20th, Rommel issued his orders: a feint in the centre, a diversion in the north, and a sweep to the south aiming first of all at Bir Hacheim. 'We realize that success cannot be guaranteed,' signalled a magnanimous Churchill to Auchinleck during the day. 'There are no safe battles.... We have full confidence in you and your glorious army, and whatever happens we will sustain you by every means in our power.' Churchill suggested Auchinleck should take command of 8th Army himself; Auchinleck declined.[69]

A small drab figure arrived in London on 20 May: Vyacheslav Molotov, People's Commissar of Foreign Affairs of the USSR – it had now, after all, been arranged he should visit London before Washington. The last time he had left Soviet soil had been to visit Hitler in Berlin. First talks began at 11.30 a.m. next morning, attended by Churchill, Attlee, Eden and Cadogan with Molotov and Maisky on the Russian side of the table. Discussions were described to the War Cabinet at 5.30 p.m. by Churchill and Eden. The Prime Minister said Molotov had come to negotiate over the Anglo-Soviet treaty and to discuss the Second Front; the Russians considered the latter to be most important, but debate during the day had mainly concentrated on the treaty question. No progress had been made in reconciling the British and Soviet drafts, with the Polish frontier issue remaining the chief stumbling-block. Churchill said a meeting would take place next morning, attended by the COS, to discuss the Second Front question. The First Sea Lord told the War Cabinet that the Russians had expressed great satisfaction at the decision to send the May convoy. 'The Russians were going to treat the arrival of this convoy as a special operation. Two hundred aircraft of the Red Army would be employed on protective measures and 50 bombers would attack the enemy aerodromes in northern Norway.'[70] Next morning Molotov immediately began by asking how the British Government considered the prospects of drawing off, in 1942, at least 40 German divisions from the Russians. The CIGS was flying back from inspecting an American training exercise in Northern Ireland, and Churchill therefore answered Molotov's awesome question: his reply was all Brooke could have wished. Britain's choice of a cross-Channel target was restricted to those few areas where the RAF could provide cover; plans were however being studied, continued Churchill, based on the assumption that the landing of successive waves of assault troops would bring about air battles which, if prolonged, would 'lead to the virtual destruction of the enemy's air power on the Continent'. With this achieved, landings could be made at other points along the coast, but, Churchill stressed, 'with all the best will and endeavour, it was unlikely that any move we could make in 1942, even if it were successful, would draw off large numbers of enemy land forces from the Eastern Front'. Britain already kept occupied considerable German strength: 11 Axis divisions in Libya, the equivalent of 8 in Norway and 25 in France and the Low Countries, totalling 44.[71] Churchill therefore refused to commit Britain to premature action; in return Molotov continued to prove stubborn over the Polish frontier issue.

Eden had already started to consider an alternative agreement, mentioned informally to Molotov on the evening of the 21st: a mutual assistance pact for 20 years, without reference to frontiers. According to Eden's memoirs, he informed the War Cabinet he intended to put this alternative idea to Molotov, but in fact no mention is made in the official Minutes on the 21st and no meetings were held between the 21st and 25th – Ministers had been given a few days' holiday over Whitsun. Eden's draft was handed to Maisky and Molotov on the afternoon of the 23rd. Initially the Soviet Foreign Ministers showed no enthusiasm, although he agreed to extend his stay in London. Also on the 23rd Brooke and Mountbatten spent three hours with Churchill, and however much the Prime Minister may have displayed caution with Molotov on the Second Front question, he now revealed considerable optimism. 'This meeting with Winston,' wrote Brooke, 'was typical of many others when all difficulties were brushed aside, and many unpleasant realities, such as resources available, were scrupulously avoided.'[72] But Molotov continued to meet with lack of official response over the subject of cross-Channel operations. He cabled Stalin for fresh instructions early on the 24th, Whit Sunday, and was probably told of latest reports of an imminent German offensive. Eden found him 'less unreceptive' at talks starting at 4 p.m. Molotov saw Winant, the American Ambassador, in the evening, and was informed a treaty on the lines of the original Russian proposal would probably make a bad impression in the United States; immediately afterwards Maisky telephoned Eden to say that Molotov was now ready to discuss the new British draft. A meeting was arranged for 3 p.m. next day, 25 May, later postponed to 10 p.m.[73]

Out in the bleak, windswept Arctic a single German aircraft droned monotonously round ships of convoy PQ 16, keeping outside effective range and sending regular reports of the convoy's position, course and speed. At 8.30 p.m. on the 25th twelve Junker dive-bombers approached from the east, peeling off from their formation to plunge whining down upon the ships. Two enemy aircraft were shot down, the rest disappeared again and the convoy sailed on. In London, Churchill, Eden, Molotov and Maisky were having a highly satisfactory conversation. The Prime Minister revealed his hopes for the Libyan operation and Molotov replied with some details of Soviet plans; and, by the time the gathering broke up late that night, Molotov said he had received authority to sign the British draft treaty. Arctic summer months were filled with perpetual light, and the sun was still shining over PQ 16. U-boats were prowling round the convoy, waiting for a gap in the anti-submarine screen, and just after 3 a.m. on the 26th the SS *Syros* suddenly exploded and sank within minutes. U-boats became bolder. Early on the 26th, with the convoy about 250 miles west-south-west of Bear Island, the cruiser escort had to leave, to place themselves between the convoy and the Norwegian coast should German surface ships venture out. PQ 16's anti-aircraft fire-power was thus seriously reduced: such was the shortage of suitable shipping that only two vessels remained which had the ability to engage the Junker dive-bombers before they swooped to attack. Anxiety mounted during this Tuesday; four days of steaming remained, and the most dangerous stretch had still to come.

Eden spent the morning of the 26th working on final details of the Anglo-Russian treaty, while the COS considered a progress report on 'Sledgehammer' planning presented by Douglas, Paget and Mountbatten: this selected a target area between Cherbourg and the River Canche, but the scheme was based entirely on the assumption that a crack in German morale had already become apparent.[74] A special War Cabinet meeting was called at 1 p.m. to be told of the Soviet treaty development. Approval for Eden's draft was willingly given.[75] Signature took place during the afternoon amidst loud mutual congratulations. 'Somehow the whole affair gave me the creeps,' wrote Brooke. Molotov prepared for his departure for Washington the following day; his London visit had failed to secure promise for a Second Front operation in 1942, but armed with the treaty, he hoped to do better in Washington. The War Cabinet held a second meeting at 6.45 p.m. 'Our relations with the USSR were now on an entirely different and far more satisfactory footing,' declared Churchill. 'The United States would be greatly pleased by the changed situation.' Ministers were told of the latest PQ 16 situation; Brooke also stated that in Libya 'there were indications that the enemy might launch an attack before the end of the month'.[76]

As Brooke spoke Rommel's tanks were already rolling forward, past dim lights concealed in petrol cans indicating the line of march south round the British positions. Soon after midnight the full German advance was underway: the Italian *Ariete* Division had been ordered to take Bir Hacheim at the southern end of the British line, while the Trieste Division plunged at the centre, leaving the *Afrika Korps* free to sweep deep south-east round Bir Hacheim to strike towards Tobruk. When the main engagement began next morning, 27 May, the British were once again caught off-guard. Far away to the north, PQ 16 was advancing apprehensively towards Soviet safety: three sailing days still remained, and now, on the 27th, the main ordeal began. Clouds lowered to 3,000 feet, allowing enemy aircraft to take up position unseen; aircraft screamed down from all sides. For three terrible hours during the afternoon the convoy battled helplessly against this multiple attack : two merchantmen were sunk, one of them an American, then six aircraft concentrated on the *Empire Lawrence* and all that remained of the 12,000 ton vessel was a wrecked lifeboat in a glistening pool of oil. Two more vessels suffered damage. The Polish destroyer *Garland* was swept by deadly fragments after a near miss had exploded three bombs just above her, and her decks were covered with maimed and slaughtered men; a Russian tanker was swept by fire, but struggled on. Another attack came at 5.20 p.m. and another at 7.45, and two more ships exploded and sank. Ammunition was now almost gone; men were dropping from exhaustion at their guns, and not until freezing fog fell next day were they allowed respite.

In London on the 27th the Prime Minister urged the COS to adopt his 'Jupiter' scheme : this, he said, would mean an end to the enemy aircraft raids on PQ convoys from the two vital North Norwegian airfields. The COS agreed to a detailed study. This meeting, which took place as Molotov flew to America on his mission to urge for a Second Front in 1942, revealed no hopes for 'Sledgehammer'. Attending the conference were Mountbatten and Paget; Churchill, with his talks with Molotov clearly in mind, asked what cross-Channel operation could be launched in 1942 if no decision was in sight on the Russian front – his question therefore removed the previous assumption of a 'Sledgehammer' operation only being undertaken in the event of a German collapse, or imminent Russian defeat. The Prime Minister was informed that in the face of un-impaired German resistance a bridgehead could not be secured, since there would be insufficient airborne forces to take coastal defences from the rear. Limited landing-craft resources would restrict the seaborne assault to about 4,300 men. Churchill admitted such a sacrifice would be of no help to the Russians; he was therefore not prepared to give way to 'popular clamour' for a Second Front in 1942 in view of the strong military arguments against such an operation.[77] So, although planning for 'Sledgehammer' would continue, the chances of the plan being acted upon were non-existent without a dramatic change in the situation – a Russian or German collapse. A clear hint of this was given in a message from Churchill to Roosevelt sent next day, 28 May: Mountbatten would soon leave for American talks, and Churchill told the President: 'Dickie will explain to you the difficulties of 1942.' The Prime Minister mentioned his 'Jupiter' scheme, but added: 'We must never let "Gymnast" pass from our minds. All other preparations would help, if need be, towards that.'

Churchill also told Roosevelt: 'Auchinleck's news tonight indicates that the battle in Libya has begun. This may be the biggest encounter we have ever fought.'[78] The battle was in fact hanging in fine balance. The *Afrika Korps*'s sweep to the south-east had dislocated British defences, but Bir Hacheim itself had still to be taken, and Rommel's supply link to his forward units was extremely vulnerable; the attempt by the Trieste Division to break through the centre minefields had still to be completed. Yet the British had still to obtain a firm grasp of the situation, and British armour was being wasted in small, unco-ordinated efforts. Rommel, seeing the danger to his supply link, ordered his armour to halt and concentrate. Fierce engagements throughout the 28th resulted in heavy losses for both sides, but Rommel's *Panzer* groups were gradually drawing together in the area between Sidra and Aslagh ridges – to be known thereafter as 'the Cauldron'. On the 29th he ordered the completion of gaps blown through the central minefields, and, during the next few days his units pulled back into these openings and plugged the gaps behind them with strong anti-tank artillery. Thus the British minefields became part of Rommel's defence; he prepared to strike again.

Although reports from Cairo were received with considerable optimism, the situation was ominous.

Molotov arrived in Washington on the 29th, and on the same day Roosevelt presented a list of supplies which would be sent to the Soviet Union by Britain and America after June 1942: as far as possible Britain and America would supply shipping for the portion of the programme which could not be carried in Soviet vessels.[79] Also on the 29th, Eden told the War Cabinet that talks were to be held on a recent Soviet demand for an increase in emergency supplies; he proposed that 'this matter should be dealt with on the basis of an increase of, say, 100 tanks in the number to be included in the next convoy (PQ 17) but of no increase in the number of fighter aircraft'.[80]

PQ 16 split into two groups during the 29th, and the Archangel section reached safety. The remaining vessels approached Murmansk next day; Russian destroyers had appeared on the 29th but only now, in the last stage, did Soviet aircraft arrive. The convoy filed into Kola Inlet, 'reduced in numbers, battered and tired, but still keeping perfect station', according to the Royal Naval escort commander. No more vessels had been lost since the 28th, although air attacks had continued: of the 35 ships which had started from Iceland, five had been sunk by bombing, one through a torpedo dropped by an aircraft and one through U-boat attack. The toll was far less than might have been expected in view of the savage and prolonged attacks; undue optimism now led to military disaster.

In Washington on this Saturday, 30 May, undue optimism was to lead to diplomatic conflict. Molotov asked Roosevelt the same question he had posed in London: could the Western Allies undertake offensive action in 1942 sufficient to draw off 40 German divisions? Churchill had not supplied a definite answer, explained Molotov, but had promised a more positive reply when he, Molotov, returned to London. He hinted that without a Second Front, Russia might collapse. Roosevelt asked Marshall whether developments were clear enough for Stalin to be told a Second Front was being prepared; when Marshall agreed, Roosevelt authorized Molotov to inform Stalin 'we expect the development of a Second Front this year'. Marshall did however stress transport difficulties. Next day, 31 May, Roosevelt held a discussion with Hopkins, Marshall and King on the final statement he was to make to Molotov; he wanted, he said, to declare something specific and at his last meeting with Molotov on 1 June the President repeated he expected to set up a Second Front in 1942, again despite Marshall's reluctance to mention the year and despite Churchill's telegram of 28 May mentioning difficulties in a 1942 operation. Nor were the British consulted, although they would have to provide the bulk of the forces; not until Molotov's return to

London on 9 June would Churchill be confronted by the stand taken by Roosevelt. Misunderstandings resulting from the Hopkins-Marshall mission to London in April were starting to have effect. On 1 June, the day Roosevelt gave this final optimistic message to Molotov, the COS in London were hearing further depressing evidence against 'Sledgehammer': Mountbatten, on the eve of his departure for Washington, told the COS that the launching of this operation would hinder preparations for the large-scale 1943 operation, owing to landing-craft shortages, and the same would apply to a small, hit and run raid for 1942, 'Imperator', which had recently been suggested.[81]

Also on 1 June the War Cabinet heard of excellent results from recent intensification of the bombing offensive. Cologne had been raided by 1,036 bombers two nights before; Eden told Ministers that Maisky had told him 'the raid had had very good morale effect in Russia'. Eden added: 'It was clear that, if these very large raids could be repeated periodically, this would have more effect on our allies than a sustained effort on lower scale.' That night massed bombers struck at Essen. Ministers were also assured at the 1 June meeting that the battle in Libya appeared favourable. 'The enemy was now endeavouring to withdraw through two gaps in our minefields. Although it was early to form a judgment, the situation appeared to be satisfactory.' Final losses in PQ 16 were revealed; Churchill warned that owing to plans for a convoy to Malta it would be necessary to postpone PQ 17. He thought consideration should be given to providing extra air cover for PQ 17.[82] This ill-fated convoy would eventually leave Iceland on 27 June.

General Eisenhower was far from satisfied with progress made on the build-up arrangements for American troops and supplies in Britain, termed Operation 'Bolero'. 'It's necessary to get a punch behind the job,' he reported from London on the 3rd, 'or we'll never be ready by Spring 1943 to attack. We must get going.' The report strengthened suspicions already growing among the American Joint Chiefs of Staff that Britain was not only reluctant to undertake 'Sledgehammer', but also 'Round-Up' for 1943. Churchill's cable to Roosevelt on the 28th had shown the Prime Minister was apparently considering diversionary operations far removed from the main point of frontal assault across the Channel.[83] Suspicions of British reluctance for 'Sledgehammer' were well founded – this reluctance had been present from the beginning; nor were suspicions entirely incorrect over the British attitude to 'Round-Up'. On 3 June, the same day that Eisenhower sent his report, Mountbatten arrived in Washington. 'What I had to do,' wrote Mountbatten later, 'was probably my most important task of the whole war. I had to try to persuade Roosevelt and his advisers that our entire strategy needed re-thinking.' Mountbatten believed 'Round-Up' would have to be put back to 1944. 'I was already reaching the conclusion that this would ... be the earliest date we could manage.'[84]

Gigantic naval forces were manoeuvring in the mid-Pacific on 3 June. Next morning, the Battle of Midway had begun. For the next 48 hours waves of Japanese and American aircraft would wrestle for naval supremacy in the Far East; and the US Navy regained the initiative. Pearl Harbour had been avenged; the offensive against Japan could begin. In the North Africa desert on the 4th and 5th the British lost their last chance on winning the continuing struggle south of Tobruk. An attempt to prise Rommel out of his position in the minefields failed; yet the seriousness of the situation was still not recognized in London. And in Washington the President was becoming increasingly attracted to the idea of 'Gymnast' in place of 'Sledgehammer' for 1942, although this plan for North African landings had first been proposed on the assumption that Rommel would be simultaneously driven back. The American Joint Chiefs and Stimson feared, in Mountbatten's words, 'that I had "put one over" on the President.... But the root of the problem didn't lie in personal preferences or differences of opinion. It lay in the inexorable realities.... Roosevelt was the first to grasp the point, and go on to the next question: what, then, *could* the British and Americans do in 1942?' 'Gymnast' provided the answer.[85] Mountbatten also had two meetings with the Combined Chiefs of Staff and gave full but noncommittal details of allied planning and training arrangements underway in Britain.[86]

Confusion had therefore replaced the clear-cut impressions which the Americans had gained as a result of the April talks in London. Roosevelt was veering towards North Africa, yet had made the dangerous statement to Molotov; Marshall and Stimson were determined 'Bolero' should result in the operations for which it was intended; Molotov was on his way to London, well-satisfied. Churchill was pressing for Norway and was meeting COS reluctance, and for 'Gymnast'. The COS again studied plans for 'Sledgehammer' and the smaller-scale 'Imperator', but concluded on 5 June that neither offered hope. On the 8th the COS approved a paper by Churchill: this ruled out the tip-and-run 'Imperator' scheme – 'it would be cited as another example of sentimental politics dominating the calm determination and common sense of professional advisers' – but the paper urged further study should be given to 'Sledgehammer'; the latter, however, would be based on two principles: '(a) No substantial landings in France unless we are going to stay. (b) No substantial landings in France unless the Germans are demoralized by another failure against Russia.' These conditions amounted to insuperable obstacles. Discussion also took place at this meeting on the 8th on Churchill's 'Jupiter' project for Norway; a draft appreciation had been prepared by the Joint Planners, and it seemed 10 airfields would have to be occupied in north Norway, not two as Churchill believed. Pound stressed that convoys to Russia would have to be stopped in order to fulfil shipping requirements for the operation. Churchill still refused to step down.[87]

Ministers at the War Cabinet meeting on the 9th were mistakenly informed that the Western Desert situation continued to be generally favourable. 'The German forces were about where they had been at the beginning of the week and must have suffered heavy casualties.'[88] A cheerful Molotov reached London during the day and dined with Churchill, Attlee and Eden; he immediately revealed Roosevelt's optimism over a Second Front in 1942. The Americans, he said, had suggested a reduction in the tonnage of supplies sent to Russia if this would make an operation more possible, and Moscow had agreed. Roosevelt, he continued, was willing to risk the sacrifice of up to 120,000 men in the first instance, despite the possibility of a 'second Dunkirk', but Molotov thought this total would be insufficient – 'a mere six or ten divisions would be ineffective'. Churchill immediately replied that Britain was preparing plans for six divisions to land in France that autumn, 'but whether it were to be actually attempted or not must depend on the situation when the time comes'. The Prime Minister was puzzled by the American suggestion that reduced supplies to Russia might help 'Sledgehammer'. 'It was not a question of providing large vessels such as those used in the Russian convoys, but of special landing craft. . . . He did not see how the President's proposal to cut Russian tonnage requirements would help towards the solution of the problem involved in effecting a landing on a highly fortified strip of coast.' Churchill might well have asked where the 120,000 troops were coming from that Roosevelt was prepared to see sacrificed: the Marshall Memorandum had declared that only two and a half American divisions would have been sent to England by 15 September. Instead, Churchill made a statement almost as foolhardy as Roosevelt's reference to 1942: 'British and American armies were fully resolved to invade the Continent in 1943 to the strength perhaps of 40-50 divisions.'[89] Molotov had referred Churchill to a communiqué drafted by himself and agreed by Roosevelt but so far unpublished: 'In the course of the conversations full understanding was reached with regard to the urgent tasks of creating a Second Front in Europe in 1942.' The British were obliged to agree to this joint statement – as Eden pointed out: 'We could not give the enemy the comfort of conflicting communiqués.' But Churchill handed Molotov an *aide-mémoire* the following evening, 10 June: although preparations were being made for a cross-Channel landing in August or September 1942, size would be limited by landing-craft shortage and 'it would not further either the Russian cause or that of the Allies as a whole if ... we embarked on some operation which ended in disaster and gave the enemy an opportunity for glorification at our discomfiture.... We can therefore give no promise.'

Churchill explained the delicate situation to the War Cabinet next morning, 11 June. He claimed the *aide-mémoire* had been 'well-received' by Molotov; the Prime Minister then gave a broad outline of possible Second Front operations. These were divided into three categories, he said: those for the immediate future, those for Autumn 1942, and those for 1943. In the first category came the proposed Dieppe raid, 'Rutter'; in the second came 'Sledgehammer', which, Churchill repeated, 'was entirely dependent on the situation on the Russian front and was only considered to be practicable if German morale had started to crack'. Two months would be needed to assemble shipping, and September would be the last month in which it could be carried out, owing to deteriorating weather conditions. Churchill said he had made no commitment to 'Sledgehammer' in his talks with Molotov. 'The conditions in which we might undertake the operation had been clearly explained and understood.... It seemed unlikely that these conditions would obtain, but it was clearly right that all preparations for the operation should go ahead.' Plans for 'Imperator' had been cancelled. In the 1943 category came 'Round-Up', but Churchill warned: 'The operation would probably not be begun at the date contemplated in the original Marshall plan, i.e. 1 April 1943. It was unlikely that the American forces would be trained in time. Some hold-up in training would be occasioned by the preparations for "Sledgehammer" and the weather would be much better a little later in the spring.' Ministers agreed that 'Round-Up' should not take place before 1 May, when, according to Churchill, nearly 50 per cent more landing-craft would be available. The Prime Minister turned to 'Jupiter': 'as it was unlikely that "Sledgehammer" would take place, it was all the more important to give careful study to what could be done in this strategically important area', and he asked the COS to give the idea 'earnest consideration'. No mention was made at the meeting of 'Gymnast' or French North Africa.[90]

Also on this Thursday the attempt began to relieve besieged Malta. The operation comprised an approach from the west with a convoy of six merchantmen and a powerful escort of three cruisers, one battleship, two carriers and 17 destroyers; at the same time an approach would be made from the east by 11 merchantmen and a strong escort of cruisers and destroyers. All went well for the first three days. Meanwhile, Rommel had gradually been extending his position from the 'Cauldron': Bir Hacheim had been taken on the

10th; by the evening of the 11th Rommel was in the El Adem area, and fierce fighting during the 11th and 12th led to German superiority over surviving British armour. As late as 11 June Churchill had complimented Ritchie on his 'dogged and resolute fighting' and the Prime Minister had believed that the prolonged battle must wear down the *Afrika Korps* faster than the 8th Army. In London on the 12th the situation was seen as confused and increasingly alarming, but not yet disastrous. Churchill spent much of the day studying Mountbatten's report on his Washington discussions; the conclusions seemed puzzling. Mountbatten had been told by the President that he 'wished to remind the Prime Minister of the agreement reached the last time he was in Washington, that in the event of things going very badly for the Russians this summer, a sacrifice landing would be carried out in France'. No reference to such a 'sacrifice' appeared in the printed report of the Washington discussions. The President had emphasized he was not prepared to send a million troops to England on the off-chance of 'Round-Up' taking place in the spring of 1943, and had to have a guarantee that they would be given a chance to fight, whatever happened in Russia.[91] At the same time, Roosevelt had been 'very struck' by Churchill's reminder of 'Gymnast'. A clear need had developed for Anglo-American consultation at the highest level; Churchill therefore telephoned Brooke the following evening, Saturday, 13 June, and told him he was thinking of starting for Washington on the Thursday next. 'He considered Roosevelt was getting a little off the rails,' wrote Brooke.[92]

Rommel's units suddenly stabbed forward again. Pressure was put on the position in the centre of the battle-area, known as Knightsbridge, which had served as a pivot of manoeuvre for the British armour, and, during the night of 13-14 June the occupying Guards Brigade was forced to withdraw with heavy tank losses. Rommel was left in control of the battlefield; British armour had been slashed to about 50 cruiser and 20 Infantry tanks. Withdrawal of the 8th Army began to accelerate, with Ritchie even signalling to Auchinleck that Tobruk might have to be temporarily abandoned: he intended to withdraw to the Egyptian frontier. Instead, Auchinleck ordered a line to be held from Acroma – El Adem – El Gubi, running south-east between the *Afrika Korps* and the port. This confusion was reflected in signals to and from London. 'To what position does Ritchie want to withdraw?' cabled Churchill to Auchinleck in the afternoon of the 14th. 'Presume there is no question in any case of giving up Tobruk.'[93] Another flow of signals came from the Middle East, this time to the Admiralty: the Malta convoys were running into increasing opposition. The western section suffered the loss of one merchant ship during the 14th, and a cruiser disabled; the heavy covering force had to withdraw during the evening as the convoy approached the Narrows off Sardinia. The eastern section received reports that the main enemy fleet had left Taranto to intercept, and British efforts to stop this fleet failed on the 15th; the convoy had to turn back for Egypt in the face of this overwhelming threat, having lost a cruiser, three destroyers and two merchant ships. The western section lost one destroyer and three merchant ships during the 15th. Only two merchantmen out of the 17 from east and west thus reached Malta on the evening of the 15th.

The War Cabinet therefore had an extremely depressing session at 5.30 p.m. on the 15th. Churchill had received apparent confirmation that Tobruk would be held, but Ritchie had clearly been outgeneralled by Rommel. Ministers were told the Germans had started a 'definite offensive' in the Kharkov area; an offensive in the Kursk sector was also expected, but the enemy seemed to be suffering heavy casualties in the assault on Sebastopol. Reference was made to the German destruction of the whole village of Lidice in Czechoslovakia, with all men killed and women and children taken away. 'The question was raised,' stated the minutes, 'whether, as an act of counter-retaliation, we should destroy a number of German villages by air attack. The main point made in discussion was that such action could only be carried out effectively by a considerable number of aeroplanes, on a clear moonlight night. Action on the lines suggested would therefore mean the use of forces which would otherwise be employed against objectives of greater importance.' Ministers decided against the idea. The meeting also heard a report by the Minister of Information, which showed 'a rising tide of optimism about the war' had been detected among the public. The War Cabinet decided: 'This should be allowed to run its course and Ministers should confine themselves to avoiding any public statements likely to reinforce it.'[94]

Churchill was anxious to start on his Washington voyage and told Brooke on the 15th that he would like to leave next day at 11 a.m., then changed his mind, and on the morning of the 17th the decision was taken to leave that night. A note was carried from 10 Downing Street to Buckingham Palace. 'Sir, In case of my death on this journey I am about to undertake, I avail myself of Your Majesty's gracious permission to advise you that you should entrust the formation of a new Government to Mr Anthony Eden....'[95] Churchill had decided he would risk flying to America, encouraged by his flight back from Bermuda the previous January – even though the first ferry-service across the North Atlantic had only been initiated by the RAF in the winter of 1940. The Prime Minister travelled to Stranraer and his Boeing flying-boat left at 11.30 p.m.

on the 17th. Departure had been delayed to avoid German aircraft patrolling the Western Approaches. The Prime Minister, dressed in his siren-suit and slippers, with gold-topped malacca cane, and black Homburg hat tilted on the back of his head, sat in the co-pilot's seat for the first two hours; Brooke noted: 'PM in tremendous form and enjoying himself like a schoolboy.' Churchill's recollection was more sombre; he sat 'revolving problems and thinking of the anxious battle'. The enemy was closing in on Tobruk; El Adem had been taken, and now Gambut to the east of the port, thus cutting the coastal road and completing Tobruk's isolation. The weary 8th Army was demoralized and suffering from disintegration; the *Afrika Korps*, equally weary, was stimulated by the sweet smell of success. Yet hopes for Tobruk remained high in Cairo and in London; Churchill was confident this port, so valuable as a forward base and for prestige, would be held. Very different problems lay ahead of Churchill's shuddering flying-boat: the Second Front, and eventually far more important, collaboration over 'Tube Alloys' – atomic bombs. Churchill wrote: 'The fact that the War Cabinet decided that I should leave the country and London with the Chief of the Imperial General Staff and General Ismay at the height of the Desert battle measures the importance of the grave strategic issues which were upon us.'[96] To be accurate, no reference is contained in the records of the War Cabinet having been consulted.

A Strategy Settled

Churchill's flying-boat landed on the Potomac, Washington, on 18 June; in Moscow, Molotov reported on his American trip to an Extraordinary session of the Supreme Soviet, and his listeners were delighted by news of an imminent Anglo-American Second Front. Next day Churchill flew to the Roosevelt family home at Hyde Park, above the Hudson, leaving Brooke and Ismay to start strategic discussions.

General Brooke believed objections to 'Sledgehammer' to be overwhelming, but full support should be given to the movement of US troops and equipment to Britain under Operation 'Bolero', to give the Western area continued priority over the Far East and prepare the way for an eventual 'Round-Up', meanwhile providing flexibility. This flexibility might even allow 'Gymnast' to be undertaken – but only if the Libyan position was restored. The CIGS had previously supported this idea for landings in French North Africa. But at that time, in late 1941, the British hold on Libya had been strong: Rommel had been forced back. A push by the 8th Army, and allied landings behind the Germans in French Africa, would seem a logical combination. The situation had now changed. The Japanese had advanced; the Germans had launched an offensive in the Crimea and threatened to sweep down upon the Middle East from the north; above all, Rommel had pushed forward and the 8th Army was reeling. While plans for 'Gymnast' must remain on the files, the reasons for its abandonment in January were now even more valid: precious shipping and resources must not be directed to one end of the Mediterranean when strength was needed to defend the other; all available reinforcements might have to be rushed round the Cape to protect Egypt and the Iranian oil supplies. Brooke therefore approached these crucial talks with the conviction that 'Sledgehammer' must be scrapped, but the Americans must not be allowed to turn their backs on the West as a result. 'Bolero' must be continued; on the other hand he agreed with the US Joint Chiefs that for the moment 'Gymnast' was probably out of the question, under existing circumstances.

The CIGS addressed the CCS at 12.30 p.m. on 19 June. He began warily, explaining various plans and difficulties involved but avoiding stating specific dislikes or preferences. 'The crux of the matter was the degree of reliance we could place on the Russian front holding.' If the Russians held, chances of a successful operation on the Continent in 1943 were good and the Middle Eastern position would be relieved. 'If, on the other hand, Russia collapsed, the establishment of a front in France would at first be difficult and further reinforcements, necessitating a strain on our shipping, would have to be sent to the Middle East.' A Russian collapse might mean the consideration of some form of 'Gymnast', if some form of western front was considered important, but Brooke warned of the strain on shipping to undertake and maintain such an operation. The CIGS then listed various operations which the COS had been considering to relieve pressure on the Russians in 1942. A landing in the Pas de Calais area had been studied, and a maximum of about six divisions could be found for this operation, 'but it was not thought that this force would be sufficient to divert appreciable German land forces from the Eastern front. Subsequent maintenance of the force through the ports of Calais and Boulogne would be difficult.' Purely air operations over the Continent had not achieved the hoped-for air battles. A bridgehead in the Brest salient had the advantages of a good port and a sufficiency of space – but would need a force of some 15 divisions. Further raids on a large-scale had been planned, including a raid to last two or three days, but the difficulties of landing in the Pas de Calais area would necessitate this raid taking place further to the west on the outskirts of the area covered by fighter protection. Operations in North Norway had been considered, but the maintenance of this operation would be difficult and a force of three divisions would be required: the plan had been to carry the expedition on a PQ convoy and divert it at the last moment, but the size of the force required would be too large for normal PQ shipping.[1]

An informal meeting took place between Brooke and Marshall in the latter's office at 2 p.m., and the CIGS believed Marshall to be coming round to the opinion that cross-Channel operations in 1942 were not practicable; Brooke wrote: 'On the whole made fair progress today, but am a little doubtful as to what PM and President may be brewing up together.'[2] He appeared before the CCS again at 11 a.m. next day, Saturday, 20 June, and referred to talks with Marshall the previous afternoon: he had been 'much encouraged to find that there was complete unanimity of opinion between the US and British staffs on general strategic policy and the merits of the

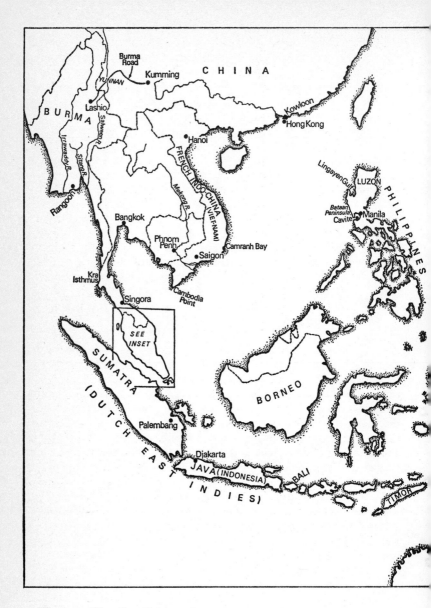

Map 4. The Far East

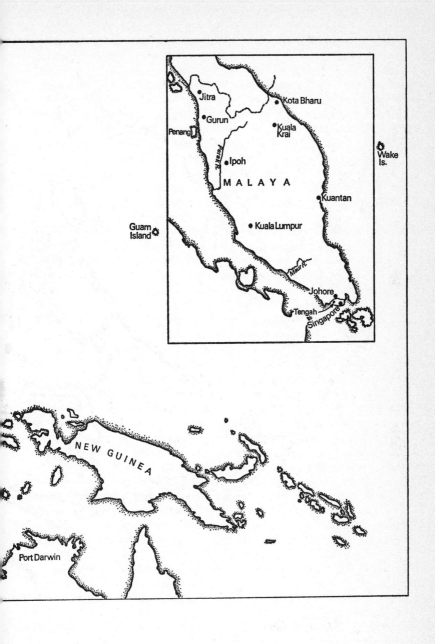

"Bolero" plan as a whole'. Brooke then asked for consideration of the situation which would arise if Russia collapsed during the summer. 'Bolero', he stressed, still held good. 'If the Germans, as a result of defeating Russia, were able to bring back large forces into France, the renewed threat to the safety of the United Kingdom would immediately become a vital consideration.' But, Brooke continued, such a massive increase in German strength on the Continent might make 'Round-Up' impracticable. 'We should have to seek an alternative to a major offensive on the Continent in 1943.' Brooke then made reference to the possibilities of 'Gymnast' – but only on this condition that a Russian collapse had allowed such German strength to build up on the Continent which would rule out 'Round-Up'. He stated: 'The issue in Russia would be decided by September 1942 and by that time, although American reinforcements would be sufficient to give a reasonable security to the UK, the number of American troops thus committed would not be so great as to make it impossible to modify existing plans in favour of an expedition to North Africa.' Brooke's tentative reference to 'Gymnast', despite his main purpose being to illustrate 'Bolero's' flexibility, and despite the fact that he did not mention a date, nor did he personally advocate this operation under existing circumstances, provoked immediate outcry. Admiral King declared he was 'entirely opposed to any idea of carrying out "Gymnast" in 1942. An entry into North West Africa would open up a new front with all the increase on overheads and escort and transportation problems involved.... Moreover, the present situation in North Africa did not augur well for the success of "Gymnast" this year. By putting all our efforts in "Bolero" we were concentrating to the maximum on one Front. In the Pacific risks had had to be taken for "Bolero".... "Gymnast" would make the position far more serious there, since it would be necessary to withdraw the naval forces.' Marshall also voiced his opposition. 'Large-scale operations on the Continent in 1943 would clearly not be possible unless all efforts were concentrated now on their preparations. If we changed our plan now, and opened up another Front, we should probably achieve nothing.... To defeat the Germans we must have overwhelming power, and North-West Europe was the only front on which this overwhelming superiority was logistically possible.' Admiral Little, the British naval representative on the CCS committee, 'felt sure the First Sea Lord would agree with Admiral King's opposition to "Gymnast". The naval situation in the Atlantic was already difficult enough without taking on a large new commitment. Even as it was we were not able to maintain our existing sea communications properly.'

Brooke switched to 'suggestions that had been made for a so-called "sacrifice" operation on the Continent to relieve pressure on Russia.

This question had been exhaustively examined by the British COS, but they had not been able to discover any worthwhile objective.... Even if a landing force gained a bridgehead, we should not have sufficient forces available to follow up.' Eisenhower mentioned the possibility of securing a bridgehead and holding it as Malta or Tobruk had been held. The CCS agreed a paper should be prepared dealing with the points made in discussion.[3] Brooke considered the meeting a success; at least the 'military men' were in agreement – continue 'Bolero', no 'Gymnast', no diversions. 'But we fully appreciated,' he wrote, 'we might be up against many difficulties when confronted with the plans that the PM and President had been brewing up.... We fear the worst and are certain that North Africa and North Norway plans for 1942 will loom large ... whilst we are convinced that they are not possible.'[4]

On this Saturday, 20 June, Churchill and Roosevelt were sitting in a tiny, sweltering room at Hyde Park, discussing the fearful possibilities of atomic energy. Before them lay papers on progress by British and American scientists; British research already showed a uranium bomb of collossal destructive power could probably be constructed before the end of the war and might be decisive; Lord Hankey's Scientific Advisory Committee had recommended that a pilot plant should be built in Britain and if possible a full-scale plant in Canada. On 11 October 1941, Roosevelt had suggested joint development, and at the same time it had become clear for geographical, strategic and above all financial reasons, America would be the most suitable country in which to build the plants. And, on this Saturday, informal agreement was reached by Roosevelt and Churchill: plants would be sited in America, but according to Churchill 'everything was on the basis of fully sharing the results as equal partners'.[5]

Also on this Saturday, Brooke's fears were proved amply justified. 'No responsible British military authority,' declared Churchill in a note to Roosevelt, 'has so far been able to make a plan for September 1942 which had any chance of success.... What else are we going to do? Can we afford to stand idle in the Atlantic? ... Ought we not to be preparing within the general structure of "Bolero" some other operation by which we may gain positions of advantage, and also directly or indirectly to take some of the weight off Russia?' Churchill concluded: 'It is in this setting and on this background that the French North-West Africa operation should be studied.'[6] Churchill's powerful note was supremely typical. The position in Libya had deteriorated. Churchill's immediate reaction in time of setback was to issue strident calls for an offensive; this had been his attitude in 1940 and at the time of the fall of Singapore – be rid of the defensive mentality, he had urged. For political, diplomatic and morale reasons the dramatic offensive had constant appeal; inactivity ill-became him. This was an attitude shared by his fellow politician and statesman, Roosevelt: a similar impetuosity had already prompted the President to tell Molotov he expected a Second Front in 1942. And the Congressional elections would be held in November. The two leaders therefore continued enthusiastic discussion on their train journey to Washington late on the 20th, an earlier return than expected, while Brooke, Dill and Marshall remained convinced 'Gymnast' was out in 1942, and while, in London, grim signals were being received from Cairo.

'Enemy attacked south-east face Tobruk perimeter early morning after air bombardment and penetrated defences.' Auchinleck's signal, dated 20 June and received at 13.15 hours on the 21st, continued: 'By evening all our tanks reported knocked out and half our guns lost.... Major-General Klopper commanding troops in Tobruk last night asked authority to fight his way out feeling apparently could not repeat not hold out. Ritchie agreed.... Do not repeat not know how he proposes to do this and consider chances of success doubtful....' A signal reached the Admiralty from the C-in-C Mediterranean. 'Tobruk has fallen and situation deteriorated so much that there is a possibility of heavy air attack on Alexandria. ... I am sending all eastern fleet units south of Canal.' At 15.05 hours on the 21st a telegram was relayed from Malta, where a signal had been received from Cairo: 'Critical situation rapidly developing on Libyan front ... must ask you to despatch forthwith 20 Spitfires.' Two hours later a telegram arrived in London for Churchill from the Minister of State at Cairo, immediately transmitted to Washington: 'You will receive a telegram almost at once from the Middle East Defence Committee telling you the grave news that Tobruk has virtually fallen, and that it is proposed to fight as strong delaying action as possible on the positions on the Egyptian border in the vicinity of Sollum, but that the C-in-Cs believe the main stand cannot be made elsewhere than at Matruh ... forces at our command in this theatre are inadequate to enable us to cope with the enemy.'[7]

Churchill was unaware of this disaster when he was told by Brooke of decisions reached by the CCS. The CIGS found him 'very upset' and 'peevish'; not until later would full discussions be held and Roosevelt's tacit approval for 'Gymnast' be revealed. Meanwhile Churchill had been struck 'one of the heaviest blows I can recall during the war'. Roosevelt handed him a pink slip of paper. Tobruk had fallen. For the first time, Ismay saw Churchill wince. A copy of the signal from the C-in-C Mediterranean to the Admiralty provided confirmation. In the sudden silence Churchill thought of the damage to the reputation of British armies, of the catastrophe in Egypt should the collapse continue – 'defeat is one thing,' he wrote, 'disgrace is another'. The Americans made an immediate offer of 300 precious Sherman tanks, 100 self-propelled 105-mm guns and air reinforcements. Churchill telephoned London and requested Ministers to meet as soon as possible.

The War Cabinet therefore met at 10 Downing Street at 10.30 p.m. on the 21st. The Vice-CIGS revealed the contents of an appreciation sent by Auchinleck before the fall of Tobruk, which credited the British forces with about 110 tanks, excluding those in Tobruk, and estimated the enemy to have between 100 and 130. The COAS said the enemy were estimated to have about 700 service-able aircraft, compared with about 550 for the RAF. Ernest Bevin immediately attacked Auchinleck's handling of the situation: 'We should not tolerate the suggestion that Rommel and his troops were superior to our own.... Nevertheless, we now seemed to be witness-ing the defeat of our forces in detail,' and he asked whether changes in the higher command should not be made. Oliver Lyttelton spoke up in defence of the Cairo command, reminding the War Cabinet that 'when General Auchinleck had been urged two months ago to stage an offensive in Cyrenaica, he had constantly affirmed that he was too weak in armour to do so with any prospect of success. Recent events might well confirm the correctness of this view. The position on the frontier would not be restored by changes in the higher command.' Nevertheless Lyttelton and other Ministers questioned the wisdom of only leaving a rearguard to hold the enemy at the frontier while the main 8th Army remnants pulled back to Matruh. The Vice-CIGS pointed out that orders had already been issued to delay the enemy on the frontier while withdrawing the main body, and he believed this decision to be correct – it had been taken 'by the C-in-Cs in consultation with the Minister of State and in possession of all the relevant factors.... By withdraw-ing to Matruh we should gain the advantage of fighting Rommel's armour 125 miles further from their base and of gaining time.' The War Cabinet agreed this decision could not be changed from London, but also decided to send a telegram to Cairo stressing the importance of a protracted defence of the frontier position.[8]

Back in Washington on this fateful 21st June – Auchinleck's birthday – discussion had been resumed on the Second Front issue. The Prime Minister's influence on the President now became fully apparent: written conclusions of the CCS talks were never even formally presented. The debate at the White House this Sunday night was long and animated; an apparent compromise decision was recorded, drafted by the diplomatic Ismay: 'Plans and prepara-tions for the "Bolero" operation in 1943 ... are to be pushed for-ward with all speed and energy. It is however essential that the US and Great Britain should be prepared to act offensively in

1942. Operations in France or the Low Countries in 1942 would, if successful, yield greater political and strategic gains than operations in any other theatre. Plans and preparations for the operations in this theatre are to be pressed forward with all possible speed, energy and ingenuity.... If a sound and sensible plan can be contrived we should not hesitate to give effect to it.' But the Memorandum continued: 'If, on the other hand, detailed examination shows that, despite all efforts, success is improbable, we must be ready with an alternative. The possibilities of Operation "Gymnast" will be explored carefully and conscientiously.'[9] This compromise was accepted for the moment; and yet, in effect, it killed 'Sledgehammer' and led to Marshall's correct conviction that 'Round-Up' was also being seriously affected by a concentration upon 'Gymnast'.

Anglo-American strategic talks continued in Washington, but the news from the Middle East had eclipsed the debate. Churchill waited anxiously for news from Cairo, passed on from London, where War Cabinet Ministers were given further depressing news in the Cabinet War Room situation report on 22 June. 'At 07.45 on the 21st wireless communication ceased and it was confirmed last night that Tobruk is in enemy hands.... The fall of Tobruk brings the enemy forward aerodromes to within 300 miles of Alexandria.'[10] 'I deeply regret that you should have received this severe blow at so critical a moment,' cabled Auchinleck to Churchill on the 24th. On the same day Rommel's formations crossed the frontier into Egypt; next day Auchinleck took over command of the 8th Army from Ritchie; on the 26th the Germans broke through the Matruh defences.

Churchill and Brooke were clearly needed in London, and they prepared to leave for Baltimore late on the 25th, where Churchill would board his flying-boat. Critics at home were in full cry, reported the American newspapers: 'Churchill faces stormy session when House convenes,' declared one headline; 'British Ire is High. Churchill under Fire,' announced another. The Prime Minister replied to Auchinleck on the 25th: 'Do not have the slightest anxiety about course of affairs at home. Whatever views I may have about how the battle was fought or whether it should have been fought a good deal earlier, you have my entire confidence, and I share your responsibilities to the full.'[11] On the same day Sir John Wardlaw-Milne, chairman of the all-party Finance Committee and the Conservative Foreign Affairs Committee, tabled a Commons motion: 'That this House, while paying tribute to the heroism and endurance of the Armed Forces of the Crown, in circumstances of exceptional difficulty, has no confidence in the central direction of the war.' Churchill's flying boat splashed down on the Clyde on the 27th; in the desert Matruh was abandoned, and the courageous New Zealand Division escaped 80 miles back to join the rest of the British forces in their new position – El Alamein; and, on this early summer Saturday, 35 brave merchant ships steamed from Iceland and headed towards the forbidding Arctic – PQ 17.

Churchill reported to the War Cabinet at 5.30 p.m., describing the 'invaluable help' being sent to the Middle East by America, and reading the agreed Memorandum on future strategy. Brooke described his discussions: the first few days had been spent clearing up 'certain misunderstandings', he said, and he referred to those 'very high quarters in Washington' who feared that 'if we concentrated on "Bolero" to the exclusion of any other projects ... if 'Round-Up' was not practicable, large bodies of American troops would be locked up in Great Britain.' Ministers discussed arrangements for the Commons debate scheduled for 1 and 2 July; they agreed any call for an inquiry into the loss of Tobruk should be resisted.[12]

Mussolini left for North Africa on 29 June to be on hand for a triumphant entry into Cairo. Eden told the War Cabinet at 5.30 p.m. on this Monday that the British Ambassador had inquired 'whether arrangements should be made for evacuating civilian personnel', and the War Cabinet agreed the Ambassador should hold discussions with the Minister of State. Brooke was feeling the strain of the constant criticisms voiced against the Army; he wrote after this meeting that Bevin had been 'full of uneducated peevish questions about the Middle East operations, continually asking questions on points that I had just explained'.[13] The Cabinet War Room Record for this day declared: '*Tirpitz*, *Hipper* and four destroyers were still at Trondheim at 12.30 on 27 June.'[14] PQ 17 was therefore still safe from an attack by these massive warships.

General Marshall warned Roosevelt on the 30th that Rommel might reach Cairo within a fortnight. Alamein was a mere 60 miles from Alexandria, and Churchill signalled the Minister of State: 'Everybody in uniform must fight exactly as they would if Kent or Sussex were invaded.... Egypt must be held at all costs.'[15] Early next morning, 1 July, Rommel threw his forces forward, urging all possible speed to maintain momentum; also on 1 July, Sebastopol fell after weeks of terrible fighting; and, at noon on this Wednesday, a *Luftwaffe* shadowing aircraft located PQ 17.

The previous day, 30 June, Churchill had told the War Cabinet that Sir John Wardlaw-Milne was prepared for the Commons debate to be postponed in view of the seriousness of the general situation. Ministers had agreed the debate must proceed.[16] The decision was correct: the proposer and seconder of the Censure Motion made a serious tactical mistake when the first, Sir John, condemned Churchill's dual role of Prime Minister and Defence Minister, while the seconder, Admiral Sir Roger Keyes, complained that the Prime Minister was obstructed by the COS and should be given a freer hand. As Oliver Lyttelton said in the opening speech for the Government: 'The mover complained that the Prime Minister had too much power and thwarted the Chiefs of Staff, and the seconder that the Chiefs of Staff thwarted the Prime Minister.' Sir John also damaged his case by suggesting the Duke of Gloucester should be made Commander-in-Chief; Harold Nicolson wrote: 'A wave of panic embarrassment passed over the House.' In both the Commons and Lords, Churchill's predominant position came under fire; Lord Winterton declared: 'We are getting very close to the intellectual and moral position of the German people: "The Führer is always right."' 'The Prime Minister is exercising a tremendous dictatorship,' declared John McGovern. 'From my experience he is the most arrogant and intolerant member of this House.' But Churchill, despite his ill-concealed distaste for the whole affair, had no reason to fear the voting to take place next day. Nevertheless, as Cripps commented in a Memorandum to the Prime Minister on the morning of the 2nd, 'there is no doubt that there is a very grave disturbance of opinion both in the House of Commons and in the country'. The most bitter and biting attack in the debate came from Aneurin Bevan; he accused the British army of being 'ridden by class prejudice', and suggested the generals should be replaced by Russians, Poles or Frenchmen. As usual, Hore-Belisha delivered his meticulous, specialized arguments. Late on the 2nd, Churchill rose to reply. 'Everything that could be thought of or raked up has been used to weaken confidence in the Government, has been used to prove that Ministers are incompetent and to weaken their confidence in themselves, to make the Army distrust the backing it is getting from the civil power, to make the workmen lose confidence in the weapons they are striving so hard to make, to represent the Government as a set of nonentities over whom the Prime Minister towers, and then to undermine him in his own heart, and, if possible, before the eyes of the nation.' Churchill rejected the dictator arguments on the very grounds his critics had used. 'The Mover of the Vote of Censure has proposed that I should be stripped of my responsibilities for defence in order that some military figure or some other unnamed personage should assume the general conduct of the war, that he should have complete control of the Armed Forces of the Crown.... It is a system very different from the parliamentary system under which we live. It might easily amount or be converted into a dictatorship.' The motion was defeated by

434

476 votes to 25. But criticism would continue; the best, if not the only, means of stilling it would be a military success, and five more months would have to pass before bells could be rung in celebration of a British victory.

And yet this dismal day of 2 July saw the start of this success. Rommel's attempt to smash through the Alamein line failed. Auchinleck had taken over direct command of the 8th Army, and, reported Rommel, 'was handling his forces with very considerable skill and tactically better than Ritchie had done'. Rommel's momentum had been checked; the *Afrika Korps* had only 26 tanks left fit for action on 3 July, while the 8th Army had almost 100, and instead of following 8th Army's previous policy of dividing into small 'battle-groups' with consequent dispersal of strength, Auchinleck ordered the British armour to stand solid south of Ruweisat. Rommel signalled he would have to move on to the defensive 'for at least a fortnight'.

Ministers meeting at noon on the 3rd heard a COS report on 'what might happen if our forces were driven out of Egypt'. The COS believed the Germans intended to attempt a push on through Egypt to take Palestine and Syria, 'freezing' Turkey; the CIGS explained preparations for demolition work in Egypt 'if the worst came to the worst', and Eden proposed to inform the British Ambassador at Cairo to prepare civilian evacuation plans, although British civilians should 'stand fast' for the moment and preparations to leave should be kept hidden from the local population.[17] Churchill wanted to fly to Cairo, first mentioning the idea to Eden immediately after the Vote of Censure debate and returning to the plan on the 3rd. Brooke was appalled: nothing would be worse than Churchill descending in mid-battle, and he spent 45 minutes successfully arguing with the Prime Minister on the evening of the 3rd.[18]

For the first three days of July, bad weather had prevented Photographic Reconnaissance Unit flights over Trondheim. Now, on 4 July, the Cabinet War Room situation report read: 'Northern waters. A PRU flight to Trondheim showed that *Tirpitz*, *Hipper* and destroyers had left their respective berths.' Next day the report declared: 'Northern waters. Yesterday evening, owing to threat from enemy surface ships, the convoy was ordered to scatter and proceed to Russian ports.'[19] This last sentence described a disaster.

PQ 17 had managed to escape casualties, despite isolated air attacks, until early on the morning of 4 July, when a lone Heinkel torpedo bomber dived through a hole in the protective fog and sank the *Christopher Newport*. Further air attacks took place during the evening of the 4th, and two more vessels were sunk. Back at the Admiralty, discussions had been taking place on the implications

435

of the disappearance of the *Tirpitz* and *Hipper*; if these war-ships were heading for the convoy, they could be expected to arrive at about 2 a.m., 5 July, and the result would be catastrophe: PQ 17's escort of destroyers, commanded by Commander J. E. Broome, and the covering force of cruisers under Admiral Hamilton, would be unmatched against the battleship *Tirpitz*, the battle-cruiser *Hipper* and the powerful force likely to be in attendance. One plan discussed at the Admiralty was to withdraw the cruisers and leave the convoy to continue with destroyer escort, in the hope some ships might get through. The cruisers would be free to harass the battleships, and the merchantmen, remaining in convoy, would be concentrated for mutual support against air and U-boat attack. They would still be vulnerable to surface attack but fog might give protective cover. Another course was to scatter the convoy; if this were decided upon, reassembly of the convoy formation would be impossible and all cohesion against air and U-boat attack would be lost, but risks from a surface attack would be minimized. Pound made the decision. A signal left the Admiralty at 9.11 p.m. on the 4th: 'Cruiser Force withdraw to the westward at high speed.' Twelve minutes later another signal was made: 'Owing to threat from surface ships, convoy is to disperse and proceed to Russian ports.' And at 9.36 p.m.: 'Convoy is to scatter.'[20]

An important difference existed between 'disperse' and 'scatter': the former instructed merchantmen merely to loosen formation; the latter meant merchantmen must follow pre-arranged plans to move from one another in star-shaped fashion, to put maximum distance between each ship in minimum time. The order to 'scatter' was only used under immediate threat of overwhelming surface attack. Commander Broome therefore believed such an attack must be imminent, and his instructions clearly specified that in the event of an attack on the convoy by a surface force greatly superior to the escort force, he must shadow the enemy and attack if possible; Broome therefore decided he must join the cruiser force so that the enemy surface fleet could be blocked. The merchantmen were left unprotected, and, once scattered, each was terribly alone. Enemy U-boats and aircraft moved in. The War Cabinet Ministers were told at 5.30 p.m. on the 6th: 'Reports showed that up to date we had lost 11 ships out of 34.'[21] The deadly game of hide and seek continued. The situation report on the 8th read: 'Northern Waters. Out of the total of 33 [*sic*] ships of the outward convoy to Russia, six ships, with nine of the escorting vessels, were reported yesterday.'[22] No sign had been seen of the expected enemy surface attack, and escorts were frantically trying to round up the pathetic-ally vulnerable merchantmen; but, later on the 7th an RAF aircraft operating from north Russia at last sighted the *Tirpitz* and the

436

warships with her – returning to Narvik. The U-boats and *Luftwaffe* continued their slaughter. The Defence Committee, meeting on 10 July to discuss future convoys to Russia were appalled by the news that 'of the 36 [*sic*] ships which had originally sailed, 16 were known to be safe, two others were doubtful, and two had turned back to Iceland. The remaining 16 were probably lost.' The next PQ convoy would leave Iceland on 23 July, under present plans; Pound stressed heavy ship cover could not be given in the Barents Sea, because of enemy shore-based aircraft and U-boats – heavy ship losses might affect naval control in the North Atlantic and even the 'Bolero' operation. But in discussion it was pointed out that 'we could not afford to abandon the running of the next Russian convoy when the great battle was raging on the Russian front' and the Committee agreed that 'there should be no interruption in the sailing of convoys'.[23]

Discussion was taken up again on Monday, 13 July, when the Defence Committee were told that 'it seemed almost certain ... a maximum of 8 ships only would be saved. About 500 tanks and 260 aircraft had been lost, together with 19 American and 8 British ships.' It would only be meagre consolation when later figures showed these losses to be over-pessimistic. Eleven ships survived; 430 tanks, 210 aircraft and 3,350 vehicles were lost. More details of the reason for this disaster were to be given to the War Cabinet on 1 August in a statement by the First Sea Lord, who described the receipt of the news that *Tirpitz* might be expected in the convoy area and continued: 'Instructions were therefore issued for the convoy to disperse. In view of the slow speed of the ships, 8-10 knots, and the short time in which the convoy had to disperse, the Admiralty had signalled an order to the convoy to scatter. This gave the impression to the convoy that it was about to be attacked at any moment. The Senior Officer of the escorts (Broome) considered the best way to deal with the surface forces was to add his destroyer strength to Admiral Hamilton's force, and asked permission to do so. This was approved by Admiral Hamilton. It is considered Admiral Hamilton acted correctly until he received the order from the Admiralty to retire to the westward. It would have been preferable had he then ordered the escort destroyers to return to the vicinity of the convoy. His failure to do so could hardly be regarded as more than an error of judgment.' The War Cabinet 'took note of this statement'.[24]

Pound told the Defence Committee on 13 July that he 'could not guarantee that a single ship would get through' if PQ 18 were despatched as planned. Ice and weather conditions would be the same as they had been for PQ 17, and no additional protective measures were possible; the Germans had improved their offensive methods and now planned to use U-boats to the west of Bear Island and surface ships to the east. Churchill commented that 'the loss of so many ships and so much material meant that the convoy, far from helping Russia, constituted a disastrous loss to the Allied Cause'. Eden found it very worrying 'to have to give negatives to the Russians at this critical time', but saw no alternative. Other Ministers present – Attlee, Lyttelton, Alexander, Sinclair and Grigg, agreed, together with Lord Leathers, who added that 'it should not be imagined that there had been any hanging back on the part of the merchant seamen.' Churchill thought there should be 'a liberal distribution of George Medals' – and he added that the situation about convoys to Russia 'made it all important ... to seize northern Norway'.[25]

Churchill therefore had the task of telling Stalin that PQ 18 would be suspended. And this cable, despatched on 18 July, dealt Stalin another blow – over plans for the Second Front, so confidently expected by the Russians in 1942. Discussions had been taking place in London which, despite misgivings by Churchill's professional advisers, had led to the logical development of the Prime Minister's discussions with Roosevelt during the Washington visit.

'Conditions which would make ["Sledgehammer"] practicable in 1942 were now extremely unlikely to arise,' declared Churchill at the War Cabinet meeting at 5.30 p.m., Tuesday, 7 July. He added that 'if it had been possible to force a lodgement in the heavily defended Pas de Calais and, at the same time, to effect simultaneous landings at many other points on the French coast, the losses which would inevitably be incurred in the Pas de Calais would be compensated by our ability to make firm lodgements elsewhere. In present circumstances, however, operations on such a scale were out of the question in 1942.' The War Cabinet agreed, and with this firmly put to one side, Churchill could advance to his next step. 'It had been agreed in Washington that should Continental operations in 1942 prove impracticable, we should immediately consider what could be done elsewhere. Operation "Gymnast" offered considerable attractions at the present time, and the President had always expressed the keenest desire to carry it out. If, as now seemed possible, the position in Egypt was held, a threat to Rommel's rear might cause the Axis considerable embarrassment.' The War Cabinet 'expressed general agreement as to the desirability of going ahead with Operation "Gymnast"'. The Prime Minister had achieved his aim, but he attempted a further success. 'Operations in northern Norway, where the most powerful elements were waiting to co-operate with us, offered such attractive possibilities from so many points of view that it seemed desirable that no effort should be spared to work out a practicable plan.' Ministers once more agreed with Churchill. But Pound stressed that 'certain fundamental and so far insuperable difficulties presented themselves'. An air striking force would have to be established at Murmansk, and 'in view of our recent experiences with the PQ convoy, it was by no means certain that this could be done', and he continued: 'We should have to gain control of all enemy airfields between Petsamo and Narvik, by separate simultaneous operations.... Naval forces required for these ∩perations were beyond our present capacity.' Even if troops managed to get ashore, they would be 'unaccustomed to Arctic conditions and would be opposed by an enemy who had become acclimatized'. But the War Cabinet still decided that 'Jupiter' should be undertaken 'if by any means a sound, sensible plan could be devised'.[26] 'A dreadful exhibition of amateur strategy by Cabinet Ministers,' complained Brooke in his diary. 'A most depressing and lamentable evening.'[27] The CIGS had continued to hesitate over 'Gymnast': the Egyptian situation might have become more stabilized, but serious dangers remained and 'Gymnast' would come too late to help the 8th Army in its present predicament; Brooke knew the Americans to be vehemently opposed to the scheme. And, despite COS objections to 'Jupiter', plans for this operation would have to continue.

On this day that the War Cabinet decided not to proceed with a Second Front in Europe in 1942, German forces smashed through to Rostov. Also on the 7th, another British plan, the Dieppe raid, was abandoned and troops dispersed, following an unsuccessful exercise and bad weather. Next day Churchill read the War Cabinet a personal telegram which he had sent to Roosevelt informing him of the conclusions reached the previous evening: 'No responsible British General, Admiral or Air Marshal is prepared to recommend "Sledgehammer" as a practicable operation in 1942.... I am sure myself that French North Africa is by far the best chance for effecting relief to the Russian front in 1942. This has all along been in harmony with your ideas. In fact, it is your commanding idea. Here is the true Second Front of 1942. I have consulted the Cabinet and Defence Committee, and we all agree.' After reading this message Churchill referred Ministers to the question of the appointment of a Supreme Commander for the 1943 cross-Channel operation, 'Round-Up'; he had gathered that 'if the Supreme Command was offered to General Marshall he would be very pleased to accept' and he added: 'The Americans were proposing to employ 27 divisions to our 21.... I think that our interests would best be served by the appointment of an American.' The War Cabinet agreed.[28] Marshall was unlikely to be mollified by this offer; his suspicions would grow that the British preference for 'Gymnast' in 1942 would damage prospects for 'Round-Up' in 1943, and these suspicions seemed confirmed by another signal sent by Churchill to Roosevelt late on the 8th: 'I hope, Mr President, you will make sure that the appointment of a US commander over "Bolero" [the code-name some Americans persisted in using for "Round-Up"] in 1943 does not prejudice operations of immediate consequences, such as "Gymnast".[29]

Rapid German victories in Russia, commented Hitler on the 9th, might confront Britain with the dilemma of either launching an immediate invasion of the Continent, or 'seeing Russia eliminated'. He gave orders for further defensive measures along the Atlantic coast. 'A telegram has come from Great Britain,' wrote a seething Stimson on the 10th, 'indicating that the British War Cabinet are weakening and going back on "Bolero" ["Round-Up"] and are seeking to revive "Gymnast".... This would simply be another way of diverting our strength into a channel in which we canot effectively use it, namely the Middle East. I found Marshall very stirred up and emphatic over it. He is very naturally tired of these constant decisions which do not stay made ... he proposed a showdown which I cordially endorsed.'[30] Marshall and Admiral King sent a memorandum to Roosevelt stating that even if 'Gymnast' were found practicable it would be indecisive, and would limit if not make impossible the execution of 'Round-Up' in Spring 1943; dropping 'Sledgehammer' would repudiate the American commitment to Russia – which Roosevelt, actually against Marshall's advice, had made during Molotov's visit. 'If the United States is to engage in any other operation than forceful, unswerving adherence to "Bolero" plans, we are definitely of the opinion that we should turn to the Pacific and strike decisively against Japan.'[31]

Churchill hastened to increase pressure on Roosevelt; instructions were sent to Dill on the 12th: 'You should draw particular attention to Mountbatten's Note showing the mortal injury that would be done to "Round-Up" by "Sledgehammer".... "Gymnast" affords the sole means by which the United States can strike at Hitler in 1942.' Perhaps mindful of Roosevelt's concern over the Congressional elections four months away, Churchill said that should the President reject 'Gymnast', 'both countries will remain motionless in 1942, and all will be concentrated on "Round-Up" in 1943. There could be no excuse in these circumstances for the switch of United States effort [to the Pacific].' Two days later Churchill addressed himself directly to the President: 'I am most anxious for you to know where I stand.... I have found no one who regards "Sledgehammer" as possible. I should like to see you do "Gymnast" as soon as possible, and that we in concert with the Russians should try for "Jupiter". Meanwhile all preparations for "Round-Up" in 1943 should proceed at full blast, thus holding the maximum enemy forces opposite England. All this seems to me as clear as noonday.'[32] Yet also on the 14th the British Joint Planning Staff reported to the COS: 'It is fairly certain that we cannot carry out "Gymnast" and "Round-Up" within 12 months of each other. A properly executed "Gymnast" in fact must be regarded as an alternative and not an addition to "Round-Up".'[33]

By 15 July the Washington debate had reached its climax. Roosevelt felt he could not override his military chiefs directly. His relationship with them differed considerably to that between Churchill and the COS: as Brooke wrote: 'The President had not great military knowledge and was aware of this fact and consequently relied on Marshall.... My position was very different. Winston never had the slightest doubt that he had inherited all the military genius of his great ancestor, Marlborough.'[34] Roosevelt continued to be convinced of the need to defeat Germany before Japan, as basically did Marshall; he was also convinced of the need for an offensive operation in 1942. To ease himself out of the direct confrontation, Roosevelt decided to throw Marshall and King to the British: these two, and Hopkins, would visit London where they would change Churchill's mind, if possible. But Roosevelt confided to Hopkins on the evening of the 15th: 'My main point is that I do not believe we can wait until 1943 to strike at Germany.... If we cannot strike at "Sledgehammer", then we must take the second best – and that is not the Pacific.'[35] The formal instructions to the American team stated: ' "Sledgehammer" is of such grave importance that every reason calls for the accomplishment of it.... You should strongly urge immediate all-out preparations for it, that it be pushed with utmost vigour, and that it be executed whether or not Russian collapse becomes imminent. In the event Russian collapse becomes probable, "Sledgehammer" becomes not merely advisable but imperative.' Yet Roosevelt's directive also declared: 'If "Sledgehammer" is finally and definitely out of the picture I want you to ... determine upon another place for US troops to fight in 1942.' The document clearly decided against a switch to Japan: 'Defeat of Germany means the defeat of Japan.'[36]

General Brooke was meanwhile becoming increasingly concerned about the situation in the Western Desert: Auchinleck made three major attempts to throw Rommel off-balance between 14 and 17 July; all failed at considerable cost to the 8th Army. The British seemed utterly weary, demoralized and 'punch-drunk'. The CIGS had already decided he must fly to Cairo to see the situation for himself; on the evening of the 15th, during a conversation with the Prime Minister in the sunlit garden of 10 Downing Street, Brooke took advantage of Churchill's mellow mood and obtained his permission. Brooke arranged to leave after the critical Anglo-American talks, scheduled to begin on the 18th.

Churchill had now to contact Stalin: the Soviet leader had to be told that the PQ convoys were to be suspended – 'PQ 18 would bring no benefit to you and would only involve dead loss to the common cause'. Churchill sent this signal on 18 July, on the day the Americans arrived to press for a 1942 cross-Channel operation; he took it upon himself to hint that such an operation would not be undertaken, only mentioning the possibility of combined operations in northern Norway in the Autumn and of air reinforcements on Russia's southern flank.[37]

General Brooke met Marshall, King and Hopkins at Euston at 7.50 a.m. on this Saturday. The Americans declined an invitation to stay at Churchill's Chequers stronghold and closeted themselves with Eisenhower and other American planners in London. The British and American camps therefore stayed separate during the weekend, although Hopkins crossed over to spend Sunday with Churchill. The British plan of action had been discussed at a COS meeting on Friday night, 17 June, and the COS had been summoned to Chequers on the Saturday night for further debate lasting until 2.45 a.m. The Chiefs were unanimous with Churchill in believing 'Sledgehammer' should be finally buried, and Brooke believed the more ambitious 'Round-Up' must depend on Russia. 'If she breaks and is overrun, there can be no invasion and we should then be prepared to go into North Africa instead.' The CIGS therefore opposed a rigid timetable. Yet with 'Sledgehammer' hopeless the COS were now bound to admit 'Gymnast' offered the only alternative for an allied offensive that year; the operation would moreover safeguard the supply route to Malta and provide a secure air link to the Middle East and India. Churchill's argument that 'Gymnast' would threaten the *Afrika Korps*'s rear had been made more powerful through Rommel's apparent inability to push on into Egypt at the moment: while the 8th Army had failed in the attempt to break the German positions, the reverse was also true, and it now seemed Auchinleck might be able to hang on until the 'Gymnast' operation could be launched. 'Gymnast' would also tighten the blockade around Europe. Faced with these facts in favour of the operation, the COS were now apparently prepared to support Churchill's bid to win over the Americans to 'Gymnast', and the Saturday night meeting at Chequers ended with satisfactory agreement that 'it would be much to our advantage to get a footing in North Africa cheaply, in the same way as the Germans got Norway cheaply, by getting there first. "Gymnast" would in effect be the right wing of our Second Front. An American occupation of Casablanca and district would not be sufficient. The operations would

442

have to extend to Algiers, Oran, and possibly farther east.'[38]

Anglo-American staff talks began after lunch on Monday, 20 July. Records of the discussions during the coming few days seem to indicate a previous agreement between the COS and Churchill as to the tactic to be followed during the debate: initially, no mention would be made of 'Gymnast'. Instead, the Americans would be allowed to present their case and would be faced by solid British opposition to 'Sledgehammer'; when the Americans realized British objections could not be overcome, they would have to recognize that one of three courses would be necessary: Anglo-American forces remaining on the defensive until 1943, which would be politically unacceptable, or the emphasis shifting to the Pacific, which was unacceptable to Roosevelt and Marshall, or some other alternative operation in the West. Like the British COS they would have to realize only 'Gymnast' offered this alternative; the British would not refer to 'Gymnast' until this realization had arrived. General Marshall and Admiral King opened the first meeting on 20 July by presenting a Memorandum, which formed the basis of the first day's discussion. The paper urged 'Sledgehammer' either as a 'sacrifice' operation to help the Russians or as the first stage of 'Round-Up'. With the first, declared the Americans, 'we would be guilty of a gross military blunder if the Germans should be permitted to eliminate an allied army of eight million men when some stroke of ours might have saved the situation'; with the second, based on the assumption that there had been a 'gradual turn for the better' in Russia, 'the allies must decide whether "Sledgehammer" should not be undertaken on the ground that it provides for the seizure and expansion of a foothold on the Continent, as a preliminary useful step towards the full evolution of "Round-Up" in 1943.' It might be that the Russian situation would continue on much the same level, with both sides trying to make maximum effort: in this case German defensive forces might be reduced to a minimum in Europe, and ' "Sledgehammer" would constitute the most effective action that the allies could take on behalf of Russia and indeed for the allied cause in general'. The British COS insisted in reply that a sacrifice operation would merely mean the loss of six divisions without any appreciable result, and, as for 'Sledgehammer' as a preliminary to 'Round-Up', the initial landing force would probably be unable to maintain itself, still less gain ground, against the German weight which would rapidly be thrown against it. Much the same arguments and counter-arguments were repeated when talks resumed at 11 a.m. next day. Marshall seemed to agree a sacrifice operation before September was impractical, but continued to press for 'Sledgehammer' after September as a preliminary to 'Round-Up'. The COS stressed weather conditions after September would make a crossing impossible. Talks lasted until 1 p.m. and although the meeting agreed to continue discussion next morning, deadlock had been reached.[39] At the third meeting, starting 11 a.m. on the 22nd, the Americans handed over a Memorandum which re-stated their views; the British repeated their objections. Marshall then said the matter would have to be referred to the President but asked to see Churchill first. An interview was therefore arranged for 3 p.m.

Churchill insisted on his support for 'Round-Up' and warned that one of the dangers of 'Sledgehammer' would be the risk of its eating up 'the seed-corn' for the 1943 operation. Marshall admitted 'Sledgehammer' was 'not at all the operation that one would deliberately choose, if choice had been possible' and he personally believed it could not be launched before October, 'which increased the hazards as to weather.... However, there was no choice.... Time was tragically against us. Without "Sledgehammer" we were faced with a defensive attitude in the European theatre.' Churchill agreed to put the whole matter before the War Cabinet. And clearly the time was almost ripe for referring to 'Gymnast'.[40] Ministers met at 5.30 p.m., and Brooke gave a detailed account of discussions so far before explaining the COS attitude towards the American proposal for a Cherbourg landing as a 'Round-Up' preliminary. 'This was a difficult operation but held out some prospect of success in certain conditions.' Maintenance and exploitation of such a landing would however be infinitely more hazardous, with the area being at the limits of fighter aircraft range from Britain, hence making continuous fighter protection impossible, and with the size of Cherbourg port restricting the offensive force to six divisions. 'The Germans had about 27 divisions in France, of which about 15 were in the coastal areas from Belgium to Brest. A force of some 6-10 divisions could quickly be built up.... The result might well be that our forces would be driven back into the sea.' Portal confirmed the difficulty over fighter aircraft range: 100 aircraft could cover the initial landings, but only for three hours, and thereafter only 36 fighters at a time could be over the area. 'The enemy air forces immediately available against us would have a first line strength of about 324 bombers and 426 fighters.' Pound completed the picture: 'The weather broke between the second and third weeks of September and the second week in October.... In heavy gales it would not be possible to get many of the transports across the Channel.'

Churchill described the Cherbourg proposal as 'attractive', but only if combined with other landings; on the other hand, 'we must not show ourselves too ready to raise difficulties'. Mountbatten even supported the Cherbourg scheme, believing it feasible, and he pointed out he had consistently taken the view that this was one coastal area upon which a successful assault could be launched in 1942. 'Detailed planning ... had however not been pursued, on the grounds that we should not help the Russians by operations in the Cherbourg peninsula.' Churchill said he had wondered whether the Americans should be told that 'while we did not share the American opinion, if they wished to conduct the operation we were prepared to carry it out with them', but he thought 'on the whole the wisest course, if we did not see our way to agree with the American proposal ... was that we should ask the American Chiefs of Staff to report to the President.' And Churchill now said that 'if "Sledgehammer" was abandoned discussion of "Gymnast" would at once be started ... planning for "Round-Up" in 1943 would, of course continue'. Ministers agreed 'Sledgehammer' should be scrapped and operations in French North Africa undertaken; Churchill said he would ask the American chiefs to inform the President that it had been found impossible to reach agreement in the joint talks – 'this would open the way for discussion on the alternative operations with the least difficulty'.[41]

Churchill was sure of his success. The Americans were informed, a signal was despatched to Roosevelt, and Marshall and King went to an excellent dinner at Claridges with the British COS. Roosevelt replied within a few hours: the American delegation was instructed to work out some other plan to bring United States land forces into the field in 1942, giving first priority to an offensive in North Africa. The President was therefore the first to bring 'Gymnast' to the forefront. Marshall and King spent 23 July in discussion with American planners in London; Eisenhower, who had been the author of the latest Cherbourg scheme as a preliminary for 'Round-Up', admitted 'my only real reason for favouring it was the fear of becoming so deeply involved elsewhere that the major cross-Channel attack would be indefinitely postponed, possibly even cancelled. Almost certainly any 1942 operation in the Mediterranean would eliminate the possibility of a major cross-Channel venture in 1943.'[42] Eisenhower was to be proved correct, indeed, British service chiefs had already reached the same conclusion.

A formal CCS meeting was fixed to take place next noon, 24 July, in the War Cabinet Offices. Meanwhile, on 23 July, the British COS discussed the German advance in the Caucasus region and possible measures to guard against an enemy breakthrough to Iran and the Abadan oilfields.[43] The situation on the southern Soviet sector was clearly desperate. Rostov fell during the day; and, on this Thursday, Hitler issued Directive No 45: Army Group A was ordered to capture the whole Black Sea east coast and to thrust along the Caspian coast to occupy the important Baku oilfields; Army Group B was ordered to 'thrust forward to Stalingrad, to smash the enemy forces there, to occupy the town....' The German General Staff pleaded either the Caucasus or Stalingrad should be the main objective, not both; Hitler's blind reaction took the form of a 'fit of insane rage'.

Also on 23 July, Stalin replied to Churchill's message of the 18th which had revealed the suspension of PQ convoys and which had hinted, prematurely but accurately, at cancellations of plans for a 1942 cross-Channel Second Front. The communication from the incensed Stalin was handed to Churchill by the unfortunate Soviet Ambassador during the evening. However inevitable the tone of the reply, the Prime Minister reacted violently, and was 'not easily soothed', wrote Eden. Two conclusions could be drawn from Churchill's message, said Stalin. 'First, the British Government refuses to continue the sending of war materials to the Soviet Union via the Northern route. Second, in spite of the agreed communiqué concerning the urgent tasks of creating a Second Front in 1942 the British Government postpones this matter until 1943. Our naval experts consider the reasons put forward by the British naval experts to justify the cessation of convoys to the northern ports of the USSR wholly unconvincing.... With regard to the second question.... I am afraid it is not being treated with the seriousness it deserves.... The Soviet Government cannot acquiesce in the postponement of a Second Front in Europe until 1943.'

In the early afternoon of the 24th the British and American Chiefs of Staff formally agreed there should be no Second Front in Europe until 1943, and tacit recognition seemed to be given to the fact that 'Gymnast' would push 'Round-Up' back into 1944. The meeting considered a Memorandum by the US Joint Chiefs concerning operations for 1943; General Marshall said the Americans 'believed very strongly' that no unavoidable reduction in 'preparations' for the large-scale 1943 operation should be considered so long as there remained any possibility of its successful execution prior to 1 July 1943, after which date the odds were definitely against 'Round-Up' for the remainder of the year. The US Memorandum did not therefore specifically advocate 'Gymnast', although it clearly stated that it had been decided 'that "Sledgehammer" is not to be undertaken as a scheduled operation.' Emphasis remained on 'Round-Up', with a North African operation mentioned as an alternative to this plan – under certain conditions. The critical section was contained in Paragraph C: 'If the situation on the Russian front by 15 September indicates such a collapse or weakening of Russian resistance as to make "Round-Up" appear impracticable of successful execution, the decision should be taken to launch a combined operation against the North and West coast of Africa at the earliest date possible before December 1942.' The Americans did not there-

446

fore declare a full, unconditional acceptance of 'Gymnast'; nor would they agree with the view previously expressed by Churchill that both 'Gymnast' and 'Round-Up' could be undertaken; the Memorandum continued: 'A commitment to the operation ["Gymnast"] renders "Round-Up" in all probability impracticable of successful execution in 1943 and therefore ... we have definitely accepted a defensive, encircling line of action for the continental European theatre, except as to air operations and blockade.' In basic terms, the Americans therefore proposed a joint agreement to scrap 'Sledgehammer', and to substitute 'Gymnast' – but only if Russian resistance had weakened to such an extent that 'Round-Up' should also be scrapped; 'Gymnast' would mean the acceptance of a defensive position in the European area. Portal questioned whether this mention of a defensive line was in fact correct: 'Gymnast' would 'open up a Second Front and might commit Germany to the occupation of Italy and Spain. It was conceivable even that she might be so weakened by this that "Round-Up" might be undertaken in 1943.' General Marshall emphasized that 'once large forces had been put into North Africa, "Round-Up", as originally conceived, was no longer practicable at all'. Brooke claimed that the British COS 'were fully determined to go ahead with preparations for an invasion of the Continent on a large scale'. Admiral King insisted the British and American Governments 'must be under no illusion. Once "Gymnast" was undertaken with all the commitments that it might involve, there was no possibility of carrying out "Round-Up" in its original form. An entirely new operation would have to be prepared.'[44] The Americans therefore refused to allow any lee-way with their rigid declaration that one or the other must be chosen: the British had preferred 'Gymnast' to 'Sledgehammer', therefore they must accept the consequences – no 'Round-Up', with all the diplomatic and political effects. If, by employing this blunt tactic, they hoped to change the British attitude back towards 'Sledgehammer', they failed – the British COS accepted the position, indeed, they had already come to this undeclared conclusion.

The COS therefore agreed to put the Memorandum to the War Cabinet – and, while they might have accepted this uncomfortable document, the War Cabinet might find it more difficult to swallow. Earlier in the day Churchill had minuted that 'Gymnast' should be renamed 'Torch': this code-name was therefore used by Ministers in discussing the American Memorandum at their 5 p.m. meeting. Brooke filled in the 'Gymnast' plan; the Chiefs contemplated the operations against North West Africa (Casablanca) would be wholly American, whereas the operation against the north coast, with landings at Algiers and Oran, would be carried out by British troops, but under 'an American veneer'. He added: 'This meant that, for political grounds, and in order to insure the best reception by the French, our troops would be proceeded by US forces.' War Cabinet discussion centred on Paragraph C of the US document, stating that 'Gymnast' would be launched if Russian resistance had collapsed to the extent that 'Round-Up' would probably be unsuccessful. Ministers felt this not only left open whether 'Torch/Gymnast' would be carried out, but made the operation dependent upon the Russian situation. 'There was thus no definite decision to proceed with either operation.' General Brooke had a hard task arguing against alterations. 'There was complete unanimity between the British and American Chiefs of Staff ... both the British and American COS believed that it was unlikely that "Round-Up" would be carried out in 1943 and that unless this expectation was falsified by the course of events later this year, Operation "Torch" therefore held the field.' He added: 'The American COS had greatly modified their views during the course of their visit ... it would be undesirable to press for further alterations.' The War Cabinet therefore instructed General Ismay to inform the Americans they had authorized the British COS to subscribe to the Memorandum. The document would now be submitted to President Roosevelt and back to the War Cabinet for formal Governmental approval.

Brooke later admitted: 'I perspired heavily ... and was engaged in heated arguments ... any change would have been fatal.'[45] The CIGS had himself perhaps been helped in his acceptance of the American document by one comforting fact: the American condition for 'Gymnast' – that the operation would be carried out if a Russian collapse had led to such an increase in German Continental strength as to rule out 'Round-Up' for 1943 – was virtually the one Brooke himself had specified in referring to 'Gymnast' at the CCS meeting in Washington on 20 June. The CIGS, like the American COS, had only recently been persuaded to support the 'Gymnast' proposal; perhaps the CIGS, like the Americans, hoped this condition would provide an escape route – if so the hope failed when Roosevelt ordered all-out progress for 'Torch' a few days later.

Ministers at the War Cabinet meeting were read Stalin's reply to the Prime Minister. Churchill referred to the first protocol signed on 1 October 1941: 'Great Britain and the USA will give aid to the transportation of these materials to the Soviet Union and will help with the delivery,' and he then told Ministers that 'it would be very easy for us to answer certain passages in this telegram ... but it was important that we should avoid a wrangle which would be of no advantage to either of us'. He had therefore contented himself with saying to Maisky that he would not have received a message in these terms but for the stern fight which the Russians were putting up, and that it would be better for Stalin's telegram to remain

448

unanswered. Eden said he had seen Maisky earlier in the afternoon and had repeated this view. 'Maisky had been disposed to agree.'[46]

The CCS met again at 10.30 a.m. next day, Saturday, 25 July, to start preliminary planning for 'Torch'. Brooke proposed an American commander should be chosen, and suggested planning should be centralized in London. The Americans agreed, and General Eisenhower was later selected for the command. The Americans travelled to Scotland that evening for their flight back to America. 'I doubt if success would have been achieved,' cabled Churchill to Roosevelt on the 27th, 'without Harry's [Hopkins] invaluable aid.... As I see it Second Front consists of a main body holding the enemy pinned opposite "Sledgehammer" and a wide flanking movement called "Torch".'[47] Also on 27 July the COS approved a new directive for a Dieppe operation – and this, to take place on 19 August, was to show what might have befallen 'Sledgehammer'.

Meanwhile, the Russians had to be appeased, and on the 27th the War Cabinet returned to the subject of the PQ convoys. Latest figures showed that the previous information on the PQ 17 convoy had been overpessimistic: 10 ships had survived, and one was still in passage. Churchill pointed out that 'practically one third of the convoy had reached Archangel. This was better than we had at one time expected. There was much to be said for attempting to run a further convoy to North Russia in September. By that time the Germans might have withdrawn their naval forces from North Norway. There would be great political advantage if we could tell the Russians that this was our plan.' Eden agreed, and the War Cabinet invited the First Lord of the Admiralty to consider the idea.[48] Next day the British Ambassador at Moscow suggested to Cadogan that Churchill himself should fly to the Soviet capital to reassure the Russians. The Prime Minister was immediately interested and obtained the King's private approval during a dinner at 10 Downing Street that night.[49] On the 29th Roosevelt signalled: 'I agree with you that your reply to Stalin must be handled with great care ... while I think that you should not raise any false hopes in Stalin relative to the northern convoy, nevertheless I agree with you we should run one if there is any possibility of success.'[50] Churchill was pushed towards the idea of a mission overseas by two other factors. Also on the 29th Eden commented on the 'poor spirit' of MPs; some dramatic initiative was necessary to revive them. And reports from the desert continued to be depressing. Next day, 30 July, Brooke was therefore told by Churchill that both would travel to Cairo instead of the CIGS going alone as planned and they would then journey to see Stalin. Churchill signalled the Soviet leader during the day, and a reply came within 24 hours inviting him to

Moscow. The Prime Minister passed blood pressure and high altitude tests on the 31st. And if he needed any further incentive, this came in a telegram from Auchinleck at 2.15 p.m. 'Reluctantly concluded that in present circumstances renewal of our efforts to break enemy front or turn his southern flank not feasible.... Opportunity for resumption of offensive operations unlikely to arise before mid-September.'

Churchill read this message to the War Cabinet next morning, 1 August, and commented: 'This seemed to be a very depressing account of the position'; he was convinced it was all the more necessary that 'the position should be considered on the spot'. He revealed his plans for a visit to Cairo where he hoped to be able 'to make arrangements which would result in a more vigorous handling of affairs'. Churchill told Ministers he was leaving that night and hoped to be in Cairo within about 48 hours' time; he would then go on to meet Stalin.[51] General Brooke had left the previous evening for Gibraltar on the first stage of his flight; the CIGS planned to make a detour via Malta to see Gort. Churchill left Lyneham at midnight, 1 August, with Cadogan. Both parties arrived in Cairo on Monday, 3 August. The Prime Minister and CIGS would be away from London for 25 days: ahead lay important strategic decisions, behind lay momentous decisions of Grand Strategy. The last few days had seen, in Roosevelt's accurate words: 'the turning point of the war'. 'Torch' was being prepared; but, as Churchill began his travels, problems of planning and outlook were already beginning to arise.

The apparent inertia of Middle East Command had pushed Churchill's impatience to uncontrollable limits. Yet in military terms Auchinleck had far from failed during these last few painful weeks; the enemy advance had been halted and the British Army had been dragged into some semblance of cohesion. This achievement had been essential, and was for the moment militarily sufficient. Auchinleck had adopted the correct strategy in prodding at the Italian divisions at various parts of the front, causing Rommel to exhaust the German units by rushing them hither and thither to bolster the positions. This, with the weak forces at Auchinleck's disposal, had been all he could do, and it had been enough. 'I am thankful for every day's respite we get,' wrote Rommel to his wife on 2 August. 'A lot of sickness ... even I am very tired and limp. ... Holding on to our Alamein position has given us the severest fighting we've yet seen in Africa.' Yet this was the victor; Auchinleck, whose future now hung so much in the balance, the loser.

As Churchill began discussions in Cairo a threat to Britain's Middle East position almost equal to Rommel's army was growing in the opposite direction. The German thrust into the Caucasus had continued; Portal told the War Cabinet on 5 August that if the advance continued and the Russians collapsed 'we might ... find that we had insufficient forces to hold the north front and to defend Egypt from the threat from Libya. We should then have to choose between deploying our resources so as to secure the Iranian oilfield with the consequential loss of Egypt, or concentrating on the defence of Egypt with the risk that we should lose the Iranian oil.' Portal said the COS had concluded that 'should the worst arise every effort should be made to hold on to the Abadan area, even at the risk of losing the Nile Delta'.[52]

By now Churchill had made up his mind on the changes needed at Cairo, after one or two diversions such as offering the 8th Army to Brooke. Late on 6 August a signal arrived in London from Churchill which led to a special meeting of the War Cabinet at 9.30 next morning. 'As a result of such inquiries as I have made here,' cabled Churchill, 'and after prolonged consultations with Field Marshal Smuts and CIGS, and Minister of State, I have come to the conclusion that a drastic and immediate change is needed in the High Command.' Churchill proposed that the command should be reorganized into two parts: A Near East Command comprising Egypt, Palestine and Syria, with its centre in Cairo, and a Middle East Command, comprising Iran and Iraq with its centre in Basra or Baghdad. General Auchinleck would be offered the latter, and General Alexander would replace him at Cairo. General Gott would command the 8th Army. 'I have no doubt that changes will impart a new and vigorous impulse to the army, and restore confidence in the Command which I regret does not exist at the present time. Here I must emphasize the need of a new start and vehement action to animate the whole of this vast but baffled and somewhat unhinged organization.' Ministers agreed with the proposals except for two points, and discussion showed they favoured action which would have led to even harsher treatment of Auchinleck; they doubted the wisdom of splitting Middle East Command into two: 'The reasons which had led to the setting up of a unified command in 1941 were felt to be even more cogent at the present time.' Ministers also felt that 'it would be inadvisable for General Auchinleck, after being removed from his present high command, to be appointed to the new Middle East Command. The impression would be conveyed that this separate command had been created in order to let him down lightly. Moreover, he would not have the confidence of his troops.' A telegram containing these objections was drafted for despatch to Churchill.

The War Cabinet then discussed PQ convoys and 'Torch'. Churchill intended to stress the importance of the latter in his

451

attempt to mollify Stalin, but it was now revealed that the operation might affect convoys to Russia. The First Lord said it would not be possible to run another PQ convoy before 'Torch' took place. The Vice-CIGS explained that the Americans had proposed 30 October as the date for 'Torch'. 'After examining the position we had reached the conclusion that it would be both practicable and desirable to fix an earlier date, say at the end of the first week in October.' The Americans had been informed but no official reply had been received and Dill had reported that American preparations were proceeding slowly.[53]

Churchill refused to alter his proposals; according to Brooke: 'They are quibbling at the split in command. Their arguments were not very conclusive, and we were able to deal with them fairly easily.'[54] Another cable from Churchill therefore reached London that evening, 7 August, and Ministers were summoned to a meeting which started at 11.15 p.m. and lasted until the early hours of the 8th. The Prime Minister had cabled: 'I doubt if the disasters would have occurred in the Western Desert if General Auchinleck had not been distracted by the divergent considerations of a too widely extended front.' The telegram described the vast distances within the existing command and the differences in character between the two areas. He continued: 'I have no hesitation in proposing Auchinleck's appointment.... He has shown high minded qualities of character and resolution.... There is no officer here or in India who has better credentials.... Nor can I advise that General Auchinleck should be ruined and cast aside as unfit to render any further service ... I must point out that when General Wavell was removed from the Middle East Command to India he in no way lost his reputation with the public at home or abroad.' Ministers now remembered that when it had been originally decided to set up a single unified command in the Middle East, 'it had been felt that the issues had been fairly evenly balanced'. The War Cabinet therefore agreed that while they were not entirely in favour of the separation proposal, 'the case against the reorganization was neither so strong, nor so clear cut that they could properly oppose the views of those on the spot'. As far as Auchinleck's appointment was concerned, Ministers repeated their doubts as to whether he would have the confidence of the troops.

Two more telegrams arrived from Churchill while the War Cabinet were still in session. 'Deeply regret Gott has just been shot down in the air and killed.' Much hope had already been built on the appointment of this tough and experienced desert fighter as Commander of the 8th Army. Churchill's second telegram read: 'CIGS decisively recommends Montgomery for 8th Army. Smuts and I feel this post must be filled at once. Pray send him by special plane at earliest moment.' The Vice-CIGS left the Cabinet Room to issue instructions, and Ministers agreed to a reply to Churchill concerning his reorganization proposals: 'Your further telegram has not entirely removed our misgivings, either as to division of command, or as to Auchinleck's position. But as you, Smuts and the CIGS who are on the spot are all in agreement we are prepared to authorize action proposed. We would however strongly represent to you that the continuance of the title of C-in-C Middle East to General Auchinleck would lead to confusion and misrepresentation.'[55] Churchill still refused to alter his decision, despite objections to the division of the command from the existing C-in-Cs Middle East, who suggested that a Deputy C-in-C should be appointed to relieve Alexander of the more pressing responsibilities.[56] The Prime Minister did however agree to change the name: Middle East Command remained at Cairo while the other half became the Persia and Iraq Command.

General Alexander had previously been chosen to lead the British 1st Army in 'Torch' under Eisenhower's overall command, and the two men had started work. On the 7th Ismay had told Eisenhower that Alexander would have to be taken from him and would be replaced by Montgomery; now, on the 8th, Eisenhower had to be informed that Montgomery would not be coming. General Anderson eventually filled the post. Eisenhower asked: 'Are the British really taking "Torch" seriously?'[57] Montgomery was told the latest news early on the 8th. On the same day General Auchinleck was handed a letter by Colonel Jacob at his desert HQ. Churchill wrote that on 23 June Auchinleck himself had mentioned in a cable to the CIGS that he might welcome being relieved of his command. 'At that time of crisis for the army HMG did not wish to avail themselves of your highminded offer.... The War Cabinet have now decided, for the reasons which you yourself have used, that the moment has come for a change.' The General was told of the new appointment now offered; Colonel Jacob reported: 'He did not move a muscle and remained outwardly calm.' Churchill's offer was refused; Auchinleck preferred temporary retirement, and a 'bleak and impeccable' interview with Churchill in Cairo next day failed to change his mind.[58] Also on the 9th, General Alexander arrived in Cairo to take up his new appointment; Montgomery left for the Middle East on the evening of the 10th, and Churchill departed for Teheran on the start of his journey to Moscow.

A convoy was moving painfully across the Mediterranean in another attempt to relieve Malta. The ships had passed through the Straits of Gibraltar on the 9th, with fourteen merchantmen escorted during the first stage by two battleships, three carriers, seven cruisers and thirty-two destroyers. Another carrier, the *Furious*, sailed independently to fly-in thirty-eight Spitfires to strengthen the island's defences. The carrier *Eagle* was sunk by a U-boat off Algiers on the 11th; air attacks began the following day and soon afterwards the battleships and carriers were withdrawn owing to their vulnerability in the narrow waters near Malta. Arguments and consequent lack of co-operation between the Italians and Germans led to a failure by the Italian surface fleet to intercept, but air attacks still caused terrible loss: when the last merchantmen reached Malta on the 15th, nine vessels out of the fourteen had been sunk. But the five survivors allowed Malta to live on, and as it happened, this was the last convoy which had to be sailed to Malta under the desperate conditions then prevailing.

Churchill reached Moscow on the 12th, accompanied by Averell Harriman, sent by Roosevelt to provide moral support. Brooke's aircraft, which also carried Tedder, Wavell and Cadogan, would arrive on the 13th after a false start at Teheran. The Prime Minister, well aware of his miserable duty in having to reveal the decision for no second front in 1942 – 'it was like carrying a large lump of ice to the North Pole' – had his first meeting with Stalin on the night of his arrival. Churchill's tasks so far could have been equally well undertaken by the CIGS or from London. But now Churchill's unique and highly individual qualities were essential, and as Harriman reported to Roosevelt after the first confrontation with Stalin on the 12th: 'The Prime Minister was at his best and could not have handled the discussion with greater brilliance.' This four-hour Kremlin meeting began sombre and bleak as Churchill explained there would be no cross-Channel operation in the current year. He carefully explained the reasons, including lack of air cover, strength of the opposition, uselessness of the sacrifice and approach of winter. Stalin became increasingly restless and accused the Allies of being afraid of the Germans and unwilling to take risks. But he was eventually obliged to admit that if a landing could not be made in France in 1942 'he was not entitled to demand it or to insist upon it', although 'he was bound to say that he did not agree' with Churchill's arguments. The Prime Minister's tactics were very similar to those used against the Americans in London: he had decided to start with uncompromising opposition to a 1942 operation against France, now 'the moment had come to bring "Torch" into action'. With typical drama he unfolded a map of southern France, the Mediterranean and North Africa, and scribbled a crude drawing of a crocodile, explaining the intention to attack 'the soft belly' at the same time as 'his hard snout'. The Prime Minister recorded: 'And Stalin, whose interest was now at a high pitch, said "May God prosper this undertaking."' Only 'Torch', insisted Churchill, would take pressure off the Russians, and Stalin seemed to grasp the advantages. Churchill returned to his quarters in State Villa No 7, drafted a telegram to the War Cabinet and went to bed well satisfied.

Satisfaction soon disappeared. Next night Stalin treated Churchill and his party, now joined by Brooke, Wavell and Cadogan, to an extended insult about the fighting qualities of the British, with accusations of cowardice and of wanting to stand back and allow the Russians to suffer. The attack was made all the more powerful by Stalin's manner in delivering it: his voice was low and gentle, he avoided looking Churchill in the face and only occasionally emphasized a point by gesturing with his right hand. Churchill reacted in typical fashion: his fist crashed down on the table and for five minutes he displayed his wonderful power of oratory. The content was wasted although the delivery was not. Interpreters sat stunned and only Cadogan scribbled a note which he started to read out. Stalin interrupted: 'I do not understand the words, but by God I like your spirit.' The Soviet leader sat back, large bent pipe in his grinning moustached mouth. Brooke was convinced Stalin had deliberately baited Churchill to find the measure of the man; this had been displayed, and Brooke wrote: 'I am certain that it played an important part in laying the foundations for a certain mutual understanding.' Churchill had a different interpretation, described in a cable to the War Cabinet late that night. 'I think most probable [explanation] is that his Council of Commissars did not take the news I brought as well as he did.... It is my considered opinion that in his heart, so far as he has one, Stalin knows we are right.'[59] Cadogan observed that Churchill's temper had still to be restored next day, 14 August, even after a sumptuous Kremlin banquet. 'He declared that he really did not know what he was supposed to be doing here,' wrote Cadogan. 'He would return to London without seeing Stalin again.'[60] Churchill stayed another day, during which Brooke was engaged in long and abortive staff talks with Soviet officers. The Prime Minister went to bid farewell to Stalin at 7 p.m. and expected a short interview; he emerged seven hours later after having been invited to Stalin's private apartment in the Kremlin. Talk ranged over a multitude of topics, including the situation in the Caucasus, Arctic convoys, the domestic situation in Russia, the possibility of a Norwegian operation, and even Soviet history. A communiqué was agreed, uninformative but – a major achievement – not hinting at any difference in opinion over strategic policy. Churchill left at 5.30 a.m. on the 16th, reaching Cairo forty hours later.

A number of telegrams began to reach Whitehall from Churchill giving further details of the Moscow visit. First to arrive was a cable describing the last talk with Stalin on the night of the 15th. 'The

455

greatest good will prevailed, and for the first time we got on to easy and friendly terms. I feel that I have established a personal relationship which will be helpful ... On the whole, I am definitely encouraged by my visit to Moscow ... It was my duty to go. Now they know the worst.' A signal dated 17 August gave details of the military talks undertaken by Brooke: the Russians had been unable to understand the reasons for delaying a European second front; in turn the Soviets supplied meagre and inaccurate military information. 'My own feeling,' Churchill informed the War Cabinet, 'is that it is an even chance they will hold, but CIGS will not go so far as this.' In fact, the Germans were gradually working their way through the Caucasian foothills, but they were also thrusting for Stalingrad – a mistake which was to prove fatal. On the day of the Anglo-Soviet military talks, 15 August, German formations crossed the Don at Kalach, 50 miles from Stalingrad. Another cable came from Churchill on the 19th, in response to signs of reluctance by the COS to support the idea of air forces being sent to the Soviet southern flank. 'I have committed HMG to this policy and I must ask the Cabinet for support.... Everybody always finds it convenient to ease themselves at the expense of Russia, but grave issues depend on preserving a good relationship with this tremendous army, now under dire distress.'[61]

Churchill left to tour the desert front on 19 August. On this Wednesday a total of 6,100 troops, nearly 5,000 of them Canadians, crossed the Channel for the raid on Dieppe, now named 'Jubilee' and formerly 'Rutter'. Hitler, always fearful of raids and a possible invasion, had long ordered defences to be extended and improved; German units had been warned to expect attacks especially at certain alert periods – one of these periods ended on 19 August. The operation aimed to effect landings on eight beaches, after which installations and strong-points would be destroyed before the forces withdrew at a pre-arranged time. German coast defences would be tested, and it was hoped to inflict heavy wastage on the *Luftwaffe* thereby giving some relief to the Russians. But only the assault on the cliffs on the outer western flank achieved complete success; on the eastern flanks some progress was made; in the centre the infantry and tanks met with far stiffer resistance than expected. Casualties were deplorably heavy – including 68 per cent of the Canadians, although many survived to be taken prisoner. Mountbatten, in his account to the War Cabinet at 6 p.m. on the 20th, managed to convey the impression of an almost satisfactory outcome. 'Our naval losses had been extremely light. Two-thirds of the total military forces ... were accounted for and had returned to this country. Although tanks had been got ashore they had been unable to leave the immediate vicinity of the beaches, owing to the exits being blocked. As a result, the objectives of the forces which had landed on the central beaches had not been reached. The personnel of one enemy coastal battery had been wiped out while another battery had been neutralized by a small party of determined men who had sniped the gun crew. Planning, organization and co-operation between all the Services had been excellent. The air support had been faultless.' Mountbatten said lessons learnt would be invaluable in planning for 'Round-Up', and the raid would be carefully examined to evolve new techniques against the very strong German coastal defences.[62] On the 29th the War Cabinet were told that the Dieppe raid had achieved complete surprise from the air point of view. 'It had been three hours after the attack had started before German fighters and six hours before German bombers, had appeared.... Final figures of enemy losses had been 96 destroyed, 40 probable, and 140 damaged. Our losses had been 107 aircraft (37 pilots safe).'[63]

Churchill had heard the news of the Dieppe raid while visiting Montgomery in the desert; the latter had been responsible for the army side of early planning for 'Rutter', and had strongly opposed the resurrection of the scheme at the end of July, on the grounds that secrecy would be difficult to maintain.[64] Churchill was by no means dissatisfied with the results. 'It was a costly but not unfruitful reconnaissance in force. Tactically it was a mine of experience.'[65] But for the moment the Prime Minister was preoccupied with the coming desert offensive; he was well pleased with the Alexander-Montgomery combination. 'I am sure we were heading for disaster under the former régime,' reported Churchill to the War Cabinet on the 21st. 'A complete change of atmosphere has taken place.' This signal added: 'It seems probable that Rommel will attack during the moon period before the end of August.'[66]

The Prime Minister left for home on the evening of 23 August, and two days later, at 5.30 p.m., he received his accolade from the War Cabinet before giving Ministers his main impressions on the visit. First he dealt with Egypt: Rommel had been expected to launch an early attack, but since returning to London the Prime Minister had been informed of evidence 'which pointed the other way and it was now not so certain that the attack would take place'. Should an enemy offensive be launched, Alexander aimed to fight with the intention of complete destruction of the enemy's armour, and 'for this purpose it might be necessary to uncover Cairo'. The 45,000 rear service troops in the Delta were being organized for defence. Brooke said that 'the steps taken to reorganize our forces had already shown good results, but would require some time for their full development. It was proposed to form a large mass of manoeuvre which could be used to exploit an advantage if opportunity offered. Montgomery had obtained a quick grasp of the situation.' Churchill said Auchinleck had been unwilling to accept the Iraq-Iranian command for two reasons. 'In the first place, he did not think that the Iraq-Iranian command was a very good arrangement. Secondly, his confidence in himself had suffered a severe shock as the result of his supercession.' The Prime Minister added that 'there was no reason why he should not recover his confidence and render further good service later on'. In fact Auchinleck returned to his old command in India in June 1943.[67]

Churchill had arranged with Alexander that the latter should send a single codeword when Rommel's offensive began; on 30 August this signal flashed to London: 'Zip'.[68] The War Cabinet situation report for 31 August declared: 'Field-Marshal Rommel is thought to have renewed his attack.... No reports of the fighting have been received.'[69]

Rommel stepped down from his vehicle on the first day of battle and told his doctor: 'Professor, the decision I have taken to attack today is the hardest I have ever taken. Either the army in Russia succeeds in getting through to Grozny and we in Africa manage to reach the Suez Canal, or ...' Rommel threw up his hands. Montgomery wrote: 'I think officers and men knew in their hearts that if we lost at Alam Halfa we would probably have lost Egypt.'[70] Rommel's plan was similar to that at Gazala in May: hold in the north, feint in the centre and punch through in the south after gaps had been made in the British minefields. This southern striking force would then sweep north on the 31st to encircle the British army. Rommel relied on speed, surprise and the assumption that the British, as in the past, would disintegrate when thrown off-balance. Montgomery's great achievement was to impose his vigorous will over the 8th Army so soon after having taken command: he gave strict orders for armour to remain concentrated and not to become bogged down in close fighting – no more wild, unco-ordinated tank charges. Horrocks, new commander of 13 Corps, was to prove a perfect subordinate. Moreover, by deploying 13 Corps at Alam Halfa ridge to the rear of the main British positions, Montgomery prevented Rommel from pushing on eastwards: to do so would have exposed his left flank. The ridge would first have to be cleared, yet an attempt would be perilous – German tanks would have to thrust through a series of depressions, hindering mobility and allowing the RAF to strike, after which the Germans would be drawn on to 22 Armoured Brigade, positioned hull down on the reverse slopes. Montgomery therefore imposed his will not only on the 8th Army, but also on the enemy. And the Germans lost the battle within the first few hours.

The offensive began on the night of the 30th. The RAF retaliated almost immediately: progress through the minefield became painfully slow. Both surprise and speed had therefore been lost, but Rommel, on the telephone at his HQ throughout the night, ordered the attack to continue. Montgomery was woken to be informed of the start of the battle. 'Excellent,' he declared, and went back to sleep. Dust storms hampered the RAF on the 31st, but although German tanks managed to regroup they found themselves stuck in the depressions south of Alam Halfa and exposed to heavy concentrated fire: 22 German tanks were destroyed during the day. The same pattern was repeated on 1 and 2 September; attacks on the Halfa ridge failed and Rommel was fast running out of fuel. Retreat began on the 3rd and was completed on the 6th. Montgomery decided to allow Rommel to run; the 8th Army would be preserved intact for the decisive battle of El Alamein. At 0700 hours on 7 September Montgomery therefore ordered all further moves against the Germans to be stopped.[71] Also on the 7th the War Cabinet were informed that 'it was thought our losses were light.... Rommel had lost about 80 tanks and very large numbers of motor vehicles. We had lost 52 tanks, but we had remained in possession of the battlefield and a number of these might be reconditioned. The enemy front was now being held by Italians while the German forces were withdrawn to recoup and re-fit.'[72]

Both British and German authorities use the same word to describe Alma Halfa – 'a turning point'. The battle must be linked to operations conducted by Auchinleck at the Alamein line in early July, when the momentum of Rommel's advance had been halted by exhausted, disorganized units of the 8th Army. Auchinleck had started to tilt the balance away from Rommel. British armour had stood firm and had allowed the enemy to be drawn on; the RAF had begun to win air superiority. Developments had now been taken further, and British morale had been boosted, and the RAF superiority had been increased. These were soon to be the means of inflicting total defeat upon the vaunted *Afrika Korps*; Rommel, suffering from chronic stomach ailments, nasal diphtheria, poor blood circulation, knew himself his desert reign was almost done.

Beginnings

The tide might turn. All depended on Alexander and Montgomery – and upon 'Torch'. Churchill and his War Cabinet were fully aware that even if they could stand the strain of further setbacks, the country might not. Churchill's stock was higher now than at any previous time in 1942, but this would slump lower than ever before if the long list of failures received merely one more addition: Dunkirk, Dakar, Greece, Crete, Hong Kong, Singapore, Burma, Tobruk – disasters which had seemed interspaced by apparent fruitless talkings and military inactivity. 'There may be trouble ahead,' Brendan Bracken warned Sir Charles Wilson. 'The Prime Minister must win his battle in the desert or get out.... There is a good deal going on under the surface.'[1] Churchill knew the danger around him. 'It is indeed remarkable that I was not in this bleak lull dismissed from power, or confronted with demands for changes in my methods, which it was known I should never accept. I should then have vanished from the scene with a load of calamity on my shoulders.'[2]

The climax approached; Russia might soon collapse and the weight of the *Wehrmacht* might bear down from the north; the shipping situation remained serious; Malta remained besieged; the Japanese still threatened India; Cripps stood ready to replace Churchill. Rommel's tanks were still massed at the gates of Egypt, despite Alam Halfa – and, critics asked, why had the *Afrika Korps* been able to retreat unmolested after this battle? So much therefore depended upon North Africa. 'I am concentrating my main thoughts upon "Torch" from now on,' cabled Churchill to Roosevelt on the day after his return to London.[3] Ten days before, the Prime Minister had signalled the War Cabinet from Cairo: 'Stalin is entirely convinced of the great advantages of "Torch" and I do trust that it is being driven forward with superhuman energy on both sides of the Ocean.'[4] Within hours of arriving back in London on 25

August, Churchill had found this trust sadly misplaced. Planning for 'Torch' threatened to collapse.

President Roosevelt had given 'Torch' his full blessing at a White House conference on 30 July: the operation was to be undertaken at the earliest possible date, would be the principal American objective, and should have priority over preparations for all other operations.[5] This firm ruling by the American C-in-C appeared to settle the problem contained in the CCS memorandum of 24 July – that 'Torch' was dependent on developments in Russia ruling out 'Round-Up' in 1943. Planners on both sides of the Atlantic had a clear directive.

Eisenhower submitted his first plan to the British COS on 10 August; this provided for four landings: Bône, Algiers, Oran and Casablanca. The first two would be handled by a British force with a strong American contingent, while American troops alone would deal with Oran and Casablanca, with divisions for the latter sailing direct from the United States. But a landing at Casablanca was considered by the COS to be dangerous, in view of the heavy Atlantic swell. Moreover, the COS had decided the date for the operation should be about 7 October: any longer would increase the possibilities of leakage and hence a German move to forestall the operation by moving into Tunisia. But the American divisions for Casablanca might not be ready until the end of the first week in November: the threat of an early Axis move into Tunisia would therefore be increased, and, as the COS declared on 11 August: 'The whole conception of "Torch" may stand or fall on this question of early Allied occupation of Tunisia.'[6] Almost immediately a new complication arose – the same difficulty which had dogged earlier discussion on 'Gymnast': shortage of shipping, both with landing-craft and escorts. Eisenhower therefore produced a revised plan which attempted to remove these three main problems – the Atlantic swell, the date, and lack of shipping; this scheme, submitted to the COS on 22 August, scrapped the idea of a Casablanca landing: the port would be taken instead by forces landing at Oran and moving in from the rear. The launching date could be 15 October, but Eisenhower warned this might be over-optimistic. And even 15 October might not prevent the Germans getting to Tunisia first: the Joint Planning Staff concluded on the 23rd that, taking into account the distances of Bône and Algiers from Tunis, any serious French resistance would delay the Allied forces to such a degree that Tunis could not be taken before the Germans built up overwhelming strength in the area, moreover, it would take up to four months to capture Casablanca from the land.[7] Also on 23 August Eisenhower described his serious misgivings about the whole operation in a memorandum to the COS. 'It is my opinion that this expedition ... is not sufficiently powerful to accomplish, against the potential opposition ... the purpose prescribed by the Combined Chiefs of Staff.' He stressed the dangers of determined French resistance, the threat to Allied communications through the Straits of Gibraltar in the event of Spanish intervention, and the weakness in naval strength. 'I believe that if the two Governments could find the naval, air and ground forces, with the shipping, to carry out, simultaneously with the attack planned inside the Mediterranean, a strong assault at Casablanca, the chances for success would be greatly increased.' But Eisenhower added: 'Such simultaneous attacks could not be made before 7 November at earliest.' The COS, discussing this Memorandum with Eisenhower on the 24th, could only conclude by expressing their opinion that the problem of inadequate naval forces would have to be put to Churchill and Roosevelt.[8]

This apparent impasse was bad enough; infinitely worse was the proposal submitted to London next day, 25 August, by the American Joint Chiefs of Staff – described by Churchill as a 'bombshell'. Eisenhower had suggested the Casablanca landing should be cancelled; the Joint Chiefs took the opposite view: landings should be confined to the Atlantic coast of Morocco, despite the risk of surf; plans for assaults at Bône and Algiers should be scrapped, despite the risk of Axis build-up in Tunisia; the furthest the US Chiefs would agree to go into the Mediterranean was Oran, over 200 miles from Algiers and 600 from Tunis. The British COS, and Eisenhower, had thought along the lines of an Allied force plunging into the Mediterranean to secure the whole of North Africa as a base for an assault on Europe. The American Joint Chiefs declared a more cautious approach should be adopted: first secure a safe base in Morocco. Next day the British Mission in Washington supplied some of the reasoning behind the American attitude: shortages of resources as a result of Pacific demands – plus the increasing influence of 'the Pacific school'; doubts over British ability to hold out in Egypt; the need for a hold in Western Africa to protect US shipping lanes in the event of a general collapse in the European theatre. Dill had already indicated that the Americans were concerned to avoid a catastrophic conclusion to the first major operation of their army in the European theatre.[9] But as far as the British Mission was concerned, this catastrophe might well result from the new American proposals: the Germans would pour in troops and the Middle East would be lost. 'It would be better to abandon whole operation rather than undertake it on such limited scale.'[10]

Also on the 26th, Brooke took over again as Chairman of the COS meetings, following his return to London the previous day – and he immediately revealed himself as opposed both to Eisenhower's idea of cancelling the Casablanca landing and to the latest American idea of cancelling the Algiers attempt. A base must be secured in Morocco, he insisted, and he wrote in his diary: 'I am afraid I was very rude to all members of the COS.'[11] And yet from this opposition to both attitudes came the motivation for compromise; next morning, 27 August, the COS began by approving the proposals on which all of them, and Eisenhower, agreed: landings at Algiers and Oran. Following Brooke's insistence, qualified approval was given for Casablanca, and a message to this effect was sent to Washington. On the same day, Churchill exerted his influence. 'We are all profoundly disconcerted by the [Joint Chief's] Memorandum,' signalled the Prime Minister to Roosevelt. 'It seems to me that the whole pith of the operation will be lost if we do not take Algiers.... Not to go east of Oran is making the enemy a present not only of Tunis but of Algiers.... We are all convinced that Algiers is the key to the whole operation.' He warned: 'I hope, Mr President, you will bear in mind the language I have held to Stalin, supported by Harriman with your full approval. If "Torch" collapses or is cut down as is now proposed, I should feel my position painfully affected.'[12]

British and American views confronted one another at a CCS meeting on Friday, 28 August. Admiral Cunningham, presenting the British case, declared that the 'essence of the operation was... the early capture of Tunisia. The capture of Tunisia would threaten the Mediterranean position of the enemy. Further advantages of clearing the whole northern coast of Africa would be that it would provide a point of departure for the subsequent entry into Europe, ease the shipping situation by opening the Mediterranean, relieve the danger to Malta and ensure satisfactory outcome to the battle for Egypt.' He admitted the existence of risks, including French opposition and Spanish intervention, but he claimed that 'the new directive proposed by the US Chiefs of Staff would produce all these disadvantages without the corresponding advantages', and he described the severe setbacks in concentrating on Morocco alone. 'Communications to the eastward were so bad that it would be months before our forces could reach Tunisia.... If determined efforts were not made to carry out the operation as originally contemplated, we would lose our one opportunity of wresting the initiative from Hitler.' Admiral Leahy, former US Ambassador to Vichy France and now Chief of Staff to the President, opened the American reply by stressing the difficulties of supporting the allied army inside the Mediterranean through the Straits of Gibraltar; but Cunningham, former C-in-C Mediterranean Fleet, claimed that 'the supply ships could be got through ... provided the south shore was in our hands. It would be difficult, but certainly not impossible, to pass convoys through.' General Marshall's chief objection to the proposals for landing inside the Mediterranean was the attrition to naval resources; he also admitted that 'success in this operation was essential, since the reputation of the US armed service was at stake'. Marshall pointed out that 'the British COS had strongly emphasized the hazards of "Sledgehammer" but were making no mention of similar hazards incident to "Torch" '. Admiral King agreed. Cunningham might well have replied that the reverse also held true: the Americans had previously insisted that 'Sledgehammer' should be undertaken, despite the risks, and now they seemed to be suffering from undue nervousness over 'Torch'. Instead, Cunningham maintained that 'a North African venture was far easier than a landing on the coast of France'. Discussion, summed up by Leahy as 'most beneficial' failed to alter either British or American views.[13]

Churchill, in his appeal to Roosevelt on the 27th, had mentioned the three landing targets as agreed upon by the British Chiefs of Staff: Algiers, Oran, and, with reluctance by all members apart from Brooke, Casablanca. These three were taken up by Roosevelt in his reply to the Prime Minister on the 31st: he insisted on Casablanca and Oran and maintained that to help avoid hostile French reaction, the initial attack should be made by an exclusively American ground force, supported by naval transport and aircraft provided by Britain: a British landing might be made at Algiers, but not until a week later. Roosevelt had therefore acquiesced to the British view that a stab should be made inside the Mediterranean; as far as necessary shipping was concerned, Roosevelt said that 'we should re-examine our resources and strip everything to the bone to make the third landing possible'. He still hoped the operation might be launched on 14 October.[14] This reply marked a definite step towards agreement, but the British COS, meeting on the 31st, objected to the interval between the American and British landings – Algiers was of cardinal importance and must be among the initial objectives. Nor were the British convinced that the Americans would receive better reception from the French – and British participation would anyway be revealed through the presence of her ships and aircraft.[15] This latter point was put by Churchill in his reply to Roosevelt on 1 September; he added: 'It seems to us vital that Algiers should be occupied simultaneously with Casablanca and Oran. Here is the most friendly and hopeful spot where the political reactions would be most decisive.... To give up Algiers for the sake of the doubtfully practicable landing at Casablanca seemed to us a very serious decision.'[16] Also on 1 September,

464

Brooke was given 'a gloomy picture' by the British Ambassador at Madrid, Sir Samuel Hoare: the Spaniards might pounce upon the Gibraltar base, which was intended as Eisenhower's HQ and the main RAF staging area. Brooke wrote in his diary: 'It is hard to maintain one's determination to carry out an operation when everybody keeps pouring into one's ears all the awful dangers.'[17] The CIGS was evidently feeling the strain; so too was Churchill, described by Brooke as 'dejected, tired and depressed'. The Prime Minister had almost made up his mind to fly to Washington, and an aircraft was being kept in permanent readiness for him to leave; his doctor, Sir Charles Wilson, feared for his health.

Roosevelt now agreed to the proposal for simultaneous landings at Casablanca, Oran and Algiers. His reply, received on 3 September, specified that 34,000 American troops should land at Casablanca, 25,000 at Oran, and 10,000 at Algiers with British troops following an hour later. The British COS were still not satisfied. Discussions held in the afternoon of the 3rd decided that landing-craft requirements would be difficult to meet unless the size of the Casablanca force were reduced by up to 12,000 men – the heavy proportion at Casablanca might anyway be a mistake in view of the surf difficulties. Churchill sought this reduction in a message to Roosevelt that night; Roosevelt replied next day: 'We are getting very close together,' and he agreed to cut the Casablanca strength by 5,000. The COS decided on the 5th that this would be sufficient, and Churchill signalled later in the day: 'We agree to the military lay-out as you propose it.' '"Torch" is now again in full swing,' wrote a relieved Brooke in his diary.[18]

The threat to 'Torch' had been removed largely through the realization by both Churchill and Roosevelt of the political and diplomatic, as well as military, necessity for the operation. Without 'Torch', Churchill would have had an even more difficult political time at home; moreover, he had committed the West to 'Torch' in his conversations with Stalin. But as far as relations with Russia were concerned, of equal importance were the PQ convoys, and, ironically, these were now threatened by 'Torch' itself. PQ 18 had sailed on 2 September after elaborate defensive plans had been carefully worked out, including the provision of an escort carrier. The War Cabinet were informed at 5.30 p.m. on the 14th: '12 ships of the convoy have been reported as lost' and on the 21st: '27 ships out of the 40 in the recent convoy had arrived in Archangel.'[19] Thirteen ships lost, despite the stronger escort, seemed a depressing result; on the other hand, no previous convoy had been subjected to such repeated air attacks as PQ 18 – and the *Luftwaffe* had suffered heavily. The loss ratio was acceptable under the yardstick of 50 per cent sinkings. But, also on the 21st, Churchill revealed to Ministers the clash between the next PQ sailing and the launching of 'Torch': one or the other would have to be severely delayed.

The Prime Minister, despite vigorous objections, had had to agree to the date for 'Torch' being fixed at 8 November: American equipment and troops, and British vessels allotted to 'Torch' from Russian convoy duty, would not be ready any earlier.[20] Churchill now told the War Cabinet: 'If we decided to send a further PQ convoy before Operation "Torch", this would mean Operation "Torch" would have to be delayed until either 24 or 28 November.' He believed that to delay 'Torch' would be 'to court disaster': rumours were already circulating about an impending operation, and the weather would worsen. He hinted that a delay might also affect American determination to see the operation through, declaring 'it was ... significant that since a week ago there had been a big change in the atmosphere at Washington, where the authorities were now full out on Operation "Torch" and determined to make it a success'. Churchill therefore said the War Cabinet must decide whether the operation should in fact be pushed forward at the earliest possible date, and if so, 'what should be done about convoys to Russia?' The Russians would be 'greatly upset' and in view of the 'very grim picture which the suspension of the convoys would present', he urged for reconsideration of Operation 'Jupiter' against northern Norway – Churchill, at this time, was considering the use of Canadian troops for this expedition. But, he told the War Cabinet, the COS 'took a rather unfavourable view of the possibility of being able to provide the necessary forces and particularly the shipping for "Jupiter" in addition to "Torch"'. He had discussed the situation at a meeting with the COS that morning, also attended by Eisenhower, at which Churchill had 'gained the impression' that 'Torch' would also push 'Round-Up' back into 1944. This delay to the large-scale cross-Channel operation had always been envisaged by the American Joint Chiefs of Staff as a necessary penalty to pay for the adoption of 'Torch', but until now Churchill had refused to accept the fact. The meeting had resulted in the drafting of telegrams to Roosevelt and Stalin, and, as Churchill proposed to tell the President, the delay to 'Round-Up' would be 'another tremendous blow to Stalin. Already Maisky is asking questions about the Spring offensive.'

The War Cabinet agreed that 'the carrying-out of Operation "Torch" as early as possible was of paramount importance', and also agreed to the despatch of the telegram to Roosevelt. This would contain the suggested message to Stalin and the President was asked for his approval. 'This is a formidable moment in Anglo-

American-Soviet relations,' Churchill told Roosevelt, 'and you and I must be united in any statement made.' He added that simply to tell Stalin there would be no more PQ convoys until 1943 would be extremely dangerous, and he suggested mention should be made of staff talks for 'Jupiter'. The message to Stalin began: 'The effect of "Torch" must be either, (a) to oblige the Germans to divert air and land forces to counter our move, or (b) to compel them to accept the new position created by the success of "Torch", which would then create a further diversion by the threat of attack against Sicily and the south of Europe.' Russia, in order to obtain the benefits of this drawing-off of German strength, would have to accept the fact that there would be no more large-scale PQ convoys in 1942, although means of sending supplies on a reduced scale were being examined.[21] The message to Roosevelt and the suggested cable to Stalin were communicated to Washington at 2 a.m. on the 22nd; Roosevelt would take almost a fortnight to consider the matter.

In addition to anxiety over this 'formidable moment in Anglo-American-Soviet' relations, Churchill was having to deal with another crisis, this time with his domestic political affairs. The Prime Minister's stress and strain were clearly revealed at a War Cabinet meeting in his room on Wednesday, 9 September: on the previous day a Commons debate on the war situation, scheduled to last two days, had come to a premature end shortly after a speech by Attlee. Cripps, Leader of the Commons, had criticized the fact that MPs 'had not wished to take part in the discussion' and some had even left while Churchill was speaking. Cripps's remarks led to his first recorded clash with the Prime Minister in a War Cabinet session – although this particular Minute was marked as 'Confidential Record, not for circulation'. Churchill said that the statement by the Lord Privy Seal 'might be construed as an encouragement to members to make speeches critical of the Government's conduct of the war. In his view, it was satisfactory that members should have found in his speech nothing on which they wished to comment. He welcomed the silent support of the House of Commons, and he deprecated the view that Parliament was not fulfilling its function unless it was actively and critically debating the war situation.' Cripps retorted that he had not regretted the absence of critical speeches but he 'thought it a matter of regret that the House had let pass this opportunity for the expression of their support of the Government's policy', and he believed 'the collapse of the debate would produce a bad effect, both in this country and abroad.... Even critical speeches could be of assistance to the Government in their conduct of the war – and it was a

467

mistake to assume that all criticism was necessarily capricious or hostile.'[22]

The incident was more than mere shadow-boxing or a display of the Prime Minister's peevishness. Churchill was in fact having to deal with a considerable threat from the austere, deadly-serious Cripps. The Lord Privy Seal was by now intensely dissatisfied with the existing machinery for central direction of the war; among other measures he suggested was the creation of a War Planning Directorate, consisting of three men working under the Prime Minister as Minister of Defence, who would concentrate on broad strategic planning and would supersede the COS for this purpose. Each area of war would have a single commander, directly responsible to the Directorate. Day-to-day administration would be left to the COS. Churchill immediately disagreed with this 'planner's dream', which would, in effect, have made him into a Supreme C-in-C directly commanding all three Services throughout the world. Churchill therefore condemned the proposal: the Directorate and the COS would have been two rival bodies; the Directorate would be in the happy position of formulating plans without having to execute them.

The two men argued throughout September, with neither prepared to compromise. By the time of the incident at the War Cabinet meeting on the 9th, Cripps was starting to consider resigning. Churchill well knew this would be a political calamity and possibly disastrous at that strained moment. The situation approached a climax in the third week of September: Cripps wrote to Churchill on the 21st intimating he might leave the Government – he claimed he felt out of touch with the Prime Minister and with the war situation. 'Problems of strategy are conceived by the War Cabinet hurriedly, without sufficient information and often in isolation'; in answer to Churchill's criticism of his Joint Planning Directorate scheme, he commented: 'It is not right, in my view, that the War Cabinet should appear to carry responsibility for the conduct of the war, since it is not in a position to discharge that responsibility.' 'I am surprised,' replied Churchill on the 22nd, 'and somewhat pained, to receive your letter.... I always do my best to see my principal colleagues. I have always found our conversations agreeable and stimulating.' He added: 'Great operations impend which are in full accordance with your own conceptions and on which we are all agreed. We must have fibre and fortitude to endure the delays and await the outcome. As I myself find waiting more trying than action, I can fully understand the uneasiness you say you feel.'[23]

This tone of studied reasonableness failed to prevent a stormy interview between Churchill and Cripps late at night on 30

September; Cripps asked to see Eden urgently on 1 October and said he had 'reached the parting of the ways' with Churchill.[24] Next day the Prime Minister persuaded him to stay, for the moment; Cripps wrote on the 3rd that his disagreements would have led him to resign, 'were it not for the special circumstances to which you and my other colleagues have drawn my attention. ... I have therefore decided that it is my duty, in the interests of the successful prosecution of the coming operations, to delay taking any further action ... until the operations are at least well launched.'[25] Churchill, according to Eden, was convinced Cripps had a 'Machiavellian plot'; Eden disagreed but also believed it would be 'crazy to have a political upheaval here, even a minor one'.[26]

'If "Torch" fails,' Eden had warned Cripps, 'we are all sunk.' Almost daily, the operations in North Africa were looming in importance, both strategic and domestic, and in late September and October suspense began to rise, even creeping into the cold official Minutes of War Cabinet discussions. Nor was it sufficient for 'Torch' alone to be a success: for strategic reasons, Rommel had also to be pushed back and defeated in the East; for political reasons it would be damaging if the predominantly American landings succeeded while the British 8th Army in Egypt remained inactive or failed again. In September Churchill therefore began to put his familiar pressure on Cairo for early action, fretting at the same time for operations in North Norway. 'I am anxiously awaiting some account of your intentions,' cabled Churchill to Alexander on 17 September. Two days later the C-in-C replied that he would attack on 24 October – Operation 'Lightfoot'. The Prime Minister immediately sought to bring this forward so that victory could be gained on the eve of 'Torch'; Alexander proved as stubborn as his predecessor. 'If I were to be obliged to carry this operation before my target date,' he signalled on the 21st, 'I should not only be not satisfied with the chance of success, but I should be definitely apprehensive as to the result.'[27] Brooke had a 'hammer and tongs' argument with the Prime Minister on the 23rd, but later in the day Churchill cabled: 'We are in your hands, and of course a victorious battle makes amends for much delay.'

Also on this Wednesday, Rommel left the desert for home, under doctor's orders. Mussolini was now back in his capital after his abortive trip to North Africa; Rommel saw him on the 24th and complained that 'he still did not realize the full gravity of the situation' in North Africa.[28] On the same day Churchill complained to Brooke that all his plans for action, in the Middle East, against Norway, were obstructed. 'Everybody did nothing but produce difficulties.' Brooke reported the emotional Prime Minister being so upset that 'tears streamed down his face'.[29] 'Mussolini is convinced that Rommel will not come back,' wrote Ciano in his diary on the 27th. 'He finds Rommel physically and morally shaken.'[30] An anxious Beaverbrook told Eden on the 29th that Churchill appeared 'bowed' and 'not the man he was'.[31]

Hitler was also feeling the strain. On 9 September the Führer had been delighted by Intelligence reports indicating all Russian reserves had been used up. Stalingrad, he believed, must soon fall. This opinion had been shared by Ministers in London; the Cabinet War Room record declared on 14 September: 'German forces are now closing in on the town' and reports for the next few days showed a steadily tightening German grip. Then a new note began to sound; Ministers were told on the 21st: 'At Stalingrad the Russians were still fighting fiercely but the situation is very confused.... It is satisfactory that the enemy has made such small progress during the week.' And on the 28th: 'In the Stalingrad area Russian attacks from the north of the city have contributed to the slowing up of the enemy's progress in Stalingrad itself.'[32] Next day Ciano commented on a speech by Hitler: 'How much he's changed. Last year, at about this time, he made an address that was a paean of victory. Now, at best, it may be said that he has made a defensive address.'[33]

Russia's incredible resistance was once again causing amazement in London and consternation in Berlin. But the terrible struggle hung in grim balance. 'I have to inform you,' cabled Stalin to Churchill on 5 October, 'that the situation in the Stalingrad area has deteriorated.... The Germans managed to secure superiority in the air in the ratio of two to one.... Even the bravest troops are helpless if they lack air protection.' He urged that the next PQ convoy should carry more aircraft.[34] Yet also on 5 October came Roosevelt's reply to Churchill's suggested approach to the Soviet leader, concerning the suspension of the PQ convoys. 'I feel most strongly that we should not tell Stalin that the convoy will not sail,' cabled the President. 'I would like to urge that a different technique be employed, in which evasion and dispersion are the guiding factors. Thus let PQ 19 sail in successive groups, comprising the fastest ships.' Roosevelt's message was read to the War Cabinet at 11.15 a.m. on the 6th, after which Churchill and the COS met to consider a reply; the draft was approved by the War Cabinet at 10.30 p.m. and immediately despatched to Washington. 'There is no possibility of letting PQ 19 sail in successive groups.... Neither can the fact that the convoy is not sailing be concealed from the Russians any longer. Maisky is already aware of the position, though not officially informed.' Churchill said that Britain was preparing 10 ships to sail individually during the October dark

470

period. 'They are all British ships for which the crew will have to volunteer, the danger being terrible and their sole hope if sunk far from help being Arctic clothing and such sheeting arrangement as can be placed in a life-boat.... I believe the blunt truth is best with Stalin.' Appended to the message was a note from the First Sea Lord: 'The voyage in anything but a full escorted convoy is so hazardous that it should only be undertaken by volunteers who clearly understand the risk. The chance of crews of stricken ships surviving when they take to their boats is remote.'[35] Next day, 7 October, Stalin appealed to Roosevelt for a minimum monthly delivery of 500 aircraft and 8,000 tanks; but, on the 8th, the President wired his approval to the original draft message to Stalin and the War Cabinet authorized its despatch.[36]

On the same day Beaverbrook again told Eden that he feared for Churchill's health, and Eden commented in his diary: 'Brendan [Bracken] also said "W. was very 'low'" yesterday when Max saw him. I told him that his powers of recuperation were very great.'[37] At least Churchill could be cheered by progress in 'Torch' planning; Admiral Cunningham gave an excellent report to the CCS on 9 October: 'The whole of the forces in Great Britain would embark in four or five days and proceed to Scotland where landing exercises would take place between 18 and 25 October', and General Marshall told the meeting that 'the telegrams he had received from General Eisenhower were encouraging'.[38] Another, delicate, aspect of Anglo-American co-operation was discussed by the War Cabinet on the 13th; the issue had first been mentioned on 31 August, when Eden had expressed anxiety about the proportion of coloured troops being sent over in the American troop build-up – about 10 per cent of the whole – and he had commented that 'having regard to the various difficulties to which this policy was likely to give rise, including the fact that the health of coloured troops would be likely to suffer during the English winter, he thought that we were justified in pressing the United States to reduce as far as possible the number of coloured troops.'[39] Now, on 13 October, the War Cabinet discussed a suggestion that a booklet should be issued to British officers, titled *Notes of Relations with Coloured Troops*, to give general guidance. Ministers agreed in discussion that 'it was desirable that the people of this country should avoid becoming too friendly with coloured American troops'. On the other hand, 'while it was right that our troops and our people should be educated to know what the American attitude was, it was equally important that the Americans should recognize that we have a different problem ... they must not expect our authorities, civil or military, to assist them in enforcing a policy of segregation.' One danger to avoid was mentioned at the meeting – 'a certain number of instances had arisen in which well-intentioned persons had extended invitations to American white and coloured troops at the same time'.[40] Cadogan described in his diary another incident mentioned at this session: Ministers were told that a black official at the Colonial Office had been barred from his favourite London restaurant because the place was now patronized by American officers; Cadogan recorded Churchill as commenting: 'That's all right: if he takes a banjo with him they'll think he's one of the band.'[41]

Also on the 13th, Stalin sent an extremely curt reply to Churchill's news of PQ suspensions: 'I received your message of 9 October. Thank you.'[42] Anglo-Soviet relations sunk abysmally. On the other hand, military news from Russia continued to improve: Stalingrad persisted in defying the Germans, and Ministers were told on the 14th that the anticipated attack on Leningrad seemed to have been abandoned.

Attending this War Cabinet meeting on the 14th was General Smuts, who gave a long report on the desert situation which was soon to be proved perceptive and wise. The South African leader had had several talks with Alexander and other commanders, but not Montgomery. 'The change in the 8th Army since General Alexander's appointment was unbelievable,' said Smuts. 'Our tank position was very strong. The training of the troops had been well carried out. We could look forward to the results of the battle with some confidence.' But Smuts said he had 'sounded a note of warning' to Alexander. 'On this occasion there was no chance of outflanking the enemy. As we were attacking on so narrow a front, only 30 miles, we would almost certainly have to fight our way through heavily defended positions.' He had therefore cautioned Alexander to be prepared not to meet immediate success and had advised him to keep on attacking to fight a way through. 'We might have to sustain heavy casualties.... But our losses were unlikely to be greater than the heavy loss which we had suffered in recent retreats. We might have to keep up the pressure of the attack for a week.' Alexander had agreed and intended to rely 'very much on strong artillery preparations and to blast his way through.... His tanks would be in close reserve and would be kept for the final blow.'[43] Churchill would have done well to remember this assessment in a few days' time.

The Russians now began to display their anger with the British. On 14 October a declaration was issued by the Soviet Government advocating the immediate trial of every war criminal already in Allied hands; within hours Molotov specifically announced that Hess should be tried by an international tribunal.[44] Next day Eden complained to Maisky that information concerning 'Torch' was being leaked by the Ambassador – on the same day, 15 October, Jodl suggested to Hitler that Vichy France should be permitted to send reinforcements to North Africa to repel an invasion. On 19 October *Pravda* published an article on Hess suggesting that Great Britain was a place of refuge for gangsters, and describing the British view that Hess was not liable for trial until after the war as an attempt to ignore his crime. The Ambassador at Moscow believed the campaign was intended to stir British public opinion against Churchill's Government.[45] The War Cabinet were told on the 20th that a question had been put down in the Commons for Eden to answer on the 21st, and Ministers approved a draft reply that 'there was no reason to apply to Hess any treatment other than that which was being laid down and elaborated for war criminals generally; and that Hess could not be responsible for any of the misdeeds for which the Germans had been found guilty in their invasion of Russia, since at the time he had come to this country Germany and Soviet Russia had still had diplomatic relations.'[46] But the only way in which Anglo-Soviet relations could improve was through a successful offensive; once again the burden on 'Torch' and 'Lightfoot' had been increased.

Churchill signalled Alexander on the 20th: 'Events are moving in our favour both in North Africa and Vichy France, and "Torch" goes forward steadily and punctually. But all our hopes are centred upon the battle you and Montgomery are going to fight. It may well be the key to the future....'[47] First 'Torch' transports slipped down the Clyde on Thursday, 22 October; next evening at 21.40 hours Operation 'Lightfoot' began – the Battle of El Alamein. Rommel was still in Austria.

All day the RAF had bombarded enemy airfields, supply lines and batteries. Now 1,000 guns roared along the British line and 8th Army infantrymen swept forward into the German minefields. 'We are ready NOW,' declared Montgomery's personal message to officers and men. 'The battle which is now about to begin will be one of the decisive battles of history. It will be the turning point of the war. The eyes of the whole world will be on us....'

The British had more troops – 195,000 against 50,000 German and 54,000 Italians; twice as many tanks and twice as much artillery. The air advantage was even greater. And morale had never been higher. Montgomery envisaged a 'dogfight' lasting 12 days: he would aim first at destroying the enemy infantry, meanwhile fending off the enemy armour. The battle would follow three stages, first, two corridors would be punched through the enemy minefields by 30 Corps infantry divisions, one in the north sector, one in the south, and armoured divisions from 10 Corps would filter through these gaps; second, enemy armour would be contained while the German and Italian infantry strength was 'crumbled' through attacks from flank and rear; third, the enemy armour would be forced to counter-attack and would be met by British tanks embedded in firm defensive positions among the enemy minefields. Much depended on the initial advance; the first few hours would therefore be critical. Ministers clustered round the daily situation report in the Cabinet War Room.

'CABINET WAR ROOM RECORD: 24 hours ending 07.00, 25 October 1942. Egypt. Northern Sector. By 03.30 hours on the 24th our troops had captured their first objective and had succeeded in the main in reaching their final objectives by 05.30. By 06.30 a portion of our armoured formations was starting to pass through the gaps in the enemy minefields created by our initial advance.... Southern Sector. By 05.25 hours on the 24th our advanced elements had reached three miles west of Qaret El Himeimat, but later were heavily counter-attacked by tanks and were forced to withdraw. Other troops in this sector were delayed by machine-gun and anti-tank gun positions....'[48]

Montgomery feared the leading tank formations were hesitating to fight out into the open at the end of the minefield corridors; he gave orders on the 24th that any commander guilty of hanging back would be instantly removed. On the 25th, considered by Montgomery as 'the real crisis of the battle', armoured formations in the southern corridor had extreme difficulty in pushing through into the open where they could manoeuvre.[49] Rommel reached the desert at dusk.

'CABINET WAR ROOM RECORD: 24 hours ending 07.00, 26 October 1942. Egypt. In the extreme north enemy counter attack was repelled, and our own troops mopped up isolated enemy resistance in their final objective. The passage of our armoured formations through the gaps in the enemy minefield was delayed somewhat ... but eventually it was completed.... There had been no major tank battles so far. In the southern sector an armoured formation passed through the gaps made in the enemy minefields but was held up by anti-tank gunfire, by 30 German tanks in hull down position and by intensive artillery fire.'[50]

By this Monday, 26 October, all fast troopships for 'Torch' were underway from the Clyde and the American convoys had left US ports. War Cabinet Ministers were told at 5.30 p.m. that on the first day of the El Alamein battle RAF aircraft had flown over 1,000 sorties; during the last seven days the enemy had lost 36 aircraft and a further 18 probables, while the RAF had lost 33. The ground situation was considered satisfactory, but Alexander had warned he would not be able to give a reliable appreciation for another week. After a pause in their offensive the Germans had resumed attacks in Stalingrad but had only succeeded in taking a few streets.[51]

Grinding fighting continued for the next three days in the terrible heat, noise and seeming confusion. Dust and smoke from the tangled armies billowed high above the desert and over the blue, cool Mediterranean. Men collapsed from heat, thirst and exhaustion and the flies settled black upon them. Montgomery had the advantage: he trusted his troops and had more of them; outnumbered Rommel had no faith in his Italian allies. Yet by the 28th even Montgomery showed some anxiety: 'I began to realize from the casualty figures that I must be careful.' He therefore ordered the southern flank to stay on the defensive, and pulled back strength from this sector ready for the final push, while 30 Corps continued the struggle in the north. The final blow would be launched by 2 New Zealand Division in a drive along the coast at the northern end of the battle line. Rommel, anticipating this move, shifted German units northwards, taking the risk of leaving the Italian formations in the south unbolstered by *Afrika Korps* strength. This deployment was identified by British intelligence on the 29th: Montgomery therefore switched the direction of the final blow to a point further south, while a feint would be made northwards towards the sea. This operation, 'Supercharge', would be launched on the night of 31 October.[52]

In London, where Ministers were unaware of Montgomery's plans, suspense had almost reached snapping-point by the 29th. Despite the warning from Smuts that the pressure might have to be maintained for a week, and despite Alexander's notification that it might be this long before an appreciation could be sent, Churchill insisted on more decisive action. And when news reached London of Montgomery's redeployment – with this news not accompanied by details of the reasons behind his decision – the Prime Minister's impatience exploded into anger. The attack must be resumed before 'Torch' he exclaimed to Brooke on the 28th. 'A standstill now will be proclaimed as a defeat.'[53] Next morning the CIGS was handed a cable Churchill intended to send to Alexander urging, in blunt terms, for better progress: 'We ... were somewhat concerned to see that on the 27th the attack on Kidney Ridge by two battalions was the only substantial thrust. And now by your Sitrep most units appear to be coming back into reserve.... We should be grateful if you could tell us if you have any large-scale attacks impending.' The battle should be pressed 'remorselessly to a finish'. A few minutes after reading this draft, Brooke was summoned to see Churchill. What, demanded the Prime Minister, did Montgomery think he was doing? Why, after three days of inactivity, were troops being withdrawn from the front? 'The strain of the battle had had its effect on me,' wrote Brooke, 'the anxiety was growing more and more intense every day and my temper was on edge.' The Prime Minister and CIGS flared at one another; Brooke objected to the draft cable; Churchill summoned a COS meeting at 12.30 p.m., attended by Lyttelton, Attlee and Smuts. Brooke tried to explain the position as he saw it: Montgomery must be withdrawing troops in order to create a reserve and must be planning a final blow. Any hint that the commanders on the spot had lost the confidence of the British Government could be disastrous at this critical moment. Smuts, Attlee and Lyttelton agreed, and Churchill was obliged to substitute his cable for a milder message – which nevertheless contained implied criticism. 'The Defence Committee feel that the general situation justifies all the risks and sacrifices involved in the relentless prosecutions of this battle. We assure you that you will be supported, whatever the cost.' Churchill mentioned a daring reconnaissance visit made by General Mark Clark to Algeria in an effort to assess Vichy feeling. 'Clark has visited "Torch" area and held long conference with friendly French generals. We have reason to believe that not only will little opposition be encountered, but that powerful assistance will be forthcoming. Events may therefore move more quickly, perhaps considerably more quickly, than had been planned.'[54] The implication was not lost on Alexander, who replied on the 30th: 'Montgomery and I fully agreed utmost pressure of our offensive must be maintained.'[55]

Brooke, for all his declarations to Churchill and at the COS meeting on the 29th, was himself suffering doubts – 'these had to be kept entirely to myself.' The Americans were also becoming increasingly concerned, and Field-Marshal Dill had to give a somewhat lukewarm explanation to the CCS on the 30th. 'A rapid advance had not been expected, as the operations were taking place on a narrow front defended in depth. The advance, therefore, was slow and methodical, designed to capture strongpoint by strongpoint, before a hole could be made through which our armed forces could pass and deploy.'[56] In response to appeals for information, Montgomery's Chief of Staff merely told the Minister of State, Cairo, 'to tell Whitehall not to bellyache'. Montgomery wrote: 'Anyway, I was certain the CIGS would know what I was up to.'[57] The final push, 'Supercharge', was delayed 24 hours and eventually went in at 1 a.m., Monday, 2 November. The enemy put up desperate resistance and Rommel was told by Hitler: 'You can show your troops no other road than to victory or death.' Casualties soared on both sides; 9 Armoured Brigade alone lost 70 out of its 94 tanks.

'CABINET WAR ROOM RECORD: 24 hours ending 07.00, 3 November 1942. During the night half an infantry division supported by tanks attacked in the northern sector to pierce a gap in the enemy defences through which our armoured forces could be passed.... In spite of strong enemy resistance and counter-attack, by 06.00 hours our forces had penetrated nearly three miles into the enemy lines on a front of 4,000 yards.... Heavy fighting with armoured formations continued throughout the morning.... Activity slackened slightly at mid-day and the battle centre shifted southwards....'[58]

And next morning:

'CABINET WAR ROOM RECORD: 24 hours ending 07.00, 4 November 1942. In the extreme north enemy movement was observed to the west of our position throughout the 2nd, and during the night of 2nd/3rd there were signs that the enemy to the east of this position might attempt to break out. No movement had, however, been reported up to mid-day on the 3rd.... In the southern sector our line has been advanced. Explosions were heard behind the enemy lines and some withdrawal of enemy infantry westwards was observed.'[59]

British armoured cars were streaking through into the open desert, turning and harrying the enemy from the rear and attacking the columns which were now trying to retreat. Hordes of Italians began to surrender. In Berlin, Hitler received a signal from Rommel: 'The enemy has almost wiped out the troops holding the front line. Our losses are so high that there is no longer a connected front.' In foggy London Churchill received a telegram from Alexander: 'After 12 days of heavy and violent fighting the 8th Army has inflicted a severe defeat on the German and Italian forces under Rommel's command....'[60] The Prime Minister wept as he dictated messages to Roosevelt, Stalin, the Dominions, overseas Commanders. 'If the reasonable hopes of your telegram are maintained,' he signalled Alexander, 'and wholesale captures of the enemy and a general retreat are apparent, I propose to ring the bells all over Britain for the first time this war. Try to give me the moment to do this in the next few days. At least 20,000 prisoners would be necessary.'[61]

'CABINET WAR ROOM RECORD: 24 hours ending 07.00, 5 November 1942. On the 3rd there had been signs that the enemy was continuing to thin out in the forward areas, especially in the southern sector, and by mid-day his troops were withdrawing along the coast road in the northern sector.... By 15.00 hours on the 4th both of our armoured forces were engaging the remnants of enemy armoured formations.... Many prisoners have been taken.'[62]

General Eisenhower left for Gibraltar during the morning of this

Thursday. During darkness that night the first ships of the Anglo-American armada passed through the Straits of Gibraltar: 400 vessels carrying the mighty 'Torch' invasion force. Listeners to a BBC piano-recital were told at 11.55 p.m. that a special message would be broadcast at midnight – 'the best news we have heard in years', said the announcer. The message consisted of a Cairo communiqué: the Germans were in full retreat.

Another telegram was handed to Churchill next morning, 6 November. 'General Alexander to Prime Minister. Ring out the bells. Prisoners estimated now 20,000.... Our advanced mobile forces are south of Mersa Matruh. 8th Army is advancing.'[63] By now rain was hosing the sand in the desert tracks into clinging mud. Both armies suffered from the downpour, but the British were delayed most: *Afrika Korps* units somehow managed to fight stiff rearguard actions, the rain accentuated British supply problems, RAF strikes were restricted. Rommel continued to display his characteristic coolness throughout the desperate hours of 6 and 7 November. Disaster was averted but the retreat continued.

Wakes from hundreds of ships curved and crossed as naval columns zigzagged towards the shore; gunfire broke out, first heavy guns flashing in the night sky to the south, then, as the vessels neared the coast almost drifting now with the swell, flickering tracers and the rattle of machine-guns. Convoy ships spawned scores of smaller craft, and the waves of 'Torch' crashed against North Africa's beaches.

'CABINET WAR ROOM RECORD: 24 hours ending 07.00, 8 November 1942. French North Africa. Operations commenced early this morning to occupy French Morocco and Algeria, in order to provide a base for an advance on Tunisia by combined British and US forces. Landings are taking place at Algiers and Oran covered by strong British naval forces and at Casablanca by US forces. Landings at Algiers were reported as being successful, but no reports have so far been received from Oran or Casablanca.... Egypt. The pursuit of the enemy has continued.... Owing to the speed of our advance accurate details are not yet available.'[64]

Algiers surrendered at 7 p.m. that day, 8 November, after two British destroyers had been sunk attempting to force an entrance in the harbour against Vichy French opposition. Fighting continued at Oran and Casablanca, with landings at the latter hampered by the 15-foot surf. War Cabinet Ministers were informed at 6 p.m. on the 9th that 'at Oran a good deal of opposition had been and was still being encountered. Although three successful landings had been made, the town had not yet been captured, and it had been

478

bombarded that morning from the sea.... French warships from Casablanca had engaged American naval forces and had suffered heavy casualties.' Brooke gave latest details of the desert campaign. 'It has been estimated that nine-tenths of the enemy tanks and three-quarters of their guns have been either captured or destroyed. 40,000 prisoners have so far been captured.' 'This is one of the greatest victories ever won by the British Empire in the field,' declared Churchill. 'Arrangements should be made for church bells to be rung on the morning of Sunday, 15 November.'[65] Fighting ceased at Oran on the 10th and at Casablanca on the 11th. Churchill addressed a meeting in the City of London: 'Now this is not the end. It is not even the beginning of the end. But it is, perhaps, the end of the beginning.'

Sources

Note. Cabinet papers used in this book are all to be found at the
Public Record Office, London; the main files are given the same
reference numbers in the sources as in the PRO index. These are
as follows:

War Cabinet Minutes: 1940: CAB 65/7-CAB 65/10; 1941: CAB
65/17-65/20; 1942: CAB 65/25-CAB 65/28. In addition, especially
sensitive material was kept in separate files, with a more limited
circulation and known as the Secretary's Standard File. Reference
numbers are: 1940: CAB 65/13-CAB 65/16; 1941: CAB 65/21-
CAB 65/24; 1942: CAB 65/29-CAB 65/32. War Cabinet minutes
in the main files are given their full reference details in these
source lists, for example CAB 65/7 WM(40) 141, meaning the
141st meeting of the War Cabinet in 1940. References to material
in the Secretary's Standard File are merely given page numbers.
Chiefs of Staff Committee: 1940: CAB 79/4-CAB 79/8; 1941:
CAB 79/8-CAB 79/16; 1942: CAB 79/17-CAB 79/24. Secretary's
Standard File, one volume only: CAB 79/86.
Defence Committee (Operations): 1940: CAB 69/1; 1941: CAB
69/2; 1942: CAB 69/4. Secretary's Standard File, one volume
only, CAB 69/8.
Other files consulted include:
War Cabinet Memoranda: CAB 66, CAB 67.
Chiefs of Staff Memoranda: CAB 80.
Combined Chiefs of Staff Committee: CAB 88.
War Cabinet Daily Situation Reports: CAB 100.
Lord President's Committee: CAB 71.
Battle of Atlantic Committee: CAB 86.
Details of papers available are given in *The Second World War;
A Guide to Documents in the Public Record Office*, published by
HMSO for the PRO. This does not however give the number of
the pieces for the particular year.

Throughout these source lists Winston Churchill's *The Second World War* is merely referred to as Churchill II, III or IV. The initials OH have been placed after an item if the work concerned is an Official History. Full details of all the books mentioned are to be found in the Bibliography.

CHAPTER 1 DUNKIRK

1 CHURCHILL II, 122, 125
2 CAB 65/7 WM(40) 141; CAB 65/13
3 WHEELER-BENNETT, *Action This Day*, 49, 220
4 CHURCHILL II, 180
5 ISMAY, *Memoirs*, 167
6 BIRKENHEAD, *Halifax*, 459
7 WHEELER-BENNETT, *op. cit.*, 231
8 LYTTELTON, *The Memoirs of Lord Chandos*, 170
9 WHEELER-BENNETT, *op. cit.*, 107
10 LYTTELTON, *op. cit.*, 294
11 WHEELER-BENNETT, *op. cit.*, 100
12 CUNNINGHAM, *A Sailor's Odyssey*, 584
13 ISMAY, *op. cit.*, 164
14 BRYANT, *The Turn of the Tide*, 308
15 WHEELER-BENNETT, *op. cit.*, 195-196

CHAPTER 2 THE BATTLE FOR FRANCE

1 WRIGHT, *Dowding*, 104
2 CAB 65/13, 235
3 WRIGHT, *op. cit.*, 107
4 *Ibid*, 108
5 WHEELER-BENNETT, *Action This Day*, 172
6 WOODWARD, *British Foreign Policy in the Second World War*, Vol. 1, 219-220 (OH)
7 CAB 79/4 COS(40) 167
8 CAB 65/13, 242
9 CHURCHILL, II, 214
10 *House of Commons Debates*, Vol. 361, Col. 795
11 GARDNER, *Churchill in His Time*, 58
12 WOODWARD, *op. cit.*, 224 (OH)
13 *Ibid*, 219
14 CAB 79/4 COS(40) 169; CAB 65/13, 251

15 HULL, *Memoirs*, I, 774, 775
16 CAB 65/13, 251
17 CAB 65/13, 252
18 CAB 65/7 WM(40) 156
19 BUTLER, *Grand Strategy*, II, 220 (OH)
20 *Ibid*, 221
21 CAB 79/4
22 CAB 65/7 WM(40) 157; CAB 65/13, 259
23 WOODWARD, *op. cit.*, 225 (OH)
24 *Ibid*, 221, 222
25 *Ibid*, 222
26 CAB 65/7 WM(40) 158
27 BUTLER, *op. cit.*, 222-223 (OH)
28 CAB 69/1 DO(40) 14
29 EDEN, *The Reckoning*, 115
30 DILKS, *The Diaries of Sir Alexander Cadogan*, 302
31 CAB 65/7 WM(40) 159
32 WOODWARD, *op. cit.*, 223 (OH)
33 CHURCHILL, II, 129, 130
34 WOODWARD, *op. cit.*, 244 (OH)
35 CAB 69/1 DO(40) 160
36 BUTLER, *op. cit.*, 256 (OH)
37 WOODWARD, *op. cit.*, 251
38 CAB 65/7 WM(40) 160
39 WOODWARD, *op. cit.*, 244
40 CIANO, *Diary*, 263, 264
41 *Ibid*, 264
42 CHURCHILL, II, 116, 117
43 CAB 79/5
44 WOODWARD, *op. cit.*, 225 (OH)
45 BUTLER, *op. cit.*, 218 (OH)
46 CAB 65/7 WM(40) 161
47 CHURCHILL, II, 136
48 CAB 65/7 WM(40) 162
49 EDEN, *op. cit.*, 117
50 CAB 65/7 WM(40) 163
51 CHURCHILL, II, 158
52 CAB 65/7 WM(40) 164
53 CHURCHILL, II, 158
54 CAB 79/5
55 CAB 79/5
56 CAB 65/7 WM(40) 165
57 BRYANT, *The Turn of the Tide*, 167, 170
58 CAB 65/7 WM(40) 166
59 ELLIS, *The War in France and Flanders*, 299 (OH)

60 BRYANT, *op. cit.*, 170, 171
61 CAB 69/1 DO(40) 16
62 BRYANT, *op. cit.*, 172, 174
63 CAB 65/7 WM(40) 167; CAB 65/13, 308
64 WOODWARD, *op. cit.*, 270, 271 (OH)
65 *Ibid*, 268
66 *Ibid*, 348
67 *Ibid*, 273
68 CAB 65/13, p. 313; CAB 65/7 WM(40) 168
69 CAB 65/7 WM(40) 169
70 LEASOR AND HOLLIS, *War at the Top*, 92

CHAPTER 3 ALONE

1   CAB 65/7 WM(40) 170
2   BRYANT, *The Turn of the Tide*, 180, 181
3   WOODWARD, *British Foreign Policy in the Second World War*, I, 292, 293 (OH)
4   CHURCHILL, II, 191
5   *Ibid*, 172
6   CAB 79/5 COS(40) 185
7   WOODWARD, *op. cit.*, 350, 352 (OH)
8   CAB 65/7 WM(40) 171
9   WOODWARD, *op. cit.*, 296 (OH)
10 CIANO, *Diary*, 266
11 *House of Commons Debates*, Vol. 362, Col. 60
12 CAB 69/1 DO(40) 17
13 CAB 65/7 WM(40) 172
14 WOODWARD, *op. cit.*, 299 (OH)
15 *Ibid*
16 CAB 65/7 WM(40) 173
17 WOODWARD, *op. cit.*, 322-323 (OH)
18 CAB 65/7 WM(40) 174
19 DGFP, ix, 512, 513-515, 521-522
20 CAB 65/7 WM(40) 175
21 WOODWARD, *op. cit.*, 307-308 (OH)
22 *Ibid*, 306-307
23 CHURCHILL, II, 199-200
24 CAB 65/13, p. 326; CAB 65/7 WM(40) 176
25 DILKS, *Diaries of Sir Alexander Cadogan*, 306
26 CAB 65/7 WM(40) 177
27 EDEN, *The Reckoning*, 119
28 DILKS, *op. cit.*, 306

29 CAB 65/7 WM(40) 178
30 CAB 65/7 WM(40) 179; CAB 65/13, 336
31 CAB 65/7 WM(40) 180; CAB 65/13, 342
32 BUTLER, *Grand Strategy*, II, 219 (OH)
33 CAB 65/7 WM(40) 181
34 CAB 79/5 COS(40) 193
35 WOODWARD, *op. cit.*, 329 (OH)
36 CAB 65/13, 347
37 CAB 65/7 WM(40) 183; CAB 65/13, 349
38 CHURCHILL, II, 148, 151
39 CAB 79/5 COS(40) 195
40 CAB 79/5 COS(40) 196
41 WOODWARD, *op. cit.*, 353 (OH)
42 CAB 65/7 WM(40) 184; CAB 65/13, 352
43 CAB 65/13, 358
44 CHURCHILL, II, 565
45 CAB 79/5 COS(40) 200
46 CHURCHILL, II, 208
47 CAB 65/8 WM(40) 189
48 DGFP, X, 82
49 WOODWARD, *op. cit.*, 401 (OH)
50 CAB 65/14, 4
51 ISMAY, *Memoirs*, 149
52 BUTLER, *op. cit.*, 223, 224 (OH)
53 CHURCHILL, II, 209

CHAPTER 4   THE BATTLE OF BRITAIN

1   CAB 65/14, 13
2   CHURCHILL, II, 209, 210
3   PLAYFAIR, *The Mediterranean and Middle-East*, I, 131-138 (OH);
    ROSKILL, *The War at Sea*, I, 240-245 (OH); BUTLER, *Grand Strategy*,
    II, 224-225 (OH)
4   CAB 65/14, 19
5   CAB 65/14, 23
6   CAB 65/14, 25
7   CAB 65/8 WM(40) 200
8   CAB 69/1 DO(40) 19
9   GARDNER, *Churchill in His Time*, 156
10 CAB 65/8 WM(40) 194
11 CAB 65/8 WM(40) 196
12 CAB 65/8 WM(40) 200
13 CAB 65/8 WM(40) 205

14 CIANO, *Diary*, 274
15 CAB 79/5 COS(40) 205
16 CAB 69/1 DO(40) 19
17 CAB 65/8 WM(40) 192
18 EINZIG, *In the Centre of Things*, 208-219
19 CAB 65/8 WM(40) 194
20 WOODWARD, *British Foreign Policy in the Second World War*, I, 361, 326 (OH)
21 CIANO, *op. cit.*, 275
22 WRIGHT, *Dowding and the Battle of Britain*, 137, 138
23 COLLIER, *The Battle of Britain*, 64, 65
24 CAB 65/8 WM(40) 199
25 NCA, 1940, 62-66
26 DGFP, X, 209-211
27 TREVOR-ROPER, ed., *Hitler's War Directives*, 74
28 CAB 79/5
29 BRYANT, *The Turn of the Tide*, 194, 195
30 COLLIER, *op. cit.*, 69
31 CAB 65/8 WM(40) 208
32 MACLEOD AND KELLY, *The Ironside Diaries*, 387
33 BRYANT, *op. cit.*, 195, 196
34 CHURCHILL, II, 229
35 CAB 65/8 WM(40) 211
36 CAB 65/14; CAB 65/8 WM(40) 209
37 EDEN, *The Reckoning*, 126, 127
38 CHURCHILL, II, 375
39 EDEN, *op. cit.*, 127
40 CHURCHILL, II, 450
41 COLLIER, *op. cit.*, 67, 70, 71
42 CAB 69/9 DO(40) 23
43 CAB 65/8 WM(40) 213
44 CAB 79/5
45 BRYANT, *op. cit.*, 200
46 EDEN, *op. cit.*, 128
47 BUTLER, *op. cit.*, 359-363 (OH)
48 CAB 65/8 WM(40) 214
49 EDEN, *op. cit.*, 128, 129
50 *Ibid*, 127
51 NICOLSON, *Diaries and Letters*, II, 101
52 CHURCHILL, II, 365
53 NCA, 1 August 1940
54 CAB 65/8 WM(40) 217
55 TREVOR-ROPER, *op. cit.*, 79
56 CHURCHILL, II, 357
57 WOODWARD, *op. cit.*, 365 (OH)

58 CHURCHILL, II, 359
59 CAB 65/8 WM(40) 218
60 CAB 65/14, 74
61 CAB 79/6; CHURCHILL, II, 420
62 CAB 79/6
63 CHURCHILL, II, 421
64 *Ibid*, 422
65 CAB 65/14, 96
66 CHURCHILL, II, 423
67 CAB 65/8 WM(40) 221
68 CHURCHILL, II, 260; BUTLER, *op. cit.*, 279 (OH)
69 EDEN, *op. cit.*, 129
70 CAB 79/6; CAB 95/2
71 CIANO, *op. cit.*, 281
72 CAB 65/8 WM(40) 223
73 EDEN, *op. cit.*, 130
74 CHURCHILL, II, 378-379; BUTLER, *op. cit.*, 308 (OH); EDEN, *op. cit.*, 130; CAB 79/6
75 CAB 65/8 WM(40) 224
76 CAB 69/1 DO(40) 25; EDEN, *op. cit.*, 131

CHAPTER 5 DAY OF EAGLES

1   COLLIER, *The Battle of Britain*, 80
2   CAB 65/8 WM(40) 225
3   BRYANT, *The Turn of the Tide*, 207
4   CAB 65/14, 90; EDEN, *The Reckoning*, 132, 133
5   CAB 65/8 WM(40) 226
6   CAB 69/1 DO(40) 27
7   COLLIER, *op. cit.*, 90; CHURCHILL, II, 286
8   CHURCHILL, II, 286
9   CAB 65/8 WM(40) 228
10 CHURCHILL, II, 383
11 EDEN, *op. cit.*, 133
12 WOODWARD, *British Foreign Policy in the Second World War*, I, 508 (OH)
13 CHURCHILL, II, 360-361
14 CAB 65/8 WM(40) 230
15 WOODWARD, *op. cit.*, 370-371 (OH)
16 ISMAY, *Memoirs*, 180
17 NICOLSON, *Diaries and Letters*, II, 106
18 *House of Commons Debates*, Vol. 364, Col. 1170-1171
19 CAB 79/6

20 CAB 65/8 WM(40) 231
21 CIANO, *Diary*, 285
22 CAB 65/8 WM(40) 232
23 EDEN, *op. cit.*, 134
24 CAB 79/6
25 CAB 65/8 WM(40) 233
26 CAB 69/1 DO(40) 29
27 WOODWARD, *op. cit.*, 375-376 (OH); CHURCHILL, II, 365
28 WOODWARD, *op. cit.*, 509 (OH)
29 BUTLER, *Grand Strategy*, II, 316 (OH)
30 COLLIER, *op. cit.*, 106
31 CHURCHILL, II, 302
32 CAB 65/8 WM(40) 234
33 CAB 65/14, 116
34 CAB 65/8 WM(40) 237
35 *Ibid*
36 CAB 65/9 WM(40) 239
37 WOODWARD, *op. cit.*, 382, 397-399 (OH)
38 *Ibid*, 381
39 CHURCHILL, II, 313, 405, 408; BUTLER, *op. cit.*, 403 (OH)
40 CAB 65/9 WM(40) 240
41 CAB 65/9 WM(40) 242
42 CAB 65/9 WM(40) 243
43 BUTLER, *op. cit.*, 288 (OH)
44 CAB 79/6; BUTLER, *op. cit.*, 288 (OH)
45 COLLIER, *op. cit.*, 130
46 CALDER, *The People's War*, 155
47 CHURCHILL, II, 276
48 *Ibid*
49 BRYANT, *op. cit.*, 214
50 CAB 65/9 WM(40) 245
51 COLLIER, *op. cit.*, 136
52 NICOLSON, *op. cit.*, 122
53 CAB 65/9 WM(40) 246
54 *Ibid*
55 CAB 65/9 WM(40) 247
56 CAB 65/9 WM(40) 248
57 BRYANT, *op. cit.*, 216
58 CAB 65/9 WM(40) 249
59 BRYANT, *op. cit.*, 216
60 CHURCHILL, II, 417
61 BRYANT, *op. cit.*, 216
62 NCA, 1940, 101
63 CHURCHILL, II, 293; WRIGHT, *Dowding and the Battle of Britain*, 202-203; BUTLER, *op. cit.*, 287 (OH); COLLIER, *op. cit.*, 140-153

64 CAB 65/9 WM(40) 250; CAB 65/16, 17; BUTLER, *op. cit.*, 318 (OH)
65 EDEN, *op. cit.*, 137
66 CAB 65/9 WM(40) 251
67 NCA, 1940, 101
68 CAB 65/15, 21
69 CAB 65/15, 23
70 CAB 65/9 WM(40) 253
71 EDEN, *op. cit.*, 138
72 NICOLSON, *op. cit.*, 113
73 CHURCHILL, II, 321
74 CAB 65/9 WM(40) 254
75 CAB 65/9 WM(40) 255
76 CHURCHILL, II, 310
77 CAB 65/9 WM(40) 256
78 CHURCHILL, II, 433
79 EDEN, *op. cit.*, 138, 139
80 BUTLER, *op. cit.*, 290 (OH)
81 CAB 65/9 WM(40) 257
82 CHURCHILL, II, 432
83 CAB 65/15, 41

CHAPTER 6   OCTOBER ORDEALS

1   CAB 65/9 WM(40) 260
2   CAB 65/9 WM(40) 265
3   EDEN, *The Reckoning*, 138
4   LYTTELTON, *The Memoirs of Lord Chandos*, 191
5   EDEN, *op. cit.*, 144-146
6   CHURCHILL, III, 102
7   CHURCHILL, II, 305
8   FEILING, *The Life of Neville Chamberlain*, 457
9   CAB 65/9 WM(40) 267
10 CAB 65/9 WM(40) 268
11 CUDLIPP, *Publish and Be Damned*, 150
12 CAB 65/9 WM(40) 270
13 CHURCHILL, II, 306-307
14 CAB 73/2
15 CAB 65/9 WM(40) 271
16 CAB 69/1 DO(40) 34
17 CAB 65/9 WM(40) 272
18 BRYANT, *The Turn of the Tide*, 224
19 CAB 65/9 WM(40) 273
20 CAB 65/9 WM(40) 274

21 CHURCHILL, II, 329-331
22 BUTLER, *Grand Strategy*, II, 411 (OH)
23 CAB 65/9 WM(40) 280
24 CAB 69/1 DO(40) 39
25 CIANO, *Diary*, 297
26 CAB 65/15, 69
27 CAB 65/9 WM(40) 269
28 CIANO, *op. cit.*, 297
29 CAB 79/7
30 WOODWARD, *British Foreign Policy in the Second World War*, I, 488 (OH)
31 CAB 65/9 WM(40) 271; WOODWARD, *op. cit.*, 489-490 (OH)
32 EDEN, *op. cit.*, 152-153
33 CAB 65/9 WM(40) 273
34 WOODWARD, *op. cit.*, 414 (OH)
35 ISMAY, *Memoirs*, 175
36 CAB 65/9 WM(40) 274
37 CHURCHILL, II, 451-453
38 WOODWARD, *op. cit.*, 414 (OH)
39 *Ibid*, 492-493
40 N-SR, 216
41 DGFP, xi, 227
42 CAB 65/9 WM(40) 276
43 CAB 65/9 WM(40) 277
44 WOODWARD, *op. cit.*, 415-416 (OH)
45 *Ibid*, 494
46 CAB 65/9 WM(40) 278
47 SCHMIDT, *Hitler's Interpreter*, 200
48 CAB 65/9 WM(40) 278; CAB 65/15, 75
49 CAB 65/9 WM(40) 279; CAB 65/15, 78
50 CAB 65/9 WM(40) 278
51 WOODWARD, *op. cit.*, 417, 418 (OH)
52 CAB 65/16
53 EDEN, *op. cit.*, 167, 168
54 CAB 79/8
55 WOODWARD, *op. cit.*, 515 (OH)
56 *Ibid*, 416-417
57 *Ibid*, 494
58 CHURCHILL, II, 474
59 EDEN, *op. cit.*, 169
60 CAB 79/8
61 CAB 65/10 WM(40) 282, 283
62 SHIRER, *Rise and Fall of the Third Reich*, 460
63 CAB 65/16, 8
64 CAB 79/8

65 WOODWARD, *op. cit.*, 418 (OH)
66 NICOLSON, *Diaries and Letters*, II, 122-123
67 CHURCHILL, II, 489
68 CAB 65/10 WM(40) 283
69 WOODWARD, *op. cit.*, 420 (OH)
70 CAB 65/10 WM(40) 285
71 CHURCHILL, II, 480
72 CAB 65/10 WM(40) 284
73 CHURCHILL, II, 479
74 CAB 65/10 WM(40) 285
75 CHURCHILL, II, 480; ISMAY, *op. cit.*, 195
76 WOODWARD, *op. cit.*, 386, 387 (OH)
77 *Ibid*, 495, 496
78 CAB 65/10 WM(40) 286
79 WOODWARD, *op. cit.*, 421, 424 (OH)
80 CAB 65/10 WM(40) 286

CHAPTER 7 'OFF TO SEE THE WIZARD'

1 HIGGINS, *Winston Churchill and the Second Front*, 44; BUTLER, *Grand Strategy*, II, 423 (OH)
2 CAB 65/16, 23
3 CAB 65/10 WM(40) 288
4 CHURCHILL, II, 483
5 NCA, 1940, 125
6 CHURCHILL, II, 518
7 CALDER, *The People's War*, 204
8 CAB 65/10 WM(40) 290
9 *Ibid*
10 CIANO, *Diary*, 307
11 CAB 65/16, 32
12 CAB 79/8
13 CAB 65/10 WM(40) 292
14 EDEN, *The Reckoning*, 175
15 CAB 65/10 WM(40) 294
16 BRYANT, *The Turn of the Tide*, 255
17 CHURCHILL, III, 74
18 CHURCHILL, II, 483
19 CIANO, *op. cit.*, 310, 312
20 CAB 65/10 WM(40) 295; CAB 65/16, 35
21 CAB 65/10 WM(40) 296
22 CAB 65/10 WM(40) 297
23 EDEN, *op. cit.*, 178

24 CAB 79/8
25 CAB 69/1 DO(40) 47; EDEN, *op. cit.*, 178
26 CAB 69/1 DO(40) 48
27 EDEN, *op. cit.*, 180
28 WOODWARD, *British Foreign Policy in the Second World War*, I, 388-395 (OH)
29 CAB 65/10 WM(40) 302; CAB 65/16, 44
30 CHURCHILL, II, 539
31 CAB 69/1 DO(40) 49
32 TREVOR-ROPER, *Hitler's War Directives*, 88
33 CAB 65/10 WM(40) 304
34 CIANO, *op. cit.*, 317
35 EDEN, *op. cit.*, 181
36 CAB 65/16, 46
37 TREVOR-ROPER, *op. cit.*, 90-91
38 CAB 65/10 WM(40) 306
39 EDEN, *op. cit.*, 181
40 *Ibid*, 182
41 TREVOR-ROPER, *op. cit.*, 93
42 CAB 65/10 WM(40) 308
43 CAB 65/10 WM(40) 310
44 DILKS, *The Diaries of Sir Alexander Cadogan*, 344
45 HARRIS, *Bomber Offensive*, 51, 52
46 CAB 65/10 WM(40) 311, 312
47 CHURCHILL, II, 507
48 NCA, 1940, 138-139
49 GWYER, *Grand Strategy*, III, part 1, 39, 9 (OH)

CHAPTER 8 INDECISION

1 YOUNG, *Churchill and Beaverbrook*, 179-181
2 CHURCHILL, III, 3
3 CAB 69/8 DO(41) 3
4 CAB 65/17 WM(41) 1
5 CAB 65/17 WM(41) 2
6 CAB 65/17 WM(41) 3
7 BUTLER, *Grand Strategy*, II, 381 (OH)
8 DILKS, *The Diaries of Sir Alexander Cadogan*, 347
9 CAB 69/2 DO(41) 1
10 CAB 69/2 DO(41) 2
11 CONNELL, *Wavell: Soldier and Scholar*, 312-313; CHURCHILL, III, 17

12 CHURCHILL, III, 21; ISMAY, *Memoirs*, 213-214; SHERWOOD, *The White House Papers*, I, 238
13 CAB 69/2 DO(41) 3
14 TREVOR-ROPER, *Hitler's War Directives*, 100
15 CAB 65/17 WM(41) 5
16 WOODWARD, *British Foreign Policy in the Second World War*, I, 519 (OH)
17 CHURCHILL, III, 19
18 *Ibid*, 52
19 CAB 69/2 DO(41) 4
20 LYTTELTON, *The Memoirs of Lord Chandos*, 165
21 SHERWOOD, *op. cit.*, 244
22 CAB 69/2 DO(41) 4
23 BUTLER, *op. cit.*, 413 (OH); GWYER, *Grand Strategy*, III, part I, 32-33 (OH)
24 BUTLER, *op. cit.*, 376, 377 (OH)
25 CAB 69/2 DO(41) 5
26 WOODWARD, *op. cit.*, 520 (OH)
27 CAB 65/17 WM(41) 8
28 CAB 69/2 DO(41) 6
29 BRYANT, *The Turn of the Tide*, 229
30 CAB 65/17 WM(41) 9, 10, 12
31 CAB 65/17 WM(41) 10
32 SHIRER, *Rise and Fall of the Third Reich*, 429
33 CHURCHILL, III, 74, 18
34 BUTLER, *op. cit.*, 382 (OH)
35 CAB 79/8
36 CAB 65/17 WM(41) 11
37 BUTLER, *op. cit.*, 383 (OH); EDEN, *The Reckoning*, 188
38 CHURCHILL, III, 32
39 KENNEDY and FERGUSSON, *The Business of War*, 84
40 BRYANT, *op. cit.*, 241, 242
41 CAB 65/21, 17
42 TREVOR-ROPER, *op. cit.*, 110
43 CAB 65/17 WM(41) 14
44 CAB 65/21, 22
45 EDEN, *op. cit.*, 306; BUTLER, *op. cit.*, 497 (OH)
46 EDEN, *op. cit.*, 307; WOODWARD, *British Foreign Policy in the Second World War* (original version), 170 (OH)
47 EDEN, *op. cit.*, 308, 309
48 CHURCHILL, III, 157
49 CAB 65/17 WM(41) 18
50 CHURCHILL, III, 158
51 WOODWARD, *British Foreign Policy in the Second World War*, I, 521, (original version, 131) (OH)

52 EDEN, *op. cit*, 189
53 CAB 65/17 WM(41) 15
54 CAB 69/2 DO(41) 7, 8
55 CHURCHILL, IIII, 58
56 CONNELL, *op. cit*., 333
57 CHURCHILL, III, 60; CAB 65/21, 24
58 CAB 65/17 WM(41) 18
59 CAB 65/17 WM(41) 19; CAB 65/21, 24
60 CHURCHILL, III, 64
61 EDEN, *op. cit*., 197
62 CHURCHILL, III, 66-68; BUTLER, *op. cit*., 442-443 (OH)
63 CAB 65/21, 26; CHURCHILL, III, 69
64 CAB 65/21, 32
65 BUTLER, *op. cit*., 451 (OH)
66 DILKS, *op. cit*., 359
67 CHURCHILL, III, 86
68 CAB 79/9
69 DILKS, *op. cit*., 360; CAB 65/18 WM(41) 22
70 BUTLER, *op. cit*., 450 (OH)
71 CAB 65/22
72 CAB 65/22, 8; EDEN, *op. cit*., 211-212
73 CAB 69/2 DO(41) 9
74 CHURCHILL, III, 90
75 *Ibid*
76 GWYER, *op. cit*., 40 (OH)
77 CHURCHILL, III, 107-109
78 BUTLER, *op. cit*., 465 (OH)
79 GWYER, *op. cit*., 10 (OH)
80 CHURCHILL, III, 106
81 DILKS, *op. cit*., 361
82 CAB 65/22, 23
83 CAB 65/22, 36
84 CHURCHILL, III, 94
85 CAB 65/22, 58; CHURCHILL, III, 93
86 CAB 65/22, 58; CAB 65/18 WM(41) 27
87 CHURCHILL, III, 111
88 CAB 65/18 WM(41) 29
89 NCA, 1941, 32
90 CHURCHILL, III, 95
91 CAB 65/22, 80
92 CAB 65/22, 89
93 CAB 65/18 WM(41) 30, 28
94 DILKS, *op. cit*., 364
95 LEWIN, *Rommel as Military Commander*, 32, 33
96 CHURCHILL, III, 178

97   *Ibid*, 141
98   CAB 65/18 WM(41) 31
99   CHURCHILL, III, 178
100 BUTLER, *op. cit.*, 500 (OH)
101 CAB 65/18 WM(41) 33
102 BUTLER, *op. cit.*, 458 (OH)
103 EDEN, *op. cit.*, 231
104 WOODWARD, *British Foreign Policy in the Second World War*, I, 543 (OH)
105 CAB 65/19 WM(41) 33
106 LEWIN, *op. cit.*, 33
107 EDEN, *op. cit.*, 233
108 *Ibid*, 235
109 LEWIN, *op. cit.*, 34
110 EDEN, *op. cit.*, 242; BUTLER, *op. cit.*, 460 (OH)
111 WOODWARD, *op. cit.*, I, 545 (OH)
112 CAB 79/9
113 CAB 65/18 WM(41) 35; CAB 65/22, 92
114 EDEN, *op. cit.*, 236
115 CAB 69/2 DO(41) 11
116 CHURCHILL, III, 154
117 LEWIN, *op. cit.*, 37
118 CHURCHILL, III, 182

CHAPTER 9   AEGEAN AGONY

1   CAB 79/9
2   CAB 65/22, 96; CAB 65/18 WM(41) 36
3   CHURCHILL, III, 183
4   CONNELL, *op. cit.*, 403
5   BUTLER, *Grand Strategy*, II, 459-460 (OH)
6   CONNELL, *op. cit.*, 405
7   CAB 65/18 WM(41) 37
8   CHURCHILL, III, 183
9   KENNEDY and FERGUSSON, *The Business of War*, 90; CHURCHILL, III, 183, 184
10   DILKS, *The Diaries of Sir Alexander Cadogan*, 370
11   WOODWARD, *British Foreign Policy in the Second World War*, I, 575-576 (OH)
12   BUTLER, *op. cit.*, 474 (OH)
13   CHURCHILL, III, 670
14   CAB 65/22, 102

15 CHURCHILL, III, 185
16 *Ibid*
17 CAB 69/2 DO(41) 13
18 CAB 69/2 DO(41) 14
19 CAB 65/22, 113
20 CAB 69/2 DO(41) 15
21 CHURCHILL, III, 212, 213
22 CAB 69/2 DO(41) 16
23 CAB 65/18 WM(41) 41; CAB 65/22, 120
24 WOODWARD, *op. cit.*, 551 (OH)
25 CAB 69/2 DO(41) 17
26 WOODWARD, *op. cit.*, 576 (OH)
27 CAB 79/10
28 CHURCHILL, III, 311
29 BUTLER, *op. cit.*, 394 (OH)
30 CHURCHILL, III, 202
31 *Ibid*, 217-218
32 ISMAY, *Memoirs*, 202; EDEN, *The Reckoning*, 242; CAB 79/10
33 BUTLER, *op. cit.*, 454 (OH)
34 CAB 69/8 DO(41) 18
35 CAB 65/22, 129
36 CAB 79/10
37 CAB 65/22, 135
38 CHURCHILL, III, 221
39 BUTLER, *op. cit.*, 501 (OH)
40 CAB 65/18 WM(41) 44; CAB 65/22, 137
41 CHURCHILL, III, 288
42 WOODWARD, *op. cit.*, 578 (OH)
43 BRYANT, *The Turn of the Tide*, 254
44 CAB 69/2 DO(41) 19
45 CHURCHILL, III, 241
46 BUTLER, *op. cit.*, 501 (OH); CAB 79/11; CAB 69/2 DO(41) 20
47 BUTLER, *op. cit.*, 502 (OH)
48 CAB 65/18 WM(41) 45
49 CAB 69/2 DO(41) 21
50 BUTLER, *op. cit.*, 502 (OH)
51 CAB 65/18 WM(41) 45
52 CAB 79/11
53 CHURCHILL, III, 243
54 LEWIN, *Rommel as Military Commander*, 40, 41
55 CHURCHILL, III, 245
56 CAB 69/2 DO(41) 24
57 CAB 69/2 DO(41) 25
58 BUTLER, *op. cit.*, 524 (OH); LEWIN, *op. cit.*, 41
59 CAB 65/18 WM(41) 47

60 CHURCHILL, III, 246
61 *Ibid*, 241
62 CAB 69/2 DO(41) 25; ISMAY, *op. cit.*, 207
63 CHURCHILL, III, 373-376
64 NICOLSON, *Diaries and Letters*, II, 163
65 CAB 65/18 WM(41) 48
66 CAB 69/2 DO(41) 26
67 WOODWARD, *op. cit.*, 564 (OH)
68 CONNELL, *op cit.*, 452
69 CHURCHILL, III, 299
70 EDEN, *op. cit.*, 250, 251
71 CHURCHILL, III, 299
72 CAB 69/2 DO(41) 29
73 CHURCHILL, III, 377
74 DILKS, *op. cit.*, 379; CAB 65/18 WM(41) 50
75 BUTLER, *op. cit.*, 525 (OH)
76 CHURCHILL, III, 302
77 CAB 79/11
78 CAB 65/18 WM(41) 51; CAB 65/22, 146
79 CHURCHILL, III, 250
80 CAB 79/11; CAB 69/2 DO(41) 33
81 CHURCHILL, III, 254
82 CAB 69/2 DO(41) 33
83 CONNELL, *op. cit.*, 462
84 CAB 65/18 WM(41) 52
85 CHURCHILL, III, 291
86 CAB 79/11
87 CHURCHILL, III, 259; CAB 79/11
88 CAB 69/2 DO(41) 34
89 CHURCHILL, III, 291
90 CONNELL, *op. cit.*, 467; CAB 79/11
91 CAB 79/11
92 BUTLER, *op. cit.*, 519 (OH)
93 CHURCHILL, III, 260, 261
94 CAB 65/22, 150; DILKS, *op. cit.*, 381
95 CONNELL, *op. cit.*, 471; CHURCHILL, III, 261, 262
96 CAB 65/18 WM(41) 54; CAB 69/22, 153
97 CAB 69/2 DO(41) 35
98 CHURCHILL, III, 304; CAB 79/11
99 CAB 65/18 WM(41) 55
100 BUTLER, *op. cit.*, 513 (OH)
101 CONNELL, *op. cit.*, 484
102 *Ibid*, 474
103 EDEN, *op. cit.*, 244
104 CAB 65/18 WM(41) 56; CAB 65/22, 155

105 CHURCHILL, III, 293
106 CAB 65/18 WM(41) 57; CAB 65/22, 158
107 BUTLER, *op. cit.*, 530 (OH)
108 *Ibid*, 526
109 DILKS *op. cit.*, 386
110 CAB 65/22, 161
111 EDEN, *op. cit.*, 261
112 MINNEY, *The Private Papers of Hore-Belisha*, 292-295
113 DILKS, *op. cit.*, 386
114 CONNELL, *op. cit.*, 492
115 CAB 79/12
116 CAB 65/18 WM(41) 59; CAB 65/22, 163
117 EDEN, *op. cit.*, 286; BUTLER, *op. cit.*, 544 (OH); WOODWARD, *op. cit.*, 621 (OH)
118 WOODWARD, *op. cit.*, 620 note (OH)
119 CHURCHILL, III, 330
120 CONNELL, *op. cit.*, 496
121 CAB 65/18 WM(41) 60; CAB 65/22, 166
122 LEWIN, *op. cit.*, 46
123 CAB 69/2 DO(41) 42; CAB 65/18 WM(41) 60
124 CAB 65/18 WM(41) 61; CAB 65/22, 171
125 CONNELL, *op. cit.*, 504

CHAPTER 10 BARBAROSSA

1 CHURCHILL, III, 332
2 GWYER, *Grand Strategy*, III, Part I, 90-91 (OH)
3 SHERWOOD, *White House Papers*, I, 303
4 CAB 65/18 WM(41) 62
5 CAB 65/18 WM(41) 64
6 CAB 65/19 WM(41) 65
7 CAB 65/19 WM(41) 66
8 CAB 65/19 WM(41) 67
9 CAB 65/19 WM(41) 69
10 CAB 65/19 WM(41) 72
11 CHURCHILL, III, 342-343
12 CAB 69/2 DO(41) 50
13 CHURCHILL, III, 344, 345
14 WOODWARD, *British Foreign Policy in the Second World War*, (original version) 153 (OH)
15 CAB 65/19 WM(41) 72
16 SHERWOOD, *op. cit.*, 341-342
17 CAB 65/19 WM(41) 77
18 CAB 65/19 WM(41) 78

19   BUTLER, *Grand Strategy*, II, 530-532 (OH)

20   GWYER, *op. cit.*, 170 (OH)

21   CHURCHILL, III, 355

22   GWYER, *op. cit.*, 178-179 (OH)

23   CAB 69/2 DO(41) 51

24   GWYER, *op. cit.*, 180, 181 (OH)

25   *Ibid*; CHURCHILL, III, 359-360

26   CAB 65/23, 7

27   CAB 65/23, 15

28   CAB 69/2 DO(41) 53

29   CHURCHILL, III, 361

30   LYTTELTON, *The Memoirs of Lord Chandos*, 244

31   CAB 65/19 WM(41) 77; LYTTELTON, *op. cit.*, 247

32   CHURCHILL, III, 424

33   WOODWARD, *op. cit.* (original version) 162 (OH)

34   CAB 65/19 WM(41) 75

35   CHURCHILL, III, 425

36   DILKS, *The Diaries of Sir Alexander Cadogan*, 393

37   CAB 65/23, 10

38   CAB 69/2 DO(41) 42

39   BRYANT, *The Turn of the Tide*, 256

40   CAB 65/18 WM(41) 62

41   CAB 65/19 WM(41) 66

42   CAB 65/19 WM(41) 78

43   CAB 69/2; BUTLER, *Grand Strategy*, II, 485 (OH)

44   WEBSTER and FRANKLAND, *The Strategic Air Offensive against Germany*, I, 178 (OH)

45   CAB 65/19 WM(41) 71

46   CHURCHILL, III, 381

47   *Ibid*, 383

48   GWYER, *op. cit.*, 132 (OH); WOODWARD, *op. cit.*, (original version) 175 (OH)

49   GWYER, *op. cit.*, 133 (OH)

50   CHURCHILL, III, 390

51   CAB 65/19 WM(41) 80

52   CAB 65/19 WM(41) 81

53   CHURCHILL, III, 397

54   *Ibid*, 396

55   *Ibid*, 394

56   HIGGINS, *Winston Churchill and the Second Front*, 66

57   CAB 65/19 WM(41) 84

58   CAB 79/13

59   WOODWARD, *op. cit.* (original version) 176 (OH)

60   CHURCHILL, III, 427

61   CAB 79/6

62 CAB 79/13
63 CAB 65/19 WM(41) 86
64 GWYER, *op. cit.*, 189 (OH)
65 YOUNG, *Churchill and Beaverbrook*, 204
66 CHURCHILL, III, 403
67 *Ibid*, 410
68 CAB 65/23, 64
69 CAB 65/20, 67
70 CHURCHILL, III, 437
71 CAB 65/23, 73
72 CHURCHILL, III, 367
73 WOODWARD, *op. cit.* (original version) 154 (OH)
74 BRYANT, *op. cit.*, 256
75 CAB 65/23, 79
76 CAB 65/23, 77
77 CAB 65/19 WM(41) 93
78 YOUNG, *op. cit.*, 208
79 GWYER, *op. cit.*, 151, 152 (OH)
80 CAB 65/19 WM(41) 93
81 CAB 65/23, 79
82 CAB 65/23, 89
83 CAB 65/19 WM(41) 94
84 CAB 69/2 DO(41) 62
85 GWYER, *op. cit.*, 155, 156 (OH)
86 CAB 65/19 WM(41) 95
87 CAB 65/23, 99
88 CAB 65/19 WM(41) 97, 98
89 LEWIN, *Rommel as Military Commander*, 56, 57
90 CAB 65/23, 107
91 ISMAY, *Memoirs*, 230
92 CHURCHILL, III, 418
93 CAB 65/19 WM(41) 100
94 CAB 65/19 WM(41) 101
95 CAB 65/19 WM(41) 102
96 CAB 69/2 DO(41) 63
97 BRYANT, *op. cit.*, 260, 262
98 CAB 69/2 DO(41) 64
99 CAB 69/2 DO(41) 65
100 WOODWARD, *op. cit.* (original version) 156 (OH)
101 CAB 69/2 DO(41) 22
102 CAB 69/8 DO(41) 67
103 CHURCHILL, III, 483
104 *Ibid*, 413
105 CAB 65/23; CAB 69/2 DO(41) 69
106 CHURCHILL, III, 465

107 EDEN, *The Reckoning*, 279
108 GWYER, *op. cit.*, 215, 216 (OH)
109 CAB 65/20 WM(41) 109
110 CAB 65/24, 12
111 CHURCHILL, III, 471
112 *Ibid*, 473
113 CAB 65/20 WM(41) 115
114 EDEN, *op. cit.*, 313
115 GWYER, *op. cit.*, 281 (OH)
116 CAB 69/2 DO(41) 21
117 CAB 69/2 DO(41) 65
118 CAB 69/8 DO(41) 66
119 GWYER, *op. cit.*, 285-289 (OH)
120 WOODWARD, *op. cit.* (original version) 178 (OH)
121 CAB 65/24, 8
122 CAB 79/13
123 CAB 65/24, 22
124 GWYER, *op. cit.*, 257 (OH)
125 *Ibid*, 228
126 *Ibid*, 229
127 CHURCHILL, III, 482
128 CAB 69/8 DO(41) 66
129 CAB 65/23
130 CHURCHILL, III, 486, 487
131 *Ibid*, 490
132 ISMAY, *op. cit.*, 271
133 CAB 65/20 WM(41) 114; CAB 65/24, 31
134 BRYANT, *op. cit.*, 256; EDEN, *op. cit.*, 281
135 BRYANT, *op. cit.*, 266
136 CHURCHILL, III, 500
137 *Ibid*, 507
138 CAB 65/20 WM(41) 118
139 CAB 65/20 WM(41) 119
140 GWYER, *op. cit.*, 264 (OH)
141 CHURCHILL, III, 530
142 HULL, *Memoirs*, I, 1056, 1074
143 *Ibid*, 1082-83
144 WOODWARD, *op. cit.* (original version) 184 (OH)
145 CAB 65/20 WM(41) 122
146 WOODWARD, *op. cit.* (original version) 184, 185 (OH)
147 CAB 65/24, 49
148 BRYANT, *op. cit.*, 277
149 *Ibid*, 278
150 CAB 69/2 DO(41) 71
151 CHURCHILL, III, 474

500

152 CAB 65/24, 64
153 CAB 65/24, 67, 72
154 BRYANT, *op. cit.*, 298, 299
155 *Ibid*, 281; CAB 79/6
156 CHURCHILL, III, 539
157 EDEN, *op. cit.*, 286
158 CHURCHILL, III, 539

CHAPTER 11 ALLIES

1   CHURCHILL, III, 543
2   CAB 65/20 WM(41) 125
3   ROSKILL, *The War at Sea*, I, 363-370 (OH)
4   CHURCHILL, III, 544
5   GWYER, *Grand Strategy*, III, Part I, 316; CAB 69/2
6   CHURCHILL, III, 511
7   CAB 65/20 WM(41) 126; CAB 65/24, 75
8   CHURCHILL, III, 553
9   GWYER, *op. cit.*, 317 (OH); CAB 79/16
10 CAB 79/16
11 GWYER, *op. cit.*, 318 (OH)
12 CHURCHILL, III, 554
13 CAB 65/20 WM(41) 127
14 CHURCHILL, III, 564
15 *Ibid*, 565
16 CAB 65/20 WM(41) 128
17 CHURCHILL, III, 513
18 *Ibid*, 574-584
19 GWYER, *op. cit.*, 339-348 (OH); CHURCHILL, III, 584
20 EDEN, *The Reckoning*, 289
21 CAB 65/20 WM(41) 131; CAB 65/24, 80
22 CHURCHILL, III, 565, 566
23 BUTLER, *Grand Strategy*, III, Part 2, 405-406 (OH); CAB 69/2
24 CAB 65/20 WM(41) 133; CAB 65/24, 87
25 CONNELL, *Wavell: Supreme Commander*, 62, 63
26 CAB 69/2
27 CAB 65/20 WM(41) 135
28 CAB 65/20 WM(41) 132
29 BRYANT, *The Turn of the Tide*, 287
30 CONNELL, *op. cit.*, 66
31 BRYANT, *op. cit.*, 288
32 GWYER, *op. cit.*, 366 (OH)
33 CHURCHILL, IV, 5, 6

34   *Ibid*, 8
35   CHURCHILL, III, 601
36   CAB 69/2 DO(41) 75
37   BRYANT, *op. cit.*, 295
38   GWYER, *op. cit.*, 368-370 (OH)
39   CAB 65/20 WM(41) 137, 138
40   BRYANT, *op. cit.*, 295
41   CHURCHILL, III, 600
42   CONNELL, *op. cit.*, 71
43   BRYANT, *op. cit.*, 360
44   STIMSON and BUNDY, *On Active Service*, 414
45   GWYER, *op. cit.*, 387 (OH)
46   CAB 65/20 WM(41) 138
47   CAB 65/25 WM(42); CAB 65/29, 3
48   BUTLER, *op. cit.*, 407, 408 (OH)
49   CAB 69/4 DO(42) 1
50   CHURCHILL, III, 607, 609
51   BRYANT, *op. cit.*, 293
52   CHURCHILL, IV, 9
53   CAB 79/17
54   BUTLER, *op. cit.*, 445 (OH)
55   CAB 65/25 WM(42) 2
56   CONNELL, *op. cit.*, 85
57   BRYANT, *op. cit.*, 289
58   CHURCHILL, III, 620-623
59   CHURCHILL, IV, 20
60   BUTLER, *op. cit.*, 439 (OH)
61   NICOLSON, *Diaries and Letters*, II, 202
62   BUTLER, *op. cit.*, 415 (OH)
63   CHURCHILL, IV, 10, 11
64   *Ibid*, 42
65   CAB 69/4 DO(42) 3
66   LEWIN, *Rommel as Military Commander*, 95
67   CONNELL, *Auchinleck*, 454
68   CAB 65/25 WM(42) 8
69   CHURCHILL, IV, 15, 16
70   BUTLER, *op. cit.*, 436, 437 (OH)
71   CHURCHILL, IV, 43
72   ISMAY, *Memoirs*, 247
73   CAB 79/7 17
74   CAB 65/29, 19
75   BUTLER, *op. cit.*, 465 (OH)
76   CAB 79/17
77   CAB 69/4 DO(42) 4
78   EDEN, *op. cit.*, 318

79 LEWIN, *op. cit.*, 99
80 CAB 65/25 WM(42) 10
81 LEWIN, *op. cit.*, 103
82 CHURCHILL, IV, 24
83 *Ibid*, 24, 25
84 *Ibid*, 25
85 CAB 65/29, 24
86 CONNELL, *op. cit.*, 122
87 NICOLSON, *op. cit.*, 207
88 BRYANT, *op. cit.*, 303
89 CHURCHILL, IV, 29
90 CAB 79/18

CHAPTER 12   SEARCH FOR A SOLUTION

1   CAB 65/25 WM(42) 14
2   CHURCHILL, IV, 83, 84; CAB 79/18
3   BUTLER, *Grand Strategy*, III, Part 2, 417, 418 (OH)
4   CONNELL, *op. cit.*, 142
5   YOUNG, *Churchill and Beaverbrook*, 224, 225
6   CHURCHILL, IV, 101
7   *Ibid*, 102
8   CAB 65/29, 36
9   BUTLER, *op. cit.*, 592 (OH)
10 CAB 65/25 WM(42) 19; BRYANT, *The Turn of the Tide*, 303
11 CHURCHILL, IV, 88
12 YOUNG, *op. cit.*, 225
13 CONNELL, *op. cit.*, 154
14 *Ibid*, 161-162
15 CAB 65/25 WM(42) 20
16 DILKS, *The Diaries of Sir Alexander Cadogan*, 433
17 CONNELL, *op. cit.*, 166-167
18 *Ibid*, 168-169
19 YOUNG, *op. cit.*, 226
20 CAB 65/25 WM(42) 21
21 CAB 69/4 DO(42) 6
22 CAB 79/18
23 BUTLER, *op. cit.*, 468 (OH)
24 *Ibid*, 471
25 BRYANT, *op. cit.*, 311
26 CONNELL, *op. cit.*, 181
27 BUTLER, *op. cit.*, 475 (OH)
28 CHURCHILL, IV, 142

29 *Ibid*, 144
30 *Ibid*, 145
31 CAB 65/29, 43
32 DILKS, *op. cit.*, 438
33 BRYANT, *op. cit.*, 376
34 CAB 65/29, 46
35 BUTLER, *op. cit.*, 449 (OH); CAB 79/18
36 BUTLER, *op. cit.*, 449 (OH)
37 CAB 69/4 DO(42) 7
38 *Ibid*
39 CHURCHILL, IV, 129
40 DILKS, *op. cit.*, 440
41 BUTLER, *op. cit.*, 507 (OH)
42 *Ibid*, 573
43 CAB 88/1 CCS 10
44 CHURCHILL, IV, 175
45 BUTLER, *op. cit.*, 586 (OH)
46 CAB 79/19; BUTLER, *op. cit.*, 567-571 (OH)
47 HIGGINS, *Winston Churchill and the Second Front*, 103
48 CAB 88/1 CCS 11
49 CHURCHILL, IV, 262
50 BRYANT, *op. cit.*, 338-339
51 CHURCHILL, IV, 262, 263
52 CONNELL, *Auchinleck*, 469
53 CHURCHILL, IV, 264
54 CAB 69/4 (Memorandum) DO(42) 35
55 CAB 69/4 DO(42) 9
56 CAB 69/4 (Memorandum) DO(42) 36
57 CAB 88/1 CCS 13
58 STIMSON and BUNDY, *On Active Service*, 413-417; SHERWOOD, *White House Papers*, II, 513; CHURCHILL, IV, 177, 280-281
59 CAB 79/20
60 CAB 79/19
61 CAB 79/19
62 CAB 79/19; CAB 80
63 CHURCHILL, IV, 160
64 BUTLER, *op. cit.*, 487 (OH)
65 CAB 69/4 (Memorandum) DO(42) 39
66 BIRKENHEAD, *The Prof in Two Worlds*, 250
67 BUTLER, *op. cit.*, 528 (OH)
68 BRYANT, *op. cit.*, 343

1 CAB 65/26 WM(42) 44; BUTLER, *Grand Strategy*, III, Part 2, 592 (OH)
2 SHERWOOD, *White House Papers*, II, 528; BRYANT, *The Turn of the Tide*, 352
3 BUTLER, *op. cit.*, 675 (OH)
4 CAB 79/20
5 BRYANT, *op. cit.*, 354
6 EDEN, *The Reckoning*, 325
7 CAB 65/26 WM(42) 47
8 CHURCHILL, IV, 283
9 MATLOFF and SNELL, *Strategic Planning*, 189
10 CAB 79/20
11 BUTLER, *op. cit.*, 577 (OH)
12 CAB 65/30, 15
13 CHURCHILL, IV, 272
14 CAB 69/4 DO(42) 10
15 BRYANT, *op. cit.*, 358, 359
16 CHURCHILL, IV, 162
17 CAB 79/20
18 CHURCHILL, IV, 286, 287
19 *Ibid*, 287
20 *Ibid*, 289
21 CAB 88/1 CCS 16
22 CAB 69/4 DO(42) 10
23 CAB 65/30, 28
24 CAB 88/1 CCS 16
25 CHURCHILL, IV, 272
26 CAB 65/30, 19
27 BRYANT, *op. cit.*, 379
28 CAB 69/4 DO(42) 12
29 BUTLER, *op. cit.*, 488 (OH)
30 *Ibid*, 489
31 CAB 65/30, 23
32 CAB 69/4 DO(42) 12
33 CAB 65/26 WM(42) 50
34 NICOLSON, *Diaries and Letters*, II, 222
35 CAB 65/26 WM(42) 52; CAB 65/30, 23
36 CHURCHILL, IV, 231-232
37 CAB 65/26 WM(42) 56
38 CAB 65/26 WM(42) 61
39 WOODWARD, *British Foreign Policy in the Second World War* (original version), 195 (OH)
40 CAB 69/4 DO(42) 8

41 CAB 69/4 DO(42) 11
42 CAB 65/30, 19
43 CAB 65/30, 33
44 CHURCHILL, IV, 312
45 BUTLER, *op. cit.*, 618 (OH)
46 BRYANT, *op. cit.*, 366
47 CHURCHILL, IV, 275; BUTLER, *op. cit.*, 458 (OH)
48 BRYANT, *op. cit.*, 362, 372
49 BUTLER, *op. cit.*, 643 (OH)
50 CAB 88/1 CCS 18
51 BRYANT, *op. cit.*, 389
52 BUTLER, *op. cit.*, 458 (OH)
53 BRYANT, *op. cit.*, 339, 380
54 CHURCHILL, IV, 212
55 CAB 79/20
56 CAB 65/30, 36
57 CAB 65/30, 42
58 CAB 65/26 WM(42) 61
59 BRYANT, *op. cit.*, 372
60 SHERWOOD, *op. cit.*, 357; YOUNG, *Churchill and Beaverbrook*, 244
61 CAB 79/20; BUTLER, *op. cit.*, 638 (OH)
62 CONNELL, *Auchinleck*, 503
63 CHURCHILL, IV, 233
64 *Ibid*, 234
65 *Ibid*, 276
66 CAB 65/30, 48
67 CAB 65/26 WM(42) 64
68 CHURCHILL, IV, 276
69 *Ibid*, 277; LEWIN, *Rommel as Military Commander*, 111-112
70 CAB 65/26 WM(42) 65
71 CHURCHILL, IV, 297, 298
72 BRYANT, *op. cit.*, 373
73 EDEN, *op. cit.*, 329; WOODWARD, *op. cit.* (original version), 196 (OH);
    BUTLER, *op. cit.*, 593 (OH)
74 CAB 79/21
75 CAB 65/30, 60
76 CAB 65/26 WM(42) 68; CAB 65/30, 62
77 CAB 79/21
78 CHURCHILL, IV, 303, 304
79 BUTLER, *op. cit.*, 587 (OH)
80 CAB 65/26 WM(42) 69
81 CAB 79/21
82 CAB 65/26 WM(42) 70
83 SHERWOOD, *op. cit.*, 550
84 TERRAINE, *Mountbatten*, 94

85 *Ibid*
86 CAB 88/1 CCS 23
87 CAB 79/21
88 CAB 65/23 WM(42) 72
89 BUTLER, *op. cit.*, 596 (OH)
90 CAB 65/30, 73
91 BUTLER, *op. cit.*, 622 (OH)
92 BRYANT, *op. cit.*, 397
93 CHURCHILL, IV, 331
94 CAB 65/26 WM(42) 74
95 CHURCHILL, IV, 337
96 *Ibid*, 336, 337

CHAPTER 14   A STRATEGY SETTLED

1   CAB 88/1 CCS 27
2   BRYANT, *The Turn of the Tide*, 402
3   CAB 88/1 CCS 28
4   BRYANT, *op. cit.*, 403
5   CHURCHILL, IV, 342
6   *Ibid*
7   CAB 65/30, 82
8   CAB 65/26 WM(42) 78; CAB 65/30
9   CAB 88/1 CCS 29
10 CAB 100/9 CWR record, 22 June 1942
11 CHURCHILL, IV, 349
12 CAB 65/26 WM(42) 82; CAB 65/30, 110
13 CAB 65/26 WM(42) 83; BRYANT, *op. cit.*, 418
14 CAB 100/9 CWR record, 29 June 1942
15 CHURCHILL, IV, 383
16 CAB 65/26 WM(42) 84
17 CAB 65/31; CAB 65/27 WM(42) 85
18 BRYANT, *op. cit.*, 419
19 CAB 100/9 CWR record, 4 and 5 July 1942
20 CHURCHILL, IV, 235
21 CAB 65/27 WM(42) 86
22 CAB 100/9 CWR record, 8 July 1942
23 CAB 69/4 DO(42) 14
24 CAB 65/31, 52
25 CAB 69/4 DO(42) 15
26 CAB 65/31, 7
27 BRYANT, *The Turn of the Tide*, 418, 419
28 CAB 65/31, 14

38 CAB 88/1 CCS 43
39 CAB 65/27 WM(42) 119
40 CAB 65/28 WM(42) 140
41 DILKS, *The Diaries of Sir Alexander Cadogan*, 483
42 CHURCHILL, IV, 520
43 CAB 65/28 WM(42) 141
44 WOODWARD, *British Foreign Policy in the Second World War* (original version), 199 (OH)
45 *Ibid*
46 CAB 65/28 WM(42) 143
47 CHURCHILL, IV, 528
48 CAB 100/9 CWR record, 25 October 1942
49 MONTGOMERY, *Memoirs*, 130-131
50 CAB 100/9 CWR record, 26 October 1942
51 CAB 65/28 WM(42) 145
52 MONTGOMERY, *op. cit.*, 132-135; LEWIN, *op. cit.*, 178-179
53 HOWARD, *op. cit.*, 67 (OH)
54 BRYANT, *op. cit.*, 512, 513; CAB 79/23; HOWARD, *op. cit.*, 68 (OH)
55 CHURCHILL, IV, 535
56 CAB 88/1 CCS 46
57 MONTGOMERY, *op. cit.*, 135
58 CAB 100/9 CWR record, 3 November 1942
59 CAB 100/9 CWR record, 4 November 1942
60 CHURCHILL, IV, 538
61 *Ibid*, 537, 538
62 CAB 100/9 CWR record, 5 November 1942
63 CHURCHILL, IV, 539
64 CAB 100/9 CWR record, 8 November 1942
65 CAB 65/28 WM(42) 151

Bibliography

Official Histories (OH); HMSO
Campaigns
COLLIER, BASIL, *The Defence of the United Kingdom*, 1957
ELLIS, MAJOR L. F., *The War in France and Flanders, 1939-1940*, 1953
PLAYFAIR, MAJOR-GENERAL, *The Mediterranean and Middle-East*, Volume 1, 1954
ROSKILL, CAPTAIN S. W., *The War at Sea*, Volume I, 1954
WEBSTER, SIR C. K. and FRANKLAND, N., *The Strategic Air Offensive against Germany*, Volume 1, 1960

Civil Series
POSTAN, M. M., *British War Production*, 1952

Diplomatic
WOODWARD, SIR LLEWELLYN, *British Foreign Policy in the Second World War*, Volume 1, 1970; Volume II, 1972
——, *British Foreign Policy in the Second World War* (original version), 1962

Grand Strategy
Volume II, September 1939-June 1941, BUTLER, J. R. M., 1957
Volume III, Part I and Part II, June 1941-August 1942, GWYER, J. M. A., and BUTLER, J. R. M., 1964
Volume IV, August 1942-September 1943, HOWARD, MICHAEL, 1972

AMERY, L. S., *My Political Life*, Volume III, The Unforgiving Years, 1929-1940, London, 1953-1955
ATTLEE, CLEMENT, *As It Happened*, London, 1954
BIRKENHEAD, EARL OF, *Halifax*, London, 1965
——, *The Prof in Two Worlds*: The Official Life of Professor F. A. Lindemann, Viscount Cherwell, London, 1961
BRABAZON, LORD, OF TARA, *The Brabazon Story*, London, 1956
BROME, VINCENT, *Aneurin Bevan*, London, 1953
BRYANT, ARTHUR, *The Turn of the Tide*, 1939-1943, Study based on

the Diaries and Autobiographical Notes of Field Marshal The Viscount Alanbrooke, London, 1957

BULLOCK, ALAN, *Life and Times of Ernest Bevin*, Volume II, Minister of Labour, 1940-1945, London, 1967

BUTCHER, HARRY C., *Three Years with Eisenhower*, New York, 1946

CALDER, ANGUS, *The People's War*, Britain 1939-1945, London, 1969

CHURCHILL, SIR WINSTON, *The Second World War*, Volume II, *Their Finest Hour*, London, 1949; Volume III, *The Grand Alliance*, London, 1950; Volume IV, *The Hinge of Fate*, London, 1951

COLLIER, BASIL, *The Battle of Britain*, London, 1962

CONNELL, JOHN, *Auchinleck*, London, 1959

——, *Wavell, Soldier and Scholar*, London, 1964

——, *Wavell, Supreme Commander*, London, 1969

COOPER, ALFRED DUFF, VISCOUNT NORWICH, *Old Men Forget*, London, 1953

CUDLIPP, HUGH, *Publish and Be Damned*, London, 1953

CUNNINGHAM, LORD, OF HYNDHOPE, *A Sailor's Odyssey*, London, 1951

DGFP – *Documents on German Foreign Policy*, 1918-1945, United States State Department

DILKS, DAVID, ed., *The Diaries of Sir Alexander Cadogan*, London, 1971

DRIBERG, TOM, *Beaverbrook*, A Study in Power and Frustration, London, 1956

EDEN, ANTHONY, LORD AVON, *The Reckoning*, London, 1965

EINZIG, PAUL, *In the Centre of Things*, London, 1960

EISENHOWER, DWIGHT, *Crusade in Europe*, New York, 1948

FEILING, K., *The Life of Neville Chamberlain*, London, 1946

FLEMING, PETER, *Invasion 1940*, London, 1957

GARDNER, BRIAN, *Churchill in his Time*, A Study in Reputation, 1939-1945, London, 1968

GAULLE, GENERAL CHARLES DE, *War Memoirs*, Volume I, *The Call to Honour*, 1940-1942, New York, 1955

GRIGG, SIR JAMES, *Prejudice and Judgement*, London, 1948

GUDERIAN, HEINZ, *Panzer Leader*, London, 1952

HARRIS, SIR ARTHUR, *Bomber Offensive*, London, 1947

HIGGINS, TRUMBULL, *Winston Churchill and the Second Front*, 1940-1943, New York, 1957

HOARE, SAMUEL, *Ambassador on Special Mission*, London, 1946

HULL, CORDELL, *Memoirs*, Volume I, London, 1959

ISMAY, GENERAL LORD, *Memoirs*, London, 1960

KENNEDY, GENERAL SIR JOHN, and FERGUSSON, B., *The Business of War*, London, 1957

LEAHY, FLEET ADMIRAL WILLIAM, *I Was There*, New York, 1950

LEASOR, JAMES, and HOLLIS, GENERAL SIR LESLIE, *War at the Top*, London, 1959

LEWIN, RONALD, *Rommel as Military Commander*, London, 1968
LYTTELTON, OLIVER, *The Memoirs of Lord Chandos*, London, 1962
MACLEOD, R. and KELLY, D., *The Ironside Diaries*, London, 1962
MAISKY, I., *Memoirs of a Soviet Ambassador*, 1939-1943, London, 1967
MATLOFF, MAURICE and SNELL, EDWIN M., *Strategic Planning for Coalition Warfare*, 1941, 1942, Army Department, Washington, 1953
MINNEY, R. J., *The Private Papers of Hore-Belisha*, London, 1960
MONTGOMERY, VISCOUNT, OF ALAMEIN, *The Memoirs of Field Marshal Montgomery* (London, 1958), Fontana edition, 1960
MORAN, LORD, *Winston Churchill: Struggle for Survival*, 1940-1965, London, 1966
MUGGERIDGE, MALCOLM, ed., *Ciano's Diary*, 1939-1943, London, 1947
NCA – *Nazi Conspiracy and Aggression*, Office of the US Chief of Counsel for Prosecution of Axis Criminals, US Government Printing Office, 1946
NICOLSON, HAROLD, *Diaries and Letters*, Volume II, 1939-1945 (London 1967), Fontana edition, 1970
N-SR – *Nazi-Soviet Relations*, 1939-1941, documents from the archives of the German Foreign Office, edited by Sontay, Raymond, and Beddie, James, US Government Printing Office, 1948
PETRIE, SIR C., *Private Diaries of Baudouin*, London, 1943
REYNAUD, PAUL, *In the Thick of the Fight*, 1930-1945, New York, 1945
ROOSEVELT, ELLIOTT, *As He Saw It*, New York, 1946
——, ed., *FDR – His Personal Letters*, 1928-1945, New York, 1950
SCHMIDT, PAUL, *Hitler's Interpreter*, London, 1951
SHERWOOD, ROBERT E., ed., *White House Papers of Harry L. Hopkins*, London, 1949
SHIRER, WILLIAM L., *Berlin Diary*, 1934-1941 (London, 1941), Sphere edition, 1970
——, *The Rise and Fall of the Third Reich* (London, 1960), Pan edition, 1969
STIMSON, HENRY, and BUNDY, MCGEORGE, *On Active Service in Peace and War*, New York, 1947
TERRAINE, JOHN, *The Life and Times of Lord Mountbatten*, London, 1968
TREVOR-ROPER, HUGH, ed., *Hitler's War Directives* (London, 1964), Pan edition, 1966
WHEATLEY, RONALD, *Operation Sea Lion*, London, 1958
WHEELER-BENNETT, SIR JOHN, ed., *Action This Day*, London, 1968
——, *John Anderson*, London, 1962
WINANT, JOHN GILBERT, *A Letter from Grosvenor Square*, London, 1947
WRIGHT, ROBERT, *Dowding and the Battle of Britain*, London, 1969
YOUNG, KENNETH, *Churchill and Beaverbrook*, London, 1966

Some Major Figures Involved

With descriptions of appointments and the roles during the period covered (where relevant the names of the previous holders of the post, and the immediate successors, are given in brackets after the dates of appointment).

ALEXANDER, Albert, V. (later Lord, of Hillsborough), First Lord of the Admiralty, 12 May 1940 (Churchill) to May 1945.

ALEXANDER, General (later Field Marshal) Sir Harold R. G., C-in-C Burma, February 1942 (Hutton) to 15 August 1942 (Irwin); GOC-in-C, Middle East (Auchinleck).

ALI, Rashid, Prime Minister of Iraq, 1940 to 31 January 1941; Iraq leader after *coup* 3 March 1941, fled 30 May 1941.

ALFIERI, Dino, Italian Ambassador to Berlin.

AMERY, Leopold, Secretary of State for India and Burma from May 1940 to 1945.

ANDERSON, Sir John, Home Secretary until 3 October 1940 (Herbert Morrison); then Lord President of the Council (Chamberlain).

ARNOLD, General Henry H., Chief of the United States Army Air Forces.

ATTLEE, Clement R., Lord Privy Seal until 19 February 1942 (Cripps), then Deputy Prime Minister and Dominions Secretary (Lord Cranborne).

AUCHINLECK, General Sir Claude J. E., C-in-C India 27 January 1941 to 5 July 1941 (when changed with Wavell); GOC-in-C Middle East until 15 August 1942 (Alexander); C-in-C India from 20 June 1943.

BAUDOUIN, Paul, French Under Secretary for Foreign Affairs until 17 June 1940; Foreign Minister until October 1940 (Laval).

BEAVERBROOK, Lord, Minister of Aircraft Production from 14 May 1940 to 1 May 1941 (Moore-Brabazon), then Minister of State until 29 June 1941, when became Minister of Supply (Duncan), until 4 February 1942 when became first Minister of Production, until 19 February (Lyttelton).

BERESFORD-PEIRSE, Lieut-General Sir N., GOC Western Desert, Spring 1941.

BEVAN, Aneurin, Editor, *Tribune*.

BEVIN, Ernest, Minister of Labour and National Service from 13 May 1940.

BLAMEY, General Sir Thomas, Commander, Australian Imperial Forces, later C-in-C Allied Land Forces, Australia.

BRACKEN, Brendan (later Lord), Churchill's Parliamentary Private Secretary until 20 July 1941, then Minister of Information (Duff Cooper).

BRAUCHITSCH, Field Marshal Walther, C-in-C, German Army until 19 December 1941 (Hitler).

BRETT, General, US Army Air Force, undertook mission to Singapore and China, December 1941, appointed Deputy to Wavell in ABDA Command in the same month.

BRIDGES, Sir Edward, Permanent Secretary of the Cabinet Office and Secretary of the War Cabinet.

BROOKE, General (later Field-Marshal) Sir Alan F., Commander, British forces in France, June 1940; C-in-C Home Forces 20 July 1940 (Ironside) until 25 December 1941 when appointed Chief of the Imperial General Staff (Dill).

BROOKE-POPHAM, Air Chief Marshal Sir Robert, C-in-C of three services in Far East, October 1941 (first to take this unified appointment), until December 1941 (Pownall).

BULLITT, William C., American Ambassador to Paris until creation of Vichy French Government (Leahy).

BUTLER, Richard Austen (later Lord), Parliamentary Under-Secretary for Foreign Affairs until 21 July 1941; became President of the Board of Education until 1944.

CADOGAN, Sir Alexander, Permanent Under-Secretary at the Foreign Office from 1 January 1938.

CALDECOTE, Lord, Secretary of State for Dominions, 14 May 1940 (Eden), until 3 October 1940 (Lord Cranborne).

CAMBON, Roger, Minister at French Embassy, London, until 5 July 1940 (de Castellane).

CAMPBELL, Sir Ronald Hugh, British Ambassador at Paris until mission withdrawn 24 June 1940.

CAMPBELL, Sir Ronald Ian, British Ambassador at Belgrade, captured by Italians 18 April 1941.

CASEY, Richard G., First Australian Minister to America, 1940 to February 1942, then British Minister of State, Cairo (Lyttelton), until 1943.

CASTELLANE, Marquis de, temporary French Chargé at London, July 1940.

CATROUX, General Georges, Free French High Commissioner and de Gaulle's representative in Near East, 1940; C-in-C Free French, Levant, 1941-3.

CHAMBERLAIN, Neville, Lord President of Council until 3 October 1940 (Anderson).

CHURCHILL, Winston, British Prime Minister from 10 May 1940 (Chamberlain).

CIANO, Count Galeazzo, Mussolini's son-in-law, Italian Foreign Minister, 1936-43.

COOPER, Alfred Duff, Minister of Information from 12 May 1940 (Reith); Chancellor of Duchy of Lancaster from 20 July 1941 (Hankey), including period as Minister of State, Singapore until January 1942.

CORBIN, Charles, French Ambassador at London until 26 June 1940. (No new ambassador appointed.)

CRAIGIE, Sir Robert, British Ambassador at Tokyo until declaration of war, December 1941.

CRANBORNE, Lord, Secretary of State for Dominions from 3 October 1940 (Caldecote) to 19 February 1942 (Attlee).

CRIPPS, Sir Stafford R., British Ambassador at Moscow 12 June 1940 (Seeds) to 4 February 1941 (Kerr); leader of House of Commons and Lord Privy Seal (Attlee) until became Minister of Aircraft Production 22 November 1942 (Llewellin).

CUNNINGHAM, General Sir Alan, Commander of British forces in Kenya and Somaliland, 1940; Commander, 8th Army until 25 November 1941 (Ritchie). Brother of Admiral Sir Andrew.

CUNNINGHAM, Vice-Admiral (later Admiral of the Fleet, Viscount, of Hyndhope) Sir Andrew B., C-in-C Mediterranean Fleet 1 June 1939 until 1 April 1942 (Pridham-Wippell); member of British mission to Washington and the CCS from November 1942 to 20 February 1943. Brother of General Sir Alan.

CURTIN, John, Australian Prime Minister, October 1941 (Fadden) to 1945.

DALTON, Hugh, Minister of Economic Warfare from 15 May 1940 (Cross) to 22 February 1942 (Wolmer), then President of the Board of Trade (Llewellin).

516

DARLAN, Admiral J. F., C-in-C French Fleet; Minister of Marine under Pétain from 16 June 1940; Vice-Premier and Foreign Minister from 9 February 1941 (Flandin) to April 1942 (Laval), when became Pétain's official successor and head of Vichy French armed forces.

DENTZ, General Henri, French High Commissioner in Syria and the Lebanon 1940-41.

DILL, Lieut-General (later Field Marshal) Sir John G., Chief of the Imperial General Staff from 10 June 1940 (Ironside) to 25 December 1941 (Brooke); then Head of British Military Mission to Washington.

DOBBIE, Lieut-General Sir William, Governor and C-in-C Malta, 1940 to April 1942 (Gort).

DOUGLAS, Sholto, Air Marshal Sir W., AOC-in-C Fighter Command 25 November 1940 (Dowding) to 25 November 1942 (Leigh-Mallory).

DOWDING, Air Chief Marshal Sir Hugh C. T., AOC-in-C Fighter Command until 25 November 1940 (Douglas).

DUNCAN, Sir Andrew, President of Board of Trade, 5 January 1940 (Stanley) to 3 October 1940 (Lyttelton), then Minister of Supply (Herbert Morrison) to 29 June 1941 (Beaverbrook), then returned to Board of Trade (Lyttelton) until 4 February 1942 (Llewellin), when he returned finally to the Ministry of Supply (Beaverbrook).

EDEN, Anthony (later Lord Avon), Secretary of State for War, 12 May 1940 (Stanley) until 22 December 1940 (Margesson), then Foreign Secretary (after Halifax).

EISENHOWER, General Dwight David, Assistant Chief of Staff in charge of Operations Division, Officer of US Chief of Staff, until June 1942; Commanding General, European Theatre, until November 1942; C-in-C Allied Forces, North Africa.

FADDEN, A. W., Australian Prime Minister 25 August 1941 (Menzies) until October 1941 (Curtin).

FRANCO, General Francisco, Spanish Head of State and Generalissimo of National Armies from 1936.

FRASER, Peter, Prime Minister of New Zealand from March 1940 (Savage), also Minister for External Affairs.

FREYBERG, Sir Bernard Cyril, V.C., GOC New Zealand Forces, November 1939 to 1945, also Commander of Imperial and Greek Troops in Crete, 1941.

GAULLE, Charles de, Under-Secretary of State for National Defence under Reynaud, June 1940; President of the (Free) French National Committee.

GEORGES, General Alphonse Joseph, French Army Commander North-East, May-June 1940.

GÖRING, Hermann Wilhelm, Reich Commissioner for Air.

GORT, General Lord, V.C., Governor of Gibraltar until April 1942; Governor and C-in-C Malta (Dobbie).

GREENWOOD, Arthur, Minister without Portfolio, 11 May 1940 (Hankey) until 22 February 1942.

GRIGG, Sir James P., Permanent Under-Secretary of State for War, 26 October 1939 until 5 March 1942; became Secretary of State for War on 22 February 1942 (Margesson) until 1945.

HAINING, Lieut-General Sir Robert H., Vice-CIGS 27 May 1940 until 19 May 1941 (Pownall); Intendant-General, Cairo, June 1941.

HALDER, General Franz, Chief of Staff, German Army, until 24 September 1942 (Zeitzler).

HALIFAX, Lord Edward, Foreign Secretary until 22 December 1940 (Eden), then Ambassador at Washington (Lothian).

HANKEY, Lord Maurice Paschal, Minister without Portfolio until 11 May 1940 (Greenwood), then Chancellor of Duchy of Lancaster until 20 July 1941 (Duff Cooper); Paymaster-General.

HARRIMAN, William Averell, special representative of President Roosevelt in Britain with rank of Minister from March 1941, in Soviet Union with rank of Ambassador from August 1941, representative in London of Combined Production and Resources Board from July 1942.

HARRIS, Air Chief Marshal Sir Arthur T., AOC No 5 Bomber Group until 1940; Deputy Chief of Air Staff 1940-41; Head of RAF delegation to America, 1941; from 22 February 1942 AOC Bomber Command (Peirse) until 1945.

HESS, Rudolf, Nazi Party Deputy Leader.

HITLER, Adolf, German Chancellor from 1933; officially C-in-C German Army from 19 December 1941 (Brauchitsch).

HOARE, Sir Samuel, Lord Privy Seal until 3 April 1939 (Attlee on 11 May) then Secretary of State for Air (Kingsley Wood) until 11 May (Sinclair); British Ambassador at Madrid.

HOLLIS, General L. C., Senior Assistant Military Secretary to War Cabinet.

HOPKINS, Harry, Presidential special adviser and representative from January 1941.

HORE-BELISHA, Leslie, M.P., Secretary of State for War in Chamberlain's Government from 1937 to 5 January 1940 (Stanley).

HULL, Cordell, American Secretary of State.

HUTTON, Lieut-General (later Sir) Thomas, C-in-C Burma December

1941 to February 1942 (Alexander).

INÖNÜ, General Ismet, President of Turkish Republic, 1938-50.

IRONSIDE, General Sir W. Edmund, CIGS until 10 June 1940 (Dill), then C-in-C, Home Forces, until 19 July 1940 (Brooke).

ISMAY, Major-General Sir Hastings L., Deputy Secretary (Military) to War Cabinet and Churchill's representative on COS Committee from 2 May 1940.

JACOB, Sir Ian, Assistant Military Secretary to War Cabinet.

KAI-SHEK, Marshal Chiang, President, Chinese Republic; Supreme Chinese C-in-C.

KEITEL, Field Marshal Wilhelm, Chief of Supreme Command of German armed forces.

KENNEDY, Major-General Sir John Noble, Director of Military Operations, War Office, 1940-43.

KENNEDY, Joseph P., American Ambassador to London until April 1941 (Winant).

KERR, Sir Archibald J. K. C., British Ambassador at Moscow from 4 February 1942 (Cripps).

KEYES, Admiral of the Fleet Sir Roger, M.P., Director, Combined Operations HQ, August 1941 (Bourne) to October (Mountbatten, with title of 'Adviser').

KING, Fleet Admiral Ernest J., Chief of US Naval Operations and C-in-C US Fleet.

KING, Mackenzie, Canadian Prime Minister.

KORYZIS, Alexander, President of the Greek Council, 29 January 1941 (Metaxas), committed suicide 18 April 1941.

KURUSU, Saburo, Special Japanese envoy to Washington, 15 November-December 1941.

LAVAL, Pierre, Vichy Foreign Minister October 1940 (Baudouin) until 13 December 1940 (Flandin); returned as Foreign Minister in April 1942 (Darlan) and as Prime Minister.

LAYTON, Vice-Admiral Sir Geoffrey, C-in-C Eastern Fleet 11 December 1941 (Phillips) until 5 March 1942 (Somerville).

LEAHY, Fleet Admiral William D., American Ambassador to Vichy 1940 until May 1942, then Chief of Staff to President until 1949.

LEATHERS, Lord, Minister of War Transport (first to have this appointment) 1 May 1941 until 1945.

LINDEMANN, Professor F. A. (Lord Cherwell from 1942), scientific adviser to Prime Minister.

LINLITHGOW, Victor, 2nd Marquis of, Viceroy of India, 1936-43.

LITTLE, Admiral Sir Charles J. C., Second Sea Lord 30 September 1938 to 1 June 1941 (Whitworth), then head of British Admiralty delegation to Washington and to the CCS.

LITVINOV, Maxim, Soviet Foreign Minister 1930 to 3 May 1939 (Molotov); Soviet Ambassador to Washington from November 1941.

LLEWELLIN, John Jestyn (later Lord, of Upton), Parliamentary Secretary to Minister of Supply 1939-40, to Minister of Aircraft Production 1940-41; President of Board of Trade 4 February 1942 (Duncan), until 22 February 1942 (Dalton); then Minister of Aircraft Production (Moore-Brabazon) until 22 November 1942 (Cripps).

LLOYD, Lord, Secretary of State for the Colonies from 12 May 1940 to 8 February 1941 (Moyne).

LONGMORE, Air Chief Marshal Sir Arthur, AOC-in-C Middle East 13 May 1940 until 1 June 1941 (Tedder).

LORAINE, Sir Percy, British Ambassador to Rome 1939 until withdrawal of mission, 11 June 1940.

LOTHIAN, Lord Philip Kerr, British Ambassador at Washington 1939 until 12 December 1940 (Halifax on 22 December).

LYTTELTON, Oliver, President of Board of Trade from 3 October 1940 (Duncan) to 29 June 1941 (Duncan); Minister of State, Middle East, until 12 March 1942, when became Minister of Production (Beaverbrook had left the Ministry on 18 February).

MACARTHUR, General Douglas, Commanding-General of the American Far East Command from July 1941; Supreme Commander, Far East.

MAISKY, Ivan, Soviet Ambassador at London, 1932-43.

MARGESSON, Captain David R., Conservative Chief Whip; Secretary of State for War 3 December 1940 (Eden) until 22 February 1942 (Grigg).

MARSHALL, General George C., Chief of Staff, US Army, from 1939.

MATSOUKA, Yosuke, Japanese Foreign Minister, 1940-18 July 1941 (Toyoda).

MENZIES, Robert Gordon, Australian Prime Minister and Minister for Defence Co-ordination, 1939 until 25 August 1941 (Fadden); opposition member of Advisory War Council 1941-4.

METAXAS, General Ioannis, President of the Greek Council and Foreign Minister, 1936-29 January 1941 (Koryzis).

MOLOTOV, Vyacheslav Mikhailovich, Soviet Foreign Minister, May 1939-49.

MONNET, Jean, Chairman, Franco-British Economic Co-ordination Committee, 1939-40; member, British Supply Council in Washington, 1940-43.

MONTGOMERY, General (later Field Marshal) Bernard L., Commander, Southern Command from December 1941; Commander, 8th Army from August 1942.

MOORE-BRABAZON, John Theodore (later Lord Brabazon of Tara), Minister of Transport, 3 October 1940 (Reith) until 1 May 1941 (Leathers, as Minister of War Transport), when became Minister of Aircraft Production (Beaverbrook) until 22 February 1942 (Llewellin).

MORRISON, Herbert S., Minister of Supply, 12 May 1940 (Burgin) until 3 October 1940 (Duncan), then Home Secretary and Minister for Home Security (Anderson).

MOUNTBATTEN, Lord Louis (of Burma), Adviser, Combined Operations (Keyes, with title of Director) October 1941 to March 1942, when received the title of Chief, Combined Operations, until October 1943 (Laycock).

MOYNE, Lord, Secretary of State for the Colonies, 8 February 1941 (Lloyd) to 22 February 1942 (Cranborne).

MUSSOLINI, Benito, Italian leader from 1925.

NEAME, Lieut-General Sir Philip, V.C., GOC in Cyrenaica, March 1941, captured April 1941.

NEWALL, Marshal of the RAF Sir Cyril, Chief of Air Staff until 25 October 1940 (Portal), then Governor-General of New Zealand.

NICOLSON, Harold G., Parliamentary Secretary at Ministry of Information 17 May 1940 to 20 July 1941.

NOMURA, Admiral Kichisaburo, Japanese Ambassador to Washington, February 1941 to December 1941.

NYE, Lieut-General Archibald E., Vice-CIGS from 5 December 1941 (Pownall).

ODEND'HAL, Admiral, Head of French Naval Mission to Britain, 1940.

PAGE, Sir Earle, Special Australian representative in London.

PAGET, General (later Sir) Bernard C. T., C-in-C designate to Far East, 1941, instead C-in-C Home Forces 25 December 1941 (Brooke) until July 1943 (Franklyn).

PALAIRET, Sir Michael, British Ambassador to Athens until German occupation, 1941.

PAPAGOS, General (later Field Marshal) Alexander, commander of Greek armies, 1940-41.

PARK, Air Vice-Marshal Keith, Commander, 11 Group, Fighter Command, 1940.

PEIRSE, Air (later Chief) Marshal Sir Richard E. C., Deputy Chief of Air Staff 1937-April 1940, then Vice-Chief of Air Staff until 5 October 1940 (Freeman); AOC-in-C Bomber Command until 22 February 1942 (Harris), then AOC-in-C India.

PERCIVAL, General A. E., GOC, Singapore, 1941.

PÉTAIN, Marshal Henri Phillippe, Vice-President of the French Council under Reynaud from 18 May 1940 to 16 June; French Premier in Vichy Government.

PHILLIPS, Rear-Admiral Tom, Vice-Chief of Naval Staff 1 June 1939 to 21 October 1941 (Moore), then C-in-C Eastern Fleet until December 1941.

PLEVEN, René, member, Anglo-French Co-ordination Committee, 1940, then Secretary-General of French Equatorial Africa.

PORTAL, Air Chief Marshal Sir Charles F. A., Chief of the Air Staff from 25 October 1940 (Newall).

POUND, Admiral of the Fleet Sir Dudley, First Sea Lord and Chief of Naval Staff from 12 June 1939 to 15 October 1943 (Cunningham).

POWNALL, Lieut-General Sir Henry R., Vice-CIGS from 19 May 1941 (Haining) to 5 December 1941 (Nye), then C-in-C Far East (Brooke-Popham).

RAEDER, Admiral Erich, Chief of the German Naval Staff.

REITH (Lord) John Charles, Minister of Transport 14 May 1940 (Euan Wallace) to 3 October 1940 (Moore-Brabazon), then the first Minister of Works and Building until 22 February 1942 (Lord Portal).

REYNAUD, Paul, French Premier from 21 March 1940 until 16 June 1940 (Pétain).

RIBBENTROP, Joachim von, ex-wine merchant; German Ambassador to London, 1936-38; Foreign Minister.

RITCHIE, General Neil, Deputy Chief of General Staff, Cairo, June-November 1941; Commander, 8th Army, until 25 June 1942.

ROMMEL, General (later Field Marshal) Irwin, Commander German forces in North Africa from February 1941.

ROOSEVELT, Franklin D., President of the United States.

SARAJOGLU, Sukru, Turkish Foreign Minister, 1938-42.

SCHULENBURG, Count Fritz von der, German Ambassador to Moscow.

SIGEMITSU, Namoru, Japanese Ambassador to London until December 1941.

SIMON, Sir John (later Lord), Chancellor of the Exchequer from 28 May 1937 to 12 May 1940 (Kingsley Wood), when became Lord Chancellor.

SINCLAIR, Sir Archibald, Secretary of State for Air from 11 May 1940 (Hoare).

SMUTS (Field Marshal from 1941), J. C., Prime Minister of South Africa.

SOMERVILLE, Admiral Sir James F., Commander, Western Mediterranean 1940-41; C-in-C Eastern Fleet from 5 March 1942 (Layton).

SPEARS, General Edward, Military Liaison officer at Paris, later with de Gaulle.

STALIN, Generalissimo Joseph, Soviet leader and C-in-C.

STARK, Admiral Harold R., American Chief of Naval Operations.

STIMSON, Henry L., American Secretary of State for War.

TEDDER, Air Marshal Sir Arthur W., AOC-in-C Middle East 1 June 1941 (Longmore) until 11 January 1943 (Douglas).

TELEKI, Count Paul, Hungarian Premier until April 1941.

TOJO, General Hideki, Japanese Prime Minister from 16 October 1941 (Konoye).

TOVEY, Vice-Admiral (Sir) John C., C-in-C Home Fleet 2 December 1940 (Forbes) until 8 May 1943.

VANSITTART, Sir Robert G., Chief Diplomatic Adviser to Foreign Secretary until 25 June 1941. (Post not re-filled.)

VUILLEMIN, General Joseph, Head of French Air Force, spring 1940.

WARDLAW-MILNE, Sir John, Conservative MP and Chairman of the all-party Finance Committee.

WAVELL, General Sir Archibald P., GOC-in-C Middle East until 5 July 1941 (Auchinleck); C-in-C India (Auchinleck) and Far East 21 June 1941 until 20 June 1943, also ABDA commander December 1941 to February 1942.

WELLES, Sumner, American Under-Secretary of State, 1937-43.

WEYGAND, General Maxime, Minister of Defence under Pétain from 16 June 1940 until October 1940, then Delegate-General, Algiers and C-in-C French Africa.

WILSON, Sir Charles (later Lord Moran), Churchill's physician.

WILSON, General Sir Henry Maitland, Commander, British Army of the Nile, 1939-40; GOC-in-C Cyrenaica, March 1941 and Commander of forces in Greece in the same month; Commander of Allied forces in Syria and Transjordan, summer 1941; GOC Persia-Iraq from December 1941; 16 February 1943 became GOC-in-C Middle East (Alexander).

WINANT, John G., American Ambassador to London after March 1941 (Kennedy).

WOOD, Sir Kingsley, Secretary of State for Air, 16 May 1938 to 3 April 1940 (Hoare); Chancellor of Exchequer 12 May 1940 (Simon) to 24 September 1943 (Anderson).

WOOLTON, Lord, Minister of Food, 3 April 1940 (W. S. Morrison) to 11 November 1943 (Llewellin).

Index of Names

Alexander, Albert, 5, 47, 49, 50, 52, 64, 66, 86, 124, 152, 217, 271, 272, 273, 278, 384, 393, 438, 449

Alexander, General, in Burma, 371, 378, 380, 382, 399, 406; completes withdrawal to India, 410; replaces Auchinleck, 451, 453, 457, 458, 460; and Alamein, 469, 472, 473, 475, 476, 477, 478

Ali, Rashid, 216, 221, 222, 224, 232, 253; see also Iraq

Amery, Leopold, 78

Anderson, Sir John, as Home Secretary, 5, 20, 58, 107, 111, 112, 113, 117, 119, 121, 122, 123; as Lord President, 127, 158, 161, 275

Arnold, General Henry H., 348, 379, 381

Attlee, Clement, 3, 4, 5, 9, 38, 40, 42, 77, 87, 120, 124, 130, 131, 165, 167, 209, 217, 240, 264, 268, 271, 278, 297, 300, 311, 325, 329, 334, 335, 343, 353, 365; as Dominions Secretary, 372, 377, 411, 438, 467, 476

Auchinleck, General Sir Claude, 95, 240, 245; replaces Wavell, 261, 268, 269, 270; withstands Churchill's early pressure, 270, 271; in London, July '41, 272-4; 284, 288, 289; and removal of Australian troops from Tobruk, 289-91, 293-5; 303; and 'Crusader', 298, 310-19, 322, 331, 332, 335, 353, 355; and German advance, January '42, 359-61, 363; 375, 376, 377, 382, 383, 384, 404, 405, 406, 407, 408, 409-10, 411-12, 415, 421; and fall of Tobruk, 430-2; at Alamein position, 435, 441, 450,

451; replacement of, 451-3, 458, 459

Baudouin, Paul, 27, 43, 45, 49, 50, 53, 70, 141

Beaverbrook, Lord, 4, 14, 19, 30, 129, 130, 131, 132, 156, 165, 167, 174, 197, 199, 234, 240, 242, 263; as Minister of Supply, 277, 278, 281, 283, 284, 285, 288; and mission to Moscow, 291, 292, 295-9; and supply to Russia, 300-3; 304; visit to Washington, December '41, 333, 338; 359, 361, 362, 364, 365, 367, 369; resignation from Production Ministry, 372; 375, 401, 408, 409, 470, 471

Beresford-Peirse, 257, 258, 259

Bevan, Aneurin, 360, 434

Bevin, Ernest, 4, 44, 99, 161, 162, 174, 288, 364, 365-6, 431, 433

Blamey, General Sir Thomas, 206, 207, 229, 252, 257, 294, 295

Bracken, Brendan, 5, 250, 374, 460, 471

Brauchitsch, General Walther von, 104, 105, 186, 219, 220

Brett, General, 341, 343

Bridges, Sir Edward, 3, 132, 223

Brooke, General Sir Alan, 28, 31, 34, 35, 36, 37, 44, 45, 46, 76, 77, 80, 92, 93, 108, 109, 112, 113, 114, 160, 162, 178, 179, 182, 185, 276, 290, 291, 299; becomes CIGS, 313-14, 321; on supplies to Russia, December '41, 321, 323-5; 325, 332, 333; during Churchill's visit to Washington, December '41, 334, 335, 342-5, 347, 348, 350, 352, 355, 359, 365, 366, 373, 374, 375, 376, 377, 378; becomes COS

525

General Index